"Required reading for women who care about our history and the fate of the world. Sjöö and Mor are revolutionary in their knowledge of women's early shamanic practices and ways of life, our deep connection to the moon, and the necessity of reclaiming the primacy of our biological blood mysteries. The book is politically forceful and deeply insightful about women and culture."

—Vicki Noble,
author of *Shakti Woman*

"A must on every goddess-worshiping person's shelf. The book will upset you. It will astonish you. It will educate you, and finally, it will give you hope."

—Zsuzsanna Budapest,
author of *The Grandmother of Time*

"Original, forceful analysis of great importance, rich with fresh, potentially shocking perspectives and much timely guidance."

—*East West*

"(Mor and Sjöö) interpret myth and symbol philosophically, psychologically, biologically, and mystically. This is exciting stuff."

—*The Women's Review of Books*

". . . Monumental and superbly readable . . . a stunning accomplishment in which all the strands of life are interwoven."

—*Mama Bear News*

"Their passionate research reveals the beginnings of matrifocal societies and shows women as creators of culture. . . . An exhaustive study of the female condition and its arising. . . . I could almost feel my cells remembering."

—*Peacework Press*

"The message of the book mirrors (Carol) Christ's (in *The Laughter of Aphrodite*) and its urgency is powerful."

—*Belles Lettres*

"This passionate exploration draws on religious traditions, cultures, and archaeological sources from all over the world to recreate for the first time the Goddess religion that is our ancient heritage."

—*Together Books Newsletter*

The Great Cosmic MOTHER

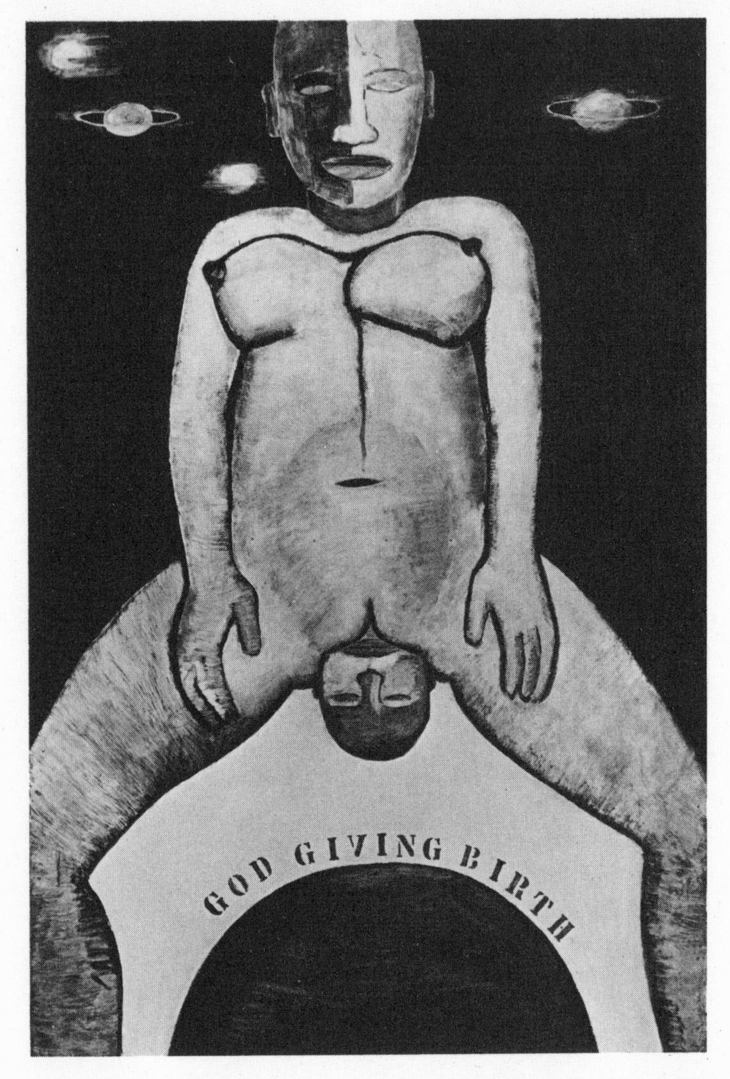

God Giving Birth, Sjöö, 1968

The Great Cosmic Mother

Rediscovering the Religion of the Earth

MONICA SJÖÖ
and
BARBARA MOR

HarperSanFrancisco
A Division of HarperCollins*Publishers*

Note:

Monica Sjöö's pamphlet, *The Ancient Religion of the Great Cosmic Mother of All,* was printed in Bristol, England, in December, 1975. In 1977, a Norwegian translation was published in book form (*Den Store Kosmiske Mor—Regnbuetrykk*). Monica Sjöö and Barbara Mor made contact through an Oregon publication, *WomanSpirit,* in 1976; they rewrote and expanded the text, adding sections and titles. This enlarged book of eighty printed pages was published under the original title by Rainbow Press, Trondheim, Norway, in 1981. A German-language edition, *Wiederkehr Der Göttin,* translated by Gisela Ottmer, Marion Kannen, and Rosemarie Merkel was published in 1985 by Labyrinth Press, Braunschweig, Germany.

This much larger American edition, completely rewritten and extended, was authored by Barbara Mor.

Photograph and illustration credits may be found on page 491.

SECOND EDITION

Cover image: *Diana, the Moon Mother,* Sjöö, 1976

Originally published by Harper & Row in 1987

Library of Congress Cataloging-in-Publication Data

Sjöö Monica.
The great cosmic mother : rediscovering the religion of the earth / Monica Sjöö and Barbara Mor.
p. cm.
Reprint, with new introd. Originally published: San Francisco : Harper & Row, c1987.
Includes bibliographical references and index.
ISBN 0-06-250792-3 (acid-free) (incorrect)
ISBN 0-06-250791-5 (acid-free) (correct)
1. Mother goddesses. 2. Women—Religion. 3. Matriarchy—Religious aspects. I. Mor, Barbara. II. Title.
[BL325.M6S55 1991]
291.2'114—dc20 90-55783
CIP

97 RRD(H) 20 19 18 17 16 15 14

The Bleeding Yew Tree at Nevern Graveyard, Sjöo, 1982

To my son Leif Sjöö-Jubb, of mixed Afro-American and Swedish descent, who was tragically killed on the 26 of August 1985 by patriarchal technology in a road accident at only 15 years of age in the south of France and to my kind and beautiful Swedish artist mother, Harriet Rosander, who "died" prematurely in her early fifties from poverty and a broken heart.

Monica Sjöö

To my mother, Mary Grace Carney, 1911–1948, and to Meridel LeSueur, 1900 to Infinity.

Barbara Mor

''Tell them as I dying live,
so they dying will live again.''

—The Moon, speaking through a
tortoise to the African Bushmen

''As the moon dieth and cometh to life again,
so we also having to die, will live again.''

—California Indian prayer

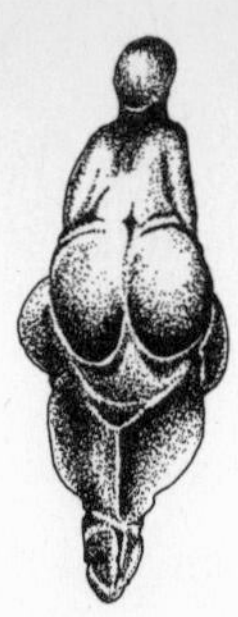

CONTENTS

III. Women's Culture and Religion in Neolithic Times 87

IV. Patriarchal Culture and Religion 229

PREFACE: WHEEL LIFE

This book is a wheel (she began). It begins and ends with the word *beginning*. Like a year, it has 4 parts, 52 chapters (4 seasons, 52 weeks: 13 lunations), though not symmetric. A She-Wheel, it unrolls Her Story: a description of the female journey through our human time on earth. Gyro-cycles of great myth and small data, poetry and numbers, dream and invention. Ice and fire: Cro-Magnon caves and Inquisitional burnings. Night and day: Her silent presence and His noisy history. And this new edition appears now in 1991: 9, the magic number of Muses, Crones, and that first mytho↔(menstrual)↔mathematically observed wheel: the Moon. *One,* which we are, and must become. Wheels within wheels within wheels: cellular, personal, local, global, cosmic: and begin again.

This is not planned; it just happens. As the world turns, as witches spin. As what disappears in the telescope reappears in the microscope; and vice versa. It seems to be organic.

I ride a bicycle: a 3-speed Schwinn (green, with food-gathering baskets), solidly built but in need of total overhaul. For 15 years, it has been my sole transportation (besides feet), and my Irish mood. (A wheel is a vehicle, a mood, a mode of direction.) My bike wheels are not precisely round: warped rims, threadbare tires, badly braked, punctured seasonally by goatheads and broken glass. Asymmetric, bumpy: my ride through life wobbles. But it moves, it works. It renews itself (strange oroboros wheels) stubbornly, to get the job done. The revolving bumps underline the rhythmic weirdness of the weather I must roll through, planetary and personal.

The earth too has its wobble.

As in winter. In the huge wobble of the Ice Age, humanity evolved itself. So most of this book's work was done in unlikely winter. It was December 1976 when *WomanSpirit* magazine, for whom I read poetry, sent me Monica's pamphlet, mimeographed earlier that year in England. I lived on welfare in northern New Mexico, with my son and daughter. Weekly, I biked 25–50 miles round trip to Taos (through wind, sage, dust, mud, lightning, snow) for food, supplies, and mail. Our adobe house, on a Spanish farm, was heated by piñon wood in an old cast iron kitchen stove; I wrote at a wheel table (a wooden spool once used to wind electric cable). Working through winter, I doubled Monica's 100 pages; rewrote, restructured, added new material, sections, and titles. *WomanSpirit* could not print this enlargement. Four years later, in 1981, it was published by Rainbow Press in Norway (distributed in America by *WomanSpirit*). True to its winter nature: this book lay long dormant, but vital, under snow.

Winter again, 1984. Monica had made contact with a Harper & Row editor at the 1984 International Women's Book Fair in London. With this go-signal, I began writing the present book. Still in Taos, still on a bicycle; but the gears of welfare existence were grinding harder. Rent, food, utilities had doubled; but benefits (under Reagan) were frozen. So were we. Taos is 7,000 feet in the Southern Rockies, with ground snow through winter; temperatures of −30°F on the deepest nights. I could afford to burn wood only 2–3 hours each evening; in daytime, the kitchen thermometer read 38–40°, from December through March. Through these months, I wrote 8 hours daily, sometimes wearing a down jacket; but the bulk impeded typing. Using material and notes from earlier writing and workshops I'd done in San Diego (on women's religion, witchcraft, global politics), I expanded the 80 printed pages of the Rainbow Press Edition into the present book. Nightly, we huddled together (2 daughters and I) in sleeping bags on the living room floor, sandwiched by blankets, dogs, and cats. Ancient creatures in our cave. Bedrooms were cold storage; from the window of my youngest daughter's room a foot-long icicle, 4 inches wide, crawled *inside* and down the wall. Our personal, microcosmic glaciation. It didn't begin to melt until mid-March. So be it.

Winter is the time of our content.

(In the Mule Mountains of southern Arizona, winter 1985, there was much cold, occult work to be done on the manuscript before it could be printed: text corrections and documentation, footnotes, bibliography, permissions, illustration selection and placement. I worked at the wheel table; 5,500 feet, no heat. The next winter, 1986, I proofed the galleys twice, sitting at a big table in a dark kitchen in a downtown barrio: a house of Tlazolteotl, Mexican Witch Goddess. Still no heat, no hot water. But by then I was in Tucson, where even winter is warm.)

A wheel is also a torture instrument, where witches were bound for punishment.

With my half of the advance, I left welfare. Publication was then delayed a year, until May 1987, to complete the manuscript and production work. Then, the first year of royalties was in the minus column, until the advance and authors' share of publication costs were repaid. Meanwhile, I had no money. My daughters went to live with their brother and his wife in Albuquerque; into their basement storage went my belongings: bike, books, notes, typewriter.

And I became a Bag Lady on the streets of Tucson. For 13 months, off and on, I was one of those statistics: no job, no income, no home. All the heat I'd not had during the icy months of writing curved around to hit me in the face. Intense 100°+ *calor* of a desert city's brick-oven streets, from May through October. Windless; or the wind blew relentlessly electric, like a laundromat of open driers. I was on foot (age 51). I carried a big purple drawstring bag, full of my life (not much). Parked cars, boarded-up houses, barrio porches and backyards; garages used as shooting galleries; booths of 24-hour restaurants: this is where I slept. Nighttime helicopter surveillance and police raids entered my real dream. Also: solicitations for sex, threats of beatings and death, abandonment to nocturnal streets or the militant mercies of charity shelters. Days, I hung out in parks, plazas, courthouses, libraries. City fountains were multiple: to bathe, wash clothes, cool off; then you collect the coins. In air-conditioned oases (Burger King, Carl's Jr.), 59¢ bought endless coffee refills, and free newspapers, i.e., "culture." Public restrooms I also used for laundry and personal hygiene. I underwent malnutrition, began menopause, learned survival from my street partner: on the litmus paper of my own flesh, I kept notes of my experience.

In my bag, I carried a 9-page resume, 20 odd years of feminist and literary activity (including this just-published book). I applied for editorial work at the University of Arizona Press, university library work, an open seat on the Tucson Women's Commission. No one could use me; except a bankrupting downtown motel (later closed by the city). Homeless people were channeled there by charity agencies to do maidwork and maintenance. We labored 10 hours daily, 6 days a week: struggled up and down in one defective elevator (4 floors), lugging one semi-functioning vacuum cleaner; running out of everything else. Our laundryroom floor, strewn with dirty sheets and towels, kept flooding with backflow from the pool. (The young manager, son of the owner, quietly partied in a 4th floor suite; cleaning it, I observed he was reading Donald Trump's *The Art of the Deal.*) When my first paycheck bounced, I quit.

For my fall into the street, I had no explanatory Bad Habits (except Poetry) to win sympathy from social agencies. I don't drink, smoke, use dope, seem officially crazy or criminal. Simply: I wrote a good book, left welfare, and hit the skids.

I.e., this wheel is surreal.

And it continues turning.

My personal events are tiny wobbles amidst huge cyclings. Global wheels revolve: vast, familiar changes. Modes of world control shift, back and forth, from Terror to Seduction. Icy political walls fall; hot markets erupt. War Gods retract oiled missiles; Money Gods open shopping malls.

Overnight, they reverse: peace is bulldozed for a new battlezone. Universal freedom to Buy (they say) means individual freedom to Be. Then the money disappears; chaos/tyranny extinct all rights, needs, dreams beyond a price tag. Or a gun. Inside these manufactured wheels, final gears grind: earth depletion, pollution, trash. Our planet of biologic forms venally redefined as functions of a thing-producing machinery. Forests, elephants, ozone: disappearing. Healthy soil, air, water: all depleting. Human place and integrity are endangered species (they won't appear again on this wheel).

For women, counter-spin. Markets are freed, businesses deregulated; but state and technological control over reproduction increases. Female bodies are used lavishly to sell goods; we still don't own our own wombs. We "freely" enter careers; and are beaten, raped, killed just as freely. "Successful" women proliferate; so do the numbers of malnourished, poor, sick, and homeless women (and our planet's children).

A wheel is direction's energy (also a steering device, a will). Among circling and exploding stars: how do we dare to live? I look in my cracked mirror. Personal↔political↔cosmic. With *The Great Cosmic Mother* I've made a journey of creative female endurance. The book, readers say, gives us back our HerStory. Women's creation of human culture, our epic struggle to imaginatively survive and transform the world to which we gave birth: *our collective story* amazes, enrages, energizes us. Individual lives are illumined and empowered by it. Women, and men, are returned to themselves. My small *epos,* the book's writing and after, underscores (I hope) this theme. Female spirit, the goddess in us, is not fragile or new; not an invention of privileged women or an escapist New Age elite. We are tough and ancient: tried by a million years of ice and fire. On enormous and minute wheels of pain and beauty we have turned. The spinning wills of witches transmute our experience into worlds: dream into real, need into art, difficult fact into daily vision. Skilled in memory, muscled by quantum leaps, we return to tell and respell our story. Sometimes, uphill; against odds and harsh winds: my metaphoric saga is Everywoman's. Knowledge of our truly *revolutionary* past can resolve our present dilemmas. Daughters of earth, all this whirling past is in us, of us. We are powered by experience. Now we can create and consecrate our globe's next turn: the magic future.

Nothing is easy. Work we thought done, must be redone. Generations of richly cynical young people need our cronish views and mythic tools. Communal action is a large wheel. Within it, each personal will must passionately spin: to face hardship, anonymous conditions; to forego (disbelieve!) apparent access/success; to defiantly redefine and redo the real work. Sacred/practical retrieval of the female/earth: a transfusion of our spiritual reality into the body politic/economic: *is not easy*. My experience is revelatory. I could change god's sex; I couldn't pay my rent. I could rewrite HisStory; I can't afford to eat. I survive; but with a grimmer face. (A stronger, more ancient face.)

Our stubborn struggle, too, is organic.

Earth, alone among known planets, wills life repeatedly from her own winter. Travels (tough Bag Lady) through conscious nights and days of her own orbit: bombarded by meteors, doubts, the terrific noise of time and human traffic. (She is solitary, and 5 billion years old!)

All of us, together. Each of us, brief and alone. Travel with her. Her survival story is ours.

This wheel is a book. She began (again). Let it roll.

Barbara Mor
October 1990

INTRODUCTION

The Great Mother in Her many aspects—maiden, raging warrior, benevolent mother, death-dealing and all-wise crone, unknowable and ultimate wyrd—is now powerfully reemerging and rising again in human consciousness as we approach the twenty-first century. Isis, Mawu-Lisa, Demeter, Gaia, Shakti, Dakinis, Shekhinah, Astarte, Ishtar, Rhea, Freya, Nerthus, Brigid, Danu—call Her what you may—has been with us from the beginning and awaits us now. She is the beauty of the green earth, the life-giving waters, the consuming fire, the radiant moon, and the fiery sun. She is Star Goddess and Spiderwoman; she weaves the luminous web that creates the universe. As earth, the great planetary Spirit-Being, She germinates life within Her dark womb.

After thousands of years of life-denying and anti-evolutionary patriarchal cultures that have raped, ravaged, and polluted the earth, She returns. The earth's immune system is breaking down and so is ours. Her soil, atmosphere, plant life, trees, and animal worlds are exhausted beyond endurance. All beings are suffering and can take no more.

Based in matricide, the death of all nature, and the utter exploitation of women, Western culture has now run itself into the ground, and there is no other way but to return to the Mother who gives us life. If we are to survive we have to attune yet again to the spirits of nature, and we must learn to "hear" the voices of the ancestors who speak to us from their Otherworld realms.

There is a growing feminization of poverty worldwide, especially in the Third World (more truly of the First World), where women's livelihoods and lands are being taken from them—much thanks to Western/U.S. imperialism and so called "development" schemes that exclude women. In the Western world, the assault on women's last remnants of autonomous powers, the destruction of our ancient knowledge of healing and of magical technology that enhanced our psychic powers as well as the fertility of the land, came about with the "witch hunts" that lasted more than three hundred years. In Europe, it has taken women until now to even dare to think our own thoughts and to articulate them, to dream our own dreams. We are the wise women returning at this dangerous hour because women worldwide are and always were the guardians of the living earth, as are all the surviving native tribal shamanistic peoples who still commune with the spirits.

I was involved with the anarchist and anti–Vietnam War movements in Sweden in the 1960s. I've also been active in the women's movement in Britain since the beginning. My political activism always grew out of my spiritual understandings of the earth as the living Mother because the Goddess is injured wherever there is injustice, wanton cruelty, poverty, and pollution. Of course, the Goddess is not just benevolent and fertile, She is also death-dealing and the destroyer. But these are natural forces, neither good nor bad, in the impersonal universal dance. But what I am speaking of here is the destruction brought about by the selfish and despotic patriarchs, male brotherhoods, who hate organic life in itself and desire to become disembodied, thereby returning to an abstract and impossible "Father" who desires sterile death with no rebirth for us all.

I do not believe that it is biologically given in men to be violent and destructive. There would never have been peaceful maternal cultures, such as we explore in this book, if this were so.

I am primarily an artist, a creator of visionary images, who also felt an urgent need to communicate through writing. The reason I originally wrote the first pamphlet about the ancient Goddess in 1975, titled *The Ancient Religion of the Great Cosmic Mother of All* and run off on stencils, was because I needed to clarify to myself and to others where my images came from.

By then I had created many Goddess paintings. My early images had a strange, archaic quality about them, as if they came from another time and space. At the time, I felt utterly alone in my work and in what I was attempting to express. *God Giving Birth* (1968) is a sacred painting in which I wanted to holistically express my growing religious belief in the Great Mother as *the* cosmic spirit and generative force in the universe. To my utter amazement, it nearly brought me to court over the years for "obscenity" and "blasphemy." The inspiration for the painting was the natural homebirth of my second son in 1961, now twenty-nine years ago, which felt to me like a first initiation to the Greater Mother and opened me to Her in visions and dreams.

I always experience my art as what can only be described as a shamanic process—entering into a state of being or mind where knowledge is available from past, present, and future.

This way of "knowing" belongs to the Lunar Mother who is both dark and light—She, of the dark nights and inner radiant light like that of the Moon, who gives us dreams and illuminations. No surprise perhaps that many of my images appear to be moonlit and that I have been sorely tested by the Dark/Light Mother who has taken back to Herself two of my beloved sons.

My youngest son (part Afro-American and Swedish) was run down and killed in front of my eyes in the Basque country in the south of France. My oldest son died from lymphoma cancer in July of 1987. And my new journey began through grief and numbing pain, truly a darkness of my soul during which I didn't want to live and, at times, hated everything alive. I have come through this still loving this beautiful earth, our Mother.

I have now returned to painting and writing, exhibiting and traveling. It gave me hope to watch the courage and the loving energy my oldest son radiated before his death in spite of his pain and illness. My sons communicate with me in dreams.

I have exhibited with other Goddess artists in Britain, Germany, and Scandinavia. Most recently, I took part in two exhibitions: "The Goddess Reemerging" in Glastonbury, September 1989, and with Chris Castle in "Stones and the Goddess" in Berkeley, May 1990. Everywhere I have traveled, I have also given slideshow talks about my art and life, ancient cultures, the Goddess, and Her sacred sites.

I live in Bristol, a city in the southwest of England, not far from Glastonbury and Avebury—ancient sacred places of the Neolithic Mother. Glastonbury Tor, or the Isle of Avalon, is a three-dimensional labyrinth with an indwelling Goddess. With Blood Well/Chalice Well in its "skirts," it's in an Otherworld place of death and magical rebirth. Silbury mound, the pregnant womb of the earth, along with the Avebury Stone Circle and West Kennet long barrow, abode of the Dark Mother, is *the* most sacred and magically powerful Goddess site in the Northern hemisphere. It was here that I had a transformative experience in an altered state in 1978 that utterly changed my life and work. It was on Silbury that for the first time I truly knew that the earth is Her living body. I also felt Her grief and pain, Her great love and rage. It was this experience that tore me apart. It also gave me joy, and I had to leave the city. I went to live in Pembrokeshire in the ancient Welsh countryside where there are so many remains of the Neolithic and Celtic past . . . so many holy wells, standing stones, and sacred trees. Here I learned to grow a garden, to live with the seasons, to follow the Moon in Her changes.

I have journeyed like a pilgrim in the British Isles, in Ireland, and in the Scottish Highlands and islands to many of the so numerous sacred sites. I have followed the trails of the Celts back to their sacred places in Germany and have visited Carnac in Bretagne. I have had powerful experiences at New Grange in the Boyne Valley in Ireland and at Callanish stone circle on Lewis in the outer Hebrides. The stone circles, wells, and mounds are trance-inducing places, window areas into other realities, where the voices of the ancestors, the blessed dead, the Shining Ones, or the Fairies speak to us in visions, dreams giving healing and prophesy from the magical Otherworld realms of the Mother.

The Great Cosmic Mother is a central part of this reemergence of the Mother and of another and far more ancient consciousness/intelligence. We are pioneers in this great movement—along with many other writers, artists, poets, and thinkers—that will have to succeed or we will die.

I want to make it clear that Barbara Mor is the book's main author. The reason for this is that when the time came to rework and extend our original work, my youngest son had just been killed, and I had moved back to Bristol to live with my other son, who was suffering from cancer. I was unable to work on the book. At that point, I even feared it.

Barbara Mor—poet, scholar, and word magician—had to spend months writing, researching, and vastly extending this book from our earlier and more collaborative *The Ancient Religion of the Great Cosmic Mother of All,* published in 1981 by Rainbow Press in Norway. That version in its turn was worked out by both of us over several years from the original pamphlet that had been written and conceived by me in 1975. Our book has indeed been a very long labor of love and has gone through many transformations along the way.

I want to thank Jean and Ruth Mountaingrove of the former Oregon *WomanSpirit* Journal, who brought me and Barbara Mor together originally, for the support they gave. They also distributed the Rainbow Press version of the book in the United States.

I also want to thank Jan Vindheim of Rainbow Press in Trondheim for having had the vision and courage to publish our book in English. Being a small alternative publisher without a great international distribution network, this was indeed a gamble. I also want to thank Gisela Ottmer and Rosemarie Merkel from Braunschweig in Germany, who were inspired by the "WomanMagic, Celebrating the Goddess Within Us" collective exhibition that I was traveling with in Europe during the early 1980's and took it upon themselves to translate and publish our book in German. *Wiederkehr der Göttin* (Return of the Goddess) was published in 1985 by their new Labyrinth Press.

Blessed Be,
Monica Sjöö
July 1990

I

WOMEN'S EARLY CULTURE: BEGINNINGS

Women's Mysteries, Sjöö, 1971

THE FIRST SEX: "IN THE BEGINNING, WE WERE ALL CREATED FEMALE"

In the beginning . . . was a very female sea. For two-and-a-half billion years on earth, all life-forms floated in the womb-like environment of the planetary ocean—nourished and protected by its fluid chemicals, rocked by the lunar-tidal rhythms. Charles Darwin believed the menstrual cycle originated here, organically echoing the moon-pulse of the sea. And, because this longest period of life's time on earth was dominated by marine forms reproducing parthenogenetically, he concluded that the female principle was primordial. In the beginning, life did not gestate within the body of any creature, but within the ocean womb containing all organic life. There were no specialized sex organs; rather, a generalized female existence reproduced itself within the female body of the sea.[1]

Before more complex life forms could develop and move onto land, it was necessary to miniaturize the oceanic environment, to reproduce it on a small and mobile scale. Soft, moist eggs deposited on dry ground and exposed to air would die; life could not move beyond the water-hugging amphibian stage. In the course of evolution, the ocean—the protective and nourishing space, the amniotic fluids, even the lunar-tidal rhythm—was transferred into the individual female body. And the penis, a mechanical device for land reproduction, evolved.

The penis first appeared in the Age of Reptiles, about 200 million years ago. Our archetypal association of the snake with the phallus contains, no doubt, this genetic memory.

This is a fundamental and recurring pattern in nature: Life is a female environment in which the male appears, often periodically, and created by the female, to perform highly specialized tasks related to species reproduction and a more complex evolution. *Daphnia,* a freshwater crustacean, reproduces several generations of females by parthenogenesis; the egg and its own polar body mate to form a complete set of genes for a female offspring. Once annually, at the end of the year's cycle, a short-lived male group is produced; the males specialize in manufacturing leathery egg cases able to survive the winter. Among honeybees the drone group is produced and regulated by the sterile daughter workers and the fertile queen. Drones exist to mate with the queen. An average of seven drones per hive accomplish this act each season, and then the entire male group is destroyed by the workers. Among whiptail lizards in the American Southwest, four species are parthenogenetic; males are unknown among the desert grassland, plateau, and Chihuahua whiptails, and have been found only rarely among the checkered whiptails.

Among mammals, even among humans, parthenogenesis is not technically impossible. Every female egg contains a polar body with a complete set of chromosomes; the polar body and the egg, if united, could form a daughter embryo. In fact, ovarian cysts are unfertilized eggs that have joined with their polar bodies, been implanted in the ovarian wall, and started to develop there.

This is not to say that males are an unnecessary sex. Parthenogenesis is a cloning process. Sexual reproduction, which enhances the variety and health of the gene pool, is necessary for the kind of complex evolution that has produced the human species. The point being made here is simply that, when it comes to the two sexes, one of us has been around a lot longer than the other.

In *The Nature and Evolution of Female Sexuality,* Mary Jane Sherfey, M.D., described her discovery in 1961 of something called the inductor theory. The inductor theory stated that "All mammalian embryos, male and female, are anatomically female during the early stages of fetal life."[2] Sherfey wondered why this theory had been buried in the medical literature since 1951, completely ignored by the profession. The men who made this herstory-making discovery simply didn't want it to be true.

Sherfey pioneered the discussion of the inductor theory; and now, with modifications based on further data, its findings are accepted as facts of mammalian—including human—development. As Stephen Jay Gould describes it, the embryo in its first eight weeks is an "indifferent" creature, with bisexual potential. In the eighth week, if a Y-chromosome-bearing sperm fuses with the egg, the gonads will develop into testes, which secrete androgen, which in turn induces male genitalia to develop. In the absence of androgen, the embryo develops into a female. There is a difference in the development of the internal and external genitalia, however. For the internal genitalia—the fallopian tubes and ovaries, or the sperm-carrying ducts—"the early embryo contains precursors of both sexes." In the presence or absence of androgen, as one set develops the other degenerates. With the external genitalia, "the different organs of male and female develop along diverging lines from the *same* precursor." This means, in effect, that the clitoris and the penis are the same organ, formed from the same tissue. The labia majora and the scrotum are one, indistinguishable in the early embryonic stages; in the presence of androgen "the two lips simply grow longer, fold over and fuse along the midline, forming the scrotal sac."

Gould concludes: "The female course of development is, in a sense, biologically intrinsic to all mammals. It is the pattern that unfolds in the absence of any hormonal influence. The male route is a modification induced by secretion of androgens from the developing testes."[3]

The vulnerability of the male newcomer within the female environment is well known. Vaginal secretions are more destructive to the Y-bearing sperm. The mortality rate is higher among neonate and infant males. Within the womb the male fetus, for the first two months, is protected by being virtually indistinguishable from a female. After that, it must produce large amounts of the masculinizing hormone in order to define itself as male, to achieve and to maintain its sexual identity. For all we know the Near Eastern myths upon which our Western mythologies are built, those which portray the young god or hero battling against a female dragon, have some analog here, *in utero*, where the male fetus wages a kind of chemical war against rebecoming female.

For now, it is enough to say that "maleness" among mammals is not a primary state, but differentiates from the original female biochemistry and anatomy. The original libido of warm-blooded animals is female, and the male—or maleness—is a derivation from this primary female pattern. Why, then, did the medical men, the scientists, take longer to figure out this basic biological fact than it took them to split the atom? And why, once this fact was noted, did they turn around and bury it in professional silence for ten years, until a woman dug it up again? Why indeed.

For about two thousand years of Western history, female sexuality was denied; when it could not be denied it was condemned as evil. The female was seen as divinely designed to be a passive vessel, serving reproductive purposes only. In one not-too-ancient dictionary, "clitoris" was defined as a "rudimentary organ," while "masculinity" equalled "the Cosmic generative force" . . . ! With Freud, female sexuality was not so much "rediscovered" as pathologized. Freud dismissed the clitoris as an undeveloped masculine organ and defined original libido as male. Clitoral eroticism was reduced to a perverse neurosis. Even after Masters's and Johnson's laboratory studies were published in *Human Sexual Response* in 1966, their findings were not integrated into psychoanalytical theory. In Mary Jane Sherfey's research during that period, she found not one work of comparative anatomy that described—or even mentioned—the deeper-lying clitoral structures; yet every other structure of the human body was described in living detail. Even today, with our relative sophistication of 1987, we are frequently whistled at by magazine headlines that promise breathless articles announcing the discovery of a new "spot"—a G-spot, an X-spot—located within the vagina. Within all these new "spots" exists the old wistful desire to deny the existence of the clitoris as a trigger-organ of female orgasm.

Why? There is the generalized, traditional fear of female sexuality. Further, there is discomfort with the similarity, with the common origin, of the female clitoris and the male penis. Women are used to hearing the clitoris described as an "undeveloped penis"; men are not used to thinking of the penis as an overdeveloped clitoris. Finally, and most seriously, there is a profound psychological and *institutional* reluctance to face the repercussions of the fact that the female clitoris is the only organ in the human body whose purpose is exclusively that of erotic stimulation and release. What does this mean? It means that for the human female, alone among all earth's life-forms, sexuality and reproduction are not inseparable. It is the male penis, carrier of both semen and sexual response, that is simultaneously procreative and erotic. If we wanted to reduce one of the sexes to a purely reproductive function, on the basis of its anatomy (we don't), it would be the male sex that qualified for such a reduction, not the female. Not the human female.

But these are only biological facts. These are only biological realities. As we know, facts and realities can be, and are, systematically ignored in the service of established ideologies. Throughout the world today virtually all religious, cultural, economic, and political institutions stand, where they were built centuries ago, on the solid foundation of an erroneous concept. A concept that assumes the psychic passivity, the creative inferiority, and the sexual secondariness of women. This enshrined concept states that men exist to create the human world, while women exist to reproduce humans. Period. If we argue that data exists—not solely biological, but archaeological, mythological, anthropological, and historical data—which refutes the universality of this erroneous concept, we are told to shut up; because something called "God" supports the erroneous concept, and that's all that matters. That's the final word.

Throughout the world, throughout what *we* know of history, something called "God" has been used to support the denial, the condemnation, and the mutilation of female sexuality. Of the female sex, ourselves. Today, in parts of Africa—predominantly among African Muslims, but also among African Christians and Jews, and some tribal beliefs—young girls are still subjected to clitoridectomy. This surgery, often performed by older women with broken glass or knives, excises the clitoris, severing the nerves of orgasm; the operation is intended to force the girl to concentrate on her vagina as a reproductive vessel. Infibulation, a more thorough operation, removes the labia minora and much of the labia majora; the girl is then closed up with thorns or required to lie with her legs tied together until her entire vaginal orifice is fused shut, with a straw inserted to allow passage of urine and menstrual blood. On the wedding night the young woman is slit open by a midwife or her husband; further cutting and reclosing is performed before and after childbirth. Complications from these surgeries are numerous, including death from infection, hemorrhage, inability to urinate, scar tissue preventing dilation during labor, painful coitus, and infertility due to chronic pelvic infection. In 1976 an estimated 10 million women were involved with this operation.[4] And something called "God" justified it; a "God" who supposedly created young girls as filthy sex maniacs who must then be mutilated to turn them into docile breeders.

The word "infibulation" comes from the Latin *fibula,* meaning a "clasp." Those civilized Romans, great highway builders, also invented the technology of fastening metal clasps through the prepuces of young girls to enforce chastity. This practice was copied by Christian crusaders during the early Middle Ages in Europe; they locked up their wives and daughters in metal "chastity belts" and then took the keys with them while they were gone—often for many years—fighting for "God" in the Near East.

And, lest through hypocrisy and racism we dismiss these practices as merely "barbaric" or "ancient," we must recall that clitoridectomies were performed in the last century on young girls and women in both Europe and America. This surgery, very popular with nineteenth-century Victorians, was inflicted on any female considered to be "oversexed," or as a punishment for masturbation, or as a cure for "madness." These determinations were all made by male relatives, male physicians, and male clerics, and the women involved had no legal say in the matter.

These are extreme examples of the repression and mutilation of female sexuality, always sanctioned, however remotely and dishonestly, by something called "God." All the other repressions and mutilations—of the body, of the mind, of the soul, of our experienced female selves—are so well known and documented that they need no numeration at this point; we can all make our own lists. The point is this: Wherever repression of female sexuality, and of the female sex, exists—and, at the present writing, this is everywhere on earth—we find the same underlying assumptions. These are ontological assumptions—assumptions made at the very root of things, about the nature of life itself. They are (1) that the world was created by a male deity figure, or God; (2) that existing world orders, or cultures, were made by and for men, with God's sanction; (3) that females are an auxiliary sex, who exist to serve and populate these male world orders; (4) that autonomous female sexuality poses a wild and lethal threat to these world orders, and therefore must be controlled and repressed; and finally (5) that God's existence as a male sanctions this repression. The perfect circularity, or tautology, of these assumptions only helps to bind them more securely around the human psyche. That they are as erroneous as they are universal seems to pose no problem to their upholders. After all, wherever we go on earth, every intact institution—religious, legal, governmental, economic, military, communications, and customs—is built on the solid slab of these assumptions. And that's a pretty entrenched error.

In the post-World War II United States—as well as in Europe and most of the world generally—we've gone through a secularizing period in which some of these assumptions have been loosened up, and even been made to crumble, under questioning. But now the backlash is upon us. Today, spokespeople for various fundamentalist religious beliefs use modern media to broadcast a very old idea: that female sexuality—i.e., feminists, and feminist demands for abortion, contraception, reproductive autonomy, childcare, equal pay, psychological integrity—constitutes a threat to "our civilization"; and this amounts to a "blasphemy against God." Whores of Babylon, Darwin's Theory of Evolution, and the "menace of world communism" all somehow get subliminally mixed up in this feminist threat—for some very good historic and psychological reasons, which we will explore later. For now, it is enough to say that "God" and "civilization" are loaded concepts (loaded with dynamite!) that can always be brought in to end an argument that cannot otherwise be refuted. Or, for those who don't lean too heavily on "God," or who major in "civilization," you can always quote an anthropologist!

For, just as established religions assume the maleness of God, just as Freud and psychoanalysis assumed the maleness of libido, so have the social sciences—and in particular anthropology—assumed the generic maleness of human evolution. Both popular and academic anthropological writers have presented us with scenarios of human evolution that feature, almost exclusively, the adventures and inventions of man the hunter, man the toolmaker, man the territorial marker, and so forth. Woman is not comprehended as an evolutionary or evolutionizing creature. She is treated rather as an auxiliary to a male-dominated evolutionary process; she mothers him, she mates him, she cooks his dinner, she follows around after him picking up his loose rocks. *He evolves,* she follows; *he evolutionizes,* she adjusts. If the book jackets don't give us pictures of female *Homo sapiens* being dragged by the hair through 2 or 3 million years of he-man evolution, we are left to assume this was the situation.

This, despite the known fact that among contemporary and historic hunting-and-gathering people, as among our remote hunting-and-gathering ancestors, 75 percent to 80 percent of the group's subsistence comes from the women's food-gathering activities. This, despite the known fact that the oldest tools used by contemporary hunters and gatherers, and the oldest, most primal tools ever found in ancient sites, are women's digging sticks. This, despite worldwide legends that cite women as the first users and domesticators of fire. This, despite the known fact that women were the first potters, the first weavers, the first textile-dyers and hide-tanners, the first to gather and study medicinal plants—i.e., the first doctors—and on and on. Observing the linguistic interplay between mothers and infants, mothers and children, and among work-groups of women, it is easy to speculate on the female contribution to the origin and elaboration of language. That the first time measurements ever made, the first formal calendars, were women's lunar-markings on painted pebbles and carved sticks is also known. And it is thoroughly known that the only "God-image" ever painted on rock, carved in stone, or sculpted in clay, from the Upper Paleolithic to the Middle Neolithic—and that's roughly 30,000 years—was the image of a human female.

In 1948 *The Gate of Horn* was published in Britain; in 1963 it was published in America, retitled *Religious Conceptions of the Stone Age.* In this pioneering work, archaeologist and scholar G. Rachel Levy showed the unbroken continuity of religious images and ideas descending from the Cro-Magnon peoples of the Upper Paleolithic period in Ice Age Europe, through the Mesolithic and Neolithic developments in the Near East, and down to our own historical time. As Levy noted, these early people are lost to us in the mists of time; but their primal visions, images, and gestalts of human experience on this planet still resonate in our psyches, as well as in our historic religious-ontological symbols. These Early Stone Age people "bequeathed to all humanity a foundation of ideas upon which the mind could raise its structures."[5] And what were these primal human images and ideas? The cave as the female womb; the mother as a pregnant earth; the magical fertile female as the mother of all animals; the Venus of Laussel standing with the horn of the moon upraised in her hand; the cave as the female tomb where life is buried, painted blood red, and awaiting rebirth. Levy shows the continuity of these images and symbols through the Late Neolithic Near Eastern rites and mythologies, and their endurance 30,000 years later in "modern" religions. In Christianity, for example, with its central image of the birth of the sacred child, in a cave-like shelter, surrounded by magic animals; and, especially in Catholicism, the icon of the great mother who stands on the horned moon and awaits the rebirth of the world.

The evidence leaves no doubt that these images *were* at the origins of what we call human psychological and spiritual expression. Levy's book is a masterpiece; it received great praise upon both its British and American publications; and has since been virtually bypassed and ignored by the anthropological-archaeological-academic establishments. Why? Because her evidence is irrefutable. It shows with clarity—and in the solidity of stone and bone—that the first 30,000 years of *Homo sapiens'* existence was dominated by a celebration of the female processes: of the mysteries of menstruation, pregnancy, and childbirth; of the analogous abundance of the earth; of the seasonal movement of animals and the cycles of time in the Great Round of the Mother. *The Gate of Horn* is as close as we can come to reading the "sacred book" of our early human ancestors. And it confirms what too many people do not want to know: that the first "God" was female.

Since Levy wrote, the tendency has been to relegate these Old Stone Age and Neolithic images to the psychological realm—they've become "archetypes of the unconscious" and so forth, while anthropological writers proper, both academic and popular, continue to explain physical, real human development solely in terms of the experiences of the male body in hunting, aggression, and toolmaking. Thus the female images—which are there, and cannot be denied—are sideswiped, reduced to "the subjective," "the mythic realms"; and thus the first 30,000 years of our human history is denied to us, relegated to a "mind trip" or "psychological software." Even among feminists, in recent years, there has arisen doubt that these images and symbols might be anything but "mythology"—i.e., unrealities.

To approach our human past—and the female God—we need a wagon with at least two wheels: one is the mythical-historical-archaeological; the other is the biological-anthropological. A strong track has already been laid down for the mythical-historical-archaeological wheel; milestones along that track, along with G. Rachel Levy's great work, are J. J. Bachofen's *Myth, Religion and Mother-Right,* Robert Briffault's *The Mothers,* Helen Diner's *Mothers and Amazons,* Jessie Weston's *From Ritual to Romance,* Robert Graves's *The White Goddess,* O. G. S. Crawford's *The Eye Goddess,* Sibylle von Cles-Reden's *In the Realm of the Great Goddess,* Michael Dames's *Silbury Treasure* and *Avebury Cycle,* Marija Gimbutas's *The Goddesses and Gods of Old Europe*; and most recently Elizabeth G. Davis's *The First Sex;* Merlin Stone's *When God Was a Woman* and *Ancient Mirrors of Womanhood*; Phyllis Chesler's *Women and Madness* and *About Men*; Adrienne Rich's *Of Woman Born*; Mary Daly's *Beyond God the Father, Gyn-Ecology*, and *Pure Lust*; Susan Griffin's *Woman and Nature*; Anne Cameron's *Daughters of Copper Woman*—and many many more, including the richly useful *Women's Encyclopedia of Myths and Secrets* by Barbara G. Walker.

The other side of our wagon—the biological-anthropological side—has almost no wheel and no track; not because there is no important place to go in that direction, but because the physical-cultural anthropologists are off somewhere else, busily mapping the evolution of Tarzan. There is no body of anthropological work based on the evolution of female biology. With rare exceptions, there have been no attempts whatsoever to study the evolution of human physiology and cultural organization—from prehominid to "modern man"—from the perspective of the definitive changes undergone by the female in the process of that evolution. Popular books on this subject, by Lionel Tiger, Desmond Morris, *et al.*, are invariably male-oriented, treating the evolution of the female as sex object only, from monkey-in-heat to hot bunny. One delightful exception is Elaine Morgan's *The Descent of Woman*; during 12 million years of dry Pliocene, Morgan speculates, the female prehominid took to the oceans, surviving in the warm and food-filled coastal waters—and during this experience underwent a sea-change from knuckle-walking, rear-sex primate to upright human sexual body, to which the male primate responded by becoming man. Morgan argues convincingly that the human species survived the long Pliocene drought through the cooperation and social invention of the evolving hominid females in their adaptation to the sea; academic "experts" ignore this theory, but they have no other explanation for our Pliocene survival, for our successful evolution from ape to human during this difficult period, or for the many ways in which our human bodies resemble the bodies of sea mammals, rather than primates.

In *The Time Falling Bodies Take to Light,* historian William Irwin Thompson points out that early human evolution occurred in three critical stages: (1) *hominization,* in which our primate bodies became human, not only in walking upright and freeing the hands, but specifically in our sexual characteristics and functions; (2) *symbolization,* in which we began using speech, marking time, painting and sculpting images; and (3) *agriculturalization,* in which we domesticated seeds and began control of food production. And, as Thompson writes, all three stages were initiated and developed by the human female.[6] The symbol-making and agricultural stages have been studied, and the originating role of women in these stages is known; it is sexual hominization which, as yet, has barely been explored.

Why? Why indeed. Because sexual hominization is almost exclusively the story of the human female. The mechanics and anatomy of male sexuality, after all, haven't changed greatly since the primates made love. The revolution in human sexuality—the revolution that made us human—resulted from evolutionary changes that occurred in the female body. These changes were not primarily related to mammalian reproduction, but to human sexual relationship. No one knows the order in which they occurred, but taken together, as an evolved cluster of sexual characteristics, they constitute a truly radical sexual metamorphosis undergone by the human female:

- *Elimination of the estrus cycle, and development of the menstrual cycle,* meant that women were not periodically in heat, but capable of sexual activity at any time. Pregnancy could occur during a part of the cycle; but for most of the cycle sex could happen without necessarily resulting in pregnancy. Among all other animals, the estrus cycle determines that copulation always results in pregnancy, and has no other than a reproductive purpose.

- *Development of the clitoris and evolution of the vagina* meant a greatly enhanced sexuality and orgasmic potential in human females compared to all other animals.

- *The change from rear to frontal sex,* we can imagine, created an enormous change in relations between the sexes; frontal sex means a prolonged and enhanced lovemaking period, and what might be called the personalization of sex. The emotion-evoking role of face-to-face intercourse in the development of human self-consciousness has yet to be evaluated (she turned around and looked him in the eye: and there was light!)

- *Development of breasts* added to woman's potential for sexual arousal; further, combined with frontal sex, no doubt the female's maternal and social feelings were also now aroused by the *personal lover,* whose body was now analogous to the infant's body at her breast.

As Thompson points out, such radical changes in the female body alone were enough to trigger the hominization of the species. Human beings, with these changes, became the only creatures on earth for whom copulation occurs—can occur, anytime—for nonreproductive purposes.

Human sex thus became a multipurpose activity. It can happen for emotional bonding, for social bonding, for pleasure, for communication, for shelter and comfort, for personal release, for escape—as well as for reproduction of the species. And this is one of the original and major, determining differences between humans and all other animals, birds, reptiles, insects, fishes, worms . . . for whom copulation exists only and solely for species reproduction.

<u>The human race has been definitively shaped by the evolution/revolution of the female body into a capacity for nonreproductive sex.</u>

This is not just a physical fact. It is a cultural, religious, and political fact of primary significance.

Many feminists today are unsure whether studies of evolutionary biology, or of religious mythology, can have political relevance for contemporary women. We believe that nothing could be more politically relevant than knowing why we got where we are now, by seeing how we got here, and where we began.

In the beginning, the first environment for all new life was female: the physical/emotional/spiritual body of the mother, and the communal body of women—young girls, grown women, older women—working together. When hunting-and-gathering people move, the infant is carried bound close to the mother's body; when they settle, the women form an "inner circle" campsite of women and children. The socialization process begins here.

Human culture is marked by a strengthening and prolongation of the relation between mothers and offspring. For its first year the human child is virtually an "embryo" outside the womb, extremely vulnerable and totally dependent. Female group behavior—the cooperative care-sharing among mothers and children, older and younger women, in the tasks of daily life—emerges from the fact of this prolonged dependence of the human child on the human female for its survival. Males help—but they also leave; the male body comes and goes, but the female presence is constant. Females train, discipline, and protect the young; beyond infant care, the maintenance and leadership of the entire kin-group is the task of women. The female animal is always on the alert, for on her rests the responsibility not only of feeding the young, but of keeping the young from being food for others. She is the giver and also the sustainer of beginning life. Among humans, males help with protection and food acquisition; but it is the communal group of females that surrounds the child, in its first four to six years of life, with a strong physical, emotional, traditional, and linguistic presence. And this is the foundation of social life and human culture.

The popular image of early human society as being dominated—indeed created—by sexist male hunters and ferocious territorial head-bangers just doesn't hold water. If the first humans had depended solely on despotic and aggressive male leaders, or on several males in chronic, ritualistic contention for power—human society would never have developed. Human culture could never have been invented. The human presence on earth would never have evolved.

The fact is that it was from this first inner circle of women—the campsite, the fire-site, the cave, the first hearth, the first circle of birth—that human society evolved. As hominids evolved into Paleolithic *Homo sapiens,* and then into settled and complex Neolithic village people on the time-edge of "civilization," these tens of thousands of years of human culture were shaped and sustained by communities of creative, sexually and psychically active women—women who were inventors, producers, scientists, physicians, lawgivers, visionary shamans, artists. Women who were also the Mothers—receivers and transmitters of terrestrial and cosmic energy.

We have to understand how and why these ancient millennia of womancultures have been buried—ignored, denied, passed off as "mythology" or "primitive prehistoric origins"—by Western male historians who insist (and often really believe) that "real history" began *only about five thousand years ago*—with the relatively recent institutions of patriarchy.

MARX AND THE MATRIARCHY

Ancient woman-oriented groupings were the original communism. Friedrich Engels and Karl Marx recognized this. Engels especially refers to the Mother-right concepts of J. J. Bachofen,[1] and both men based their analyses of social development on the primary existence of ancient matriarchies—i.e., communal matrifocal systems.[2] In this they were influenced by the writings of Lewis Morgan, an American anthropologist. Morgan lived with and studied the tribal society of the Iroquois; in their kinship structure, language, and customs he found evidence of early communal and blood relationships based on different stages of group marriage. In *Ancient Society,* written in the 1880s, Morgan offered his conclusion that such a society was matrilinear, and matrifocal, of necessity, since within a group-marriage structure only the mother can be definitely known as the parent of a child.

We now know that similar evidence can be found all over the world; for example, many kinship systems distinguish between the biological father of a child and the social father, who is usually the mother's brother, or other male relative. The social father is considered the "real father" in these societies; identity and inheritance are passed along through the female bloodlines.

But, pioneers that they were, neither Morgan, Engels, nor Marx were fully aware of women's real functions and achievements in past cultures. Nor were they tuned in to the total gestalt of early peoples. With Marx and Engels—and in particular with their dogmatic interpreters and followers—a narrowing of focus to strictly economic and class analysis has totally obscured the original human state of being, which was more profoundly spiritual than economic. This Marxist narrowing of focus, and its consequent denial of human spiritual experience, has had tragic repercussions throughout the world.

How did this happen? Karl Marx (Engels as well) was a deeply compassionate man; his "opium of the people" statement, which is never fairly quoted, is evidence of this:

> Religious distress is at the same time the expression of real distress and the protest against real distress. Religion is the sigh of the oppressed creature, the heart of the heartless world, just as it is the spirit of a spiritless situation. It is the opium of the people. The demand to give up the illusions about its conditions is the demand to give up a condition that needs illusions. Criticism has plucked the imaginary flowers from the chain, not so that men will wear the chain without any fantasy or consolation, but so that they will break the chain and cull the living flower.[3]

No one has said it better, or more clearly recognized the human being's absolute *right* to cling to "spirit" in "a spiritless situation," and to "heart" in "a heartless world." Because spirit and heart *are real;* and they alone have helped millions of human beings survive in otherwise unsurvivable situations.

The tragedy of Marx—and of Marxists—was to confuse spirit with established religions. They saw clearly, and historically, that established religion aligned itself with the oppressor—the oppressing class, the oppressing monarchy, the oppressing social and economic systems. They saw the seeds of oppression in religious doctrines: doctrines that rationalized poverty and enslavement, and excused brutal tyranny and greed, by setting "God's seal" on social systems based on hierarchies of rich and poor, hierarchies of rulers and the ruled. They saw the wealth and power of the churches and the wretched passivity of the believers. They saw that "the church" was in fact a very manmade institution that gained and retained power by exploiting the reality of the spirit versus the reality of physical need; they heard sermons condemning "material wealth" and "earthly pleasures," while the churchmen and their rich supporters lived in opulent security, and the mass of believers lived on their stony knees, in rags. And they heard these conditions justified as "God's plan for man." They saw that religious establishments take it upon themselves to define "spirit" and "God" and "human destiny" always in their own elitist terms, and only to their own worldly advantage.

Seeing these things, Marxists rightly condemned the collusion of established religions in the historic oppression of human beings. Tragically, they also denied the reality of the human spirit and its genuine longings. They rightly wanted to save humanity from religious exploitation; but in their narrowing of focus, their economic and class reductiveness, they split the human being into two conflicting parts: material existence versus spiritual existence. This split was just the mirror-image of the already existing religious dualism. As dogmatic Marxist communism unfolded in country after country, this split reinforced the same "alienation" of the human condition that Marx had wanted to resolve. It has created the dreary "state capitalism" of Soviet Russia and its satellites, in which the state works, dourly and mechanically, to enforce its definition of human life as spiritless mechanism. It has given fuel to the propaganda engines of the reactionary systems in all countries, so that the world is ripped apart in a false dichotomy between "Godless communism" and "divine capitalism." For if communism is atheistic, its opponents can claim to be mandated by God, however phony this claim might be.

Finally, it has turned away untold millions of oppressed human beings who need the economic and social analysis of Marxism to clarify and change their situations, but who fear they are being asked to buy this analysis at the price of their living souls. No matter how corrupt and collusive the established religions of the world are known to be, they still stand there, offering themselves as the only sanctuaries of "spirit in a spiritless world." Marxism stands—unfortunately, in the perception of too many people—as a total, fanatical repudiation of spiritual reality. And this perception of Marxism has helped to fuel the equally fanatic revivals of fundamentalist religions throughout the world today.

Marx and Engels confused spirit with established religion—as their doctrinaire followers continue to do—because, as Western white males, they could not see the total paradigm of ancient women's original communism. Coming from this linear, fragmenting, and reductive Western tradition—which has historic roots in the Judeo-Christian Bible as well as in Aristotelian-Platonic, Greco-Roman hyper-rationality—they could not comprehend the primal holism of human experience on earth. As a result Marxism tends to reinforce, rather than oppose, Western capitalism's notorious strategy of alienation. Marxist analysts generally are obsessed with isolating economic/productive development from magical/religious/sexual development. As Paul Cardan, a "Libertarian" thinker, writes:

> There is the Marxist assumption that throughout history human societies have always aimed first and foremost to increase production and consumption. But the human being doesn't at birth bear within itself the finishing meaning of [her] his life. The maximization of consumption . . . or of power or of sanctity, are not tendencies inherent in the newborn child. It is the prevailing culture in which [she] he will be brought up which will teach [her] him that [she] he "needs" these things. . . . The cultivation of maize among the Mexican tribes, or the cultivation of rice in some Indonesian villages is not only a means of ensuring food. Agricultural labor is also lived as [Goddess and child] worship, as festival and as dance. And when some Marxist theoretician comes along and claims that on these occasions everything which is not directly productive labor is but mystification, illusion or "cunning of reason," it must be forcibly pointed out that he is himself a far more complete personification of patriarchy and capitalism than any mere boss could be. What he is saying is that everything that humans have done or sought to do in history was only crude prefigurations of the factory system.[4]

If the Marxist in this case was denouncing or trying to eliminate patriarchal religion, founded on privilege and property and mystification of reality, and functioning through the exploitation of human labor and human sexuality, that would be fine. But he is also denying what is the very truth of human existence, and the essence of the original matriarchies: the experienced unity of psychic/productive/sexual/cosmic power and activity in the egalitarian collective of women.

For this is precisely what patriarchy sets out to do: to split material production from spiritual experience, science from magic, medicine from herbal knowledge and psychic/seasonal environment, sexuality from the sacred, art from craft, astronomy from astrology, language from poetry—and to place the resultant "specialized," abstracted, and mechanistic knowledge in the hands of a privileged male elite organized into professions, hierarchies, and classes. To reduce the ecstatic dance of muscle, blood, and soul to factory assembly lines, production output schedules, and the gross national product.

Patriarchy divides life into higher and lower categories, labeled "spirit" versus "nature," or "mind" versus "matter"—and typically in this alienated symbolism, the superior "spirit/mind" is male (and/or white), while the inferior "nature/matter" is female (and/or black). This false dualistic symbolism arises from an enforced order of male domination. With the aid of such phallic psychology, men can then go about the earth raping nature, exploiting resources and human labor, manipulating and "improving" *her* with technological-mechanical inventions and "progressive goals." In patriarchy man separates from earth, emulating some aloof and disconnected Sky God of his own creation, and this intellectual separation makes him feel "free" to devastate the natural world without any sense that it belongs to a common ecosystem with himself. He exploits "it," totally alienated from the fact of his own continuity *with* "it." For the deluded profit of the few, and the existential pain of the many, patriarchy exists by destroying the original holism.

When it refutes or opposes the reality of human spiritual experience, Marxist communism does not resolve this destruction; it only compounds it, with a different rhetoric. It gets rid of "God" and "church" only to substitute another tyranny: that of "the state" or "the machine" or "the party" or "the production quota." It does not truly free human beings; it only changes the brand-name of the chains.[5]

A truly human politics must study the entire history of the world's religions and spiritual beliefs. It must try to return to, or move toward, spiritual systems that are harmonious with all our visions of creative communal life. Because this is what is missing under both of the competing "world powers": a creative communal life. Both systems—Western capitalism and Soviet communism—are based on the denial of communal celebration. For celebration is a play of the spirit, and there is no profit in communal existence. But human evolution, human creativity, is a real miracle, and a cosmic fact. We need a politics that participates in this biological-spiritual adventure. Neither the God of the Dollar nor the God of the State—nor any of the alienating patriarchal gods from which they descend—allow for this participation.

Wilhelm Reich is not commonly connected with Marxism, but this is where he began. His early work was an attempt to link the Marxist economic-class analysis with a psychoanalytical understanding of the significance of sexual repression in the development of Fascist patriarchal society. This attempt was mostly successful—and for it, he was excommunicated by both the European Communist Party and the Freudian psychoanalytical circles. I.e., he was on to something.

In *The Mass Psychology of Fascism* and other work in the 1930s, Reich chronicled the successful manipulation of the German people by Nazi ideology. On the deepest psychological and biological levels, he argued, the people had already been conditioned by generations of religious and culturally directed psychosexual repression to respond obediently and to cooperate unquestioningly with sadism, tyranny, and genocide. An anti-sexual religious morality, paranoid concepts of "blood purity," and a rigid sense of ethnic superiority had already "wired" the nervous system of the torturer and clenched the muscles inside the black gloves and boots. As Reich showed—predicted, in fact—a "hypnotic" leader like Hitler does not create these conditions; he only exploits them. Fascism is not a wild "barbaric" phenomenon that appears suddenly and without reason in the midst of "civilization." It is the result of a long conditioning process, and the institutions that do the conditioning are those of the "civilization" itself. One of Reich's major points was that Marxist communism, and European socialism generally, narrowed down to an "objective" focus on economic and class relationships, were unable to anticipate, analyze, or prevent the Nazi triumph, which was a massively subjective explosion of a pathologically conditioned people into brutal expression. Further, the syndrome of fascism was not confined to "the Germans." Fascist thought and behavior is not a national aberration but a historically ingrained feature of the psyche of all Western "civilized" people—a feature clearly visible in the history of Western colonialism and imperialism.

Reich's political point was this: At this point in history, changing the objective economic-social systems alone is not enough. Repressive behavior, sadistic power relations, competitive greed to exploit, dominate, and humiliate—and our accomodations to these insults—are by now conditioned into the nervous systems of each member of our "civilized" societies; both oppressors and victims are damaged by the experience. The repressive wiring of the nervous system occurs at the most intimate levels—of sex and of the spirit. The re-creation of the human being must occur on these levels also if we desire a truly human revolution—one that does more than just change the guard.

This point is of importance to feminists, who have already observed that sexist, dominating male behavior can occur along the entire political spectrum, from right to left. The repression, control, and exploitation of female sexuality is a major tool of patriarchy, because it goes hand in hand with the exploitation of female labor. Left-wing males who see no connection between labor exploitation and sexual exploitation have failed to make a total analysis—or, in Reich's terms, they have failed to undergo a total revolution; on the neuron level they are still wired for oppression.

Reich pointed out in the 1930s that the prevalent male sexual fantasy, in male-dominated society, is one of rape. And he knew that this was not a personal fantasy, but a political one—with political repercussions. He was very clear on how sexual repression of women has been the most powerful patriarchal weapon in creating social victims—females who have been weakened, made dependent, fearful, or ashamed of our own bodies and punished for their functions, sexual-psychological prey to any predator—such creatures are easy to exploit politically and economically; people who do not own their own sex cannot own their own labor. Unfortunately, Reich was a strict heterosexual, unsympathetic to homosexuality and too influenced by Freudian ideas of female sexuality; and these problems have been passed along to us at the expense of his gifts. Reich missed the connections between bisexuality and psychic wholeness; but in his comprehension of the profound and intentional links between sexual repression and political repression, he was always right on target.

Marx said, "Human power . . . is its own end."[6] Reich was devoted to the liberation and enjoyment of healthy human power as the only valid political goal. Biological energy—unrepressed and undistorted—he saw as a continuum of cosmic energy, with no nonorganic distinctions made between "the physical" and "the spiritual." He saw both as forms of one energy—he called it Orgone—manifest throughout the universe, the same in nerve cells as in stars and in human consciousness. This evolutionary energy surging through all life-forms, and as an energy field in space, he defined as a spiritual reality as well as a physical force; and he believed that politics included the realignment of the repressed human being with this original creative flow. I.e., Reich was no mechanistic ideologue, but a political mystic. Therefore he was banished from the Communist Party and psychoanalytical professional circles in Europe; he had to flee Nazi Germany; he ended up in the United States with his books destroyed by the federal government and his work outlawed; and he died in a federal prison. I.e., he was probably on to something.

Another problem area, among Marxists, is the assumption that matriarchal society, where it existed, occurred only at very low stages of production and under only "primitive" conditions. This assumption echoes the generalized linearity and chauvinism of Western history, which tends to see all "other" cultures—"other" in space or in time—as mere preliminary stages on the way toward "modern development," or as sadly failed attempts to achieve the freeway and the ball bearing.

In fact, the evidence shows that some of the most "advanced" societies of the ancient world—technologically as well as culturally advanced—were also matrifocal, i.e., woman-oriented and led by women. The early Cretans were worshipers of the Goddess, and Cretan women were priestesses, judges, doctors, artisans, athletes, business entrepreneurs—cultural leaders on all levels. Crete was the major cultural and trading center of its day, with ships traveling to Ireland, Spain, Africa, and the Near East for gold and tin; one of the things exported was the Cretan lineal script, whose syllabary was then passed on through the Greeks to the Phoenicians.[7] At home, the Cretans had indoor baths, with hot and cold water running through ceramic pipes; Cretan plumbing, in 1700 B.C., was far superior to anything achieved in Europe until well after A.D. 1700. The graceful and artistic Etruscans were also matriarchal, and so were the early Egyptians; traces of matriarchy existed in Egypt down through the later empires and dynasties.

In these cultures, as in many others, the family group lived on land that belonged collectively to the mothers. A woman's husband or lover lived with the woman and her kin-group; children, regardless of the father's identity or legal relation, lived with the mother's family group. Ancient Egyptian law clearly designated that all family property—land and household goods—belonged to the woman, and that she, married or unmarried, had total disposition of her own belongings, including herself. No one, studying the Cretans, Etruscans, or Egyptians, could refer to these cultures as "primitive." Very advanced cultures were also developed by the matriarchal Dahomey and Ashanti peoples of West Africa, and by the Naya people of Kerala in southern India. Among Native Americans, it is largely the matrifocality of the Pueblo people that has allowed them to endure so long in their old ways, with strong architectural technologies developed among them. The dwelling places of all these people—from portable grass huts to multistoried "apartment" buildings—were not simply maintained by women; women built them. Everywhere, homesite technology was originally seen as women's province.[8]

We are not saying that "matriarchy" was a system in which the women went around "ruling" everyone with a big stick. Matriarchies are not built on dominance principles, but on the facts of blood-kinship, including the primacy of the mother. Women owned their bodies, their children, and their living properties; women made vital decisions affecting the survival and well-being of their people. There was no way by which an elite group of men could set up laws to restrict women's movements, ideas, or sexual activities. Economic relations were not experienced as separate from religious and social relationships; they were originally based on gift exchange, which served a communal-bonding function, not a competitive or profit-making one. Material goods had value only in terms of the social or spiritual uses to which they were put.

If Marxists tend to underrate ancient matrifocal cultures as "primitive" or "underdeveloped," this is only because Marxists share Western prejudices about "development"; they are assuming that all cultures, ancient and modern, are to be judged according to how close they come to approximating the industrial factory system, with its quantitative production—regardless of the life-quality of the cultures being evaluated. In this prejudice, Marxists and stock-market men seem to share equally.

Women of the Third World,
Sjöö, 1967

THE ORIGINAL BLACK MOTHER

It is possible that the religious ideas of ancient Crete and Egypt originated in black Africa. During 7000 to 6000 B.C., the Sahara was a rich and fertile land, and a great civilization flourished there. Images of the Horned Goddess (who became Isis of Egypt) have been found in caves on a now-inaccessible plateau in the center of what is now the Sahara desert. When the earlier fertile land dried out, probably as a result of climatic change, the people spread out from this center, and wherever they settled they brought with them the religion of the Black Goddess, the Great Mother of Africa.

Great importance has always been given to the Queen-Mother across the continent of Africa. The original Black Goddess was regarded as bisexual, the instrument of her own fertility; she was the ancient "witch" who carried a snake in her belly. Africans worshiped her many manifestations. The creator of the gods of Dahomey, for example, was Mawu-Lisa, imaged as a serpent; Mawu-Lisa was both female and male, self-fertilizing, seen as the earth and the rainbow. Africans believed that the earth is ultimately more powerful than the sky and its gods; the sky can withhold rain, but earth is the source of the life force itself. The Gaia hypothesis of modern environmental science confirms this ancient concept: The sky, with all its dramatic life-giving movement, is in fact created by the earth—the envelope of air and moisture surrounding us is really the earth's "breathing." As in the ancient African beliefs, the sky gods are creations of the Mother Earth; she breathes them out, and can breathe them back in again.

Great work needs to be done in the study of indigenous African mythologies and religious beliefs, especially in linking these with the development of other world religions. For just as physical humankind probably began in Africa, so no doubt did our concepts and images of the sacred originate there. One black historian who has investigated the African origins of Egyptian, Mediterranean, and Near Eastern religions—including Christianity—is John G. Jackson; though his 1972 work on African origins of world culture is titled *Man, God and Civilization,* Jackson fully acknowledges the matriarchal origins and influences of African society. He quotes Lewis H. Morgan, Sir James G. Frazer, and Robert Briffault and points out that their investigations of early group marriage and also of the primacy of lunar-based religions throughout the world are confirmed by early African matrifocal cultures.

Not only the royal families of Egypt were matriarchal, but also all the common people. The Greek historian Diodorus Siculus, circa 100 B.C., wrote of the Egyptians: "Among private citizens, the husband, by the terms of the marriage agreement, appertains to the wife and it is stipulated between them that the man shall obey the woman in all things." As Jackson notes, "These customs seemed strange to the Greeks, but they were normal features of African societies."[1]

Jackson has devoted his life's work to pointing out that these ancient African societies were neither "primitive" nor "undeveloped," but formed the creative cradle of the world. For example, of early technologies: Remains of graded roads and cultivation terraces are found throughout Uganda, Kenya, and Tanzania, and there are megalithic structures in West Africa. In the opinion of many anthropologists, including Franz Boas, iron smelting originated in central Africa; the ancient people of Mashonaland, in Zimbabwe, were extensive miners and iron workers. Herodotus reported that iron tools were used in building the Egyptian pyramids, and these tools were mined and smelted in Africa.[2]

Another example is writing. Sir Wallis Budge, renowned Egyptian scholar, believed it was clear that Egyptian hieroglyphs derived from symbols used by native Africans on painted pots and boat banners.[3] And we must add that the pottery-painters and banner-makers were women.

In fact, the legendary Atlantis could have been West Africa. The Greek historian Diodorus Siculus referred to the western Ethiopians as "Atlanteans." Trade between sixth century B.C. Phoenicians and Ethiopians living on an Atlantic island called Cerne (the Canary Islands?) beyond the Pillars of Hercules is recorded.[4] Leo Frobenius, the great twentieth-century archaeological explorer of Africa, was convinced that Atlantis had been located on the West African coast; in Yorubaland he found remains of great palaces and statues, and heard the Yoruba people recount legends "of an ancient royal city and its palace with golden walls which in the past sank beneath the waves."[5] Frobenius concluded:

> Yoruba, with its channeled network of lakes on the coast and the reaches of the Niger, Yoruba, whose peculiarities are not inadequately depicted in the Platonic account—this Yoruba, I assert, is Atlantis, the home of Poseidon's territory, the Sea God by them named Olokun; the land of peoples of whom Solon declared: "They had even extended their lordship over Egypt and Tyrrhene."[6]

Frobenius also saw links, physical and cultural, between the West African Yorubans and the culture of the Mayans in Central America. In *Africa and the Discovery of America,* Harvard professor Leo Wiener also traced this African-Mayan connection, finding documented evidence that, in pre-Columbian times, West African mariners and traders made over fifty voyages across the Atlantic to Central America.[7] This connection would explain the early Olmec statuary found in the Veracruz region of Mexico, with its clearly Negroid features, and also the legend that Mayan glyphs were originated by the Olmecs.[8]

In connection with ancient West African mariners, it's also interesting to note that, according to Irish historical legends, the Celtic island was invaded and dominated for a time by sea-rovers from Northwest Africa, called Fomorians. And, on the other side of Europe, in India, evidence shows that the early inhabitants of India, the Dravidians, were black Africans, with "Ethiopoid features." These Dravidians founded the first Indian civilization in the Indus Valley, with large cities, two-story brick houses, bathrooms with drains leading to brick sewers under the streets. . . . The Dravidians were extremely skilled in iron technology; a Dravidian-made column of welded iron in a temple courtyard in Delhi has stood for over four thousand years without showing any rust. The renowned Damascus blades were made of this Dravidian iron. And, once again, the pictographic script of two hundred signs used by these fourth-century B.C. Dravidians is almost identical to that found carved in the ruins of Easter Island—two thousand miles west of Chile in the Pacific Ocean.[9]

All this far-flung evidence supports the probability that the ancient Africans were global mariners, traders, and settlers, sailing both West and East, the Atlantic and the Pacific, and spreading their advanced culture everywhere like seeds. And we must remember that this was a matriarchal culture!

What all these scholars of Africa and their data are telling us is that "human development" does *not* proceed in a straight line, from "the primitive" to "the advanced." Nothing in nature proceeds in straight lines, but in circles; and human cultures too, like individual human beings, go through cycles of development and regression. Empires *do* rise and fall; and cultures that now appear "primitive" or "never developed" could well be sitting on the rubble of great past civilizations, once built by their ancestors, once flourishing, and then disintegrating under a multitude of pressures. This point is important for women investigating the past existence of matriarchies, as well as for students of ancient African glories: For the same patterns apply to both. The contemporary Western world, ruled by an essentially white patriarchal elite, sees itself as the peak of human development; in its linear view, all past cultures were by nature "inferior"—simply because they came earlier in time—and existed mainly, not on their own right or in their own terms, but as mere steps on a grand stairway leading up to the "supreme white Western maledom." This linear developmental process is rarely questioned, no more than white male dominance is questioned; in the official view, it just "comes from God," or derives from Newton and the internal combustion engine. Confronted with evidence—from archaeology, anthropology, mythology, *strange dreams!*—of the existence of great past cultures, whether of black Africans or of Central American Mayas, *or* of Mediterranean matriarchies, for example, in Anatolia, Crete, Malta, Etruria—the historical tendency of white patriarchy has been absolutely to deny these early cultures, and mock their evidence; or, if they can't be denied, to treat them with chauvinistic contempt, as some form of lavish "barbarism." And the detractors quickly rush to point out that these early cultures, despite their esthetic and spiritual qualities, were "limited in technology" (i.e., didn't have smog or home computers), or "practiced human sacrifice" (as though twentieth-century Western "civilizations" don't), or some other stigma of inferiority, which always adds up to saying, "They weren't us."

No, they weren't. But they were viable cultures within their own terms. And because they were earlier in time, most of the arts, crafts, technologies, and religious insights we boast about were invented by them.

When historians like John G. Jackson point out that many contemporary African village people live among the ruins of ancient graded roads, farm terraces, iron smelters, and megalithic monuments which they no longer use, or would not even know how to construct, they are referring to a phenomenon known as cultural regression. People can go backward in cultural and intellectual development, as well as forward (as any student of the European "Dark Ages" can testify). Backwards or forwards, the movement is always along a spiral, not a straight line. Many factors can be responsible for such regression—including climate change, environmental damage from new technologies (i.e, cattle-grazing helped create deserts), and internal cultural change.

By all accounts, the major cause of cultural regression during the past two thousand years has been political invasion, and the cultural colonialism that follows. The invaders try to destroy the existing social forms, by force and punitive colonial practices, and attempt to impose their own cultural and religious patterns on the conquered. Culture is a people's own vision of themselves in relation to the world, created by themselves through a blood-continuity of time and space. Political invasion, via cultural colonialism, weakens the creative will of the conquered by destroying the people's coherent vision of themselves. Guns, police, and the invader's law help in this process; but imposition of alien cultural symbols and religious ideas are the most effective tools, in the long run, for obliterating or distorting a people's self-image—because they are aimed at the most intimate parts of human beings: sex and the spirit.

By the time European and Arabic slave traders and colonial invaders reached Africa, that continent's great period of cultural development and extension had peaked; but the matriarchal social patterns, at least along the West Coast, were still intact, and the people still worshiped Black Goddesses with bisexual powers, and still participated in the cyclic processes of Mother Earth as a sacred year-cycle ritual. And it was these matrifocal social and kinship patterns, and these Goddess-oriented spiritual participations, that the colonialist invaders had to break in order to impose imperialist domination and exploitive slavery on the people. "Wherever Islam or Christianity impinged on the life of the Africans it was introduced by the invaders in whose interests it was to detach the local inhabitants from the dependency on the rules of behavior demanded by agricultural and seasonal change."[10]

This pattern, the paradigm of patriarchal imperialism, we find repeated again and again throughout the world—in Africa, in Asia, in South and North America. (What many people don't realize is that the same pattern was successfully imposed by Imperial Rome on its colony, Europe, at the beginning of the Christian Era; a process we will investigate in Part 4.)

To break up the ancient maternal kinship groupings, and the sacred life-patterns they followed, for the purpose of robbing the native people of their land, stealing the earth's raw resources, and exploiting human labor—the colonial armies sent the missionaries in to introduce the abstract and alien concepts of "father-right" and a Father God who was the enemy of the Great Mother. Christian missionaries preaching of the heavenly Father and his son, and Moslems carrying the message of Allah and his prophet Muhammed, performed the same colonizing functions: They found the Mother's people, who were alive and well within the holistic Now, and they denounced these people's ways and redefined them as backward children of a distant, aloof, paternalistic power. All exploitation follows, quite easily and self-righteously, from such a redefinition. Colonialist powers really convince themselves that they are doing their victims a favor, lifting them up from Mother Earth—through whips, degradations, imprisonments, hunger, and slaughter—so they can glimpse through tears a far-off shining palace, the abode of the heavenly Father (i.e., the exploiting home country). Imperialist colonialism always sees itself, officially, as an instrument of spiritual enlightenment. What this means in practice is that the Mother—the people's blood-identity—is denounced, in the name of some superior Father God who always happens to live somewhere else.

Because, in maternal cultures, the "father" is a social rather than a biological role—and because this father role is defined in terms of its relation to the mother (i.e., it is her brother, or her uncle)—this enforced redefinition brutally attempts to pull the ontological rug out from under all basic social relationships and the emotions surrounding them. We must consider the effects of this.

In some matrifocal cultures, such as the pre-Aryan Toda people of India, who practice polyandry, a woman will choose one among her many husbands to be a "social father" for her child. The more common practice is for the mother's brother to act as social father. In these arrangements, the man acting as "father" must win the children's affection and respect; he cannot expect it as his "right." He protects and cherishes the children, among some people receiving them into his arms when they are born; but they are not "his" in the sense that he is seen to have had a share in their physical procreation. Among most preliterate people—as among the ancient Paleolithic and Neolithic peoples—the man's role in procreation is seen as one of "opening" the womb; but it is believed that children are placed in the mother's womb by spirits—perhaps the returning spirits of dead kin. The man cannot relate to the children as his property, in other words; they come *from* the mother, *through* the mother, and *belong* to the spirit world. There are fewer emotional conflicts in such cultures; the neurosis-producing, ego-festering hothouse atmosphere of the Victorian-type nuclear family is entirely avoided. After spending early childhood close to the mother's body, the young child then moves out into the group's life, guided by the social father. The child belongs to the whole people, and feels this belonging. Because he does not relate egoistically or possessively to the children, the social father is much better prepared to let his own nurturing talents develop truly; there is no question of property right, personal ambition, economic responsibility, sexual jealousy, or social status involved in his relationship to women and children. These cultures are not perfect, but the notorious soap opera of Western domestic life is avoided. Most of all, these matrifocal cultures weave a webwork of non-possessive intergroup relationships, which supports a growing being through every phase and crisis of unfolding life.

Colonialism tries to rip this network apart with the artillery fire of patriarchal concepts: concepts of women's inferiority, of misogynistic and antisex morality, of possessive fatherhood, of competitive greed and alienated individualism, and of women, children, and land existing as the property of dominant males. A major rip involves splitting the human spirit away from the Mother Earth and her cyclic processes, and forcibly reattaching this sundered spirit to the "sky"—i.e., to some aloof and abstract source of dominance and power. A result of all this is the destruction of a people's blood memory, its past identity; especially since colonized people tend to keep oral histories, and patriarchy insists that only written-down history is real. As Franz Fanon says in *The Wretched of the Earth:*

> . . . colonialism is not simply content to impose its rule upon the present and the future of a dominated country. Colonialism is not satisfied merely with holding a people in its grip and emptying the native's brain of all form and content. By a kind of perverted logic, it turns to the past of the oppressed people, and distorts, disfigures and destroys it. This work of devaluing pre-colonial history takes on a dialectical significance today.[11]

Colonialism is a form of vampirism that empowers and bloats the self-image of the colonizing empire by draining the life energies of the colonized people; just enough blood is left to allow the colonial subject to perform a day's work for the objective empire. And these drained energies are not only of the present and future, but of the past, of memory itself: the continuity of identity of a people, and of each individual who is colonized.

No one should recognize this process better than women; for the female sex has functioned as a colony of organized patriarchal power for several thousand years now. Our brains have been emptied out of all memory of our own cultural history, and the colonizing power systematically denies such a history ever existed. The colonizing power mocks our attempts to rediscover and celebrate our ancient matriarchies as realities. In the past women have had to accept this enforced female amnesia as "normal"; and many contemporary women continue to believe the female sex has existed always and *ab aeterno* as an auxiliary to the male-dominated world order. But we continue to dig in the ruins, seeking the energy of memory; believing that the reconstruction of women's ancient history has a revolutionary potential equal to that of any political movement today.

One interesting fact in the reconstruction of both African history specifically, and ancient matriarchies generally, is that there was a great explosion of scholarly interest in these subjects between the two world wars. Between 1920 and the mid-1930s, Helen Diner, Robert Briffault, Margaret Murray, and Jessie Weston were passionately digging up evidence of women's ancient cultures and religion, building on Jane Ellen Harrison's great work of the 1910s. During this same period W. E. B. DuBois, Carter G. Woodson, Leo Wiener, and the German Eugen George, among others, were exploring black African history, building on the 1913-published work of Frobenius and the work of Joseph McCabe, who explored pre-Christian world history, including ancient African history, from 1917 to 1935. Because ancient women's cultures existed everywhere, including Africa, and because Africa was originally matriarchal, there was a great deal of overlap in some of these studies, with most students reaching the same conclusion: Women—and furthermore, dark women—were the originators of most of what we know as human culture.

With the eruption of World War II, these studies were cut off; and they were never picked up again, at least in the mainstream academic world. Since the 1950s, all research into women's past history, as well as into black African history, has been initiated and carried through by highly motivated independent women and black researchers, functioning outside the academic establishment and in an atmosphere of subversive investigation. And, in our *sub rosa* research, we have found these great pioneering works of the 1920s and 1930s consigned to the academic dustbins, as "eccentric" and nonreputable histories.

What was the devastating effect of World War II on these earlier studies? Apparently, the reputed alignment of Hitler and Nazism with paganism has had long-lasting results: they are still equated in many minds, especially in the United States. "Pagan" remains a code word for everything evil, brutal, and willfully destructive; i.e., a code word for Nazism, seen as a deliberate revival of the pre-Christian "orgiastic" and "bloodthirsty" Teutonic spirit. This equation occurs despite Wilhelm Reich's clear and irrefutable analysis of German Nazism as a predictable eruption of puritanical patriarchal culture. People who indulged in five hundred years of Inquisition, led by both Catholic and Protestant churchmen, jurists, and local magistrates, erupted again two centuries later in the Nazism of the 1930s. As we will show later, the European Inquisition and German Nazism were based on the same patriarchal principles, and used the same hysterical scapegoating and mass-manipulation techniques. I.e., German Nazism was an expression of European Christian development, and cannot in any historic sense be blamed on pre-Christian paganism. Nevertheless, the equation has occurred; and this, combined with Western sexism and racism with their chronic fears of "the dark," "the contaminating female," and "the lurking bestial jungle forces," has created an official academic as well as public hostility toward any serious investigation of "the pagan"—i.e., the non-Christian, the non-white, the non-good. This hostility has been the excuse, if not the motivation, for a general refusal to recognize the importance of research into both ancient African cultures and ancient matriarchies. The "pagan," the "female," and the "dark" are still interpreted as attributes of the Devil, and the desire of too many people is still to push them out of sight and out of mind.

In one area alone Westerners allow themselves to explore this material—to explore the pagan, the dark, and the female—and to admit its familiarity; its intimate familiarity, as the stuff of dreams. This is the area of psychoanalytical and in particular Jungian study. Erich Neumann especially, in *The Great Mother: An Analysis of the Archetype,* has gathered together powerful statues, paintings, and other icons of the Great Goddess as she was worshiped for thousands of years worldwide, and attempted to analyze the meaning of her many manifestations—as Good Mother, Terrible Mother, White and Black Mother, Lady of the Beasts and Plants, and so forth. To avoid the controversial existence of *real* matriarchies, Neumann and other Jungians say it is not relevant whether a belief in the Goddess arises out of a society shaped by women or by men. But they clearly assume the beliefs, as well as all these icons, were shaped by men. The Great Mother exists for them as archetype only, as the classic mental object of the male mind struggling to develop and understand itself.

The real historical existence of real matriarchies in which women created Goddess symbols and images out of their own female experience, worshiped by women and men alike—this interpretation would be revolutionary, and Jungians go out of their way to avoid politics! Their studies concentrate exclusively on the individual in isolation—a solipsistic paradigm deriving from the privileged economic status of both the analyst and the client; focusing on the disconnected individual ego in the modern world, they cannot understand the political content of the ancient myths, their economic and social backgrounds, and the female communal environment from which they emerged.

Also, using without question the nineteenth-century developmental models of inevitable and linear "progress," Jungians theorize that Mother Goddess religions—*if* they existed—existed only near the temporal origins of human culture. Therefore they must express only the "infancy" of the race, or of the individual psyche. Psychoanalytical arrogance corresponds to Christian theology's view of all pagan religions as "spiritually underdeveloped" by positing Mother Goddess archetypes as "infantile," or as "inchoate subconscious material."

When Jungians say that the unconscious belongs to the realm of the Mother, they are right; but they do not draw the enormous sociopolitical conclusions from this:

> Contemporary man . . . is possessed by "powers" that are beyond his control. His gods and demons have not disappeared at all, they have merely got new names. They keep him on the run with restlessness, vague apprehensions, psychological complications, an insatiable need for pills, alcohol, tobacco, food—and, above all, a large array of neuroses.[12]

Modern sickness is that of disconnection, the ego unable to feel an organic part of the world, except via chemical and popular culture addictions. But when the healers—the physicians of mind and body—do not know themselves what it is we need to be connected to, how can they solve the syndrome of disconnection? When the ego lets itself go, sinks down into the oceanic all-oneness of the beginning, and its peace—the shrinks call this "regression"! They have virtually defined "mature-mindedness" as a state of permanent alienation—the *I* chronically differentiated from the *All*. What this amounts to is that "the mature mind" is the male mind, rejecting his mother. Within Western culture, whenever the "doors of perception" open ever so little to let us catch a glimpse of the holographic cosmic mind within us—we are in danger of being locked up for psychiatric observation, and given tranquilizers and other "cures." The established patriarchal institutions all have a vested interest in keeping the individual mind disconnected from the experience of cosmic oneness, because this disconnection *is* patriarchy. The bulk of patriarchal industries—drugs, alcohol, entertainment media, fashion and cosmetics, pornography, the tourist business, polyester-suited politics, drive-in religious sermons, interstate freeway systems, you name it—exist and profit solely by selling momentary diversions to multitudes of "quietly desperate people," seeking anesthetic escape from the pain of personal alienation.

What in ancient times was experienced as our "super-consciousness," within which we perceived the I-Thou of the ego dissolving into the cosmic being of oneness, and whereby we received understanding, wisdom transcending dualism, magic perception, and healing powers—is now wholly submerged within us and termed the "unconscious." And the psychotherapeutic establishment, including Jungians, portray this "unconscious" as essentially a frightening and threatening realm—"the dark jungle within," "the place of orgiastic desires," "cannibal land," "the black, hairy forest full of beasties"(!)—i.e., the pagan, the female, the dark. A ring of terror is placed around the unconscious for patriarchal political reasons: to keep us in a permanent state of fear and distrust in regard to our own innermost beings, and vis-à-vis the vast cosmos. Patriarchy manipulates and profits from this chronic state of fear and alienation; and Western religious and social history can be read as one long attempt to repress the cosmic female by keeping this fearful alienation institutionally alive and intact:

> Students of mythology find that when the feminine principle is subjected to sustained attack, as it was from the medieval Christian authorities, it often quietly submerges. Under the water (where organic life began) it swims through the subconscious of the dominant male society, occasionally bobbing to the surface to offer a glimpse of the rejected harmony.[13]

Patriarchal politics, religion, and psychotherapy are always there, militant and quick, to tell us that this "rejected harmony" is childish, illusionary, crazy, blasphemous, or unpatriotic. And we should know, by now, its reasons for doing so.

But—a breakthrough? In some very interesting clinical experiments conducted between 1975 and 1979, a variety of female, male, and adolescent psychotherapy patients who received the subliminal message *Mommy and I are one* flashed on a tachistoscope screen were much more successful—and permanently successful—at losing weight, stopping drinking and smoking, and overcoming emotional problems to improve reading skills, than were patients receiving neutral or no subliminal messages. Designed by psychologist Lloyd Silverman of New York University (and described in his book *The Search for Oneness*), these studies show that successful overcoming of problems—i.e., mature development—does not come from severing the early infantile sense of unity with the Mother, but from reestablishing it.[14] The holistic point of ancient women's religion was that the Mother is not one's personal maternal parent solely, but the entire community of women, the entire living earth, and beyond this the entire surrounding and ongoing cosmic process. One could not be alienated because one is always within this process, as it is always within the self. Unless, of course, such knowledge is suppressed from the outside, by patriarchal conditioning.

Truly, our very sanity is at stake with continuing patriarchy and the denial of the cosmic self—the Goddess—within us all, and us within her.

The Great Mother was the projection of the self-experience of groups of highly aware and productive women who were the founders of much of human culture. In this sense the Great Mother is not simply a mental archetype, but a historical fact. Ancient icons, symbols, and myths cannot be understood if they are disembodied from this fact. They cannot be understood as "mind trips" alone, but must be seen in the context of ancient political realities.

Robert Graves, Welsh poet, essayist, and historical novelist, was one of the few modern students of mythology who took those ancient female political realities seriously. In his two-volume work *The Greek Myths*, Graves showed that the major theme of Greek myth was the gradual historic reduction of women from sacred beings to slaves. The dramatic core of Greek myth and drama is the actual transition, circa 1300 B.C., from matriarchy to patriarchy in the Aegean and the repercussions of this transition on the psyches of the Greek people. In *The White Goddess* Graves traces the origins of the European Great Goddess, her connections with world mythologies (and world alphabets, always a Goddess invention), and her attempted obliteration by the Roman Empire and the Christian religion. Many feminists dislike Graves's interpretation of the Goddess as—occasionally, at least—a white bitch. But Graves's main concern is to relate to the Goddess as a male poet, and to rediscover the European roots of Goddess-worship. It remains for women to interpret the Goddess as women relating to Woman; and only black women, Oriental women, and Native American women can completely rediscover and reanimate the original Goddesses of Africa, Asia, and the Americas for us. It's the job of white Europeans and Americans, after all, to stop "explaining" everyone else and to begin trying to understand ourselves and our own history. But when Graves shows, in his exploration of early Greek and European goddesses, that the loss of our mythic history is the loss of our sociopolitical history, he speaks to all of us.

Probably the greatest student of ancient mythology as ancient female political history was Robert Briffault. An anthropologist, gynecologist, and Marxist, Briffault spent ten concentrated years of his life (thereby ruining his health) researching and writing his enormous work, *The Mothers*, probably the most thorough collection of evidence for the early existence of matrifocal cultures and Great Goddess religions throughout the world. The data Briffault collected is global, and irrefutable; once we read Briffault, and Graves, we can never again look at the Great Mother as an apolitical archetype—as some power-image that exists in our minds only, but never in historical reality. Because the Great Mother was a historic reality, her psychological suppression also must be seen in historical terms, as a political suppression of an earlier female-oriented world order by a later male-dominated one.

Throughout Europe—especially Eastern Europe, but also in Spain, France, and Italy—we can find Black Madonnas. People have local legends to explain the blackness of these Virgin Mary statues, including the ingenuous idea that the icon is charred, the miraculous survivor of a terrible fire. Jungian interpreters would see the blackness as a "subconscious" reference to the dark side of something or other—the moon, no doubt. It is rarely speculated that a real, historic blackness of the early goddesses of Egypt and Africa is being recalled. But when we read Briffault, and the other researchers into early mythic history, and see not only the black African origins of the Great Mother but the extent to which early matriarchal Africans traveled throughout the ancient world, spreading the Black Goddess, her pyramid technologies, stone and clay arts, and hieroglyphic scripts everywhere, then it is easy to understand the existence of these Black Madonnas. They are not "psychological symbols of the dark side of the mother of Christ"—or not solely, or originally. They are solid iconic remains of the ancient time when the religion of the Black Goddess ruled Africa and from thence, much of the rest of the world.

Here's another: In *The Adventure of Mankind* the German scholar Eugen George argued that the Atlanteans were Ethiopians, "supreme in Africa and Asia," who also penetrated into southern Europe. It was only after thousands of years of battle that these black Atlantean invaders were finally pushed out of Europe, but the genetic memory of Europeans still bears traces of this experience. George suggests that this ancient memory survives in the European dread of dragons . . . ! who are, after all, loved and celebrated everywhere else (throughout Asia, India, Africa, Mexico, Central and South America). For, as George points out, "the dragon painted on the insignia of the kings was carried in the van of the black armies."[15] The dragon that represents dark earth energies to those converted to white Sky God beliefs; the curled dragon with its tail in its mouth that represents the ancient female holism to the all-conquering linear male—such a dragon also, historically, was carried into Europe on the banners of the matriarchal Atlantean-African invaders.

The archetype is an archetype because it represents a past reality; its power over us as internal image is so profound because it was once an experienced fact of the external world. Our history as a species is stored in our genes; and no matter how hard patriarchy tries to suppress our past matriarchal history, it keeps "bobbing to the surface"—in worldwide archaeological ruins, icons, and myths, as in our dreams.

WOMEN AS CULTURE CREATORS

When we say that women created most of early human culture, we are not trying to sound radical. The evidence is there, quite tangible. When we realize how many basic life industries were the inventions of women—cooking, food processing and storage, ceramics, weaving, textiles and design, tanning and dyeing, everything related to fire (e.g., chemistry and metallurgy), the medicinal arts, language itself and the first scripts and glyphs, grain domestication, animal domestication, religious imagery and ritual, domestic and sacred architecture, the first calendars and the origins of astronomy, and on and on—then we don't need to project our imaginations far back into the past to confirm these inventions. They are still all around us today, they constitute our world. Stolen and mechanized by several thousand years of patriarchal exploitation, most of these inventions have been turned into grossly alienated and profiteering mass-market industries. We do have to use our imaginations to remember that all were once warm, personal, and lovingly tended arts and crafts, originated and sustained by early communities of women.

This information is radical in the true sense of the word. "Radical" came from *radix*—root, and means "going to the root of things." These cultural inventions of early women were at the very root of human existence—they created what we know as human life.

Evelyn Reed, an anthropologist, Marxist, and feminist, has written extensively about women's early social forms and inventions. In *The Myth of Women's Inferiority* and *Woman's Evolution,* Reed describes how human culture developed out of women's labor groups, interrelations, and first crafts.

> It was the female of the species who had the care and responsibility of feeding, tending and protecting the young. However, as Marx and Engels have demonstrated, all societies both past and present are founded upon labor. So . . . it was not simply the capacity of women to give birth that played the decisive role, for all females give birth. What was decisive for the human species was the fact that maternity

> led to labor—it was in the fusion of maternity and labor that the first human social system was founded. It was women who became the chief producers; the workers and farmers, the leaders in scientific, intellectual and cultural life. In the language of "primitive peoples" the term "mother" is identical with "Producer-procreatrix."[1]

It was a society where power was linked with real love. Among the earliest examples of "Stone Age" peoples found living today, such as the Kalihari Bushmen and the BaMbuti Pygmies of Africa, the same linkage occurs; female authority is valued, and both sexes are "mothers" to the young. Contrary to the "bloody tooth and claw" theories of popular aggression-oriented anthropologists, evidence shows that the farther back we go in human history, the gentler our species was. This is because the early matrifocal groups were concentrated on maintaining, rather than exploiting, life.

Evelyn Reed shows that during the food-gathering epoch, stretching over hundreds of thousands of years, the human group's main nourishment was supplied by the women collectors, who dug the earth for edible roots, plants, and grubs, collected fruit and nuts, and hunted such small animals as lizards and hares. Large-game hunting kept the men away for long periods of time, and didn't always bring in enough meat. Among hunting-and-gathering people today, the women's food-collecting activities provide 75 percent to 85 percent of their group's daily nourishment.

Over these thousands of years of food gathering, women's keen knowledge of herbs and plant properties was developed, through trial-and-error testing and practical experience, into the arts of medicinal healing. Ultimately, women's food collecting developed into agriculture, as women observed the relation between scattered seeds and plant growth. This female invention, based on generations of experimentation with seed cultivation, cutting and grafting, and grain storage, brought about the vast Neolithic Revolution circa 10,000 B.C. The women's digging sticks were humanity's first tools, and women's work the prototype for all the industry that followed.

Much of the small game that women hunted and snared was brought back alive to the camp; sometimes the young of animals killed by the male hunters was captured and brought back alive too. These animals were often kept as pets, and provided the first experiments in animal training and domestication, which finally led to stock breeding. Motherless animal young often suckled the women's breasts, as captured bear cubs do today among the Ainu of Japan. So, even the domestication of animals had its roots in women's maternity.[2] Later, cattle breeding became an extremely male-oriented activity, like so many others; but originally it was woman's. Among the ancient Arabs women not only made and owned the family tents, they also owned the herds.

World myths, folk traditions, and anthropological studies agree that women first discovered how to use and produce fire.[3] In a survey of 224

Womencultures, Sjöö, 1977

modern tribal societies, it was found that fires were made and tended always or usually by women in 84 societies; almost all these societies have legends telling of the early times when women were the exclusive "owners" of fire. Ritual maintenance of fire remained entrusted to women down through historic times, such as the Vestal Virgins of ancient Rome, or the Irish nuns of St. Brigid (from the originally Celtic Goddess Brigid, or Bride), who tended a perpetual fire at Kildare until the suppression of the monasteries under Henry VIII. Fire is sacred to the Moon Mother. Cooking—boiling, roasting, baking, steaming—was only one of the techniques women acquired from their mastery of directed heat. Fire was the tool of tools; through its use foods could be dried and conserved for future use, and some poisonous plants and fruits made edible. It was women who developed all the early associated industries of cooking and ceramics in which fire was the critical tool.

Women built the first granaries and storehouses for provisions; some of these were sunk into the earth, while on marshy ground they were upraised on stilts. Women domesticated the cat to protect these granaries from rodents.[4] Cats, since immemorial time, have had a special relationship with women; among European witches, cats acted as "familiars" and were believed to have telepathic powers (which is why special bonfires were erected during the Inquisition to burn all the cats in town, along with the women).

Industry, science, and human need were combined in women's work, and the daily tasks were infused with magical meaning. Women converted plants and herbs into medicines—some substances discovered by women are still used today for their narcotic properties; and World Health Organization figures show that 95 percent of the world's health care today is still provided by women, using many of these ancient remedies. Women designed and produced containers and vessels out of materials like wood, bark, fibers, and leather. Fire was used to hollow out wood, a technique that could then be used to make canoes and boats from tree trunks.

All these tremendous discoveries were related to daily survival. Yet they were also experienced as magic transformations of raw material into something completely different, especially through the alchemy of fire. Consider the chemistry of bread-making: the planting of the seed and its growth through combinations of moon, sun, rain, and tilled earth; the careful harvesting, and grinding the grain into flour; then, with the correct combination of water, yeast, and fire, the original seed is transformed into bread, the human food.

The original beehive-shaped or domed ovens, found all over the world, could be used *only* by women; the oven was seen symbolically as the belly of the Great Goddess. Many miniature pottery models have been found in Southeast Europe, depicting Neolithic shrines. In the shrines there are ovens, clay altars (originally covered with wooden planks), horned thrones, figurines of women worshipers, and wall images showing rain symbols and the magical grinding of grain. In these regions there are still women's rituals of celebration involving the sacred New Year bread dough, which is held communally in the upraised arms of the elder women of the group.

The textile industries also originated in women's work. Women developed cordage techniques, the weaving of bark and grass fibers into baskets and textiles. Women were the leather-makers, tanning and working the skins (softening the skins by chewing them, as the polar Eskimos still do). The skin-scraper, along with the digging-stick, was a woman's tool everywhere—and is so still among the Eskimo people. The cured leather was then made into tents, clothes, boots, straps, and cords. These were brightly ornamented with vegetable and mineral dyes, another complex chemical process invented by women.

Women were everywhere the first potters. In *World of the Maya*, archaeologist Victor W. von Hagen writes:

> Pottery was woman. All we see of the remains of the Maya ceramic art was done by women. It is a fact that should be stressed. In almost every place where pottery making was on an archaic level—Africa or Melanesia—pottery was womanmade and its design woman-inspired. Throughout the area of the Amazon, pottery was a woman's task. Women were the potters, so far as we know, in ancient Peru. Early Greek and early Egyptian pottery was also womanmade until the introduction of the potter's wheel. Sir Lindsay Scott is "certain" that it was only after the introduction of the potter's wheel that pottery became—as the drawings on the walls of Thebes show—exclusively masculine. This suggests that all the superbly beautiful patterns found on pottery (as well as weaving) were conceived by woman. Perhaps, then, Art *is* a woman.[5]

Pot-making involved the creation of entirely new substances that did not already exist in nature. The beginnings of pottery are unknown, insofar as the first pots were unbaked and didn't survive. But the earliest fired ceramics found so far, including fine burnished and painted wares, date from the late seventh millennium B.C. These already reveal a mastery of ceramic technology. Mixing special kinds of earth with water, in exactly the right proportions; molding a piece of clay into a shape; then heating it to over 600° C in ovens or kilns built by the women—the change must have seemed a magic transmutation, from dust or mud into a substance almost as hard and durable as stone. And a substance, made with water, that could hold water. Women decorated their pots, the coloring changing with the firing process. "Art" developed out of the potter's "craft"; and out of the pottery decorations developed, there is little doubt, the written language.

Some pots were used for daily life, others for ritual purposes. Sacred pots were painted with mystic symbols that became standardized over millennia, and these acted as a kind of shorthand language, understood by all. Among the people there was a common understanding of the commonly held mythic tradition; material fact and ritual activity were shared daily between the women who made the pots and those who used them. The artist could therefore communicate abstractly through the magic signs, and over the ages these symbols evolved into glyphs, and then character or phonetic scripts.

Graphic designs—ideograms—were used for thousands of years in Old Neolithic Europe. Marija Gimbutas, in *Goddesses and Gods of Old Europe—6500–3500 B.C.*, says that there were two categories of ideograms: those signifying water and rain (Vs, zigzags, chevrons, meanders, and spirals), all related to the Snake-and-Bird Goddess; and those related to the moon, to becoming, to the vegetal life cycle, the rotation of the seasons, the birth and growth essential to life. These moon signs were the cross, the encircled cross (signifying the four quarters of the world, the year as a journey embracing the four cardinal directions of the cosmic cycle), the crescent, the horns, the caterpillar, the egg, and the fish.[6]

All were symbols of the continuum of life—which the ideograms were meant to ensure—and of the Great Moon Goddess of Life and Death, of cosmos, earth, and vegetation. The horns, the lunar crescent, and the cross were all originally alternative symbols for the waxing and waning moon.

Sequences of inscribed linear signs have also been found; these are a form of very ancient and until recently unknown Neolithic-Chalcolithic script dating from circa 5000 B.C.—which is two thousand years before the development of Sumerian "literate" civilization. According to male historical tradition, the earliest examples of written language were found at the temple of the Queen of Heaven in Erech, which was the sacred city of the Sumerian Goddess; these were clay tablets inscribed about five thousand years ago.[7] But even then the Goddess at Erech had long been known as the "inventor" of clay tablets (clay was sacred to women and the

Goddess), of language and of the original alphabet, or picture script. It is known that a special sacred language was used by women initiates of the Goddess until late in Neolithic time.

In 1973 the Peruvian ethnologist Dr. Victoria de la Jara proved to a congress for Andean archaeology at Lima that the Incas had had a script. She spent ten years doing research on the geometrical "patterns" of Inca pottery and urns, and had come to the conclusion that these patterns were in fact characters with a content ranging from the simple to the highly complex; they were language-symbols relating historical events, myths, and poetry, with a grammar based on groupings of complementary colors. Generations of male scholars had claimed that the Incas had used no language script; in fact, they were not looking in the right place, or in the right way.[8]

THE FIRST SPEECH

Did women also develop the spoken language? From the earliest hunting-and-gathering times, we know that the men spent long, silent, and often solitary days away on the hunt. It takes silence to track animals. Meanwhile, the women worked collectively in or near the camp, surrounded by children, talking and singing. Language must have developed in the first intimate relations between mother and child, and between women working together for the kin-group's daily sustenance.

Alexander Marshack, renegade student of the Paleolithic period, has already proposed the thesis that human speech developed, not among male hunters, but in a childhood setting among females working together.[1] We can't go back in time to confirm this thesis, but we can confirm its probability by looking around us at everyday life, and at the development of individual speech. As William Irwin Thompson writes: "Food sharing in a home base sets up the ideal conditions for communication, babbling, clowning, and play."[2] We've all seen how speech begins, for each human child, in this home atmosphere of babble and play. *Sound communication* begins, between mother and child, at the very beginning, during the intense gazing between them in the days after birth. Thompson refers to recent studies of newborns, one or two days old, who move their arms and legs "in rhythmic synchrony with the pulse of [their] mother's words. . . . The newborn is literally dancing *to* language before [s]he can utter a word."[3] Even earlier, the child in the womb can hear its mother's voice, and comes to recognize it, a few months before birth. We also know that growing girls, of all cultures and linguistic backgrounds, are much more language-proficient than boys of the same age. Finally, many mothers have the strong feeling that, following birth, it is speech that takes the place of the umbilical cord; it is speech that continues to bind us quite viscerally to the growing child, and through which passes the social food of instruction, warning, and communication with a growing consciousness.

It makes sense that we women, who give birth to human life through our sexual, or vaginal mouths, would also give birth to human language through our social, or facial mouths.

What kind of language? Thompson has a fascinating idea that women's plant-collecting activities were related to the development of a kind of mental vocabulary-dictionary and classification system: "The gathering of useful plants is an exercise in establishing a cultural taxonomy of nature, precisely that kind of activity likely to establish a list and a grammar of discrete items."[4] Plant-gathering women would be involved in highly detailed tabulations of various plant and herbal properties—what is edible, what is poison, what is medicinal, what is hallucinogenic—and in transferring this information on to others; over generations an incredibly complex and replete botanic and pharmacopoeic catalog would be filed in each female mind. If you are a male hunter, it is not too hard to tell the difference between a mammoth and an elk; if you are a female food- or medicine-gatherer, the distinction between a poisonous and a nonpoisonous mushroom, or between two varieties of herb, one toxic and one curative, can be very subtle, requiring most minute observation—and a lot of educated guessing; a mistake could be lethal for many loved ones. So Thompson's observation makes sense; an important part of women's early language use would be a detailed observation and classification of the floral and mineral environment—an experimental classification that was the origin of science.

But no women, Stone Age to Rock Age, ever lived by head alone. The constant pattern of women's existence has been the need (and the talent) to link mental activity with physical activity with emotional activity—all encircled, in these beginning times, with the aura of spiritual activity. So, early women's scientific language (because that's what plant-gathering is, a science) would be uttered side-by-side with the emotional language of social relations, and the physical language of the body moving through daily tasks. And surrounding all of these would be the symbol language of sexual-spiritual celebration.

The first symbols did not arise from the mind alone, but from the holistic experiencing of mind, body, sex, heart, soul, and world all moving together, all one. This is the dream-body language of women's ancient rituals. Dream-body language is the deepest type of thinking; it is right-brain thinking[5]—it is the thinking of magic and poetry, in which left-brain language is used for nonlinear, nonlogical expression—and it is a mode of perception and power that Western culture has scorned, to its own harm. A good deal of Robert Graves's research into the defeat of Mediterranean and European matriarchy by patriarchy focuses on the suppression, by male linear logic, of the earlier synthetic-holistic language process. Graves says in *The White Goddess:*

> The language of poetic myth anciently current in the Mediterranean and Northern Europe was a magical language bound up with popular religious ceremonies in honour of the Moon-goddess, or Muse, some of them dating from the Old Stone Age, and . . . this remains the language of true poetry. . . . The language was tampered with in late

> Minoan times when invaders from Central Asia began to substitute patrilinear for matrilinear institutions and remodel or falsify the myths to justify the social changes. Then came the early Greek philosophers who were strongly opposed to magical poetry as threatening their new religion of logic, and under their influence a rational poetic language (now called the Classical) was elaborated in honour of their patron Apollo and imposed on the world as the last word in spiritual illumination: a view that has prevailed practically ever since in European schools and universities, where myths are now studied only as quaint relics of the nursery age of mankind.[6]

Once again, this academic contempt of myth and magic poetry is analogous to the attitudes of psychoanalysts and Christian theo*logicians* towards what they call "primitive" or "infantile" or "pagan" thought processes. But in fact, it was in this Nursery Age, guarded, led, and elaborated by women, that all the basic inventions essential to human culture were born. And these primary industries, tools, arts, medicines, daily objects, and alchemic processes did not arise from the logic centers of the brain alone, but were the products of dream-thinking, of holographic thinking, of mythic, ritual, and poetic communication between women and their environment. "Man's" hard-headed, pragmatic civilizations have been living off these first, enchanted female inventions ever since.

Poetic thinking is nondualistic. Paradox and ambiguity are not exorcised as "illogical demons," but are felt and synthesized. The most ancient becomes the most modern; for in the holographic universe, each "subjective" part contains the "objective" whole, and chronological time is just one aspect of a simultaneous universe. Subjective and objective merge into an experience of cosmic oneness. Such a thought mode, of course, does not build huge political and corporate empires like Rome or General Motors. For these purposes men have devised a language of logical precision, in which words can be used like knives to chop up one continuous life into mechanically unrelated parts; in which the visible—i.e., the intellectually possessible—dimension is stressed at the expense of the aural, tactile, affective, and mystic dimensions. With such a partial language, all kinds of destructive manipulations are possible: Against the earth and her creatures, and against the psyche itself. Rationalistic language is used to make lying, exploiting, enslaving, torturing, and murdering seem "nice and legal," not to mention "God's will" and "great material progress."

The languages of "primitive" peoples, though not written, are as complex as the languages of "literate" peoples; preliterate people's brains are in no way inferior to the brains of the "civilized." (In fact, their memories and powers of concentration are much stronger; no African Bushman or Australian aboriginal child could ever be dismissed as having only a "ten-minute attention span," as teachers characterize American schoolchildren today.)

But primal people do see the world in a different way. The practical and the sacred are not separated by the knife of logic; the individual soul is not severed from the world-womb of the Mother. And this is where we all began. What has happened to us? Our primordial and practical, material-magical perception of oneness between ourselves and the universe is the innate female state which, in this modern patriarchal world, we are all supposed to "grow out of" in order to become . . . men. In the place of our ancient female mode of being, now referred to as "primitive animism," the academic psychotherapists, God-logicians, existential poetry technicians, and new car salesmen offer us their own product, called "the agony of alienation," otherwise known as everyday life—which you can fix temporarily by buying something.

This is how they talk: "Man" has struggled for centuries to free his divine spirit from "the paralyzing fetters" of the material cosmos. (I.e., in his mind he is disembodied.) Imagination, the mother of human memory and creative mental powers, is assigned to the female realms, to biology and childhood. Jehovah, Socrates, modern hardware, and the GNP bid "men" to leave these picture-forming but infantile habits of the soul and turn to "abstract thought."[7] As *men*, we are to be given new bodies and new worlds by the Father Logos (batteries included)—while Mother Nature remains at work as a servant of this enterprise, her energies and resources used to realize his thought-forms and achieve his goals. The earth, the body, the soul, and the imagination will be allowed to survive *only* as handmaidens of the great male mind up in the sky.

So the patriarchs have been talking—in their religions, their philosophies, their physical sciences, their politics and economics, their behavioral and psychoanalytical systems—for over two thousand years. What are they really saying? We have only to look around us, to see *his* vision for us: Robots. Computer hearts. Satellite missiles. Ground zero. Cruising nuclear penises targeting cities in barbed-wire bondage. Our flesh has never been good enough for him; his babies are all quite metalloid. And these are our new bodies and our new worlds. He has so abstracted himself from the female imagination and the cosmic-material "fetters" of Mother Nature that he is just about to blast himself entirely *out of the picture*. And everything with him. "Abstract thought," after all, was the condition of the universe *before* the female imagination began its childish picture-forming activity; another word for it is *entropy* (the static show on the TV screen in the absence of an image). Will we get a glimpse of his ultimate "flesh-free" vision of ourselves just as he and his boys push the final button—as we get to watch ourselves, the world, and everything in it dematerialize before our eyes, courtesy of his advanced (b)anal techology?

For the ultimate feeling of the master ("male mind") for his servant ("female nature") is not love, but necrophilic contempt; and the apotheosis of contempt is a brutal will toward total annihilation.

So, how did we get here? On the ground-level of being, the average adult member of a hunting-and-gathering culture—even in some environments called "sparse" by our standards—worked only fifteen hours a week to fill sustenance needs. The rest of the time was spent in leisure activity: arts and crafts, spiritual ecstasy, running, swimming, making love, laughing, eating, goofing around.

In our "advanced Western culture," the average male's work week is forty-five hours; the average female's is seventy-seven hours.[8] A lot of employed people seem to be working more and more, and enjoying it less. The unemployed and underemployed are working less and enjoying it less. Certainly there is less joy, grace, creativity, and wonder in our average daily life than there is in the daily experience of the average Kalihari Bushman or Australian outback Martukuja—those who are left. We don't have to "prove" this statement; we believe we all know somewhere deep in our beings that it is so. "Modern existence," in the long run, "profits" very few, at the expense of too many.

So, how did we get *here* . . . and how do we get out?

II

WOMEN'S EARLY RELIGION

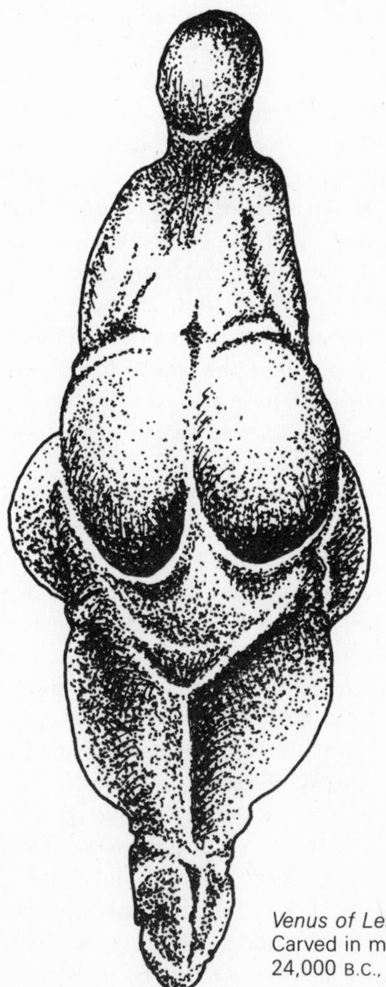

Venus of Lespugue, France.
Carved in mammoth ivory,
24,000 B.C., reconstructed version

THE FIRST MOTHER

Biology is not destiny—but, like the sea, it is a beginning. The mysteries of female biology dominated human religious and artistic thought, as well as social organization, for at least the first 200,000 years of human life on earth. The first human images known to us are the so-called Venuses found in Upper Paleolithic remains (35,000–10,000 B.C.). From the way these statues are positioned and located in cave hearths, niches, and graves, they are interpreted as cult images—the Mother Guardians of the daily life, death, and rebirth of the people. These Venuses, carved from stone, bone, and ivory, and shaped from clay, are very fleshy, more or less stylized to represent pregnancy and abundance. Though named after Venus, the Roman Goddess of Love, they are no longer seen by archaeologists as Cro-Magnon "bunnies"; they are not sex objects. They are magic images of the mysterious power of the female to create life out of herself, and to sustain it. The statues have no feet; the legs taper to a point, so they could be stuck upright in a soft hearth or niche—they were placed everywhere.

These statues appear in Europe with the appearance of the Cro-Magnons. But much earlier, during the Neanderthaloid period (dating from at least 200,000 B.C.), evidence shows that great magical power was attributed to the earth as Mother of Life and Death. Neanderthals buried their dead curled in fetal position, painted red; bones were painted with red ochre. Analogically, the dead were to reenter the earth (the tomb, the womb) to be reborn again. A Neanderthal corpse found in Shanidar Cave in northern Iraq had been laid to rest on pine boughs and strewn with wild flowers. Even earlier than this, a remarkable find at La Ferrassie, in the French limestone country, shows the beautiful resonance that was felt in the minds and hearts of these earliest people between life, death, and the Mother. In a rock shelter, a child's grave was found covered with a large stone slab. On the underside of this slab small cupules had been scooped out—these were all in pairs, to symbolize the mother's breasts. These breast-shaped cupule markings were made throughout prehistory; they are found over great areas of outcropped rock in Europe. But on this stone slab in France, covering a Neanderthal child's grave, is where they first appear.[1]

Mircea Eliade, the great student of aboriginal religious symbolism and shamanism, speaks of "a primary intuition of the earth as a 'religious' form."[2] The earth was seen by all primal people as the source of nourishment, protection, power, and the mystery of cyclic recurrence. Perhaps the first human analogy made was between the earth and the female, who performed the same functions on an individual level. Especially awesome was the woman's ability to bleed rhythmically with the moon's phases, and her periodic swelling up and dramatic expulsion of a new being. Paintings of the mother giving birth, with the expulsed child still connected to her via the umbilical cord, are found throughout the Cro-Magnon caves. Childbirth *is* a powerful drama and ritual. To imagine the enormous impact of pregnancy and childbirth on our human ancestors, we have to remember that Paleolithic people, like many aboriginal people today, did not know the connection between intercourse and pregnancy; the male role might have been seen as "opening" the womb, but the pregnancy itself was seen as resulting from a magical intercourse between the mother and the spirit world—or it was seen as a parthenogenetic act, the woman as spontaneous and autonomous creator of life.

Rock drawing of a woman giving birth, from Sha'ib Samma in Yemen

In these cave drawings of childbirth and in the Venus statues, as well as in many images of gravid animals, the fertility of earth and woman was imaged and celebrated as a spiritual-magical act, to ensure the year's abundance of game and fruit. The seasonal return of vegetation and young animal life following winter and apparent death gave early humans the idea of a magical-cyclical rebirth of their own kind. Entombments—whether cave graves or the later underground vaults and collective burial mounds—were ways of returning bodies to the womb of Mother Earth, where they waited for rebirth. In the later megalithic "porthole tombs," holes were laboriously chiseled out of the portal slabs at the grave entrance, to simulate the birth-canal opening. Even later, in Egypt, the overarching Sky Goddess Nut was painted on the inside of coffin lids; this is a lovely echo of that first stone slab placed over the Neanderthal grave, with the Mother's breasts protectively covering and nourishing the dead child, as it waited to be reborn.

Death is the powerful dramatic mystery equal to Birth—and both are overarched and contained by the Great Mother. This concept of a female earth as the source of cyclic birth, life, death, and rebirth underlies *all*

Cosmos within Her Womb, Sjöö, 1971

mythological and religious symbology; it is the source of all religious belief. It is important to grasp the time dimension involved: *God was female for at least the first 200,000 years of human life on earth*. This is a conservative estimate; wooden images of the Mother God were doubtless carved long before the stone Cro-Magnon Venuses, but wood does not survive. And long before those first breast shapes were carved in the Neanderthal grave-slab, or the red-ochred bodies were placed fetal-position in the cave earth, the idea, the symbolic image, the resonant analogy preceding all icons, was in the minds and hearts of our earliest ancestors.

In the world's oldest creation myths, the female god creates the world out of her own body. The Great Mother everywhere was the active and autonomous creatrix of the world . . . and, unlike the aloof and self-righteous patriarchal gods who only recently usurped her mountain-throne, the ancient Goddess was always there—alive, immanent—within her creation; no ontological scapegoater, *she* was wholly responsible for both the pain and the good of life. Here is one of the oldest world creation myths, from northwest India:

> At first Kujum-Chantu, the earth, was like a human being; she had a head, and arms and legs, and an enormous fat belly. The original human beings lived on the surface of her belly. One day it occurred to Kujum-Chantu that if she ever got up and walked about, everyone would fall off and be killed, so she herself died of her own accord. Her head became the snow-covered mountains; the bones of her back turned into smaller hills. Her chest was the valley where the Apa-Tanis live. From her neck came the north country of the Nagins. Her buttocks turned into the Assam plain. For just as the buttocks are full of fat, Assam has fat rich soil. Kujum-Chantu's eyes became the Sun and Moon. From her mouth was born Kujum-Popi, who sent the Sun and Moon to shine in the sky.[3]

"Mount Everest," in nearby Nepal, was only recently affixed with the name of a nineteenth-century British surveyor. In reality, this tallest breast of earth was always known by the native people who live with her as Chomo-Lungma, "Mother Mountain of the Universe."

THE ORGANIC RELIGION OF EARLY WOMEN

The first God, Mother Earth, was a human concept—or, the sign of a human response to an experienced fact. The first arts and religions, the first crafts and social patterns, were designed in recognition and celebration of her. But what were real human females feeling and thinking? We can only see the attributes of the Great Goddess as the projections of women's experiences of themselves. As we read the powerful magic signs of the Great Mother's celebration, we can read these first women's powerful discoveries and celebrations of themselves.

The religious beliefs, the mysteries and rites developed by ancient women, grew organically out of women's supreme roles as cultural producers, mothers, and prime communicators with the spirit world. The mysteries of creation, transformation, and recurrence—the primal mysteries of all religions—emerged from women's direct physical and psychic experiences of these mysteries: in bleeding, in growing a child, in nursing, in working with fire, in making a pot, in planting a seed.

In pottery-craft and myth alone, we can see the development of a religion. The pot was seen to have the body shape and internal womb of the Mother. In Neolithic Europe, clay was said to have "a woman's soul," and no man was allowed to see the female potter at work. Clay, sacred to women and the Goddess, was often marked with the maze-like windings of the magic underworld, a place of transformation. Aruru-Ishtar, the Cosmic Creatrix of Babylon, was imaged as a potter. A divine potter, shaper of life. The making of cult vessels was like this shaping of life, and the Babylonian words for rebirth were, "We are as fresh-baked pots."

From this, we can see the absurdity (and the political cooptation) of the notion of a male God-Father making human beings from clay, or dust. The biblical image is stolen without shame from the earlier Sumerian and Babylonian *Goddess* creation stories. Such a patriarchal version of creation is very recent; the facts of women's experience of life are primordial. It is *woman* who goes through the sacred transformations in our own body and psyche—the mystery-changes of menstruation, pregnancy, birth, and the production of milk. It is woman who first shaped a seed into food, earth into pottery, fire into a tool, the struggle for survival into human culture. Woman as procreator and producer-creator. Women's mysteries are blood-transformation mysteries: The experience of female bodily transformations magically fused with her conscious and willed transformations of matter. Matter: the mud: the Mother. *She transforms herself.*[1]

Religious rites were combined with industry. Women's religions were organic, a unity of body and spirit, of daily life tasks and cosmic meaning. Among the women weavers of the matrifocal Navajo, for example, this is still so. The women experience themselves as being directly inspired by the Great Spider Woman, the original weaver of the universe. They use no set patterns and feel no separation between art (sacred) and craft (secular, profane). The woven blankets are valued as organic expressions of the special powers of the makers. Each blanket with its inspired design has a spiritual significance, and is thought of as giving power and protection to the person who wears it.

In ancient textiles, a highly charged symbol language was used to communicate herstory and myth. Spinning and weaving were imbued with magic powers, and inscribed spindle-whorls are found in innumerable Neolithic sacrificial pits sacred to the Goddess. The Greek Artemis was seen to "spin the thread of life," and the Three Norns of Scandinavian mythology sat spinning the web of life, destiny, fate at the roots of Yggdrasill, the cosmic world tree.

The subtle energy-form of the human body may be seen as a subtle energy-form of cosmos, relatively miniaturized, but no less vast and totally alive. The cosmos that we know is a construction (perception/projection) of the energy currents in our own bodily systems. Cosmic mind and human mind are not essentially different, or separate, nor are cosmic body and human body. Everything is interconnected in a vast webwork of cosmic being—a universal weaving—in which each individual thing, or life-form, is a kind of energy knot, or interlock, in the overall vibrating pattern. The Latin root word for "religion" is *religare,* which means "a bond; a binding back to something." (*Yoga,* interestingly enough, means the same thing: a yoke, or yoking of the individual soul to the All.) William Irwin Thompson writes,

> The sacred is the emotional force which connects the part to the whole; the profane or the secular is that which has been broken off from, or has fallen from, its emotional bond to the universe. *Religare* means to bind up, and the traditional task of religion has been to bind up the pieces that have broken away from the ecstatic Oneness.[2]

True religion is the original umbilical cord that binds our individual selves back to our larger, universal source. That source, in women's religion, is the Great Mother, who is the great cosmic weaver, the divine potter, the carrier of the heavenly water jar; we participate in her substance, her nature, her processes, her play, and her work. In her are both the lower regions of the tomb (the world of the dead), and the upper regions of the celestial sky, whose stars are her eyes. Groundwater belongs to the belly-womb region of the lower female; the heavenly rainwater belongs to the great breast region of the upper female. As divine water-jar, she is mistress of the upper waters (the rain), and of the lower waters (the brooks, springs, and rivers flowing from the womb of the earth). The Egyptian Sky and Water-jar Goddess Nut nourishes the earth with her milky rain. (In fact, our word "galaxy" comes from the Greek *galaxias*, meaning "milky circle," and the Milky Way describes the thick white stream of stars pouring from her breast.) As uterus, she is a vessel that breaks with childbirth, pouring forth water like a wellspring.

These are all symbols of creative life and of ecstatic participation in it. The self-representation of the Goddess is a form of divine epiphany, and the parts of her body are not understood literally as physical organs, but as numinous centers of whole spheres of life. Her navel is the center of the earth—of us—from which the universe is nourished, by our conscious participation, as we are nourished by it. Such symbolism expresses the nondualistic, poetic mind of ancient women, who could experience their bodies as whole worlds or universes, and the universe as their own body.

Ecstasy is the dance of the individual with the All.

Ek-stasis means standing outside "one's self," and so canceling out the conditioned mind. All life was experienced as partaking of a material-spiritual wholeness that was her. In this magic unity, ecstasy and responsibility (i.e., responsiveness) were one. And so the earliest communicators with her, of her essence, were ecstatic women—shamans and seers. In their trance states, they were responsible for keeping the energy channels open and flowing between each individual, the group, and the cosmic source. They healed, balanced, and translated the life forces from one energy manifestation to another. It is significant that to this day, within almost all the patriarchal world religions, women's robes are still the official priestly garb, and male priests function as a kind of "male mother" to the believers. Among the Siberian tribes, male shamans have always worn ornamental and symbolic "breasts" on their robes. When "civilized" men become the moralistic priests of the new Father God, women (and pagans of both sexes) remain the shamans (the witches) of the ecstatic Mother.

The reality implicit in the Universe—in each one of us, in the self at the heart of being—is her way. It is very ancient, and has no time.

"*My me is God, nor do I know myself save in Her.*"[3]

Ecstasy is the only way through which the soul can lose itself in union with her. Some male mystics have also understood this. Martin Buber describes prenatal life as the original state of ecstatic consciousness within a sexual-spiritual universe, "a flowing toward each other, a bodily reciprocity." The mother's womb is a condensed experience of the cosmos. At birth we forget this undivided world, but we never forget completely. The memory lingers as a "secret image of a wish," a desire for total reintegration, and this is the real meaning of the human longing to return to the womb. It is not at all a sign of pathology or inadequacy, not a backward craving, but an urge to expand, to reestablish the cosmic connection.[4]

Contemporary researchers have found neurological connections between religious or trance experience and female sexuality. In women's brains there are unique neural links between the forebrain and the cere-

Universal Creation/Sheela na Gig, Sjöö, 1978

bellum, which allow sensations of physical pleasure to be directly integrated into the neocortex, or high brain center. This explains why some women experience orgasm so intense that they enter "religious" trance, or altered states of consciousness. And this ecstatic female orgasmic experience, in which the physical and the spiritual are fused and realized as one, is at the core of all mystical experience. This is why, in the original religion of the Great Mother, body and mind and spirit are always integrated. Because human male brains do not seem to have these neurological connections (just as human male sexuality has not evolved radically beyond primate sexuality, while human females, through the shift from estrus to menstrual cycles, have evolved a nonreproductive sexual capacity that functions primarily for affectional bonding), the researchers conclude that it is women who must take the lead in further human evolution—"toward the integration of the conscious and the unconscious mind and to a more profound understanding of the spiritual nature of the species."[5]

What these modern researchers are now "discovering" is something ancient women always knew. The warring dualisms of "matter vs. spirit," the hostile antagonisms of "sexual body" versus "religious truth," are recent patriarchal inventions, destructively forced on the world and the soul. They had no place at the beginning of things, for they are neither natural nor true. For women, at any rate, they can never be true; and that is why the first religion, originated by women, was a sexual-spiritual religion, the celebration of cosmic ecstasy. Among these early women, though some more receptive psyches might have acted as shamanic trance-channels, we can imagine no real leaders, no followers, no hierarchies—just as there was no hierarchic distinction made between ordinary daily tasks and the most exalted rituals—because we can see these women sharing experience as a kind of ecstatic rite in itself. They knew *life* as an ecstatic rite—and as their right to ecstasy.

FEMALE COSMOLOGY: THE CREATION OF THE UNIVERSE

The universe exists as sleeping darkness, unknowable, unknown, wholly immersed in deep sleep. Does she dream in sleep or only when she wakes? We know not. She sleeps. And then in her sleep the divine self appears with passionate creative power. She stirs, dispelling darkness. She who is subtle and full of desire, imperceptible and everywhere, now and eternal, who contains all created beings, wakes—then the world stirs. When she slumbers tranquilly, the universe sinks into sleep. Thus she, the imperishable one—who seems always perishing, always changing—alternatively waking and sleeping, incessantly revivifies and destroys the whole of creation. . . . [1]

She is the dark night and the black soil that holds within itself the intense powers of light, the secrets and the forces of all life. She is the mouth, the vagina, the passionate and wise source from which all comes and to which all returns. . . .

The black-winged night laid a silver egg (the moon) in the womb of darkness, in the dark waters. The divine one resided in that egg during a whole year. Then she by herself alone divided into two halves and out of these halves She formed heaven and earth. . . .

The most holy one created the world like an embryo, as an embryo grows from the navel, so she began to create the world by the navel, and from there it spread, grew, multiplied in all directions . . . she was both seed and flower, both primordial and final. The first vibrations of the egg of the world which unfold to the edges of the universe are both expanding and contracting, emerging from the source and pulsing outward to disappear into a spherical vortex. The still center (the heart) is the axis of creation—the universal continuum perpetually unfolds, pulses outward, contracts—perpetually spinning through its own center. . . .

The egg is a symbol of female creation, female generative energy. At the pole of contraction, our universe existed as an invisible point of dark light, of compacted *potentia* and energy. This was the world egg.

The spiral movement that creates a center and a moving, continuous whole is also that which, combined with gravitational contraction, creates the solar system, and the atom—and on a large scale, the galaxy. Galaxies seem to be created by the inward spiraling of interstellar gas, and the outward spiraling of heat. The same vortical laws govern the movements of water, which composes nearly three-quarters of our physical bodies—and three-quarters of the physical body of the earth. Water is pure, potential, and unformed matrix from which all life on earth takes its being—water that is not a thing, but a flow, a dance. It is from the involution of the unformed but *forming* Waters that the egg crystalizes, takes shape, by the turning-in on itself of energy, of matter, of consciousness. The macrocosmic cyclic and spiraling movements are mirrored in the spiraling cycles of the human microcosm—our waking and sleeping, our sexuality and solitude, our emotions, our wisdom, our conceptions of time itself, which moves continuously around an unmoved center.[2]

All these ideas, of the original Goddess, were incorporated into ancient Hindu belief (and are contained within modern physics and physical cosmogony). Within later Hindu thought, the Goddess Shakti-Kali, joined with the God Shiva, dances the world into creation—continuously, orgiastically expanding and contracting together. But the spiral, and later the labyrinth, are everywhere and from the beginning associated with her original cosmology—*all* religion and cosmology, in all their forms, originate in the great laws of life spiraling around the mystery-center of creation:

> The mysteries of life, birth and death
> —violence, love and beauty
> out of body-tearing blood-pain
> comes tenderness-in-a-whisper-said *Love*
> for created being.[3]

(In later Hindu mysticism the egg is identified as *male* generative energy. Whenever you come upon something like this, stop and ponder. If it is absurdly inorganic—male gods "brooding on the waters" or "laying eggs"—then you know you are in the presence of an original Goddess cosmology stolen and displaced by later patriarchal scribes.)

THE COSMIC SERPENT

This is a Pelasgian creation myth:

> In the beginning, Euronyme, the Goddess of All Things, rose naked from Chaos, but found nothing substantial for her feet to rest upon, and therefore divided the sea from the sky, dancing lonely upon its waves. She danced towards the south, and the wind set in motion behind her seemed as something new and apart with which to begin the work of creation. Wheeling about, She caught hold of this north wind, rubbed it between her hands and behold! the great serpent Ophion. Euronyme danced to warm herself, wildly and more wildly, until Ophion, grown lustful, coiled about those divine limbs and was moved to couple with her . . . so She was with child.[1]

This Pelasgian myth is much older than Greek legend. Still it comes from the transition period when the Great Mother is no longer believed to give birth parthenogenically; there is now a perception of the male part in conception. In this myth, Euronyme is fertilized by the North wind; the wind is the subtle body of the serpent, its movements through the air. Ultimately, though, she is still seen as the creator of male sexual energy—the generative force of the wind and the great serpent—as an emanation from herself; from her passion and her dance.

Great live snakes were everywhere kept in the Goddess's temples during the Neolithic. In wall paintings, bas reliefs, statues, she was often represented carrying snakes in her upraised arms or coiled around her. Or, she was imaged as a serpent herself, with a woman's body and a snake's head. Of one Near Eastern Goddess it was said, "Paghat, She who observes the water, who studies the dew from the drop, who knows the courses of the stars, Her heart is like a serpent."[2] The Sumerian Goddess was known as the Great Mother Serpent of Heaven, perhaps another image of the Milky Way, the great spiraling galactic arms.[3]

Everywhere in world myth and imagery, the Goddess-Creatrix was coupled with the sacred serpent. In Egypt she was the Cobra Goddess; the use of the cobra in her ceremonies and icons was so ancient that the inscribed picture of a cobra preceded the names of all goddesses, and became "the hieroglyphic sign for the word *Goddess*."[4] Isis also was pictured as a Serpent Goddess. Far away, in Australia, the aboriginal Goddess Una, who established the earth, was pictured, sometimes as three sisters, with the rainbow snake held up in her arms. And this is a Venezuelan creation myth, from the native Yaruros:

> At first there was nothing. Then *Puana* the Snake, who came first, created the world and everything in it. . . . *Kuma* was the first person to people the land. . . . Everything sprang from *Kuma*, and everything that the Yaruros do was established by Her.[5]

Australia, Venezuela, the ancient Middle East . . . the distribution of the Goddess and her Serpent is global; on South Pacific islands with no snakes, the eel is mythologized. Ancient Celtic and Teutonic goddesses were wrapped with snakes. The Chinese celebrated the dragon power, and the Aztecs and Mayas of Mexico and Central America imaged the feathered serpent, or flying snake, a form of dragon. Both the monumental Karnak of Egypt and the mysterious standing-stone alignment called Carnac in Brittany are magic snake alignments; both names mean "serpent's mount."

When we see this worldwide occurrence of the Goddess and her Serpent, and then recall the ancient African Black Goddess, the Black Witch, imaged with the snake in her belly—we can see the profound power as well as universality of this cosmological symbol, its range of endurance in the human mind. And we begin to see why the upstart patriarchal religions based themselves on the utter destruction of the goddess/serpent, pictured by the Babylonians as "primeval chaos"—an image picked up later by the Hebrews and used in the biblical Genesis, where Eve linked with her serpent become the symbols of ontological evil. Among patriarchal Hebrews, the serpent was portrayed as Samael, the brother of the "evil" first woman, Lilith. When Old Testament reformers like Hezekiah went around destroying "brazen serpents"—cult images made of brass—as "pagan abominations," what they were really doing was attacking the primordial Goddess religion followed by all their neighbors. The Hebrew patriarchs tried to destroy the world's original, most widespread, and enduring religion by branding it as "evil," and by portraying the Mother Goddess and her magic snake-lover as the source, not of all life, but of "all wickedness"—hated and condemned by their new tribal god Yahweh. To the degree that they were historically successful in this attempt, Western biblicized peoples have lost their original concept, and memory, of what the Goddess and her Serpent really meant—to all people, and all time.

The snake was first of all a symbol of eternal life (like the moon), since each time it shed its skin it seemed reborn. It represented cosmic continuity within natural change—spiritual continuity within the changes of material life. Gliding as it does in and out of holes and caverns in the earth, the serpent also symbolized the underground, abode of the dead who wait for rebirth. Its undulations symbolized the serpentine earth currents of the underground waters. The serpent path on earth was the terrestrial energy-flow; the serpent path in the sky was the winding spray of stars in the galactic spiral-arm, or Milky Way.

The connection between snakes and birds is evolutionary: the bird species evolved directly out of the reptile species, the shining scales becoming feathers. Some snakes are born alive, but reptiles generally, and many snakes, lay eggs—as birds do. And the egg belongs to the Goddess. The formation of the world, and of life itself, took its beginnings from a double egg (the chromosome and its polar body?) in the midst of which a germ resided, the life embryo. Some of the most ancient Paleolithic engraved and sculpted Goddess-images show her as a divine water-bird, with a long, snaky, phallic neck and bearing the cosmic double egg in her protruding buttocks—so expressing, in the Upper Stone Age, a nonphysical reality through these material symbols of becoming.[6]

The mystery of earthly life has its origins in water—in oceans, deep lakes, and shallow pools, cave grottoes, streams, and rivers; in the sea-like pulse and taste of blood. Before a child is born, water flows out of the ruptured womb-ocean within the mother. The very ancient Bird-clawed and Horned Goddess was born in the womb of the mythical waters. The cosmic egg was created by the cosmic horned (lunar) snake, or laid by a mythic water-bird—both bird and snake vehicles of an energy which has its source, both evolutionary and magical, in terrestrial water. She is one, she is two—mistress of waters, and of sky and air. In Egypt, in Babylon, in Crete, India, and ancient Europe, it was believed that her abode is beyond the upper waters, beyond the meandrous labyrinths. She was ruler over the waters on earth, in the skies, and beyond the clouds, where the primordial waters flow. To represent all this, the Bird-and-Snake Goddess was pictured: Her body is decorated with snake spirals, her arms and legs are snakes, her eyebrows are horned—and the magical source of life, the double egg, lies within her.

The Goddess was also she who gives life to the dead, aided by her magic serpent who winds in and out of the earthly tomb-womb. The snake—with its stylized image, the spiral—was seen as the vehicle of immortality, and the image of spontaneous life energy, its continuous flow. The snake could shed its skin but still live, as the Moon birthed herself from her own darkness, and the womb bled periodically without being wounded—all were seen as miraculously interconnected transformations. To the serpent was attributed power that can move the entire cosmos. And does.

The cosmic snake winds over and around the cosmic egg like a continuous flow of water, of energy; the beginning of life within the egg is caused by the orbiting of two snakes within it, their interaction causing and sustaining a tension-field which becomes form.

Bronze female head from Benin, Nigeria, with snakes issuing from nostrils, birds on head

The symbolisms of snake, egg, horns, fish, and doe, along with the female images of vulvas, triangles, spiraling circles—all related to water—originate in Stone Age times. Egg-shaped sculptures with the vulva engraved on them have been dated from circa 6000 B.C. The horned rams and bulls of Neolithic ritual were sacrificed to the ancient Bird-and-Snake Goddess. Marija Gimbutas points out that the sixth millennium B.C. saw centuries of drought, and from this comes an obsession with rain and water symbolism, which is everywhere present in ritual, on vessels, and in ideograms of that time.[7] The snake spiral was *the* basis of ornamental composition in ancient Europe, its peak expression being circa 5000 B.C.

So we have here some extremely ancient and mysterious connections, or psychic resonances, involving snakes—spirals—waters and the tides—menstrual periods—the moon—the dead—oracular powers—psychic healing—bisexuality—the magnetic earth-current—the womb—the stars—immortality and ever-renewed life.

In Africa "snakes issuing from the nostrils" indicated clairvoyant powers—doubtless related to the third eye, the pineal gland behind the nose—and the snake-hair of Medusa had the same significance (one legendary-historic Medusa was an Amazonian queen in the region of present-day Morocco-Algeria, North Africa). According to Merlin Stone, snake venom (injected into people who have previously been immunized against it) has highly hallucinogenic qualities; some venom is chemically similar to mescaline (peyote) or the psilocybin of mushrooms. Reported effects were clairvoyance, extraordinary mental powers, enhanced creativity, prophetic visions, and illumination about the primal processes of existence. As Stone remarks, the sacred snakes kept at the Goddess's oracular shrines "were perhaps not merely the symbols but actually the instruments through which the experiences of divine revelation were reached." And so the Egyptian Cobra Goddess was also known as the Lady of Spells.[8] We can be sure the ancient women shamans worldwide were aware of this property of snake venom—and that this was one of the recognized meanings of the snake symbols and images inscribed everywhere.

Rudolf Steiner, founder of Anthroposophy, spoke of the innate clairvoyant power of ancient humanity, a power lost by "modern man," who is now unaware of his primordial connection with universal Life and its magic energies. Reduced to a mere mechanism, a physical recording apparatus, "he" lives in a void of utter loneliness and alienation. For it is precisely the astral-lunar region, the psychic world of supersensual perception—called by occultists "the astral serpent"—which partriarchy tells us to destroy, to overcome in the name of an abstract, static, asexual, hyperrational, and mechanistic system.

Finally, the snake came to symbolize the phallus, male sexual energy, which was understood to be originally contained *inside* the Goddess—born from her, and returning to her again, when at the end of each world cycle (expansion-contraction) she curls up in dark sleep. Though Upper Paleolithic images of copulation between women and men occur, icons and myths of the Great Mother do not show her actually mated with a human son/lover until Middle Neolithic times, circa 5500 B.C. At this time, and especially after the peak period of Çatal Hüyük, there seems to have begun a divorce of male attributes from the Mother; and quite a "phallic obsession" developed, shown in representations of phallic cups, standing phallic stones, and ithyphallic gods (though pictures of shamans in trance, with huge erections, go far back into the Upper Paleolithic). But these are not aggressive or misogynistic phallic images; rather, they seem to represent the phallus *serving* the Goddess, women, and the life processes of all. This is really shown in the tradition of Goddess-phallus stones, with the Goddess-figure carved on phallic-shaped bones or rocks; this phallic-form of the Goddess is found continuously from the Paleolithic, thru the Neolithic, and into "the proto-urban period in Mesopotamia."[9] Marija Gimbutas sees these Goddess-phallus icons, deriving from the Old Stone Age, as suggesting the "androgynous nature" of the Great Mother.[10] This is so. They also suggest the potential unity of the sexes, in mutual love-service, before their disastrous splitting apart by patriarchal misogyny and puritanical sex-codes.

At any rate, from the period of patriarchal cosmological texts (circa 4000–3000 B.C.) the serpent comes down to us as a narrowed and pejorative symbol—of male sexuality, or "immoral sex," and of evil.

The Egyptians believed that from the union of chaos and the wind (the life-breath, the All-Goddess dancing with her own breath) came forth Maat, in the form of an egg. *Maat* was the Egyptian word for both "mother" and "matter"; it was the primordial mud of the Nile from which life grew. It also meant "truth" and "justice," and was often symbolized both as a feather and a vulture—the feather weighed in the balance scales

Yin & Yang within the Goddess, Sjöö, 1980

against the soul at death, and the Vulture-Mother who swoops down to pick the dead bones clean for rebirth. Maat as the ultimate truth contained within herself the potential existence, and nonexistence, of all things, all polarities. She was also pure Nothingness, having no identifiable characteristics, but the eternal potency—and potential—of everything.

Another symbol for this same complex of ideas is the oroboros, the serpent curled with its tail in its mouth, forming the perfect circle, or female O, or zero—the cycle of all, and of nothing. The continuous eternal wisdom-cycle of all coming from nothing and returning to nothing again. The hallucinated dream-circle of sleep, waking, and sleep; and who can say which is the dream, and which is not?

THE WORLD EGG: YIN/YANG

The ancient Great Mother of All Living gave birth parthenogenetically, to herself and the entire cosmos. She was the world egg, containing the two halves of all polarities or dualisms—the yin/yang of continuity and change, expansion and contraction of the universe. This process is symbolized by the spiral turning continuously in on itself, by conscious breath waking from sleep and sinking back into sleep—Kali (or Euronyme) dancing the universe into being and then to destruction and death. The ascending spiral is matter transforming into spiritual/psychic energy. Simultaneously, from the descending spiral, the materialization of the spirit, comes the differentiation of the whole manifest world. The spiral involution of energy into matter is the primary movement of the universe, into created beings; the spiral evolution of matter into energy is the creative movement of these beings, consciously evolving back to their source. Inhaling and exhaling breaths of living Cosmos spirals the Universe into creation and dissolution. Energy↔Matter. World↔Spirit. Radiant energy can be transformed into massive particles, and vice versa. The Spiral is the symbolic key to immortality—or eternal process—and is identified with the moon.

Ancient as this cosmology is, it remains the most accurate statement of cosmic process yet made. Twentieth-century physicists, using their very different mathematical language, have only been able to confirm these ancient conceptions of how the universe creates and recreates itself.

The world egg's two halves were white and black—light and dark, day and night, hot and cold, life and death. It contained within itself all oppositions but it also stated the union of opposites, as the continuum is contained and synthesized within the spiral. In the Orient, some early time in the millennia before our era, this idea was formalized in the concept of *yin/yang. Yin,* or negative principle, originally referred to the dark or shadow side of a mountain; it shared attributes with the earth, moon, and water. *Yang,* or positive principle, signifying bright banners in the wind, or the light side of a mountain, was linked with the sky, sun, and fire. After several generations of Eastern philosophers, everything became classified under these categories, including the sexes: *yin* was female, *yang* was male.

But this Eastern dualism differed originally from the moralistic dualism of the Christian West. *Yin* and *yang* were not seen as hostile and irreconcilable opposites, vying for control over the universe. Nor was one "good" and the other "evil." On the contrary, *yin* and *yang* constantly complement each other, to maintain cosmic harmony. And they are not fixed, static principles but transform each other, and transmute into each other, in an ongoing process. Without the eternal movements and interchanges of these forces, life wouldn't exist. Winter, which is *yin*, changes into summer, which is *yang*. Both *yin* and *yang* can create; both can destroy. The life-giving sun, which can also scorch and kill life, gives way to the dark barren cold of the earth, in which new life-seeds will invisibly germinate.

The *yin/yang* images and conceptual categories are *pagan*: "from the land," since they emerge from close prolonged experience and observation of natural processes. These processes are not linear, but cyclic: Life transmutes into death, which turns into life again, in a great revolving wheel. The moon goes through its changes, dies, and is reborn—because it circles in a circling cosmos—and so the moon, like the serpent, is the avatar of these processes. The psychic focus is not on the mutual antagonisms, but on the subtle interchanges and permutations—the dance—of the polarities. Later mandarin-philosophers, like Confucius, used the *yin/yang* principles to serve the hierarchic politics of the Chinese court and the patriarchal state, emphasizing dominant *yang* over submissive *yin*.

Earlier Taoists, though, gave full value to the negative force, or shadow side, *yin*, as a creative power equal to the *yang*. Taoism, a mystic and sexual religious philosophy, originated in ancient Chinese matriarchy, which saw the male as the "earth-animal," and the female as the "animal of change," or transforming principle. The original *I Ching* characters for the female and male principles—the Receptive and the Creative hexagrams—contained these matrifocal meanings also.[1] As Western alchemists and later Western physicists were to confirm, it is the negative pole that initiates the creative activity of matter. Some physicists theorize that the universe began to organize, gathering shape and motion, in the shadow sides of randomly scattered particles. Also, until recently, scientists have assumed that the "weight" of the universe was in bright stars and speedy particles. But now they have found enormous amounts of dark, cold matter circling the stars and all galactic bodies, and this matter is preponderant and responsible for the "weight" of the universe, which functions as gravity. As they report, " . . . the structure of the whole universe appears to be shaped by the gravity of dark matter."[2]

What has been called the dark, the negative, the female, in both the celebratory and the pejorative senses, is now seen to be the original creating and sustaining force of the universe. If the expanding universe is ever to contract again, it will be from the gravity of this dark matter.

The corruption of the original *yin/yang* oracular-mystical synthesis into a dualistic system of hierarchy, dominance, and oppression occurred, in the East as in the West, in the shift of human culture from land-tribal to court-hierarchic—i.e., in the shift from matrifocal-rural to patrifocal-urban social structures. In the patriarchal struggle for property and power, the *yin/yang* equation became a tool, a weapon, of inequality and repression, both economic and sexual. Now the yin, as receptive-feminine, was interpreted as sexual, intellectual, and spiritual passivity, inferiority, and subordination; *yang*, as active-masculine, was interpreted as sexual, intellectual, and spiritual aggression, superiority, and dominance. In the West also these religiously institutionalized sexual dualisms have created the ideal of heterosexual patriarchal marriage, in which a sexually oppressed and economically dependent "wife" serves a sexually and economically dominant "husband." These concepts are highly political and serve to maintain and justify patriarchy and the subjugation of women. *Yin*-wisdom is scorned by men as "irrational weakness," and *yang*-power is used to justify any kind of exploitative action, no matter how unjust and brutal.

But these are not the original meanings of these terms. The original meanings apply to the interworkings of rather impersonal, and certainly nondomestic forces—much like the negative and positive electrical poles in a battery. As R. Buckminster Fuller put it:

> Energy,
> when its potential is built to sufficient voltage
> must arc over to the dominant negative—[3]

THE GYNANDROUS GREAT MOTHER

In truth, Western Christianity's stereotypes of "weak femininity" and "strong masculinity" are among the most extreme in history. Many of these sex-role traits originated among the privileged classes—the only people who could afford passive and dependent women, and for whom a bored and indulgent lifestyle made sex-role playing "an amusement." Bound feet among the wives of wealthy Chinese men of the past served the same "esthetic" and entertainment function, and were a sign of privilege. In the modern West, with its relative economic abundance, many strict sex-role traits once indigenous to the wealthy have been passed on, via the media, to the "masses." So we see female office workers tottering to the job on spiky high-heeled shoes; such shoes were once worn only by royalty, by "courtiers and their ladies"—and were originally devised to be worn by sacred priests, to keep their *mana* from escaping into the ground. One thing "democracy" does is spread the silliness around. Unfortunately, with many of the silliest sex-roles, people tend to forget their origin in culture and class, and believe they come directly "from nature," or "from God"—and so we see the silliest of customs enforced with humorless severity, and sometimes the most punitive laws.

Extremely sex-biased roles are the product of rigid heterosexuality, intellectual dualism, and a labor-exploitive culture. They didn't exist in early societies. And many of the sex customs that did exist were just the reverse of "ours." For example, among hunting-and-gathering people worldwide, the "home" is not only the property of the woman, but is built by her—and, if it's portable, carried around on her back when she moves. Among traditional Chinese the women wore pants, men wore skirts. Among people with *couvade* customs, the women usually give birth in relative ease, while their husbands writhe and howl and grind their teeth. And, among the still-pagan twelfth-century Irish (to the horror of their chronicler, Giraldus Cambrensis), it was the females who pissed standing up, while the males squatted—![1] With sex-roles and customs, it is very hard to make an absolute statement—"women always do this," "men exclusively do that"—without having it immediately contradicted by some culture, some place, at some time.

Indeed, the further back one goes in time the more bisexual, or gynandrous, is the Great Mother. As Charlotte Woolf says in *Love Between Women*, perhaps the present-day Lesbian woman is the closest in character to ancient women—with their fierce insistence on strength, independence, and integrity of consciousness.[2]

The first love-object for both women and men is the mother; but in patriarchy, the son has to reject the mother to be able to dominate the wife as "a real man"—and the daughter must betray her for the sake of "submitting to a man." In matriarchal society this double burden of biological and spiritual betrayal does not occur. For both women and men there is a close identification with the collective group of mothers, with Mother Earth, and with the Cosmic Mother. And, as psychoanalysts keep repeating, this identification is conducive to bisexuality in both sexes. But homosexuality in tribal or pagan men was *not* based on rejection of the Mother, or the female, as is often true in patriarchal culture; rather, it was based on brother-love, brother-affinity, as sons of the mother. And lesbianism among women was not based on a fear and rejection of men, but on the daughter's desire to reestablish union with the Mother, and with her own femaleness. The collective of mothers, identified with by both daughters and sons, was made up of strong, creative, productive, sexually free, and visionary women. And so the ideal of womanliness, for both sexes, was *not* the enforced and mindless submissiveness of the oppressed, as it is in patriarchal culture.

In many of the most ancient images of the Goddess, she is shown with both breasts and phallus, as hermaphroditic—e.g., "Bearded Ishtar." Divine bisexuality stressed her absolute power—especially over her own sexuality, which was a spiritual as well as an emotional-physical expression. Male shamans in many primal cultures wore women's clothes and lived like women, often in homosexual relationships. The Neolithic Goddess was served in her temples by bisexual or Lesbian priestesses and by bisexual or homosexual priests. In the disorder of the Late Neolithic, in the transition from matriarchy to patriarchy, eunuch priests served her, men who had castrated themselves in an orgiastic identification with the Goddess. (One branch of the Essenes, the Semitic sect with which Jesus was later associated in Qumran on the Dead Sea, served as eunuch priests in the Temple of Artemis at Ephesus, on the west coast of Turkey.) With what we know of this period, men were feeling under extreme pressure to identify either with the Ancient Great Mother, or with the militant new male gods, and devotion on both sides went to extremes—because such acts had become politicized with the rise of patriarchal misogyny, a fanaticizing sex phobia new in the world.

Creative women and men in all ages have found rigid heterosexuality in conflict with being fully alive and aware on all levels—sexual, psychic, and spiritual—because it is a mental and emotional limitation, as well as a physical one. It is as if, on all levels of our being, we are split in half—locked into one half, and forbidden the other. We are split against ourselves, and against the "self" in the other, by this moralistic opposition of natural polarities in the very depths of our souls. And the result is war, necrophilia, alienation at the root. And if we don't resolve this, we will all die—of a mutual murder that is total suicide.

As Esther Harding says in *Women's Mysteries, Ancient and Modern,* modern woman, at the core of her being, is cut off from the source of life.[3] With rigidly imposed heterosexual roles, women (and men also) are emotionally and mentally stunted. Women are also physically stunted—compare us with statues and reliefs of the Amazons, or of the huge Celtic warrior women!

In ancient Scotland, land of the Picts—who were later invaded by Celts from Northern Ireland—some very mysterious and legendary warrior women lived. They were Amazonian battle-fighters and witch-shamans, a Lesbian/bisexual sisterhood entrusted with the guardianship of their tribe's secret powers and visions. According to Jean Markale in *Women of the Celts,* all the great Celtic warrior-heroes were initiated into the profession of arms, and also into the sacred mysteries of sex, by these women. The Picts were the naked shock-troops of all the Celtic nations; they went into battle—women and men side-by-side—wearing only their blue body paint (woad), sacred to the Earth Mother. They were called Picts (Indo-European *Peik*, "tattooed," Goidelic *Qict*, and Latin *pictus*, "painted"), as they decorated their entire bodies with these blue tattoos of all the magic birds, beasts, and fish belonging to the Great Mother. They practiced communal sex rites, and sometimes ritual cannibalism. The Celtic women, generally, were known for their great physical strength and ferocious bravery in battle. Roman historians wrote that among the Gauls, the women were almost as tall as the men, and equal in courage. The Teutonic as well as Celtic tribes were often led into battle by Warrior Queens, and the invading Roman soldiers reportedly feared the fighting women more than their male companions.[4]

As Briffault noted again and again, among "primitive" people not yet contaminated by the physical habits and role playing of "civilization," it was common to find the women equal in stature, often larger than the men, with greater musculature and endurance capacities. Among Stone Age skeletons of Neanderthals it is often impossible to determine sex by size or weight of bones; early females and males were almost equal in stature, equally strong. As seen in the most ancient Paleolithic images of the Goddess, the solid strength and massiveness of the female body was an ideal. And certainly the human race, and earlier hominids, couldn't have survived two to three million years of catastrophic earth changes if females had been as physically weak and mentally dependent during those long, hard ages as we are supposed to be today. Anne Cameron's *Daughters of Copper Woman,* stories of Northwest Pacific Indian women from Vancouver Island, gives us a real picture of the strengths needed by early women. To

Cromlech Goddess, Sjöö, 1980

be fit—as mothers, as lovers, food and shelter producers, as wise women, as visionaries, as creators and guardians of a whole people's culture—these females began undergoing rigorous physical training programs, long before puberty, to develop every strength of mind, of heart, of leg and arm muscle, and of spirit needed by them to be—grown women! I.e., fully evolved human beings.[5] And so the young women of ancient matriarchal Sparta also developed skilled and athletic bodies. When they married, the "wedding ceremony" included a wrestling match with their new mate.

In "civilized" patriarchal society, on the other hand, a physically undeveloped, lobotomized, and desexualized woman can live what is called a "normal life." Here are the memorable thoughts of the psychosurgeons:

> Lobotomized women make good housekeepers. . . . it is more socially acceptable to lobotomize women (than men) because creativity, which the operation totally destroys, is, in this society, "an expendable nullity in women."[6]

There is no such thing as a partial liberation. No one can be "economically free" while sexually repressed and bifurcated; no one can be "sexually liberated" while an economic slave. No one can enjoy "mental freedom" while the body's labor and sexuality are exploited and conditioned by oppression. And if we pretend that we can "free our spirits" while the bodies, minds, and emotions of humanity are still straightened by bio-phobic and exploitive sexual, social, and economic ideologies, we delude ourselves. Freedom is all or nothing. And there is no freedom for males, of any class or color or ethnic group, while the female remains unfree.

Ancient bisexual woman was inventor, scientist, builder, artist, healer, producer of craft and culture, shaman, ecstatic visionary, warrior, and leader. *This* is our total potential, when our life energies are not divided against themselves, and against us, blocked and distorted by cultural and religious stereotypes. This is just the beginning of our potential, when our energies are able to flow out freely to create the world—as symbolized by the self-sustaining power of the gynandrous Great Mother.

MYSTERIES OF THE THRONE, THE CAVE, AND THE LABYRINTH

To return to our beginnings: *All religion is about the mystery of creation.* If the mystery of birth is the origin of religion, it is to the woman that we must look for the phenomenon that first made her aware of the unseen power. Primeval woman, like the animals, probably first *knew* she was pregnant when she felt the first movement within her, at the quickening. She was not aware of the male's part in conception, nor of the moment of inception of pregnancy. Of course she would notice breast-swelling, perhaps nausea. But doubtless she would understand this first quickening movement as the beginning of the process leading to birth. Among people worldwide who believed that a woman is impregnated by the spirits, or by the wind, this first movement would be the kinetic announcement of the entrance of the new spirit-being into her body.

Woman's awe at her capacity to create life *is* the basis of mystery. Earliest religious images show pregnancy, rather than birth and nurturing, as *the numinous or magical state.* Numerous Paleolithic figurines of women representing the pregnant Goddess go back over 30,000 years. It is not until the Middle Neolithic, circa 6000–5000 B.C., that figures of the Great Mother holding a child appear. These are fascinating figures from Çatal Hüyük and Hacilar, in the region of modern Turkey. The first, carved in gray-green schist, shows the Goddess as two female bodies, back to back, one nursing an infant and the other embracing a lover. The Hacilar clay statuette shows a nursing male child with his genitals near the Mother's vulva.[1] In both statues the female is larger than the male; both show the beginnings, within the Great Mother religion, of a companion worship of a young male who is both her son and her lover. For many Neolithic centuries this son/lover of the Great Goddess is the only thing approaching a male god to be found. And, coupled with the Mother, it remained a central image in later Near Eastern religions—e.g., Isis and the child Horus in Egypt, Mary with both the newborn and the dead Jesus in her arms.

In predynastic Egypt, the Goddess of the women was Ta-Urt, the "Great One," who was imaged as a pregnant hippopotamus standing on its hind legs. Figures of Ta-Urt are among the earliest Egyptian amulets,

Labyrinth carved on stone in Ireland, Sjöö collection, 1978

and her worship continued until the coming of Christianity—and probably secretly among women for centuries after. Christian and other patriarchal priesthoods have never been any help to women in the great female experiences of menstruation, pregnancy, childbirth, and nursing. Clearly the pregnant Goddess of the Cro-Magnon caves, Ta-Urt, and later goddesses of pregnancy and birth were shaped out of women's needs and experiences and beliefs. This is the original transformation mystery: primordial birth, in which we struggle alone facing death and pain in order to create life within the cosmic womb of the unknown. Only women are ever truly alone, as the universe is alone with herself. And birth is the supreme paradox of aloneness, when a woman in sweating and groaning solitude brings forth the continuity of human life. Men can only imitate this experience by participating in the Goddess-mysteries of rebirth in the sacred caves; and in fact, worldwide, men's original rituals were imitations of the female mysteries of menstruation and childbirth.

Images of the pregnant Goddess were also found in the excavations of Tell Haraf, dating from 5000 B.C. This Goddess is shown sitting on the earth, embodying the earth that belongs to her. In ritual and custom, to sit on something has the symbolic meaning of "taking possession."

In later matriarchal times, *she was the throne*—the throne symbolized her lap. The Queen came to power by sitting on this lap or womb of the Goddess, so becoming one with her power. Among the Ashanti of West

Africa there was a cult of the throne, and giant throne-replicas have been found in the Ashanti graves. The Black Goddess was worshiped throughout the Ashanti territory.[2]

All the great mountains were seen as the Goddess "sitting" on the earth. The mountain was the original throne-womb; it combines the symbols of earth, cave, bulk, height, and immortality. In the towering mountain overlooking the land is embodied the enormous strength of the Goddess. Throughout Thracian, Macedonian, Greek, and Cretan lands are mountains with huge thrones at their summits, carved laboriously from the rock. These are the "empty thrones," waiting for the Goddess to take her seat.

This custom was taken over by later patriarchal kings. To be "enthroned" is to be empowered, i.e., to receive the power of the Great Mother and her mandate to rule. This is why Egyptian paintings and statues depict the small, mortal king sitting on the throne-lap of the huge Goddess Isis. In this way the king was reborn, or made immortal, and thereby given the sacred power to rule over the people. He had true power *only* as her son.

The cave, as the womb of the Earth Goddess, was considered by the ancients to be the repository of mystic influences. In the original cosmology, a cave was the symbol of the whole world, providing passage for the dead and for the rebirth of souls. Many tribal people today still hold the belief that their first, mythic ancestors emerged from caverns, or mounds in the earth. The cave was the home of our Ice Age ancestors, when they were making the transition from hominids to *Homo sapiens.* Paleolithic caves were the matrix of internalized consciousness: womb-like, skull-like, tomb-like. Animal souls were believed to live in the dark, echoing caverns. This is where one went to commune with the deepest, most resonant, and awesome powers. The wall-paintings of animals and humans, in the innermost sanctuaries, could be reached only with great difficulty, along winding paths, narrow ledges, slippery and dangerous passages, often crawling on hands and knees. These were the narrow winding passageways of birth, and rebirth.[3]

I am the Way and the Life.

This was the primordial revelation of the Great Mother. As G. Rachel Levy observes, early people conceived the divine body as "the road travelled by itself and its seeker."[4] The Great Mother was the body of life; she was also the way that must be traveled to realize life.

It was in the spiral, or labyrinth, that the way had to be danced or walked—in all the rites of the Mother throughout the ages, and the world, the way is always connected with a cave/womb, and with a maze-like spiraling entrance and exit. Labyrinths, situated at cave entrances, are always presided over by a mythical woman. Among ancient Cretans, as among present-day Hopis in the American Southwest, the earth womb is depicted as a maze, and the mythic place of emergence of the whole people, and of the individual soul, is called the place of birth, or rebirth. Visually, the Cretan maze-womb and the Hopi maze-womb are identical. In Hindu tradition, both the convolutions of the brain and the eightfold stages of

Cromlech & Serpent Goddess, Sjöö, 1980

the mind (the *manas*) are identified with the winding spiral form of the labyrinth.

A labyrinth both creates and protects the still center (the heart), allowing entry only to the initiated. Before larger knowledge is revealed, old preconceptions must be dissolved by the psychic and ecstatic reentry into the original cosmic womb/cave of the Mother. The pathways between the two worlds were trodden by humans in magic dances and rituals. Perhaps the human collective actually generated as well as absorbed the life forces of the Goddess in these rites, since the roads taken by the divine power are themselves currents of energy. Among hunting-and-gathering peoples, the shamans still go into caves to experience visions, dreams, and spiritual rebirth, and to gain healing powers through resonant communion with the dead. The dead are especially sacred to the Goddess since they directly partake of her being, spirits awaiting rebirth through her physical manifestations. The familiar bull-roarer, still in use among aboriginal people, produces the terrible whirring sound of the spiral—the strange whirlwind of passage between the two worlds.

Extremely complex ideas were expressed through the symbol of the labyrinth. First, the initiate had to find the way through the underworld—the womb of the Mother—going through symbolic death to be reborn again through her on a larger psychic level. Simultaneously, by dancing the winding and unwinding spiral, the initiate reached back to the still heart of cosmos, and so immortality, in her. The dance would have been combined with sexual rites and the taking of some hallucinogen like the legendary soma. In the resulting illumination soma and self were experienced as one with the cosmic self in orgasmic ego-death. The ecstatic center of the labyrinth was the no-mind center of orgasm experienced as death, creative madness, and loss of the conditioned "self." Sexual magic was not practiced for the sake of fertility—especially in early times when no necessary connection was seen between the two. Sexual magic was practiced for the sake of ecstatic self-transcendence, a sexual-spiritual fusion of the human with the cosmic All.

Prana, or life current, in mystic Indian thought, is interrelated with sexual energy, and can be directed by breathing techniques. Mind and breath, united and rhythmically directed towards a chosen goal, is the basis for sexual magic. Breath/air is linked with mind, the creatrix of ideas; they are experienced as identical. The breath (*prana*) is used by the yogi to compel the upward surge of *kundalini,* the sleeping serpent at the base of the spine (the sexual *chakra*). *Kundalini,* the serpent power, is dormant cosmic fire, and she, activated through controlled and concentrated breathing, rises through the six lotuses or body-centers (*chakras*) to unite in the seventh, highest center with pure consciousness (*samadhi*). With this union, liberation is attained, which is true nature and union with cosmic self.

Kundalini, the mystic fire, is also expressed sexually, as in Tantra yoga. Here is the awakening of the great magic power which is shakti-*kundalini*—the cosmic movement which is Shakti, and her movement in the human body which is *kundalini*—their ultimate union bringing great power: the eternally spiraling serpent-force, through which is experienced cosmic timelessness.

In Tibetan mystery schools, the breath plays a vital part in the process of dying. If consciousness is retained to the last, through proper knowledge and concentration, then the breath or soul passes over consciously to the after-death of the organism. There is similar thought in the Egyptian *Book of the Dead,* based on the mysteries of Isis and Osiris. Consciousness must be retained to—and through—the moment of death, to enable the soul to take the right path, the *way*, through the underworld. Concentrated unity of the psyche brings release from the power of death. The same method appears in *The Secret of the Golden Flower,* a Chinese book deriving from ancient matriarchal Taoist ideas.

Jungians pay respect to these mystic and symbolic perceptions of ancient peoples, but still fear the "female realms." This Western rationalist prejudice and fear distorts Jungian commentary on the timeless ritual transformations of the labyrinth: "In all cultures, the labyrinth has the meaning of an entangling and confusing representation of the world of matriarchal consciousness; it can be traversed only by those who are ready

Cailleach & Brigid—Dark Mother & Light Daughter, Sjöö, 1984

for a special initiation into the mysterious world of the collective unconscious."[5]

In Indian mystic symbolism, the multiplicity of this world is shown by the interpenetration of the upward male triangles (phallic) and the downward female triangles (vulva)—the ascending and descending vortices of creative energy. This vulva image, the descending triangle, which signifies cosmic energy spiraling down into manifestation through matter, is a very ancient symbol. It has been found in Paleolithic caves, inscribed on stone blocks lying face downwards on the ground, and within engraved stone circles in the caverns' depths. Ancient people believed that power resided in images themselves—or rather in the resonance between the image and the thing imaged—and this belief still lives in all of us; symbols continue to have great power over the human mind and heart. Contemporary hunting-and-gathering people, such as the Australian aborigines, maintain connections with mythical ancestors by tracing sacred paintings and dreamtime maps on the walls of secret caves. We can imagine that ancient women gained cosmic energy by touching and tracing the sacred vulva-sign of the Great Goddess; just as initiates gained the power and insight of ecstatic death and rebirth by tracing and retracing the sacred spirals of the labyrinth, the womb-tomb-maze of the Great Earth Mother.

THE CULT OF THE DEAD

The idea of the "living dead" can be traced far back also, to Paleolithic times, where it existed first among the Neanderthals, who buried their dead wrapped in fetal position, the bodies and skeletons painted red. Neanderthals also set up bear-skull shrines deep in their caves. Next came the Cro-Magnons of western and southern Europe; they displaced the Neanderthals but also interbred with them, and followed many of the same burial practices. They had a cult of the dead and a cult of the skull, also burying their dead curled up and daubed with red ochre. This ochre-painting of bodies and bones with the magic life-color of blood (*mana*) was for countless millennia believed to give life to the dead, who were buried lovingly, with cherished possessions, in the floors of the caves where they had lived. The cave was the womb of the Mother, and she who gave birth would also give rebirth. Human religious ideas of death and resurrection go back at least this far.

From these burial practices of the Neanderthals and Cro-Magnons, we can assume their belief in themselves as indivisible spiritual entities. Though their material lives were "primitive," by our standards, in their esthetic and spiritual iconographies they are revealed as deeply feeling and evolved beings. They conceived, and experienced, a union between the divine cosmic cycle, the cycles of animal, plant, and human life, and the recent dead. All ancient and contemporary aboriginal people conceive death as naturally continuous with life. Perhaps the need for unity and reunion, expressed by these ceremonies, is a first acknowledgment of a conscious sense of separation, in the evolution of human consciousness. At any rate, in the first human religious rites, rebirth-resurrection-reincarnation were believed to occur within the body of the Mother, as birth, death, and rebirth occur in the great cycles of nature.

The further back one goes into ancient cultures, the more the holy enters nearly every phase and activity of life. Being born, giving birth, making pots, digging food, planting seed, making tools, hunting, building a fire . . . all are acts whose major aspects fall within the sacred sphere. Social groups have magic-religious foundations. Rites of transition from one life stage to another required group participation in ritualized expression, all designed to keep the individual's psyche united and in balance while passing through crises. Death was one of those major life events requiring ritual participation by the group—aimed at reharmonizing the survivors as well as easing the passage of the dead.[1]

Even after people left the caves and took up living in small, settled villages, the dead continued to be buried close by. In the matriarchal town of Middle-Neolithic Çatal Hüyük, generations of the dead were buried under the floors of the homes, beneath the sleeping platforms; in this way they continued to participate in the everyday lives of the living. Their presence was a recognized part of the ongoing life of the matrifocal group, and women shamans performed the death ceremonies. Like magic weavers, they connected the collective dream state, in which past, present, and future psychic and physical realities merge, with the textured realms of the dead. Drugs such as hallucinogenic mushrooms were used as one means of perceiving the underlying realities of the mystic connection.[2] Funeral rites also always included some form of self-wounding, since blood accompanies birth, the moon's cycle, food killing, and other crucial life stages, as well as death. Blood is the physical counterpart of the mysterious terrestrial and cosmic life-flows, and so women's transformation mysteries were all blood mysteries.

THE MOTHER OF WILD ANIMALS AND THE DANCE

Commenting on the almost total blindness of male historians via-à-vis the obvious female orientation of the Upper Paleolithic, William Irwin Thompson writes:

> Because we have separated humanity from nature, subject from object, values from analysis, knowledge from myth, and universities from the universe, it is enormously difficult for anyone but a poet or a mystic to understand what is going on in the holistic and mythopoeic thought of Ice Age humanity. The very language we use to discuss the past speaks of tools, hunters, and *men*, when every statue and painting we discover cries out to us that this Ice Age humanity was a culture of art, the love of animals, and women. . . . Gathering is as important as hunting, but only hunting is discussed. Storytelling is discussed, but the storyteller is a hunter rather than an old priestess of the moon. Initiation is imagined, but the initiate is not the young girl in menarche, about to be wed to the moon, but a young man about to become a great hunter.[1]

What the historians leave blank, our imaginations can fill in, with bright pictures like those covering the sacred cave walls. We know that women's religious rites were never separable from a totality of art, magic, and social and physical realities. The matrifocal group organized its power into a religious and cultural human expression through the medium of art. Art was the tool of the connection, the manifest vision, expressing experience of a single life-giving principle conserved in the changeless Otherworld of the deep caves—where there is perpetual darkness, and time becomes spatial: resonant and static. In such a standing silence, as within a giant, living skull, the dream images make themselves known.

The Great Goddess was the Mother of Wild Animals. The inner recesses and womb-walls of the caverns were alive with magic pictures of her beasts. She was herself an animal, all the animals; in many of the early images she wears an animal mask. As in ancient Chinese Taoism, so in Western pagan religions, the female principle was the transforming animal, the energy of metamorphosis and hence evolution. The brilliant rush of European animal imagery, from Cro-Magnon through Celtic, Nordic, and Teutonic art, and incorporated into medieval bestiaries and illuminated manuscripts, expressed this primal dynamic vision of evolutionary energy as a surge of spirit into multitudinous forms. The Goddess kept her various animal shapes for many thousands of years, among them the doe, the owl, the hare, the vulture, the pig, the cow, the wild mare, the lioness, the crow, the crane, the salmon, the jackal, the hermaphroditic snail, the serpent, the wren, the butterfly and the chrysallis, the spider.

Early human attitude toward animals was totemistic. "Totem" means "related through the mother." The blood-clan's solidarity was identified with some specific plant or animal. Through the totem the life of the human group and the ongoing life of nature were made inseparable. This is the meaning of "sacrament": the absorption by humans of the non-human, or cosmic flow of forms. The secret spirit lives in—and through—the multitude of plant and animal forms which the Goddess can assume at will. This means that any tree or beast, bird or fish or insect, is symbolically/potentially her, and must be related to with magic and respect.

Individual members of a species die, but the group form remains, is permanent, is one of the Great Mother's ideal forms. This is the primal conception of reincarnation. Later European pagans believed in individual soul reincarnation—through many forms, animal and human and demonic—as the mechanism of biological as well as spiritual evolution.

The animism of primal peoples has been called "childish." In fact it is a profound, experiential perception of the evolutionary relation between all life forms as manifestations of the original *one*—the first cell from which all life multiplied, the original cosmic egg. When human survival depends on such a sensitive rapport with the environment—as it always has, and always will—such a conception is not infantile, but crucial. Human survival does indeed depend on a sacramental relation to nature. Now that this relation has been betrayed, and destroyed, we know how important it was. And is. A sacramental bond between our earliest human ancestors and the natural world was the primary factor in our evolution—not simply as a physical species, but as conscious beings. For this bonding set up a resonance in which all art, all religious ritual, all magic-alchemic science, all spiritual striving for illumination was born. As primal people have always experienced it, when you look and listen to nature, something appears, something always speaks. Animism is still a valid relationship. If "modern man" neither sees nor hears, the fault is in his dead sensorium.

In primitive belief, no animal can be killed against its wish. When a member of a species is struck down, the *one* is wounded. Therefore the hunter must fast and pray to the animal-spirit before the hunt, not simply to ask its pardon but to gain its assent to being killed. The hunted animal is seen to give itself to the hunter, as human food, while its spirit returns to the group form. Because men did all the large-game hunting, and felt themselves to be tracking and slaying brother and sister animals, magic children, like themselves, of Mother Earth—we know they felt guilt, and sought its resolution. After the spilling of blood one must restore harmony with the dead animal, and with the Mother of Animals, as its soul persists through the multiplicity of lives and deaths.

Cave paintings from the Upper Paleolithic show stick-figure male hunters, or entranced shamans, alongside beautifully rendered bison and other game animals; the hunter's or shaman's spear may be shown juxtaposed with the vulvas of female animals. They were seeing the animal's wound as a magic vulva of the Goddess, and trying to establish a union or symbolic resolution within the violence of killing: as penis to vulva (which bleeds and heals itself), so spear to wound. Rock carvings and paintings found in North Africa, identical in theme to the European cave paintings, make this analogy between penis and arrow, Goddess's vulva and animal wound, with circular lines returning the energy in a vulva-to-vulva cycle. In all these Stone Age depictions of the hunt, there is not one image of aggressive or "bloodthirsty" hunters engaged in wanton slaughter; there are only images of "prayerful petition and worshipful observation."[2]

As Thompson points out, these Paleolithic paintings of vulvas as "magic wounds that heal themselves, or give birth to new life" continue, as symbolic images, through Western religious history. Medieval paintings show Christ exposing his wound, from which blood and water flowed during the Crucifixion, as from a uterus in childbirth.

> The labial wound in the side of Christ is an expression that the male shaman, to have magical power, must take on the power of woman . . . the magical labial wound is the seal of the resurrection and an expression of the myth of eternal recurrence. From Christ to the Fisher King of the Grail Legends, the man suffering from a magical wound is no ordinary man; he is the man who has transcended the duality of sexuality, the man with a vulva, the shamanistic androgyne.[3]

These pagan meanings were kept alive, not in orthodox Christianity certainly, but in the Gnostic tradition, which recognized magic bisexuality, the alchemical androgyne, the necessity of the male to experience his female wound. The Grail legend has been traced back to the Neolithic Near Eastern Goddess religion, but in fact it goes back much further—to the sacred Cro-Magnon caves, and the Stone Age hunter's attempt to resolve bloodletting guilt symbolically, and ecstatically, through a fusion of his sex-spirit with the magic vulva-wound of the Mother Goddess.[4]

Ritual cannibalism began with the same symbolic desire: not solely to propitiate but to participate in the magic life-death-rebirth process. Among primal people the totemic animal is sometimes eaten as a sacrament by the group; or, it is totally avoided as a group taboo. Either way, human hunger, killing, and eating are felt as unbalancing acts, which must be reharmonized through sacramental rites. Ritual cannibalism doubtless began with shared eating of the totem animal—a taking in of the animal's life force by the group; to participate in its death, in its lifeblood, is to partake of its eternal rebirth in the Mother. Where it occurred in the world, ritual cannibalism—like hunting—was predominantly or exclusively a male activity. We can see in it early man's desire not to separate himself, and to reestablish magic bonds with the Mother, after the spilling of her blood. This sacred cannibalism is still practiced, symbolically, in the Christian communion.

Another mode of group intoxication, of ecstatic rebalancing, is the dance. Sacred circles made with stones are found in the deep Paleolithic caves, and in them the traces of human feet that danced around and around. Cave paintings show the shaman dancing in animal skins and antler headdress; the footmarks on the cave floors reveal generations of ritual dancing by all, women, men, children. Dancing to—and with—the spirits of the animals is the most ancient human ceremony that we know. Masked dances, like dancing the maze, were a deliberate means of approach to the biomystical animal world, and to the Great Mother within and beyond all forms.

"Pantomimic dance is of the essence of each and every mystery function." In *Themis,* Jane Ellen Harrison describes how the primal dancing group projects its aroused energies outward into the creation of a god. Beginning with mimetic rites—wearing animal masks, feathers, horns, and claws, dancing to a common rhythm, common excitement—members of the group become emotionally supercharged and one. Initially, no "god" concept is involved, but the collective emotion is overwhelmingly felt as "something more than the experience of the individual, as something dominant and external." *Dithyramb* meant originally "song of birth"—the ecstatic "choric dance" literally gave birth to the god; group emotional energy becomes "the raw material of the Godhead." In time, a leader of the dance is slowly differentiated, the dancers become audience, worshipers of something "beyond." Prayer and sacrifice reveals that severance is complete. The community of emotion ceases, restructured into hierarchic observance, and the primal chorus loses all sense or memory that the god is themselves. *We* forget the god is always ourselves.[5]

Harrison's description shows the social and sheer biological origins of religion: the creation of "divinity" not from private prayer or individual moral abstraction, but from its chthonic roots in physical, collective, ecstatic energies. Like many early twentieth-century students of ancient mythology, however, Harrison's thought reveals a Freudian influence: a belief the creation of "God" is only a one-way process. Like Freud, Harrison sourced human cultural expression—art, dance, religion—in "unsatisfied desire," and seemed to agree that all experience of the sacred was reducible to psychological "projection." Witness the analytic urge to demystify the mystery: the Freudian school knew no quantum physics or energies beyond the human. But there *are* other dimensions than the

The Venus of Laussel, from Dordogne, France, circa 19,000 B.C.

spatially-temporally tangible, even though the linear mind is not structured to perceive them.

Spiritual or magical experience is an impingement of these other dimensions, other force fields, into "our" ordinary rational reality. A dancing group can project its entranced emotion into Godhead. Through a tranced and rhythmic "opening" of psychic channels, it can also introject the Godhead—"pulling down" transhuman powers; both directions of this process can really occur, simultaneously. The group generates and renews the power; the power generates and renews the group. The spiraling process gives birth in both directions. Later priestly ideas that the "gods" demand constant human supplication, obeisance, and abasement are wrong, and exploitive; but they derive from this genuine primordial perception of an energy exchange between humans and transhuman powers—a vibratory field-communication that must go both ways for the connection to work. Chimpanzees do rain dances, for no logical reason other than to reconnect their animal energies with the transhuman energies of rain, thunder, and lightning: the original chemical dance of life.[6] And the Apocryphal Jesus says: "The Whole on high hath part in our dancing. . . . Who danceth not, knoweth not what cometh to pass."[7]

This idea is incorporated in the Gnostic round dance; but its origins are not in Christianity by any means, but in the earliest pagan Paleolithic sacred cave dances—even beyond that, in the dances of chimpanzees; and beyond that in the first circling dances of molecules, of atoms, of quarks around the cosmic spiral. The sacred dance takes us beyond the God of Morality and back to the Goddess of Ecstasy; beyond obeisance to social hierarchy and back to an original communion with sheer evolutionary energy. That is why such Gnostic texts were branded "apocryphal," and why the medieval Gnostics were persecuted and burned at the stake by the orthodox church: because they spoke a pagan and primordial truth, old as the universe, who is the first dancer.

One of the earliest images we know of the Mother of Wild Animals and the Dance is the Venus of Laussel, a bas-relief from a cave in the Dordogne Valley, France, dating circa 19,000 B.C. This icon shows the Great Mother standing with a bison horn upheld in her right hand; the horn is a lunar crescent, and the relief is painted with red ochre, the magic color of menstruation and birth. Such a figure presided over the masked shamanic dances and the circle dances of communion with all animals, all life, in which blood-woman-moon-bison horn-birth-magic-the cycle of life are analogized in a continuous resonance, or harmony, of sacred energies. This Laussel Great Mother holding the lunar horn became the virgin and the unicorn (one-horn) of medieval legend. The marvelous tapestries of the Middle Ages, all woven by women, frequently tell the story of "the unicorn who may be touched and tamed only by a chaste virgin." As Thompson notes, the unicorn is "a lunar symbol of the ancient religion of Europe," the Great Mother religion, and the ritual-drama of the macho hunter chasing and slaying this magic beast represents a trace memory of the shift from the moon-worshiping matrifocal European pagan society to the patriarchal sun worship of the Roman Empire and the Christian church.[8]

Such traces of the Paleolithic Hunt Goddess and her magic relation to all the beasts can be found throughout European folklore, art, alchemy, witchcraft and other "heresies." They can also be found throughout the world: Asia, Africa, the Americas. They are found everywhere human beings are found because they represent our original heart and mind. Among the Stone Age cave paintings are images of great women with upraised arms—some with their arms supported by smaller male figures on either side. Legendarily, sacred women stood in this position during the hunt, acting as receivers of cosmic energy. Among the African Stone Age cliff paintings found by Mary Leakey in central Tanzania, the hunt dancers are almost always women, who move their bodies in the shapes and gestures of the animals.[9] Among the Kalahari Bushmen today a shaman-woman performs a special invocation-dance on the dawn of the hunt day, invoking the protective Dawn Star (Venus) who is called the Hunter, and communing with the spirits of the animals who will voluntarily die to feed humans. (Among these Kalahari aboriginals, also, the Milky Way was created by a young girl in menarche, who, feeling lonely, threw the ashes of her fire

The Crane Dance, Sjöö, 1976

into the night sky, to create a friendly light for her people.) The African Hottentots sing and chant to the rain spirit, who is a pregnant Moon Goddess called Goro, "Thou who has painted thy body red . . . Thou who does not drop the menses." Before their invocation dance they paint their bodies red with ochre, which is called "gorod" after her blood-red color. Australian aboriginals pour blood over their sacred stones, and ritually paint themselves red after their dances, saying the paint is really women's menstrual blood.[10]

When we think of the 21,000-year-old Venus of Laussel, stained with red ochre and holding up the hunter's lunar crescent horn in the sacred cave, we know what all these same rites, images, and analogies mean, and where they come from. They come from our original selves, as children of the Great Mother, as sisters and brothers of all her magic animals. The rites, icons, and dances conceive the earth as the body of the Mother, and try to restore the harmony lost when she is wounded. They aim to relate the beasts' wounds to her magic vulva, which bleeds with the moon, and heals itself, again and again. In this way the species spirit of the animals may be renewed through rebirth, after the killing of individual members. Surely in these dances and rituals we see the world meaning of all religious symbolism—but more clearly, and beautifully, because closer to the source.

Western history does not show us any evolution toward greater spirit, greater meaning, greater culture. The Western Roman-Christian contribution to the world, when we look at it, has been almost entirely in the area of technology, and of analytical intellect; combined with a notorious spiritual and cultural alienation, and perhaps the loneliest individuals the planet has ever seen. What there still is of spirit, of poetry, of coherent meaning, of symbolic truth in the world did not come from "us." It was there at the beginning, among our Stone Age ancestors. Their vision, their cosmology, their intuited truth and sacred analogies run like bright red threads through the tapestry of Western history; whatever is still alive and vibrating in patriarchal religions, especially Christianity, when traced to its source, is found to be one of these bloody living fibers retained (stolen) from the original Paleolithic cosmology, woven by these Ice Age people out of their primal pagan experience of the Great Mother and her magic world.

What has followed them, in the mythic, religious, spiritual, and psychic realms at least, has been no great advance, but a devolution—a corruption, a narrowing and hardening, an atrophy of vision and heart. Our Stone Age ancestors would have no trouble understanding the words of Smohalla, a Nez Perce who sang the primal truth to the "white man's world" of nineteenth-century business- and resource-development-oriented America:

> My young men shall never work. Men who work cannot dream and wisdom comes in dreams. You ask me to plough the ground. Shall I take a knife and tear my mother's breast? Then when I die She will not take me to her bosom to rest. You ask me to dig for stone. Shall I dig under Her skin for bones? Then when I die I cannot enter Her body and be born again. You ask me to cut grass and make hay and sell it and be rich like the white man. But how can I cut off my mother's hair? It is bad law and my people cannot obey it. I want my people to stay with me here. All the dead humans will come to life again. We must wait here in the house of our ancestors and be ready to meet in the body of our mother.[11]

III

WOMEN'S CULTURE AND RELIGION IN NEOLITHIC TIMES

The Triple Goddess, Sjöö, 1973

THE FIRST SETTLED VILLAGES

The Neolithic revolution, occurring circa 10,000 B.C., was the creation of women. Through the long generations of human evolution, it was the females who had dug the earth for food, gathering roots and grasses, wild grains and berries to be used for nourishment, medicine, and clothing fibers. Women were the skilled observers of plant nature, passing on from generation to generation their knowledge of food, medical, toxic, and mind-changing properties of the wild plants, fungi, and herbs in their environment. And it was women who had a special relation to the earth, as daughters related to the body of the Great Mother. Where groups of women and their children settled, culture took root, growing slowly into Neolithic villages.

During the Paleolithic, or Old Stone Age, the centers of the cave culture (that we know of) were in western and southern Europe. As the last glaciers receded and human migration increased, centers of human culture shifted to the moist and fertile valleys of the Near East, where the first systematic cultivation of grain occurred. Wild wheat and emmer grew there, water conditions were good, and there were wild goats to be domesticated. By 7000 B.C., agriculture was well-established in Jordan, Iran, and Anatolia (modern Turkey). These New Stone Age people were matriarchal and Goddess-worshipers; they entered Anatolia and the Near East via Thrace (the Balkans).

There were three centers of settled agriculture in the Near East: on the western slopes and valleys of the Zagros mountains, where the Tigris empties into the Persian Gulf; in the hill country of Turkish-Syrian Mesopotamia; and on the South Anatolian plain, now western Turkey. Some of the oldest-known settlements, and the oldest-known grain sickle, have been found in the area of Palestine. These are the remains of the Natuffian Neolithic culture, which lasted until circa 6000 B.C. The people of the most ancient city of Tell es-Sultan (now Jericho) practiced a cult of skulls, and buried their dead in deep pits under the floors of their houses. The first layer of the city dates from 8000 to 7000 B.C., and was built in the shape of the crescent moon. At its earliest levels, the culture seems very advanced.

The houses were built in beehive shape, constructed with sun-dried clay bricks. Floors were sunk into the earth, strewn with sand and covered with clay. Timber was also used in construction; remains of a wooden staircase have been found. The city is surrounded by an 18-foot-high wall of regularly shaped stones, and this is surrounded by a protecting ditch or moat 27 feet wide, cut 9 feet deep into the solid rock. Architecture and building techniques at Tell es-Sultan are at least as advanced as those of medieval European fortresses. The strange thing is that no tools for cutting such huge stone blocks—no axes, picks, chisels—have been found. In the rooms of all the houses were found images of the Goddess.

Jericho was founded at the site of a sacred spring, and the original structure, beneath many layers of debris from later buildings, has been identified as a shrine to the local spirit. Successive cities were built around the same sacred place, the spirit of which became the founding deity. She received the sacrifices offered by the settlers, perhaps in expiation for "using" the earth body in this new agricultural way, and she gave the law by which the city was governed. Implicit in this law was a contract between humans and the Goddess; the people permitted a conditional use of the land for farming and building, in return for observances paid to the Goddess.

The next oldest settlement in the area dates from 6500 B.C. These people built triangular houses, with rooms more than 21 feet long and 12 feet wide, around a courtyard with a central hearth. The bricks were given a plaster coating, and there are no corners or broken lines in this architecture. The walls are gently curved, molded by hand—as the Pueblo houses of the American Southwest are still hand-adobied today by the women. The walls were painted red or yellow and were highly burnished. These houses had drains. Spindle-whorls and loom-weights were found in the ruins, but no traces of pottery—the women used stone vessels. A chapel has been found, containing a stone menhir—a carved stone pillar with oval point and breasts, representing the Great Goddess.

The best-known of these Anatolian cities is Çatal Hüyük, excavated by James Mellaart in the 1960s. This complex town, a ceremonial center for the Goddess religion, flowered between 6500 and 5650 B.C. Çatal Hüyük was very large for its day, 30 to 35 acres in extent. Twelve successive layers have been excavated, and no signs of warfare or weaponry have been found. There are also no signs of animal slaughter within the town, though there are murals depicting the old ritual of the hunt. The people were peaceful agriculturalists, mostly vegetarian. Çatal Hüyük was situated near the obsidian trade routes, and was a major trading center for grains and probably also religious icons. Women's skills as gardeners and agriculturalists are manifest here; the presence of numerous querns, mortars, pounders, grinders, storage pits, and sickle blades shows a growing abundance of food. And burial sites containing luxury objects indicate a surplus of goods and therefore trade—there are many obsidian objects and cowrie shells (Goddess symbols) from coastal regions.[1]

At Çatal Hüyük, the most honored burials were of women and children. Before burial, bodies were exposed so their bones could be picked clean by vultures, the sacred bird of the Death Goddess. Women and children were buried in central graves directly under the sleeping platforms inside the houses, with signs of ritual respect and love, amulets and icons, obsidian mirrors and toys, buried with them; men were buried in smaller corner sites, never with children, and with their Stone Age hunt weapons.[2]

The whole town seems to have been dedicated to the Great Mother religion and to religious artisanry. At least forty shrines have been found in Çatal Hüyük, all of the Goddess. Murals on temple walls show shaman-women as vultures; women's breasts are molded in relief on shrine walls, surmounted by cow horns, and surrounded by imprints of human hands (the same handprints found throughout the Paleolithic caves). Here the Great Goddess is shown, in mural images and statues, in her triple aspect: as a young woman, a mother giving birth, and an old woman or crone accompanied by a vulture. These are the three phases of the moon: waxing, full, waning.

Çatal Hüyük also was built over a sacred well, and the site designed in coordination with natural and cosmic laws: the lines and centers of the earth's energies, and the positions of the stars. To build at a place was to share the life of that place; it was an organic and spiritual location. Earliest agriculture must have grown up around the shrines of the Great Mother, which were social and trade centers as well as holy places. The priestesses of the Goddess were also administrators, scribes, and traders; The Goddess of the Neolithic became the teacher of planting, harvesting and storage methods, as well as healer and dispenser of curative herbs, roots, and plants.[3]

Erich Fromm, in *The Anatomy of Human Destructiveness,* speculates on the meaning of this culture: the fact that among hundreds of skeletons, covering at least eight hundred years of continuous culture, not one shows signs of violent death; the fact that women seemed to outnumber men and are buried with greater honor; the fact that the religion of Çatal Hüyük, administered by priestesses, stressed the renewing and protecting powers of the Great Mother. He writes:

> The data that speak in favor of the view that Neolithic society was relatively egalitarian, without hierarchy, exploitation, or marked aggression, are suggestive. The fact, however, that these Neolithic villages in Anatolia had a matriarchal (matricentric) structure, adds a great deal more evidence to the hypothesis that Neolithic society, at least in Anatolia, was an essentially unaggressive and peaceful society. The reason for this lies in the spirit of affirmation of life and lack of destructiveness which J. J. Bachofen believed was an essential trait of all matriarchal societies.[4]

SOUTHEAST EUROPE: THE BIRD-AND-SNAKE GODDESS

The Goddess religion was carried into the Near East by descendents of the European Old Stone Age. They entered Anatolia via the Bosporus and the Dardanelle straits, bearing with them countless generations of cultural, social, and spiritual development centered on the worship of the Great Mother. The Balkan region of Southeast Europe, known in the ancient world as Thrace, was one of the sites of this development.

It was previously assumed that agriculture and Neolithic culture generally originated in the Near East and spread from there to Europe in the fourth millennium B.C. It has now been shown that the movement could have been in the other direction: an independent Neolithic culture existed in Southeast Europe circa 7000–3500 B.C.[1] This matristic culture was similar to those in Anatolian, Near Eastern, and Egyptian regions, but did not derive from them; it is likely that all were seeds dropped on the way of the outward migrations of Paleolithic cave people following the recession of the Ice Age.

The Southeast Europeans lived in small townships with laid-out streets; they farmed, domesticated animals, developed pottery, and used sophisticated bone- and stone-carving techniques. Located on five seas—the Adriatic, the Ionian, the Aegean, the Marmara, and the Black Sea—these people traded at great distances on seas and inland waterways, transporting many items, including native obsidian, alabaster, and marble. They might have traded obsidian to Çatal Hüyük as early as 7000 B.C.

The Vinča culture, near present Belgrade in Yugoslavia, flourished circa 5300–4000 B.C. These people built large settlements, of two- and three-room houses. Two thousand figurines of the Goddess have been found in the excavations. And the first attempts at linear writing appeared there, not later than mid-sixth millennium B.C., on spindle-whorls, figurines, and vessels—all related to women and the Goddess.

The Bird-and-Snake Goddess reigned supreme. As archaeologist Marija Gimbutas notes, she was a "combined snake and water bird with a long phallic neck" descended from the Magdalenian Goddess of the European Old Stone Age, and she was "the feminine principle."[2] In the Vinča

"Lady Bird" goddess from Vinča culture, circa 4000 B.C., late Neolithic

houses were sacred corners with domed altars, the altarpieces in the shape of the Bird Goddess with upraised arms. She wore a bird-beaked wooden mask, the receptacle of invisible forces. While some of her mysteries were enacted in natural caves, miniature replicas of temples have been found, showing whole buildings made fantastically in the shape of the Bird Goddess.

The Vinča and surrounding Southeast European cultures were largely destroyed by invaders from the East. These were seminomadic pastoralists, Aryan ancestors of the Indo-Europeans, who disturbed most of central and eastern Europe during the fourth millennium B.C. In their aggressive infiltration and settlement, these invaders destroyed a good deal of the Goddess culture and incorporated what they could not destroy. They also interbred, producing the mixed Gauls, Celts, Teutons, and other later invaders of western Europe.

Only around the Aegean did the earlier matriarchal European Neolithic culture survive unbroken into the end of the third millennium B.C.—and on Crete, in the form of Minoan culture, until the mid-second millennium B.C.

But Thrace remained a major center radiating ancient knowledge down to Pythagorean times. In *The First Sex,* Elizabeth Gould Davis notes that the Classical Greeks found evidence there of an ancient technology far beyond their own. Herodotus wrote:

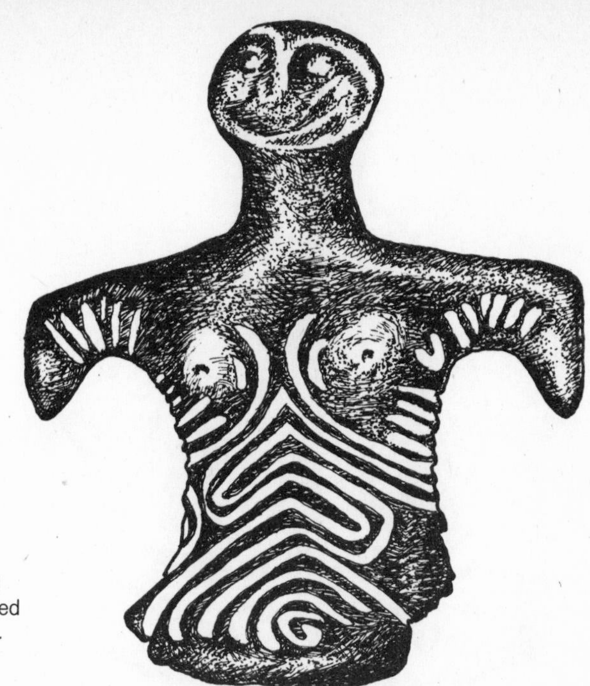

Vinča figurine with owl mask and wings, marked with a labyrinth design. Northwest Bulgaria, 5000–4500 B.C.

> The Thracians dwell amid lofty mountains clothed with forests and capped by snow. . . . Their oracle is situated upon their highest mountain top, and their prophet is a woman.[3]

According to Apuleius,[4] Thrace was the original home of witchcraft—woman wisdom. It was also the home of the Nine Muses, called "mountain goddesses" by Herodotus; thus the legendary home of magic poetry, the wild and mysterious Maenads. And it was also the homeland of one of the original Amazon tribes, warrior women who later fought in Greece against the patriarchal armies. Davis speculates that Thrace was the germinating center for all the later civilizations of Sumer, Crete, Egypt (this may or may not be so); at least it was a strong link between original European Goddess cultures and the matriarchal centers of the Neolithic Natuffians, Çatal Hüyük, Hacilar, and other Anatolian and Near Eastern sites.

In Thrace the Goddess was worshiped as the moon (Diana, Selene), and the Nine Muses, or Mountain Goddesses, were her nine magical aspects. The Maenads were her oracular priestess-shamans, custodians of her primal wisdom—and legendary teachers of the later Celtic Druids, who worshiped Cerridwen, Mountain Goddess of Inspiration. Orpheus, the mythic poet-shaman, came from Thrace; Davis thinks he was murdered by the Maenads for revealing their ritual secrets. Thracian Maenad teaching

Beaked vase with breast spouts and painted zig-zags. From the cemetery of Mallia in eastern Crete, end of third millenia B.C.

on the immortality of the soul and the theory of reincarnation influenced Pythagoras as late as the fifth century B.C.[5]

Some years back there was an exhibition on "Thracian Treasures" at the British Museum in London. The catalog describes a rich culture in Thrace between 6000–4000 B.C.:

> This culture belonged to an unknown and mysterious people, scholars cannot explain it. . . . Walls were made with lath and plaster. . . . Local pottery, gracefully made from its very beginnings, was often brightly coloured and richly ornamented. In Thrace, as in Asia Minor, it is images of the Mother-Goddess which predominate in the idols made of clay and bone. . . . About 2800 B.C. far-reaching changes took place throughout the Bronze Age, changes which contributed to the disappearance of all graces of this culture and were strongly connected with centralized rule. . . . [6]

What is never spelled out is that "centralized rule" was introduced with patriarchy. "Culture declined for hundreds of years. . . . " etc., etc., during which the ancient magical science was destroyed and forgotten and patriarchal rapine ruled.

Everywhere in the exhibit where images of the Goddess appeared (and there were plenty dated from 4000 B.C. and earlier), she is called an "idol" or "fertility figurine." There was a pottery model of a circular shrine enclosing three huge images of the Goddess with arms upraised. There were many goblets and vases decorated with heads of warrior women! Yet the catalog does not once speculate on the meaning of these objects. Instead, one is given plenty of information about patriarchal Thrace in later times: " . . . men had many wives. . . . the women did all the work both at home and in the fields. . . . the men considered it shameful to till the land and their noblest occupation was to go to war and to be tattooed. . . . "

So is our herstory taken from us by male archaeologists and historians posing as "objective" researchers.

THE MEGALITHIC TOMB: THE MOON AND THE STONE

Most High Neolithic cultures in the Near East developed gradually from village settlements into city-centers around 5000–4000 B.C. Perhaps this was the Golden Age in this part of the world, a time of peaceful and creative life in the Jordan valley, kept alive in later myths and legends. And perhaps the same peaceful, settled existence was ongoing at the same time in other parts of the East, in India, in Africa, in western Europe.

From diggings, we know that the dead were no longer buried deep under the house floors, nor entombed in oven-shaped chambers cut in the rock of caves. Now they were given more monumental habitations in the form of rock chambers or stone structures built on the ground, covered with artificial earth-mounds. These are the megalithic tombs or dolmens. The dolmen itself, a chamber formed of great upright stones "roofed" with a topstone, was seen as having great healing powers. Stones, shaped by water, wind, the earth, were believed to be the habitation of the Goddess. In some stone chambers the portal stone was carved out to resemble the birth canal. The dead, still buried in fetal position, were placed in the womb of the Great Mother, awaiting rebirth.

Still later, women—being the farmers, gardeners, and keepers of the grain—buried their dead in great egg-shaped *pithoi* or clay storage urns under the ground. Always a connection was made between the miraculous growth of the plant from a seed buried in the earth, and the dead body, planted also in the earth, with the hope of regeneration through her womb-powers. The women drew on their daily practical experiences as agriculturalists to create elaborate new myths of cyclic birth, death, and resurrection.

With the spread of settled agriculture, this new culture and its religious symbols blossomed everywhere—the Middle East, India, through Europe into Scandinavia, Britain and Spain, the Mediterranean Islands, North and West Africa. The ancient primordial symbols remain, but in a much more elaborate and permanent form.

The Great Cosmic Mountain Mother, who was the Mother of Wild Animals—who was the dark ocean, and the night and day sky—begets the silver egg, or fruit of her night sky, the moon. She is both moon and earth. And the ancient Bird-and-Snake Goddess of Water and Air begets a daughter, the pregnant earth, Goddess of Vegetation. The green child.

Both Mother and daughter are linked with the moon. The massive Great Mother of the Old Stone Age begins to share her powers with a new Goddess, the strong young daughter of agricultural skills, ruled by the moon.

The moon, as daughter of the Great Mother, is known as the Triple Goddess. She presides over *all* acts of generation, whether physical, intellectual, or spiritual. Her triple aspect expresses the three phases of the moon: waxing (growth), full (rebirth), and waning (periodic death).

> She is, as the New or Waxing Moon, the White Goddess of birth and growth.
> She is, as the Full Moon, the Red Goddess of love and battle.
> She is, as the Old or Waning Moon, the Black Goddess of death and divination.[1]

These are the three phases of a woman's life, all natural and all magical. Biological phases are also spiritual phases. Transcience and immortality are different aspects of the same Goddess. The moon as the daughter-fruit of the Great Mother's sky expresses the essential unity-in-perpetual-change of her cosmos. Moon and sun are the eyes of the heavenly Mother, the all-seeing one. We still talk of "heavenly bodies" and of "stars looking down on us." And we still experience the universe as a larger symbolic body, as macrocosm to microcosm, or as mythic Mother to daughter. The three cyclic phases of the ever-turning moon should remind us that our minds are *not* primordially dualistic, but structured to flow through changes, always conscious of the One, while experiencing the whole range of diverse psychic manifestations. *Mens,* the word for mind, is also the word for moon.

On ancient images of the Goddess we find the spiral symbol, one end rolling upward and the other downward, by the genital triangle. When represented by this double-spiral, she is never solely the Goddess of Fertility, Pregnancy, and Birth; she is always at the same time Goddess of Death and the Dead. Bearing on her belly the continuous rising and descending spiral, she expresses the constant double motion of the cosmos. In megalithic art, the Goddess as giver-of-life is depicted naturalistically and sensuously. But as ruler over the spirits and the dead her form stresses the unnatural, the surreal, and the psychic-spiritual. She is then figured in weird, fantastic, hermaphroditic or phallic shapes. She is hallucinated into composite monster-animals, like the Sphinx, or the later griffin and Abraxas.

Or, in a stylized form called the Eye Goddess, she becomes simply a double spiral representing her cosmic, magic eyes. This Eye Goddess design is found on pottery, on statues, on clay and bone implements all over the Near East and Europe. On the New Grange burial mound in County

Owl goddess. Grave stele, Aveyron, France

Meath, Ireland, the double spiral marks the main stones; the Goddess receives there the first rays of the sun's rebirth on winter solstice. And the same design appears on stones on Malta, Crete, and in Scandinavia, and inside burial chambers through France and Brittany. The eye spirals are often mistakenly called "cup and ring marks" and assumed by male archaeologists to be "Sun wheels."[2]

Carved in grim relief inside burial mounds in Brittany, the Eye Goddess stares forward, seeing death and life equally. The funerary mood is expressed in the stylized abstraction of her gaze, reducing complex existence to the stark essentials of seeing and the invisible. Nature is both growth and decay, and life cannot be without death: such is the unblinking vision of the Eye Goddess.

Stone, in Neolithic times as in the Paleolithic, remains the powerful abode of the Great Goddess. Stone, of all earth forms, is immortal and unchanging, symbol of permanence. As the bones of the earth, the pelvic walls of caverns, it gives off a profound vibration or resonance—both subhuman and supranatural. All "primitive" people carry wishbones and healing-stones, talismans painted with magic symbols. Animals as well as humans seem drawn to tall, standing menhirs, or stone pillars; sick livestock rub against them in the countryside, and it is timeless folk custom to touch menhirs in order to become fertile, or to be cured of illness.

Legends often refer to stone circles (e.g., in Brittany and Cornwall, in Ireland and England) as nine maidens or merry maidens; nine is the magic number of the moon, and the Thracian muses. To explain these circles, it is said that nine naughty young women were turned into stone, by the avenging Christian God, for dancing on *his* sabbath.

It has been suggested that a specific number of women/girls dancing in a circle at certain speeds, and all singing or humming the appropriate note (young women having high piping voices), might set up a vibratory resonance in the stone circle, subjecting each stone to a burst of sound-energy as each woman passed it . . . and this energy traveling from stone to stone . . . ! The ultrasound in the voices or music would act on the crystal structure of the stone.

It has recently been found that the quartz content of such stones is an electrically active crystal and that certain standing stones associated with the stone circles generate ultrasound when stimulated by the elements in the electromagnetic spectrum radiated by the sun at dawn. In England geologists and "ley-line hunters" (why *hunter,* why not *seeker?*) are working together in the Dragon Project, physically monitoring and measuring radiation and energies emanating from standing stones and stone circles . . . at different times of day and night, lunar and solar risings and settings, and at different seasons.

In Neolithic times, the moon and the stone symbols were combined in one characteristic shape: the horned altar. Anything shaped like a crescent moon was considered, by analogy, to belong to the Triple Goddess. Thus, where horse's hooves struck crescent marks on the earth, the moon ran—and the wild mare belonged to her. The curving lunar horns of cows and bulls, goats, oxen, and other herd animals were held sacred, and adorned; and the horned crown became the magic adornment of warriors, rulers, and priests of the Late Neolithic. Horned Teutonic warrior women and the horned Pan, pagan god of Nature (*pan* means *all*), belong to this tradition; and this is why the Christian Devil is depicted wearing horns.

From Upper Paleolithic times we have the Venus of Laussel and other cave images of women wearing or holding horns, and figurines of horns with women's breasts. There were also images of the pregnant doe and her magic antlers. Northern hunting people still see the Mother of the Universe as a doe, elk, or wild reindeer. There are myths of pregnant women who rule the heart of the world, covered with hair and with branching deer's horns on their heads. The deer was still sacred to Artemis and Diana, Goddesses of the Moon, in later times. The Doe's udders were seen to be sources of rainwater and the growth of her antlers was magically connected with the growth of the crescent moon, both symbolizing growth and regeneration. The symbol of the Sumerian Goddess of Childbirth was a stag. Apparently there was a synchronicity between the growth cycle of the stag's antlers and that of spring-grown Neolithic cereal grains. In later Celtic and Teutonic myth, the fairy transformed herself most commonly into a magic deer, and she lived within an earth-mound, the pregnant womb of the Goddess.

A whole complex of symbols is associated with this Neolithic religion of the Great Goddess: the sacred pillar; the horns; the cosmic snake and egg; the labyrinth; the world tree; the dove; the swastika; the sacrificial double-ax or labrys; the bee; the butterfly and chrysallis.

The *horned altar,* the cow's horns shaped in stone or clay, the likeness of the young crescent moon, stood for new growth and fertility. It also meant the simultaneously waning crescent, the dying moon. These altars are found in megalithic tombs. But agricultural rites of the horned altar were also performed for the living group, just as earlier Paleolithic people had performed magic cave rituals to encourage the birth and capture of the hunter's animal quarry. In the settled Neolithic, where people depended on cultivated crops, the seasons, and the weather, horned altar ceremonies were enacted to help the rebirth of the new moon, to assist crop growth and harvest, to renew the fertility of the fields each year, so bringing about the resurrection of the daughter vegetable life through the Mother Earth and Moon. When ploughing developed, it was a part of funerary rites.

The *sacred pillar,* along with the horned altars, were sacred stone objects standing in the open country, along roads, and in the village. Also descended from the Old Stone Age, they were phallic pillars with the Great Mother carved on them. Stone pillars with breasts are found throughout the Near East; as Gimbutas suggested, these ancient phallic Mother stones symbolized shamanic bisexuality, and the unity of the sexes—a Neolithic ideal stressed in ritual and imagery.

The *cosmic snake and egg* derive from the original Goddess cosmology, and continue to represent wisdom, immortality, continuity within change, and the magic germ—or still-heart center—within the whirling negative-positive spiral field of cosmic energy. The *labyrinth* also continues the earlier Paleolithic rituals of the underground cave, the initiation maze-dance through life and death. Serpent and maze designs are common symbols on Neolithic pottery worldwide, and in urban times they were incorporated in floor mosaics. In Neolithic western Europe—and in Neolithic North America—giant burial mounds were built in the shape of serpents, with spirals engraved on their stones.

The *world tree* is another worldwide symbol. Found everywhere among Neolithic agricultural people, the world tree also existed among earlier Old Stone Age hunting-and-gathering cultures. Shamans in trance climbed the world tree—which is the human spine, and the spine of the world—to receive illumination. The Neolithic world tree appears in a garden, abundant with fruits and grains. It reflects the agricultural concerns of settled people, when the energy bonds between human society and the cycles of vegetable life were stressed, and also coming under human control. The world tree incorporates serpentine and lunar symbolism, shedding bark and leaves like skin or light, being reborn in the spring, growing rhythmically with the monthly moon phases. At least two thousand years before the Hebrew patriarchs wrote of the Garden of Eden, the Neolithic Great Goddess had her magic Garden of Immortality. Clay seals and figurines from Sumer and Crete show her sitting in her garden, the branches of the world tree overspreading bundles of fruits and grains, a crescent moon over her shoulder . . . and somewhere twined around the tree trunk, or stretched on the ground at her feet, the cosmic serpent. In some, fertilizing rivers, meander lines, pour in from the four directions. Such images of peaceful abundance are the apotheosis of the Neolithic. The *dove* is often pictured there too, perched in the world tree as the symbol of the Great Mother's all-giving love (as the vulture meant all-taking death); doves continued through Roman times to be the companions of the Love Goddess, Venus, as well as biblical symbols of peace.

In the image of the *cosmic tree* penetrating the three sacred zones of heaven, earth, and underworld, the threefold structure of the universe is expressed. Also the threefold structure of the human brain: the original reptilian brain stem, surrounded by the mammalian cerebrum, and all enveloped by the human neocortex. The reptile brain is the secret dream underground; the mammal brain is abundant earth; the human neocortex is the flying bird who sits in the world tree, and can climb the sky. Wherever bird and snake appear together (as in the Thracian Bird-and-Snake Goddess), they are to be seen as the upper and lower symbols of the world tree. And it is understood that the world tree—which is the spine, the arousal of *kundalini* through the *chakras*—connects them. In the presence of this Neolithic world tree symbol, one is in the presence of the most ancient shamanistic trance power, and of yoga. Both are magic techniques of the Great Mother.

In the Hebrew Genesis, Eve and Adam are driven from the Garden of Immortality by Yahweh because they consort with the cosmic serpent under this magic world tree. The Genesis tree was not an apple but a fig tree; Eve and Adam cover their nakedness with fig leaves after eating of its fruit in Eden. Hathor, the Cow Goddess of Egypt, was anciently identified with the fig tree, which was known as the "living body of Hathor on earth." To eat of its sweet pulpy fruit, its very vulva-like fruit, was to eat of her flesh and fluid. The fig tree was also sacred on Crete, considered the food of eternity and immortality. The biblical Garden of Eden was in fact the entire Near Eastern, North African, and Mediterranean Neolithic agricultural world of the Great Goddess. And the forbidden tree and evil serpent represented her ancient magic powers of illumination and immortality. And earthly peace.

The *swastika* is one of the most ancient abstract symbols. It is found

Bee Goddess on Boetian amphora, circa 700 B.C.

scratched on Siberian clay figures of wild geese, on the underside of their wings, from the earliest Neolithic excavations. The *cross* originally represented the earth (the Great Mother's body, her outstretched arms, the four directions); the swastika means the earth in flight. It is the cross with feet, or wings, set in motion: the earth and its moon are wheeled through their changes. Later seen as a sun-wheel, the swastika was first a moon-wheel, and like the double crescent (the labrys) it could signify both directions of the cosmic spin: into creation or dissolution. The right-spinning wheel (clockwise) was used to build, encourage, maintain; the left-spinning wheel (counterclockwise) was used to destroy, prevent, or transform the nature of something; just so, the witch-circle turns clockwise to *do*, widdershins to *undo*. The swastika can be found worldwide, from old relics dug up in Iran to the pottery decorations of present-day Zuni Indians in the American Southwest. Typically, as on a seventh-century B.C. terra cotta amphora from Boeotia, and other statues and pots from the Aegean, the swastika was associated with the Lady of the Beasts, the New Stone Age version of the Paleolithic Mother of Wild Animals.[3] It is one of the magic signs on the foot of the Buddha. Taken over by patriarchy, the swastika has meant only destruction; Hitler read it as an Aryan fire sign.

The *double-ax*, or *labrys*, was the instrument used by women in ceremony, agricultural work, and battle. It is an ax with two heads, the two moon crescents, waxing and waning. A practical version was used by women in daily agricultural work. In the form of the battle-ax, it was used by Amazonian warriors of North Africa, Thrace, and Macedonia, and the Caucasus. As a sacred sacrificial ax, it could be used only by priestesses, who alone could cut down the Goddess's ceremonial trees. Our word labyrinth comes from the Minoan *labrys*; it refers to the Hall of Double-Axes, or Labyrinth, dug up by archaeologists at the Palace of Knossos on Crete. Crete was the great matriarchal culture-center of the Mediterranean; its murals and mosaics, pottery designs, seals, and amulets show the labrys wielded only by women, and it appears extensively as an icon-symbol of the Great Goddess.

The *bee* was always a sign of the Goddess. Honey was the only sweetener of the ancient world and its maker, the honeybee, is both industrious and magical. Only the female bees build hives and make honey, and they communicate with each other via dance-language. Bees appear in the spring, at the rebirth of grasses and flowers. The Goddess was also pictured as *chrysallis* and *butterfly*, who emerges from its self-spun "tomb" totally transformed; as the bird once emerged from the reptile, and as the "new soul" emerges from ritual death, on wings of illumination. The butterfly is, like the *cowrie* shell, a vulva symbol. According to Marija Gimbutas, the butterfly-winged Goddess was slowly merged with the double-ax image during the Bronze Age.

The megalithic tomb *was* the body of the Great Mother. It was her temple where religious rites were performed at night, by the light of her moon. The stone menhirs were designated as females—colossal upright blocks, some ten feet high, and often grouped in threes. They embodied the Triple Goddess of Birth, Death, and Rebirth, and were associated throughout the Neolithic with vast circles, marked out by stones, which were ritual enclosures and sacred dance-grounds. These stone circles, or the traces of them, are found worldwide.

The rites enacted in the menhir-circles represented the spiritual understanding of the Neolithic people, their wish for union *with* the Goddess, and for immortality through her. The ceremonies were presided over by women shaman-priestesses, whose spheres were vision, sacrifice, poetic and magic lore, the ritual calendar and the law, and astronomical-astrological observation. (The later Druids inherited much of their knowledge, lore, and ritual.) These priestesses were also healers, rainmakers, midwives, and the keepers of soma, the sacred mind-expanding drink.

Beehive-tombs with passage-entranceways have been found from Greece to Ireland, dating from the close of 3000 B.C. All have huge circular enclosures, amphitheaters for funerary games. Their entrances are ornamented with eight double spirals: the circle that has no end, the point that breathes itself into a universe, and back again.

On Crete, cult shrines enclosing small stone pillars, or clay pillars molded around tree trunks, were set up to ceremonialize the dead and the magic tomb.

The Egyptian pyramids were an elaborate culmination of the megalithic tomb, guarded by the giant Sphinx who is the Goddess, guardian of the dead.

THE EARTH MOUND AS COSMIC WOMB OF THE PREGNANT GODDESS

Silbury Hill, situated on the Wiltshire Downs in Southwest England, is the largest surviving image of the Goddess from Neolithic Europe. It is 520 feet in diameter and 130 feet high, and it is over 4,500 years old.

For hundreds of years male archaeologists have been excavating the mound, desperately hoping to find within it the Bronze Age burial remains of an ancient Essex king. But, as Michael Dames points out in *Silbury Treasure: The Great Goddess Rediscovered*, Neolithic culture was based on kinship, *not* kingship. In Dames's view, the Silbury mound expresses a vision of cosmic unity long lost to patriarchy.[1]

Silbury Hill was the primordial belly: the omphalos or navel of the world, the sacred mountain emerged from the waters of chaos, the world egg born from the primordial sea of night. It is the throne who is the squatting Goddess, the white mountain, the navel of waters. The Indo-European root for "hill" (*kel*) also meant "a concealed, sacred place" (Germanic *haljō*), and was probably related to *halig*, meaning "holy." The mountain was always a generator of energy, inspiring the high state of madness and prophesy, giving oracular powers. It is the world axis where the different levels of psychic/physical experience interpenetrate—the threshold between underworld, earth, and sky, from which all creation emerges. From the mountain the shaman begins her/his ecstatic journey.

In Britain, there are 1,500 hilltops with large enclosures on their summits, encircled by earthen banks. These earthworks look like coiled serpents, and were used as ritual mazes.

According to Michael Dames, Silbury Hill contains a vegetable core surrounded by layers of chalk, gravel, soil, and clay. Radiating from this core are spokes of twisted string, looking like umbilical cords, or snakes. This central axis is surrounded by sarsen stones, which are covered with earth dug from the surrounding quarry, originally filled with water. The surface of the Mother's body *was* water, and she contained within herself earth, water, air, and fire (sunlight reflected in the moat). The hill and its ditch—a convex hill and concave hole—create together the image of the Goddess squatting in the Neolithic birth position, tranquil and stable, ready to give birth to the world.

The Neolithic farming communities had a nonlinear sense of time, believing that time began anew with each new year. The pregnant Mountain Mother gave birth in August when the seeds, spring-planted in her womb, had grown large. At that time the entire community came to be with her: the divine birth is the harvest of the wheat, and the first fruits were offered to the Goddess. Similar mysteries were enacted in Eleusis around Demeter, the Grain Mother. In Britain she was known as Bride, Ana, or Danu, and she was celebrated on her womb/mounds in August as late as the seventeenth century A.D. Great assemblies of witches traditionally gathered on Lammas Eve (August 1), the people believing that their welfare in the coming year depended on the performance of these sacred rites of the Corn Mother, or Harvest Queen. (The Christian church throughout Britain finally took drastic action against this "pagan cult worship." The Christian priesthood preaches linear, not cyclic time, hoping to separate "man" from the Goddess of Nature, and "God" from the great cosmic rhythms of creation. As many wise people have observed, the way to control human life is to control the rhythm of life. Pagan life was ruled by natural cyclic rhythms. The church opposed these female rhythms with linear-historic ones, thus trying to change human rhythm from natural to mechanical—which serves the industrial process but leaves human life and labor, including agricultural life and labor, quite alienated.)

As Dames says, both lunar and solar phenomena (particularly the solstices and equinoxes) were studied by the Late Neolithic farming communities, who used a solar calendar to determine annual agricultural events, while the months (from the word "moon") and the daily rhythms were linked to the more ancient lunar calendar. In the ancient world the full moon was birth-time for all life. The ceremonial birth at Silbury was celebrated on the night of the full moon closest to the fixed solar quarter-day (or sabbat) of Lammas.

Silbury Hills drew up power (water) from the underworld, and drew down power (light) from the sky. When these elements were joined within her earth body, the universal birth took place. The birth and death of light could be witnessed from her summit, both occurring at the same moment: as the sun rose and the moon set, and, after twelve hours, the reverse. All equinoctial settings of sun and full moon, according to Dames, mark the positions of the Goddess's moat eye.

At Silbury, the interaction between the Hill Mother and the River Mother is one and bisexual. The moon is born from the water, and gives birth on the water. The Goddess at Silbury is also the Eye Goddess, as the moon and sunlight are reflected in the moat, an image of the indivisibility of mind and matter (eye and womb), as well as their transformation through the tomb. When death was formed by the Mother, everything was both dead and alive, in process, by nature. Earth was seen in its totality,

The Goddess at Carnac in Bretagne, Sjöö, 1980

and the people recognized death as one of the sources of first-fruit ceremonies. This was the psychic orientation of pagan agriculturalists, long before (in Dames's words) "war was declared on the human body with the emergence of patriarchal warrior societies in the Bronze Age."

Silbury Hill is comparable to the temples on Malta: "To sleep within such a Goddess-shape would itself have been a ritual act."

Recent excavations in the Orkney Islands of Scotland have revealed whole Neolithic villages, up to sixty houses, designed in the shape of a Goddess-body. Individual houses made of stone and mud, on Skara Brae, are shaped like uteruses with vaginal entranceways. Stone temples in Malta are carved and built in the shape of the massive Paleolithic Great Mother, and small clay figurines of the Great Goddess in this same form are found throughout Malta. The West Kennet long barrow, in England, is built in the same identical shape. The large Medamud Temple in Egypt and the Bryn Celli Ddu mound in Wales are the same body: the great earth-mound belly, open thighs of stone, the entrance-portal open for the passage of birth and death.[2]

Worldwide, architecture was the mother of arts, as women built to live *within* her body-shape. Dogon villages in Africa are constructed in the shape of a bisexual human figure lying on its back. The village represents the first vibration of the cosmic egg. It is built in the center of fields cut in spirals. At the southern end is a cone-shaped shrine, the penis. A hollowed stone nearby, on which the fruit is pressed for oil, is the vagina. Menstrual huts, to the east and west sides of the village, are hands. Both sexes carry out the agricultural work of these bisexual villages. Primal people understand quite clearly that the shape of one's dwellings is the shape of one's life.

The White Goddess of pagan Britain was the mother of the good and fertile soil of the chalklands, white as the full moon. All her creation, including stones and minerals, was organic and animated. Her body permeated all the later Avebury monuments on the Wiltshire downs. This area is rich in sarsen stones, massive blocks of hard sandstone which lay on the surface of the hills and didn't need to be quarried. These stones were called bride stones—Bride (Brigid) was one of the Goddess's names.

The White Horse, a large turf-cut figure on the hillside at Uffington in Berkshire, is an evocation of Epona, the Celtic Horse-Goddess. Dragon Hill nearby was a Neolithic first-fruits ceremonial site; folklore tells that the white sterile patch on its summit was caused by the execution of the lifegiving Dragon Goddess at the hands of a patriarchal solar-hero. Where her blood fell, nothing will grow.

One such dragon-slayer, or serpent-killing "hero," is St. Michael. Many of the earliest Christian churches in Britain, dedicated to St. Michael, were built precisely on the ancient mounds and high-places of the Great Goddess. In Christian lore, St. Michael was the head chief of a band of angels (read "patriarchal invaders") that went to war with the Mother Dragon and her people. In folklore, St. Michael is thought to be the successor of Wotan, the Anglo-Saxon god who was a warlike slayer of dragons. In fact, an abnormal number of Christian churches dedicated to St. Michael and St. George, the other British dragon-slayer, are built on high places along the ley-line (or dragon path) that runs from Land's End in Cornwall through the Goddess monuments at Glastonbury and Avebury in southwest England.[3]

Such a St. Michael's church was built on the summit of Glastonbury Tor! . . . but in the year 1300 A.D. it was destroyed by an earthquake. As Elizabeth G. Davis notes, all the Christian male angels were originally the Great Goddess, with her wings. When the image of the Winged Goddess "continued to be engraved on Roman coins, in defiance of the new Christian hierarchy in Constantinople"—who had smashed or taken over all her Roman temples—the Church fathers just changed her name to "the Angel of the Lord," Archangel Michael.[4]

Glastonbury Tor is a spiral mound with a processional way, along which a dance was performed by the community, circling around and up to the top. Glastonbury means glass castle: "glass castles" in Welsh, Irish, and Manx legend were island shrines or "star prisons" ruled by the White Moon Goddess of poetry and ritual death; in medieval legend they were made of glass.[5] In Neolithic times, they were Goddess mounds of birth and death. Original rites at Glastonbury were aimed at restoring the bird and flower life of spring, perhaps. The mound was a magnetic center for the absorption and refraction of generative energies, to which animal, bird, and plant life responded. And women, as the ancient farmers and bee-keepers, performed the rites. Glastonbury was probably the enchanted Isle of Avalon.

Lands "flowing with milk and honey," eulogized in the Bible as original Edens, were in fact the lands of the Neolithic Goddess. Milk belongs to the Mother, and since women were the first bee-keepers, the honeybee has always symbolized matriarchy. North African and Thracian Amazons legendarily fed on honey and mare's milk, along with blood, raw meat, and reed marrow. The Indo-Europeans inherited bee-keeping from the Minoans of Crete, who practiced it from the beginning of the Neolithic. Cretans believed that at the death of the sacrificial bull the Goddess was reborn, as a bee. Thus the "bull-born" Goddess of transformation and regeneration—both bee and bull belonged to the moon. The bull, because of its crescent horns; while the bees make the sweet light of honey within the night-darkness of the hive. At Ephesus, where the many-breasted Artemis-Diana was worshiped, the bee appeared as her cult animal. Her temple at Ephesus was a symbolic beehive (built by priestesses, and known as one of the wonders of the ancient world). Her priestesses were called Melissal ("bees"), and the eunuch priests were Essenes ("drones").

Thus the beehive-shape of so many Neolithic earth-mounds was quite intentional and symbolic. Bee-keeping was a metaphor for settled agriculture, and for the peaceful abundance of the earth in those times. And the honeybee was like the full moon, making illumination in the night.

In Ireland, in Brittany and Wales, and in Scandinavia, the fairies with their Fairy Queen are still believed to be living in earth-mounds, or tomb-dwellings. The Swedish sagas about trolls are obviously distorted tales about ancient moon-worshiping people. The trolls are said to live inside mountains, to be dressed in skins, to eat human flesh, to exist in both human and animal form, and to die if caught in the rays of the sun . . . they live by night, by moonshine. So in Ireland, the fairy people said to live inside the burial-mounds are Tuatha De Danaan, people of the Goddess Danu, displaced and driven underground by later patriarchal invaders. The Danaans were matrilinear, and their Goddess was the Mother of all magic, art, and craft. Hallowe'en was originally Samhain, one of the four great "cross-quarter days," or sabbats, of the witch-year in pagan Britain. Originally, on this Night of All Souls, priestess-oracles sat at the stone portals of earth-mounds, or mass burial chambers, while the spirits of the heroic dead passed in and out, visiting the world just once before the great death of winter.

In North America, Neolithic farming cultures also built earth-mounds. The earliest, dating from 1000 B.C., were found throughout the Southeast by early explorers: from Florida and Georgia into West Virginia, Kentucky, and the Tennessee Valley, and west into Arkansas and Oklahoma. Ohio was the site of two great mound-building Native American cultures. The Adena, dating circa 800 B.C. to A.D. 900, built conical mounds; the Hopewell, 600 B.C. to A.D. 1500, elaborated on the earlier structures, building huge mounds and earthen embankments covering hundreds of acres. Both these cultures built burial mounds; later people in the southeast built temple mounds, large earthworks with temples on the top, but no burial chambers within. Ohio is the site of the great Serpent Mound of the Adena culture. The Serpent Mound is 1,400 feet long, made of Earth in the shape of a snake winding around the cosmic egg, the maternal ovum.[6]

Many American Indian cultures were not mound-builders, but most believed their ancestors emerged from such mounds, or from some such structure symbolizing the earth's pregnant belly. The Hopi and other Southwest tribes still go into *kivas* (underground chambers) for initiation into the presence of the earth spirit. And the great pyramids of Mexico and Central America were built up, generation after generation, over original earth-mound structures. *Mexico* means "navel of the moon."

THE ISLANDS OF MALTA AND GOZO

On the islands of Malta and Gozo in the Mediterranean can be seen the clearest connection between the cave, the tomb, and the temple—all three *being* the body of the Great Mother. Sometime in the third or second millennium B.C. (or maybe earlier) an incredibly advanced culture developed on these small and isolated islands—which, situated between Sicily and the Libyan coast, were really right at the center of the ancient world. Malta and Gozo were an ancient sacred center for the religion of the Great Mother. From Europe, from Africa, from the Aegean and the Near East, pilgrims traveled here, and the sick came to be healed.[1]

Over a period of perhaps one thousand years, up to thirty huge megalithic temple structures were built on these islands. But there are no remains of houses; only the caves show any trace of habitation. The amazing architecture of the temples was far beyond its time. Pottery and carvings are found in the ruins, but there is a complete absence of metal, the only tools being rough stone implements and the horns of oxen and goats. Perhaps there was a religious taboo on the use of metal; no weapons were made or used on the islands.

(Metallurgy began, in fact, as a sacred technology of the Goddess. Only ceremonial metals were cast at first; there was much taboo around the use of metals and, no doubt, secrecy about smelting methods. Pagan European witches and Native Americans share an ancient belief that metal interferes with magic. These were stone-oriented people, who felt metals blocking and distorting psychic-spiritual energy currents. Witches were not supposed to touch iron. Guy Underwood, a British water-diviner, says his experiences have shown him that placing a metal object on a "blind spring" obliterates, for a short time, all geodetic reactions around it. Water is extremely sensitive to metals, especially heavy metals.)

The Malta and Gozo temples imitated the rock-cut megalithic tombs of the mainland. They were built in roundish chambers, in cloverleaf and crescent designs, around an inner courtyard, with long connecting courtyards between them. No dead were buried in these temples; bodies were still interred in caves and rock-cut tombs. But there was only a step from

Mother Goddess at Malta

performing ceremonial rites at the cave-tombs to building special temples for the veneration of the spirits of the dead. The temples were built with enormous double walls, rubble and earth piled in the space between the inner and outer wall—so, in effect, the temple was still *inside* the earth, as inside a mountain, surrounded by powerful earth-currents (similar to a Reichian orgone chamber, in fact).

In myth, Gozo was the island-realm of Calypso, the daughter of Uranus. It was on Gozo that the patriarchal hero Ulysses was believed to have stayed, enchanted by the sorceress Calypso, for seven years. In myth, the huge temple of Ggantija, fourth millennium B.C., was built by a giant Titan-woman with a baby at her breast. Single-handedly, in one day, she hauled the huge blocks of stone to the building site—and built the temple walls by night. This temple is 90 feet high, and some of its great stone slabs measure 5 yards by 4 yards. Mortar was used on the inside walls, which were then painted with red ochre, the color of rebirth. Some of the megaliths weighed 50 tons, and stone rollers that must have been used to transport the huge blocks have been found by the temple site. The entire population of the island must have worked during many generations to produce this single temple.

What were they seeking? Probably what we could call "the living

Shaman Priestess Sleeping within New Grange, Listening to the Voices of the Underworld, Sjöö, 1981

darkness"—the stillness of the tomb, the breathing silence of the womb of the Earth Mother. The chambers, painted blood-red, had no sharp angles; all the shapes are rounded, or molded in curves and waves. There was no worship of the heavens in these temples, and no human sacrifice. There are traces only of animal sacrifice and the pouring of libations. Here, the living and the dead were as close as possible to each other.

But the strangest thing is that the temple on the surface of the earth was only the entrance to a still vaster shrine beneath. Legends tell of a huge labyrinth, catacomb, or rock necropolis built under the temple, a "city of the dead" in which the whole island population ultimately resided. In fact, an enormous labyrinthine cave-sanctuary has been found, the collective burial tomb of seven thousand bodies. This mass tomb was built in several stories out of the subterranean rock; at its entrance is a trilithon gateway giving access to the underground city, the abode of "the perfect ones." Long vaulted corridors, "bloodstained" with red ochre, led to a sacred deep temple area; with its altar, pillars, gateway, and spiral-designs painted in red on the roof, it mirrored or echoed the temple built aboveground.

This was the center of something—as Malta and Gozo are indeed at the geographic center of the Neolithic Great Goddess culture, stretching from Africa to Scandinavia, from Sumeria to Spain (or to the sunken continent of Atlantis, as some believe). In this sacred space priestesses of the Great Goddess contacted the spirits of the dead, consulted oracles, prophesied, and performed ritual healing.

In the temple are huge squatting images of the Goddess. These are of the same bulging, rounded shape as the temple. In later images she wears a flounced skirt, with small figures hiding in it for protection. She holds her arm raised to her breasts—her head is smaller, proportionately, than the body, and made of a separate material—and she wears a blissful expression: peaceful, gracious, and still. She meditates with closed eyes, sitting on a throne, and she has small, delicate hands. The blood of sacrificed animals was poured into a stone vessel with a hollow base standing on the altar, and burning-fire ceremonies were also enacted. These secret chambers of the Great Mother, where timeless mysteries were performed, are guarded by her eyes—the cosmic symbol of the double spiral, inscribed on the ceiling stone. Plant, flower, and animal motifs are carved in relief on the walls and altars, and they show strong Cretan influence, evidence of much contact between these islands.

The temples were also healing centers: The sick came to sleep in the huge stone chambers. Priestesses in clairvoyant sleep listened to the voices of the Underworld. Divination and also acoustic conjuring were practiced—the priestess's disembodied voice, from her little chamber hidden in the thick walls, reverberated through the vaults via clay pipes and mouldings—seeming the voice of earth itself. People came on pilgrimage to sleep in the temple, to have dream-communion with the powers of the underworld and the dead, to obtain counsel, wisdom, healing, and clairvoyant knowledge of the future. The temples contain two small figurines of sleeping women . . . sleeping to dream, to die, to wait for birth and rebirth. They echo the huge, pregnant shape of her who was both impersonal and kind, both familiar and terrible—the earth, embodying cosmic strength, mystery, abundance, paradox.

We don't know anything about the people who built these island temples. They were weaponless and so defenseless against warlike pirates who overran them, using metal weapons. These conquerors probably came by way of Sicily, bringing a culture much inferior to that of Malta. They still practiced some form of Goddess-worship, but they burned their dead—showing that they were in transition from matriarchal to patriarchal orientation, since the Sky Father-worshiping nomads from the East also practiced cremation; i.e., they sent the body-spirit up to the sky rather than returning it to the earth-womb.

It is quite possible that Malta and Gozo were schools for priestesses. Such island-schools are common in legend. Ancient Celtic myth tells of sacred islands inhabited and ruled by women, where the mysteries were kept and taught. According to Irish texts the Tuatha de Danaan came from such an island in the North, where they had learned science, magic, art, and ancient wisdom from priestesses of the Goddess Danu. Druids were buried in ceremonial groves on distant islands. According to the Roman Pomponius Mela: "Facing the Celtic coast lie a group of islands which take the collective name of Cassiterites. . . . *Sena* (off the Breton coast) was renowned for its Gallic oracle, whose priestesses, sacred for their everlasting Virginity, were said to be nine in number." These priestesses were called Gallicians and had magic powers:

> . . . to unleash the winds and storms by their spells, to metamorphose any animal according to their whim, to cure all disease said to be incurable, and finally, to know and predict the future. But . . . they reserved their remedies and predictions exclusively to those who traveled over the sea expressly to consult them.[2]

They were nine in number because nine is the triplicity of three, the sacred number of the Moon Goddess. Girls who were to become priestesses were chosen at the age of nine. Nine priestesses are pictured dancing around an ithyphallic young man in a cave painting at Cogul, in northeastern Spain, dating from the Old Stone Age Aurignacian period. Arranged in a crescent, the dancing nine represent the moon's phases, growing older in a clockwise direction: three young girls, three strong grown women, three thin dark crones (the oldest, with an old moon face, dances widdershins, counterclockwise). This painting could be 30,000 years old! So primordial is witchcraft.[3] On the sacred island of Avalon, Apple Island, Morgan La Fay ("the Fairy") ruled over nine sisters, and taught how plants can be used to cure illness. She knew the art of changing her outward form and could fly through the air with the aid of magic feathers. She was one of many renowned shamans, practicing ancient women's wisdom on an enchanted island. The temples of Malta and Gozo reveal that such legends were based on reality, as legends usually are.

All that remains of the Maltese island people are their resonant stone temples. But their religious ideas and rites were similar to those surviving in the mystery cults of classical Greece; such survivals show that early Christianity's belief in the body's immortality grew from very deep and ancient pre-Indo European, prepatriarchal roots.

Delphi was another oracular shrine-tomb. Located on the Greek mainland, it was ruled over by a spiraling python-serpent and a prophetic priestess who served Gaia, the Earth/Death Mother. The python was housed in the omphalos, or "navel-shrine"—the navel of the earth—built underground in beehive-shape (originally perhaps deriving from the African *masabo,* or "ghost house"). The name "Delphi" comes from "Delphyne," the great snake of the Mother. The Goddess's most ancient name at Malta had been Delphyne, since she was part serpent—and the name comes from an ancient word, *delphys,* meaning "womb." (And is now the brand-name of a contraceptive foam!)

Apollo, the patriarchal Sun God of classic Greece, was a mythological latecomer to the oracular shrine at Delphi, though now he is always associated with it. Apollo began as an underground oracular hero, in fact, and his name means "apple-man." In classic myth, he could not rule at Delphi until he had slain the sacred python with his arrows (or phallic sunbeams), as Zeus had also killed the dragon-offspring of the Earth Goddess, at Dodona. But even after the slaying of the symbolic python, the prophetic Sibyl at "Apollo's Delphi" remained a woman. Bending over her tripod, inhaling smoke and entering trance, she pronounced her judgments on past, present, and future acts of the Greeks. (But Apollo, as harbinger of patriarchal/Sun God technology, increased the production-demand on the oracle beyond her endurance and human capacity, driving her mad. As John Michell has noted, the same policy of artificially inducing and mechanically increasing the earth's fertility—attempting to mass-produce earth's fruits for profit rather than accepting what is given organically by Nature—can be found wherever the Solar gods assumed management over the ancient shrines of the Goddess.[4]

Blood was used in the Delphic shrine to feed the ghosts and make them return, to speak and prophesy through the Sibyl. The Sibyl drank the blood, producing in herself prophetic ecstasy. Sounds of peepings and mutterings, and eerie batlike voices speaking through her, were believed to be the voices of ghosts. This was the function of ancient human and animal sacrifice: the recently dead were more easily recalled from the other world, and not so potentially dangerous as those long dead. Through these dead confidantes, the priestess gained knowledge of healing and the future.

The bull, with its lunar horns, was associated with the underground rituals. Bull's blood was believed to be the most potent magic, and diluted with water it was used to fertilize the fields and orchards of Crete and Greece. Drunk straight, it was considered a deadly poison to anyone but the Sibyl or priestess of the Goddess. Archaically, bull-sacrifice took place in a ritual circle of twelve stone herms (pillars) at the foot of a sacred hill. Half the bull's blood was sprinkled on a thirteenth herm in the circle's center. The rest was poured into a large basin from which the priestess drank. The Celts also used bull's blood for divination; Irish poets had to drink bull's blood—and then lie down to dream—in order to tell the truth.[5]

TWELVE CIRCLING DANCERS

Again and again in the religion of the Great Mother, one comes across twelve dancers in a circle. "Even the passion that I revealed to thee and the others in the round dance, I would have it called a mystery . . . "[1] These are supposedly the original words of Christ leading the twelve apostles in a hymn to the biblical Father. And the following comes from the Gnostic round dance, taken from the Apocryphal Acts of St. John:

> And we all circled round him [*her*] and responded to him [*her*]: Amen.
> The twelfth of the numbers paces the round aloft, Amen.
> To each and all it is given to dance, Amen.[2]

Both the dance and the number twelve are taken from the original Goddess religion—the Old Religion, as witches and pagans would say. Everything *alive* in Christianity (especially its heresies!) is taken from the Old Religion.

Within the witches' covens there are twelve members and a high priestess. Women and men in alternating positions dance around the magic circle that has been drawn on the ground or floor and blessed by the high priestess. The witches take their sacrament and jump over the holy fire, to stimulate the lifegiving energies of the moon. The witches or wiccan (wise ones) practice an ancient women's religion, the Dianic cult, whose rites and beliefs were passed down directly from the earliest Paleolithic and Neolithic religions. (It has apparently been determined that the secret language used now in the covens is Neolithic Basque. Very interesting, since Basque is believed to be a remnant of the language used in Atlantis.[3]) During the Christian Inquisition and witch-hunts, which went on for over five centuries, the wiccan chose hideous torture and death at the stake rather than forego their ancient ways—inherited from the beginning of things. They believed that the fertility of the countryside and the health of the people ("pagan" means "peasant") depended upon the performance of their sacred rites; they also knew they were involved with the irreducible truth, the "unimproveable original."[4]

In a Neolithic cave located in Sacro Monte, Spain, thirteen skeletons, all in priestess dress and holding amulet bundles, were found. They sat in a circle and apparently had participated in a ritual death; the floor was strewn with "beads and seeds of the opium poppy." The High Priestess wore a leather tunic engraved with geometric symbols. We don't know why they chose to die in this cavern north of Granada, but they were sister-members of the world's oldest religion.[5]

On Crete, the sacred ring-dances were performed. Naked women dancers, arms linked, circled within an area enclosed by the sacred horns of consecration. Perhaps they danced to raise the *kundalini* powers, the collective free flow of their mental, biological, and spiritual energies directed at a common task or vision. The dance is a recreation of the Goddess's original cosmic dance of creation (clockwise) and dissolution (counterclockwise). We don't know what kind of power was generated by these dances, but we can guess. Some other form of energy—real technological power—can be produced by tapping the terrestrial and cosmic energy currents, and consciously directing their flow.

When the psychic powers—body, mind, and spirit—are correctly concentrated, magical results are possible. All existence is the result of vibrations of the elements. All matter consists of cosmic light and sound waves vibrating at different speeds—"the pure sound of the element in the elemental composition." Sufis believe that by sound one is able to affect and perhaps control the elements. Elizabeth Gould Davis suggests that ancient women shamans were able to control, by group sound, the elemental vibrations with very practical results. Indeed, legends from the Near East, Europe, and Britain tell of great stones being raised, huge megalithic structures built, by magic use of sound alone. In one legend large stones are set floating in the air by women playing sacred pipes. Rocking stones, poised in such a way that they moved at a touch, perfectly balanced, were used for divination and magic. Oracles, always women, were inspired by the sound of the stone's rocking and the energy it generated. Such rocking stones can still be found throughout the countryside of Britain and the Breton coast of France.

How were those cyclopean walls of Jericho and Malta built? Remember the builders used no metal tools. Remember the recurring images of the Goddess, her priestesses, and dancers with upraised arms. Perhaps this was the posture of the cosmic moment when the Goddess appeared—the moment of simultaneous time/nontime when galactic and earth forces fuse and flow together, directed by the human spirit. Women in a dance circle with upraised arms are pictured in Stone Age cave and cliff paintings throughout Europe and Africa, the first homes of humanity. Millennia later, in patriarchal legend, Moses with supported, upraised arms helped bring victory to the Hebrews. This iconic posture of a power-figure with upraised arms supported by the people goes back to the first human experiences of the Goddess, and the concept is always related to the fusion of material and spiritual energies in a charged, or magic body.

The Goddess with upraised arms and parted legs gave birth to the

Prehistoric Egyptian terra-cotta figurine fashioned from Nile mud, circa 4000 B.C.

universe and the world. Ancient images also show her as magic musician, blowing sacred pipes or conch shells. In the Tanzanian cliff paintings found by Mary Leakey, some estimated to be 29,000 years old, all the groups are dancing women, some carrying musical instruments. A tall, wonderful red-ochre piper plays, with dashed lines falling from the end of her pipe. A singer's open mouth has the same lines falling from it.[6] These lines are song, and could also be rain. (A South African Bushman painting shows a naked woman in the sky, with magic rainmaking lines coming from her body, and the rain falling on a reclining woman and a man standing with upraised arms.[7] Ancient rainmaking was a woman's activity, or rain was seen to fall from a woman's body, e.g., the moon.)

As the possessor of the secret of life, woman's music, dancing, and utterance had magic and binding significance, helping to release the life forces not into chaos but into harmonious activity. Women, in their dances, imitated the animals, especially birds and snakes, and resonated with natural energies of earth and weather. In women's art and pottery design, also, connections were made between meanders, rhythm, music and dance, rippling waters, the motions of snakes and water birds. In this way women originated dance, music, art, and ritual as a magic linking of physical and symbolic forces. Young women of the Bavenda tribe in South Africa identify with the serpent force. Older female initiators kneel in the center, as pivots, around which the young dancers spiral in the rhythmic coils and undulations of the python. "Collapsing and reviving, they rest like the forces of nature in the seasonal round of death and rebirth."[8] Dahomean priestesses in West Coast Africa still perform a very similar python dance, as an energy-raiser and communication with departed spirits. These women are invoking more than personal fertility; their dances are ritual linkings (*religare:* "to bind") of the individual and tribal energies with the entire musical pulse of the earth, and with the dance cycle of cosmic energies. This primordial and continuous linking, or symbolic binding, always took place within, through, by means of the female body. The health, well-being, and experienced ecstasy of a people depended on the health, well-being, and experienced ecstasy of this female body—of individual women, of Mother Earth, of the cosmic dancing woman.

Sufi dervishes claim that their hand-clapping, dancing, whirling, and singing are involuntary expressions of the divine power manifesting itself through their bodies. They say this is a way of life handed down from remotest antiquity. This training in ecstasy was designed to produce the perfect woman or man, *within this world,* not out of it. Sufi dancing is a vehicle for self-realization, an experience of the self's joyous union with the larger Self of the universe. The dervishes developed their ecstatic rites against the background of a moralistically strict and misogynistic Islam. Were they reconnecting, in a patriarchal milieu, with ancient matriarchal rites of ecstatic women shamans? Their teaching is based on the concept of Essence: "S/he who knows her/his essential Self, knows God." The dervish is called "knower," "lover," "follower," "traveler"; *dervish* itself means "poor man" or "waiting at the doors of enlightenment." Are Sufis the inheritors of some of the rites of the ancient Great Goddess?

They are! (Even as the Essenes were originally ecstatic worshipers in the Temple of Artemis at Ephesus.) The Sufi ceremonial ax is an Amazonian labrys—a bronze double crescent of the Goddess, direct descendent of the double-axes used by the priestesses on matriarchal Crete.[9]

In Sufi belief, there is a form of superior mental activity available to human beings, and its power can be manifested on the plane of daily life. But most people cannot open to this mental power because our psychic energies are blocked by rigid, conventional, and dualistic thought habits. This "superconsciousness" includes precognition, telepathy, and bilocation (the ability to exist in two places at once). Sufis encourage poetic thinking and language, and specialize in making startling and cryptic utterances; this has given them a reputation as socially unrealistic, even mad. In fact, they are *female!* They teach techniques to help free the mind from cultural preconceptions and conditioned ideas, and their methods are not linear and verbal, but multisensory, using auditory, tactile, kinetic sense-impacts as well as visual. Sufis believe that their teachings constitute the inner reality of all religions—the core truths and techniques of all human spiritual-psychic experience. And so it seems to be: Elements of their teaching can be found in the early Troubadour culture of Europe, in the witch cults and mystic rites of the Knights Templar, in alchemic and Gnostic ideas—i.e., in all those pagan European remnants of the Great Goddess worship which the Christian church worked for so many centuries to destroy. Many of the same core techniques are found among Native Americans, Siberian shamanic cultures, Haitian voudun cults, and what remains of African magic religion, especially among the Dahomey and other West Coast African Goddess people.

As Sufis believe in communication without physical presence, they could be spread out everywhere—wandering musical Sufi jesters and *ariakeens* (harlequins) in patchwork costumes traveling on foot from city to city, teaching by songs and cryptic words, sometimes not speaking at all. No matter how much physical distance separates them, all Sufis feel themselves linked by a force they call *baraka,* meaning grace, lightness, and beauty.

In their ecstatic dance rites, Sufi dervishes go into swoons—they sing, sigh, weep, cry, sway from side to side, thrust knives into their flesh, burn themselves in the heat of delirious passion. In *The Mystic Spiral,* Jill Purce describes a Dervish dancing in flowing robes:

> The Dervish starts his dance with his arms crossed over his breast, suggesting a junction in the heart of the descending and ascending vortices [the ancient attitude-posture of the Goddess]. He has his left foot firmly earthed, representing the still axis. By moving his right foot, he begins like a planet to turn on his own axis, while revolving with his fellows around a central sun, the leading Dervish. He gradually expands, uncrosses his arms, and, lowering his head over his right shoulder, he raises his right arm (of and in consciousness) to receive the Divine Emanation, and lowers his left to return his gift to the earth. He spins gradually faster, as if by his own revolutions he were connecting Heaven and Earth by actually turning the spirit through himself and down in the ground, while his axis and heart remain absolutely still and his own spirit soars to its Divine Source. The greater his ecstasy, his expansion and speed, the wider his skirt extends. When his arms are both outstretched to Heaven, it is as if the union in his heart, delineated in its state of contraction (spirit into matter) by his crossed arms, has reached its fullest expression (matter into spirit) by the opposing gyres of arms and skirts: the outer expression of the bliss of the Divine Union in the very stillness of his heart.[10]

If at one point in this dance, with right arm pointing to sky and the left to earth, the dervish seems very much like the Magician in the Tarot cards, it is because they come from the same place and have the same meaning. The Paleolithic male shaman in animal skins and mask stood in the same posture, holding up "the lunar *baton de commandement* borrowed from women's mysteries to be his androgynous ensign of power."[11] This magician's baton, misnamed by a male archaeologist, was a women's lunar calendar stick, the first time-measuring device known, dating from the Ice Age. A male magician or shaman cannot be *magic,* i.e, *female,* without it.

Other forms of ecstatic dancing come down to us from the Near East, Thrace, the Mediterranean, preserved in Greek legend. One of these is the ecstatic dance of the Bacchantes, wild women intoxicated by chewing ivy leaves and also the mushroom, sacred to Dionysus. The Bacchantes or Thracian Maenads ("mad women") were the daughters of the Great Mother—her "white wild maids," possessing the magical power to make the whole earth blossom. Rites were performed on mountaintops, and at the touch of these wild women's wands (the original lunar calendar sticks) streams of wine and water, milk and honey, broke free and flowed from the rocks. In their ivy-induced fury, at the dark of the moon, they would tear any man in pieces who happened to cross their path or enter their sacred precincts. Dionysus himself, who some would call "basely effeminate," was torn apart ritually and eaten as a sacrament (this story could apply to the magic mushroom itself, which was called "Dionysus").

The cult of Dionysus and the wild women was popular with the common people, especially those in the countryside, far into Roman times. Central to this cult were the ancient mushroom mysteries, the communal eating of hallucinogenic psylocybin, called "the body of Dionysus." The spotted scarlet flycap, *Amanita Muscaria,* was referred to as "Christ's body" by Hebrew and early Christian cultists. There is no doubt that all ancient religious experience was associated with, if it did not originate in, hallucinogenic experience, and that this was under the tutelage of women, the great Stone Age pharmacologists.

Anthropologist Jacquetta Hawkes also believes that the ecstatic mystery religion of Dionysus, the "tender-faced and curly haired" son of the Cretan Great Mother, was originally the cult of the Great Goddess herself, and her wild orgiastic women.[12] When we think of the Love and Death God Dionysus surrounded by white, wild madwomen, our minds fly back immediately to that Old Stone Age cave in Northeast Spain, with the hugely genitaled young man surrounded by a crescent of nine moon-phase women, all dancing. This was the young man who became the Neolithic son/lover of the Goddess, and eventually Christ.

In Cretan myth, Dionysus was the bisexual son of the Mother, raised as a girl among women. Throughout the Near East and the Aegean he was known by many names—Attis, Adonis, Tammuz, Damuzi, Osiris. Jesus was called *Adonai,* "Lord," after his erotic prototype, *Adonis.* As a Vegetation God he was ritually sacrificed, usually on a tree (prototype of the later crucifix). His flesh was eaten as bread, his blood drunk as wine—Dionysus is the God of the Vine, Wine, and Divine Intoxication. This ritual sacrifice, in the harvest season, was believed to be necessary for the land's fertility. The immortal son's "mortal part," his flesh and blood energies, were cut up and sprinkled on the fields. (The Christ-idea was in

Women's Music, Sjöö, 1975

no way original with the Hebrews of Bible times, but inherited by them, along with paradise/garden myths, flood myths, and an entire birth-death-rebirth ritual cosmology, from the entire Neolithic agricultural Great Goddess religion of the Near East. They added to all this just one new twist: the incorporation of the Mother's son into a strictly patriarchal ontology.)

In *From Ritual to Romance,* English scholar Jessie Weston traced the red thread from these Neolithic Mother Goddess and son/lover/sacrificed god mystery cults into early Christian mysticism, and also into pagan European legends of the Grail, the sacred quest, and the healing of the wasteland, which became merged with Christian Romance. Twentieth-century poets like T. S. Eliot drew heavily on her discoveries and ideas (without giving her much credit), but turned the spirit quest into one of patriarchal-Christian despair and resignation, rather than a courageous and ecstatic return and reintegration with the Goddess.

Poetry was originally oral, the chant of ecstatic dance and entranced prophecy. Long before the "Song of Songs," Near Eastern erotic poetry was the expression of the love-cycle of Innana and Dumuzi, Ishtar and Tammuz, the Goddess and her son/lover. The "Song of Songs" itself is clearly a prepatriarchal chant of ecstasy to the Black Goddess.[13] Among the North African Berbers and other pre-Islamic Moorish peoples in the region that is now Morocco and Algeria, it was the women who traditionally made, chanted, and sang the lyric love poetry. This tradition was undoubtedly once spread throughout western and northern Africa. According to Briffault in his fascinating book *Troubadours,* these Moorish women's song-forms and erotic love poetries were carried by the Moors into Spain and the French Provençal region, and were the seeds of the Troubadour tradition that flourished in the Middle Ages. This tradition became European lyric poetry.

EARTH SPIRIT, SERPENT SPIRALS, AND BLIND SPRINGS

To all ancient people, the earth was *alive*, a great animal inhabited by a life-spirit, or "soul-substance." All phenomena were manifestations of this divine force, and after death all forms returned to this source before passing into another animate existence. The earth spirit was the "central transformer" of all life-energies into the multiplicity of life-forms, all protoplasmically connected with each other as in the same body, the same imagination. In the Gaia hypothesis, earth is defined as a living, breathing, and co-responding body, creating its own atmosphere, filling its own needs, relieving its own stresses. Far from the patriarchal-mechanical model of earth as a merely passive receiver of stimuli from the sun and sky, this new model shows us an intentional organism, exhibiting will and direction, and quite capable of reciprocal relations with all its creatures.

In *The Pattern of the Past,* Guy Underwood tells of his wanderings around Britain in search of ancient roads, animal tracks, stone circles, and other megalithic sites. Underwood, a water-dowser, describes the "earth force"—like a magnetic current—emitted by underground waters in motion and under pressure. This force is affected by the movements of the stars, the moon and the sun; in turn, it has great penetrative powers and affects the nerve cells of animals and humans. Modern Western science has not yet begun to study this force, but the Russians seem to be on its track, particularly in their studies of water-divining.

Generated within the earth, this "force" causes wave-motions perpendicular to the earth's surface. It forms spiral patterns (also mazes and labyrinths), and the spiral coils are based on multiples of seven. "When manifested in Spiral forms it was seen as a catalyst with the construction of matter and with the generative powers of Nature; it was part of the mechanism by which what we call life comes into being."[1]

She the joyous spiral.

What Underwood calls primary lines—water lines, aquastats, and track lines—were in ancient times considered healing/holy. They have remained stationary since time immemorial. Among the Celts, Elen-Helena, the Goddess of the Ancient Tracks, was considered the first and oldest of all deities. Animals follow these tracks, and use them to find suitable places to sleep and give birth. Migrations of birds and fish also follow these geodetic-magnetic lines, finding their way "instinctively" over vast distances. Most ancient roads were aligned with these irregular and winding animal paths, along the underground force lines.

Another system of forces contracts and expands daily, making the earth "a breathing animal" indeed. Underwood found that some of these secondary lines, along with the geospirals, reverse their positions at each phase of the moon, every fortnight.

> The ancient calendar was lunar and among the Celts the months commenced on the 6th day after the first new moon, while the year began on the 6th day after the first new moon following the vernal equinox. Each month was divided into 2 fortnightly periods. It would seem that the Celtic calendar was based upon the phenomena of fluctuation in secondary lines, since this provided an exact time once every fortnight in relation to which dates and times for rituals and religious observances could then be fixed.[2]

The spiraling force forms an energy network all over the earth's surface, affecting the germination and growth of trees and plants, as well as animals. Here is the practical side of Goddess mythology and symbolism: the moon, spirals, earth, water, all related to the right time to plant different kinds of seed, according to the moon's phases. Further, the magic earth current is known as the serpent force—or in China, the dragon current. Raising the serpent force is a common and ancient rite among Native Americans, Hindus, Asians, Africans, and the Celts of pagan Europe. These sacred serpentine paths were followed "instinctively" by the first nomadic tribes. Australian aborigines make ritual journeys along these current-paths, "in the steps of the gods," who created the original divine landscape. They believe that each place the gods "stopped" became manifest reality. A spiral-center of energy.

The dragon—the serpent on legs—was everywhere associated with creation and life-giving. As Underwood says: "The serpent is the one land-living vertebrate which naturally and frequently reproduces all the geodetic spiral patterns and so it seems reasonable to assume that both the serpent and the spiral are representations of the geodetic spiral."[3] And serpents and spirals were always associated with the Goddess. Eileithyia, Cretan Goddess of Childbirth, was always accompanied by snakes; the umbilical cord is itself a serpentine connection between the mother and new life. The mythic relation between serpents and earth-water is also ancient: Sacred pools and underground springs were always legendarily guarded by magic snakes.

A blind spring is a spot from which a number of underground streams flow, forming a radiating pattern of energy. Underwood noted that cows will break out of a field to reach a blind spring and give birth to their young there. This is true of all animal mothers. Perhaps the spiral energy patterns found over blind springs can ease labor, and produce healthier offspring.

Doubtless, ancient women also sought out the blind spring as a place for childbirth. According to Erich Neumann in *The Great Mother:*

> *The earliest sacred precinct of the primordial age was probably that in which the women gave birth.* It is the place where the Great Goddess rules and from which—as still in later female mysteries—all males are excluded. Not only is the place of childbirth the sacral place in female life in early cultures; obviously it also stands at the center of all cults that are dedicated to the Great Mother as the Goddess of Fertility. The mysterious occurrence of menstruation and pregnancy and the dangerous episode of child-bearing make it necessary for the inexperienced women to be initiated by those who are informed in the matters. This precinct is the natural social and psychological center of the female group, ruled over by the older, experienced women . . . [4]

The blind spring was the "esoteric center" of the Old Religion, as well as being the physical center of its monuments. It was "holy (healing) ground," a place of harmonious power where the Goddess dwelt. Blind springs were to be found at the center of every "prehistoric" temple, as well as every medieval church in Britain and Europe, according to Underwood. Gates of cities and temples were also set over blind springs, giving "divine protection" to those entering and leaving. Holy, healing, and oracular wells were sunk on blind springs, and the most ancient cities of the Near East, such as Jericho and Çatal Hüyük, were built over such sacred wells. The subterranean well-water was medicinal for a short season each year, when the animated spirit traveled through like an electrical current. Stones placed nearby probably served as "storage batteries" for its magnetic energies.

The ancient idea of divine protective sanctity was expressed by encirclement. Monuments were enclosed by protective underground spirals, mirrored aboveground in the foundation-maze or labyrinth. All burial places were surrounded by underground streams. In mythology and fairy tale, all magic castles are surrounded by a circular moat, or a rushing stream; and no magic rite can safely occur unless first a protective circle is drawn around it and the participants. There is a general association of important "prehistoric" sites, geodetic lines, and underground water.

Guy Underwood was a water-diviner. This art, along with geodesy (measurement of the earth's surface), was part of the training of Celtic Druids. It was also practiced by the Scythian Ennares, who were legendarily hermaphrodites; they wore women's clothes and received their gifts of divination from Aphrodite. The Druids prophesied with the aid of willow-wands, a tree sacred to the Moon Goddess; the Ennares with a wand made

St. Non's Well in Bride's Bay, Pembrokeshire, South Wales, Cymru, Sjöö collection, 1981

from yew or mountain ash, trees sacred to the Death Goddess. Both willow and yew are used in water-divining.

John Michell in *The Earth Spirit* theorizes that a stream of life-giving magnetic current passes through the land once a year, following certain paths—the season determined by positions of the stars. Legendarily, this super-energy transit was described as "the god passing through." Sacred calendars related to local topography, and myths and customs were based on a once-unified system of awareness of the pathways of the earth spirit.[5]

Worldwide, the sacred energy pathways were marked by some human means: mounds, banks, ditches, dolmens, menhirs and stone crosses, stone circles, terraces, and roads. In some places the energy circuits were known as "fairy paths," roads of psychic activity; and local peasant celebrations were timed to coincide with the current's passage. Processional and holy ways were located along raised serpent-paths. Stone avenues, representing the serpent, lead up to Stonehenge, which is an ancient temple of the moon and the serpent—as Michell describes it, the mercurial earth current glides toward it like a serpent toward an egg, moving through the earth's

St. Non's Well, Sjöö, 1981

crust. All stones in such monuments are believed to have strong healing powers, the rocks and boulders acting as vessels of the Vital Spirit.

In all ceremonies, the Goddess was seen to approach her shrine by a particular route: She both followed—and made—the energy path. Once she was accompanied by her nomadic celebrants; with permanent settlements and agriculture, these sacred journeys were imitated in religious processions. All these ceremonies were intended to energize and harmonize the people, as together they followed the path of the earth's magic life-flow.

And this is the real difference between ancient science and modern: Modern technologies tend to cut across the lines of the earth-force, arbitrarily and unconsciously separating human activities from the energy radiations of the earth. And so setting humans and earth against each other in a force-field of antagonistic vibrations. The old science and technology found ways to locate and tap the earth's natural force-flow, integrating human and earth energies, through ritual, in a strong, harmonious field.

New Grange burial mound, Co. Meath, Ireland, Sjöö collection, 1978

Corn Mother at New Grange, Sjöö, 1981

Celebrating Ancient Celtic Wales/Cumry, Sjöö, 1984

The operating principle of the ancient beliefs was the analogy between macrocosm and microcosm. What was true of the earth body was also true of the bodies of all creatures on earth. And so, analogous with the ancient science of geomancy, is another ancient technique: acupuncture. As Michell writes, "Chinese . . . acupuncture treats the human body by regulating the currents of vital energy that flow through the skin [as] the geomancer treats the body of the earth."[6] Kirlian photography has shown us that all the ancient acupuncture points are identical with points of great energy explosion on the skin's surface. We will find ways to take Kirlian photos of the whole Earth Body, the globe's etheric body, and perhaps learn again to follow the energy-charged serpent-paths to the benefit of all life.

"*It is Cosmos to those who know the Way and Chaos to those who lose it.*"[7]

UNDERGROUND CAVERNS AND ALCHEMIC MYSTERIES

The power and effectiveness of shamans—witches, sibyls, Druids—emerges from their ability to communicate with the *nonhuman:* extraterrestrial and subterranean forces, and the spirit-world of the dead. The megalithic chambers of Malta and Gozo were places of such communication. And in Britain also there are rumored to be subterranean caverns, chambers of initiation and incantation, under Stonehenge, Glastonbury Tor, and other stone monuments. Underground chambers, called *fogous* or *souterrains,* are often found within enclosures of ancient villages in the western parts of Britain, and especially in Ireland. There is much speculation about their purpose. Three-dimensional underground mazes, called weems, were built by the ancient Picts of Scotland. The word *weem* relates to the word *wamba* (cave) and also *wame* (womb). The Old English word for "womb" is *wambe.*[1]

The mysterious Tuatha de Danaan, "children of the Goddess Danu," knew all the magical arts, which they brought to Ireland. Driven underground by later Celtic invasions, they are still believed to dwell in earth-mounds, and are the Irish "fairies" who serve as communicators of energy between the mortal and invisible worlds. All "prehistoric" monuments in Britain, and globally, are associated with the cult of the dead, a very exact ancient science of spiritual invocation and conscious direction of natural forces. The Irish "fairy realm" is the "otherworld" of the Mexican *nagual,* the "dreamtime" of Australian aborigines, the summerland of the immortal dead who live on in other dimensions of our total reality. It is the *potentia* of all possible energy and form. (The Tuatha de Danaan were also called *Aes Sidhe. Sidhe*—pronounced *shee*—is a Gaelic word meaning "fairy mound," or realm of the magical powers, and it no doubt corresponds to the Hindu yogic term *siddhu,* which also means magical or occult powers.) Far from being "crude and carnal," as Christianity has labeled paganism, the sacred mysteries of antiquity were of a subtle psychic nature, introducing initiates into the invisible world by means of heightened consciousness. In these rites, the human psyche experienced physical death and the transcendent state of future being.

The mysteries were enacted in underground chambers from which all light was excluded, built to focus the earth's powerful energies on the chamber and its occupants. "Behind this animated current is the Mystery, hinted at in the catacombs of Eleusis, that may not fully be comprehended within the natural limits of human experience."[2] As the child is conceived within the mother's womb, so is the spirit conceived within the subterranean depths. Recent experiments conducted in caves suggest that conditions for ESP—telepathy, precognition, clairvoyance—are more favorable in an underground environment. Perhaps the moist earth, wholly surrounding such caverns, dampens the electromagnetic radiation with which the brain is normally bombarded, allowing the psyche to receive other, transdimensional radiations. At any rate, as John Michell writes,

> . . . the oldest branch of alchemy . . . was concerned to bring about the earthly paradise through the fruitful union of cosmic and terrestrial forces. . . . alchemy . . . geomancy . . . astrology were originally united in a system that recognized correspondences between planetary influences and the spirits of the earth's metals . . . [3]

Alchemy was a major continuation of the ancient mysteries and their symbols. The dragon, in alchemy, represents the "flame of spirit," and the dragon's "fiery breath" signifies transmutation of matter through intense heat. The Philosopher's Stone was the mystic condition through which all things could be transformed. All modern chemistry has its roots in both practical and philosophical alchemy. Some kind of atomic theory was known to the ancients who, working always by analogy, believed in total correspondence between material and psychic processes, and thus their mutual influence and interaction.

In Egypt, and as late as Roman rule there, many of the renowned inventions within the science of alchemy were created by women. Maria the Jewess, in particular, circa first century B.C., invented practical instruments for laboratory research, including the alchemical "still." She is credited with improving all the essential appliances that would be necessary to alchemical and chemical research for the following two thousand years.[4]

What we have left of alchemy, in addition to modern chemistry, are its symbols of psychic death, change, and rebirth through the process of alternating fusion and dissolution of opposite elements. This is a psychic rite, an earth-spirit ritual, retaining much of the ancient Goddess mysteries in distilled form, within each individual psyche. The Tarot cards also retain a pictorial record of these ancient rites of transformation and their process-symbols.

THE GODDESS AT AVEBURY IN BRITAIN

Avebury, on the Wiltshire Downs in the south of England, was the sacred center of megalithic culture in Britain. Avebury's stone circle is the largest yet found in England. It dwarfs Stonehenge. (There are seventy-seven other stone circles, or *henges*, dating from the late Neolithic and early Bronze Age.) Avebury was built by pre-Celtic people, living in a farming community circa 2600 B.C.

For thousands of years before its construction, the entire landscape of the surrounding area, stretching for about 37 miles, had been seen as the outline of the body of the Goddess. Every hill, mound, stone, and long barrow was believed to form part of her maternal body. The three stone circles at the "causewayed camp" at Windmill Hill nearby predated Avebury by more than six hundred years.

The Avebury monuments, which include Silbury Hill and West Kennet long barrow, form a "condensed sequence of visual sculpted images within the center of the larger and more ancient presence. They express together journeys of cosmic range and the entire yearly agricultural cycle within the space of three fields."[1]

The monuments are aligned within the "pubic" triangle of two rivers meeting. These rivers were seen as superhuman bloodstreams gushing from the earth womb of the Goddess.

Here, every year anew, the Goddess was born, grew into maiden and lover, became mother, and finally the old hag of death. The temples were her seasonal reality, and the people moved with her from place to place in rhythm with the changing farming year.

Our solar year is divided by solstices and equinoxes, but in the ritual calendar the quarter-days in between were used as the major days and nights of celebration. To the ancients, the lunar and solar manifestations of these days were equally important. The celebration nights fall in early August, November, February, and May on the appropriate lunar phase nearest to the solar quarter-day. These are the witches' sabbats of Lammas, Samhain, Imbolc, and Beltane. At the August (summer) and February

Avebury Stone Goddess,
Sjöö, 1978

(winter) quarter-days/nights the moon and sun rose and set in alignment with the axis joining the two sacred springs at Avebury.

Avebury circle originally had 98 stones, some up to 18 feet high, enclosing an area of 28½ acres. Two smaller circles stand within the large outer one. The earthworks surrounding the horseshoe or circular space are bounded by a ditch, with a bank beyond. Using only red-deer-antler picks and shovels made of ox shoulderblades, the people raised the earth-bank nearly 50 feet above the ditch bottom, stretching almost a mile in circumference.

Two serpentine stone avenues led into the circle. They were 1½ miles long, 50 feet wide, and were defined by 100 pairs of stones set at intervals of 80 feet. In shape, the stones were broad-hipped and long forms of the Goddess, alive and powerful in her stance.

The Christian church began its long fight against the Avebury stones in 634, smashing them or "exorcising" them with the sign of the cross. Both inner circles were destroyed sometime after 1700, and many of the other stones were demolished or simply buried. This was at the height of the witch-hunts, and these ritual stones of the Goddess—just like her priestesses, the witches—were actually "tortured" and "exorcised" by Christian priests: the stones were burnt, chipped, mutilated. The institution of private property finally brought about the end of the sacred stones, with the enclosure of common land by private, wealthy farmers. The emergence of the landless proletariat and the modern notion of individual progress at the expense of the community fittingly coincided with the fall of the Great Mother at Avebury.

Of the original stones in West Kennet avenue, 72 were left in 1722; by 1934 only four were still standing, with nine left fallen. In 1937 a Scots industrialist bought up the land, restored the ditch and earthworks (which had been serving as a rubbish dump!), and dug up and reinstalled 43 of the buried megaliths.

The long Avebury avenues represented the bisexual Snake/Dragon Goddess, female and male in one. The West Kennet avenue originated, at the serpent's tail-end, from the "sanctuary," once a circular temple-labyrinth of complex timber structures covered with a conical roof. This might have been the puberty temple, where young women of the community were initiated into the mysteries of farming, sexuality, and childbirth in the springtime season of ploughing and preparation of the seed bed. The young women reentered her womb within the sanctuary, which *is* Silbury Hill at a different season.

Here the Goddess is the hibernating spring-quarter serpent, just reawakening from her long winter death/sleep. On February 1, at Imbolc, the "Feast of Lights" was celebrated, torches carried processionally in the night to help the Goddess return from the underworld and to be reborn again.

At the tail-end of Beckhampton stone avenue, with its more phallic-shaped stones, was the male counterpart to the "sanctuary," doubtless a temple for male initiation.

Avebury circle is where the young women and men met, after dancing and winding their way up the avenues in imitation of the serpent, at midnight of the waxing moon of the May quarter-day. This stone circle forms both an enlarged cunt *and* a great head, the inner circles forming the lunar and solar eyes. It is also a world island surrounded by the cosmic ocean, and its hidden power and secret is the sacred underground water that seeps into the ditch in the spring. Here the unborn fetuses dwell.

Avebury henge was the Goddess of Love incarnate, the proper place of conception. Here was celebrated the communal yearly May festival-wedding in orgiastic rites, the entire community dancing with upraised arms on the outer banks, in imitation of the horned new moon. This was Beltane.

The maiden becomes a mother, and so the next stage of the cycle was centered at Silbury Hill, the pregnant womb of the Goddess, "the Creation Cone." Here, as already described, the people gathered on the summit on the night of the full moon at Lammas, the August quarter-day/night, to watch the harvest child being born.

With oncoming winter, the Goddess becomes the Lady of the Tombs, the Hag of Death, the Mother of the Dead. Her dwelling is now at West Kennet long barrow, where she retreats into the underworld after Samhain, or Hallowmas. This barrow is 340 feet long and shaped in her gigantic image. The image of the Silbury Mother is repeated within the chambers that represent vagina, birth passage, and uterus—but here is made hollow to receive the dead, who were buried within her in fetal position. The 30 chamber stones of West Kennet might form a lunar monthly count. There is no water associated with this barrow, no spring, no stream; all is dryness and barrenness. There are only rivers of stone.

West Kennet long barrow was built in 3500 B.C. It is a Stone Age horned grave/tomb/womb/temple, and it is older than Avebury and Silbury Hill. The people were buried within it collectively, without distinction of class or hierarchy. It was ritually frequented by the living as well as by the dead.

Megalithic culture is far older than was once supposed. Traces of a megalithic farming community have been found in County Tyrone, Ireland, dating from 4500 B.C. Patriarchal Bronze Age culture was first brought to Britain circa 2000 B.C. by the taller, warlike, and aggressive Beaker people.

In 2600 B.C., the entrance to the West Kennet long barrow was sealed off with huge megaliths (great stones). These stones form the body of an ox. The Goddess was moon and ox, one and bisexual. She is the Ox-Lady. She emerges miraculously out of death through the sacred bull. There was continued veneration of the tomb during late Neolithic culture. On Samhain in November—the winter quarter-day—a winter eve ox was sacrificed here on the night of the no-moon. The ox was ridden by the Queen of Death, and this ox is miraculously reborn with the spring.

The Winter Goddess lived on in folk memory as Black Annis. She was remembered as a great mountain builder, and was a gigantic hag. There are also sacred hills in Ireland named for her: the Paps of Annu, or Annu's Breasts.

Pervading all the earthworks and stoneworks of Avebury was the desire to be close to the earth. The people drew strength from her in birth, in life, and in death. The monuments could clearly *not* have been built with slave-labor, but were the love-labor of farmers, women and men, who were in tune with great psychic-physical powers. To carry through such a task, they lived a peaceful existence. Perhaps natural magic-energy was released from the earth, and used on an everyday basis by the people.

Ancient myths of the dragon-serpent guarding a mysterious and symbolic treasure perhaps refer to lost secrets of crop fertility—a hidden power running in fertility currents through the countryside. The story goes that anyone who tastes the dragon's blood becomes at one with nature, and

The Goddess at Avebury/Silbury, Sjöö, 1978

forever understands the songs of birds. Perhaps this is the bloodstream of the Mother gushing from the earth at sacred wells.

The ancients knew that some wells and stones, drunk or touched or embraced in a certain way, and at certain times of the year, could regenerate and revitalize people and animals. Sacred stones seem to contain and emit a force that periodically waxes and wanes. Beneath each "active" standing stone, there appears to be a crossing of underground water streams. The movement of water through a tunnel of earth—particularly through clay soil—creates a small electrical field, for which the stone acts as an amplifier. When this energy/power emerges from the ground, it does so in the form of a spiral ascending in seven coils, the lowest two beneath the ground. This is not a stable phenomenon, but waxes and wanes, changing polarity every month. After waning it dies away for a few days, and then waxes in the opposite direction; it cyclically increases and decreases until the end of the lunar phase.

The study of the moon's orbit was essential to megalith builders—the people of the moon, the stones, and the Serpent Goddess. The stones might also have functioned as a means of communication over long distances, since the magnetic force that activates the stones also links them in a continuous chain of vibrations. The ley-lines, paths for the force, interlock in a cobweb of stones, circles, mounds, and barrows all over the earth.

But the stone circles would not have been fully activated unless the calendrical events were accompanied by human rituals and dance, sometimes sacrifice, which focused the forces and fixed them in the stones.

Fire, like water, was essential to the workings of the monuments and their hidden power. At May Day/Night was the moment when Beltane fires were lit from hilltop to hilltop, to celebrate the coming of the new moon. On May Day the people drank from the sacred well and circled it nine times.

The May Day sunrise links Avebury in a direct line with Glastonbury Tor some 40 miles away. Glastonbury looks as humanmade as Silbury Hill, but it was actually shaped by volcanic rock violently thrown into the sky, in an otherwise flat and marshy land. Glastonbury's spiral path, however, was molded by human hands; it is a three-dimensional labyrinth, rising up the Tor in seven circuits. Nearby is sacred Chalice Well, anciently called "Blood Well" because of its miraculously healing red-stained waters.

Not far from Glastonbury is Wookey Hole, an ancient cave where the rites of the Winter/Death Goddess were probably enacted. According to the myth, in this cave lived a terrible and bloodthirsty "witch" who demanded human sacrifice. She was supposedly finally exorcised by a Christian monk from Glastonbury.

The persistent British myth of the slumbering giant Albion, and the return of King Arthur and the Golden Age, is really the legend of the reemergence of the Goddess and her people, the Great Mother and cosmic harmony we lost with Avebury. Today we live truly in the mythic "waste-land" of patriarchy, awaiting her rebirth and return with the spring of reemerging womencultures.

MOON TIME: THE GREAT INTELLECTUAL TRIUMPH OF WOMEN'S CULTURE

To interpret the flow of terrestrial magnetism—the dragon current, the serpent path—it is also necessary to watch the night sky. Night, to ancient people, was not an "absence of light" or a negative darkness, but a powerful source of energy and inspiration. At night cosmos reveals herself in her vastness, the earth opens to moisture and germination under moonlight, and the magnetic serpentine current stirs itself in the underground waters—just as the thick, snakey spray of stars, the Milky Way, winds across the night sky. Moon phases are a part of the great cosmic dance in which everything participates: the movement of the celestial bodies, the pulse of tides, the circulation of blood and sap in animals and plants. Observation of the night sky, of the stars, and especially of the moon, was the beginning of mathematics and science.

Stonehenge, on Salisbury plain—16 miles south of Silbury Hill—does not exist in isolation. Its structure also represents a seasonal and human life cycle. It was probably the center—or head—of an earlier, much larger configuration of long barrows that together portrayed the squatting Goddess. The Avebury monuments and Stonehenge, taken together (as Michael Dames says) may have been arranged to share and perfect the celestial environment, just as they share the river Avon.

Stonehenge was elaborated over a long period of generations, and was rebuilt many times. Stonehenge I (circa 2750 B.C.) is contemporary with Silbury; it consists of the earthworks of the outer banks and the 56 "Aubrey holes." Its four "station posts" are in lunar and solar alignments; the latitude of Stonehenge is practically optimum for moon/sun rectangular alignment.

The midsummer sunrise stones in the West Kennet avenue at Avebury, and the heel stone at Stonehenge, were both erected circa 2600 B.C.

The function of the Aubrey holes was to predict lunar eclipses.

It is infinitely more difficult to study the orbit of the moon than that of the earth around the sun. The moon describes an arc around the earth that varies from month to month. The arc is slightly tilted in such a way that over a period of 18.6 years the moon first rises and sets very far in the north and south, and then it gradually moves its rising and setting points further inwards from these extreme positions. After 9.3 years it begins to move back again, retracing its steps.

We now know that the megalithic stone circles of England and Brittany were, among other things, giant observatories. Running its dimensions through computers, modern astronomers have confirmed that Stonehenge was used to calculate the solstices, equinoxes, and future eclipses of sun and moon. Some have called it a "solar temple," but the major concern of the megalith builders seems to have been precise observation of the moon. The moon's eclipse cycle is measured by a period of 18.61 years; the 56 Aubrey holes are set to mark this cycle over a period of time: 19 + 19 + 18 years. More remarkable, many of the stone circles and alignments throughout Britain were built to calculate precisely the slight periodic 9′ oscillation of the moon—its "wobble" of amplitude 9′ or 0.15 degrees. The period of this tiny wobble is 173.31 days, or half an eclipse year. Such accurate knowledge of this small lunar oscillation—familiar to Neolithic moon-people—was lost to the Western world and not rediscovered until Tycho Brahe's observations in the sixteenth century. (The moon's wobble *was* known and accurately measured by ancient Arabic astronomers, whose traditional knowledge was not destroyed by Christian book-burnings, library-razings, and persecutions of intelligence. The Mayans observed it also.)

At this point, let's quote Pliny, a writer of the first century A.D.:

> True it is (I confess) that the invention of the ephemerides (to foreknow thereby not only the day and night, with the eclipses of Sun and Moon, but also the very hours) is ancient: howbeit, the most part of the common people have been and are of this opinion (received by tradition from their forefathers) that all the same is done by enchantments, and that by the means of some sorceries and herbs together, both sun and moon may be charmed, and enforced both to lose and recover their light: To do which feat, women are thought to be more skillful and meet than men. And to say a truth, what a number of fabulous miracles are reported to have been wrought by Medea, queen of Colchis, and other women; and especially by Circe our famous witch here in Italy, who for her singular skill that way, was canonized a goddess.[1]

The "charming" of sun and moon to lose and recover their light refers, of course, to eclipses; and apparently the knowledge needed to predict them, including the ephemeris tables,originated with women, and with a female cosmology, dating far back into the Stone Age.

The chalk banks of Stonehenge avenue meander for nearly two miles from the river Avon to the henge. There was even an enclosure nearby very much like the Avebury sanctuary; it is called Woodhenge, and its egg-shaped ring has five concentric circles.

At Stonehenge I, in the concentric circles of ditch, bank, and Aubrey holes, the image of the Eye Goddess was created.

At Stonehenge II (2000 B.C. to 1800 B.C.) the "station posts" are still standing; a half-circle of U-shape (vulva-shape) design was created with precious blue-stones brought from the Prescelly Mountains in Wales, more than a hundred miles away. That part of Wales was itself an ancient sacred center of the Celtic Goddess Cerridwen, abounding with stone circles. The blue-stones are about 6 to 8 feet high, delicately colored and finely shaped. Nearby stands Pentre Han, the large gateway cromlech anciently called "the womb of Cerridwen" by the Druids. Originally covered by an egg-shaped earth mound, it was a dark interior space where Druids practiced initiation rites.

Stonehenge is precisely positioned so that the distant hills align astronomically with the great stone arches. It was built to keep the rhythm of the agricultural year in synchronization with the movements of the astronomical year. Even in historic times, according to Michael Dames, the stones were still related to the wheat harvest. In folk memory and custom, the stones could be counted correctly only by laying a loaf of bread beside each stone.

The thirty upright stones of the Sarsen circle probably represented the 29.5 days of the lunar month, with the smallest stone (II) as the half-day.

In the final version of Stonehenge, built by the Beaker people, the blue-stones were repositioned. The new feature is the unique use of stone lintels. Perhaps at this point the alignment was turned more specifically into the "solar temple" that most male historians and writers so urgently want to find there.

But even from this later Beaker period, Goddess carvings are found on the stones. It is possible that the elevation created by the later trilithons was trodden at the first-fruits ceremony, people climbing up by ladders or scaffolding. What appears to be a libation bowl, carved with Goddess eyes, is sunk into the upper surface of the great trilithon lintel.

Stonehenge is very majestic, but harsh and gloomy. Avebury is open, deeply maternal in feeling, and the heart of a beautiful rolling countryside. Which is presumably why Avebury was condemned to oblivion for centuries, until rescued in the 1930s. And there was *no* thorough written account of Avebury between 1743 and 1977! Stonehenge, as soon as it was described as a "solar temple," took all the attention, and later became particularly popular as a "Druid temple."

The megalithic stone circles were used for the most delicate lunar observations. Alexander Thom, a British civil engineer who measured hundreds of megalithic sites, believes that all the impressive alignments in Britain were lunar. The geometry of the stone circles is derived from the extreme positions of the moon, stars, and sun as they cross the horizon; in particular the moon could be measured against a distant hill-slope, with

Shaman/Goddess at Callanish, Sjöö, 1982 (stone circle on the Hebrides off the northwest coast of Scotland)

all the lunar back-sites marked by the tallest stones. The great 60-foot-high menhir near Carnac, in Brittany (the Breton coast of northwest France), when viewed from other megalithic sites, acted as a marker of extreme positions in the moon's orbit. And this lunar-observatory stone dates from four thousand years ago.

Lunar sites, according to Thom, were often built in very remote and inaccessible places, particularly along the wild coasts of Britain and France, and in Northern Scotland. Night after night, the ancients used foresights on the great horizon-circle to calculate a curve on the ground, marking positions with stakes or rods. Stepping back each night, the curve obtained on the ground is, to a smaller scale, a graph of the moon's declination plotted on a time base. Thom notes that the megalithic people were mariners, traveling the seas to the far ends of the Scottish Isles and further; sailors in those dangerous waters needed some means of predicting tides. Knowing from lunar observations when to expect an eclipse, they could then calculate the resultant direction and violence of the tides.[2]

There is no longer any doubt about the advanced astronomical nature of these lunar-observatory sites. What no one mentions is that *women* were the first observers of lunar cycles. As the first agriculturalists, women related moon phases to planting and reaping times. Even earlier, women watched the moon to know the optimal time to conceive, to abort, to give birth. It is women who live the lunar cycles in our bodies. Becoming and changing are the lunar order of things. The moon exerts an identical influence on the magnetic serpent current in the earth, the tides of the sea, and women's menstrual flow. The lunar body is mirrored in nature, and it synchronizes with the flow of menstrual blood.

LUNAR CALENDARS

The first engraved rocks and stone tools yet found date from 300,000 B.C. This was at the very beginning of *Homo sapiens,* during the early Neanderthal period in Second Interglacial Europe. These permanently marked stones are believed to be time markers—moon-time markers—and were without doubt engraved by females. So early, as Thompson notes, "the human is . . . miniaturizing her universe into symbolic form."[1]

Thousands of similar pieces of stone and bone have been found, dating from the later Old Stone Age, circa 30,000 B.C. These are marked with long and often complex sequences of notches and scratches—an elaboration of the earliest Neanderthal engraved stones. Many "prehistorians" have dismissed these marks as decorations (does this sound familiar by now?). But Alexander Marshack, an American archaeological writer, decided to study these marks systematically under a microscope. He found the signs to be deliberately made, the tiny grooves cut in differing depths, widths, and shapes. Scratches on one pebble or bone were made with differently shaped tools. Marshack concluded that the marker changed to a new tool, often cutting at a new angle, with each change of moon phase. One piece of bone records six months on one side, six months on the other.[2]

This system had been undergoing refinement since the Neanderthal engraved rocks of 300,000 B.C. It was a complicated notation for recording factual data—time-keeping, phase- and cycle-marking—and it was in use in Europe tens, indeed hundreds of thousands of years before what is called "true writing" appeared in the Near East sometime in the late fourth millennium B.C. This notation, and the lunar calendar it recorded, was the invention of women.

Marshack has studied another form of time-keeping, the lunar calendar stick. Originally perhaps carved from bone, later of wood, the sticks were an elaborate "record of the lunar year." One such calendar stick that Marshack spotted in an 1828 portrait of a Winnebago Chief was 53 inches long, with four sides, or faces. "Vertical marks are etched into it at regular intervals; above them are small crescents and dots." These sticks were complex lunar tally sticks that marked the lunar year, brought the lunar year into phase with the solar year, and noted the times of rituals. So far, Marshack has found at least five calendar sticks from three different Native American tribes.[3]

Such sticks appear in Paleolithic cave paintings dating from 50,000 B.C. They are held by women and shamans. (And later became the magician's wand.) Abbé Breuil named this stick "*le baton de commandement,*" suggesting it was an insignia of male rulership or power. But in fact, as a lunar measuring instrument, the stick derives from women's earliest moon-phase engravings on rock and bone. In Thompson's words, "the owner of the baton is not man the mighty hunter but the midwife."[4]

The midwife. Of course! Because it was her job—and the job of every pregnant woman—to know exactly when babies were due. Anthropologists have described the keeping of lunar calendars, specifically by women, among Australian aborigines, six Siberian tribes, and the Yurok Indians of North America. Australian women used notched sticks. Among past and present-day Siberians—Nganasans, Entses, Dolgans, Chuckchi, Koryaks, and Kets—"pregnancy has the duration of exactly 10 lunar months," and it has always been women who kept the lunar calendars marking those months off toward a safe full-term birth. Yurok women kept menstrual calendars (and were certainly typical in this of other Native American women of both hemispheres). The Yurok count was kept by "dropping a 'month' stick each Lunar month into a second basket until they reached a count of ten." With this method they could predict births to within a day—a crucial accuracy among early hunting-and-gathering people on the move. The count was also useful in connection with abortion.[5]

As Thompson says, "it is perfectly reasonable to assume that menstruation, lunar calendars, and midwifery are as much or more at the foundation of human science than man the great killer so celebrated" by the macho-anthropologists.[6] And in fact, this does make sense—the kind of clear, simple sense that is so easily overlooked. The biblical idea that humanity began with a crime of disobedience is wrong. The Capitalist-Darwinian notion that human intellect begins with a clever act of self-interested murder and plunder and self-aggrandizement is wrong. The macho-anthropological belief that human life and the human brain evolved through the inventions, discoveries, and experiences of the male hunter alone, is all wrong. Human life begins with birth. And human culture and intelligence began with birth, with the female's experiences of surviving pregnancy and bearing children and keeping them alive.

The possession by the Winnebago Indian Chief of a lunar calendar stick as part of his insignia of power, along with an ax and a neck pendant, shows that this ruling power derives from the ancient time of female power. Thompson, again, points out that priests and shamans must *always* dress as women to take on woman's original magic, and that aboriginal men worldwide were put through imitation childbirth and menstruation rituals for purposes of initiation. "The fact that the baton was taken over by men in the militarist cultures of patriarchal civilization may, in fact, indicate that they took it over *because* it was a most ancient symbol of feminine power."[7]

So: at the very beginning of the Upper Paleolithic, women—Neanderthal women—apparently knew that lunar periods were of a certain length, were repeated regularly, and that the phases were roughly predictable within a day or two. Cro-Magnon women, in 30,000 B.C., had formed a conception of a lunar year and were working out a lunar calendar. By the end of the Paleolithic age (circa 10,000 B.C.) they could predict the seasons of the year, the phases of the moon, the annual migrations of animals, birds, and fish.

When Neolithic people settled in village sites, they began building their calendars, stone circles that were to be used for lunar and solar observations as well as religious ceremonies. Or perhaps it was the other way around: Perhaps the ceremonial observatories, these power centers formed of fixed points of stone, were the loci that gave rise to the settled farming communities that replaced the nomadic food-gatherers and hunters.

It is not far-fetched to think women invented symbolic and abstract notation, observational science and early mathematics. Early woman's thought processes (early man's too) were still organic, still rooted in nature and practical experience—not alienated or born of a desire to "conquer Nature." Organic rational thought emerged from a desire to cooperate with the natural world, and from a real integral observance of the needs and rhythms of the personal self and the human community. It also emerged from a mind free of the inhibitions, blocks, and dogmas imposed by later patriarchal religions and cultures.

> The implications of this association of women and the moon would suggest that women were the first observers of the basic periodicity of nature, the periodicity upon which all later scientific observations were made. Woman was the first to note a correspondence between an internal process she was going through and an external process in nature. She is the one who constructs a more holistic epistemology in which subject and object are in sympathetic resonance with one another. She is the holistic scientist who constructs a taxonomy for all the beneficial herbs and plants; she is the one who knows the secrets of the time of their flowering. The world-view that separates the observer from the system he observes, that imagines that the universe can be split into mere subjectivity, and real objectivity, is not of her doing. She expresses "*the withness of the body*" that Whitehead tried to rediscover in his philosophy of organism and process. Here is the philosophy that stood before the speculations of the presocratics; she is the "Holy Mother Church" which Descartes challenged when he cut the umbilical cord between philosophy and the Church and split reality into the *res extensa* and the *res cogitans*. The reason the Venus

of Laussel or the modern Virgin of Guadalupe are pictured with the crescent moon is that woman and the moon are a single mystery.[8]

This mystery is, and was, a reality, and all original real mystery was observed, studied, pondered, and participated in by original real human beings. Mystery was not used as a tool of fear or oppression, of obfuscation and power, but was used gratefully as ceremonial food by the evolving human intelligence, led by the observational intelligence of women.

In *The Woman's Encyclopedia of Myths and Secrets,* Barbara G. Walker reminds us that *mathesis* (*Ma-thesis*) means "mother wisdom," and originally referred to divination by the stars. Worldwide, in ancient and modern languages, the word "ma" means "mother." The first astrologers and mathematicians, meaning "learned mothers," were women.[9]

The Lunda people of African Angola tell of a girl who discovered a method for measuring long distances in boundary disputes. In her daily tasks she wove wicker-work doors for huts from leather strips, measuring them a thumbnail wide. She noticed that an ox-hide could be cut into a continuous strip to cover a great distance, and that all ox hides produced strips of similar length. So she suggested the strips be used as standard units of measurement by her tribe.

Certainly measuring amounts of stored food, and estimating how much could be used on a daily basis to feed a certain number of people through the lean months of the agricultural year, gave Neolithic women profound experience in mathematical calculation. Life depended on it.

Geometry and the human image were originally two expressions of the same divine image—the body of the universe. Number emerged from sensory matter. To the ancients, number was always founded in real and concrete human experience, and did not possess abstract universality, or "objectivity." The megalithic yard of the stone monument builders was 2.72 feet—the measurement of the human stride. Throughout classic antiquity measurements were based primarily on parts of the human body, e.g., the foot, the hand-span, the finger-joint.

The Chinese word for "mathematics," *suan,* is no older than Confucius, circa 600 B.C. Units of linear measure were codified into abstractions gradually, a process perhaps begun in Babylon circa 2500 B.C. In Western artistic creation, we have inherited a tradition of ideal forms and measurements that uses a numerical system exploited during the European Renaissance. This tradition can be traced back to Pythagoras (circa 550 B.C.), who developed a kind of mathematical mysticism out of megalithic philosophy. He acquired his knowledge and perhaps his methods also from Thracian wise women. Pythagoras, like mathematicians after him, came to believe that mathematics is not just a language describing Nature, but is inherent in nature. "All things are numbers." "Numbers are the first principle, indeed the very elements of the things of Nature."[10]

Thus, for the Western world, a description was abstracted from substance and deified into an "objective system." Thus Pythagoras introduced

Moon Birds, Sjöö, 1978

"logical reasoning," (rather than organic reasoning) into the domain of religion and ritual, laying the foundations for the later "intellectual theology" of Christian scholars and the Western world in general. This combination of mathematics and theology characterizes religious philosophy in Classic Greece, in medieval Europe, in Reformation and modern times. Consequently, "God" was no longer intuition or ecstatic vision, not profound ontological experience, but a kind of rational machine "explained" by a few scholarly men. Plato, St. Augustine, Thomas Aquinas, Descartes—all inherited this numerical philosophy, and shared a logical admiration of the "timeless" and static, utterly transcendent and aloof "pure spirit" of the Father God. Utterly abstracted from flesh and earthly cyclicity, this Father God was as unappealable as pure number. Pure number is always elevated above the messy world of mere life. During three hundred years of witch-hunts in Europe, this rationalistic theology was used as a legal and clerical weapon against what still remained of the ancient womencultures. Medieval scholiasts not only debated endlessly, and in dead earnest, about how many angels could dance on the head of a pin; during obscene torture, priests and civil judges also hounded their female victim with obsessive questions about the precise number of imps she employed, the total number of times she had intercourse with the

Devil, the exact size and length of his "member," and so forth. The dogmatic insistence on *number* was supposed to cast an aura of "rationality" and "objectivity" around their otherwise bizarre and sick proceedings. In modern forms—e.g., psychological measurements, behavioral norms, notions of quantifiable "sanity" and "adjustment"—deified number is still used as a power-tool against "social deviants."

In contrast, Eastern mysticism—like European pagan orientation, and primal orientation everywhere—understands mathematics as one part of our conceptual map—a means of apprehending one part of reality, but not an abstractible feature of reality itself. Reality is undifferentiated, constantly moving and cyclic—like the moon.

MOON MINDS

The slightly bulging equatorial region of our globe is closer to the moon than other parts of the earth. Probably for this reason, women who live near the equator tend to ovulate during the full moon.[1] Because of the phenomenon of menstrual synchrony, in which women living together tend to have their periods at the same time,[2] a synchronous full moon ovulation would mean a synchronous menstruation near the dark of the moon. And mythology has in fact always associated the two. Women living together in small gathering-and-hunting bands in the equatorial regions would have their bleeding times together, at the same time of the month, when the moon was dark and the earth devoid of her light. Our human ancestors lived for millions of years in equatorial Africa; and perhaps this means that human consciousness began evolving in synchrony with this powerful observed fact of all females bleeding together, bleeding mysteriously, in time with the mysterious disappearance of the moon.

Among early women, no one experienced menstruation in private. It was not a "personal" phenomenon, but an awesome *datum* of the female group. Group initiation rites were held when the young girls reached puberty; this is still true among all aboriginal people worldwide whose customs have not been totally suppressed by Christian patriarchy. Originally, female puberty rites of first menstruation were not meant to punish girls with shame for the "crime" of becoming women, or to restrict their new lives as women in any punitive way. The rites were a celebration of female power, and an initiation of the young girl into the wise and careful use of that power for the benefit of all.

The first menstruation was a transition into partaking of the nature of the Cosmic Mother, and of her full face, the moon. Women's monthly cycle being seen as of the same duration as the moon's cycle, and women's bleeding synchronous (actually or legendarily) with the dark moon, it was easy to believe that the moon mother was bleeding also. The witches' sabbats were originally observances of the sacred or taboo days at the new and full moon, critical days of her cycle—days, and nights, of great power, for good or for harm. Women originally went into menstrual huts in order to gather the dark moon power, to focus it and study it, in solitude. In both group and solitary meditation, moon power became mind power.

In most languages there is a common root word for "moon" and "menstruation." Our own word for menstruation comes from *menses*, the Latin word for "month," which was measured originally by the moon. And both words are related, through Indo-European roots, to the Old English word *mona* (moon), deriving from *me*, which meant both "mind" and "measurement." All are cognates—moon, mind, measurement, month, menstruation—since it is the moon mind that establishes measurement, including calendars. This cluster of meanings can also be found in the Egyptian Moon God, who was worshiped as the creator of the alphabet, the art of writing, literature, numbers, counting, and wisdom; though the Egyptian Moon God was male, he was seen as the lover of the Goddess, and thus assigned her attributes.

Menstruation also means "moon-change," also "mind-change." The Mother was seen to rest at full moon, when she was neither waxing nor waning. *Sa-bat* means "heart-rest"; the witches' sabbats were first held once a month, but later at each quarter of the moon. All witches' celebrations, all pagan rituals, were acts of cognizing a revolving process: change-within-continuity, continuity-within-change, around and around forever.

Pregnancy, as well as menstruation, was believed to be caused by the moon. Menstruation came from the new moon (or dark moon) while the full moon impregnated—a folk-belief that correlates very well with the fact of equatorial ovulation during the full moon. Many mythological and folk heroes, and religious founders, were supposedly conceived by the moon, including the Buddha—(and Jesus, when we think about it, whose Mother still stands on her moon).

Physically, the moon exerts a gravitational pull which, combined with that of the sun, deforms the earth's surface by as much as a foot. The surface of the ocean is pulled into a bulge measuring several feet, causing the tides. Recent studies have shown, however, that it is the light of the moon, perhaps even more than its gravitational pull, that influences reproductive behavior in organisms. Like most animals and plants, humans evolved in a light and dark world, day and night, alternating regularly. But periodically the night is not dark: around the time of the full moon. Perhaps the human species evolved a genetic response to moonlight, if all early women ovulated at the full moon. Light is a potent trigger of biological rhythms. And it is not an impossibility that artificial light has affected our body rhythms (there is never real darkness in a city), destroying our ancient understanding of our menstrual month/moon periodicity—perhaps destroying also our knowledge of natural contraception, as suggested provocatively by Louise Lacy in her book *Lunaception*.[3]

The power of fertility in plants, as well as in humans, was seen to emanate from the moon. Many people still hold the ancient belief that plants grow mostly at night, under the polarized moonlight. Agriculture began in very warm Near Eastern climates, where the sun can be a force hostile to life, scorching young shoots, burning leaves and the soil into arid dust. Plutarch, in his *Isis and Osiris,* argued that: "the Moon, with her humid and generative light, is favorable to the propagation of animals and the growth of plants, while the sun, with his fierce fire scorches and burns up all growing things, renders the greater part of the earth uninhabitable by reason of his blaze, and often overpowers the moon herself."[4] In such lands, summer with its unrelenting heat was conceived as a return to chaos, the end of the world through heat and fire. Early people saw the sun as the lesser fruit of the Mother Sky; it was female night, with her cool moisture and magical moonlight, that gave life and fertility. (In the cold North, though, where the sun is benevolent and welcome, the sun was seen as a Mother Goddess—perhaps this was so for the Celts.[5])

Ancient people knew that a child is not only the product of human sex; children are also the offspring of the earth spirit joined with the astrological influences existing at its conception and birth. Earth was considered to be the home of children *before* they were born. In Africa and Australia, for example, souls waiting to be born were believed to live under the earth or in rocks. Unborn children lived in fountains, springs, lakes, and streams, or in trees, bushes, and flowers, waiting to be born as human beings through the joined energies of the earth and moon. Festivals dedicated to the Goddess were the favorite times to conceive children. The moon's monthly waxing was beneficial to an infant's growth, and there were baptism rites where the baby was exposed to the moon, sun, and earth, incorporating the newborn within this celestial sphere, or "family." In this way, both Bantu Africans and Native Americans linked the social, biological, and spiritual worlds.

Among people for whom sex does not imply impurity, or hold magico-religious danger, the taboo on the sexual act does not occur in relation to ceremonies. Rather, ceremonial sex was always a powerful act leading to spiritual perfection. Within the stone circles of the Neolithic, perhaps the entire human community celebrated the creative power of the Goddess, in festivals coinciding with those magic times when the energy-tides of the unseen flowed strongly around and through the earth. Earth-channels were then wide open to receive her spirit, giving enhanced consciousness, healing, and fertility to the people. These are the ceremonies that have been so condescendingly labeled "fertility rites" by prurient patriarchal anthropologists, and "satanic orgies" by the missionaries.

And what were those children like who were born with the blessings of both the Moon Mother and their human mothers? Were their psyches wide open, communicating easily with the greater Self? Was the psychic/astral/lunar body more vibrant and aware? Were they able to communicate and resonate with the animals and plants, the stones and whole earth, and also tune into cosmic vibrations of moon, sun, and stars? What were moon minds like!

The vast silence of dark space lit by the clarity of the moon, and stars, became a metaphor for deep thought and creative vision. The Moon

Goddess was the judge and giver of law. Crimes, challenges, problems were investigated by the women by moonlight. Bright nights were spent sitting around the fire thinking, contemplating, envisioning. This is why words that have to do with mental activity are, in most languages, cognate with names for the moon, e.g., *mens:* mental, measure, month, mind.

"They call the moon the mother of the universe," having both female and male powers and reproducing herself alone.[6]

Sowing and reaping were reckoned by the moon, sowing at the new moon and reaping at the old. All agricultural proceedings had to be timed with the moon's changes. Planting, cultivating, and harvesting were originally women's work, since only women are under the direct guardianship of the Moon Mother. Many agricultural people still believe that only women can make things grow.

Water, like fire, was anciently sacred, and specially related to the Moon Mother. Rainmaking and magic control of the weather were secret rites performed by naked women—not to be seen by men. Witches have the same customs still, and it was traditionally said of them that "tender girls of eight to ten years can raise up rain and tempest." In recent studies of psychic phenomena made in Russia, it was found that dowsing rods work twice as accurately in the hands of women than in those of men. More dramatically, the dowsing rod *always* responds to the polarity of women's bodies, no matter from what direction the body is approached; this is not the case with men's bodies.[7]

Since the tides are regulated by the Moon Mother's cycles, she was believed to give all moisture—from the morning dew, natural springs, and rain to the great rivers and oceans. The Moon Queen was the tribe's rainmaker. The moon also controls the fluids of the human body, and the brain, as the moistest part of all, was particularly subject to its influences. Words like "lunacy" and "moon-madness" show negative traces of this belief.

In the Stone Age caves there had been darkness, and seemingly changeless stability. Following wild game and gathering wild plants, Paleolithic people lived in "dream-time." Perhaps movement in time was not intellectually experienced, as we do, until reaping of wild grain was replaced by the punctual observance of seed-time and harvest-time—the development of a calendric time-sense. Seasonal inundation of land helped mark these planting and harvesting periods. Shepherds learned to reckon the periods of river-height increase by watching the moon's phases cross the higher pathway of the stars. Out of primordial "dream time" emerged this new and revolutionary conception of seasonal advance and regression, the complex interplay of opposing forces and their regularity.

Until recently, duration of time was reckoned by nights, rather than days—this can still be seen in time-words like fortnight, honeymoon, month (moon). Originally the month was a triplicity, like the moon's cycle: waxing, full, and waning. The month was divided into three periods of ten days each, and this division is retained in the astrological division of a zodiacal month into three decans. The first of each month fell on the night when the lunar crescent appeared. The crescent of the waxing moon came to symbolize increasing power, and was later adopted as the emblem of Islam, for this reason; pre-Islamic Arabic people were all moon-worshipers.

Even the summer and winter solstices were calculated by the moon. The zodiacal constellations were called the houses of the moon, and the zodiacal belt was named "the Girdle of Ishtar." This Neolithic time-calculation is quite different from that of the Paleolithic cave peoples, who reckoned cycles by the breeding seasons of animals. In the agricultural Neolithic, people developed a new consciousness of their own being in relation to the universe. This new consciousness is much closer to what we call "modern." The understanding of numerical relations made it possible to make brick-units from sun-dried mud, units of definite size and shape. The many industries developed by women, the willed transformation of matter brought about by women's discoveries in experiments with fire and water, led undoubtedly to increased activity of the "logical mind." Just the notion of movement returning on itself, the building up of shape around emptiness—as in the making of a pot, so different from the carving of wood, bone, or stone—was an amazing feat of abstract thinking.

A conception of cyclic symmetry developed, which in the end led to the invention of the wheel. There was a striking geometric tendency in Neolithic design, as in the repeated patterns of woven cloths, and the repeated signs and symbols of pottery. This abstract and repetitive patterning was very different from the naturalistic animal and human forms of the Old Stone Age cave cultures. And it had its dangers: With the development of the pottery wheel, as has been said, in many cultures men took over ceramics entirely and began the "mass-production" of items that had once been very lovingly handcrafted for local use.

What kept this Neolithic intellectual development still within the matriarchal context was that all magic symbols, the lunar calendar, the daily industries occurred within a ritual, religious framework belonging to the Goddess and the human collective. Techniques and signs were not to be manipulated for personal profit, or exploited for personal power, until the full establishment of patriarchy in the Bronze Age, or Late Neolithic.

MOON MOTHER

The earliest representations of the Moon Mother, and perhaps the most universal, were in the form of a cone, or pillar of stone. This is the column on which the Death-in-Life Goddess perches, the "Anointed One." The stones themselves were considered sacred, sometimes they were meteoric, and they were anointed by having ritual oil, blood, or fermented liquor poured over them. The great Semitic Moon Goddess Astarte was worshiped on Mount Sinai by the Canaanites, in the form of a stone pillar, long before Moses received the stone tablets of the Law there. *Mount Sinai,* in fact, means "Mountain of the Moon." And it is interesting to note that the Hebrew Levite priests were originally serpent priests—i.e., *Levi:* "great serpent," as in Leviathan.

There is a close resemblance among Moon Mothers everywhere. In this form the Great Goddess is always the law-giver, the orderer of time, the judge of the dead, and the eternal source of wisdom and ecstasy. She was Ishtar of Babylon long before 3000 B.C. As the Hindu Moon Mother, Kali sits in her lotus posture, breathing the rise and fall of our earthly tides. The Irish Goddess Cailleach (pronounced Kali) sits in her lotus position also, and does the same. Even Mary of the Catholic church is called "the moon" and is turned to by women in childbirth, as was her original, Diana-Artemis-Astarte.

In her form of the great whale-dragon (Babylonian Tiamat, Hebrew Leviathan), Ishtar brought about the Great Flood, an earthly disaster-story the Hebrews borrowed from Sumerian and Babylonian accounts. But Ishtar also lamented her drowned children, comparing them to fishes in the sea. And it is always in the form of the great serpent or dragon or sea monster that the Moon Mother was slain by later patriarchal heroes—as Tiamat (Tehomet), Vritri of the Vedas, the Gorgon-Medusa, the dragon slain by St. George, or the snakes driven from Ireland by St. Patrick. (In fact, there never were any, or many, snakes in Ireland; the Christian saint *symbolically* killed a female "fiend" in serpentine or dragon form, whose Irish name was Caorthannach, or Corra, called "the Devil's mother" by the pious.)

Drawing by Albrecht Dürer, title page from *The Life of the Virgin*, woodcut, 16th century Germany

The Threefold Goddess of Arabia, Magna Dea, was enshrined in the sacred Black Stone, the Kaaba at Mecca, where she was served in ancient times by her priestesses. The sacred Black Stone at Mecca, site of so many pilgrimages, is imprinted with her vulva/yoni sign, and covered with a black pall called "the skirt of Kaaba." The male priests who serve her today are called *Beni Shaybah,* which means "the sons of the Old Woman," i.e., the moon. Present-day Muslim pilgrims to this shrine, the most holy place of all Islam, are mostly unaware of the pre-Islamic significance of the Kaaba.[1] They circle the Black Stone seven times "to attain the summit by spiraling around it." Seven is the number of the moon, and the ancients always danced "the Way" in spiral processions to the summits of her earth-mounds.

Moon shrines and sanctuaries were situated in forests, in caves and on mountaintops, and by lakes, sacred springs, and wells that were also healing centers. Priestesses guarded the water supplies, as well as the sacred fires. This was true in even Roman times, where the priestesses were called Vestal Virgins. Water springs, originating deep in the earth, were believed to have magic and healing powers. And fire was the fertilizing power of the moon, the sacred flame representing the moon's light. Torches, candles, and bonfires were burnt to help keep the moon's fertilizing light shining. The bonfires, torch-processions, and candle-burning at Christmastime originated in these fire-rituals of the Goddess. On December 13 in Sweden, St. Lucia travels in procession as the Queen of Light, with a crown of candles in her hair, surrounded by her maidens. Even now. And of course the evergreen tree, the gift-exchange, and the midwinter festivals of Christmas all derive from ancient pagan midwinter rituals of the Goddess.

Earth Is Our Mother (with Nerthus—Nordic Mother Goddess), Sjöö, 1984

(St. Lucia of Sweden on December 13th. The festival of the Greek Hecate on August 13th. Thirteen members in a witch coven. Is the number 13 seen as unlucky because of its association with matriarchal religion? Among pagan Scandinavians Friday the 13th was celebrated as a beneficent day; Friday is Freya/Frigga's day, the Great Goddess of the north, and thirteen is the number of lunar months in a year. Many patriarchal "bad omens" are simply reversals of what was sacred to matriarchy and the Goddess religion. The left-hand path, in patriarchal religion, is called the path of evil, of woman, of black magic. The left side of the body, where the heart beats, was considered by the ancients to be the seat of divine feminine power; all life comes from her heart. The word *sinister,* which originally meant "left," has come to mean everything suspicious, evil, ominous; while *dextra,* meaning in Latin "right," or "right-handedness," has acquired wonderful meanings like skillful, mentally clever, correct. In Europe, an "illegitimate" child was long signified as *bar sinister,* meaning "child of the left side," i.e., the mother's side. The right-hand path is supposed to be the path of goodness, or of white magic; and children are

Egyptian Isis with Horus, whom she conceived without husband or lover

encouraged to favor the right hand, the hand of righteousness. In Christian imagery, the "good sheep" sit on God's right hand in heaven while the "bad goats" go to the left. That these connotations remain with us in modern politics is not accidental; the right is father-fascistic, the left is mother-communal.)

Ancient moon priestesses were called virgins. "Virgin" meant not married, not belonging to a man—a woman who was "one-in-herself." The very word derives from a Latin root meaning strength, force, skill; and was later applied to men: virile. Ishtar, Diana, Astarte, Isis were all called virgin, which did not refer to sexual chastity, but sexual independence. And all great culture heroes of the past, mythic or historic, were said to be born of virgin mothers: Marduk, Gilgamesh, Buddha, Osiris, Dionysus, Genghis Khan, Jesus—they were all affirmed as sons of the

The Goddess in Her Garden with Tree, Serpent & Her Son/Lover, the Green Man of Vegetation, Sjöö, 1971

Great Mother, of the Original One, their worldly power deriving from her. When the Hebrews used the word, and in the original Aramaic, it meant "maiden" or "young woman," with no connotations of sexual chastity. But later Christian translators could not conceive of the "Virgin Mary" as a woman of independent sexuality, needless to say; they distorted the meaning into sexually pure, chaste, never touched. When Joan of Arc, with her witch coven associations, was called La Pucelle—"the Maiden," "the Virgin"—the word retained some of its original pagan sense of a strong and independent woman.

The Moon Goddess was worshiped in orgiastic rites, being the divinity of matriarchal women free to take as many lovers as they chose. Women could "surrender" themselves to the Goddess by making love to a stranger in her temple. This has been called, by male historians, "sacred prostitution," but the word is totally misleading. This was not any kind of service to men, nor did any woman have to do this to live. It was a way for women to participate, for a ritual moment, in the transindividual being of the Goddess. The Goddess comes into being "in the moment of union"—a moment of psychic as well as sexual union. This was one way that men could partake in her essence also, through the body of a woman. The rite was meant to recharge the living Goddess, and to enlarge the woman's ego-consciousness into an experience of cosmic sexual power and flow. It was a way for each woman to experience herself as "the moon."[2]

Persephone & Demeter within New Grange, Sjöö, 1982

THE COW GODDESS AND NEW FOODS

In the Neolithic religions of both Egypt and Mesopotamia, as G. Rachel Levy noted, the horned cow appears, with a significance going back to the Old Stone Age. "For the cow-heads of the Sumerian Copper Age, like the sacred calf of Egypt, had a triangle between the horns inlaid in mother of pearl." That Paleolithic female triangle later "stood as an upright cone or little mountain between the horns of Syrian altars."[1] In both Egypt and Mesopotamia also, the symbolic attribute of the Goddess of Birth was the bicornate uterus of a heifer; i.e., the cow-head horns were echoed in the "horned" cow womb.[2]

Even more wide-ranging, throughout Asia and Africa, the Moon Goddess wore the cow's horns—the same horns that appear in later Europe on the helmets of Teutonic heroines. She was the cosmic cow, who produced galactic milk, human milk, and the new foods, and who ruled over the sacred herds. "She who gives you blessings from Heaven above and from the Abyss below, blessings of Mother-Life." Her gifts were seen to pour from the sky, from the dark abyss of the unknown, and from humanity. *I have breasts therefore I am,* says the Great Mother. These are her words carved in a stone inscription from dynastic Egypt.

She was the Goddess of the Pasture, and the sacred queen or king was ritually nourished from her milk. She was also the enclosure that protected the calves: "I am the Fold, he the Lamb."[3] She was the gate of the enclosure, as well as the winged and horned gate of the temple. She was the gate of the dolmen-womb—two stone pillars with a transverse stone resting over them, as a kind of ritual doorway. Entrance and threshold rites were always performed to her. The enclosure, the gate, the door, the pillars of the temple—all these were her body and were thought to have magic and healing powers.

Wild goats were probably the first animals to be systematically domesticated, as they were native to the areas where the first Neolithic cultures seem to have originated. Human children have been suckled by she-goats, whose milk is very similar in consistency to human mother's milk. In the myths and folklore of many people are tales of human babes reared by animal mothers. A Spanish legend says that the Milky Way of the stars is really milk dripping from the udder of a fabulous goat. The galaxy is indeed her milky circle. Women domesticated many animals, and surely women—who can produce milk from our own breasts—were the first to think of using milk from goats and cows as human foods. These new foods meant an increase in nourishment, and so a great advance in human practical and cultural development.

Remember the clay reliefs of women's breasts surmounted by cow's horns on the temple-walls of Çatal Hüyük? Those matriarchal people were vegetarians living on "milk and honey," suggesting that their cows were venerated for their milk, but not slaughtered for their meat. In matriarchal Crete, every cow was known by her personal name! But it seems that bull-calves, who were unproductive, were ritually killed and eaten. This could be the origin of the religious sacrifice of the sacred bull—son of the Cow Mother—his annual death and resurrection being a widespread celebration throughout the Mediterranean and Northern Africa. Surely the veneration of cattle among East African peoples to this day is a remnant of the widespread Neolithic Mother Cow and bull worship. Though cattle herds have now become a symbol of specifically male wealth, especially in East Africa and Asia, still even today on farms in many countries it is women's work to milk and tend the cows, and money from milk sales belongs to the women.

In matrifocal cultures the human communities lived in harmony with nature's ecosystems. With the introduction of settled farming came a serious danger of upsetting the balance that nomadic food gatherers and hunters had maintained with the environment. The women farmers and gardeners of the Neolithic had to learn to cooperate with the earth through crop rotation; they learned to fertilize fields with human and animal excrement (where human excrement has been widely used to fertilize soil, as until recently in China, people build up resistance to its bacteria). In the Neolithic, at the origin of agriculture, everything went back to nature in an eternal cycle—in a natural ecosystem one dead organism becomes energy for another life—and the cultivated fields and farmlands developed their own ecocycles. In Indonesia, for example, up to forty different kinds of plants will grow in the same fields: vegetable bushes, root vegetables, beans, herbs, fruit trees, and so forth. People develop these wise systems for a simple reason: They are living directly with the earth's capacity, for survival, not for profit.

With patriarchy, however, with male-dominated farming and animal husbandry, the plants, animals, and soils began to be forced to produce beyond their natural capacities. In the beginning of patriarchy, profit was in the form of ego and power: ownership of large herds, domination of agricultural space and labor. Even before money was introduced, this kind of personal-profit system took precedence over the natural balance of the ecosystem. Healthy cycles were ignored and destroyed. With the growth of cities and large, landless urban populations, more people had to be fed, with less respect paid to the land. Finally, with advanced technology, farming became a business-industry, and specialized monoculture methods were introduced. Growing just one kind of plant, like wheat, on vast areas is more immediately profitable, saving machinery and human labor in the short run. But in the long run, with the same crop year after year in the same fields, the soil is exhausted. Insects also multiply in monocultures, and chemical pesticides become a global business, introduced to kill pests violently—but they also kill off the birds, who are the natural insect-eaters, and the bees. (And, over longer spans, they kill the workers.) Without bees the fruit trees and other plants are not pollinated . . . and so it goes.

Nature works in coordinated cycles, and when a harmonious cycle is destroyed, a cycle of destruction will take its place. Because patriarchal men have refused to cooperate with nature, following religions and secular ideologies based on defiance and contempt for the earth, they have now almost destroyed our chances of survival on earth. It took 1,500 million years for the first living organisms to change the atmosphere so that animal life could begin to be possible. But patriarchy has destroyed so much in relatively no time at all: roughly in two thousand years. At increasing speeds today, forests are cut down, water is poisoned, the air polluted, the soil ruined. The point is that such devastation could happen only by way of male-dominated religions and cultural ideologies based on hostility toward the earth's cyclic processes. For at least 500,000 years human beings survived as pagans, not because they were savage and stupid, as the missionaries of all patriarchal religions would have us believe, but because "pagan" means "of the land"—it is a spiritual orientation that linked people, body, mind, and soul, with the intelligence of the earth. In contrast, patriarchy assumes that the earth is stupid, and proceeds to "replace" her ways with manmade ways. With what result?

The European Black Death, in the fourteenth century, is now thought to have been caused or exacerbated by wanton tree-cutting all over England. The rats and mice who normally lived in the forests could no longer survive there with so many trees decimated. They invaded the cities, infecting urban house-rats with plague bacteria. Fleas became carriers, and spread bubonic and pneumonic plague bacteria to human beings—and nearly one-third of Europe's human population was destroyed.

Pagan Europeans, Teutons, and Celts worshiped trees. Large numbers of trees were designated sacred, and there were penalties ranging from mild to severe for anyone cutting down a sacred tree. Anyone found cutting an oak, for instance, had his navel removed; his intestines were then pulled out and wrapped around the tree, his body thus roped to the tree with his own guts until he died. Was this savage? Or was it a way of guaranteeing that no mortal could destroy the life and heritage of a whole people, a whole living world, for his own brief personal profit? If any of our pagan ancestors were to view the current decimation of entire forests, *with our permission,* to turn them into cardboard boxes and toothpicks—certainly they would think of us as something worse than "savage."[4]

In A.D. 1000, African men accumulating larger and larger herds of cattle as symbols of personal wealth and status began to graze tame cattle on the savannah—where normally only wild animals had ranged, in balance with the region's fragile capacity. The cattle were male property—the more cattle, the more status; women also were bought with cattle. But because these cattle were used only for their milk and blood, and not slaughtered for meat, they multiplied rapidly, eating all the grass. And the savannah was turned into a desert.

It takes 20 million tons of grain-protein to feed cattle, which in turn give back only 2 million tons of protein in the form of meat. So all the land used to feed cattle is used inefficiently. This is a major cause of world famine today: Land that should be producing grains to feed many people are instead being used to feed cattle that will become food for a relative few. And the way 80 percent of American cattle are raised, by the cattle industry, their excrement does not even return to fertilize the fields.

Under patriarchal animal breeding, the animal mothers—cows, sows, hens—are reduced to mechanical units of mass-production, in grotesque denial of their motherhood and the laws of healthy growth:

> Few people realize that cows have to be subjected to yearly pregnancies so that milk, cheese and cream that form a substantial part of the diet of the lacto-vegetarians and meat-eaters (the majority of the population in the Western World) may be produced. Hardly any cows in the dairy herd are allowed to suckle their calves for more than three days, if at all. The calves are then reared by hand. Cattle are highly intelligent and attachment between the calf and mother is particularly strong. The calves, the inevitable by-product of these continuous pregnancies, if male, go to the slaughter almost immediately to be made into veal. The Rennet used to make most commercial cheeses has to be taken from the stomach of a newly-born calf and 80% of the beef-industry is a by-product of the dairy-industry. The modern dairy cow leads a life of hell in continuous childbirth (made painful by the cow's unnatural life-style and forced passivity), separation from her calf, pregnancies and being milked all through the years.[5]

Poultry also is force-fed and force-bred, and all meats artificially fattened with steroids. The mass antibiotics injected into commercial animal feed also remain in the meat, leading to wide-scale disruption of the helpful bacterial growth in the human intestine. Not to mention all the other chemicals—flavorings, preservatives, and color dyes—pumped in to make something long-dead seem freshly killed. If we are what we eat, then what are we when we eat foods produced in these ways?

MOTHER AND DAUGHTER, AND REBIRTH

In later Neolithic times, she—the Heavenly Cow—begot a son/lover who was seen as the sacrificial bull. The bull as the moon's son/lover was ritually killed in Crete by priestesses even in the Bronze Age. He was the bull called Minotaur ("Bull of Minos") in the Cretan Labyrinth. Remaining frescoes show the ritual sport of bull-leaping, with young Cretan women and men somersaulting naked over the horns. The *corridas* of modern Spain, France, and Mexico are Western remnants of this Neolithic matriarchal bull ceremony in Crete.

In Dahomey, West Africa, black Amazon priestesses practiced bull sacrifice with ritual dances and sacred swords. Dahomey had Amazon warrior-troops well into the nineteenth century, and a version of their ritual is still performed by Dahomean women. They dance in serpentine coils around a sacred tree, where the bull is tethered. As the priestess kills the bull with her sword, the women's chorus chants: "Thou the great, who presents thy saber to cut a throat . . . My hand itches . . . What our ancestors have done . . . We the strong . . . We are alive . . . We knock at the door of your house . . . We are the only ones left."[1] These women are priestesses of the voudun, and much of this ritual survives also in the voodoo cults of Haiti.

But long before the bull-son was born, she gave birth to the first daughter. The Corn Mother of North American Natives sacrifices herself—her limbs severed and her blood given to the earth—to bring about the cultivation and many uses of corn by humanity, her children. Iatik was a Native American Corn Mother who called the maize "the very milk of my breasts." Among the Central American Mayans, the Mother and her daughter were two aspects of the One Goddess, and women were annually sacrificed to her to ensure the corn harvest. It is possible that before the ritual sacrifice of the vegetation deity, the son/lover of the Goddess, the Mother sacrificed her daughter, who was also herself, for the sake of the renewal of all vegetation. Perhaps there were sacrificial queens who died for the tribe's benefit before there were sacrificial kings.

Demeter-Ceres, the Great Grain Mother of Greek and Roman legend,

Doubleheaded ceremonial ax of the Yoruban Shango cult, Nigeria, West Africa

was reaped as the grain with her own moon-shaped sickle. Reaping meant death, later castration. The Goddess was the white-raiser, the red-reaper, and the dark-winnower of the cereal grain. The Eleusinian Mysteries celebrated in Attica and Sicily were holy grain mysteries of Demeter and her daughter Persephone. The rites were originally enacted by women only, in underground chambers, and were kept profoundly secret.

Demeter's festivals in Greece coincided with all the real seasonal rituals of grain cultivation: with the ploughing, the sowing, the threshing and reaping, and the storage of the harvest. One of the most important festivals was the Thesmophoria, in late October, which included ceremonies to ensure the fruitfulness of the seed and the fertility of women. Only women took part in the Thesmophoria; they sat on the ground in sacred circles and fasted. The rites concerned the hidden powers of the earth, life after death, and rebirth.

Persephone, Demeter's daughter (or other aspect) is the grain harvest who dies once a year and goes to the underworld. There, as the awesome, dreaded, and terrible Death Goddess, she rules over the dead for six months of every year. At the end of this time, in the spring, she is resurrected by her Mother and becomes Kore, the maiden, once again. Kore was the deity of youth and gaiety, and leader of the dancing nymphs. In these three female aspects—the young Maiden, the benevolent Mother, and the Death Goddess—we can see the Triple Goddess of the Moon. In later myth it was said that Persephone was carried off and raped by the male god of the underworld, kept as his queen for six months in the land of the dead against her own wish and will. In this patriarchal version of the legend, the Goddess and her vegetation processes are seen as passive functions, subject to male will and manipulation. In the original legends, the whole process is *active*: the Goddess is intentional, she sacrifices herself.

It is Demeter's annual grief at the loss of her daughter that causes the death of the crops. Demeter goes searching for Persephone, mourning, while all lands and animals go barren, nothing can grow, and "terrible despair falls upon the earth." When she at last finds Persephone and restores her to life, there is a renewal, a spring, reawakening sexual desire in humans and animals. All nature is reborn in celebration. Demeter gave the gifts and techniques of agriculture to humans, with the sacred Eleusinian Mysteries, in thanks for the mortal help she received in her search for her daughter. In return, farmers always offered their harvest first-fruits to Demeter. The same ceremony was enacted by the Neolithic people of Britain at Silbury Hill, in worship of Danu.

But Persephone, as her own death-aspect, must return to rule as Queen of the Underworld, during the dark time every winter when vegetation dies. As Kore, the maiden, she returns each spring, the fruits of the fields. And so there is an eternal cycle of birth-loss-mourning-searching-rebirth.

Feminists have read the Demeter-Persephone myth as a paradigm of contemporary woman, struggling to escape the death clutch of patriarchy in a search for her original, fruitful self. As the grieving, determined mother she descends to the Underworld—into social rebellion, role-reversals, personal madness, the dark journeys of introspection and disintegration that precede creative, visionary power—to rediscover her own soul, retrieve the joyous daughter of self-determining life. Once empowered by this reintegration of mythic and real female energies, women could then rendezvous with male energy—as lovers, procreators, friends—without undergoing the suicidal capitulations so long required of us by patriarchal sexual tradition. In the view of writers like Jill Johnston, it is the modern Lesbian especially who experiences within herself the conflict and union of ravaged Persephone and brave, sorrowing Demeter: social outcast and social conscience.[2]

Ceres, the Roman Demeter, was the Goddess of Grain, and of the Earth's creative powers. She was worshiped by the common people, who always worship the more ancient and original earth powers, while aristocrats and ruling classes turn to new-fangled gods designed to justify their illegitimate power. As the provider of bread and guardian of sacred laws, Ceres was the protectress of the common people in their early struggles for liberation under the Roman Empire. All laws were recorded in her temple, inscribed in bronze. Cities were founded amid her rites, the walls rising symbolically from the womb of the earth. During festivals of Ceres in patriarchal Rome, neither father nor son could be named out loud, lest the mystery of the Mother be desecrated by the memory of masculinity, marriage, or father-right—all aligned with the hated innovations of the new military regime.

In the Eleusinian, Orphic, and other mysteries of the Mother, the small dung mushroom was eaten by worshipers (it is still used by Portuguese witches). It has an effect similar to mescaline, giving the participant an experience of universal illumination. Demeter, in one myth, attempts to make a child immortal by anointing it with ambrosia and hiding it in a fire, to burn away its mortality. Many such stories were originally related to ritual use of natural hallucinogens, combined with Tantra yoga techniques.

When the Goddess begets a son, and he becomes the moon hero and the newborn spirit of the vegetation (the green child), he is then the origin of all the dying and resurrecting male gods. And she, like Inanna of Sumer, or Ishtar of Babylon, journeys to the underworld to save him. As Inanna-Ishtar passes through the seven doors guarding the land of the dead, her amulets, jewels, combs, and belt are stripped from her, and her garment-veils, one at each door. This ritual stripping of the Goddess Inanna-Ishtar is the origin of Salome's legendary dance of the seven veils. She arrives in the ultimate place of death naked and weakened, and is hung up on a nail, corpse-like, by the Sumerian Death Goddess, Ereshkigal. In these Mesopotamian original versions of the legend, the significant ritual action is all performed by the different female aspects of the Goddess herself. Inanna-Ishtar must herself undergo a terrible kind of spiritual-psychic death in order to restore the world. (How do gods die? Only ritually, by their own hand.) In megalithic graves from Asia to Scandinavia, Inanna-Ishtar was always imaged as the two cosmic eyes, grim and staring, and below them a torc, or necklace of power.

She herself kills her son/lover Dumuzi-Tammuz, in her form of wild strength, the she-bear or she-boar. Then, as Inanna-Ishtar, she mourns Dumuzi-Tammuz in the Fast of Lamentation or Ramadan. Rites of Dumuzi-Tammuz-Attis-Adonis-Osiris-Dionysus were always attended by wailing, mourning women, smeared with ashes and head-shorn. Inanna-Ishtar ultimately finds and restores her son/lover to rebirth and immortality.

In Egyptian mythology it is Isis, the original Great Mother, who goes over the Earth seeking her sacrificed brother/lover Osiris. (Sister-brother marriage among Egyptian royalty was common, and desired, because both shared the Mother's blood.) Isis finds and pieces together the severed parts of Osiris's body, renewing the world. Osiris was her moon-fruit, the vegetation that was yearly destroyed and then regenerated by her. In still later legend, Osiris was murdered by his own dark aspect, a twin brother Set. In some myths the Moon Hero fights his own way out of the underworld. And still later, showing the complete reversal of meaning under patriarchy, the ritual of the Moon God becomes that of the Sun God, who saves the male-dominated world by slaying the Great Goddess herself in the form of a dragon/whale/serpent monster.

Robert Graves in *The White Goddess* writes about the Goddess in her

Mexican Moon Goddess Tlazolteotl giving birth to herself, as "the old moon gives birth to the new"

orgiastic aspect—how, at midsummer, she demands human, male sacrifice. (This is the aspect of the Goddess that has most fascinated male poets.) She is the Queen of the Mountains, of Summer, of the Wind, and of the Wild Oxen. And the hero Hercules is her son. Hercules means "The glory of the Death Goddess." (Hera-kles. *Hera/E-ra*—the female aspect of the sky and air, encompassing her fertility—was ruler over the pasturelands. Her hair was curled like snakes, her eyebrows were shaped like horns—she was called the "cow-eyed," the "noble one," "giver of all." Hera was pursued through three hundred years by Zeus, the Indo-European Thunder God, and finally agreed to become his "wife" during the Grecian Bronze Age. Then, at Zeus's bidding, Hercules slayed the serpent Ladon, who was the guardian of Hera's sacred fruit tree. This signals the triumph of patriarchy over the Goddess in Greek myth, as does the similar story in Hebrew Genesis.)

In the midsummer sacrifice, Hercules was made drunk with mead, and led into the middle of a circle of twelve stones arranged around an oak. The oak has been lopped into a T-shape (her tree of crucifixion), and an altar stands before it. Hercules is bound to the oak with willow-thongs (willow is the moon-tree), and is then beaten, flayed, castrated, and finally impaled, his flesh hacked into joints on the altar. His blood is caught in a stone basin, to be sprinkled on the fields and the whole tribe, to make all fruitful. According to Graves, Hercules was the male leader of the midsummer orgiastic rites, together with his twelve archer companions. These twelve men danced in a wild figure-eight around the ritual fires. Hercules led the people in war and hunting, but, as his name shows, he was subservient to the Goddess. As Queen of the Woods, she had sacred union with him, the tribal queen choosing a male to participate in these sexual-rites with her. The priestess of this Goddess of the Woods was the tribal lawgiver. Later the male-sacrifice ritual was abandoned, and the agricultural king reigned alone for a sacred number of years, a bull being sacrificed in his place. Or, in some versions, for each year of his reign he offered a child victim in his place.

What all these myths are about is the core of all religion: birth-death-rebirth. *The moon is the Goddess who dies and rises again.* The fruit that produces itself out of itself, with the power of life over death. The moon dies, and then conquers darkness to rise again as the new moon, small at first but with energy within to recreate herself. The serpent sheds its skin and is reborn. The grain harvest—the daughter, the son as vegetation deity—dies, and is reborn in the spring. These are all the original, ancient, and matriarchal ideas of cyclic birth-death-and-resurrection—ideas many millennia older than the doctrines of Christianity, which simply coopted them, because of their universal resonance and power, and attributed them to a male God.

But, the first and ultimate world-saver is the female. The original resurrecting god is the moon. As the Moon Mother says, from the beginning of human time: "Tell them as I dying live, so they dying will live again."[3]

THE MOON TREE

A magic tree grew in Northwest India, from which a wine with a narcotic effect was made. The yellow soma plant was plucked by moonlight and bathed in water and milk, becoming thereby identified with the yellow, swelling, and water-cleansed moon. One ate soma with the ritual words "swell and increase," becoming oneself the self of nourishment, free from all the warring opposites. Inspiration and ecstasy led to the final initiation through the moon into a higher consciousness. And this was to become like the Goddess, to transcend death and be immortal, with the power to envision and create what had not been manifest before. "Those who verily depart from this world to the moon, in truth they go. . . . This verily is the door of the heavenly world."[1]

In the Hebrew-Christian Garden of Eden, the human race is punished for desiring transcendent knowledge, sexual awareness, and immortality—for wanting to be "like gods." In the much more ancient, original, and beautiful Garden of the Goddess, human beings are asked to participate in her immortality, to know and enjoy the ecstasy of divine oneness. That's what all the symbols are for, that's why she gave us the natural hallucinogens, for wise use.[2]

The Great Mother, being the truly original Creatrix, is not threatened by human transcendence, ecstatic illumination, and full sexual consciousness. What genuine Godhead could be threatened by such things? The new patriarchal deities of the Bronze Age, like Yahweh, as secular-political usurpers of sacred power, *need* human beings to be under strict psychic control. As gods, they represented new secular power elites who wanted to horde the agriculturally created abundance of earth for themselves, for their ruling royal and priestly and military classes. So they erected gods as police, to uphold spiritual taboos rationalizing the rule of the rich few over the enslaved many, taboos designed to keep "mortals" from the Sacred Garden—to keep all humans from sharing in the earth abundance that once belonged to all, but now represented what must be called class wealth. This ruling elite created jealous gods who promised punishment to any mortals who tried, spiritually or physically, to share in the old epiphanies.

These ruling-class patriarchal religions no longer invite participation, as did the Mother Goddess religions. Instead, they demand obedience—a fearful obedience which keeps human beings out of touch with our natural transcendent centers and magical techniques. An unthinking and alienated obedience which keeps us dependent on their hierarchic-logical punishment-and-reward systems for our lives. The only way any tyranny can maintain control over the human psyche is to set up a false god, a police god, which in the guise of "religious morality" interposes punitive and manipulative dualistic systems between our daily beings—and the source of being.

The cup of soma is also the mind (mens:mind:moon). It is mental perception and knowledge conveying the psychic-cosmic inspiration of the moon. "When the understanding, of its own motion, forms ideas within itself, it then comes to be called *Mind*."[3] Through the loss of ego-personal, self-conscious "control," one reaches the still center that is true Self. Spiraling the body-psyche through sexual rite, ecstatic dance, and the drinking of soma, one reaches the still center of all.

Soma is distilled from the primordial waters, and is the dark fruit of the moon tree. Soma is the mind-fruit of the spine tree. Coming from the dark moon—from Cybele, Hecate, *kundalini,* Kali, Coatlicue—soma gives visions, but also madness. (Lunacy, as it came to be called by the culture of solacy.) Moon is the magical powers, the mind, *manas,* inspiration, and ecstatic trance. Being a moon force it is double-edged, like the double-ax labrys; it can spin in either direction, like the moon-wheel. Its spiraling gives knowledge and energy for both creation and destruction. The moon tree is the place of generation, the place of the dead, the place of regeneration, the spine. Spirit is the fruit (daughter/son) of the maternal tree. *Kundalini*—the vital serpent, the world mother—is an electromagnetic force. The fiery breath of the dragon is an actual power which when roused into action can as easily destroy as it can create. What is true of any natural power—lightning, fire, water, wind—is also true of spiritual power: Great energy is also great danger. Within the Goddess, everything is real. Spirit and matter are equally potent forces, and their intertwining action is constantly magic, constantly real.

By separating spirit and matter, patriarchal ideology has reduced physical existence to a mere observable mechanism, so-called "practical reality," while spiritual existence is discarded or abstracted into "the imagination" or "the ideal." Or, as in the Apollonian solar-cults—and in theological tendencies of Buddhism, Judaism, Islam, and Christianity—spirit becomes "sheer being" or "pure existence in eternity" or "absolute good" or some other intellectual abstraction wholly unrooted in cosmic process. Wholly extracted from life, like some sublime tooth.

Spirit, in matriarchal religion, does not negate its bond with the Mother. It is generated out of the living process in time and space: She creates, dissolves, and transforms herself as she goes. Spirit and matter spiraling together are both herself and equally real. And this is the spiritual reality of evolution, in which matter creates itself into consciousness, as spirit-consciousness has created itself into matter.

Women were everywhere the original mantics—the shamans, the ecstatic oracular prophets, the visionary poets. Mantism is the natural art of prophesying, divining, receiving, and channeling psychic-biological energy from the earth and from the moon. This is woman's original and organic province. The moon-fruit is the highest transformation form of the Earth-seed, the place of physical rebirth, sublimated seed, integrated power. All witch technique, all pagan orientation, was a biomystical discipline designed to help the individual and the group channel and direct the real power of the universe, radiating into and from all of us. Women were the first bearers of this technique, since it emanates from our own bodies and psychic processes. Women are tied directly to the mantic moon by both a mental and a blood cord.

Even after the Apollo cult took over the shrine at Delphi and declared that "god" was henceforth the sun, the resident mantic remained a woman, the Sibyl. A woman inspired only at night, by moonlight. Shamanism, inspiration, mysteries of drunkenness, vision, madness, ecstasy leading to expansions of consciousness—these are the transformative processes of the Goddess. They can all be quite dangerous. The patriarchy has forbidden, outlawed, repressed these activities for millennia and for political reasons: While claiming to protect us from the dark moon, the destructive edge of the crescent-ax, it also prevents us from making contact with the creative powers of the Moon Mother.

The dark side is real. Spiritual and psychic death from the drinking of soma. Poisoning; loss of ego; negative orgiastic rites; extinction and madness; experiences of dissolution, rejection, utter deprivation in the death mysteries of the Terrible Mother—all are real. As Inanna-Ishtar was hung up on the nail in hell by Ereshkigal, the withered Death Goddess. And this is the importance of the ancient symbols, myths, and techniques, of all rites of initiation and occult doctrines: They can help one get through the danger center of the spiral and emerge transformed on the other side. They help turn personal psychosis into sacred transformation. It is precisely at the extreme negative point that the dark moon turns, and shifts into its opposite pole of ecstasy and illumination. It is at this point that the moon journey can lead either to madness or a luminous experience of immortality. At the fusion of the double spiral there is a vortex, and winds of dissolution; beyond is a still center and the bliss of union. Transcending the opposites, one can experience the shift from one pole to the other and contain, within consciousness, an active understanding of this process. And *this* constitutes the core teaching of the ancient mysteries.

As has been said wisely many times, "Without the Devil, there is no Christianity." With the good God forever at one pole, and the bad Devil forever at the other, the human mind under Christianity is locked forever into a battlefield of dualistic antagonisms, with no hope of transcendence; i.e., no hope of maturity. The Christian mind remains undeveloped, the eternal spectator at the cosmic football game between heaven and hell, good and evil, defined as two irreconcilable teams: One must win, one must lose, and the spectator never knows wholeness. The forbidden fruit of the moon tree gives knowledge of the paradox good *and* evil, life *and* death, a mature knowledge of the reconciliation of opposites in the experience of cosmic oneness. If human beings eat this fruit, patriarchal religion is out of business. A world free of psychic alienation would need no Christian salvation, or "salvation" of any kind. When dualistic opposites are allowed to fuse in the mind, the psyche saves itself.

The moon tree, like all symbols of the Great Goddess, is double-sided: e.g., the double-ax, the double spiral; the moon-wheel spinning right and left; the lunar horns of cows, waxing and waning; the gate or doorway, womb and tomb, where one enters and leaves, is born into and dies out of. And so the moon tree is double-edged, with roots in both earth and sky—branches in both sky and earth. But this symbolism is not dualistic. The Moon Mother is a Triple Goddess, and her symbols have a triple aspect; for in each the two polar sides are *joined* in the center, joined by her body: the trunk of the tree, the handle of the double-ax, the center hub of the wheel and still center of the spiral, the cow who bears the crescent horns, the space and the lintel stone itself joining the directions of the doorway.

It is the Mother Goddess who stands herself in the center and joins the opposites in her being. As the third and magic, evolutionary term of the triplicity, she mothers the opposites: good *and* evil both born from her, there can be no psychic alienation. There can only be understanding, and a will to evolve.

All through the Neolithic, the matriarchal consciousness in both women and men was still open to the processes of the self (called, by Jungians, the "*un*conscious"), and therefore to psychic wholeness. Soma was brewed in the cauldron of inspiration and regeneration, the sacrificial cauldron of the Great Mother. The cauldron, like the other symbols, is the Mother's body. It received the ritually spilled blood of death, but also produced the drink of immortality. In the form of the crucible, it was inherited by the alchemists; in it base metals were changed into gold, matter into spirit, mortal into immortal. This "mother-pot" appears among early European pagans as the great Celtic cauldron of inspiration—the cauldron of Cerridwen central to later Druidic belief and practice. In early Christianity, mingled with medieval pagan iconography, it is the chalice of the Last Supper, the Holy Grail containing the Blood of Christ, i.e., the blood of the Mother's sacrificed son. It also appears as the suit of Cups in the Tarot cards.

Isis and her priestesses carried a musical instrument called the Sistrum. Legendarily, it contained the four elements of the universe: earth, air, fire, and water. Each is the opposite of the other, and they are all resolved into harmony within the body of the sistrum. Nature is released by the movements of Isis, vibrated into music and vision. The roses of Isis are pure passion, love redeemed from lust by the energy of understanding. "I am she of ten thousand names—I am all that has been and is and shall be, and no mortal has ever revealed my robe."[4] The robe of Isis is the multicolored veil of nature which hides the mystery-truth from uninitiated human eyes. The sons/lovers of the Goddess—Dionysus/Osiris willingly, but even Buddha/Christ against their will—are the same. The Goddess of Crete wears three opium-poppy seeds on her head. And Buddhists twirl the wheel (*chakra*) to achieve inspiration and luminous integration. All this churning of the cosmic ocean finally produces the magic drink of soma, the moon-fruit—the mind.

THE DARK OF THE MOON AND MOON BLOOD

Much of what comes to us from Great Mother mythology is her aspect as Terrible Mother. Historians and psychoanalytical researchers stress this aspect, as though it illustrates the "darkness and savagery" of all those millennia unenlightened by patriarchal order. There was blood sacrifice; but nothing approaching the scale of patriarchal mass murder. Nor was the sacrifice wanton. It was highly ritualized, and people believed there were deep reasons for it. Our human ancestors could not have survived the millennia as "brutal savages," nor could they have created all the seeds of all the cultures that followed unless they were highly complex beings. To know them, to know our own history as earthlings, we need to understand their complexity and their reasoning.

The ancient people believed that the fetus was entirely formed and fed from the mother's blood—and this was why women didn't menstruate during their pregnancies. (This perception was half-correct, though the entire menstrual cycle is only recently understood.) Menstrual blood was valued for its power. African and Australian aboriginal people painted themselves red and poured blood on sacred stones, celebrating the menstrual power of the Moon Mother. The great and terrible Goddess Mother of India, Kali, was covered in bloodstained clothes during her monthly "periods," and these garments were prized as strong medicine. Kali's devotees also slashed themselves and covered her statues with their blood; these ceremonies still occur in India.

Expanding on the perceived power of menstrual blood, it was believed that the Mother as earth body needed strengthening and renewal through blood sacrifice; as her blood created creatures, so the blood of creatures was cycled back to her. What was taken from her by humans in the form of harvest had to be returned in human or animal sacrifice. So the Neolithic funeral rites were not only connected with the deaths of human beings, but also acknowledged the death of all earth vegetation. Blood sacrifice and sexual rites were interwoven with mourning the dead, ploughing the fields, harvesting crops—all to aid the rebirth of the seed and the dead body, through a ritual renewing of the Great Mother through the

Aztec Earth & Moon Goddess Tlazolteotl giving birth to both Life & Death, Light & Dark. Page from Codex Borbonicus, folio 13, date unknown

mingling of blood, sex, and spirit. The moon also was seen as weakened and devoured by the powers of darkness during its waning phase; the dark of the moon came to symbolize the awesome underworld. Ancient Hindus believed the dark moon descended to Earth, to wait in the sacrificial place. These two to three nights of darkness are full of terrible power, as darkness and as the bleeding time of women. During this time humans once fasted and prayed, and performed rites to keep themselves concentrated and intact during the passage of darkness.

In later Neolithic times some cultures saw the moon as male, as the son/lover of the Goddess. As the vegetation deity died once each year, to fertilize the crops with his blood, so the male Moon God died each month. He disappeared for three days, locked up in her underworld. This myth was continued in the ritual of Christ being closed up three days in the tomb. In Polynesian belief the dying moon journeyed to a faraway paradise where it bathed in waters of immortality, and restored to vigor, returned in three days.

Mother Goddesses of Mexico and Central America contained very clearly this double aspect of continuing life as the fruit of death, and vice versa. Among the Mayans, the primordial gods were bisexual: "Lord and Mistress of the Two." Earth and night sky were the original unity. But the Earth Goddess falls from her embrace with the dark heaven and is torn asunder; from her two halves come heaven and earth. By this painful rending she becomes the source of all life, all food—but she also thereby becomes the Terrible Mother. "Sometimes the Earth Goddess cried out in the night, demanding human hearts, and then She would not be comforted until She had been given human blood to drink."[1]

Strong evidence suggests that mass human sacrifice among Mayans and Aztecs, in particular the offering of hearts to the sun, was a late development, initiated by the warrior and priest classes under a militant patriarchy. Blood sacrifice occurred worldwide; we never know for sure how much of it occurred within Goddess worship, and how much was attributed to the Great Mother religion by later male-oriented priesthoods. Mass human sacrifice is definitely linked everywhere with ruling priest and warrior classes in elite male service to a Sun God. Individual sacrifice, often voluntary, undoubtedly occurred under the Great Mother, under the moon; and it occurred only among settled agricultural people. Why? Because settled agricultural people, during the Neolithic, were taking control of the growing processes of earth. They were deliberately planting, deliberately reaping. And they felt this intentional use of the Mother's body might be a violation; it needed propitiation, which is a form of acknowledgment of use. Their need was for rebalancing, for reharmonizing, above all.

The Mayan Earth Goddess gives all life, all food—and then cries out in the night for human blood, her food. Here, at the place of origin, is a profound fusion of positive and negative symbols, and this is always related to food. Not to sex, but to food, which is the first taboo. Sex does not require an act of death, an act of murder, for its fulfillment; but eating does. From the beginning there was a primary human perception that our living is sustained by death; by the death of other life forms, animal or vegetable. For all the world was seen to be alive, and humans lived by eating the world. The Mother's creatures lived by eating each other, within her body. There is a kind of ontological pain in this perception that can be resolved only through ritual, which was always a fusion of sex and eating, of fertility and death, of life through death and vice versa. In fertility ritual, as in funeral rites, sex and nourishment are related through ritual cannibalism: The constant recycling of life through death and back again, dramatically signifies a human need to harmonize these poles. Especially the woman's need to harmonize our production of children with their consumption of food. This harmonization was always a major concern of women's religion. It is only after the introduction of the patriarchal sun cult that the polar symbols of eating and sex become irreconcilable. Under patriarchal control, child production and food consumption have never been in harmony for long; and so mass human sacrifice appears—via religious ritual or warfare—as the Sun God's attempt to harmonize them.

In Mayan mythology, after the symbolic one tree of the original home, the one body of the original bisexual being, has been shattered into separate spheres, the primal Mother is dismembered to become the source of all life. Later, she was further personified as the Corn Daughter, and women were sacrificed as her, after several days of ritual in which she blessed the crops. The woman's body slain by the obsidian knife, the ritual knife itself, and the priestly hand wielding it, were all seen as her. The husking of corn was analogous to the tearing out of the ritual victim's heart. Mating, renewal of vegetation through the sex act, and ritual killing of the Corn Daughter were identical, death and fecundation symbolically one. Fecundation relates to sex, and death relates to eating; the human heart becomes food for the Earth Mother, for the Sun God. In the cult of the Mayan Mother under the later priesthood, prisoners were shot with arrows symbolizing sexual union with earth. (Just as in the Paleolithic caves the hunter/shaman's penis-spear united with the vulva-wound, to guarantee the rebirth of slain animals.) Prisoners were shot in the genital region, or they were killed in the fetal position, tied up with a "food-stuff" rope—this rope was an umbilical cord attaching the prisoner-victim to the center of a stone which represented the center and entrance place, the womb, of the earth.

Both Mayans and Aztecs had a "Goddess who died in childbirth." She was the young Moon Goddess, daughter of the primal Mother of the Beginning. The souls of women who died in childbirth went to live in the West (where the moon and sun both "die"), along with the souls of heroic warriors who died in battle. Identity was seen between birth and the cutting out of hearts, Mayan art showing simultaneous scenes of human sacrifice and birth. All such images are attempts to symbolize the continuous feeding of a process, the continuous process of feeding. Life feeding death which feeds life. The Mother Goddess dies to become food for life; her children—her daughter as Corn Maiden or as moon especially—die to feed her. Another way to show this concept is through the Two-Headed Goddess, the Mexican Coatlicue.

> The colossal Aztec statue of Coatlicue fuses in one image the dual functions of the earth which both creates and destroys. In different aspects she represents *Coatlicue,* "Lady of the Skirt of Serpents" or "Goddess of the Serpent Petticoat"; *Cihuacoatl,* "the Serpent Woman"; *Tlazolteotl,* "Goddess of Filth" [and Redemption]; and *Tonantzin,* "Our Mother," who was later sanctified by the Catholic Church as the Virgin of Guadalupe, the dark-faced Madonna, la Virgen Morena, la Virgen Guadalupana, the patroness and protectress of New Spain; and who is still the patroness of all Indian Mexico. In the statue her head is severed from her body, and from the neck flow two streams of blood in the shape of two serpents. She wears a skirt of serpents girdled by another serpent as a belt. On her breast hangs a necklace of human hearts and hands bearing a human skull as a pendant. Her hands and feet are shaped like claws. From the bicephalous mass which takes the place of the head and which represents Omeyscan, the topmost heaven, to the world of the Dead extending below the feet, the statue embraces both life and death. Squat and massive, the monumental 12-ton sculpture embodies pyramidal, cruciform, and human forms. As the

art critic Justino Fernandez writes in his oft-quoted description, it represents not a being but an idea, "the embodiment of the cosmic-dynamic power which bestows life and which thrives on death in the struggle of opposites."[2]

The resemblance between the Aztec Coatlicue and the Hindu Kali (including their names) is profound. They represent the same primal perception: the continuity of life/death. However strange or terrible (i.e., causing terror) such rites and icons might seem, they show the original human mind trying to come to terms with the paradoxical reality of the Primal Mother—she who bleeds with both life and death, she who dies and returns again cyclically, *she who gives us all to each other as food,* as blood kin, as co-creators of our ecstasies and our destructions. As Carlos Fuentes notes in *Terra Nostra, terra* (earth) and "terror" are related.[3] They have the same origin because the source of life and the source of death are the same; and this is both a frightening and an awesome recognition. It is very hard to endure without ritual resolution. Moderns who neither kill nor grow their own food nor bury their own dead would seem to have solved the problem by avoiding it; but in fact the resolution is simply delegated, nowadays, to nightmare, slaughterhouses, torture rooms, death squads, and "snuff" films, in which criminal priests perform obscene sacrifices to the gods of displaced responsibility. No one can truly avoid the paradox of life/death as one continuous god, or process. Such a perception arises from the deepest labyrinth of our psyches, where there is no distinction between "primitive" and "modern." The only real difference is that "primitives" strive to be conscious of the paradox; "moderns" strive to escape it. But the paradox shows us an ontological maze we cannot sanely deny, destroy, or overleap; we have to learn to walk it again, to dance it, as our ancestors did, with grace, strength, and awe-full wisdom.

The Goddess in her death aspect is the earth in which things rot, "the devourer of the dead bodies," the great underground vessel. The Eleusinian Mysteries of the ancient Aegeans, Cretans, and Egyptians contained symbolism of the burial of the dead in great stone jars, the *pithoi,* as grain seed was buried and stored under the earth. Women were the keepers of the seed jars and of the dead. The black night sky also was identified with water, and with the devouring darkness of the underground. Hell, the abode of the dead, was entered through the all-eating mouth-cavern of the earth; Hel/Helle was the Scandinavian/Germanic Goddess of the Living Dead. The womb was the hungry mouth, organ of cannibalistic life and death. The hungry earth-mouth takes the blood-seed of living creatures and, once fertilized, gives birth again, by way of death. The point to be made is that ancient people had no trouble cognizing these dual or polar aspects of the one Goddess, these two faces of the same source. They had no trouble so long as their lives remained bound up, on a daily basis, with the cycling paradox of earthly process, where food is

Double goddess figurine,
Cypress, 2300–2100 B.C.

born from the sleeping ground of the dead, where the tomb of death and the womb of life are analogous, and one. And female.

In Late Neolithic times, the death aspect of the Goddess broke loose, becoming dominant and morbid. Women's industries and settled villages had prospered, had grown into city-state cultures with complex social organization and removal of religious function from daily life, creating specialized labor and hierarchic structures. The creation of surplus wealth gave rise to the profession of marauder; males, no longer employed as hunters, began organizing more and more professionally together—and separately from the women—as grain guardians, then armies, then urban "police," then imperial plunderers. The Great Goddess was still worshiped into the Bronze Age, but increasingly by an urban male priesthood and an urbanized populace once removed from the real earth. Between producer and consumer, ruler and ruled, living and dead, sacred and daily life, there was a growing gap—call it "urban secular life"—historically filled with structures of nervous alienation and psychological, personal fears. This marks the rise of patriarchal consciousness, in which humans experience earth-magic and cyclic process less and less in their daily lives, and are forced to rely more and more on urban-hierarchic priesthoods and specialists to give them secondhand words of faith and moral advice. When religion leaves the land, leaves ecstatic dance and prophetic chant, it becomes increasingly a matter of verbal exhortation, of moralistic rhetoric, where people are told what to feel and believe: because they no longer feel and believe it.

At the same time, male metallurgists were introducing a technology aimed at altering the natural powers and channels of the earth spirit. Metallurgy detached from the Goddess, and was no longer a sacred art; it was being used to mass produce offensive war weaponry, the war machines of large bands of highly organized men who were inventing the profession of conquest and plunder. The profession of imperialistic power, armed with rolling metal. This was the patriarchal shift. The Furies cried: "He made man's way across the place of the ways of the Goddess and blighted age-old distributions of power!"[4]

Male priesthoods made the shift by concentrating more and more on the Negative Goddess. Once her devotees, they expressed increasingly obsessive fears of the sexual and death-dealing powers of the Great Mother. They did not, as women priestesses had always done, identify with the dark side—the Great Mother had always had her dark aspect, for this is the truth of the universe; and her priestesses resolved it through ritual expression of the fury. Under Bronze Age priesthoods this aspect was *projected,* morbidly and exploitatively emphasized and unrelieved. No longer simultaneously experiencing the luminous benevolence, beauty, and rightness of the Mother's natural world, the male priests began to rule by fear alone. Fear of death, fear of female sexuality, fear of natural process.

Thus Kali, the Hindu Great Mother, became "dark, all-devouring time." She was depicted as the bone-wreathed lady of the place of skulls, smeared with ashes, squatting among jackals and bats in the burial grounds. Served in bloody rites, Kali had many names, all negative; all bad times, in the human cycle, are named for her: the Kali-Yuga. Statues show her crouching in a halo of flames, devouring the entrails of her mate Shiva—the guts strung from the corpse to her mouth like an umbilical cord. Kali's temple in India functions as the people's slaughterhouse—the people take the meat, and the blood is left to her. Everyone has seen this Kali, the Black Mother. She dances on Shiva's dead body, wearing a necklace of hacked-off human hands, her tongue rolled grotesquely out to lap up human blood from the ground. "All creation is the sport of my mad Mother Kali," said the Hindu poet Ramprasad.[5] She also has her benevolent aspect, but the functions become increasingly severed: *Paradox is split into dualism, an act characteristic of patriarchal consciousness.* No doubt as men engaged more and more in wanton slaughter of their own kind for plunder and power, the more they needed to project this split in their own psyches onto the Goddess. The benevolent Kali becomes virtually a separate pale goddess, a passive mother, a sex-partner without power. At her best she is the divine Shakti, the creative energy of the male god, coming into manifestation at the moment of sexual union with Shiva. The Bronze Age Kali is split into the Death Goddess, or the Sex Goddess, or the Mother Goddess—but is no longer the one cosmic process containing all aspects and polarities. And it is only as the terrible destroyer, time, that she has any authority or power left.

Hair has always been connected with the idea of cosmic power. Hair is electric, radiating energy, a symbol of vitality and spiritual illumination. Witches believed their magic power was in their hair. During the European witch-hunts, the first thing the church did to captured witches was to shave them from head to foot, thus "driving out the Devil-power" that lived in their body hair. American Indians have fought hair-clipping missionaries for centuries. To mourn a dead person the hair was cut, signifying a life-offering to death. With the increase of urban priesthoods, and the unbalanced obsession with the death aspect of the Great Mother, the more we find symbolic connections occurring between death, the shaving of the head, sacrifice, and castration. The priests of Isis had bald heads. And still today we have tonsured monks, shorn nuns, and the Christian notion that a woman's hair is a seductive—witchy—insult to God, and must be covered in his church. And thus traditional Jewish brides cut off their long, glorious hair, sacrificing original female power to be subordinate to a male in marriage.

Among the Greeks, the Goddess of the Dark Moon was Hecate. She was Queen of Ghosts and of the Crossroads, where many midnight rituals took place. Hecate was the destroyer; newborn children and animals were sacrificed to her. She was the giver of rain, as well as harvest storms. Her major festival was celebrated on August 13th. In one Hecate legend, the Mother in her terrible aspect takes the form of a bear or boar, killing her own son/lover; but as the new moon she restores him to new life. Dark Diana of the Romans, Goddess of the witches, wore a necklace of testicles, echoing the castration nature of Kali. And the Gorgon-Medusa, her magic hair composed of writhing snakes, petrified all who looked at her into rigidity and death—into stone. Thus many of the primal aspects of the Cosmic Mother were turned into aspects of: the enemy.

But, from the beginning, and even far into patriarchal times, the dark of the moon symbolized divination, illumination, and the powers of healing. Soma, the mind-expanding potion, was the dark fruit of the moon tree. It opened the gaping depths of darkness from which magic incantation rises up. Darkness is the time of tactility, and of the voice. So the Dark Goddess, or dark moon, presided over love-magic, metamorphosis, wonder-working, and medicinal healing. Her sexual aspect was not separated from these other powers until the solidification of the patriarchy; only then was she fragmented, and reduced, to simply a "sex goddess," or "the wife."

The Neolithic Near Eastern Goddesses Isis, Astarte, Ashtoreth, Ishtar, Artemis, Diana—all have their dark nature, one-half of the cosmic process. In that aspect they were imaged as half-snake or half-fish. To men who were, and are, in opposition to her ever-changing cyclic nature, she appears dreadful, hostile, arbitrarily destructive, moody, "negative"—the yawning mouth of the womb-tomb, abysmally prolific with children and with death, threatening castration coming and going. During the Neolithic Age, men who saw the Dark Moon Goddess in a dream had to put on women's clothes and give themselves to other men; the dream image was a message that they needed rebalancing. To women, and men, in accord with her nature, she gives magic power and cosmic insight into the life process, forever revolving from light into dark and back again.

From earliest Stone Age times, the process of birth was the prototype for the process of spiritual rebirth, of "higher birth" into the heavens as an immortal, or star. But with increasing male domination of religious ideas, and the priestly projection of hostile fears onto the Great Goddess, this "higher birth" was seen increasingly as a break away from the Mother. The first birth was into mere flesh, but the second was into manhood, a state of nonmaterial immortality uncontaminated by the female process. At this point, the spirit begins to be defined as everything that is not earth, is not nature, is not female; i.e., it becomes an exclusive possession of males, as elitist as it is abstract.

In the early small kin-group structures, the custom of exogamy had led women to take mates from outside the mother-clan, so the childbearing women were always the cohesive group within the community—their mates tended to be visitors, blood-strangers to the matrifocal group. Among the matriarchal Hopi (where the women propose marriage to the men), the husband moves into the woman's home, which she inherits from her mother; but he spends most of his time at his mother's home, where *he* is blood-related.[6] The same customs were found throughout precolonial Africa, and no doubt existed among all our European pagan ancestors.

To gain some cohesion and sense of participation, these "outside" males bonded together in rituals in which they imitated female processes. As Bruno Bettelheim writes in *Symbolic Wounds*, it is probable that all men's initiation rites were originally based on the men's desire to imitate, to participate in, women's menstruation and childbirth, which were overwhelming magic events (magic because of their periodicity as well as their blood-power). Australian aboriginal males cut wounds in their penises, inserting stones to keep the wound permanently open. This rite imitates female bleeding, and the wound is called, in their language, a "vagina." During this rite young men pass through the legs of older men, being "reborn" from the "male womb." *Nowhere* can we find any rites or mysteries in which women have tried to imitate a male process or function; this alone tells us about the source of original *mana*, or power. All blood rituals derive from the female blood of menstruation and childbirth.

This is why, in the Bible, Jehovah's covenant with Abraham was ritually sealed with the lifeblood of Abraham, and this covenant is kept by circumcising the foreskin of every Hebraic male infant. The Hebrews, like everyone else, were originally Goddess-worshipers, and it was her magic blood that symbolically sealed covenants. As the patriarchy solidified its power, however, many of the blood ritual imitations of women's functions were turned into taboos against women's functions—taboos of avoidance and "hygiene." As the biblical Old Testament illustrates, patriarchal society places heavy taboos and penalties of shame on menstruation, and on women during and after childbirth. Such taboos were originally restrictions made by women themselves—menstrual-hut customs—to protect their bodies and guarantee their sacred solitude during the moon functions, their separateness from men and children. But as male power structures and religious reactions against the Goddess rise, seeing the Great Mother more and more as the castrating other, the terrible devourer, these moon-blood taboos are given negative connotations: Women during their menstrual periods and childbirth are defined as "unclean" and dangerous, especially threatening to "social manhood" and its coopted assumptions of "sacred wounds" and "higher powers" gained through the second ritual birth via an elder male body. The female body, which actually does these things, becomes an embarrassing threat to the males' metaphorical assumption of the blood-powers of menstruation and childbirth. No male priest can compete with a woman in these areas!

So, the menstruating woman is often totally excluded from group life, cast out into the bush or forest to fend for herself. She must be ritually cleansed before she can return to the tribe. Women in labor also must be secluded, to protect men from contamination, and must undergo periods of "purification" following childbirth; among biblical Hebrews a longer period following the birth of a daughter (of course) than a son. What was once seen, among original humans, as sacred and magically powerful to the whole kin-group or tribe, becomes under male religion impure, filthy, dangerous, negative, and evil. The source of life (female) is redefined and now hated as the enemy of male life. What was once woman's power is now to be woman's curse, woman's shame. Woman's estrangement from God. In the Bible we can see the original Orwellian Newspeak occurring, in which false male imitations of menstruation and childbirth (the circumcised foreskin, the wounds of Christ) are made sacred and holy, while the real thing done by women is made filthy, sinful, and bestial.

This terrible and unnatural split in the human psyche is still with us, of course; patriarchal religions are based on it. Under patriarchy this split was projected everywhere, into the cosmic-spiritual realms, into human culture and customs, into "scientific" perception of the mental and physical worlds. Under Bronze Age urban priesthoods the Terrible Mother was worshiped more and more with painful rites and punitive exorcisms; she became in fact "the debased flesh" which must be flailed and disciplined into submission, a religious practice that served very well as a rationalization for the mass exploitation of human slave labor by the growing urban states and their ruling elites. If human flesh and blood is "nothing but . . . ," then by all means, use it. With the devaluation of the Great Mother's female bleeding came the debasement and exploitation of human life itself.

Women's menstrual blood always was, always is of the essence of the creative power of the Great Mother. Blood is the physical counterpart of the mystical life force spiraling throughout the cosmos, nourishing the universe, sustaining its breathing in and out, its manifestations and dissolutions. Ancient women withdrew during their menstrual periods to meditate, fast, pray, and communicate with her. Women living together in cooperative groups do begin to coordinate the time of their periods; ancient women bled and meditated together, under the bleeding and meditating moon. Even under the punitive taboos of patriarchy, women withdrew to their menstrual huts with some feeling of voluntary seclusion—a chance to get back in contact with their own nature for a few days each month, apart from the demands of children and men. In *Women's Mysteries, Ancient and Modern,* Esther Harding suggests that one of the prime causes of neurosis, illness, depression, and pain suffered by many women in modern cultures during our menstrual periods—the premenstrual syndrome especially, as it is known today—is that we now have no menstrual ceremony of any kind. Menstruation is just each woman's private affliction, or annoyance; it has no positive value or function. We cannot withdraw into contemporary menstrual huts, to listen to our bodies, minds, and needs, to establish contact with our cyclic and primal cosmic selves, to experience ourselves as sacred animals. And ironically, while being deprived of ritual solitude while we bleed, we are also isolated from the communion of other women who are bleeding. Each woman must go through each life stage, transition, and crisis, in silent aloneness, unsupported by either ritual or the women's group. This combination of meaningless isolation and lack of ritual solitude is the final patriarchal taboo against women—a major cause of mental illness, and a major barrier against self-realization. Thus was women's ancient collective power broken. Women under patriarchy, isolated from each other and from themselves, could no longer threaten male dominance of "life," or question male cooptation and imitation of our original female processes.

But some faint traces of the ancient beliefs and practices remain, even in the modern world, even if in sometimes grotesque form. A continuing belief in the potency of women's menstrual blood is ritualized in Tantric yoga. A man can only reach the ultimate Tantric goal by having intercourse with a woman "power holder" at the time of her menstruation. This is when her "red energy" is most magically potent and intense.[7] And, among American motorcycle gangs like the Hell's Angels, a male cannot become a full member until he performs the blood rite of cunnilingus with "his woman" during her menstrual period. This is how he proves his macho-toughness to the other males. He probably doesn't know that he is worshiping the Great Mother . . . !

"From hidden dirty secret to symbol of the life power of the Goddess, women's blood has come full circle."[8]

Until recently, there have been no books on the psychology of menstruation, the rhythms and cyclicity of our woman-lives. In the 1970s, however, two such books were published: *Female Cycles* by Paula Wiedeger in 1975, and *The Wise Wound, Menstruation and Everywoman,* by Penelope Shuttle and Peter Redgrove, in 1978. Paula Wiedeger is an American feminist health worker and holds an advanced degree in psychology. Penelope Shuttle and Peter Redgrove are British poets influenced by Jungian psychoanalysis. They came to write their book as a result of Penelope Shuttle's own severe premenstrual depressions and her menstrual pains, and her attempts at finding their reasons and cure through in-depth dream analysis.

The two books complement each other; *The Wise Wound* is poetic and religious, while *Female Cycles* is more medical and immediately "practical." Together they chronicle the atrocious violence done to us women in societies ruled over, and defined by, "wombless men" who do not experience the lunar, cyclic rhythms in their bodies.

The Wise Wound shows how the human female's menstrual cycle was the critical evolutionary advance that initiated human society and culture. As we said in the first section, the fact that the human female is freed from the estrus cycle of other primates means that in woman sexuality is distinguishable from, separable from, fertility. In woman alone, among all creatures on earth. This shifting of sexual-hormonal action led to increased alertness of the brain and its electrical activity; i.e., women have sexual energy at our disposal separable from reproductive energy. For woman biology is not destiny in the narrow reproductive sense, even if patriarchy has tried, through the dogmatic suppression of our autonomous sexuality, to reverse this evolution. (Patriarchal religion is, in this sense, a primate religion, trying to pull the human female back from her evolutionary advance over other primates; for in this one aspect alone does human sexuality differ from primate sexuality. And it is for this subliminal reason that all hardcore patriarchal fundamentalists oppose evolutionary theory so vehemently: because the "Godhead" of human evolution, its trigger, its energy source, is, and only can be, female.) The sole function of the clitoris is sexual pleasure, and it is the only organ in the human body devoted to pleasure alone (the penis carrying both reproductive semen and sexual response in every erotic act). This means that woman's sexual capacity is enormously enhanced and multiple. And it is present in us from birth to death, clitoral sensation being determined neither by puberty nor menopause. When freed, woman's autonomous sexual capacity is a great source of psychic, productive, creative, and magical powers. It was at the origins of human culture, and it is necessary to any further human evolutionary advance.

Human life and evolution are explained in many ways. We are indeed producers and toolmakers, as the Marxists and anthropologists say, and creators of symbolic culture. *But we were not human until the appearance of the menstrual cycle.* With it came the possibility of all evolutionary developments that are specifically human: extraction of mental energy from reproduction and survival, social bonding through human emotion, symbolism (symbols are mental children), recognition and valuing of the individual as a being with rights to pleasure and subjective exploration, social organization and sexual affection leading to the development of cultural and economic cooperation for the purpose of enhancing, rather than just maintaining, human experience. Otherwise, why evolve?

Women have got to understand the importance of the switch from primate estrus to human menstrual cycle, because this was the mechanism of female evolution. It is also the target of patriarchy. Female sexuality and female evolution are—have been, for 2 or 3 millennia at least—in a lethal deadlock with patriarchal ideology, religious, economic, and political. This is because patriarchy, as a system, wants to enforce and maintain male primate power-dominance-control over our species. The rise of patriarchy was an evolutionary step backwards, in this sense. The only thing blocking or neutralizing this patriarchal-primate urge toward dominance-control of the human species is the more advanced capacity for human creative communal process via social-sexual bonding evolved by the women of our species. I.e., we are still trying to evolve from the primate to the fully human; and in this long attempt autonomous female sexuality represents an advance, while patriarchal control over female sexual process represents regression.

This is why all patriarchal religions try to define menstrual and childbirth blood—the source of life—as a filth, a shame, and a crime. Because it represents the creative power of the evolutionary female. "She who," as Judy Grahn said . . . she who, with her blood, created the human world.[9]

MOON AND WOMB

The ancient people believed, with their usual biological accuracy, that the Moon Mother created human society. If the moon were to vanish, all mental activity on earth would cease. In their languages, words for wisdom, knowledge, spirit, soul, and time are always cognate with words for the moon. In Dakotan, *wakan* means "spiritual," "wonderful," and "menstrual."

Names for the Goddess usually have their roots in words for "womb" and "vulva." The original magic was always the woman's and was associated with a change of power, or energy field, at the time of the menstrual period. The most ancient moon cults were menstrual cults. Menstrual blood is liquid flesh; both sacred and biological, i.e., magically powerful. Within it dwells the life spirit. So the ancients painted their dead, and their womb-like underground burial chambers, with red ochre—the color of rebirth within the Mother.

The human womb is strongly supplied with conscious sensory nerves; it is a sense organ, complex, thin-walled, and raw like a wound. In second-stage childbirth, it has a powerful one-hundred-pound thrust. At menstruation the inner skin is shed, and this was once seen to be similar to the shedding of the snake's skin and the eternal renewal of the moon out of herself.

Women who were in especially strong resonance with the moon-mind became shamans, oracular priestesses, witches. They were chosen by their group, or were self-chosen, for their special psychic powers and divinations of the blood at their first menstruation. Shamanism, an ecstatic lunar technology, relies on the natural psychic descent into body consciousness that menstruation brings each month to women. Shamanistic states of possession are still practiced among North Pole Innuits, Native Americans, Siberians, the Sames of Lappland . . . and pagan people everywhere trying to revive the techniques. Shamanic possession and all ecstatic trances are hysteric states. "Hysteria" means "womb" (*Hustera:* "womb-consciousness"), and hysteria is a hypersensitive state during which "occult" or "transnatural" phenomena occur, the apparent suspension of physical laws—

as in fire-walking, cuts that do not bleed, stigmata, suspended breathing, levitation, flying objects, etc. The suspension of physical law is apparent because in reality such phenomena occur within physical law, in so far as it can be manipulated or bent by a mind with the proper techniques. A part of this technique is a talent for ecstatic trance, in which very strange things happen, and happen for all to see. In our society this is called "madness." In more sophisticated cultures it was recognized as a fascinating skill. In any case, shamanic hysteria is a female-womb state—just as the Delphic oracle and her python were named after the womb, Delphine.

MENSTRUAL RITES: RIGHTS AND TABOOS

The first measure of time was menstrual time, and from this women developed lunar calendars and ancient astrology. Colleges of women (moon colleges of Hera: womb-giver of laws) were able to influence conception and birth through dream control. Communion with the body through dreams gave them self-knowledge through the cycle. It is possible to have dream knowledge of conception, of pregnancy, before any physical signs appear; in the experience of one of the authors, within two to three days after intercourse the body tells one, in a dream, that conception has occurred, along with the correct future sex of the fetus. (It happened, three out of three times!) All this is chemical information, which our brains as electrochemical information centers have access to. Translating chemical information into consciousness, via dreams, is a matter of receptivity and technique: a technique ancient women surely practiced, because it works.

In *The Wise Wound,* Shuttle and Redgrove speculate that primal women might even have *learned* to menstruate from the new moon, or dark moon. Further, that perhaps they used drugs that were not only mind-expanders but also contained steroid substances related to the human sex hormone, a steroid that could abort the uterine lining—this giving women great sexual sensitivity and also independence from unwanted reproduction, and from men. We do feel the lunar tides in our bodies, and the water in our bodies "sees" the moon as the crystalline structures of water alter or resonate with the moon passing overhead.

Women unconditioned by pejorative patriarchal taboos against the menstrual cycle were surely in fine tune with all its phases. They knew, in their bodies and dreams, the possibilities of the moon. To know something is to be it. We neglect her rites at our cost! We no longer contain our cycle; under patriarchy we are chained to it, in fear, shame, annoyance—and under constant threat of unwanted pregnancy.

Under patriarchy, menstruation is a punishment rather than a gift (i.e., an advantage and a talent). Christianity, Judaism, Islam, and other

Father God religions trace the evil of women to menstruation. Menstruation is the visible bloody sign of the serpent, of the Devil, in the female body. Patriarchal ontology states that all evil flows from this original female evil: moon blood. Menstruation was seen by biblical men as the curse of God laid upon woman for her sin in Eden—and "the curse" it is called, even today. The European Inquisition probed into women's blood-cycled dream life and trance experiences, declaring that any woman possessed by a pythonic (oracular, menstrual) spirit must burn. This idea also originates in the Bible; the Old Testament patriarchs quite intentionally set themselves against the lunar psyche in women (and in men, who are half-female), in their desire to destroy the Goddess religion, and the Goddess within us all. Because of this, the menstruating womb became the Devil of patriarchy—"the only good woman is a pregnant woman," etc.—and the three-hundred-plus years of European Christian witch-hunting has been accurately called "9 million menstrual murders."[1] Women were burned for practicing our natural moon-crafts of midwifery, hypnotism, healing, dowsing, herbal and drug use, dream study, and sexual pleasure. Crafts that go back to the Stone Age, and were passed down from mother to daughter for over 50,000 years. Since this persecution, European women at least have suffered an extreme nonalignment with their internal lunar processes; European and American women, however hard we try, rarely get back in touch with the lunar-chemical information—because we live in isolation from each other and the moon, in an environment hostile to the moon as anything but a rocket-launch base or a gigantic neon billboard in the sky.

Men in patriarchal societies learn, or reveal, a great jealousy and fear of natural women—of the sexual, mental, and spiritual abilities of fully evolved women living in harmony with the consciousness of our own bodies. The menstrual taboo is the consequence of this fear and resentment, as they are projected back on women's lives. Under patriarchy all life is dualized; women also are dichotomized, cut in two. There is the "good little ovulating wife," who is supposed to be passive and not very sexual; it's hard for even a woman to feel sexy cleaning the toilet bowl. And then there is the "witch," the sex-fiend, whore, scarlet woman! (*red* again) of active, dynamic, menstrual sexuality.

As both *Female Cycles* and *The Wise Wound* show, there are two poles to women's sexuality: the pole of ovulation, which tends to express itself in terms of wanting to surrender (its white, clear discharge is called "the river of life" and it is acceptable in patriarchy because it is receptive and fertile); and the pole of menstruation, before, during, and after, which expresses itself in wanting to take erotic initiative, to capture and demand (the red flow is called "the river of death" and its multiorgasmic and aggressive sexuality is taboo in patriarchy). Our menstrual sexuality, which is nonfertile, is called "masculine and castrating" by Freudian types who share in the cultural fear of mature women.

In early patriarchy, and in some contemporary indigenous cultures that have been colonized by misogynist religions, the menstrual taboo is openly punitive; it codifies sexual hostility in societies where women are treated as currency in men's affairs. Under the menstrual taboos women were to be punished for our powers—sexual, reproductive, and psychic powers. We were banished to the menstrual hut, called unclean and dangerous to the man and his laws and his gods. In some tribal communities we were imprisoned in dark cages or rooms for months, for as long as three years, with the first menstruation. In American Indian cultures, on the other hand, the menstruating woman is seen for what she is: a powerful life source. As *Daughters of Copper Woman* shows us, Native American women have worked to keep alive for generations their affirmative and celebratory customs surrounding female puberty, including years of physical training to make women strong in both body and mind; they did this despite constant opposition from Christian missionaries and preachers, who always view women's blood customs as "savage" and "satanic." Underneath the colonializing misogyny of Christianity and Islam, black African women too have managed to keep alive ancient puberty and menstrual customs which are energizing for women.

Worldwide, much of women's sacred blood rites and magical instruments have simply been stolen by patriarchy, or if not coopted, repressed. Male initiation rites can express an envy and awe of women, as men cut or wound their penises in imitation of bleeding vaginas. These rites reenact birth and menstruation; but they also symbolize a violent separation from women, earth, and the maternal, more a guilty theft than a true participation.

As Margaret Mead and others have shown, the more warlike and authoritarian a society is, the stronger is its menstrual taboo. In such societies, a paranoid emphasis is placed on women's "corrupting and debilitating influence" and men's need to overpower, dominate, and devalue her. Male training in aggression is linked with taboos, for both men and boys, against any knowledge of or contact with women's natural functions. It would seem that when there is no acknowledgment of women's bleeding, then there is instead a male acting-out of ritual and violent bloodshed in war. Warlike, aggressive male societies are in rivalry with women over which sex sheds the most sacred blood. War is men's response to women's ability to give birth and menstruate; all three are bloodshedding rituals. Women's blood rites give life, however, while men's bloody rituals give only death. To compensate for this, such authoritarian societies culturally repress and degrade women's blood functions, while elevating murderous war to a holy act. The women's menstrual "mysteries of inspiration" become, in war-god worshiping patriarchy, the "mysteries of resisted knowledge"—repression, madness.

Patriarchal societies are founded upon a crime. This crime is not the murder of the father, as Freud would have us believe. It is the rape and scorn of the mother. This is the unconscious horror that each girl-child inherits and, unlike male "castration anxiety," rape anxiety is all too often reinforced by the daily reality of the act and threat of rape. (Men's so-called "fear of castration" is simply a fear of losing command over women in patriarchal society, which equates domination of women with "manhood." If Western males have any legitimate fear of castration, it derives from the act of circumcision, which is a terrible thing to inflict on a male infant; but this custom comes from the Father God of the Bible, it doesn't come from women or any Great Mother religion.) Living constantly under the steel roof of patriarchy's criminal misogyny, women are forced to bend to, and accept, on pain of ever-reverberating punishment and terror, men's paranoid projections. Women, as long as we fear punishment for our powers, and as long as we are economically dependent on men, must accept that our bodies are unclean and deficient. Under patriarchy, the mother is feared and hated, quite crazily, both for her power and her weakness; everything a man cannot courageously accept about himself is projected onto his mother, or his wife. Or onto any random woman walking down the street.

Until yesterday, women were policed by the professionals, also—gynecologists and psychiatrists who acted as cultural reinforcers of the rules of "femininity"—who blamed our ills, like menstrual depression and pain, on our "failure to be feminine." How many men have grown rich, being in the business of telling women what we are supposed to be! Obviously, patriarchy wants us to be something that is not natural for us—otherwise, we wouldn't become crazy and sick trying to achieve it. Until yesterday, "once-a-month witches" were given drugs and electroshock treatment by the modern inquisition—members of the psychotherapeutic professions. Now, thanks to feminism and more women doctors, menstrual depression and pain, including the premenstrual syndrome, are being seriously studied and treated; with intelligence and concern, not the traditional contempt. But we can't forget how many women, just yesterday, were thrown into psychiatric wards by husbands and physicians because our cultural menstrual taboos rendered everyone stupid about basic life functions.

Women must understand that the object of taboo is also the object of strong desire. Menstrual blood is a powerful sexual element, and ancient men responded to women's rhythms. But to unyielding patriarchal man, whose entire self-concept depends on the fact that he is not a woman, any primal response to women's blood and rhythms is frightening. He fears to lose "control," he fears loss of his "ego," he fears empathizing with a woman, he fears melting into the other in the sexual act. He has a lot of fears. And so the heterosexual act inevitably becomes a reaction to fear—it becomes violation and rape. To repress his fears he takes on military terminology; he sees himself "invading" the woman's body—she becomes his sexual victim, his "prisoner of war." Simply because she had sex with him (engaged in battle, "allowed herself to be invaded"), he must treat her with contempt, as he would treat any "loser."

Few men in patriarchy are perceptive enough to realize that they have themselves lost a great deal, including the pleasures of sex. Men have mutilated their own sexuality, along with trying to mutilate women's. Ejaculation is not necessarily the same as orgasm. Reich was trying to investigate the difference between a genital reflex and a total mind-body response. Ancient Taoist and Tantric teachings, originating in Chinese and Indian matriarchies, taught men sexual techniques that suited women. Ancient women had strong genital pride and knowledge, and in no way envied, feared, or imitated men; women were the initiators of sexual knowledge. Women's collectives, no doubt, at the time of their menstrual flows, withdrew from the men to meditate, to practice Lesbian love, to commune with the Goddess in body-prayer. For women there is no separation between sex and spirit. Patriarchy exists by demanding that sex and spirit be opposites, and then repressing and punishing women for contradicting such a fiat.

Even in the menstrual huts, a custom enforced and twisted by patriarchy, women could still gather together to confirm their own identity, to sing and tell stories. At least they knew that their menstrual "uncleanness" was a misogynistic taboo. But in *Female Cycles* Paula Wiedeger makes it very clear that in the modern Western world, because there are no outward ritual signs of the menstrual taboo, it is even more insidious and harmful to us women. At her first menstruation the young "modern" girl is abandoned by her culture. She is made to feel that her body and its rhythms are a biological impediment to "freedom" and "fun." The subliminal message she receives from her culture is that a properly functioning body is male and noncyclic. On the job (at school, also) "work" is defined as a male activity; if she wants to be "equal" at work she must function like a male, i.e., noncyclically. (All legal and cultural disputes about women being pregnant or nursing at work, or nursing in public, derive from the fact that all workspace, all public space, in the West is defined in terms of the noncyclic male body. Women cannot "enter the workforce," or "enter public life," unless they agree to act as though their bodies were functionally male also.) To act as though one could function like a male is to suppress the fact that one is actually female. The menstrual hut is no longer to one side of the village; it is now constructed in women's own hearts and minds, as a very secret place where we take care of all our female functions while trying to act as though they weren't happening. When it comes to menstruation, we are female in secret, posing as male in public; in fact, with the popularity of panty-shields, the entire cycle from ovulation discharge to menstrual blood can now be kept so "discreet" (i.e., hidden) that any woman can become vice president of IBM. In our secret hearts and minds, though, which are our menstrual huts, continues a very real fear of men's (the male world, the world as a possession of men) negative and punitive responses to menstruation, to our whole female cycle. Female sex objects abound, but they are all manmade; when is the last time you saw a centerfold with hairy armpits, hairy legs, and a bloodflow?

The young girl of the modern West learns from all these subliminal signals to distrust, to dislike, and be ashamed of her own body and feelings, and those of other women. The femaleness she knows—body hair, sweat, monthly bloodflow, menstrual odor, ovulation discharge—must be hidden, taken care of in secret; while the femaleness men want to see (their own?) must be enhanced, publicly flaunted. Whether she really feels like doing this or not, she sees all the other women doing it. The message is that she must depend on something outside herself (men, male taste) for her self-definition. And she is on her own, isolated. The modern "community of women" exists only to show her how to hide her femaleness. She comes, crazily or with resignation, to associate menstruation with hurts, wounds, body waste, disabilities, shame, curtailment of her freedom. She comes to believe her "lack of freedom" comes from nature, her own biology, rather than resulting directly from patriarchal oppression and male fear.

And so the menstrual taboo has been one of the most successful methods devised by men to undermine self-acceptance, self-understanding, and self-confidence in women. It acts as a constant confirmation of a negative self-image. Most complaints about the advertisement of "personal products" on television come from women. Unfortunately, their complaints are not directed at the commercial exploitation of women's bodies by male industries. No. Women complain such ads are "in bad taste." They do not want their shame, their secret femaleness, discussed in public. Those ads belong in the menstrual hut.

Only dependent motherhood is celebrated and recognized as "legitimate" in patriarchy, and sexuality is presented as reproduction (or naughty sin) rather than as profound emotional experience. Sexual passion is not seen as an attribute to "femininity"; the only way our culture can handle women's sexuality is in pornography—a male distortion that reveals patriarchal puritanism and fearful fastidiousness like a fun house mirror reveals your face. Women who cannot, or will not accept the taboos are still punished, as we've been punished for two thousand years in the patriarchal world—as Lesbians, unmarried mothers, thinkers, artists, witches. One form of punishment is culturally mandated rape, which is clearly increasing as women struggle for freedom. The message is clear: Only when we women give up our sexual autonomy and our right to be independent and creative, only when we give up ourselves and accept patriarchal male definitions of "femininity" as passive, negative, and receptive—only then will we be treated humanely. Only then will we be treated, with patronizing smiles and door-openings, as something just a little less than the male. It is male fear, hatred, and envy that has for so long tried to turn our female abilities into incapacities; and despite all suave veneer of "advanced Western culture," it is gut-level male fear, hatred, and envy that women must fight to reverse this field.

Both *Female Cycles* and *The Wise Wound* speak at great length about the "menstrual epidemic" among "modern, civilized" women: as much as 90 percent of all women suffer from some form of distress (pain, cramps, depression) in connection with menstruation. Severe cramping is now being treated with prostaglandins; some depression is related to menstrual edema. But depression is also anger turned inwards or knowledge withheld. When violence is done to our nature it talks back in irregular and disharmonious ways—the attempts at detaching oneself from it simply lead to the body language of illness.

When we menstruate we are more psychologically open and vulnerable, and because of this more unable to accept injustices, deceits, and distortions; and so our stored-up rage and sexual frustrations are likely to burst out at this time. Penelope Shuttle claims that painful bleeding, backache, and cramps can be relieved by orgasmic experience. But, because of the menstrual taboo and men's fear of women's blood, most heterosexual women are not able to live out their heightened and powerful menstrual sexuality.

The menstrual cycle deeply links body, soul, and mind, but traditionally male doctors have viewed women as hormone robots; they have a hard time conceiving us as souls/minds. The menstrual tension is also caused by an increased need to dream and to meditate. This was the time, remember, when ancient women experienced prophetic dreams and went into trance-states. This is the monthly transformation and rebirth of the ego-self. *The Wise Wound* talks of children's awareness of the mother's "menstrual clock." The breath and taste of blood is our first experience at birth, and we can smell our mother's blood each month. We are aware of her unhappiness and frustration; our children are aware of ours. Men also are influenced from childhood by their mothers' cycles. If menstruation were not a taboo but an open primary life experience for all people, we could all deal with it.

Long overdue is research into male behavior and sexual attitudes to menstruation (menopause as well). It does no good to educate girls and boys about the clinical aspects of puberty, menstruation, sex, and reproduction, while never tackling the *psychological, cultural, and religious attitudes* that make these natural experiences into such a problem for everyone. The very religions that have turned human sexuality into pathology and nightmare should not be allowed to determine how public school children learn about sex! Most of our American misogyny, especially ideas about menstrual "uncleanness," comes from the Bible; for this reason alone the Bible should be kept from public schools, as a major source of the cultural defamation of women. Surely the First Amendment should protect young girls from being told "God" made them to be "unclean" and in need of monthly "purification."

More study needs to be done, also, on the effects of the birth control pill and IUDs on premenstrual symptoms, and on cyclic experience in general. It has been assumed that women will tolerate any menstrual upheaval in exchange for effective contraception, and in the short run this might be true. We have yet to see the long-term effects of reproductive technology on women's whole being—body, mind, and soul.

Menopause is the end of the menstrual cycle. In patriarchal culture it is also treated as the end of a woman's sexual identity. This reveals how totally female sexuality is equated with reproduction in the patriarchal primate brain, and in opposition to the facts of female evolution. The menopausal woman is portrayed, almost exclusively in Western culture, as a sad, ridiculous, and powerless creature. This is not so in many other cultures, including Native American, Hindu, African, where the older woman is accorded great respect and actually comes into her own in middle age, enjoying maximum freedom, independence, authority, and community influence after her childbearing years are over. With feminism, European and American postmenopausal women are also enjoying a renaissance of sorts—starting new occupations, returning to school, traveling, and experimenting with nontraditional lifestyles. Whether the reawakening and enjoyment of new powers extends to her sex life, however. . . . The contradiction, in our culture, is that women are seen by men as sexually attractive when young and fertile, precisely during the years when we are menstruating and also seen as sexually dangerous. Women must, however, not show any disturbing signs of that menstruation or cyclicity. We are taught that we *are* our reproductive functions, and that we are valuable only as long as we can reproduce. All the suppressed fear and envy of women that men feel for us during our fertile years is let loose in the form of male mockery and outright hatred of older women. Men of middle age, on the contrary, are often at the peak of their professional, economic, and cultural powers; sexually, they are much less empowered than middle-aged women, and often they attempt to mask this by becoming even more insufferably egotistical and dominant. Or, with their cultural and economic empowerment, they "buy" younger women, or a younger wife. It is not that the postmenopausal woman has become less sexual—the opposite is true—but that men lose their sexual interest in her; one reason being that male sexuality is still primate sexuality, and primate sexuality is obsessively reproductive. "Dominating" fertile females is the badge of macho primatehood. Traditionally, older women have ended up pretending they have no sexuality; they have become sexually invisible, or culturally sexless. Recently, also with feminism and the discovery that older women can be very interesting people, it has become trendy, if not always acceptable on Main Street, for older women to be coupled with younger men. This is a very ancient pagan situation! And good for us. Another option is a Lesbian relation, and a long-term relation, with another woman. This is another pagan solution, always subliminal in Western culture.

With current life expectancy, the average woman in the West has about twenty-five sexually active years in front of her *after* the decay of the ovaries and the ending of the fertility cycle. Women, and society, must adjust to this. We cannot go back to spending one-quarter of our lives, perhaps the sexiest time of our lives, as asexual zombies. "Our" culture—if it is to be ours—will also have to begin adjusting, responding positively, to women's monthly rhythms and sexual and emotional changes—the whole range of female being and potential. For this to happen, of course, we women must utterly transform life and society, to be able once again to tune in to the Goddess within us. Such a transformation will have to be genuinely bloody—i.e., it must affirm women's blood.

THE ORIGINAL WOMAN: WITCH, REBEL, MIDWIFE, AND HEALER

What would it have been like if patriarchy had never happened? To get an idea, we have to comprehend the first law of matriarchy: Women control our own bodies. This would seem a basic premise of any fully evolved human culture; which is why primate patriarchy is based on its denial.

Children were generally welcome in matrifocal society, as there was enough food for all, and children could help in agricultural and craft work. When childbearing is not a punishment, but self-chosen, and when raising children is not an economic-survival disaster, most of us enjoy being around children. Most men do too. In prepatriarchal cultures, children were raised communally—not closed up within four nuclear walls, not as property—but as the fruit of all. Most of all, childbearing and childraising were a part of each woman's life, a nourishing as well as nurturing part—but not her whole life. When women control our bodies, our daily lives, our environment, and our goals, we don't inflict on ourselves the terrible split between motherhood and self-realization that patriarchy and the nuclear family inflict on us. This split is a structural one, indigenous to male-dominated environments. In matriarchy, women could be mothers—and also enjoy other energies and interests. (Men who envied women our capacity to bear children and also do other things, turned around and invented patriarchy, in which motherhood is structured as an all-consuming burden. Men knew they could never bear children; but they could try to keep us from doing anything else.)

But women don't always want children, for a multitude of reasons best determined by women. So, in matristic cultures, there were a number of magic rites and techniques in use that contributed to fertility control. Women always had knowledge of herbal contraceptives and abortifacts, as well as narcotics and muscle relaxants (like raspberry tea) that could ease childbirth. When women are in natural control of our own fertility, population is always kept in practical relation to the needs of the group and the abundance of the environment. That, after all, is what it's all about. Since time immemorial, since the beginning of human time, the arts of gynecology, midwifery, and holistic herbal healing (including birth control) were wholely female domains, guarded by the Neanderthal women, the Cro-Magnon women, the Neolithic women and priestesses of the Great Goddess.

Contraception and abortion can become illegal only when, in patriarchal class society, church and state define it so for their own purposes. And what are their purposes? Large populations that drive the wages and value of labor down, masses of people kept in ignorance and wretchedness out of which come male cannon-fodder and female prostitutes and broodmares to service their wars. Patriarchy is based on cynical male control of female reproduction, and the resultant ugliness of such a "culture" is there for all to see. When women practiced their own medicine, thus controlling their own bodies, such a state could not come into existence. One of the major weapons of patriarchy was the establishment of a closed male medical profession that barred women from practicing their ancient herbal medicine and gynecological skills. In medieval Europe, this elite male medical profession was the joint creation of the royal courts and the Christian church, which joined together to create the European court-state as the political machinery to break the power of the people on the land—the peasants, the "pagans," the people of the witches.

Because women value the quality of life experienced by their children, women throughout history have done what they could do to keep population in balance with environment. Herbal and mechanical contraception is one method, abortion has been another. Tribal women throughout the world nursed their babies for four years, and during this time might have no sexual relations with a man; using such means to space out children, tribal women averaged four children in their reproductive lifetimes, each child receiving the maximum of intense maternal physical and emotional care during the critical early years. No method is ideal; some are extreme. But when contraception and abortion are not practiced, the results are even more extreme: infanticide, malnutrition, infant starvation deaths, mass famine. No woman, making her own choices, would deliberately bear children only to see them starve to death. Among people practicing abortion, even infanticide, the spirit of the dead child was returned to the earth-womb to await new birth, partaking still in the substance of the Great Mother. It was not lost; but the well-being of the living group was maintained.

Patriarchy arose among cattle breeders who had discovered the male role in conception; they believed that the entire life force was in male semen, and that the female womb served only as a "vessel" for the male seed, which was elevated into the Father God. So, among Near Eastern Father God religions, the child had value only as proof of male potency, and only insofar as it had been given into his ideological power. Catholics and fundamentalist Protestants believe that children dying without baptism into *their* religions have no souls and no salvation; the unbaptized dead infant remains forever in limbo. In the past, Semitic Jewish or Muslim

Sisterhood Is Powerful,
Sjöö, 1972

children who died without being named, circumcised, or otherwise ritually recognized by the fathers, were buried or burnt without ceremony. I.e., these children had identity only as the father's property. Today, the Catholic church maintains that humans, including fetuses, receive life entirely from God the Father. The ten months of biological labor put into this child by the mother mean nothing; she is just a "vessel." Pope Paul VI announced in 1972 that no woman has the right to abortion even if her life depends on it; even if she has other children who might need her; even if she is a fully grown conscious human being who might desire to live.[1] He was thereby claiming that the fetus, always considered potentially male, is more sacred than the human mother who bears it within her body. Why? She is only female; but the fetus comes from God (the big bull stud in the sky).

In March 1984, a pregnant Irish woman in Dundalk died from a recurrence of cancer, surrounded by Catholic doctors who refused to give her any treatment for fear of damaging the fetus. At the time of her death she had tumors on her legs, neck, and spine; but the doctors had refused to X-ray her, refused to give her any pain killers, refused all treatment absolutely. She died two days after delivering a premature baby who died at birth.[2]

Can we really believe that celibate priests care so much about the lives of infants? Or is it that their true concern is to maintain absolute control over the bodies of women, since it is upon this control that their entire religion is based. Feminists say: "If men could get pregnant, abortion would be a sacrament."[3] Women must understand that because men cannot get pregnant, their next move is to establish patriarchal religion, whose major sacrament is to make childbearing a punishment. A punishment for sex, a punishment for being female. Certainly it was not so in the ancient matriarchies.

The earliest recorded abortion recipes yet found date from circa 2700 B.C. They were inscribed on Egyptian papyrus scrolls. From Egypt come the first known medical texts also, and among them were prescriptions for contraceptive substances meant to be inserted into the vagina. Very likely they knew of temporarily sterilizing herbal potions that women could take. After all, the hormone progesterone, now used in the birth-control pill, exists naturally in various plants; today's multibillion-dollar birth-control industry was originally built on two yam roots found in Mexico. The Talmudic Jews invented the vaginal sponge, which was in use—soaked in oil—until the invention of the "Dutch cap" by a woman doctor in Holland in the 1880s. "Pessary" means "stone"; Oriental farmers and travelers knew that if a small object, like a stone, was inserted into the womb of a female camel, or other domestic animal, she would not conceive. Native healers on Java traditionally inserted a small object into the wombs of women for the same purposes—the original IUD. In ancient Rome and Greece vinegar or lemon juice were used as acid spermicides, and one-half of a squeezed-out lemon is a pretty good "cap." Native American women knew plants and root concoctions to take for temporary sterility, for abortion, as well as childbirth ease; all African and worldwide aboriginal people the same. It would seem that at no time in history have women been so totally oppressed in their sexuality, kept so ignorant of contraceptive methods while forced into compulsory and yearly childbearing, as in the so-called civilized societies of the Christian West.

As Dr. Margaret Murray pointed out in the 1930s, modern ideas of the witch are based entirely on Inquisition trial records of the sixteenth to eighteenth centuries, when the European Christian church was totally mobilized to crush out the remains of Western paganism. The stereotype was eagerly reinforced by the European medical professions, who saw the witches (who were also herbal healers and midwives) as economic rivals. Before these wholesale purges and repressions, many of the great early European doctors of medicine and pharmacology, like Paracelsus, claimed openly that they had learned all they knew of healing and drugs directly from women's witchcraft.[4]

The wiccan or "wise women" practiced the ancient Dianic religion, and functioned as midwives and healers to the common people and the peasantry. Throughout the European countryside, the *sage-femme* was called in at childbirth. These women were highly skilled; it is on record that some could perform Caesarean sections with complete success for the mother and child.

But during the late Middle Ages, dominated by the Christian Inquisition, the delivery of a pregnant woman was no longer considered a sacrament but a dirty business, and the women who attended the poor at childbirth were frequently considered social outcasts, or worse. They were charged with "witchcraft," tortured, and burned. One "witch" was burned alive in Scotland for the sole crime of bathing some neighborhood children, for hygienic reasons, in the midst of an epidemic. Healthcare and healing were publicly discouraged by the Christian church, which officially believed that life was supposed to be diseased, wretched, and painful—this was God's will, as punishment for human sin. People who tried to alleviate suffering or cure illness, especially through ancient folk and herbal medicine, or simple hygiene, were suspected to be agents of the Devil.

In Egypt, circa 3000 B.C., both female and male "priest-doctors" had helped women in childbirth. But in medieval Europe, midwifery was considered a crime for men, and probably a sign of witchcraft for women. The witch-hunts coincided with the rise of a specialist male medical profession, and were instigated by celibate monks whose minds were inflamed with the most psychotic sexual hatred of women. During the early Renaissance, medicine claimed to be more "scientific"—a new male profession—subject to government and professional control. Eventually these male professionals discovered the "goldmine" of obstetrics; even midwifery began to be surrounded by educational requirements, from which women were excluded. Male midwives appeared in Europe, and doctors insisted on being consulted during childbirth. (These were the same professional medics who later demanded that laboring women enter hospital wards, and then moved from corpse autopsies to childbirth beds, spreading infection to women, and causing higher mother-mortality rates than had ever existed in "pagan" Europe.)

The modern male medical professions rose on the ashes of the burnt witches. These women were villified in every way that clerical tongue, or pen, or torture instrument could inflict, and luridly accused of everything: of making men both lustful and impotent, of helping women in labor, and of depopulating Christendom by strangling newborn babies. In 1486 it was officially declared that "No one does more harm to the Catholic faith than midwives."[5] And there was truth in this accusation: European women, living in wretched poverty and condemned to unending pregnancy by the Church's celibate male priesthood, had no greater friends than the *sage-femmes*, the wise-women midwives who told them how to prevent conception, what herbs to use for abortion, and how to ease labor pain. As the church rightly suspected, the midwives also often "neglected" to properly baptize the newborn into the Christian faith. All this gave women a certain autonomy and control over their own bodies, and this power threatened the power of the male priests, the father church and father state. Midwives were witches, and witchcraft was high treason against God's *nouveau* male majesty.

The Christian male hierarchy, both Catholic and Protestant (which was developing during this time), was intent on establishing total domination over the innermost thoughts of the European people. The Inquisition was the instrument of this domination. Witches were independent of mind, they were of the people, and they served the Goddess, the native Goddess of Neolithic Europe, not a male god imposed by Roman imperialism. Their covens were correctly suspected to be meeting places for revolutionary peasants. Joan of Arc was legendarily a member of a witch-coven. In every small village or city neighborhood, the witch was the spiritual and political rival of the local priest and the imperial church. She offered real healing through anciently tested herbal knowledge, while the priest could only give slogans, promising relief in heaven or punishment in hell. Medieval Christianity taught that this world was the Devil's excrement—our flesh the home of Original Sin, and our lives an evil to be despised and endured. With the church's disruption of the old ways, human life in Europe was indeed becoming quite ugly. Countering this, the witch kept alive the ancient pagan nature-wisdom and cyclic rhythms—dances, songs, beliefs, lore, and skills celebrating the sacredness of life and the ecstasy of earth. The people followed the witches, who always had "better Music, and more Delight."[6]

The Hebrew God Yahweh, in Genesis 3:16, had condemned Eve for her disobedience: "I will greatly multiply thy sorrow and thy conception; in sorrow shalt you bring forth children." And so, according to the church, it should be. To the male priesthood and celibate monks, woman alone was sexual. Her genitals were fearsome and unclean, and childbirth was disgusting and unholy. To Christian clerics, "original sin" adhered intrinsically to orgasmic experience, to the fact of female genitalia, children were born "dirty" as a result of the "dirt" of sexual conception. ("Testament," on the other hand, comes from the Latin *testis:* testicle, male witness.)

In *Childbirth Without Fear* (1942) Dr. Grantly Dick-Read declares that there can be no more horrible stigma upon "our civilization" than the history of childbirth. Long after anesthetics were medically available, and as late as the mid-nineteenth century, the clerical and medical authorities opposed any methods that might relieve women's suffering during labor. Women were meant to suffer greatly as God's punishment for our collective sin. Witches were accused and arrested, and tortured and burned, for the "crime" of helping women in labor with herbs and muscle-relaxing techniques. Such womanly help was "a dreadful and impious act against the will of God." And as Martin Luther, founder of Protestantism, stated: "If a woman grows weary and at last dies from child-bearing, it matters not. Let her die from bearing, she is there to do it."[7]

In ancient society and among "primitive" people still, laboring women sit in a squatting position, actively in charge of the body's creative work.

In the "modern" West, until yesterday, the Christian tradition of "passive suffering" prevailed in the labor room: the woman lying on her back, usually strapped down, in cruelly impersonal hospital environments, while a male doctor "delivered" her child. Woman bears the pain, but man takes the credit for deliverance. (We now know that this strapped-down, legs-in-stirrups position was the invention of French King Louis XIV, who mandated it throughout his kingdom, because he was royally turned-on by watching women in labor.[8]) With feminism and women's rediscovery of homebirth, midwifery, and drug-free delivery, this situation has in the past decade radically changed. As recently as 1971 midwifery and homebirth were virtually illegal and/or practically unobtainable in almost all American states; now, women have heroically revived the occupation of midwife, established comfortable birthing centers, and forced hospitals to compete by offering women more comfort and autonomy in hospital delivery wards. Though midwifery and homebirth have been common practices in twentieth-century Western Europe, the American medical profession fought them vigorously; perhaps accounting for the fact that America in the recent past ranked *seventeenth* in newborn mortality rates among the Western nations. American women's successful fight (so far) to return childbirth to mother and child is reversing this statistic; and also helping to reempower women on the most basic level of becoming acquainted with our own bodies. One giant step for womankind.

During the time of Catholic-dominated Europe, it was also a crime against "God" to miscarry. Even if a woman miscarried after an accident, or after being beaten by her husband, she could still be put to death for her "sin" against the Father—because all miscarriages were suspected by the clergy of being intentional abortions. The celibate clergy always tended to believe women were "guilty until proven dead." When Spanish Catholics colonized the American West, forcibly missionizing the Western tribes, it was the custom for Native American women who miscarried, for any reason, to be punished by being whipped and publicly humiliated for their "sin" before the church door. It was believed, sometimes correctly, that Indian women would practice abortion in order to rob the church of Indian slave-labor; and the priest of "God" could not allow this. The same mentality was practiced against European women for centuries by the father church. Wherever male religious and political systems are based on the control of women's reproduction, women must live like this.

According to the Bible: "Rebellion is as the sin of witchcraft" (Samuel 15:23). All those who follow the ancient and original religion, refusing to be dominated and dichotomized by Father God ideology, are defined as evil rebels, belonging to the "Devil," and are to be put to death according to "God's will." In the Bible, for the first time, we see "God's will" (i.e., the male primate will to control female reproduction) used as a political tool to crush believers of other religions—women's religions. The fanatic misogyny of both Christianity and Islam originated, as did both these religions, in the Bible. Or, as women of the women's movement of the

1970s said: "You are a witch by being female, untamed, angry, joyous, and immortal."[9]

The wiccan nature, or witchcraft, is the original nature of all women, deriving from our primary biological experience, our psychic relationship with the earth and cosmos. It is this experience, this relationship, that patriarchy sets out to destroy. But women cannot change our nature—we can only try to forget it, repress it, or follow it under constant threat of punishment by the dominating male order. About a modern day African witch it is said, "If she is lucky enough that her psychic powers are quiescent, then she can live a normal life." There is a constant fear among her husband's relatives that she will use her powers to revenge her humiliating situation as "wife," isolated as she is among hostile strangers in the patriarchal land, in the patriarchal family, removed by patrilocal custom from her own maternal kin-group. With quiescent psychic powers, of course, any woman's "normal life" is one of submission. In parts of the West Coast of Africa, tribes remained matriarchal until well into the tenth century. When forced into patriarchal organization from the outside, through Islamic invasion, many African women chose to run away with Muslim slave-traders rather than become "wives."

So, the witch alive under patriarchy is always under suspicion for having caused the sterility of her husband, or death, disease, and bad luck among her in-laws, or bad weather or bad crops. Or, in more fundamentalist situations, she is always under suspicion as a willful seductress of "good men," a tool of "evil nature" or "the Devil," designed by death and darkness to undermine and destroy what men call their "civilization." Her genuine range and depth of creative powers are denied or forbidden. She lives in a manmade situation where she can use only her negative powers—and for that she is punished and damned! Patriarchy sets her up as the universal scapegoat for all problems, imagined or real, thus removing from all men in her vicinity the terrible burden of thought.

During the five hundred years of Inquisition, representing the triumph of Christian imperialism over pagan Europe, a woman could either become a totally subservient "wife"—beaten and bullied by her husband, her eyes to the ground as the priests and preachers condemned and blamed her sex for all things—or she could stand straight, proud in her own woman-wisdom, and be burnt as a witch.

GODDESS OF THE WITCHES

Diana-Artemis, Goddess of the Witches, was the Great Goddess of the lengendary Amazons—the wise women, and women warriors, of ancient Thrace, Macedonia, North and West Coast Africa, Libya.

She was Queen of Heaven, the pure Huntress of the Moon, and the protectress of wild animals. She was a Lesbian, scornful of men, and her followers were young women. No man could enter her temple. As the Moon, she rides the clouds, very cool, untouched by man, filling the nights with psychic brilliance. But she was also Asiatic Artemis, the orgiastic and many-breasted Mother of All; in this form she was honored at the Temple of Artemis at Ephesus, built by Amazons, and considered one of the wonders of the ancient world. And, after this temple was destroyed by fire, Amazons built it up again. In her third form she was Hecate, Dark Goddess of the Night Sky, giver of plagues and sudden death. Hecate, worshiped at midnight, at the crossroads.

All these paradoxical aspects were hers, as the moon has changing faces. Diana the Virgin Huntress, untouched by men, was also the Goddess of Childbirth. Legendarily, Diana was born of her mother without pain, and she taught women the techniques of painless childbirth: She was a midwife.

Her cult had major Bronze Age centers throughout the Mediterranean—at Marseilles, Syracuse, and Ephesus. Her temple at Ephesus was built by Amazons circa 900 B.C.; after destruction by fire it was rebuilt by another generation of women warriors. This temple was in the "beehive shape." And at this beehive temple, Dianic rites were conducted by Melissal priestesses (worker bees) and self-castrated Essene priests (drones).[1] Here was the famous image of Black Diana. A small shrine on her head, the diopet, contained a magic stone—possibly a very old Neolithic implement. This statue was smashed to pieces in 400 by a Christian, who boasted that he had finally torn down the "Demon Diana."[2]

In Rome, Diana was the protectress of the plebians, and in particular the guardian of slaves, outlaws, and thieves. Her temple stood in their city quarters, the Aventine. Roman slaves celebrated Diana's festival in mid-August (which is also the sacred festival day of Hecate, and of the Irish Triple Goddess Brigid). To the Christians, Diana the Moon was the Devil incarnate. Ninth-century church fathers in Europe condemned "deluded women who believe that in the dead of night they ride upon certain beasts with Diana—or the Witch Queen Herodias—and fly through the sky, among multitudes of women." Long into the Renaissance, she was imaged as a terrible demon. (Christians sometimes call the devil "Lucifer"; Lucifer, the "light-bringer" was in early legend Diana's twin brother, the morning star. The morning star, also the evening star, is Venus, which along with the moon was observed with very accurate calculations by ancient astronomers worldwide. To the Aztecs it was Quetzalcoatl, to the Mayans Kukulcan; to the Sumerians and Babylonians it was Inanna-Ishtar. Whenever Christians encountered astronomical-astrological observations and texts on Venus and the moon, they saw only "Devil-worship"; hence they destroyed library after library containing ancient wisdom and knowledge, including the Mayan astronomical library at Mani, as well as the library of Alexandria. Mayan astronomical knowledge was probably the most advanced in the ancient world; they invented the zero long before the Arabs did. In 1552 the Spanish Friar Diego de Landa, confronting all these texts containing Mayan intellectual brilliance as well as spiritual data, stated that they "contained nothing in which there was not to be seen superstitions and lies of the devil" and so "we burned them all."[3] Early Christian smashing of Dianic cults in the Mediterranean, as well as later church persecutions of witches in Europe, must be seen in this global context: wherever Christians saw knowledge—herbal, medical, astronomical, symbolical—they saw demonism, and moved to destroy it. The witch persecutions were not simply aimed at "Devil-worshipers," but at ancient human knowledge of the world.)[4]

Another group of Amazons and witch women was centered around what is now Morocco in Northwest Africa. They called their Moon Huntress Goddess Anatha, a name related to the Egyptian Goddess Neith, and the Greek Athene. The Amazon tribes in this area were called Gorgons, one of their queens was named Medusa, and their Warrior Goddess Anatha wore the original legendary *aegis*, a goatskin chastity tunic, along with a Gorgon mask and a leather pouch containing a sacred serpent. Probably all the Amazons ("moon women") wore these magic belts, and any man who removed one without the wearer's consent would be killed. The Greek legends of heroes slaying the Gorgon and the snake-haired Medusa could derive from actual battles fought by patriarchal Greek soldiers against these women's cultures; just as Greek males fought Macedonian Amazons on the Greek homeland. The Gorgon is a very moon-faced woman with her tongue stuck out. Even though the later Athene became the Goddess of the Greek patriarchal state, and in Greek drama was portrayed as siding with the new father-right against the ancient Mother Goddess religion, still she always in her statues carried the *aegis*, with the Gorgon's head on it, as her shield. Northwest African warrior women wearing a magic belt with a pouch suspended from it, containing a sacred serpent, sounds very close to the Dahomean Goddess, the Black Witch Mawu-Lisa, who was bisexual and carried a snake in her belly. And to corroborate the legends that ancient matriarchal Africans sailed to Central America, Frank Waters in *Mexico Mystique* mentions this interesting information: In the Mayan Temple of the Sun at Palenque is a carved tablet "identified by Pythagoreans as the *aegis* of Zeus" (who stole it from Athene). This *aegis* shows the Gorgon head with tassels that Homer described as Athene's shield, and it is backed by the carved numerals 77, the magic number of the Egyptian Goddess Neith.[5]

The original witch was undoubtedly black, bisexual, a warrior, a wise and strong woman, also a midwife, also a leader of her tribe. The many faces of the moon. The nature of the Goddess was in no way the pale, meek, mild, and solely maternal one that has been associated with "femininity" in patriarchal culture. The Goddess of unrestrained sexual love—Astarte, Ishtar, Ashtoreth Cybele—was also associated with war and death, with natural magic and primal wildness. She was also a mother, and a helper of women in childbirth. Under the Greco-Roman and Hebrew-Christian patriarchy in the West, these many aspects were separated out into the "good woman" stereotype of the Virgin Mary, versus the "bad woman" Eve. She was the Love Goddess, *or* the Good Mother, *or* the Hag of Death, *or* the Virgin Huntress. But never again *All*. It can be hard for us to remember that the original Goddess was not a fixed dualism, but a revolving triplicity. She of the moon-changes.

Whether she is seen as the benevolent Mother of All Living, or the Goddess of bloody battle, or the Death Goddess, or the prophetic witch—the attitude toward life in matriarchal society remains the same. All life is created out of the Mother and is one with her. Therefore no life can be taken without her permission. All lifeblood belongs to her and must be returned to the earth sacredly. And so life can only be taken in the form of ritual individual sacrifice. This is how and why ritual sacrifice could occur among people who were *not* "bloody savages." They did not kill, either, at a logically rationalized distance, by machine; ritual death happened up close, by a living, bloody, and responsible hand. When the biblical Hebrews opposed ritual human sacrifice, they were on the right evolutionary track; human beings needed to go beyond that. But to replace ritual, individual sacrifice with mass random slaughter, by mechanized weaponry, in the ideological name of "holy war" or "modern political war," was no advance. At least the ancient ritualists knew what they were doing, and took responsibility for each kill.

Every human is born from a woman. And so, in a society ruled by the council of older women, meeting at night in the moonlight after the day's work was done, it was not possible to see human beings in terms of statistics and ideological units—as so much raw material to be used and manipulated, as is the case in patriarchal societies. Sacrifice was voluntary, and service was seen as mutual. And, as among the American Iroquois, even the male war chief, or chief of hunting, was not free to make his own "specialist" decisions about life and death. He was bound to abide by the decisions of the council of women, the mothers of life and death.

CRETE AND THE BRONZE AGE

Crete was the last, full flowering of matriarchal culture. We are taught that Western civilization begins with Greece, but in fact the imagination of the Greeks came from Crete. All Greek religious ritual, all Greek mythology, was of Cretan-Mycenaean origin. Rites performed at Eleusis in utter secrecy were, in earlier Crete, celebrated in sacred groves. The ecstasy cult of Dionysus originated in Crete. It was the cult of the Great Goddess, Lady of the Beasts, surrounded by her wild dancing women. Later, as Bacchantes, these ivy-chewing women performed the death-and-resurrection ritual of her son, Dionysus-Bacchus.

Most of the later, famous Greek Goddesses originated in Crete. In fact, the whole progress of Classic Greek mythology involved breaking down the one, original Great Goddess into her many aspects, and stereotyping these into the partial Goddesses that we have come to know: Aphrodite the Love Goddess, Athene the Goddess of Wisdom, Demeter the Mother, Persephone the Daughter, Artemis the Virgin Huntress, Hecate the Death Crone. In these partial forms, the "goddesses" were often set at war with each other, as in the Trojan legend when Paris was asked to choose which one of three—Hera, Athene, or Aphrodite—was most beautiful. His choice precipitated a war. This story is a paradigm of how the Greek male mind, in the rising patriarchy, played with women and with the ancient Goddess: breaking her into fragments and then setting the fragments against each other, in jealous bickering. Greek mythology is full of this intellectual game, revealing the detachment of the Greek mind from what had once been sacred. Under the original Great Mother religion this fragmentation could not happen, for each different face of the Goddess was recognized as an aspect of the one being.

The Great Goddess of Crete is familiar. Statues show her standing in a flounced skirt with bare breasts, ecstatic, holding up coiling snakes in both hands. She was worshiped among early agricultural peoples of the Mediterranean region and Southwest Asia; in Northwest Coast Africa she was called Ngame. Her cult was perhaps carried to Crete in ancient times by Anatolian settlers from the Asiatic mainland; or it might have originated in Africa, or in Thrace. The wonderful flounced skirt was worn by both the Maltese and Sumerian Goddess. The Cretan Goddess is one with the Ephesian Artemis-the-Many-Breasted, with Ishtar of Babylon, with the Triple Goddess Morrigan of Ireland, with Mawu-Lisa the Black Witch carrying the snake in her belly, with the Great Mother of the Paleolithic caves. She almost always appeared with serpents, with bare breasts, and with the moon; she was the first god, always one.

The Great Goddess kept her supremacy throughout the Mediterranean, the Aegean, Turkey and the Near East, Northwest Africa and Europe through Neolithic times, until the very end, the Bronze Age, in changing forms. She survived into the rise of high civilization in Crete, when a form of class-society developed based on a palace-culture of advanced technology, but still patterned on the matrilinear family. There are no figures of male gods in all of Cretan culture. Even into the predominantly patriarchal, warring, and priest-ridden world of the Bronze Age, the Cretans—unlike most of their contemporaries—had no temple or temple-figures. Their sanctuaries were in the countryside, they worshiped among sacred trees, and even as they celebrated the birth of the young male God Dionysus in the birth cave, he was always known as the son of the Great Mother. The rites involved hiding and protecting him from the cannibalistic wrath of the neighboring Father God, who saw him as a rival for power. Dionysus was raised among women, dressed as a woman—as an ecstatic shaman—and he represents the naturally androgynous nature of the true son, who identifies with the Mother. As G. Rachel Levy wrote, the Cretans

> . . . developed a religion unusually detached from formal bonds, but emotionally binding in its constant endeavour to establish communion with the elemental powers. Perhaps this was the reason why they never built temples, but performed their rites, through the most splendid epochs of their material achievement, on mountain peaks, in caves, in household chapels and rustic shrines. Their ritual remained primitive, preserving its relations with cavern, pillar, Goddess and tree, so that they could draw profoundly on the past, and bequeath something fundamental to their more intellectual successors.[1]

The Cretans appear to have been gentle, joyous, sensuous and peace-loving. From the evidence of ruins, they maintained, like the Maltese islanders, at least one thousand years of culture unbroken by war. The only other peoples we know of with such a long peace record—e.g., those of the Indus Valley and of Southern India—were also Mother Goddess cultures.

In Crete, the uncovering of the breasts was a sacred gesture, symbolizing the nourishing lifestream of the Mother. The Goddess was the One, "whose Godhead, single in essence, but of many forms, with varied rites and under many names, the whole earth reveres." In later times her young

Cretan Mysteries, Sjöö, 1982

Cretan Goddess, Sjöö, 1982

Bee Goddess Rising; Minoan Seal Ring circa 1500 B.C.

son emerges as a deity, the leader and embodiment of the war-dancing Curetes (Korybantes). All the Cretan rites included ecstatic dancing and mystery, and in the Dionysian rituals these trance-inducing activities were not intended to prepare actual warriors, but to defend the spirit of the Mother's young son from the rising patriarchy.

At first the Indo-European Sky God, Zeus, was identified with the young Cretan God. Zeus was introduced into Greek-Mycenaean mythology by nomadic-pastoral invaders from the North, called Aryans by some historians; they could have come from the Russian steppes. Among Greeks, Zeus was first seen as a Serpent God, a consort of the Goddess and manifestation of her power. In reliefs and seals he was imaged as a serpent. When the young Zeus-Dionysus was born and concealed in a Cretan cave on Mount Ida, the holy rite of the new birth involved all the people in celebration. The Curetes danced and beat their shields—figure-eight-shaped shields ornamented with serpents and spirals—to help save the child from his devouring father, bent on secular power. All this was an accepted part of Greek mythology. But influenced by the solar cults and Apollonian "rationalism," Classic Greeks elevated the sacrificial son to Olympian immortality. (Just as early Christians were to do with Jesus.) Eventually the story of Zeus's birth and death in a Cretan cave, as the son of the Great Mother, was denied as heresy by the Greeks.

Lady of the Beasts; terracotta plate from Rhodes

There is a striking difference between the colorfully flowing and curving wall paintings and pottery ornaments of the Cretans and those of the Bronze Age Babylonian palaces and huge temples, all bearing angular, rigid, and aggressive scenes of warfare, enslavement, and the hunt. These Babylonian architectures were setting a new patriarchal standard the world was soon to follow. But whatever is gracious and beautiful in Greek art derived not from patriarchal style, but from the early Cretans.

At the service of the Great Mother of Mount Citheron on Crete, the whole of Creation was believed to stir, live, and dance. The Great Mother's mountain-flame was kept alive by nymphs in torchlight dances and winding mountain processions. There was a ritual feast of raw flesh, and a long, magical sleep of initiation in the cave, a visionary trance and rebirth. Funerary rites expressed the concept of rebirth through the Mother. Blood-sacrifice of the bull was performed by priestesses with the ceremonial labrys. The palaces contained pillar-crypts where offerings were made, and the pillar as a symbol of the Goddess was anointed with perfumed oils. In the low, dimly lit throne room of Knossos were stone basins, and the throne was flanked by griffin murals. The Palace of Knossos is a vast labyrinth in its design. "Labyrinth" names its hall of double-axes, the ceremonial ax of the Goddess.

Cretan art and religion were a vivid celebration of life. The Goddess was joyously worshiped as the Lady of the Beasts—reliefs, paintings, frescoes, and countless seals depict her on mountaintops, surrounded by her wild animals or carrying magic snakes in her uplifted arms. In Cretan homes, walls and ceiling were lavish with flowing lines and bright curves, plants and flowers, birds and forest animals, and sea creatures—purple octopi!

Cretans were mariners, traveling and trading as far as Scandinavia, Ireland, Syria, and Northwest Africa. Traces of their art and influence were carried over the seas. They worshiped cowrie shells and other vulva-like sea shapes of the Goddess; these sea spirals and convolutions were universal symbols of female creation and organic growth, of eternal continuity and change. The cowrie in Africa retained its symbolic value into patriarchal times, being used as money. In Buddhist Tantra, spiral shells are symbols of the root-mantra OM.

No one knows what happened to Crete. Its bright millennium of matriarchal culture ended suddenly and mysteriously, with no clear sign of a cause. There is no evidence of war or invasion; some believe it ended in earthquake and flood. Robert Graves speculates that Crete was the legendary Atlantis.

The Bronze Age marks a revolution in social organization. There was a break with the religion of the megalith builders. The Great Goddess still ruled, but no longer supreme. Her son/lover became more and more a dominating War God and Father God, taking over some of her functions and powers as his busy priests remade the old mythologies into his new image; in this they had the help of alphabets and script-writing invented by women of Goddess cultures. The transition from matriarchal to patriarchal organization seems to have come about in Mesopotamia, as elsewhere, through the political-social revolt of the queen's consort. She traditionally conferred executive powers on him by allowing him to adopt her names, robes, and sacred instruments and regalia. For example, the widespread custom of the king wearing artificial breasts and long robes, acting as sacred agent of the Goddess; the "crown" on his head was the "crown of birth" from the Goddess—as babies are still said to "crown" at birth. When the king revolts against his sacred role, in order to exploit the secular power of the matriarchal domain, the Mother Goddess religion begins to be distorted. We see the rise of the Father God as secular male usurpation of social, political, and economic power as well as a rewriting of all the old mythologies.

With the decay of matriarchal cultures, the mystery rites lost their pristine significance as female participation in a female universe. The relation of women worshipers to the young male God, grown from the Goddess's infant son to an adolescent, to a War God, changes. The relation of son to Mother becomes misconstrued as that of a lover to a bride, then a dominating lord to a servant. And the wild women dance-companions of the androgynous Dionysus are "legalized" into submission, becoming weak and fawning followers of a macho-warrior Godhead—or a crucified Christ who denies the Mother.

There was an era, before the patriarchal revolution took effect, when women and men cooperated in equality, producing and creating and worshiping together. The son of the Mother was her mature lover and mate. Wherever the worship of the Great Mother occurred, ritual emphasis was on the sacredness of life. Sexual union fuses the separate emanations of the divine. And so sexual rites, worship, and ceremonial union—not to be confused with fertility rites—were a part of her mysteries everywhere. The *hieros gamos* ("sacred marriage") between a high priestess representing the Goddess, and the sacrificial year-king (later permanent king) is, however, no older than circa 6500 B.C., to our knowledge. But the idea of a sacred mating between new initiates and the ritual priestess or priest still lives among some witches.

With patriarchy, this ceremonial view of sexual union ends. Patriarchy is based on secular not sacred relationships, and on property possession, which utterly excludes the experience of ecstatic communion. It is also of course based on the sexual passivity, weakness, and dependence of women. The sacred marriage becomes the ugly business of domination and humiliation between the sheets—or in the harem, the male paradise filled with sexual slaves. And now the sacred relation of mother-child is closed indoors, psychologized, and publicly diminished, as the child comes to be viewed, like the wife, as part of the father's property—neither having social, economic, or political rights except through him. With patriarchy we are in the world of male display, with males strutting and boasting before each other, and women and children, as well as religious and cultural artifacts, existing solely as material items in the assembled wealth.

TANTRA AND THE WORLD SPINE

What remains? Many real things. Witchcraft in the Western world, our indigenous Goddess religion. In the East, in Tantra yoga (and to some degree in Taoism), survive some of the ancient matriarchal beliefs, techniques, and ritual worship. The female-energy symbolism used by Tantrika—the vulva, caves, the earth, the community of women—can be traced back to the Paleolithic cave culture of 30,000 B.C. Probably in ancient times the special potency of Tantra was transmitted through a female line of "power-holders"—a mysterious sect of women called the Vratyas.[1] This female transmission of the tradition would account for the way in which female-energy symbolism has survived in later religions, such as Tibetan Buddhism and Brahmanical monastic Tantra, which are otherwise male-oriented in their dogma, and not at all likely to have discovered the female principle for themselves.

All such transmission was bound to have happened entirely outside the Hindu caste system, which depends on strict adherence to patriarchal rule for its existence. The Sanskrit word for "caste," (*varha*) means "color." The Hindu concept of lawlessness originally meant "the corruption of women," which was believed to lead to social chaos, or "caste-mixture." So, female Tantric practitioners and transmitters would have been outcastes (pariah), and considered defiling as sexual partners.

The Tantra was originally matriarchal, emerging from and belonging to the collective, classless early Goddess society of the Dravidians. India was invaded circa 3000 B.C. by the lighter-skinned Aryans, or Indo-Europeans from the north, who went on to conquer the darker-skinned matriarchal agricultural Dravidians, ending at least one thousand years of peaceful cultural development in southern India. The Aryans called themselves "the people of the sky" (i.e., inherently light, good, superior, and mighty), and the dark-skinned Dravids they called "the people of the earth and of the serpent" (i.e., inherently dark, evil, weak, inferior, etc.).

Danu, or Diti, the Great Goddess of the non-Aryan Dravids, was the Cow Goddess of India. She was undoubtedly related to the European Goddess Danu, who gave her name to the Russian River Don, to the

German Danube, and was the Goddess of the Irish Tuatha de Danaan. In Indian mythology she was murdered by the god Indra ("he who overthrows cities"), who was the god of the invaders. Danu and her son, Vrta, are first described as serpent-demons; later, as they lie dead, as cow and calf. After Indra's murder of Danu it was said that "the cosmic waters flowed and were pregnant" with her blood, giving birth to the sun of the new patriarchal order and its Brahmanic elite.

Following this conquest, over the ages, the male Aryans established the caste system, the most powerful among them establishing themselves as the "light" Brahman class at the top. They placed tight restrictions on the women, in order to preserve their own "racial purity," property line, and privilege through the patriarchal family. *Purdah*, women's imprisonment in the "domestic sphere," and harems of wives were introduced later by the Muslims.

The priestly Brahman caste presided over the temples and ritual worship, and laws of hierarchic social conduct. A Brahman was considered "pure," and to maintain his "purity" he had to be protected from all other work. The next class, the warriors, were good for nothing but war. The work of society was carried out by the lower castes, and by the "untouchables" whose duty it was to empty the latrines and do the cleaning. These "untouchables" were the original dark-skinned matriarchal Dravidians, in the new patriarchal order assigned the role of housemaid, or wife.

Brahmans are called the "twice-born," i.e., reborn out of the father. This is the aim of men's "initiation rites" all over the world: to incorporate the boy-child into the world of the fathers while exorcising all memory of the child's bond with the mother—a bond that is both erotic and mystical and thus a challenge to established power. The Indian mystic, Rabindranath Tagore, spoke often of the Shakti power of the female: "In our language we call women's power over men *Shakti*. If Shakti disappears, the creative force in society is inhibited, the men lose their virility and become mechanical in their habits." He believed that the relation between the sexes in India under patriarchal religion was so distorted that the Shakti power could not function.[2]

Distinguished contemporary Tantrika have stated their belief that many of the miseries in modern India are caused by the world-hatred that traditional Brahman philosophers have instilled into the majority of the population. World-hatred is designed to make people accept miserable conditions and injustice, as though these were functions of life itself, rather than specific results of specific manmade systems, such as the caste system in India. A good deal of India's suffering, like that of most of the world, results from Western imperialism and exploitation of native labor and resources. But such Indian problems as child-marriage, dowry-murders, and the ritual burning of widows (*suttee*) cannot be blamed on modern European imperialism. The burning alive of so many young brides by husbands' families dissatisfied with dowry payments comes directly from patriarchal religion's devaluation of women into property. Dowry-murder among lower-caste Indians seems to have replaced the longstanding custom of *suttee*, now illegal, which was practiced by the wealthier upper classes. Why? In *suttee* custom, with the immolation of the widow on her husband's funeral pyre, the Brahman priesthood inherited all the worldly property of the couple. Thus no upper-class wealth or land could ever pass into the hands of women. In the same way, the land and goods of every European burned as a heretic or witch, during five centuries of Inquisition, passed directly into the hands of the Christian church. That was a lot of property, much of it still held by the various denominations. Thus does the patriarchal priesthood consolidate its earthly domains.

Living traces of the ancient aboriginal matriarchal people can still be found in India. The Purdja of the south still do not farm the soil, but only burn wood and sow in the ashes. Purdja women wear no veils and remain proud, sexually free, and strong. The matriarchal Nayar people of Kerala in southern India enjoy high culture, no poverty, no prostitution; they practice gift-exchange economy and are noted for their highly educated and active women. The Indian women's art of yogic massage, practiced on babes from one month and small children, originated in Kerala. It has been handed down through generations of women. In this massage the left hand is dynamic energy, the right hand is static energy. The exercises require great strength and sensitivity, the women's hands—joined with controlled breathing—communicating intelligence, dignity, freedom, power, and tenderness. A cosmic dance emerging from the rhythmic movement, a silent dialog of love and union between mother and child, is designed to open the child's joints and release the sensuous power of life. This is done by all animal mothers, in fact, when they lick their newborn intensely immediately after birth.[3]

The sexual misers and misogynists of Buddhism, practicing a secret and dangerous self-indulgence in the form of spiritual nihilism, leading to institutionalized sadism, neglect, and hatred of their fellow creatures, are very similar to the patriarchal monastic Christian world of the European Middle Ages. Both terrible worldviews show the fallacy involved in any assertion of the nature of being (Brahma, or Christ-God) which fails to take into account, first of all, *that which is* and its relation to human life. The nihilistic incapacity to say yes instead of no comes from the incapacity to recognize the female principle at the source of being.

The Tantrika, on the other hand, teach that pleasure, vision, and ecstasy should be cultivated and used by all—not suppressed and damned, not hoarded for the corrupt thrills of the few. Tantra proclaims that all things—the crimes and pains as well as the joys and benefits of life—are the active play of the female creative principle: the Goddess of many forms, sexually penetrated by an invisible, indescribable, seminal male. The Tantrika use prolonged acts of ecstatic meditation in sexual union with a partner. They use liturgies, mantras, inner visualizations, yogic postures, and manipulation of the joined female and male energies. The Goddess is perceived as the energy which makes real the outer and inner worlds, the complementary images of object and subject, spinning them out from the still center—as a spider spins a web from her body—into the open space of being.

In Tantric thought, creation is time—the Goddess in her function as "measurer" (*maya: mens:* moon) weaves the substance of events in time, just as she does in space. Time is the field of the Goddess's play. While manifest in form, she is also potential energy, the yet-unrealized. In this sense she is void—the Void—because what contains everything specific cannot be in itself specific. Yet this voidness is not the Brahmanic abstraction of being which is presented as somehow superior to immersion in life. Brahmans preach that the psychic-lunar body is to be transcended; that all formal consciousness is to be transcended and despised. Such an attitude carried about by real men in the position of dominating real life can be devastating. The void of the Goddess is the real energy potential of the as-yet unmanifest; and it is the ultimate relation or union of all manifest energies. Individual consciousness is released from the prison of dualism through realizing that she/he is one with both principles.

Tantra exists in a patriarchal world, however, and has for a long time; and so its doctrine has been accordingly modified. Today it believes that the ultimate still center is, not the yoni of the female, but the self-originated lingam (male seed). Tantrika say that the lingam conveys into all Kali's play-activity the seed of being hidden beyond and within. Originally, though, there is no doubt that the still center of the universal spiral is as it always was the female yoni, the womb-tomb of the Great Mother. And there is no doubt that the origin of energy is the spiraling *kundalini* serpent who lives in the human spine, the sexual energy that powers flight.

Many Westerners have turned to India for the study of Tantra and the *kundalini* power, because here the ancient techniques have been most completely retained. Was there ever anything like them in the West, indigenous to Western people? The answer is yes, because the same Goddess ruled all. The Dravidian Danu was the Irish Danu. The Indian Kali was the Irish Cailleach, both portrayed sitting in the Lotus Posture. As William Irwin Thompson points out:

> the religion of the Upper Paleolithic is not simply the parochial superstitions of one tribe; it is the first universal religion, and its universality as an iconic system based upon the mysteries of menstruation and a lunar calendar cuts across cultures with different languages or tool kits. It is a universal religion whose range of influence even in the Upper Perigordian extends from Spain to Central Asia. By the time of the Neolithic, it had diffused throughout Africa and Eurasia.[4]

And by the Middle Neolithic at least it had everywhere developed techniques of ecstasy and illumination. Some of these techniques, especially related to shamanism and drug use, were kept alive by European paganism

Goddess of the Mound/ Magical Fairy Queen, Sjöö, 1980

and witchcraft. Others can be reconstructed and revived through study of *kundalini* yoga and Tantric techniques, while remaining dubious of the patriarchal doctrines that have accumulated around them. The ancient holism must be reconstructed in our own minds, by our own minds, helped by historic knowledge and imagination.

Remember the Snake-and-Bird Goddess worshiped as early as 6500 B.C. throughout southeastern and central Europe. To the later patriarchal Indo-European pastoral nomads, the earth was the receptive Great Mother corresponding to their active Sky Father. But the Neolithic agricultural-matriarchal people had created the original maternal image composed of both water and air divinities as well as earth: the Snake-and-Bird Goddess, a three-part totality. Who was she?

She was the three-part human brain. She was the world tree, the world spine, with the snake and the bird as the lower and upper symbols;

Mexican Winged Goddess. Terracotta from preColumbian Colima Culture

where they appear it is understood that the arousal of *kundalini* up the spine, through the *chakras*, connects them. In Mediterranean and European imagery, the divine child, or green child, was the reborn energy created in this mystic-magical process. This reborn energy was imaged as the cub of the Wild Bear Mother, the baby snake or baby bird of the Snake-and-Bird Goddess. The green child (reborn psychic energy) was not reared by the Earth Mother, but by the Wild Goddess Artemis. European paganism, like all others, always understood natural wildness as spiritual energy, the clue to illumination. Religious technique is not meant to tame this energy with moralism, but to channel it with creative understanding, which comes from the human neocortex.

Variations of the Snake-and-Bird Goddess appear everywhere, even in places we might not at first recognize. Their universal similarities are not accidental but the evidence of a universal idea, a universal recognition. In India and China, the world tree is the lotus. In Mexico and Central America, it was a jungle tree topped with the quetzal bird. Quetzalcoatl, the Aztec god of learning and peace, was imaged as a feathered serpent winding about a world tree. "To teach the snake how to rise up the trunk to become a bird or a plumed serpent—a Quetzalcoatl—is how yoga was expressed in ancient Mexico."[5] The Mayan Kulculcan was the same; both gods were Venus, the morning and evening star. In Egypt, in the religion of Isis and Osiris, *kundalini* rising up the spine is symbolized by raising the *djed* pillar of Osiris. As Thompson notes, in Gnosticism also, the mind is called "serpent-formed"; there was a universal recognition, symbolized in all these snake-tree-bird iconographies, that the human mind is not fully activated until the serpent energy is brought up the world tree-spine to flood the brain with illumination. The energy of the reptilian dream brain powers the soaring bird of the neocortex; if it doesn't, the neocortex functions only as an intellectual mechanism. In all these symbols is a genetic memory of evolution, and evidence of the ancient people's world-wide knowledge of yoga techniques. "What is expressed in the lotus, the plumed serpent, or the staff of Osiris is the yogi's knowledge of the 3 brains of man."[6] Except that the techniques were developed by women, devotees of their own processes and of the world's first and universal religion. It is women, remember, whose brains are evolutionarily structured to experience sexual and spiritual illumination as one.

This is what the Snake-and-Bird Goddess meant, symbolized; and the Thracian Maenads and all other legendary schools of priestesses in service to the Goddess were guardians of these original yogic-shamanic techniques. In pagan Scandinavia, shamanism (called *sejd*) was originally practiced by the priestesses of Freya, and they wore magic bird-costumes belonging to her; with these, they "flew" into other realities. And, on the cavern ceiling of the Paleolithic Hall of Hieroglyphs at Pech-Merle, France, are the images of three dancing women—two are headless, one has the stylized head of a bird. She has been called, by art historian Siegfried Giedion, "the earliest known representation of the fusion of a human being with an animal."[7] The consistency and ancientness of these images, of ecstatic dancing and the pulling of the serpentine bio-mystical energies up the human spine to achieve "wings," or illuminated consciousness, argues for an intuitive knowledge of shamanic-yogic techniques among our earliest ancestors. They were the techniques of the religion of the Great Mother.

Thompson describes how these techniques were desecrated by the literalism of male priesthoods in service to secular power.

> In the yoga of Quetzalcoatl, the initiate spoke of the opening of the heart to the light of the sun, and what was meant by this was the opening of the chakras in the subtle body; the Aztec priests . . . took the esoteric words literally, ripping out the victim's physical heart and holding it up to the sun.[8]

Such a grotesque literalist misreading of esoteric spiritual texts is at the heart of fundamentalist fanaticism in all religions, and of all "holy wars." In ancient Mexico the priests conducting mass heart-ripping sacrifices day after day were no longer in the service (needless to say) of individual spiritual illumination. They were trying to keep a giant patriarchal religious-military machine running using buckets of blood as fuel; using the fearful resignation of the people as fuel. Bronze Age priesthoods throughout the Near East, the Mediterranean, and Europe entered upon the same gruesome project. As patriarchal governmental, military, and architectural systems grew into gigantic edifices of stone representing secular power, crazed priests called for blood, sacrifice, castration in the name of the terrifying aspects of the Great Mother. They began to rule by fear alone—their own fears stimulating the fears of the multitudes. In atmospheres of mass fear, mass human sacrifice begins to make a kind of numbing sense. The real fear is stimulated by buildup of secular power, signalized by military power, in the hands of a human elite; people tend to respond to this by propitiating their gods.

Among the European Celtic peoples, the Druid priesthood inherited the magic-shamanic techniques (as well as the alphabet) of the earlier Goddess religion. They organized a spiritual technology that involved transcendent power for themselves alone, and so violated the cosmic law of the Mother, which demands recycling on all levels, including the spiritual. Under threat of Roman invasion and the breakup of their world the Druid priests, like the Aztecs, ended up performing more and more bloody mass sacrifice, with less result.

With the Indo-European infiltration of southern and central Europe circa 4000 B.C., the Snake-and-Bird Goddess begins to disappear. Her triple aspect disappears, her sky aspect disappears, and the Mother is deprived of her ancient bisexual nature. As shamanism and bisexuality always go together, this means the disappearance of the shamanic techniques, or their absorption into the new male-dominance religion as secret power tools of a ruling elite. The Snake-Tree-Bird Goddess, the multidimensional she of water, earth, and air, becomes under the patriarchal Indo-Europeans the monodimensional Ge, flat on her back, passive receptacle of male seed. Earth Mother who never flies. And the magic dies.

During the long millennia of the Upper Paleolithic and the Neolithic, our human ancestors—led by women—developed communal meditation techniques which led to individual knowledge and experience of human psychic powers. With the agricultural buildup of the mid-Neolithic, increasingly complex settlement, and specialization, these techniques and powers became increasingly the secret knowledge of a spiritual elite, a priesthood, just as the Neolithic increase of material abundance gave rise to a ruling secular elite, a palace royalty. This combined royal-priestly elite, armed with the new class of professional warriors, saw clearly how this communal wealth of humanity—the earthly abundance and the spinal-spiritual knowledge—could be appropriated and exploited for the elite's advantage, and toward the profitable enslavement of the masses of people.

The Bronze Age represents this elite cooptation of communal female invention by the male few in power. Royalty, priests, warriors, and other specialists took the life technologies, arts, symbols, yogic-shamanic techniques, and total agricultural wealth developed by the female collective, by thousands of generations of human cooperation in exploration, and absorbed them into the new patriarchal class system, with the king and priest on top, guarded by the professional warriors, who began systematically to visit "the wrath of God" (i.e., the religion of plunder, rape, and conquest) on the masses of newly disinherited and powerless common people—i.e., those who had once lived quite happily together in common.

"War was declared on the human body with the emergence of patriarchal warrior societies in the Bronze Age."[9] War was declared on the human body by declaring war on the female body—on the reproductive bodies of women, on the fertile body of Mother Earth, on the body of knowledge and techniques accumulated by women over the generations. Just as universal legends tell of males banding together to steal fire from the women, who collectively discovered its magic uses; just as Pythagoras stole Maenad trance-knowledge of rhythm and mathematical signs to invent an objective number system used as a "logical" weapon against ancient female holism—just so the Bronze Age patriarchies stole the practical and spiritual inventions of the female sex and the female god, and turned them into power weapons which have been used ever since to make the few rich and the many impoverished. To give males a pathetic illusion of "freedom" via the enslavement of females. To give men the delusion of "mental superiority" via the total historical plundering of the female brain. To speak continuous slogans of "progress" and "civilization" while the entire human race is dragged evolutionarily backward into the dominance-submission systems of the primates.

The magic sexual-spiritual techniques of the Snake-and-Bird Goddess still remain on earth, in traces, even though she is forgotten. Even the coopted Goddess Athena of Classical Greece, though proclaimed "motherless" and "reborn" from the forehead of Zeus the Father, still wore the magic bird wings and the sacred snake coils of ancient matriarchy. Even though we no longer know what they mean.

In *The Time Falling Bodies Take to Light,* Thompson refers to the male horror of returning to the matriarchy, of returning to the female communal order of the past. No matter how bad things get in the "modern world"—and how much worse can they get?—men (and women) are still conditioned by all patriarchal political, religious, economic, and cultural institutions to believe that humanity is much better off now than we ever were in the dark, inchoate, and anonymous (read: female) past. The Christian essayist and novelist C. S. Lewis has defined this "male nightmare" in fastidious words: "You might add that in the hive and in the ant-hill we see fully realized the two things that some of us most dread for our own species—the dominance of the female and the dominance of the collectivity."[10] Forgetting, of course, that that hive makes honey. And that that female collective once made the world.

IV

PATRIARCHAL CULTURE AND RELIGION

Patriarchy, Sjöö, 1973

GOD AS FATHER

If God is the Mother of the Universe, then the Creation is of the same substance as her—it is of her, as the child is of its mother's substance, and this means that the whole Creation is divine, and divinely related.

> We should have imagined life as created in the birth pain of God the Mother, then we would understand that—we would know that—our life's rhythm beats from Her great heart torn with agony of love and birth . . . Then we should understand why we Her children have inherited pain and we would feel that death meant a reunion with Her, a passing back into Her substance . . . the blood of Her blood again . . . Peace of Her Peace.[1]

Human females and males are not equal genetic parents. The female X-chromosome is three to four times longer than the male Y-chromosome; it carries the overwhelming preponderance of critical genetic information unrelated to sex needed to create a human being. Further, while only half the population has a Y-chromosome, all of us—female and male—contain an X. It is our primary genetic bond as a species.[2]

The female egg, even before it mates with a sperm, generates an electrical field that becomes the shaping energy of the embryo as it develops into an independent being. The mother field is both the biological environment and the shaper of form within the environment. These biological facts are also experienced as spiritual facts.

But, when the cult of the male god was established, there must have been difficulty in explaining how *he* could be the giver of life to all creation—since the man, unlike the woman, cannot produce from his body either the child or the food for the child. The whole attitude of humans towards the God had to be altered—violently altered. There could not be that same vital biological and magical link (the I-Thou) between the child and the father, as there is between the child and its mother: two beings evolving in and from the same body, the same rhythms, the same dreams.

From the religious point of view, this means the loss between the human and the divine of direct, continuous physical-emotional-spiritual relationship. Oneness is dualized, the "self" is isolated within, and the rest of the universe, including God, is displaced and objectified without. The evolutionary, protoplasmic connection between the experienced self and the All is broken, and the new relation becomes: I-the Other; or worse: I-It. The father is *not* of the same all-containing, all-infusing, shaping and nourishing substance, and so the relation between humans and the Father God becomes abstract and alienated, distant and moralistic.

The abstract God is inorganic. Equally inorganic, relative to the preceding 300,000 to 500,000 years of communal Stone Age life, was the rigid class system of royal masters served by slave labor that quickly coalesced around the ruling patriarchal elite. The few can rule the many only with the help of punitive religious ideologies, by means of which the unjust advantage of the few and the raw exploitation of the many are somehow justified by "God," by a class theology.

And so this new male God must be enforced, on the people, by the punitive and guilt-projecting ideologies of a privileged priesthood. In their writings and doctrines, flooding the Bronze Age, creation now comes to be seen as evil—the creator is above and apart from his creation, and while he is perfect, the world is flawed. And so the idea of Original Sin can be conceived, for the first time, to rationalize the unnatural new relation between the human soul and the aloof God. This lays the basis for all further alienated relationships—between people and God, between people and people, between people and the natural world. Between rulers and ruled. For now the primary relation is not that we share the same divine substance, but that we share the same material corruption. And the entire priesthood exists to "redeem" us from the "sin" of being born from the Mother. And to rationalize class disparity by preaching that the new class system is "God's design," his method for creating "civilized order" out of the "corruption and chaos" of human flesh. For an unjust system to work for any prolonged period of time, it is necessary that the masses of people believe they deserve the injustice.

This is why the Father's way—in all patriarchal world religions—is absolute. So pure, it is separable from us and from the world, and perceptible only through largely verbal abstractions that attempt to describe His emanations or manifested attributes. He is "perfect," "good," "disembodied Spirit" (the Logos). He is seen as purely "spiritual generation," totally freed from matter (because the priests must insist he is "free" from the Great Mother), and having no participation in material processes. It then becomes difficult to explain the existence of death, illness, pain, and decay—since they have nothing to do with "God"! Rather, it becomes too easy to explain them: Everything is blamed on the corrupt Mother and her human children—and her heathenish lover, the Devil. It now becomes possible for the Hindu mystic to confuse the Goddess-as-Time (*maya*) with evil on the one hand, and with the whole natural universe on the other—

so making all creation the product of evil, while "God" remains "uninvolved."

Under ontological dualism, the mind becomes more and more confused by paradox, and to work their way out of their confusion patriarchal theologians seek abstract escape from the natural world, defined as a seductive trap. The world of *maya* is called mere illusion, a veil hiding true being, and so the Hindu, the Buddhist, and the Christian seek liberation from nature in search of a state of consciousness bereft of all sense-experience (*nirvana*, or angelic heaven). It was to correct this amaterial floatiness, in fact, that Zen developed, out of ancient Taoism, to reinsist on the reality of the real. Alan Watts, in *Nature, Man and Woman*, describes the ancient female way of fusing spirit and matter in noncoercive union: a way of flowing along with events, while at the same time cooperatively molding them. It is the way of the dance, and the unfolding of plant, animal, and mineral forms: the desire of energy to form itself, according to its own rhythms. At some historic point, in an aggressive act of self-definition, the male mind interpreted this energy, this organic Will, as *Other*, and mentally separated himself from it. It became "Maya," "illusion," "evil," "mere matter," "inferior object." Denying and fighting it, man tries to artificially or ideologically impose his own contrary ego-will; in the process he "destroys nature," and thereby—for he too is nature—himself.[3]

And Taoism says:

> *Tao*—there is a thing confusedly formed, born before heaven and earth. Silent and void, it stands alone and does not change, goes round and does not weary. It is capable of being the Mother of the world. I know not its name, so I style it "the *way*." I give it the makeshift name of "the Great." Being Great, it is further described as receding, receding it is described as far away, being far away, it is . . . turning back . . . Tao is that from which one cannot for a single minute depart. That from which one may depart is not Tao.[4]

As the Father God is seen as entirely good, light, and static, like the sun at noon, the Hebrews and Christians had to invent the Devil. In the Bible, the Old Testament Hebrews refer to Satan, which means "enemy"—any enemy of the Hebrews or the Hebrew God was "satanic." Early Christians, who were mostly Hebrew and inheritors of the Hebrew tradition, expanded on this quasipolitical definition of embodied evil until the Devil became the source of all things called evil, of decay, darkness, illness, pain, and death. The Jewish Essenes, who were evolving Christian concepts a hundred years at least before the reputed birth of Christ, also took in many Persian-Zoroastrian concepts of good-versus-evil as the cosmic battle between light and dark: between "the children of light" and "the children of darkness." And so an extremely dualistic good/light versus evil/dark ontology was incorporated as the rational framework of Christianity, with an aloof cloud-dwelling God representing all that is good and light, while a very busy, world-hugging Devil represents all the bad, dark stuff. Once Christians had invented this monster, they became totally obsessed with this invention of theirs—fanatically obsessed, since "the Devil is the curse of those who have abandoned the Goddess," and fanaticism is a mental curse. So now the Devil is projected on half the world, as "the Other," by the crazy half that considers itself "good." Islam inherited the same biblical tendency toward dualism and Devil-projection, and has historically elaborated on it also. Under these religious systems, half of life is seen as the enemy of life, and is no longer experienced as an inherent and organic part of the life process. In patriarchy, the *mater* character of the symbol *materia* is devalued. Matter is no longer revered as the foundation substance of the world of growth and experience. Matter is no longer intuited as an evolutionary phenomenon, as a form of spirit-energy, as the potentia of consciousness. Matter is now the stupid dark female, despised as something of inferior value in contrast with the male ideal. In Muslim and Christian doctrine, matter has become inert, wholly negative, demonized, and hostile to spirit. It is the female world, as opposed to the divine spirit heaven that males are born to inherit.

With the Industrial Revolution, however, and the rise of science as the dominant patriarchal religion or mind technology, an ironic crossover occurred. Without canceling out the earlier negative associations, materialism becomes the dominant and manly ideology, while spirituality is consigned to an increasingly ethereal, irrelevant, and peripheral sphere of being: the afterworld, or "feminine vapors." But still, matter is viewed as dumb and inert; materialism does not glory in matter, but in the male's ability to manipulate it. The new materialism is machine-worship, and product-worship, not the vital and ecstatic celebration of spirit-matter that characterized the Goddess religion. The current "thrust" of materialism is to escape the earth's orbit, to flee the knowledge and the problems of our messy, bloody, hungry, and waste-producing bodily origins—to dwell on wholly sterile and manmade stations (stasis, static) in space, where the astronaut, the modern priest of the techno-phallic religion, realizes his ancient dream: to utterly escape the earthly processes the rest of us remain wallowing in.

In the patriarchal heaven of the Hebrew cabala, the world tree lost its paradox. It began to be pictured as one-sided: with its roots above, in the sky only. The earth-side of the process—of life, of illumination—is utterly negated. Not there. Interestingly enough, according to Mircea Eliade in his study of shamanism, modern-day male shamans worldwide rarely undertake the journey to the underworld common in old times. They have come to fear and avoid the realms of the living dead, of magic darkness and necessary worms as the domain of the Dark Mother. They eschew it; instead they concentrate on the journey to the sky, which involves considerable prestige for the shaman, being a trip into the home of the celestial patriarch, the Big Clean Father in the Sky.[5] Anti-earth, anti-natural symbolism is distinctly related to religious dualism. From it arises a purely abstract worldview, as in mathematics, in which the "manmade" symbols are not comprehended as part of a larger reality; they are comprehended as *the* reality.

Dualism is a spectator sport. No one wholly involved in an ongoing life process can conceive of it in dualistic terms, or objectify the experience. Dualism first arose among men who were functional spectators of the life created by women. These were the male priesthoods—men who did not give birth to creatures who would experience both ecstasy and pain, and who would die—men whose whole self-appointed task was the uninvolved organization and manipulation of life into abstract and systematic terms, for the sake of secular control and power. Male priesthoods are characterized by their dogmatic attempts to control a process they do not themselves, as spectators, participate in.

Such mechanical, anti-natural, remote-control concepts of life have choked the springs of the living waters. The patriarchal cabalistic world tree with roots exclusively in the sky is wholly cerebral and unreal. To erase the earth side of the spiritual equation is to deenergize the equation. To deny the earth roots of the world tree is to deny the serpent roots of the spine. And indeed the biblical Hebrews set themselves against the serpent; in so doing, they were deliberately opposing the *kundalini* powers of the spine, the sex *chakra* and the ancient brain stem. And so the Father God becomes both anti-sexual and anti-evolutionary. This is our grotesque situation today. *An anti-sexual God is now worshiped as the creator of life.* (And wherever you find a puritanical God you find also a pornographic God, for the human mind *will* strive for balance.) And an anti-evolutionary God is now worshiped as the goal of human progress—to be achieved not by organic growth of consciousness, but by worship of "developmental" machine programs and technologies.

The immortality promised by the Moon Goddess was not a state of perfection or stasis in eternal light. She offers an ever-renewed life like the moon's own, in which diminishing and dying are as essential to spirit growth as birth and becoming. Her "redemption" is not from "sin" and matter, but from mental traps that block the self from its source. It is union of the opposites within the psyche which brings release from the final power of death, which allows consciousness to pulsate from one dimension to another in the cosmic field. This is the only "redeeming" experience: To be lived by an inner presence—the creator behind the ego.

Indwelling Goddess at Glastonbury Tor, Sjöö, 1988, Alice Walker Collection

Lionheaded Solar Sekhmet & Callanish Stones, Sjöö, 1990

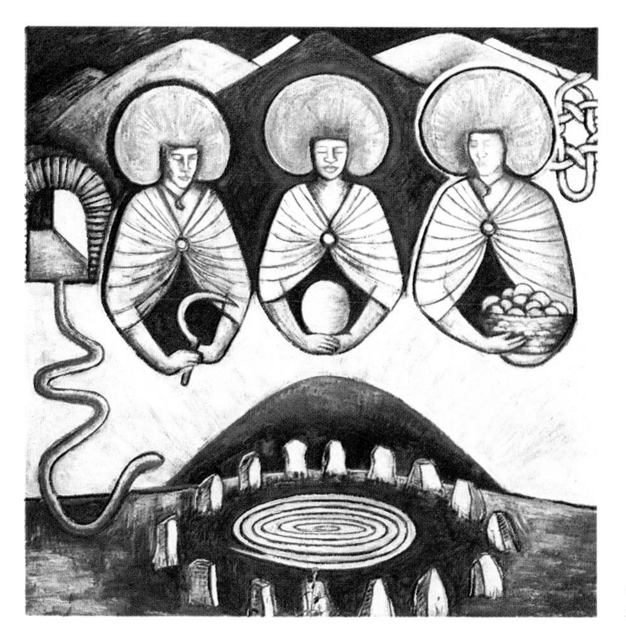

The Matronae—The Mothers, Sjöö, 1983, Alice Walker Collection

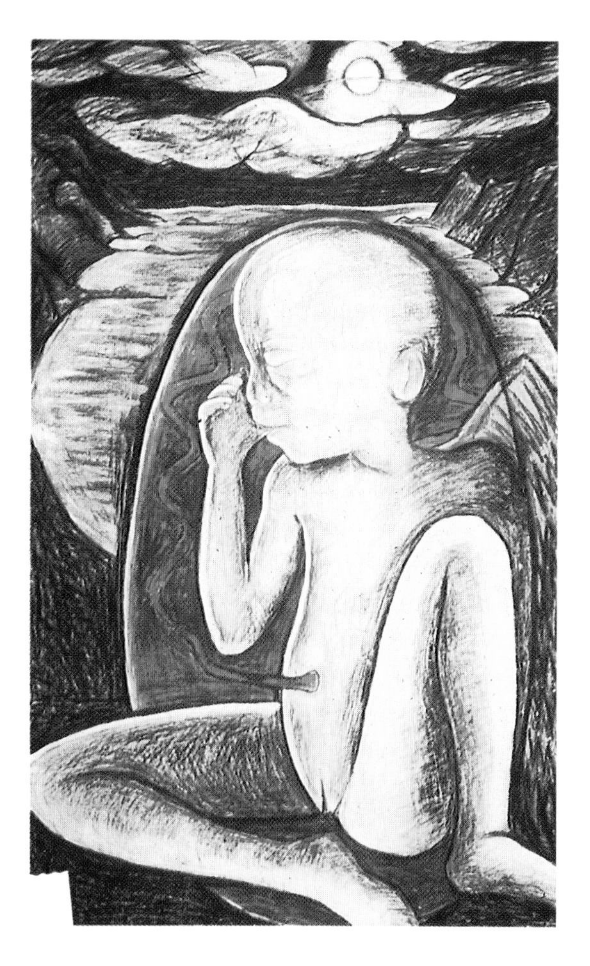

Lunar Child of the Sea, Sjöö, 1981

Bride/Brigid with Her Well, Tree & Stone, Sjöö, 1988

Vision of the Otherworld, Sjöö, 1987

Universal Yew Tree Mother, Sjöö, 1985

Rock Giantess/Gaia, Sjöö, 1984

My Sons in the Spiritworld/Spiderwoman, Sjöö, 1989

Earth Is Our Mother (with Nerthus—Nordic Mother Goddess), Sjöö, 1984

THE OLYMPIAN MALE

If Father God religions are reactionary and anti-evolutionary, the reason is simple: They are built in reaction to the original Goddess religion, which dominated human thought and feeling for at least 300,000 years. By contrast, God has been conceptualized as a complete male for only about three to four thousand years. For this reason, patriarchal religions must begin by denying evolution; for, if that long stretch of human growth time was acknowledged, it would have to be credited as the evolutionarily creative time of the Great Mother. To avoid this the Father Gods just somehow appear, as it were, by spontaneous generation, and human life just suddenly appears with them, fully formed, sprung arbitrarily from the forehead of the He-God, sometime around 2000 B.C.

The characteristic of an Olympian god (patriarchal) in contrast to a mystery god (matriarchal) is that the Olympian's form is rigidly fixed, and always human. He has lost his animal forms and his magical ability to transmute from one energy shape to another. He has lost his alchemical properties. The Olympian is idealized, rationalized, aloof, deathless—and so ultimately he seems too *geometric* to move us. All poets have had trouble making him interesting, because he isn't. The Olympian does not evolve, he apotheosizes—to the blare of trumpets. This means he is not born from woman, or earth, or matter, but from his own absolute will. He represents a static perfection, in human form, incapable of transformation or ecstatic change; as a God, he is an intellectual concept. And so the energy exchange between all creatures and their magically shape-changing deity is lost. The mystical-evolutionary power connection is broken: God becomes mere idea, and his world mere mechanism.[1]

In earlier Greek myth, the full sun was still Dionysian, though described as phallic fecundator of the receptive earth. The legend and drama of the Greek Dionysus raised fatherhood over maternity, but still yearned ecstatically for the Mother—as befit his Cretan origins. But in Classic Greek mythology, Apollo—the Platonic intellectual, "ideal" homosexual lover—was transformed into the static and immutable "light," which is no longer cyclically rising and setting, coming into being and passing away;

it exists absolutely, never changing. Apollo and Athene, "redesigned" as the motherless daughter of Zeus, together usher in the new law of "paternity," Apollo declaring that the Mother is no parent of that which is called her child. She is only "nurse" of the new-planted seed that grows within her, while the real parent is "He who mounts." Apollo "freed" himself from the bond with women, and so he is called "immune from the night of death," which still and always confronts the all-too-human, phallic, and ecstatic Dionysus.[2] Apollo becomes "the Spirit that rises above all change . . . away from the earlier subordination of Spirit to physical laws and the dependence of human development on cosmic powers." Even Pallas Athene, who still retains traces of the Cretan and Libyan Great Mother, as a remodeled Greek goddess proclaims her purely Olympian existence "free from all material desire and free from labor-pains." As she boasts, she recognizes no woman, but only her father, Zeus. Thus was the gestalt of the new patriarchy expressed by Greek male poets and dramatists. Athene's freedom from "labor-pains" not only means that she refuses childbirth; the Olympians were gods of the newly established ruling elite, which did no communal work but was serviced by slave labor.

The social structure represented by the Greek Olympians was patrilinear and class-hierarchic; thus it lifted itself above the age-old laws of biology and evolution, to base itself on conceptual property-power. But, once the cult of the mother was overthrown, the cult of the infant Zeus needed a new rationalization; for a baby is a divine attribute of a divine mother, not a father. And so we have the ludicrous spectacle of the Olympian God trying to make himself into the mother: "Enter this my male womb." Greek rebirth ceremonies thereafter occurred through the father. They were correspondingly more and more connected with urban temples and social-hierarchic political relations, less and less with the seasonal blood-renewal of crops and herds.

The Greek Olympians were a worldly ruling elite rationalized into deities. They were the gods of the urban upper classes—just as Christianity in Europe was originally, and for many centuries, the court religion of the colonizing Roman invaders and the native aristocracy that rose up through cooperation with them. But such an abstract Father God and his nonmagical rites did not appeal to the common sense of the common people. The peasants who worked the land in ancient Greece, just like the later European peasantry, knew very well from daily experience where life came from and where it went. The Greek common people, in town and country, continued to worship the Mother Goddess and take part in the mystery rites of Dionysus, of Demeter and Persephone, of Artemis the Moon. The commoners of later Rome worshiped at shrines of Diana, and the European pagans (Latin *pagani:* "peasants, of the land") continued well into the seventeenth century to celebrate the rites of the Great Mother, of the wiccan, of Diana (Bride, Danu) with her many names and her brother the Goat God, Dionysus-Lucifer, the Horned One.

But the signature of the new Olympian male was that he represented, not the peasants on land, not the masses of people, but the ruling elite—who had the secular power to back him up. Where did this power come from? The triumph of patriarchy in the Bronze Age corresponded with the development of heavy metals, and their connection with professional warfare.

Metallurgy, when it first appeared, was a highly ritualized and sacred art under guardianship of the Goddess, with strong taboos attached to it. Metals were light—gold, silver, tin, copper—and were mostly shaped into jewelry, ornaments, ceremonial vessels. Undoubtedly, the mystery-transformation of running hot metals into ornaments and tools, using fire, molds, and ovens, was first developed by women incidentally to their experimentation with pottery. Once developed into a distinct art, mining and smelting seem to have been the special tasks of men who lived apart, under religious restriction or taboo. The only male figures found on Cretan seals were tiny bodies of smiths, scratched beside the larger figure of the Goddess. Sacred metallurgy served the Neolithic Goddess and the people wisely, but in the Bronze Age the ritual controls were broken; metallurgy passed into the male sphere entirely, becoming a secular industry (or a religious industry in service to the God of War). This opened the earth up for the first time to violent exploitation, including struggles between male groups for control over the earth's ores.

Some evidence suggests, as John G. Jackson wrote, that iron-smelting began in central Africa.[3] According to Merlin Stone, the process of mining and smelting iron ore was discovered by the Aryan Hittites, circa 2500 B.C. We don't know. The significant fact is that, compared with the copper, gold, and bronze of the Goddess cultures, iron was a much stronger and more abundant metal; in particular it provided more efficient, heavier weapons. The Aryan people kept their iron-smelting process secret for many centuries, as on it depended their technological supremacy and sole power over the more culturally and practically developed matriarchal peoples. The Indo-Europeans, for example, had no written language of their own, but adopted the script of the peoples they conquered. In this adapted script, the sign for "man," "iron," and "Mars"—the War God—are the same. Further, the Goddess people used the wheeled wagon (their invention), pulled by a donkey, for daily use and trade; the Anatolian Hittites and later Near Eastern warrior-people were the first to harness up horses, turning wagons into war chariots.[4]

T. C. Lethbridge, in *Witches,* speculates that it was the development of metallurgy as a male art that brought the end of the Mother Goddess cultures. Larger and heavier metal weapons radically changed men's experience and techniques of war, giving advantage to the emerging "professional warrior"—and changing warfare from a defensive tribal skill to a whole new game stressing aggressive offense, and the spoils of victory.[5] The new weapons mounted on wheeled wagons also allowed war to be carried on much farther from home; war became a specialty of roaming mercenaries, while the women remained at the home village, maintaining the culture. (In contrast, among Neolithic agricultural people, as among African tribal gardeners until quite recently, both women and men carried spears and other weapons with them into the fields, and if attacked, both sexes fought defensively.) So, *iron*ically, matriarchal culture was overthrown with the help of the new heavy artillery mined and stolen from Mother Earth. Perhaps this is why, even today, witches must not touch iron. Metal mining and smelting remain the most male-dominated of all professions, and access to ores remains a major criterion of male power states.

So long as Stone Age hunting was a major survival occupation, it kept men busy on the peripheries of the women's camp. Hunting kept men away from the home base sometimes for long periods, but it also provided a ritual focus in the cave religion. Hunting gave men a spiritual and group identity within the worship of the Great Mother. But women's invention of agriculture and domestication of animals, together with settled village life, created a steady food abundance that rendered hunting more or less obsolete. There was suddenly a large male labor force hanging around, needing occupation. Wall paintings found at Çatal Hüyük, in the most recent levels (5400 B.C.), show men engaged in ritual hunting, dressed in leopard skins and accompanied by musicians; as Thompson notes, these paintings aren't of real Stone Age hunting but of deer-baiting and bull-baiting, and are commemorations, or images of nostalgia for "the good old days of the hunt."[6] Hunting was no longer necessary, and men could no longer find purpose and spiritual identity through it. Men's work around the settled village was at first unskilled labor, helping the women. They cleared away brush, prepared the ground for cultivation by women—this is still so in Africa, where farming remains traditionally women's work; it is so among some Native Americans, Indonesians, and many others. Men felled trees and prepared timber for construction. Only later did they begin to take over the work of construction design itself, as they also slowly began to take over the care and breeding of livestock.

With the buildup of stored grain, with ever-increasing Neolithic abundance in settled village sites, appeared a new male profession: grain guardian. Organized marauding began in the later Neolithic, and as stored wealth increased, and marauding increased, the males guarding grain supplies organized more and more into a kind of standing army. Stock breeding also led to the discovery of paternity—of the male's role in breeding, and the importance of genetic selection. Originally, as Thompson points out, the domestication of animals was a "religious act. . . . an emotional act in which the animals were first domesticated because of their symbolic connection to the great universal religions" of the Goddess.[7] As men took over stock breeding, the cattle herds took on a secular aspect: They became symbols of male wealth, power, and potency. (It cannot be an accident that the word "capitalism" comes from the Latin *caput*, or *capitellem*, originally referring to a head of cattle.)

This new, probably awesome male sense of paternity was the seed that was to grow into the Father God. But the actual growth of male power derived from men's increasing takeover—and what can only be called industrialization—of women's ancient crafts and tasks. Unlike the women, the men did not have to start from scratch. Millennia of women's work laid the groundwork for the "male revolution" of the Bronze Age. In a relatively brief time men began not only to learn the skills and crafts of the women, but to make improvements in tools and methods, always in the direction of mass-production. Men invented the plough, men invented the potter's wheel. It is very likely that women had *not* made these "improvements" because they were reluctant to break their direct connections with their materials. Craft was, like sacred ritual, a matter of rhythm and movement, of tactility. Women worked earth with hands and digging sticks, women worked clay with their hands, shaping the clay spirals for bowls on their breasts. The more "advanced" tools and techniques developed by men interposed themselves between the body of the worker and the body of the mother substance; they objectified the task and secularized it—which women wouldn't do. All Bronze Age male "improvements" on women's ancient crafts were in the direction of speed-up, mass-production, quantity over quality, the factory and the assembly line.

For a time, as men shared tasks but did not take them over, there must have been a truly egalitarian society, with women and men working side by side in the same jobs, furthering together the abundance of food, textiles, building materials—consolidating the first towns and small cities with their surplus production. But this was not to last. One of the strangest, and bitterest, facts of later male domination over women is that the major tools and industries of this domination were the inventions of women, and first given to the men by the women. The ceramic, textile, and clothing industries, the medical and healing professions, farming and the food industry, animal domestication, writing and calendric science, numbers and chemistry, religious symbol and ritual—all women's creations—were taken over by men and then closed to women's entry, except under slave conditions. In the same way men took over women's menstruation and childbirth rites, and then kept women away from these rites under taboo of death. We are told that men created "civilization." But it was women's achievements in the areas of craft, cultural, and intellectual production that made that "civilization" possible. It was women who were biologically endowed to create human society, language, and culture. And then it was men, who were socially endowed by women, who turned around and declared women unfit for culture, using women's biological endowment as a justification for our oppression.

Along with the pottery wheel and the plough, men in the Neolithic did invent one more thing: professional warfare.

The more insignificant male activities were, and the more women's

> activities produced wealth, the more some men were attracted to steal and other men attracted to defend the new acquisitions. The men discovered a new way to get together and warfare was born. . . . [8]

This was not, as Thompson describes it, "the stylized *agons* of hunters over grievances," which ended in no or few deaths. This was "institutionalized violence," this was *WAR:* the legal art of mass slaughter. In warfare, men refound the group and spiritual identity they had lost with the loss of the Stone Age hunting life. A new god, the male War God, could be erected to numinize it, to make it seem "holy." But no one could deny warfare had its very secular, practical side: it was the primary builder of male wealth, and thence of a ruling elite. Most of all, for the first time, it gave men the power to control women; i.e., professional warfare allowed organized and iron-armed males to destroy the ancient female collectivity.

> The period 6–4000 B.C. is the *Magnus Annus* of the Neolithic Great Goddess. . . . Women had been at the top of traditional, Neolithic society, but with the shift from religious, magical authority to masculine, military power, their influence collapsed and they became private property in the new trading and raiding society. Mesolithic society may have seen the domestication of animals, and Neolithic society may have seen the domestication of plants, but what the age after the Neolithic sees is the domestication of women by men.[9]

The Great Mother of All, in the Bronze Age, was reified into "a mere vessel of Male Seed." Woman, in male eyes, was no longer a powerful creator in her own right, but a piece of property. His new wealth, his new power over life, his new military ability to maim, terrify, and slaughter by the hundreds and thousands gave man a haughty contempt for life; once he had been in awe of life, but now he found how easy it was to push life around, to kill it. Man's new contempt for life extended to woman, of course, since for millennia she had stood as the numinous symbol of life's sacredness, life's holy power. But now *he* had the power, and he found he could also easily invent his own sacredness, by fiat. God became male—a warrior male—in his image.

In early patriarchy, women's ancient community tasks were turned into slave labor. Women produced the surplus products on which men based their secular power and control. In the next stage of economic development these slave tasks became the industrial occupations of the workers, while the ruling men (and their "wives") were exempt from labor. The ruling men reserved for themselves the "manly" occupations of war, hunting, sport, and priestly observances—while "workers" kept the world going. Women's forced labor, and later working-class labor, freed elite males to become lawyers, judges, doctors, artists, priests, and warriors—specialized, privileged occupations that all others are barred from. And whole bodies of law, religious doctrine, and custom are then assembled to forcibly maintain these men in these positions of power. Patriarchal law, often called "the Will of God," is in fact a wholly secular cynical legal system designed purposely to maintain male power through institutional control of female energy. Under patriarchal legal, religious, and economic-social systems, some men dominate others. But all men benefit from their organized domination of the community of women.

Which is no longer a community. Patriarchy breaks up the female collective by forcibly capturing and imprisoning each woman's female energy within the patrilocal family. Within this isolation cell, each woman's creative energy becomes servant energy, directed and owned by men. In the Hindu Code of Manu—typical of all patriarchal family law—the woman must never be free, from birth to death, of subjugation to a male relative. She passes from the guardianship of her father, to that of her husband, and finally to her oldest son. They control her education, her property, the total disposal of her mind and body, in life and in death. The ignobility of this male obsession with control is equalled only by its effectiveness. Under the Code of Manu, the Hindu woman becomes a nonperson. The breaking up of the powerful ancient women's collectives was the only way by which men could have broken women's strength and independence—but still keep a vaguely living body around to do the dirty work in bed and bathroom. What better way to turn the Great Goddess into a sex-serf than by isolating each individual woman, keeping her under total control within the male-dominated and defined family household—where she is never allowed freedom of movement, of thought, of desire—where her body, her mind, her labor, and her children are seen as property, wealth belonging to the man. Where the only thing she can do with her sex-serfdom is pass it on conscientiously to her daughters.

Confucius, circa 600 B.C. in China, advocated the patriarchal totalitarian state. The functional basis of this state was defined as women's "Three Obediences" to father, husband, and sons. In the twentieth century Adolph Hitler in Germany articulated the "Three Spheres of Women: Children, Christian Church, and Kitchen." Codified in these slogans (which were also laws) is a simple fact: Between these two men lay over 2,500 years of patriarchal society built and maintained worldwide entirely by the exploitation of women's biological creation and physical labor. Whatever we see of "male civilization" seems to be built fascistically on women's backs.

The Goddess had been all-powerful, but she was the mother of sons as well as daughters. Sons came from her body, were nourished by her breasts, and it was not her desire that men should be degraded or destroyed. Under matriarchy men were not reduced to mechanical units, to slave labor, or to subhuman objects. She knew that *she* was the parent, and did not have to enforce unnatural religion with unnatural law. "It is I who adorneth the male for the female."[10] Her son was also her lover. His

Celebrating the Goddess on Crete, 2000 B.C.*— Europe, 1973, Serving Men,* Sjöö, 1973

systematic degradation would have degraded her, who desired only free and graceful worshipers. In *no* Goddess religion known were people ever depicted on their knees.

But patriarchy must maintain, by force, an unnatural system. Since the supreme creator is a male, woman must be redefined as "male property," i.e., as "wife." In fact the very idea of a male Creator God carries within itself the necessity for some kind of tightly controlled class-caste society. Because it is only through the creation of life through human mothers, now passive and powerless, that the male God can claim glory for himself. He cannot, he does not go through the dangerous episode of childbirth in his own person. He uses women to do it for him. Then, contrary to the truth, he claims that *he* is the all-mighty creator. The woman, at best, is patronized for her role as "divine housewife."

The sacred sphere of women's daily communal work and ritual is destroyed, as women are isolated individually in men's households and women's industries and labor are exploited to build male empires. With the further destruction of the rites of the Death Goddess, with their prohibition and/or cooptation by the male churches—with moral and legal suppression of the ecstatic ceremonies of soma, pythonic divination, and pagan cults of celebratory rebirth of all things—little remains of the Goddess in patriarchal culture but a "wife" of tamed or nervous sexuality, and utterly desecrated—because isolated—mind.

SUN'S VICTORY OVER THE DARK MOTHER

Sumerian culture can be traced back to circa 5500 B.C. in the alluvial plains of lower Mesopotamia. Sumerians wrote on clay tablets. Archaeologists have proclaimed that "History begins at Sumer" for that reason only—the Sumerians wrote it all down. Their inscribed myths thus qualify as the world's oldest known "literature."[1] What does this Sumerian literature record? As Thompson says, the clay tablets reveal "the remains of a revolution, a shift from the dominant female gods of the Neolithic village to the organizing and controlling male gods of the literate city."[2]

One of these transitional myths gives us the story of a fabulous character, who can fairly be called Enki the Prick. Enki was the Water God, and the Sumerian word for "water" also meant "semen." In a lavish ode to his indistinguishable phallus, Enki virtually floods the Sumerian plains with semen. Enki is a funny guy; he also inseminates all the Sumerian people, including his own daughters and their daughters. The ancient Earth Goddess Ninhursag can't take it any longer: her daughter Utu also is inseminated by the new ebullient All-Father. Ninhursag removes Enki's semen from her daughter and turns it into plants . . . which Enki eats, of course, becoming pregnant with his own semen. He gets very sick. Only by crawling into Ninhursag's vagina, with her help, can he then give birth to eight goddesses, all named for different parts of his body.[3]

This myth is "profoundly ambiguous," as Thompson says—it is also grotesquely funny—because it is recording, in one story, the midstride shift of worldview, from matriarchy to patriarchy, in ancient Sumer. Sumer began as a Goddess-oriented agricultural village; it ended as a "civilization," which grew "not from a city but from a fortress, the fortified granary."[4] Real life changes slowly, but in a myth like "Enki and the World Order," complex changes over time are compressed into a simultaneous image, showing the proud, all-propagating potency and "world-ordering" power of the new male regime still entangled in, and ultimately dependent upon, the wisdom and physical capacity of the old order, the Earth Goddess, to get the job done. The "job," of course, is an impossible one, a mythic delusion: to turn the Father into a Mother. It could only be done,

Sumerian Goddess Ishtar/ Inanna, Queen of Heaven. Terracotta, 2nd millennium B.C.

in Sumer anyway, as a kind of slapstick comedy with Enki as all three stooges.

But he learns. In later stories the Great Goddess Inanna, Queen of Heaven and Mother of 300,000 years of human time, must come humbly to Enki, petitioning him for a place in the new male order—there is nothing for her to do, or be, man has taken over everything. As Enki boasts, "Enki perfected greatly that which is woman's task."[5] Men had indeed coopted all of women's craft and "improved" upon it—and, as Enki demonstrated, he's trying hard to do the same with childbirth and motherhood. As Thompson notes, with increased militarization and urbanization through the new male world came a revealing change in the mythic character of the Goddess; from an all-powerful and open Great Mother, she becomes a seductive and wily Sex Goddess. No doubt this is because men were writing the myths, but the mythic shift also reveals the change real women had to undergo. The Goddess becomes "eroticized" for her life. The new male God is armed and arrogant, and no longer in awe of her reproductive powers or her cultural creations; to survive, she must seduce and lure and petition him.[6] But still, the humbled Inanna in this

Achilles Killing the Amazon Queen Penthesilea; an amphora, black figure painted by Exekias, 530 B.C.

story gets nothing from Enki but an impatient brush-off; he tells her she has lots to do—she can tend sheep, observe his wars, and twist thread.

In the "Epic of Gilgamesh," the hero kills the sacred bull of heaven, Inanna's bull. The bull symbolized earth's fertility, the moon, so many things . . . the horns surmounting the breasts on the walls of Çatal Hüyük, the crescent horn in the uplifted hand of the Venus of Laussel. What does Gilgamesh do with the horns of the sacred bull of heaven? He hangs them up in his room, like a hunting trophy, a decoration for his male clubhouse. In this act, "the old conservative religion of the women is being mocked in a celebration of male ambition." The Gilgamesh Epic dates from 1600 to 2000 B.C. Thompson calls this four-thousand-year-old story "the very foundation of Western literature, for what we are witnessing here is to set the pattern for all Hebrew and Greek literature to come."[7]

This new individuating, mocking, arrogantly alienated ego of Gilgamesh, established in defiance of the Old Religion of the Goddess and the earth, becomes in Western religious and secular history the ego of man. "Mocker of the past, builder of tomorrow," etc.

This effort to displace the female seems to be the archetypal foundation for civilization, for mankind has been at it ever since; whether he is challenging Mother Nature in flying away from her in rockets, or in changing her on earth through genetic engineering, man has not given up in the attempt to take away the mystery of life from the Great Mother and the conservative feminine religion.[8]

There were women who fought the patriarchy. Tribes of Amazons in Syria, Thrace, Macedonia, and Africa defended themselves from invasion, and fought to preserve their matriarchal religion and culture against the onslaughts of the rising Sun God. We know these warrior women through Greek myth mostly—one of their last battles was fought on the Greek mainland, against Greek male soldiers. The Amazons lost, fighting to the death. Memorials to them were set up all over the Greek countryside, marking each place an Amazon had fallen in battle, and their valor, beauty, and strength were long depicted in Greek art. Even the male Sun God warriors praised them as ferocious and fearless fighters.

J. J. Bachofen, in *Myth, Religion and Mother-Right,* declared that the rise of Father-right began with the wars against the Amazon cultures. He also says that after the wars the surviving Amazonian women settled down, built cities, engaged in agriculture.[9] Their nomadic horse-life was over, but they still accomplished great things. From the Nile banks, the shores of the Black Sea, from central Asia to Italy to West Africa, Amazon names and deeds are interwoven with the historical founding of famous cities. Hiera fought at Troy as leader of the Mysian women warrior troops; she goes unmentioned by Homer, in Bachofen's opinion, because she was more beautiful and more interesting than Helen, the "star" of Troy.

Because what we know of Amazons comes down to us as "myth," we have been taught to doubt their actual existence; but myth records the real history of the ancient preliterate world. Its accuracy is proven when real Troys are dug up at the legendary sites of legendary Troys. Ancient legends tell that the wild horse was first tamed and ridden by Amazons of old Libya (which is now Morocco). The Moon Goddess is therefore everywhere connected with the horse, the white mare—this is where the "nightmare" comes from. Moroccan leather was originated by the Amazons, who fashioned it into tall, pliable, dark red boots. Julius Caesar in his historical memoirs speaks respectfully of the Great Queen Semiramis, who ruled Syria and led its Amazon troops into battle. Caesar also notes that Amazons once ruled most of Asia. When Roman troops entered Europe, they were commonly confronted by tribes of both female and male warriors, led by great warrior queens like Boudicca of the Brittains and Vellada of the Gauls. African Amazon warrior-women were still alive and well in nineteenth-century Dahomy, and an elite Amazon corps of five thousand women was instrumental in winning the independence of African Malawi in 1964.[10]

It wasn't Amazon women alone who wanted to retain the ancient matriarchal cultures. There were men, too, with a living Mother Goddess consciousness, who did not voluntarily give up the practice of her ways. Death, rebirth, and ecstasy through her being, experienced in joyful, fearful, and orgiastic rites, are crucial to the psychic balance and health of men as of women. All legends indicate that the reciprocally gynandrous/androgynous nature of female and male relationships in Goddess cultures was split apart by force: the force of heavy patriarchal arms and ideology. Here is a Hebrew myth telling how God the Father separated the originally bisexual twins:

> God found the male Upper Waters and the female Lower Waters locked in a passionate embrace. "Let one of you rise," he ordered, "and the other fall." But they rose together, whereupon God asked, "Why did you rise together?" "We are inseparable," they answered with one voice. "Leave us to our love!" God now stretched out his little finger and tore them apart. The Upper he lifted up high; the Lower he cast down. To punish their defiance, God would have singed them with fire. . . . The divided Waters then voiced their agony of loss by blindly rushing towards each other and flooding the mountain tops. But when the Lower Waters lapped at the very feet of God's throne, he shouted in anger and tramped them [her] underneath his feet.[11]

And so the War God Yahweh came to power.

When the official Genesis of the Hebrew Bible was written, the ancient Goddess was described in negative abstractions: "chaos," "darkness," "the deep" (*Tehom, Tehom-et.*) Tehom, the Mother of All, is biblically defined as mud, the swamp, some mindless beast of matter who must be kept under paranoid patriarchal control and always subject to the Father's logos, or word.

> Tehom (the Abyss, the Dark Night, the Lower Waters) has always since crouched submissively in Her deep abode like a huge beast, sending up springs to those who deserve them, and nourishing the tree roots. Though She thus influences human fate, none may visit Her recesses.[12]

The Goddess-Creatrix that Yahweh displaced was a Goddess of the Moon—and so of fertility and water. Her *fertility* involved more than protoplasmic multiplication; it involved the entire cosmic creation and all of life, as well as psychic rebirth, the energy of the mind, imagination. The women's cultures are portrayed in these myths as a chaotic commingling of the two sexes (of humans, animals, and vegetation in ecstatic spiritual-poetic animism)—which messy commingling delays and obstructs the establishment of patriarchal social *order*. As rain pouring down into the sea delays the appearance of dry land. "Under the ancient rule of Water, such disorder and Chaos prevailed that wise men avoid all mention of it."[13] *Tsk!* So the female and male principles must first be decently separated and "put in their places"—as when the Egyptian Father God Shu lifts the Sky Goddess Nut from her embrace with the Earth God Geb. When the Babylonian Sun Hero Marduk sliced Tiamat in two, he was really parting Her from Apsu, God of the Upper Waters.

Tiamat, the formidable Babylonian Mother Goddess, was the model for the Hebrew Tehom(et). Tiamat was Mother of the Deep who fashioned all things; she displayed herself as night, truth, and justice. Tehom-Maat. (Maat, the Egyptian Goddess of Truth and Justice.) Tiamat gave birth to the gods. Then, in later patriarchal epic, the gods rebel against her, and she is finally conquered by the Sun God Hero Marduk, who had been promised supremacy over the other gods if he did so. He slays her in her form of the great whale-dragon, or cosmic serpent. And she then surrenders her own body as building material for the universe. Note that in the original matriarchal creation myths, the Great Mother always sacrifices her body herself voluntarily, to create the world from her substance. In patriarchal myth the basic idea is maintained, but the Mother Body is not actively but passively surrendered—the Father God world is essentially created through male conquest and an act of matricide.

This is what Elizabeth Gould Davis has to say about Tiamat:

> In Sumerian myth the creator-goddess Tiamat appeared out of the waves of the Erythraean Sea (the Persian Gulf . . .), as a "fish-woman," and taught men the arts of life: "to construct cities, to found temples, to compile laws, in short, instructed them in all things that tend to soften and humanize life. . . . From that time, so universal were [her] instructions that nothing had to be added."[14]

Davis believes Tiamat "may have been a matriarchal Queen of the Thracian-Anatolian remnant of the ancient lost civilization" of Atlantis; that she might have sailed down the Euphrates River from Thrace or Anatolia, perhaps circa 9000 B.C., in "a ship whose figurehead was the mermaid-like creature" of many ancient legends—half-fish and half-woman. Because myth was both a historic record and a psychic-gestalt of universal symbols, the line between historic literalism and mythic-symbolic interpretation is often blurry; and that's what makes archaeological and linguistic evidence important.

Most Near Eastern myths that have come down to us derive from a time when at least part of the matriarch's divine functions had been delegated to her male warrior consort. These myths date from 2500 to 1500 B.C. The solar hero in all cultures corresponds with the establishment of patriarchal order. And order everywhere means the suppression and negation of the Great Mother religion. The Greek Sun God Apollo represents "purification" and renewal through the male: The sun-son bringing light, life, and spring back to the world by killing the python-serpent of the Mother, represented as the dragon of darkness, now; exclusively dark, chaotic, evil.

These are our classic dragon stories. The serpent of chaos is originally and always a woman's body. As the Great Mother of Chaos, of matter still unformed and undifferentiated, she holds the earth like an egg in the pure energy of her coils. She represents the time "before the gods," before the establishment of patriarchal hierarchies and distinctions. As the dragon of matter, the Undivided One older than the individuation of forms, she also signified the common flesh and blood-bond of the people. This is why the snake/dragon everywhere is identified with the indigenous "masters of the ground"—the matrifocal peasantry—who are invaded, conquered, plundered, coopted by the "dragon-slayers" of patriarchal history.

In Indian myth, the Indo-European Sky God Indra comes upon the Goddess Danu and Her Son Vrta, the two Dravidian serpent-creators, or the Great Cow Goddess and her calf. They are described as "undivided (bisexual), unawakened, sunk in deepest sleep, outstretched." Indra hurls his phallic lightning and decapitates them. This murder generates the "act of Creation," since in the Indo-European view the dark, serpentine Danu and Vrta had "withheld the Waters in the mountain-hollows," and so hindered the world from coming into Being. The Indo-European patriarchal world, that is.[15]

Tehom, Tiamat/Apsu, Danu/Vrta were obviously names for the magnetic serpentine spirit of the earth and its underground waters; the bisexual power "who was absolute mistress of all chaos before creation." Her/his sacrifice then enables patriarchal creation—i.e., "law and order"—to appear.

It is the custom in India, before a single stone is laid in the foundation of a sacred building, for the local "astrologer" to determine the exact spot of ground which is situated above the head of "the snake that supports the world." Construction rites begin with an imitation of Indra smiting the serpent Danu/Vrta in her/his lair. A wooden peg is driven into this spot to securely peg down the serpent's head. It is said in the *Rig Veda* II,12,1: "if this Snake should ever shake its head violently, it would shake the world to pieces." So, with patriarchy, it is the death of the world snake that supports male world building. But patriarchy needs the serpent energy, which is the subterranean energy that powers all life. Everyone knows the serpent is not really dead, but repressed; and the paranoid patriarchal obsession with "law and order" is the necessary mechanism of this repression.

This worldwide attack and conquest of the cosmic serpent is called in patriarchal story the "victory over the waters," through which emerged "stable forms" and the "organization of the world." That is, the male political world. The Rock of Jerusalem reached deep into the subterranean waters (Tehom) it was said; the Jerusalem Temple is situated directly above her, its Holy Rock containing "the Mouth of Tehom." Babylon was built above the "Gate of Apsu," the serpent waters before creation, Apsu the other half of Tiamat. Everywhere, this mythic rite of building the holy male city on the conquered body of the Mother-Serpent is enacted as the *origin* of patriarchy. The sun-worshiping pharaohs of later Egypt slay the dragon Apophys, Apollo slays Gaia's Python. The Greek hero Perseus slays the Amazonian Medusa—who is described as three-headed (the Triple Goddess) with snakes writhing from her three heads. St. George slays the dragon in England; even St. Patrick must drive the snake from snakeless Ireland. And in Hebrew Genesis, the serpent is doomed by the War God Yahweh to be forever the enemy of the human race: to be crushed under our heels, and to give back to us only poison. In Christian prophesy, in Revelation 12-21:1, the final extinction of the dragon is promised when a king-messiah kills the watery cosmic snake, and then takes over the world throne unchallenged: "and there was no more sea." This event is prefigured in Psalms 74:13: "Thou breakest the heads of dragons in the waters." The consistency of all these myths is commensurate with their reality.

To the ancients, the cosmic serpent—the spirit of earth and water—was everywhere known as the energy source of life: of healing and oracular powers, fertility and maternal blessing. This energy-spirit, with emerging patriarchy, was redefined as the dangerous enemy, to be reviled, defeated, destroyed. Then it was said by the new holy men that "Chaos has been ordered and the serpent-force has been mastered." And what was to be the new source of world energy? Slave labor, military force, the rule of the fist, threats of punishment and coercion by fire-breathing, guilt mongering male priesthoods, in service to the God of War and Wealth.

In Babylon the combat between the God-Hero Marduk and the great sea dragon Tiamat was ceremonially reenacted every New Year. Marduk's victory was celebrated by the priests as "an end to chaos and darkness." Marduk creates the cosmos (again) from the torn fragments of Tiamat's body, and he creates "man" from the blood of the "demon Kingu"—to whom Tiamat had entrusted the tablets of destiny. "May he continue to conquer Tiamat and shorten Her days!" exclaimed the celebrants. The cosmic combat, the hero's victory, and the new creation were imagined to take place at that same moment every New Year. The "chaos and darkness" conquered by Marduk had clear social-class implications; in Mircea Eliade's words, the slain body of Tiamat symbolized "universal confusion, the abolition of order and hierarchy, 'orgy,' chaos." According to the fourth-century-B.C. historian Berossus of Babylon, where Tiamat prevailed, "the slaves became the masters," and all power of rank was abolished.[16]

Probably the ancient moon rites were still celebrated on the last twelve days surrounding the last moonless nights of the year. These days were sacred to the dark moon, full of oracular power, before the birth of the New Year's new moon. And these last days were described as "precreation Chaos": the laws of time were suspended, Hecate roamed the black countryside, the dead rose up and came to the living in hope of new birth, orgiastic rites were held. Then, with the appearance of the new moon, the recreation of the world magically occurred: New fires were lit, the earth and her cycles were reaffirmed. First-fruit ceremonies took place, and the people sought prevention of sorrows and diseases for the coming year. The god-hero New Year celebrations were simply overlaid on these ancient rites.

In the most ancient times, Goddess shrines were in groves, by sacred wells, in caves, on mountaintops. During the Megalithic, large stone chambers were built over blind springs, and the builders consulted astronomical and earth forces, to understand their ever-changing currents. With the building of huge cities and enormous solar temples, architects were attempting to fix and permanently control the flow of the earth current. In Babylon and Egypt, patriarchy built vast, rigid monuments to the god-kings in urban centers where excess grain and other products extracted from the countryside in taxes were piled up to the greater power and glory of the ruling priesthoods. No longer sensitive to the earth's spiritual energies, these priesthoods were no longer themselves channels of real cosmic and terrestrial power. Instead, they resorted to conscious, deliberate manipulations of human fears—more and more frantic invocations and bloody mass-sacrifices—to no avail. The real spirit was wandering elsewhere. But the *buildings* became more grandiose, imposing, and expensive.

One thing the patriarchal orders of all times and places have in common: huge and square-cut blocks of stone that no longer have spiritual resonance or healing power for the human psyche. The cosmic serpent no longer lives in these stones—these rock metropolises, Iron Age or modern; only secular ambition lives there. The ancients warned that attempts to direct and fix the earth-force for selfish gain are doomed. Earth energies, artificially trapped to serve the special interests of the ruling class of men, create the tension field, the anxiety grid, of modern life. Like a fault-stress in the earth, or a great serpent underground, something seems about to recoil and unleash terrific energy. The spirit will always break loose and take its own path . . . once again.

THE SUN GOD

The sun cult—the worship of the Sun God and an all-male priesthood—was typically established, as in Babylon and Egypt, by the edict of a military dictatorship.

In prepatriarchal Egypt the Goddess Nekhebt, the Vulture, was worshiped in Upper Egypt, and Ua Zit, the Cobra Goddess, in Lower Egypt.[1] Nekhebt was the inventor of agriculture, a great healer and physician, and the bringer of laws and justice. Egypt was strongly matriarchal, and women entered and achieved in all professions. Even in later Egypt women and men studied together in the medical schools, and many famous physicians were women. After the invasion of Egypt by Indo-Europeans circa 3000 B.C., Lower and Upper Egypt were united under a newly instituted kingship, and the Dynastic Era began. The invaders, calling themselves the "Followers of Horus," formed an aristocracy, or master race, that ruled over all Egypt. The word *pharaoh* (*par-o* means simply "great house") was applied to the royal male alone.

Male deities quickly then rose to power over the Egyptian Goddesses. Horus, the "God of Light," was transformed into the official son of the Great Mother Isis. (Isis comes from Au Set, "the throne" and Immortal Queen of Heaven.) Isis incorporated the more ancient Ua Zit, the Great Cobra Goddess who created all existence; she also wore the vulture wings belonging to Nekhebt. Together with her brother and moon-lover Osiris, Isis was worshiped by the common people far into Roman times. Her cult became the most important mystery religion of Rome itself, and Isis with the Horus-child is reflected in the Roman Catholic worship of the Madonna and Child. Isis, like the Great Goddess everywhere, was the "still point of the turning world." Crowned by the lunar disc, she rises from the ocean at night to say: "I am Nature, the Universal Mother. . . . single manifestation of all gods and goddesses am I."

In Bronze Age Egypt the cult of the Sun God Ra was introduced by a privileged male priesthood for their own political and military purposes. The older lunar calendar was changed into a solar calendar through the introduction of five intercalary days. To accommodate this new belief the

Egyptian Goddess Nut as Tree Goddess, with sun disk; bronze vessel, 633–525 B.C.

resurrected Moon God Osiris was reidentified, by the priesthood, with the sun.

The people were now supposed to forget what was written on the gate of the ancient Goddess Neith (Nut): "What there is, what will be, what has been is me. Nobody has uncovered my chiton, the fruit that I bore was the Sun." Instead of being the fruit of the Great Mother-Tree, the male governors of the Egyptian dynasties now pretended to have been created by a Father God. He, Ptah, was supposed to have created the other gods through an act of masturbation. Right on, Ptah.

Ramses II, "the Great," was a Bronze Age pharaoh, probably identical with the pharaoh of the biblical record. Ramses II declared himself "born by the Sun God Ra." During sixty-seven years of fascistic rule, he hammered his superiority into the heads of the people, and built (had built for him) countless temples and palaces stretching from the Nile Delta through Luxor and Karnak to the Sudan. He controlled a victorious army, and troops of cheap workers. His political-religious edifices already had the characteristics of mass-production. And at the age of eight he "owned" a harem of women who subsequently bore him one hundred children. Moses, the founder of the Jewish-Christian patriarchy, received his education and

Egyptian Goddess Maat, with Osiris, guarding sacred lintel. Roman Egyptian period

moral conceptions at the palace of this Ramses and his predecessor, circa 1300 B.C.

Ra—the sun—was believed to fight daily the serpent of darkness, known as Zet (later Apophis). Zet was originally the ancient Cobra Goddess Ua Zit of matriarchal predynastic Egypt. It was officially declared that "law and order" were possible only so long as the Cobra Goddess was kept under the direct control of the pharaoh and his priests. In this way, they were "saving the people" from the dark serpent, the Dark Mother. But just as attributes of the Snake-and-Bird Goddess Neith were retained in the Classic Greek Athene, so attributes of the ancient Cobra-and-Vulture Goddess Ua Zit-Nekhebt were retained in Isis. She wore a cobra on her forehead, with cow horns flanked by feathers. Hat-hor, also, continued to be worshiped by the people as the Great Cow Goddess. Maat, the ancient mud-matter-mother goddess who symbolized the order of the universe, now became known as the eye of Horus, that is, the eye of the sun, of Ptah and of Ra. The Egyptian word for "eye" was *uzait* (very like Ua-Zit), and Maat was the embodiment of the primordial Uraeus cobra. To her was assigned ultimate wisdom and danger, rebellion and "chaos," and she was allowed to retain these qualities so long as she was firmly contained within a male Godhead (his "eye"), and magically guarded by the king. In other words, Maat embodied the "dangerous" elements of the ancient classless culture of the native Egyptians, who worshiped the ecstatic Goddess and her energy—they had constantly to be held in check by political-military force and priestly dogma.

All the religious, spiritual, and cultural values that had been symbolized by the moon of Isis were now strategically transferred by the priests to the sun cult, coming under male control. The surviving moon religion in Egypt remained in the hands of women, but it was the Sun God and his stolen powers that publicly ruled.

This was the pattern. The sun hero who vanquishes "evil" in the form of monster serpents or dragons was originally a moon hero, like Hercules, and as such the son/lover of the Great Goddess. In moon mysteries, he overcame death in ecstatic self-transcendence, experiencing luminous oneness with her. But when he becomes the patriarchal sun hero, he kills the Mother Goddess in Her dark underworld-serpent aspect. Instead of transcending his ego, he "transcends" the whole world, cosmic union giving way to worldly conquest and destruction of the sources of life. He destroys life in the name of "conquering death." Jungian psychoanalysts interpret this process as the liberation of the individual ego—the male ego, of course—from the "forces of darkness" and "the unconscious," i.e., the mother. The hero's action in rescuing the "maiden" from the dragon symbolizes, Jung says, the freeing of his own anima—his essential self—from the "devouring" aspect of the mother. This almost suggests that woman, in herself, is merely a projection of the male anima; and indeed that's what women are in most psychoanalytical systems. Jungians have never shown an awareness of the politics of mythology—or of mythology as the history of the preliterate real world. The sun hero is doing more than "liberating his ego" from the mother; he is "liberating" his being from responsibility to the being of the world. He liberates himself by arrogantly and recklessly destroying the interconnecting webwork of which he is a part—and then the "tragic hero" is surprised when he looks around himself, and sees nothing but wasteland and death.

Alexander the Great slew no dragons; instead he slashed through the Gordian knot with his sword. Knots symbolize the Goddess, as great weaver of the life-web. Knots are sacred to witches and used in magic spells. Rhyme and meter, in fact, and other poetic, chanting devices are linguistic knots used to bind up, to concentrate the magic energies of language. The necktie was originally a magic device, a spell-knot against throat colds. By impatiently and arrogantly cutting the magic knot with his sword, instead of going into a trance, or waiting until he *knew* how to untie it, Alexander was historically signaling the triumph of patriarchy. The sun hero slashes through the timeless web of interconnecting life energy and lays it all waste, in order to enjoy swift satisfaction, fame, and conquest. Conquest of what? Of the fact that life is paradox: (1) the fact that psychic powers are deeply hidden and dangerous, needing to be guarded by wisdom (the serpent guarding the treasure); and (2) the fact that their release can cause destruction as easily as integration. The sun hero wars against the double-edged reality of the cosmic process, slashing through paradox, denying cyclic recurrence and the serpent wisdom that comes with it, refusing to believe that his ego must die before the true magic power can be safely revealed. From Marduk to Superman, he is a little boy warring against the subtle (serpentine) nature of life: demanding it be made neat, simplistic, logical, unambiguous, designed as a flat stage for his triumph—and nothing more.

In *The Second Sex* Simone de Beauvoir catalogs male hatred and fear of woman because she presents him with the ambiguities of life and death; his classic response to these ambiguities is denial and conquest.

> . . . the organ [the man] penetrates is the same as that which gives birth to the child. . . . man finds it repugnant to come upon the dreaded essence of the mother in the woman he possesses; he is determined to dissociate these two aspects of femininity . . . [and] tends to keep away from woman . . . during her menses, when she is pregnant, in lactation. . . . The old woman, the homely woman . . . arouse hatred mingled with fear. In them reappears the disquieting figure of the Mother, when once the charms of the Wife have vanished. . . . man wishes simultaneously that woman be animal and plant and that she be hidden behind an artificial front. . . . He is delighted with his domination of her. . . . [2]

Born from woman's flesh, entering her womb in love, entombed in a female earth in death, man's horror of his "own carnal contingence" is projected on women and on the world in "heroic" acts of slashing denial and domination. Patriarchal religions and political states are the institutions of this dominion, and warfare is its tool, its mechanism. Among the Bronze Age warrior tribes spreading over the Neolithic earth, the acquisition of wealth through raids and conquest became a powerful factor in dispossessing women (matriarchal cultures) and keeping them dispossessed. The loot from raids and battle belonged to the victorious men, as did the land conquered by sword and broad-ax. Women were an important part of the victor's loot. The Bronze Age warrior's world was neatly divided between the victorious male and his spoils, and everything—women, children, animals, land, and resources—all the rest of life constituted the spoils.

This is why patriarchy's inaugural epics and myths, from the Mahabharata of Vedic India to the Greek Illiad to the Heroic Age epics of the Hebrew, Teutonic, and Celtic peoples are all the same: an endless glorification of war. These warrior tales clearly describe a new battle-loving aristocracy that was breaking up the old established matriarchal world-order with ferocious conquest and formidable iron weaponry. All the ancient unwritten laws of human intercourse were broken up also, as the warrior made his own rules—fiendishly designed to make himself come out on top every time. The Sun God or Sky Father of the invaders was everywhere imposed on the indigenous earth- and moon-worshiping people; where the Great Mother was not eliminated entirely she was "married" to the conquering Sky Father—in epics, folktales, and customs she was "retold" into a harmless, powerless wife. She never appears again with any power, except the pejorative powers of "the jealous, nagging wife" or "the seductive bad woman," Jezebel, Whore of Babylon, and so forth.

The pattern was repeated everywhere. The Sumerians who invaded Mesopotamia circa 3000 B.C. plundered the superior civilization of the settled matriarchal inhabitants, and put their own solar king on the throne. The solar king was surrounded by solar priests, who "rewrote" religion into a mythic-spiritual rationalization of war, conquest, and "royal" hierarchy. Since the Sun God rose to power through war and conquest, it follows that the mythology, popular epics, and religious doctrine of worldwide patriarchy should stress and glorify the virtues of warriors. Fascism is inherent in a patriarchal worldview. Life came to be seen as a battleground in which the victor *deserves* his spoils.

The Indo-European Aryan peoples were tall, big-boned, and light-skinned. They entered history with a superior war technology. Where wagons drawn by donkeys had earlier been used only to transport goods and travelers, the Aryans turned them into horsedrawn war chariots. Driving these chariots, using iron weapons, nomadic Aryans swept down in huge hordes from the regions of the Russian steppes and the Kazakh. In several migrations over millennia, into India, Mesopotamia, Greece, Europe, they looted, killed, and enslaved the smaller, darker, agricultural Goddess-peoples, who were trying to live in their bloody pathway. Everywhere they settled, the Indo-Europeans established themselves as a priestly, intellectual, and warrior elite, concerned mainly with military activities and administration of conquered territories. The conquered did the work. Racist theories, equating darkness-evil-women-earth-passivity-impurity-inferiority, etc., in a grand master-slave equation, with Aryans as the masters, are everywhere closely bound up with the defeat of the Goddess-worshiping womencultures of the southern regions by these iron dynamos from the north.

The Celts were perhaps of, or related to, such Aryan origins. Called Keltoi by the Greeks, who first recorded them in 900 B.C., they were tall, blue-eyed tribes that entered Europe from the East, and swept across to the Atlantic. By the third century B.C., much of the territory from what is now Turkey to Scotland and Ireland, and south through Spain, was Celtic. Invaders that they were, they were not patriarchal. Robert Graves has traced their *Ogham* script back to Anatolia, and relates the original Celtic people to the remains of the Neolithic matriarchies of the Near East.[3] Since ancient Anatolia (now Turkey) was once called Galatia, and branches of the Celts were called Galateans, or Gauls, this connection makes sense.

The Roman historian Tacitus wrote of the Celts:

> Their wives are to every man the most sacred witness to his bravery. Tradition says that wavering armies have been rallied by women. . . . They believe that the sex has a certain prescience, and they do not despise their counsels or make light of their opinions.[4]

The Celts did not own slaves or believe in capital punishment. Their tribal councils were attended and often presided over by women, and their inheritance of property and also kingship was matrilineal. Their male leaders were elected, and they had a reputation for democratic practices.[5] Whether they had origins similar to the Indo-Europeans or not, as the Celts moved into Europe they assimilated much of the native Neolithic culture. Ancient pre-Celtic influences survived liberally among Celticized people in Ireland, Wales, Brittany, and the Basque country—where survivors of the Stone Age matriarchies gathered around the North Atlantic.

In Celtic law and custom, women were relatively free and powerful. They enjoyed greater economic, social, and sexual autonomy than women in present-day Britain, France, or America. The early Celtic Christian church was suspect to the Roman Catholic orthodoxy precisely because it was pro-woman—women celebrated mass. Women priests, called *conhospitae,* administered the sacramental wine while male priests distributed the wafers. St. Patrick and Roman Christianity finally ended Druidic worship in Ireland, as in England and France, but the Irish church retained much of its pagan mysticism. Wales and Ireland, even in medieval times, preserved Celtic language, art, and literature, including the visionary *ollave* and bardic tradition of the Goddess with its sacred tree-alphabet.[6]

Jean Markale in *Women of the Celts* notes that the Gauls of France were Romanized very early, and accepted Roman patriarchal law along with Roman Christianity. This was not the case in Ireland, Wales, and Scotland; probably because Roman soldiers were never heavily stationed in these British outposts. The *tuath* (tribe) was the basic political unit in Ireland, owning the land communally. Cattle, not land, was the basis of wealth and the medium of exchange. Women also owned herds. The ruler of the *tuath* was commonly a man, but the queen was entitled to one-third of all war booty. There were many famous queen warriors, like the British Queen Boudicca in 61 B.C. Powerful legendary women, like Queen Maeve of Connaught, were undoubtedly based on real people.

Celtic women owned their own property and were free to choose their mates, or "husbands." In marriage, women didn't enter legally into the man's family, but retained independent status and property. Desiring divorce, the woman simply took back her belongings and dowry. Marriage was not a religious ceremony, and there was no concept of adultery. There were even "annual marriages," entered into by both women and men, in which both parties agreed to be bonded for one year; at the end of each year the bond was mutually renewed, or abolished. Polyandry was practiced by some tribes; children belonged to the *tuath*. Legal contracts were made by the "wife" independently of her mate, and women were often the economic "heads" of families, with daughters inheriting equally with sons. Celtic heroes were named after their mothers—and "heroism" was not confined to men. When upper-status Celts officially mated, she gave him a fine horse and a sword—and he gave her a fine horse and a sword. The mutual exchange of nobility was the ceremonial bond. Homosexuality was common among Celts, and accepted; male warriors were frequently lovers. Since sex was not related to religious moralism but to honor, bisexuality was considered normal. This is a signature of shamanic people. Celtic priests, the Druids—and Celtic oracular priestesses who followed more ancient traditions of ecstatic prophecy—were often homosexual, or bisexual. The Celtic priestess was similar to the Nordic Volva, who traveled

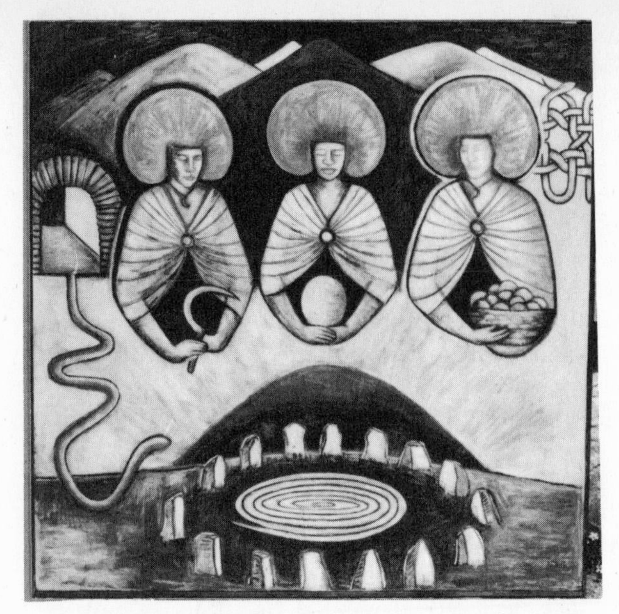

The Matronae—The Mothers, Sjöö, 1983, Alice Walker Collection

the Scandinavian countryside, setting up large platforms covered with pelts from which she uttered prophecy and, in trance, answered questions about the future. The Voluspá Saga ("Soothsaying of the Volva") is such an utterance by a legendary seeress.[7] All these practices link the Druids, Celtic, and Nordic priestesses with the present-day shamans of Asia, and the ancient techniques of mantic utterance going back to the European Stone Age caves.

When the all-male, highly patriarchal Roman troops entered Europe, as their historians tell us, they were often confronted by Gallic, Teutonic, and Celtic tribes led by warrior queens. Roman soldiers engaged in hand-to-hand combat with armed women, who they described as equal in size to the tribal men, and "fiercer in battle." The tribal bond of identity between the European women and men made them hard to persuade, or to defeat. One of the clever devices used by the Roman military to divide and conquer the barbarians was to mock the tribal males for being "ruled by women." Romans took captured men aside and laughed at them for "allowing their women" to be powerful and influential. The Roman army sold its bill of Roman goods to many Teutonic and Gallic males, promising them enhanced power and pleasure in the new regime if they would only turn against their women and become dominators of women, like the Romans were.[8] When the tribal males succumbed, and disavowed their strong women as leaders and equal partners in war and love, the native tribes of Europe collapsed into disarray, and Rome moved into the continent without further serious opposition.

From the beginnings of Sun God patriarchy to the present day, imperialist invaders have used this sex ploy to divide and conquer an indigenous people. To drive a wedge between women and men is the best way to demoralize a people; to get men to despise and control "their women" is to turn them effectively against the very source of their being—against their mothers and their partners, and the earth itself (earth as a being, rather than a "piece of property"). Wherever and whenever it can, imperialism attempts to coopt the belief energy of colonized males in this way, by challenging their "manhood" vis-à-vis powerful and independent women. The Sun God's troops can always be identified by their manipulative misogyny, and by their political relation to women as slaves, not as partners. This characteristic of imperialistic armies then becomes a device, a tool, to further demoralize and rob the energies of a colonized people. Through imposition of patriarchal law, religion, and custom, imperialists try to create among the conquered two hostile classes of humans—the male versus the female—no longer bound to each other by mutual respect and common history, but by mutual fear antagonized by mutual guilty need. The manhood energy of conquered males is diverted away from rebellion and revolution and channeled into aggressive macho behavior toward women. Conquered, colonized, and enslaved males are told by their conquerers, in effect: "You can't beat us, but you can beat your women." The history of imperialism is the history of this device in operation; on the heels of the woman-mocking Roman army came the woman-cursing Christian missionaries, blaming all the conquered males' troubles on their "evil women." Governments and religions manipulate colonized males into a betrayal of their own lives and their own people by first persuading young men to prove manhood by despising the female; and then native males are enrolled in the armies of their conquerors, as terrorist national guards or death squads upholding fascistic dictators in power. These young men are "rewarded" by being allowed to rape, torture, and slaughter their own people, whom they have been persuaded to despise. Thus does the Sun God enlist male troops in his war against the female earth, and the earth's women.

Why does this device work? Because the relation between the sexes is always very delicately balanced, very fragile. Balance is maintained by generations of ritual and custom; these are easily destroyed when people are invaded and colonized. The male ontological situation, in particular, is very fragile. In both hunting and war, men experience the acquisition of things they have not themselves produced. This can swell the ego's sense of power. Among Mother Goddess Stone Age people, as among aboriginal hunting-and-gathering people everywhere, this danger is balanced by ritual propitiation, and by the strong intact spiritual perception that life is given, not taken. The aggressive War God ideology of patriarchy counters this perception, this humble sense of life, with another: To the victor belongs the spoils. Under the Sun God, for the first time, the male ego is given power over the source of life; weaklings wait for the gift to be given, real men just take it. The Bronze Age celebration of war and hunting, seen as "manly virtues" and "male sport," became precisely the celebration of power over women, and over the female earth.[9] It is the products of women's labor, women's bodies, the body of Mother Earth herself, which are the spoils.

Even Freud could see it, subliminally. Through her sexual power, he analyzed, woman is dangerous to the community, i.e., the male ego; all social structure rests on *her* ontological fearsomeness displaced to the father. Kings and other authority figures are slain by the people not so they may be free, but so they can take on themselves a heavier yoke: one that protects them more absolutely from the Terrible (i.e., exploited) Mother. The evolution of paternal domination into an increasingly more complex and powerful state system administered by men is thus, in Freud's view, a continuance of the primal repression, which has as its primal purpose the ever-wider exclusion of women. Freud saw this, but in his patriarchal eyes, such a misogynistic repression and exclusion was *necessary* for the maintenance of "civilization."

Historically, imperial troops and native armies do not maintain this repression and exclusion of women by external force of arms alone. Patriarchal religious doctrine is the internal mechanism of oppression: God's pistol in the skull. European pagans were conquered ultimately not by the Roman eagle but by the Hebrew Sun God, Christ. In his name, missionaries preached the ultimate nihilism: the God-willed evil and worthlessness of earthly life, made foul at its source by woman's sin; and the apocalyptic goal of complete spiritual absorption into the heavenly sun/son, whose holy fires burn away all flesh. The bomb, of course, is the apotheosis of the patriarchal Sun God. Man no longer needs to worship the sun—he can make his own, and force the entire earth to bow down before it.

The American hemisphere has its own Sun God. In legend, the Mexican Aztecs originated to the north of Mexico. Their tribe was ruled over by a witch, Malinalxochitl, who had magic powers over all wild animals, birds, spiders, and plants. In a dream, her brother Huitzilopochtli appeared to a priest, telling him to destroy the witch; Huitzilopochtli promised that the Aztecs would win power and glory not through the old female ways of sorcery and enchanted being, but through male willpower and ruthless conquest—through "strength and valor of heart and arm." Huitzilopochtli was the Aztec War God. Following his priest, the Aztecs overthrew their women and their witch; in one legend, as the moon, "a very wicked woman," she is beheaded and dismembered. Some speculate that Aztec rites of human sacrifice began here, at the origin of Aztec identity as sun warriors, with the ritual sacrifice by the War God of his sister the Moon-Witch. At least here began the Aztec trek south toward Mexico City and many generations of conquest and dominion.

Nahuatl thought was great and complex. In its highest reaches, the original bisexual Ometéotl, "the Dual Lord," creates the world for pleasure. Life is a magic spectacle, Ometéotl's divine dream, in which human beings perform and entertain her/him. In this ontology, the Aztec's intellectual origins as the people of the Moon-Witch are very clear. Quetzalcoatl, also, was one of the world's most advanced gods, of peace, poetry, and learning. As the plumed serpent, he represented the shamanic-yogic values of the Snake-and-Bird Goddess: self-knowledge and transcendence through luminous experience of the three brains. But with growing secular abundance and power, the Aztec Sun God, the War God, prevailed; Quetzalcoatl, the God of Peace, fled Mexico as a fugitive. The mystic-militaristic worldview of Aztec Sun God religion was elaborated by a priest and royal counselor, Tlacaélel, in 1398; Tlacaélel declared that the whole purpose of human creation was to provide blood to feed the sun. And the Aztec empire was the official provider of this blood. As a military dictatorship, the Aztec empire engaged in continuous war for the sole purpose of capturing victims for sacrifice—at the peak of this priestly sun-feeding, hundreds of people a day had their chests slit open and their hearts torn out. The bloody bodies were tossed down the temple-pyramid stairs and piled up at the base, on top of the Malinalxochitl-Coyolxauhqui Stone, a giant circular carving showing the Moon-Witch totally dismembered. Tlacaélel had proclaimed that the tribes of Mexico were to be plundered for their flesh, the bodies rolled up and offered "like warm tortillas" to the sun.[10] This was rule by terror; for some time, the entire social, economic, cultural, and religious life of Mexico was very effectively organized around this terror.

Lest we dismiss it as "barbaric," we should remember that under the reign of the Nuclear Sun God, attended by his global military-priesthood, the entire modern world is ruled by the same terror.

THE JEALOUS GOD

In ancient Sumeria, "sheep fold" also meant "vulva." In Sumeria and Near Eastern myth and custom, the shepherd king was consecrated in a sacred marriage to the Queen of Heaven, Inanna-Ishtar. Under the eroticized veils of the beautiful young queen was the primordial Great Mother, she of the fruitful Neolithic Garden. As Thompson points out, the shepherd king Dumuzi ensures the prosperity of his people by "being a good lover to the Goddess Inanna."[1]

The biblical King David was also a sacred shepherd. His sensual and ecstatic songs of earthly love, so untypical of the Bible, derive from the ancient love rites of the shepherd king and the Goddess—her Canaanite names were Asherah, Astarte, Ashtoreth. The settled people of the Old Testament, like everyone else in the Near East, practiced Goddess worship. The Old Testament is the record of the conquest and massacre of these Neolithic people by the nomadic Hebrews, followers of a Sky God, who then set up their biblical God in the place of the ancient Goddess.

The biblical Hebrews were a nomadic pastoral and patriarchal people, tribes of sheepherders and warriors who invaded land belonging to the matriarchal Canaanites. Both Hebrews and Canaanites were Semitic people. The Canaanites lived in agricultural communities and worshiped the orgiastic-ecstatic Moon Mother Astarte. As Old Testament stories relate, the Hebrews sacked, burned, and destroyed village after village belonging to the Canaanites, massacring or enslaving the people—a series of brutal invasions and slaughters described typically by theologians and preachers as "a spiritual victory." In this way the Hebrews established themselves on the land, along with the worship of their Sky-and-Thunder God Yahweh (Jehovah), calling themselves his "chosen people." Yahweh's male prophets and priests, however, despite their political victory over the Canaanites, had to carry on a continuous struggle and fulmination against their own people, who kept "backsliding" into worship of the Great Mother, the Goddess of all their Near Eastern neighbors. For she had originally been the Goddess of the Hebrews themselves.

This constant fight against matriarchal religion and custom is the

Canaanite Mother Goddess (Phoenician-Hittite) holding scribe on her lap. Funeral stele from Anatolia

primary theme of the Old Testament. It begins in Genesis, with the takeover of the Goddess's Garden of Immortality by a male God, and the inversion of all her sacred symbols—tree, serpent, moon-fruit, woman—into icons of evil. Of the two sons of Eve and Adam, Cain was made the "evil brother" because he chose settled agriculture (matriarchal)—the "good brother" Abel was a nomadic pastoralist (patriarchal). The war against the Goddess is carried on by the prophets' rantings against the "golden calf," the "brazen serpents," the "great harlot" and "Whore of Babylon" (the Babylonian Goddess Ishtar), against enchantresses, pythonic diviners, and those who practice witchcraft. It is in the prophets' war against the Canaanite worship of "stone idols"—the Triple Moon Goddess worshiped as three horned pillars, or menhirs. One of her shrines was on Mount Sinai, which means "Mountain of the Moon." Moses was commanded by "the Lord" to go forth and destroy these "idols"—who all had breasts.

We are told monotheism began with the Jews, that it was the great "spiritual invention" of the religious leader Moses. This is not so. The

Two winged female deities with sacred tree, representing the goddess Beltis (Baaltis), consort of Bel (Baal). Assyro-Babylonian bas-relief from palace of Nimrod, circa 900 B.C.

worship of one God, like everything else in religion, began with the worship of the Goddess. Her universality has been duly noted by everyone who has ever studied the matter. "Monotheism, once thought to have been the invention of Moses or Akhnaton, was worldwide in the prehistoric and early historic world," i.e., throughout the Paleolithic and Neolithic ages.[2] As E. O. James wrote in *The Cult of the Mother Goddess,* "It seems that Evans was correct when he affirmed that it was a 'monotheism in which the female form of divinity was supreme.' "[3] The original monotheism of the Goddess is perhaps most clearly shown by the fact that, in Elizabeth Gould Davis's words, "Almighty Yahweh, the god of Moses and the later Hebrews, was originally a goddess." His name, Iahu 'anat, derives from that of the Sumerian Goddess Inanna.

Yahweh, like all male gods, was first the bisexual Goddess herself, then her son, then the lover of the Goddess (a shepherd-king). In his process of individuation from the Goddess, he first appeared alongside her, as "in the time of Jeroboam, the Goddess shared the temple with Jehovah."[4] Eventually, he was turned by his priests and warrior followers into the supreme and only God; to enforce this new regime, the old Goddess religion was damned, her people slaughtered, and the (mostly stolen) mythology of the new male God was written down by male prophets (a word that also meant "poet"), and thus given textual authority as "the word of God." But still, the "unimprovable original" maintained her influence in the hearts, bodies, and minds of the people. "So deeply ingrained was . . . the goddess cult in Palestine that it survived all attempts at drastic reformation by the . . . Yahwists until the end of the monarchy."[5]

Baal is one of the "gods" hated so drastically by the biblical Hebrews. *Baal* is "Lord," *Baaltis* means "mistress" and "fair one"; and this Goddess was directly related to the Bel of the witches' Beltane in pagan Europe. Whatever the Old Testament prophets have to say about these "heathen idols" we must take with very large grains of salt, remembering that the prophets were the leaders of a holy political war against the people who worshiped the Goddess. Moses, then, was not the inventor of monotheism or the recognition of one God; he was rather one of the chief male priests and architects of the new religion of one male God *against* the Neolithic Goddess.

In *When God Was a Woman,* Merlin Stone suggests that the ruling Levites—the Hebrew priest-caste—were in fact of Indo-European Aryan origin and lineage, belonging to that pastoral warrior tradition of male sky gods, gods of "light." In the biblical Leviticus, these Levite priests introduced the earliest, most punitive and misogynistic laws against women yet written down in those times. They seem consumed with hatred of the Goddess and of women, especially the Canaanite and other neighboring matriarchal women who in sensual joy and freedom practiced their ancient moon rites. The Levite priesthood were intent on instituting patrilineal property and inheritance rights and the father-dominated family, based on women's total submission, social degradation, and spiritual disinheritance. It follows that *any* sexual, economic, spiritual, or cultural freedom and autonomy in women—their own tribal women, or any women in the neighborhood—was seen by the Levite priests as a threat to their new regime. The Levites were themselves an elite class, like the Hindu Brahmans, living in luxury and serviced by slaves.

It is also true that Moses, the tribal leader and chief priest of the Old Testament Hebrews, lived at the palace of Ramses II, the "great" pharaoh-dictator of Egypt. Ramses II was the secular architect of the Sun God political regime in Egypt. Moses resented the captivity of the Jews under this pharaoh, and based a good deal of his religious-political ideology on this understandable resentment, as the Bible records. But Moses was also well treated in the pharaoh's palace, and was educated there; doubtless it was the political success of Ramses's secular-spiritual Sun God organization that inspired Moses to try to construct the same kind of male God political order for his own people. It is also true that the Hebrews spent generations of captivity in Babylon, and the major myths of the Old Testament—the Garden story, the Flood story, the mythic-historic struggle between the ancient agricultural Goddess-people and the new Bronze Age War God elites—were not original with the Hebrews, but taken by them from Semitic Babylonian legend and literature.

Prepatriarchal Levite priests (and priestesses) originated in Sinim, which meant "Land of the Moon," and they wore headdresses in the shape of lunar crescents. Sinn was the Babylonian Moon God, and Sinim might have been Babylon, or Sumer. Both Yahweh and the Islamic Allah began as lunar gods, consorts of the Goddess.[6]

Indeed, the Levite priests were originally serpent priests of the Great Mother. *Levi* is related to "serpent," "Leviathan," the World Dragon of the Goddess. Whether the biblical Levites derived from Aryan, Indo-European roots, or were Semites influenced by the all-conquering Indo-European warrior influences of the Bronze Age, we don't know. But just as the later misogynistic and ascetic Essenes were once ecstatic priests of Artemis, it is very possible that patriarchal religion in the Near East, including the biblical religion of Yahweh, began in a violent revolt of these newly wealthy male priesthoods against the Goddess they once served.

In *The Gate of Horn,* G. Rachel Levy analyzes the character of Yahweh as the psychological-historical projection of a Bronze Age people growing apart from their ancient ways. The Hebrew tribes were pastoralists on the move, showing the restlessness of mind and ego characteristic of the Bronze Age. They were no longer immersed in the "mutual effort of ritual," the cyclic Goddess rituals designed to "maintain the equilibrium of seasonal recurrence, and the growth and renewal of man and beast." Their concept of "God" correspondingly became detached from earth, as they were experiencing themselves as detached, becoming separated, individuated, "chosen" as a people no longer bound to the earthly cycles of the Mother. "As a result of this separation of the divine idea from its natural and animal affinities, the means of contact becomes gradually ethical."[7]

It is ironic that the concept of the male God, and people's relation to him, becomes more "ethical" as the behavior of his Bronze Age male followers becomes correspondingly more greedy, violent, plundering, and corrupt; but this is a paradox we cannot resolve. Except to say that "ethics" can be a substitute for "being there." The means of contact between the Hebrew tribes and their God was ethical in the sense of becoming more rationalized, linear, individual, and intellectual. The old ecstatic-holistic experience of oneness with the earth and the Goddess was gone. God could no longer be known, but instead had to be thought about, and thought toward. The patriarchal priesthood must design verbal descriptions of God, in the form of rules for how to act to get this God's attention. Because God is no longer all-pervasively there, looking out from the inside and in from the outside. Ethical maps are written down to tell the mind and soul how to reach something that is acknowledged to be distant. As people separate more and more from oneness *within* the body *within* the earth *within* the cosmos, religious doctrine takes on the form of instructional maps on how to get there, how to get back. But maps based on "God" as a misogynistic male cannot take people back to the female source. Nor can an anti-earth, anti-physical "God" return us to the holistic epiphany of body, mind, and spirit inhabited as one.

In Deuteronomy 16:20 it is said: "You shalt not plant any tree as an *asherah* beside the altar of God."

The *asherah* was the Neolithic Goddess (Inanna-Ishtar, Astarte-Ashtoreth-Asherah) or the symbol of the Goddess. It was a conventionalized or stylized tree, perceived as she, and planted therefore at all altars and holy places. This *asherah* represented the Goddess as Urikittu, the green one, the Neolithic mother-daughter of all vegetation, of agricultural knowledge and abundance. Yahweh's absolute hostility to the *asherah* was the political hostility of the nomadic-pastoral Hebrew people, or their priesthood at least, to the settled matriarchal cultures and their Goddess beliefs. It became a psychological hostility to the entire living earth, doctrinalized in the biblical texts:

> You must completely destroy all the places where the nations you dispossess have served their gods: on high mountains, on hills, under a spreading tree. You must tear down their altars, smash their pillars, cut down their sacred poles [*asherahs*], set fire to the carved images of their gods, and wipe their name from that place. (Deuteronomy 16:20)

(This hostility to the living earth, to its deities and symbols, and to all free manifestations of its life, can sometimes be seen in the way some fundamentalist and especially Mormon churches are built, at least in the American West; every green tree, flower, or bush is stripped away from the stark stone anti-terrestrial arrogance of the buildings.)

The Old Testament texts record the Heroic Age of the Hebrew people, the War God epics of their priestly and warrior castes. The Bronze Age saw an explosion of such epics, throughout the Near East, Egypt, and India. Gilgamesh appeared as the ego of man, a new male being building a hostile identity vis-à-vis woman, mocking and dismissing the ancient Mother Goddess in acts ranging from ritual desecration and mythic rewriting to the sacrilegious rape, massacre, and plundering of whole settled peoples. In the Old Testament of the Bible, written circa 900 to 300 B.C., this ego of man is set up as the Hebrew's new God. Yahweh, the pastoral god of cattle breeding, warfare, moralistic wrath, and misogyny, is the newly militant, self-aggrandizing and righteous male ego enthroned as God the Father, enemy of the Mother. Bronze Age raiding, mass slaughter, and secular conquest of settled matriarchal peoples by the mobilized patriarchal war machine were ubiquitous activities, not confined to the Hebrew tribes. The new element added by the Old Testament writers was the concept that became holy war: The Father God not only justified but commanded the slaughter of religious enemies, i.e., of people who believed differently. In particular, of people who believed in the Old Religion of the Neolithic Goddess. The Hebrew warriors then were not just seeking conquest and wealth for personal glory, like other Bronze Age Sun God warriors and epic heroes. No; their righteousness comes from the fact that they were also seeking to impose the right god—their new idea of the right god—

on all their neighbors. Textually, the Old Testament becomes the first handbook of holy war, i.e., the first time such an ideology was written down, as the rules of the game—as the game itself—for a whole people. Both Christianity and Islam recognize the Old Testament as a sacred text. The historic fanaticism of both religions derives its holy war fervor and rationale from the words of the biblical prophets, presented as "the Word of God." These words incite and justify religious war as the will of God.

Yahweh is called the jealous God. What was Yahweh jealous of? Of the Goddess, and her lover, of their sacred-sexual relation itself, and of its domination over the minds and hearts and bodies of generations of Neolithic people. This is why the God and religion of the Bible are identified so clearly from all other preceding gods and religions: The Bible God and his religion are based on a violently asexual, or antisexual morality never before seen on earth. Sex—the source of life and pleasure of love—becomes the enemy of God.

All the ancient people of the world embodied the fused birth- life- and death-giving powers of earth in a Mother Goddess. Recognition of this paradoxical functioning of earth was universal. The Bronze Age Hebrews apparently perceived this primordial paradigm of earth as Birth Mother, Sex Mother, and Death Mother, all three in one, and couldn't handle it. They feared and/or resented it so profoundly that in their religion, unique among all world religions, they wholly exterminated the Mother, and her earth, and thereby evolution itself, and the cycles of its processes, from their concept of deity. Nothing of sacredness remains but Yahweh the War-and-Morality God. Yahweh who, alone among all male gods of the earth, never has intercourse with a female. The *yang* has its *yin*, Sky Fathers have Earth Mothers. Even the Vedic and later Indian male gods have "female principles" or "other halves" or wives, with which they copulated. Not Yahweh. Yahweh is the only male God in the history of the world who never made love to a female or to the earth. In Christianity this extraordinary phenomenon is continued in a son born without sex, from a sexless virgin mother, who counsels his male followers to eschew sex and femaleness forever if they want their spirits to reach heaven. Thus did the ancient Hebrew Bible writers deal with their male fear and hostility toward the female sex: by eliminating the female sex entirely from the creation or purpose of the world.

Biblical misogyny was not exclusively a spiritual opposition to the Goddess on the part of Yahweh's priesthood. It also was part of the Bronze Age political project of dominating large numbers of people via a royal-priestly elite. Female blood was a sacred element in the agricultural rituals of all Neolithic people, including the matriarchal Canaanites. Blood was poured over sacred stones. Female blood, menstrual blood, was the signature of the psychic-physical bonding of humans through the blood of their mothers, and of the Mother. Thus, in Leviticus, the Levite priests wrote down extremely punitive taboos and spiritual laws against female blood—

menstrual blood, childbirth blood. What had been sacred for so long, the Mother's bleeding-for-life, was rewritten as a process of filth, shame, and physical-spiritual corruption. When we know the significance of the ancient complex of woman-moon-menstrual blood in the Neolithic religions of humanity—and stretching back beyond even the Paleolithic, no doubt—then we can see the biblical portrayal of menses, woman, and sex as icons of filth and evil as a preeminently political move. This move was designed to take control over human life and the burgeoning Neolithic abundance by destroying the original communal bonding of people through the blood of their mothers, and to replace this with an enforced new hierarchic-bonding based on the pastoral idea of a Father God, keeper and breeder of herds (i.e., heads of cattle: capital). Female blood is tabooed, is no longer the medium of a spiritual-communal bond. The new covenant is made with male blood: blood from the foreskins of circumcised male infants. This new tribal bond was elitist as well as sexist. The tribal god Yahweh was elevated to a one and only universal God; but still Yahweh was believed to recognize *only* the blood of Hebrew males in this special bonding; i.e., only Hebrew males can achieve this special relationship with God.

For something like sacred group-bonding menses to be denigrated to a corrupt process, as it is in the Bible, required a psychic overturning that was enormous. It wrenched the sexes out of balance, to this day. We have still not recovered, in the West, from that act of primary alienation from the source of our earthly lives. No matter how sophisticated our technologies or how "secular" our lifestyles, we in the West, because our culture is so historically saturated with biblical imagery and worldview, still tend to be ruled by archetypal models of a male pastoral god whose power comes not from giving birth, or enhancing life, but from dominating and breeding cattle herds as a sign of egoistic individual wealth. And dominating women as unclean but profitable cows, as well.

The puritanical morality of the Old Testament comes in some part from a misconstruing of ancient ritual and taboo. As Theodore Roszak points out in *Where the Wasteland Ends*, the Hebrew prophets looked at "epiphany" and saw "idolatry."[8] Just so, they looked at ancient sacred technologies and saw moralisms. Pagan Neolithic people did not have sex-morality systems per se. Sex was sacred, flesh was a manifestation of spirit. But spirit was related to energy—human and divine energy—and energy was experienced as easily imbalanced, mischanneled, or wasted. Pagan people designed rites of purification or energy concentration for special activities or occasions in which the soul energy was at risk; at risk through the intensity of the encounter or change it would be undergoing. The soul as the sense of personal identity and belonging was at risk in archetypal-ontological situations: birth, puberty, mating, killing, eating, death. So, men would undergo at least three days of sex-abstinence before a hunt or battle. Ritual abstinence and purification were undergone before a mating or birth, or at puberty, or after a death. These purifications/concentrations of spirit energy were a way of encountering any major life change or soul transformation which could threaten the balance of identity (personal) and communal life (transpersonal).

Whether these were or were not related to sexual activity, these ritual purifications were not moralisms. They were, in the phrase of Mircea Eliade and Jerome Rothenberg, technologies of the sacred: ritual means of focusing and maintaining spirit energy in all crises or archetypal transformations. The sacred, among pagan people, is related to magic simply because both are experienced as energy arts: techniques of gathering and directing energy toward a numinous or transphysical goal.

When the Hebrew prophets overthrew the Great Goddess and her pagan religion, they kept many of those purification techniques—but divorced them from magic or spirit arts. In doing this, they created moralism: i.e., one abstains from sex at certain times, not to focus mind-body-spirit energy, but because sex is bad, immoral. The Judeo-Christian religious systems, in their own worldviews, have wholly denounced and extirpated the magic rites and reasons behind purification ceremonies, but retained the purification technologies themselves—ending up with a psychological fetish for cleanliness, purity, etc. ("Cleanliness is next to God," and so forth. Really, since God is everything, cleanliness runs a very poor second.) Sexual moralism builds on this fetishism to a pathological degree, filling people with an alienating sense of their own and others' "bodily filth," with a fear and abhorrence of the body and its activities, and with projective systems that insist on the "uncleanness" of strangers and others—including the doctrines of "racial purity" and "racial impurity." These sex moralisms and purity fetishes, originally a misreading of pagan energy-channeling techniques, have laid the basis for racism as well as misogynistic sexism; they also lead to revulsion against the sick, the elderly, the disabled. In the Old Testament, priests of Yahweh were required to be "pure," i.e., physically perfect. No person with an illness, with a handicap or blemish or nonmale body-style—no blind or deaf person, no lame person, no epileptic, no incontinent person, no dwarf or hunchback, and no woman whatsoever—is allowed to approach the altar of God. Not because their energy might be temporarily or accidentally diffuse or unbalanced, but because they are unclean in the eyes of God, i.e., spiritually inferior.[9]

Biblical homophobia is another manifestation not only of sex-moralism but of the Hebrew prophets' political hostility toward the people and practices of other religions, specifically Goddess religion. As Thompson writes, "The image of bisexuality is universally stressed in shamanistic practices."[10] The excessive Hebrew condemnation and punishment of homosexuality—which was, after all, a common and universal Neolithic practice—was not simply a revulsion toward a particular "unnatural" sexual activity. It was an attack on all shamanistic-ecstatic religion, against the bisexual image, theory, and practice of the Great Goddess. The balancing of female and male energies was always the goal of Upper Paleolithic and Neolithic religions; bisexuality, male homosexuality, lesbianism are the symbolic and real enactments of this balancing vision—to live the "other" in the self, to live the self in the other, to free oneself from gender by enlarging gender experience to total experience. As stated in their texts and doctrines, the spiritual goal of the pastoral Hebrew prophets and kings was the separation and mutual hostility of the female and male energies; their ultimate political goal was the punishment of the female by the male (to the degradation of both). Biblical homophobia—the condemnation of people engaging in homosexual acts to death by stoning, the cursing of homosexuals beyond the grave—was a direct consequence and mechanism of the Hebrew prophets' project to vilify and destroy Goddess cultures as "evil," while setting up their own antisexual god in her place. Homophobia is a necessary psychological attribute of the religion of Yahweh; i.e., if Yahweh never has sex with a female (Goddess or mortal), nor never has sex with a male . . . then what is Yahweh? He is "pure spirit"—that is, a Hebrew male above sex, above life. This is supposed to indicate Yahweh has transcended—or outployed—the Neolithic Great Goddess.

What effect did this new Yahweh of the biblical prophets have on the lives of Hebrew women—who, like all other Neolithic women, had once enjoyed the freedom, dignity, and dynamic energy of living as women in the universe of the Goddess? That is a story for Jewish women to tell. It seems historically true that, as Christian feminist theologian Rosemary R. Reuther writes, Hebrew women of biblical times were the first to undergo a God-willed social, physical, and spiritual oppression that has since become the experience of all women in the West, and in the East, under various forms of the same patriarchal misogynist worldview. "The picture of woman obtained from the Old Testament laws can be summarized in the first instance as that of legal non-person; where she does become visible, it is as a dependent and usually an inferior, in a male-centered and male-dominated society."[11] Under the purity taboos of Leviticus 12, it was ordained that Hebrew women who gave birth to sons were "unclean" for seven days, and must "purify" themselves for thirty-three days following childbirth. A woman bearing a daughter is "unclean" for sixty-six days, and she must then make a sin offering as an atonement for bearing a female.

In 1 Samuel 21:4 it is said, "Men are holy who stay away from women."

Yahweh and his prophets had a strong urge to punish Hebrew women for their sensuality, vivacity, and autonomy under the Goddess. Here is one of many such passages, from Isaiah 3:16,17.

> Moreover the Lord saith, Because the daughters of Zion are haughty, and walk with stretched forth necks and wanton eyes, walking and mincing as they go, and making a tinkling with their feet: Therefore the Lord will smite with a scab the crown of the head of the daughters of Zion, and the Lord will discover their secret parts.[12]

Goddess with pomegranate, 6th century B.C.

Meaning . . . ? Sexual punishment, sexual humiliation, and pejorative sexual epithets are disturbingly common in this book of male prophets and "holy men." As Ruth Hurmence Green says in her wonderful book, *The Born Again Skeptic's Guide to the Bible,* "the prophets are faithful in recording the Lord's propensity for humiliation of the female sex by comparing sinful cities and nations to it."[13] The trashing of "evil" cities—cities following other religions—as "whorish" and "harlots" and "places of fornication" is common to Yahweh and his prophets, but Hebrew cities do not escape the continuous flow of misogynist cursing either, as in Lamentations 1:17, "Jerusalem is as a menstruous woman."

When "holy war" mentality is joined with such woman hatred, there is the targeted slaughtering of women and children as blood-bearers of the hated neighboring religions and cultures; the Book of Ezekiel reeks with it: "Slay utterly old and young, both maids and little children, and women: but come not near any man upon whom is the mark. . . . fill the courts with the slain" (Ezekiel 9:6–7).

In the Old Testament is the metaphor of the king who builds his house above a "privy." This seems to refer to ecstatic-orgiastic rites practiced by the Canaanites in honor of the Goddess, which the Hebrew patriarchs and prophets could not see as anything but "prostitution" and "vile whorishness." The opinion of the Hebrew patriarchs that human sexual activity is basically vile and of the gutter, ultimately of the Devil, was echoed centuries later by Tertullian, an intellectual father of the early Christian church, who proclaimed that "Woman is a temple over a sewer."[14]

SPLIT IN THE GARDEN

The biblical myth of Eve and Adam and their expulsion from the Garden of Eden is another tale of the separation of the female from the male, at Yahweh's command. According to Hebrew and Christian teachings, Eve—the "first woman"—is the cause of the "fall" of humanity from paradise into earthly suffering. She is the source of "Original Sin."

In Genesis are all the recognizable elements of the much more ancient Mother Goddess myth, symbol, and ritual. Here is the Garden of the Goddess and her wise cosmic serpent, the tree of knowledge with its dark soma fruit, the fig of the Cretan Goddess—which became, for Westerners, the magic apple of the European "White Goddess." Here also is a strong trace of Near Eastern creation mythology, which tells how the Great Mother shaped the first human beings from earth dust and her own saliva, and then breathed her breath of life into them. *Eve* means "life," and Eve is called the Mother-of-All-Living. *Adam* means "son of the red Mother Earth." These legends, these creation myths, go back thousands of years before the Hebrew patriarchs wrote the Bible.

But in Genesis, it is a Father God who creates all life. And the first woman is born from a man's body. A very interesting biological reversal! In this opening book of the Bible, the historic-political ideology of the patriarchs is clearly stated: The new male God forbids Adam and Eve to participate in the sacred mystery rites of the Great Goddess. They may not eat of her fruit and gain transcendent knowledge. Of course Eve, who was the priestess of the Goddess, disobeyed Yahweh's command. She tries, with the magic aid of her serpent, to persuade Adam to partake with her of the narcotic fruit and sexual rites leading to ecstatic illumination and rebirth in the Goddess's Garden of Immortality. And *this is* "Original Sin" in the established doctrines of the Hebrew and Christian religions.

Lilith, in Hebrew legend, was the rebellious woman created before Eve. She was portrayed as part snake and wearing wings—"the winding serpent who is Lilith"—and was blamed by Yahweh for having tempted Eve to reveal and initiate Adam into the mysteries of the garden. Lilith represented the ancient Canaanite worship of Astarte-Asherah, and also

Ishtar of Babylon. Her relation to the very old Snake-and-Bird Goddess is obvious, and her rebellious naughty mysteries were those of yoga, of *kundalini* and spinal illumination (mysteries and techniques indigenous to the Near East, as well as to Europe and India, until the Hebrew patriarchs set out to censor them). Far into medieval European Christian imagery, the serpent in paradise is pictured with a woman's head and breasts.

Significantly, Eve's punishment for her "sin" consists of patriarchal marriage. Her desire must be only for her husband, she must leave her Garden and follow him over the barren male-ordered earth, condemned to unwanted pregnancies and painful childbirth. In other words, patrilocal marriage, in which she is isolated from the women's collective and deprived of her ancient knowledge of herbal contraception and narcotics used for painless labor. She is no longer priestess and midwife to the Goddess. She will now bear children bitterly and they will "belong" to the man. She must also passively make love to Adam on her back, he enacting the male Sky Father over her meek female Earth. She must play the role of "corrupt matter" chained to a husband forever striving to "free" his immortal spirit from her.

Eve is still Everywoman. With other world creation myths reduced to "only fairy tales," the Old Testament Genesis is still treated with seriousness and respect in the Western political and cultural world. Even people who are not practicing Jews or Christians are affected by it, for the patriarchal notions enshrined in Genesis are at the base of all our cultural, political, and economic institutions. In contradistinction to the U.S. Constitution, we might add, American law and custom have always been heavily influenced by the Bible, because the men who make law and custom have been raised to believe the Bible is "the truth." No need to point out to women, in the 1980s, that anti-abortion legislation, job discrimination, pay inequity, and marriage laws against women are still roundly justified in the U.S. Congress as "God's will." Genesis is quoted to "prove" that God designed women to be dependent helpmates to men. Any legislation or custom that might free women from such economic or biological or social dependence, anything that might further women's autonomy of choice, is bulldozed by the Bible-quoters as a "threat to the family"—i.e., the biblical patriarchal family, which has indeed historically depended on female slave labor. Sex inequity, otherwise known as "God's plan for man," has for two millennia been a major bastion of support for a class-economic system designed to profit the few by underpaying the many. "God" is used to justify this system because all else fails to justify it; and the God of Genesis, who wrote the rules for sex inequity in our part of the world, now sits in the executive boardrooms of most global corporations, making sure these archaic but lucrative discriminations are interwoven tightly into our high-tech futures. Indeed, in July 1969, an American manned spaceship left a microfilm of the Bible buried in the dust of the moon—at taxpayers' expense. One giant step backward for womankind. And the moon.

The Genesis story of Cain and Abel, the sons of Eve and Adam, continues the process of the Hebrew patriarchs' political struggle against the Goddess. As already noted, the "good" brother Abel was a shepherd, like his nomadic Sky Father-worshiping prototypes. The "bad" brother Cain was an agriculturalist, representing the settled farmers of the neighboring matriarchal people of Canaan. Throughout the Near East and Mesopotamia generally, the agricultural abundance of the Neolithic *was* the Garden of Eden, a fertile and long-sustained paradise of earthly and spiritual existence. The Bronze Age raiding, plundering, and spreading warfare by Sky God warriors and nomadic pastoralists was breaking up this garden into fortressed cities, and destroying Eden. Perhaps the nomadic sheepherders and cattleherders deeply coveted the settled agricultural life, as much as they officially despised it. At any rate, ritualized Goddess-oriented Neolithic agriculture was "bad" until the new male order could take it over, and work it for gain.

Generally, when men took over control of agricultural work, developing the plough and other large-scale earth-working tools, they also began to develop ideas of the male as the cosmic generative principle. Watching grain seed germinating as if of itself in the Earth, they could conceive of the male seed as containing already, in itself, the whole germ-energy of life. (Long into the Middle Ages, people believed that a drop of male semen contained a complete miniature fetus—some notable scholars claimed to be able to see this teeny being, and even drew pictures of it.) Until the Bronze Age, the growth of the grain seed was believed to be caused by emanations of the moon, combined with nourishment from rain and the earth. The law of matriarchy had governed agriculture: all produce gathered *not* according to the right of the seed, but the right of the soil. The seed takes on the nature of the soil, not the soil of the seed.

But male-dominated agriculture evolved the concept of the earth as inert matter, simply a nourisher of the male-generated life-seed. By analogy, the human (or animal) mother was simply a passive receptacle for the father's seed, which contained the child, they believed. "When seed is thrown into the earth or into the womb, there is no difference," wrote Galenos. Ploughing was experienced by men as forced sex, a rape of the earth—the rape of dumb matter by enlightened spirit—and woman was as the humble furrow where proud man sows his seed.

The female ovum, or egg, wasn't discovered until 1827. So for two thousand to four thousand years of patriarchy all religious, philosophical, biological, and medical theories were based on the assumption of the male as the sole generative physical and cosmic force. From being seen, for so long, as little more than "openers of the womb" so fertilization could occur between women and the spirits, men in the Bronze Age came to see themselves as sole parents of life. The male God swelled and erupted with this heady recognition; and like the Sumerians drowned in Enki's semen, we still live in the ontological fallout. Elaborated by generations of male brains, the Bronze Age vision of women as earth to be conquered and "made" fertile remains intact. Freud saw libido as wholly male, and from that theorized that all creativity is male also.

Marriage, under patriarchy, was then seen as a symbolic union of sacred spirit (man) and profane matter (woman). Patriarchal marriage is, conceptually, a kind of legal-mechanical attempt to reunify the original male-female principles split apart by the Father God. But the reunion is all on his terms: dualistic role-playing rather than organic, gynandrous fusion in the psyche of each partner. "Husband and wife are one, and the one is *him*." Women have been made to act out the unintegrated negative aspect of *yin/yang:*

> Woman is earthbound. . . . Through her you grow roots in the dark, the hidden, in earth and magic. . . . The flesh is sinful, sinful is she. . . . Deepest inside man is spirit, and spirit wants to climb, climb into freer spheres. . . . Because of this the spirit fights the body, the flesh, and is ashamed when he lets himself be led astray.[1]

The Classical Greeks practiced "ideal homosexuality"—Platonic love. The Goddesses Cybele and Ishtar had allowed ecstatic sodomy in their temples, and made no prohibition of physical love between males. But, as Robert Graves points out, ideal homosexuality was an attempt by the male intellect to free itself spiritually from the Goddess, to make itself cosmically self-sufficient. It was a philosophical extension of patriarchal cultural strategy: If the physical (female) world can be reduced to meaningless material, then the idealizing mind (male) is justified in manipulating, exploiting, and even destroying it. And thereafter the male mind is defined by its ability to organize the natural world into rational categories. For "objective" study, and use.

Socrates, the proponent of ideal homosexuality, was contemptuous of mythic and poetic thought processes. He turned his philosophical back on ancient mysteries and trained himself to think "scientifically." In fact, Socrates thought verbally, turning multidimensional, multisensual life process into a linear dialog between aristocratic male minds. Socrates, the world's most famous obsessive talker, complained publicly that his wife Xantippe talked too much. She is famous, justly, for dumping a pot of piss over his head. When Socrates once did ponder the nonverbal unknown, however, he appealed to Diotima, the inspired Pythia, to reveal what lay beyond him—and she disclosed to him the essence of the Goddess.

In Socrates's time, the realities of the ancient Cretan and Mycenaean cultures were remembered only as legends of a past "Golden Age." What remained of Mother Goddess symbols and rituals were practiced in secret cults, by women and country peasants. The Aryan invaders from Central Asia had, in Late Minoan times, already begun a systematic falsification of the existing myths. Apollo's priests proclaimed that "rational poetic language and thought" were to replace the inspired poetic language of the Goddess. From then on, poetry—language itself—ceased to be mantic utterance and became a social ornament and political device: rhetoric. Socrates thought that the understanding of myth and symbols was irrelevant to "self-knowledge." He was also—of course—a townsman. He talked endlessly about "life," but was far removed from the sources and consequences of his own living, eating, breathing, shitting, and dying. Ancient myths and rituals were based on tree-lore, on seasonal observations of life in the fields, on the body's direct and rhythmic relation to nature's rhythms. But from the time of Socrates, "culture" in the Western world has meant male urban elite culture, based on an intellectual contempt for the revelations and customs of country life.

J. J. Bachofen, the first modern researcher into matriarchal societies, was also quite eloquent in his justifications of patriarchal culture. To him, the maternal society was also "the undifferentiated unity of the mass." He found "exclusivity and privilege abhorrent to Mother Earth," her children living communally and practicing orgiastic sexuality. Paternity, on the other hand, introduced "the principle of differentiation and restriction" leading to "Higher Spirituality":

> The triumph of Paternity brings with it the liberation of the spirit from the manifestations of nature, a sublimation of human existence over the laws of material life. . . . while childbearing motherhood is bound up with the earth that bears all things. . . . The Father, begetter, stands in no visible relationship to the child . . . he discloses an immateriality over against which the sheltering and nourishing mother, appears as matter and as place and nurse of generation. . . . The son's self-sacrifice to his begetter [the father] requires a far higher degree of moral development [because the relation is mainly an abstract idea] than mother-love, that mysterious power that equally permeates all earthly creatures.[2]

Bachofen speaks of "the formless and orderless freedom of Aphrodite, without private rights and property, subservient to matter and natural life . . . [and] to the harmony of the universe which they had not yet outgrown." Under the moon the law of matter prevailed, the world of endless becoming with death as the twin of life. She who awakens life works for death—death is the lot of children born to a mother. But with patriarchy, "Mother-right is left with the animals" and "mortality is restricted to matter," while male "Spirit purified from the slag of matter" rises up to immortality and immateriality, a "supramaterial life belonging to the regions of imperishable Light in the halls of the Sun. . . . " Bachofen gets very elaborate in his praise of the new disembodied Apollonian male soul, in its triumph over the ecstatic Mystery God, son of the Great Mother:

> Apollo frees himself entirely from any bond with woman. His paternity is motherless and spiritual, as in adoption, hence immortal, immune

to the night of death which forever confronts Dionysus because he is phallic.[3]

Consistent with this, Bachofen praised the emergence of the male individual ego at the cost of the human community: "The individual leaf has no importance on the Mother-Tree . . . all that is begotten belongs to the Mother-soil that encloses it."

To the patriarchal Greek and Roman, the glory of the city was that it separated him from the fields. It defined him as a political animal: He could completely structure his world with his mind (and slave labor), and so free himself from nature. "Political" is from *polis:* "city." The city was man's number one tool, with which he could achieve the manipulation and subordination of the natural world: she.

Bachofen accordingly glorified Rome: "Rome started the struggle for freedom from Nature [and natural needs], that marks the historical trend of Christianity, and replaces it with a political idea that overruns everything and molds everything to its own needs." Rome indeed carried on a ruthless struggle to raise the patriarchal political State above religion, and imposed a "historical" linear view of the universe instead of the former cosmic-cycle view. The "prestige of maternity" was "banished from the law of the State." Rome cast off "natural law"—annihilated matriarchal Carthage, and eradicated every trace of the great matriarchal Etruscan culture. Irreplaceable knowledge and experience were lost through this destruction. Bachofen says, however: "What justified the colossal destruction Rome brought was the spiritual liberation following the ascendancy of historical consciousness over the Natural idea (and Cosmic law). . . . Western life truly begins with Rome!" Indeed. Great highway builders. Rome "rejects the law of material necessity" and "upholds the superiority of the human mind" over the messages of nature, earth, and cosmos. "Everywhere *he* [the Roman male] regards himself as the first factor in historical life." Among Rome's first edicts was the subjugation of women and children to the complete control of the fathers, who were given life-and-death power over all members of "the family." This is called by Bachofen "an eminently ethical achievement."[4]

But King Servius, who founded the Roman community, was himself probably an Etruscan. He was conceived at a sacred festival of the Goddess—the son of his mother—and the Latin League was dedicated by him to the Aventine temple of Diana. Upper-class Roman patricians were solar-consecrated, while the plebs (the common people) were dedicated to the Magna Mater, the Primal Mother. Ceres was their protectress, and the community confided its treasury, its laws, and the decisions of the Senate to her temple, believing nothing could be falsified there. In Athens also, the Popular Assembly was identified with Demeter, the Earth Mother.

So the city emerges as man's ultimate attempt to become manmade, born from himself rather than from Mother Nature. The feeling of self-sufficiency he achieves through the city is largely abstract and spurious:

The sources of our biological lives remain the same as they always were—they come from Matter and Land. But city-man maintains contact with his natural life-sources not through immediate body experience, but through an artificial medium of exchange: money. He no longer works with the earth, he buys it. The ancient energy exchange between humans and nature becomes a money exchange between humans only.

Norman O. Brown writes in *Life Against Death:*

> Money is at the heart of the new accumulation complex; the capacity of money to bear interest is its energy, its body is that fundamental institution of civilized man, the city. The archaeologists note the complete rupture with the previous style of life which marks the foundations of the first cities. . . . the institution of interest-bearing capital is the key to this abrupt reorganization. . . . A city reflects the new masculine aggressive psychology of revolt against the female principles of dependence and nature.[5]

So there arose the city-states, seeds of the modern nations, organized around a professional male priesthood, politicians and specialist workers living off an often artificially forced agricultural surplus (forced by slave labor in the past, forced by chemicals today). The centralizing ideal of the city-state was an identification of the divine king with the Sun God. This new male God-Ruler was seen as the dispenser of divine justice, order, and measurement—all the ancient functions of Maat and the Moon Goddess. The Sun-Father was the Lord of the crops and measurer of the new solar seasons. It was the Sun now who was seen to germinate the seed with his phallic sunbeams. (A false notion; the sun is a necessary but not a sufficient cause of life. All planets receive sunlight, but only the one with earth and water grows anything.) The sun king also determined the agricultural taxes, by which the production of the country was hijacked to support the growing urban elites, who lived luxuriously while the landed farmers and peasants were impoverished. Around 3000 to 2000 B.C. the life of the citizen began to displace and dominate that of the country villager. (The earliest solar-wheel was found in Mesopotamia, dating circa 4000 B.C.)

By the time of the Roman Empire, every aspect of life was dominated by the demands and lifestyles of the urban centers. The famous Roman roads, built by slaves, were meant to transport armies and weaponry outward into tribal territories; the wealth of the plundered earth, in the form of food, metals, and human slaves, was then transported back into Rome to support the increasingly complex way of life at its imperial urban heart. Rome was the central Sun, with lines radiating from it in all directions: highways of power allowed conquest and spread "the Roman way," and highways of expropriation carried all the earth's bounty back into city coffers. "All roads lead to Rome."

The city broke down the organic life of the tribe and the agricultural village. It brought about the final destruction of the matriarchy and instituted the patriarchal rule of abstract urban "law and order." Phallic psychology led to aggressive manipulation of life-materials, life-styles, and life-energies, and the rape of nature by technical-mechanical means. All this was understood as the conquest of male mind over female matter.

Living, as we do, in the full apotheosis of the intellectual Sun God's victory over matter, with its results ticking over our heads every second in the form of global annihilation, the boyish enthusiasm of the past four thousand years over its newly discovered male mind and male seed-power can leave us a little queasy. The taste of victory has turned more than a little sour. In the four-thousand-year-old "Epic of Gilgamesh," our hero sets out on a sacred quest to slay the Sumerian forest demon, Huwawa. The purpose of this "sacred quest," for Gilgamesh and his friend Enkidu, is, in Thompson's words, "to make a name for themselves, a name that can live on after them, . . . a monument to the ego."[6] Because, Gilgamesh reasons, this is the only way men can conquer death. Because he has established the ego of man on a linear, phallic course, he can no longer return to the cycles of nature, or be a part of the organic life-and-death cycles of the Great Mother. Man's ego, and its victories, now constitute his whole, isolated identity. A historic identity.

Gilgamesh does slay the forest demon, who is the Mother, and is left alone with his famous name. Civilized, morbidly self-conscious man's desire to overcome earth, and death, and the bondage of flesh and woman, only creates a vaster kind of death for himself. For he has killed off everything sacred, now he must truly die alone. As Thompson writes:

> The ego has definitely arrived on the scene of history, and it is screaming out against its cosmic isolation. . . . Before, all the processes of culture were connected with the cycles of nature; in death, tribal man simply returned to the Great Mother. But when civilized man sets up walls between himself and the forest, and when he sets up his personal name against the stars, he ensures that the now-isolated ego will cry out in painful recognition of its complete alienation in the fear of death.[7]

Significantly, the murder of the forest always leads to the desert. Deserts always seem like ancient environments, but in fact they are the youngest environments on earth. Most deserts are manmade. They are what's left after everything else has been "conquered," or used up.

In the Qumran and Marabba'at caves, in dry cliffs on the shores of the Dead Sea, hundreds of scrolls have been found, since 1947, some of them dating a thousand years older than any Hebrew copy of the Old Testament seen before. These scrolls constituted the library of a Jewish monastic community that was located in the area before and during the time of Christ. It is believed by some that the historic Christ—the man who was Christ—spent time in this community and incorporated many of its doctrines and worldviews into his teachings. Others believe that the idea or figure of Christ was based on several men, "teachers of righteousness," who came from this or similar communities of that time.

As the Dead Sea Scroll texts and other extrabiblical writings dated centuries before Christ show, Jewish religious mystics of radical sects, such as the Essenes, were approaching and ennunciating a vision of the Jewish messiah many generations before Christ, a messiah in strong contrast to the orthodox teachings of the Old Testament prophets, though fulfilling many of their ideas. The messiah of the Jewish Dead Sea Scroll sects was not only to be a political-historic redeemer of the Hebrew people. He was also being shaped, in their visions, into a divinely appointed and apocalyptic savior figure. In the order of the Qumran community's Messianic Banquet, it was ritually stated that God (Yahweh) would "beget" this messiah. According to a major authority on the Dead Sea Scrolls, John Allegro: "We appear, then, to have in Qumran thought already the idea of the lay Messiah as the Son of God, 'begotten' of the Father, a 'savior' in Israel."[8] The messianic banquet was reserved for the male, initiated elect of the community, and was seen as a pattern or rehearsal of the divine banquet that would be held for the elect "who survive the great purging of the world in the last days."[9]

This Messianic Banquet, of course, prefigures the Last Supper. So many basic elements and ideas of Christianity are written down in the Dead Sea texts, in fact, that many Christians were very upset when the scrolls were first revealed and their contents published. They did not want to give ancient Jews credit, not simply for the birth of Jesus, but for almost the entire ideological substance of their Christian religion. Study of the scrolls reveals, however, that this credit is due. The scrolls contain hymns of the Qumran sect, hymns which refer to angels and the Devil ("Belial," "the angel of darkness," "Satan"), to heaven and burning hell, to the God-ordained dualisms of truth versus perversity, of debased flesh versus redeemed spirit, of "the children of light" versus "the children of darkness," and to the hope of redemption by God from the sins of the world. The scrolls speak of the Prince of Light who was about to come and save the faithful Jews not only from Roman domination but most of all from the corrupt orthodox Jewish priesthood in Jerusalem, apparently the major enemies of these monastic desert communities. In hymns and other texts, the Qumran initiates spoke of the redemption of human sin by God's grace, and elaborated their doctrine of human perfection: i.e., the new covenant of Christianity. In fact, the sect called itself the "New Covenant."

The Qumran sect began sometime between 135 and 104 B.C. and ended in A.D. 70. Their ideas of the Christlike "teacher of righteousness"—referred to also as the "anointed one" (*messiah*)—predate the New Testament by at least a century.

In a world seemingly falling apart through incessant warfare, social and political corruption, the Qumran community practiced strict ascetic discipline, regulating every aspect of daily life. They were communal in all things, practicing humility, opposing lying and negligence. Some of their penalties were extreme: For "indecent exposure during bodily movement" the initiate was penalized by thirty days' deprivation of rations (which were thin enough). "Foolish laughter" brought down the same thirty days. For "unnecessary self-exposure" of the genitals, the penalty was six months. Such practices were designed to wean the male spirit from all attachment to or identification with the earth, or the human body; indeed, they conditioned a revulsion to these things. Though the Jewish Essenes were traditionally celibate, apparently there were some female initiates in some of these communities. But the hymns, doctrines, and customs of the Qumran communities were very misogynistic. In Allegro's words, women were seen essentially as "potential seducers of men from the strait and narrow way," and the documents show an obsession with "whores" and the snares of the flesh. In one scroll from the Fourth Cave is a hymn warning about "harlots":

> In perversion they handle her befouled organs of lust,
>   they penetrate the orifice of her legs in wicked acts,
> and behave with guilty rebelliousness.
>   [. . .] pits of darkness,
> the sins within her skirts are many;
>   her garments are the murk of twilight,
> her adornments are tainted with corruption.
>   Her bed is a couch of defilement,
>   [. . .] depths of the Pit. . . .
> She is the foremost of the ways of sin
>   and alas! all who take her will come to ruin. . . .
>
> Her eyes glance keenly hither and thither
>   beneath her voluptuous heavy lids,
> looking for a righteous man to seduce him,
>   a perfect man to make him stumble;
> upright men to lead them astray,
>   those chosen for rectitude to shun the commandment; . . . [10]

As Allegro notes, all such warnings against the "wiles of the harlot" were in reality denouncements of pagan religions. They also record a general attitude about women, and sex, that led most of these desert monks to renounce marriage.

Who was Jesus Christ? Clearly, the New Testament Messiah came from, or was at least deeply influenced by, these Jewish Essene and Essene-like monastic communities. Somehow, the New Testament writers melded the Qumran concept of a "teacher of righteousness" with the Hebrew prophetic tradition of a historic messiah, or political redeemer of the Hebrew people. Most of the New Testament disciples, including the gospel writers, were Jewish males who could easily have absorbed this mixture of

Dark Virgin Mother of Guadeloupe, Sjöö, 1982

orthodox and radical Jewish messianic ideas, including their Qumran elaboration into a divinely appointed savior, or son of God, who promised redemption of the soul from sin and even "salvation of the elect" at the end of the world—which was seen to be imminent. These Jewish messianic ideas were then interwoven—by the gospel writers or by the time itself, which was volatile—with the ancient pagan images of the dying god. For the gospel stories of Jesus are thick with symbols pulled from Babylonian, Sumerian, Egyptian, and, in general, Neolithic rites of the vegetation deity (Tammuz, Dumuzi, Adonis, Osiris, Dionysus, etc.) who is sacrificed on the Mother Tree for the renewal, or rebirth, of the life of the world. The Passion, the self-sacrificing ritual of Christ, does not have its roots in intellectual ideas but in the primordial passion of the Great Mother, who dies—or whose beloved daughter or son dies—to ensure that the world will grow green again, with spring. (It is not an accident that the "birthday" of Jesus is at the winter solstice, when the sun is reborn, or that his "death and resurrection" correlate with the spring equinox, when the world is reborn.)

Jesus Christ was the last vegetation deity of the Near Eastern world, or all that remained of one, pitting himself against the rational corruption of urban Rome, as it extended into the ancient "Holy Land." But a vegetation God makes no sense separate from earth, ecstatic cycles, and the female moon. The Jewish Essene-like communities had broken utterly with pagan vision and rhythms; they were anti-earth, anti-body, anti-woman. In the ascetic aridity of the desert they raised up disembodied male spirit against the flesh, the world, and the Devil. The Neolithic garden of oneness with the Goddess was gone. What was left was a dry and fervid patriarchal "war of the spirit" against everything alive.[11]

Jesus Christ, the last vegetation god of the Neolithic Near East, bloomed in a desert. He bloomed as a devastating sun, withering to all life. All he could die for was an afterworld.

LIFE AS A MISTAKE

It is typical of Westerners to view all Eastern religions, especially Buddhism, as nihilistic, or life-negating, while flattering ourselves that the Western Christian worldview and culture is positive and life-affirming. In fact, both Christianity and Judaism, as well as Islam, are Eastern religions—they swept from the Near East, along with the Indo-Aryan Sun God beliefs, and eventually stamped out the truly Western, indigenous pagan religions of all Europe. And whether of East or West, all patriarchal religions are inherently nihilistic, and fascistic. They condemn the earth as the source of material life (while exploiting her resources and creatures greedily for their own advantage), and seek abstract "spirit" somewhere in the sky. They desire "illumination" or "salvation" not within the ongoing life-and-death process, but by denying it, striving to escape it, or being "redeemed" from it through a male Godhead who acts as ersatz Mother. In its concepts of Original Sin and the need for "salvation" from fleshly life—and in its strange elitist belief that only one man has ever been of "divine birth"—Christianity is perhaps the most nihilistic religion yet to appear on earth. Certainly its impact on European culture, throughout the years of the church's domination, was almost entirely necrophilic and destructive.

In the "house of the Lord," ruled by the Christian hierarchy, man came not to live but to prepare for death. Life was corruption and evil; life was to be lived merely as an expiation for being born. Death was the only hope of "salvation" from bodily existence. Beyond death lay the hereafter: unspoiled by suffering and sin, unlimited by time, space, and flesh, pure heavenly bliss floating around at the feet of the Lord. This life on earth was not to be celebrated but despised—a passing moment of wretchedness and pain on the threshold of angels. The more such doctrine was preached, the more accurate it became. What four thousand years of increasing patriarchy had made of human life on earth was indeed hell. Christian Europe, in the span of its "glory," was the fluorescence of hell.

Much of the Western world's secular rip-off of the earth's people and natural resources has been inspired and justified by this Christian "religious" attitude: that earthly life is debased and unreal anyway, and earth exists merely to be used—with appropriate contempt—by spiritually ambitious men. In fact, throughout the European Middle Ages, the world was pictured literally as the Devil's excrement. Christian paintings and drawings of the time show cities, fields, animals, humans, trees, dogs, babies, flowers—all falling, like masses of shit, from the ass of Satan, who squats above us all grinning. It's interesting, in this context, that Martin Luther had his great Protestant vision while sitting, as he tells us in his own words, "on the privy."[1]

The matriarchal attitude to biology and sexuality—positive celebration and ritual ecstasy—was not acceptable to the Lord. If sex and human biology were good, then women were good. And ecstasy can only be initiated by women who are equal and free partners, daughters of the Cosmic Mother. But this utterly contradicts Yahweh's wrathful theology, where women, as the carriers of sexuality, are the *cause* of the Fall and Original Sin. Both Old Testament and Christian priests saw physical love as the archenemy of the spirit; it was Anti-Christ, it was Satan—female snares lining their male path to the disembodied hereafter. Long before Freud, the cosmic serpent was reified into a "bestial" symbol of sexual love. Counseled that women were the "tempters"—unclean deceivers of the male soul—young boys were trained to be constantly on guard, even in dreams, against "female wiles." Until the trumpet announced Judgment Day, and the male spirit would be transported to a heaven in which women were safely unsexed. This training in sexual paranoia was all-pervasive in Christendom; without it, the Inquisition could never have happened.

Eating of the paradise fruit of sexual consciousness is forbidden by Yahweh in the Bible, and this ordinance was carried out by the Christian priesthood in Europe. "Original sin" was intrinsically linked to orgasmic experience. Love, to be made pious and useful, had to be sanctioned by the Lord, blessed by a celibate male priest—and then it was to be practiced only for the purpose of procreation. Righteously, not ecstatically. Men should use women for the Lord: to be fruitful and multiply his followers. El Shaddai, God of the early Hebrews, was a relentless punisher of "sexual deviation"—and "deviation" was any sexual activity not directed toward making children. Nonreproductive sex was considered a capitulation to "bestiality"—a strange error for the original Hebrew pastoralists to make, since they should have observed it was beasts, and beasts only, who copulate solely for purposes of reproduction. The error doubtless derived from the newly discovered "divinity" of human semen. He who "wasted" his semen was a murderer, to be punished accordingly. Onan, in Genesis 38:8–10, is killed by Yahweh for *coitus interruptus*, spilling his seed on the ground to prevent conception; this is the origin of the term onanism, meaning male masturbation, a crime punishable by death in the Old Testament. The command of the Hebrew tribal God against "waste" of male seed is the source of all Western laws against abortion, contraception, masturbation, homosexuality, oral sex, and so forth, none of which were considered "sins" or "crimes" in pagan Europe.[2] From the Old Testament the Christian priesthood inherited the idea that to "waste" semen (to use it nonreproductively) was to waste the life-seed of the divine Father Yahweh, diminishing his essence. It was also to "use" women as something other than seed-ovens or breeding cows. Hindu religion is also obsessed with semen, seeing it as Atman, "the Cosmic Seed."

Above all, the woman was not to enjoy the sexual act. The husband's orgasm was allowable, as he "worked for the Lord." But to give woman pleasure was to give flesh its due—tantamount to working for the Devil. If a woman enjoyed sex, she was corrupt. Further, she might seek it outside the patriarchal household; the man's property might pass to a child not his own. Most of all, the mutual ecstasy of both partners would be cosmic union with the Goddess—they would then "backslide" into the ancient matriarchal religions and social ways. Patriarchal dogmas of fleshly sin and corruption are always threatened by the imminent fact of earthly ecstasy. So is patriarchal property, which is built up so painfully via the denial of ecstasy.

(Islam, which also derives from the Bible, has gone to terrible lengths to prevent female enjoyment of sex. Infibulation and clitoridectomy, still practiced in parts of Yemen, Saudi Arabia, Sudan, Egypt, Iraq, Somaliland, Ethiopia, Togo, and probably other East African regions, is practiced on seven- to twelve-year-old girls, to make sure they will not be interested in sex. In the most extreme form, infibulation, still practiced in Sudan, the child's labia minora are sliced off, the clitoris cut out, and the vagina sewn up, leaving a straw for urination and the passage of menses. This prevents the girl from considering intercourse until her wedding night, when she is sliced open to fit the size of her husband's penis; for childbirth she is sliced open further, and then resewn. Reasons given for this "operation" are hygiene, beauty (women's natural genitals are seen as "very ugly"), and "prevention of prostitution." It is believed that girls who have not been "purified" in this way will go with many men; or, they might experience sexual love with other women, especially when living intimately together in polygynous households. Protests against this female mutilation have been brought before United Nations' agencies and repeatedly tabled, U.N. officials seeing it as a "cultural custom" with which they have no right to interfere.[3] We can imagine that if thousands of young boys each year were being castrated in these countries, the UN might make a statement, but perhaps not; world diplomats, overwhelmingly male, continue to pretend that sexual politics has nothing to do with world politics.)

The Christian church combined Old Testament insistence on sex-for-procreation with the classic Greco-Indian ideal of sexual abstinence, or homosexual misogyny. The result was a form of marriage involving the greatest possible restriction of sexual feeling. The doctrinal union of "male spirit" with "female dumb matter"—seen as a legal union, under God's Will, of two incompatible opposites—was of course not a union at all, but a cultural and physical enslavement of one sex by the other.

In patriarchy, concepts of "self" and property are linked—while *ek-stasis* means "standing outside one's self." And so there is a very deep repression of ecstasy in patriarchal society. Men fear leaving their social status as master or husband, and returning as a son to the Cosmic Mother. Men fear the no-mind (cosmic mind) center of orgasm, its similarity to death experience (ego-loss) and to madness (lunacy, moon-surrender). And so men, having divided mind from body, then manipulate the body (or penis) as an instrument of "uninvolved" experience. This mechanistic distancing debases sexuality in order to ward off the challenge of love. The deepest I-Thou among humans cannot exist under patriarchy—the almost-death orgasmic experience where the ego surrenders its defenses and becomes one with the cosmic self—because the God of patriarchy condemns and rejects such ecstasy in his creatures. Instead, the man maintains his self-enclosed, often self-righteous ego, while the woman is depersonalized into a flesh object.[4] Further, women are defined as "sexually passive" and "naturally masochistic"—all of this for highly political reasons: Depersonalized sex allows the man to keep his ego, i.e., his property. And patriarchal conditioning ensures there is no strong and healthy woman there to challenge him in the name of a higher transcendence; if such a woman should appear, she is dismissed as "evil." Beyond the wastelands of despair, suffering, and alienation are Goddess realms of intense joy and illumination—but the War and Morality God stands at the border and will not allow the male ego to cross over.

In Christianity, the only love-ecstasy allowed is beyond the body: One may love the "pure, disembodied spirit" of God, or of Christ. "Spiritual orgasm" is the only type allowed to the "lovers" of the Christian God, the ascetic male and female saints and martyrs. Indeed, saints and ascetics may experience genuine "thrills of passion" for this divinely abstract lover. But most Christians have lived lives of chronic guilt, unable to close the gap between "heavenly love" and bodily experience.

Every attempt to escape from sexuality transforms itself into prurience. Nowhere has sex been so debased—and pornography so profitable—as in the realms of Christendom. The moment of life's origin, the moment of the fusion of the female and male energies in nonreproductive ecstasy: It is in treating this moment as a bestial convulsion that patriarchal religion reveals its utter separation from life. Matriarchal identification of sexuality with the sacred—of body with spirit—threatened the manipulative dualism of patriarchal rule. Sexuality had to be ideologically debased, while reproduction was encouraged. This was accomplished by acknowledging male lust, while condemning female flesh: fuck, then repent. To this day, Christian religious doctrine exists to punish us for a "bestiality" which it has itself created.

A most unholy trinity dominates the patriarchal tradition: rape, genocide, and war. This trinity is an ideological machine, grinding out incessant warfare, power politics, exploitation of everything exploitable as some kind of objective historical process. And God the Father, in doctrine and in function, legitimizes all earthly patriarchs—bosses, slave owners, global corporations, male-controlled institutions and professions of church, state, university, law, medicine, military—which exist to capture and reify life process. This secular-imperialist tradition has for its model the domination of female matter by male mind. It is piously rationalized by theological doctrine, and exploited endlessly by business and political interests. Its existence requires the sexual and intellectual destruction of women. And any life-form—humans, animals, plants, jungles, mountains, seas—seen as female, i.e., corrupt dumb matter, may also be blasted, bulldozed, exploited, or otherwise "improved" by the all-conquering male mind; with the blessings of all male priesthoods. Women, in the Judeo-Christian-Islamic-Buddhist-Hindu-Confucian traditions, are seen as some kind of functional mistake. Nature is a mistake. Life is a mistake. And the male mind was born to correct it.

"Every woman should be overwhelmed with shame at the very thought that she is a woman," said St. Clement. "To be fully developed as a human being is to be born a male," said Thomas of Aquinas; Aquinas believed the female sex was produced by a defect in nature's "active force," or even by a wind shift, "such as that of the south wind, which is moist." The Orthodox Jewish man thanked his God every morning that he wasn't born a woman. "If the world could be rid of woman, we should not be without God in our intercourse," said Cato of Utica. "Among all savage beasts none is found so harmful as woman," said St. John Chrysostom. "What a misfortune to be a woman! And yet the worst misfortune is not to understand what a misfortune it is," said Sören Kierkegaard.[5]

The civil death of married women became fundamental law in Christian Europe. Whereas in pagan codes, such as the Irish Seancchus Mor, a married woman retained both property and civil rights, under Judeo-Christian law her "Original Sin" was punished by total civil and personal disenfranchisement. The Ecumenical Council at Macon in 900 decided with only a one-vote margin that women had souls! Our souls were voted to us by some radical bishops of the Celtic church. In still later times even this faint concession would seem heretical. To the Christian fathers of the witch-hunting centuries, if there was such a thing as a "female soul," it existed entirely as a tool of the Devil.

The five hundred years of European Inquisition were a systematic and intensive punishment of this "female soul." To understand how such a grotesque phenomenon can happen, we need a brief overview of the development of the European mind, body, heart, and soul under the Christian religion. The best analytical survey of this time is provided by Michel Foucault in two works: *Madness and Civilization,* and *Discipline and Punish, The Birth of the Prison*. Though not a feminist per se, Foucault is a superb analyst of how the body, its rhythms and energies, became the subject/object of the Western machinery of total domination.

Rome was the world's first imperial power, and Europe was the first colony. The patriarchal machine, set in place by Roman conquest and well-oiled by Christian ideology, ruled Europe by a threefold subjugation of mind, spirit, and body. It took the raw resources of land, existing cultural customs and inventions, human energy and labor capacity (including female reproductive capacities), and ran these through the intellectual, religious, and social-processing gears of state control, wealth-based patrifocal class systems, and ontological theories of "earthly evil" meant to rationalize the very new and manmade evil of imperial domination. Rome could not control Europe forever by armed force, it had to control European mind and spirit—to condition the pagan people to exploit and police themselves. Christianity was the tool of this conditioning. Generation upon generation of Europeans underwent what amounted to political brainwashing, or the first colonial-conditioning process. People were told from childhood that they were born evil, born in sin, and that life was meant to be full of suffering. They deserved this suffering, as punishment for their human corruption. The elite few who did not seem to be suffering much, but lived in luxury and in domination over the wretched many, were said to be placed in domination by "God"—and their rule was not to be questioned. Those who rebelled against earthly injustice and inequity were rebelling against God's will for man, and would be punished both on earth and forever after in hell. Those who submitted meekly to all wretchedness, injustice, and misfortune, and did not rebel or seriously question their misery, would also be punished on earth with long-suffering—but after death they would get theirs in heaven. What such Christian indoctrination amounted to was a fiendishly effective training program for voluntary self-repression. It was designed to keep the natives busy, on their knees, weeping buckets of blood. While the elite few carried off all the marbles.

How did European people endure for hundreds of years living inside a system which ground them up like daily hamburger in a sin, guilt, and punishment machine? So long as the bulk of the European population lived on the land, under the feudal system, the combined church-court power was, by necessity, loosely exercised. With the development of centralized wealth and growth of urban centers, under royal and clerical domination, more people were pulled into the cities, where control over populations was maximized. This was the origin of the European state, the collusion of court power and church power forming the control center over the lives of the people. Although our history books highlight the power struggles between the religious and ruling elites of Europe, in everyday life and most of the time they colluded as one spiritual-secular power to keep the masses of people subjugated. The church dogmatically upheld the court-state by fulminating against all political rebellion, labeling "troublemakers"—including labor organizations—as "heretical" and "satanic," and in general throwing God's weight on the side of submissive loyalty to the crown, and against "demonic" revolt. The state then scratched the church's back by using civil law and police power to uphold one religion, and punishing anyone who spoke otherwise as a "heretic" or "blasphemer." Throughout the formation of the European nation-states, religious definitions systematically became legal categories. For example, a French Edict of 1347, published by the state, stipulated punishment for anyone who criticized or questioned the church, spoke against clerics in any way, or "used God's name in vain." Such "blasphemers" were to be locked into the public pillory every day "from the hour of prime, to that of their deaths."

> And mud and other refuse, though no stone or anything injurious, could be thrown at their faces. . . . The second time, in case of relapse, it is our will that he be put in the pillory on a solemn market day, and that his upper lip be split so that the teeth appear.[6]

So much for blasphemers. As the centralized church-state drained away more wealth from the land and into city environments, and more wealth was wasted via the luxury living of the court and church elites, and endless war (one way to absorb and divert the intrastate revolutionary energy of a suppressed population is by using it up in interstate conflicts), there was of course more poverty. Poverty among large crowded city populations was disruptive of the "public tranquility," with crime, prostitution, and disease rampant. So, for the first time in history, the poverty problem was "solved," in Europe, by blaming poverty on the poor. The secular and religious powers enforced this blame by declaring the poor sinful and insane, and locking them up in "hospitals," which were in fact prisons. This was the origin of the "mental institution," as Foucault describes it in *Madness and Civilization*. From the pulpit there were moral denunciations of the poor, declaring them all to be unbaptized, living in sin and adultery, spreading demonism in their squalor, and so forth; all to stigmatize the victims of the economic system for the problems of the system. Rounded up and thrown into places like the Hôpital Général, the poor were removed from the city streets and also subjected to punishment for their economic condition. Directors of these "hospitals" had total control over the inmates, with "stakes, irons, prisons and dungeons" at their disposal for the task of teaching morality to the indigent.[7]

As Foucault points out, under imperialist-class labor exploitation, and Christian doctrines of innate human corruption, the whole idea of *work* had changed. Work was man's just punishment for being born sinful. Daily work was no longer seen as seasonal-cyclic-ritual participation in the life of earth (because it was no longer that), or as sheer productiveness of wealth, but as a moral exercise or expiation of mortal guilt. "Since the Fall, man had accepted labor as a penance for its power to work redemption. It was not a law of nature which forced men to work, but the effect of a curse."[8] At least, this is how the religious and courtly elites interpreted human work, for such a definition worked to their advantage. People had to bend their backs in endless unrewarding labor—not to provide the few in power with unearned luxury and idleness—but to pay back their debt of guilt to God. Therefore the poor, seen as refusing to work, were also refusing to be moral, refusing to be righteous, refusing to pay their debt of sin to God. This concept of human labor has ruled the Western world for centuries. The religious ideology of work as divine punishment adjusts people's minds to accept the idea of work as an exploitation of one's life energies.

The definition of the female body and female energy under patriarchal systems corresponds to the definition of the body/energy of the poor and workers under Capitalist economics. The bodily capacities and energies of some people are exploited, used as tools by others; and this is the development of all true classes, which can be simply categorized as "the users" and "the used." Foucault writes that the body's "constitution as a labour power is possible only if it is caught up in a system of subjection (in which need is also a political instrument meticulously prepared, calculated and used); the body becomes a useful force only if it is both a productive body and a subjected body."[9] Thus the political use of the body: the female body, or the body of the working class. The body cannot be used or exploited unless it is both oppressed and still functioning. This "useful tool" conditioning of females and workers is achieved by repressing the body's vital sexual energy, forcing it to sublimate in piety and drudgery. And this conditioning, as Reich clearly saw, is always achieved through religion and religious indoctrination; because, in fact, the spiritual and sexual energies are always subliminally linked.

The church-state ruling elite needs obedient workers to keep the economic and military organizations which service its power running. It also needs obedient (or at least powerless) female bodies to mass produce the workers, the armies, the police, and so forth. Foucault, again, writes that "a population will be precious in proportion to its numbers, since it will afford industry a cheap labor force, which, by lowering the cost price, will permit a development of products and commerce."[10] By doctrinally controlling the reproductive processes of women—forbidding contraception and abortion, making the multiplying of bodies an act by which the male simultaneously serves his God while subjugating his woman, etc.—the church upholds and furthers the state's power and its busyness, by assuring a continuous large and exploitable population, guaranteeing (1) overspill of numbers to make armies, i.e., "cannon fodder"; (2) a cheap labor force which is divided against itself via endemic competition of its numbers; and (3) a disorganized and malnourished mass which is more vulnerable to political manipulation from the top.

Another means of controlling large numbers to their detriment is the invention of madness, and its institutional punishment. Among all ancient, pagan, and shamanic people, "madness" is a spiritual category; exotic behavior, "schizophrenia," or hallucinations can mark a person destined for seership or shamanic psychic powers. Such people are treated as Ronald Laing has counciled us to treat the schizophrenic experience:

Make the person as comfortable and safe as possible, and then allow them to go through their inner journey to the end. Consequently, primal societies do not have "unabsorbable crazy people" who must be locked up "to prevent harm to themselves or others." Such people are a relatively recent "invention" of Western societies. Christian culture has strong taboos against the "crazy behavior" its own repressions have created; especially it telescopes "sin" into "madness" in its horrified treatment of perfectly natural behavior—masturbation, sexual urges, mischievousness, and so forth. And the state wields strong taboos against nonconformity of any kind, seeing the lack of a will to conform socially as always a potential for political rebellion. As Thomas Szasz showed in *The Manufacture of Madness*, the category of "madness" in the Western world was created to officially stigmatize and control those recalcitrant people who were, in effect, "sinners" and "rebels."

In *Madness and Civilization*, Foucault further shows that the definition of what is mad has evolved, through Western societies, in perfect tandem with their political and ideological evolutions. In the early Middle Ages, the "madness" inside human beings was defined as the remains of "natural bestiality," as yet unsalvated by "spirit." During the Inquisition, madness was the satanic process within the human soul, punishable as sin. With the "Age of Reason" that followed the Age of Witch-burnings, "madness" was socially and therapeutically redefined as the instinctive rebel within against the external authority of the bourgeois father. Changing interpretively as it did, however, in all cases the fact of madness was the same. It was the appearance of antipatriarchy: as animality, as wildness, as rebellion against legal and economic structures, as rebellion against religious assertion of male authority as the norm. Madness, as defined in Western Christian-state societies, has always been a throwback to paganism, to nature, and to the rule of women or to what was remembered as the ambience of female nature and culture, in the prepatriarchal, pre-Christian world. I.e., "madness" is a political definition, and a political state of being; as an "atavistic" throwback, it refers to actual historical and prehistorical conditions before the dominance of the patriarchal church-state over the psyche.

So, we have a religious-economic-political system which creates poverty, and then legally punishes the poor for being poor; which forbids females all control over their reproductive processes because its power depends on state-church control of these processes; and finally a system which is legally empowered to define and punish as mad, as insane, anyone who is foolish or brave enough to rebel against such a system—or who simply breaks down into understandable lunacy under the insane oppression of such a system. Further, you have large numbers of human laborers subjected to a religiously derived idea of work as punishment, as a day after day after day grinding and straitening of the born sinner into moral submission to the ruling machinery. And when the very long day's work was over, the masses of people go home—to what? To a personal life that has introjected a rigid repression of sexual ecstasy, of emotional epiphany or mental joy, a repression of all holistic vitality by the will of God and order of the king. This was the milieu of Europe even before the eruption of the Inquisition—the milieu of hell. A world in which public torture and executions, and "the dance of death," were major popular entertainments. A world in which every town center exhibited a pillory, an execution block, assorted chains, whips, and other chronically inhabited instruments of individual straitening by the combined powers of church and court. Over all of which loomed the ubiquitous image of the Devil, squatting and defecating the entire world as "immorality" and "filth" from his cosmic anus.

From such a milieu five hundred years of Inquisition was inevitably born. If life is such an error (and what else would such a milieu feel like?), then it must be corrected. If life is nothing but sin (and what else could such a world be?), then it must be punished. The church-court machine defined human life as sin, error, and madness, and then empowered itself as the "divinely appointed" appropriate apparatus for the correction, cure, and punishment of human life. As Foucault puts it, in historically chilling words: "The law of nations will no longer countenance the disorder of hearts."[11]

THE WITCH-HUNTS

If life is inherently evil, the church fathers needed someone to blame; and who is better to blame than woman, who creates life from her own body? Living women, also, can be publicly punished, as the iconic and illusory Devil can never be.

The myth of "feminine evil," which has dominated the Western world for over two thousand years, led logically and directly to the religiously targeted murder of women as witches during the Great Inquisition of Europe. Until recently, the number of deaths from the Inquisition was euphemistically underestimated, as a way of denying about five hundred years of systematic persecution and slaughter by the Holy Christian church. Now, perhaps, deaths are overestimated. We don't know; the estimates range from 1 million to 9 million people burned as witches between the fifteenth and eighteenth centuries (between 1200 and 1484, people were officially killed as "heretics"). One number is certain: Of people punished for "witchcraft" in Europe, 80 percent of those accused, tortured, and burnt were women. Town records from Germany and France reveal that whole villages were emptied of their female populations during the peak of the fire-frenzy—including very young girls and very elderly women. Travelers of the time reported countrysides hideously littered with stakes and pyres. Large numbers of homosexual men were also tortured and burnt at the stake. In fact, this is the origin of the term "faggot" to denote a male homosexual: Homosexual men were bound together at the foot of witch pyres, their bodies used as "faggots" to kindle the flames.

In Europe, at first, Christianity was a religion of the elite. It was an affectation of feudal lords and later kings who made Latin the official court as well as church language, and who kept Christian priests around as "house clerics."[1] The large masses of people remained as they were: pagan, i.e., peasants, on the land, practicing the ancient agricultural Goddess rites.

Unexpectedly for the Roman church, however, its three centuries of Crusades to the "Holy Lands" had an ideological side-effect: Returning feudal lords brought back "exotic" religious and lifestyle ideas (including the Tantric sexual arts) from the "lands of the infidels," i.e., Islam with strong Moorish-pagan undertones. The European elite, nominally Christian—especially those in the most "civilized" parts of Europe, which were southern France, the wealthy cities of central France, Italy, Belgium, and the Rhinelands—were abandoning the "fad" of Christianity for more sensual and joyful spiritual amusements, including communal sex and bisexuality (not to mention Golliard and Trouvère— Troubadour—poetry and romantic lute music—"lute" from Arabic *al-'ud,* "the wood"—which was often composed and sung by wandering ex-monks in celebration of wine, women, and song; their lyrics often mocked the church by turning hymns to the Virgin into erotic love songs to Venus, and portrayed Christian clerics as drunken bums).

The Roman Catholic church was uneasy in Europe at this time, being constantly accused of priestly corruption, luxuriousness, and political-religious chicanery. Europeans were "backsliding" into their indigenous paganism, Gnostic beliefs were circulating *sub rosa,* and communities of medieval "hippies" were springing up everywhere. The threatened church could not tolerate the mass "apostasy" of its rich southern feudal elites. Engaging in shady political deals with some northern feudal lords, it arranged for the massacres of the Knights Templar and other sexual-mystical communes of southern France. Thus, circa 1200, was the Inquisition invented. The church claimed it was punishing "heretics." In fact, in these first slaughters of the playful and poetic southern French aristocracy, the Roman church was declaring its political intention to stay in power in Europe by any means necessary—including the murder of anyone who questioned its power, or simply adopted a lifestyle of which it did not, politically, approve.

Originally, the church had no punishment for "witchcraft"; in fact, it was considered heresy to believe in the possibility of bewitchment. People were simply condemned for the delusions of flying, enchantment, and the like. But, in the mid-fifteenth century, Roman Catholic-dominated Europe was in hideous turmoil once again; it had undergone the Black Plague, the Hundred Years' War, and so many other physical manifestations of its spiritual morbidity under Christianity. Nations were beginning to mark borders and gather secular power, under kings, vis-à-vis the "universal" power of the Roman pope and his archbishops throughout Europe. The church had already established a pattern of accumulating and tightening its secular power by way of religious purges, heretic-hunting. By this means it terrorized and eliminated its political-ideological enemies, and at the same time diverted or coopted the seething sexual-revolutionary energies of the masses of people.

In 1484, therefore, Pope Innocent VIII pronounced a Papal Bull against the now-suddenly-discovered crime of *witchcraft.* He denounced witchcraft as an organized conspiracy of the Devil's army against the peace and common order of the Holy Christian Empire (a peace and common order which people living under that empire had rarely experienced). And thus the war against women was officially launched by the Christian papacy, as a diversionary tactic to keep itself in power through the strategy of sheer terror.

Two years later, in 1486, two Dominican monks—Heinrich Kramer and Jakob Sprenger—published a book called *Malleus Maleficarum (Hexenhammer, "The Hammer of Witches")*. This book, in which *Femina* is derived from Latin *fe minus*, "lacking in faith," was the official handbook of the witch-hunters, who found in it priestly and psychological justification for their already religiously aggravated hatred and fear of women.[2] It became the indispensable authority for the Inquisition during the next three hundred years of mass terror and persecution throughout Europe. The *Hammer* stated that human females were, by nature, agents and tools of the Devil, and it gave explicit instructions for recognizing "signs" of Devil-possession. Any wart, mole, or freckle, or other skin blemish, was a "sign" that a woman had been kissed by Satan, and was evidence enough to send her to the stake. Behavior also was stigmatic: The way a woman (or young girl) dressed, the way she walked or talked, her hairstyle, the way she moved her eyes, any suspicions (or envy) that she might arouse in neighbors, any uniqueness, creativity, authority, or stubbornness of mind she might display for any reason whatsoever—all, *all* was the signature of the Devil in her flesh. For wasn't woman born, in God's own words, to entertain Satan in her private parts, and thus to endanger the souls of men? In Kramer's and Sprenger's professional opinions, only the rarest of females (and dead ones) were proof against demonic seduction and inhabitation.

Thus was tumultuous Europe given a reason for all its woes. *Cherchez la femme*—and burn her. The *Malleus Maleficarum* inflamed the paranoia and hatred of the male mind against female flesh (and mental autonomy), and in the hands of the local priest, preacher, and judge, sanctified the arrest, torture, and burning of any woman who was denounced. Millions of European women, among them the best and bravest minds of their day (for these were days of cowards and fools, the only type who survived in large numbers).

The Christian witch-burners were obsessed with sex, and the *Witch-Hammer* constantly equates the Devil with sexual activity: "the power of the devil lies in the privy parts of men."[3] It was also believed that all material life sprang from semen; bodily speaking, sons (and less-valued daughters) were owned by the father, as much a part of the master's property as were servants and animals. Women, with their devil-inspired power over sex, were thus a major threat to a man's possessions: not only his soul, but all other worldly goods. Witches were accused of instigating extramarital sex, of inhibiting potency, hindering conception, slaying infants in the womb—all threats to patrilineal property inheritance. For every impotent man, a woman could be tortured and burned. Within the grim Inquisition torture chambers, also, prurience and piety were two joined hands. Women were raped and sexually abused by their official torturers—as they lay chained to dungeon walls or spread out naked on the racks—all with the blessings of the priests, who readily rationalized these activities as "Devil exorcism." The torture instruments were blessed by the priests before they were used.

Kramer and Sprenger, the two Dominican monks who wrote the *Hammer*, were eventually "chastised" by the Catholic church for their habit of going around to German villages and fabricating evidence of "witchery." For example, Kramer paid an old drunk woman to hide in ovens and make weird noises, thus "proving" to her neighbors that the woman of the house was "possessed." But of course, this chastisement was not severe; even if evidence against a woman was fabricated, she probably *was* a witch—or could be one, someday. An ounce of prevention . . . and so many women had already been burned, or would be burned, there was no way to stop it. Originally plotted and engineered by the Catholic church, the European witch-burnings took on the atmosphere of a natural holocaust—spiritual fires, set by God, burning out the evil plagues of the human soul.

Witchcraft was unavoidably political. It was what remained of the native pagan European religion, kept alive through one thousand years of Roman church imperialism and imported Christian ideology. Witchcraft was the religion of the country-people, and served as the tribal core around which potential—and actual—revolt could be mounted. King Richard I was a witch; he dreamed of leading a pagan uprising against European Christian courts and churches, but the Crusades drained off resources and energy from his plans. Too many feudal lords chose to go off to fight in the Palestinian "Holy Lands" rather than remain at home fighting for their own pagan lands, the "holy soil" of the Old Religion. Witchcraft was why the church allowed Joan of Arc to be burned: She could not only lead France against its secular enemies, she might *also* lead the people against the oppressive dominance of the French church-crown. For Jeanne D'Arc was a native European witch, resonating to the needs and dreams of the peasantry. In the wrestling match for power between the Catholic church and the new Reformation (Protestant) sects, witches were made scapegoats by both sides. In German Catholic villages and towns, priests directed the people to burn Protestants and witches; in German Protestant towns and villages, preachers called for the burning of Catholics and witches. In these endless sectarian games which make up so much of European history, people's conditioned biophobias—the endless paranoias and hatreds produced by dogmatic repression—were systematically directed by the Christian church against witches, women, and other scapegoats, and thus diverted from rebellion against what was truly oppressing them: the unearned wealth, power, and corruption of the Christian church itself. Martin Luther has been ballyhooed as a "freedom-loving reformer"; in fact, he was the same tyrant in stubbornly unpriestly garb. All the Reformist men were fanatic haters of witchcraft. Shouted Luther: "I would have no compassion on the witches! I would burn them all."[4] Martin Luther raged against the peasant rebellions that were breaking out everywhere, because the peasants were pagans; Luther believed the revolts were instigated and led by witches and Satan. He saw clearly that these indigenous uprisings threatened the imperialist Christian church-crown control of Europe, which he fully supported. He called for the merciless slaughter of all the rebellious peasants, in God's name.

Five centuries of Holy Inquisition, especially the intensive three hundred years of witch-hunts following the Papal Bull of 1484, were a means of increasing the real wealth as well as power of the Christian church. The property of every person burned passed into the church's possession: lands, goods, money. And it wasn't just the poor who were burned. On the contrary, the Inquisition was finally ended because, more and more, whole towns were being ravaged and depopulated, with leading citizens arrested and brought to the stake. Thousands upon thousands of acres of land, homes, farms, and businesses, personal wealth and goods—all were stripped from the accused witch, and absorbed into the Church. Children of the condemned were forced to stand before the stakes, watching their parents burn; as they watched, they were whipped by the priests, as punishment for being spawn of the Devil. These children, orphaned and robbed of all inheritance except shame and grief, were sent to wander as beggars or imprisoned in Christian orphanages. We can wonder how many of *us* are descendents of these church-disinherited orphans, who numbered in the millions.

This didn't all happen so long ago. Witches were still being burned daily in seventeenth-century Europe.

The Inquisition gave itself license to use any means to force confessions out of the accused. Judicial torture, not allowed under native European law, was imported directly from old Roman law for the express purpose of extracting confessions from witches. The "proving" of Devil-possession was cunning: for the refusal to confess companionship with Satan was seen as a sure sign of guilt, while confession was heard as clear admission of guilt (though most "confessions" were extracted only by the most hideous torture). Both denial and confession were punished with death. In some "trials," witches were bound hand and foot and thrown into deep ponds: if they drowned they were pronounced innocent; if they managed to float they were hauled out, pronounced guilty, and dragged to the stake. Professional men called "prickers" made a living going from town to town, sticking needles into women. Accused women were exposed naked from the waist down in the public square for this purpose. The "prick" was a tool with a hollow shaft, allowing the "pricker" to appear to stick a woman's flesh; if she didn't bleed from the wound, she was a witch. Of course with his secret retractable needle, the "pricker" could guarantee that many women did not bleed; and for each "witch" he thus exposed to death, he was paid money by the local church and town government. Many male professionals profited from the witch trials and executions: Local judges, bailiffs, guards, and doctors all got their cut, as well as the torturer and scaffold-maker. In some cases, the accused witch was actually charged for the cost of searching her/his house, transportation to the trial, the cost of the paper used to record the trial, all food eaten during imprisonment, the cost of the wood consumed during the burning, "and the travel expenses for two judges to escort the burnt body to a gravesite."[5]

The witch-trial transcripts are hideous but sobering reading. From such transcripts Ann Forfreedom gleaned the story of Frau Peller. It seems a notable German judge, Franz Buirmann, lusted after Frau Peller's sister. The sister refused to sleep with him. In retaliation, Frau Peller was arrested.

> She was arrested in the morning, and by 2 pm, she was tortured: she was exorcised, shaved, searched—and raped by the torturer's assistant—and further tortured. To silence her cries, Judge Buirmann himself stuffed a dirty handkerchief into her mouth.

After being tortured into naming her "accomplices in witchcraft," Frau Peller was indeed convicted, and "burned alive in a hut of dry straw." Her husband, a court assessor, protested her trial and was thrown out of the courtroom; he died a few months later. Judge Buirmann was a busy man. In two visits to three small German villages near Bonn, in 1631 and in 1636, he managed to burn alive 150 people from a total of 300 households.[6]

Some of the simpler torture instruments used were eye-gougers, branding irons, metal forehead tourniquets, and spine-rollers with sharp metal protrusions; there were the usual thumbscrews and leg vises, stocks with iron spikes, and boards with sharp pegs on which people were forced to kneel for hours. One of the more exotic instruments was called "the pear." It was roughly the size and shape of a pear, constructed in two metallic halves, each attached to a handle and hinged to open—like scissors or forceps. The pear was heated to red hot, then inserted in the prisoner's mouth, anus and/or vagina, and spread open as far as it would go. One renowned trial judge in France, Jean Bodin, boasted of torturing very young children and invalids; a lawyer, philosopher, and demonologist, considered one of the best minds of his generation, Bodin specialized in "cautery and hot irons, and then cutting out of the putrified flesh." Feathers were dipped in burning sulphur and clamped in armpits and groins. People were given scalding baths in water mixed with lime. Bodies were stretched on racks and ladders, or suspended by the thumbs with weights attached to the ankles. In the strappado, considered a mild torture, the arms were tied behind the back with a rope attached to a pulley, the body was hoisted up and weights were attached to the feet; in squassation, a more severe punishment, this trussed body was suddenly allowed to drop several feet, then jerked up, then dropped again. The point, frequently achieved, was to separate all the joints in the body. Even after people had confessed, been sentenced, and were waiting to be burned, they could still be subjected to random torture; hands, tongues, noses, and ears were cut off, and women's breasts were torn with red-hot pincers.[7] Girls as young as nine or ten were persuaded, through such tortures, to confess they had had sexual relations with the Devil. (In the American colonies, where an estimated three hundred people were killed as witches, some burnt but most hung, torture was also used against young and old. In Salem, Massachusetts, in 1692, two young boys were tied up from the neck and heels until blood dripped from their noses; then they confessed—accusing their mother, who was hung.[8])

Some of these activities took place in dungeons, to the private titillation of torturers, judges, and priests. Other tortures occurred in public, with much pious fulmination, supposedly to "edify" (terrify and entertain) the general populace. And of course the design, manufacture, and sale of torture devices was big business, especially in Germany, but also in France and Spain, where the Inquisition was at its worst, and longest.

All this hideous activity, we must remember, took place in the name of Christ and "by the will of God," and was said to be aimed solely at the "discipline" and "salvation" of the human soul. The Exodus 22:18 injunction, "Thou shalt not suffer a witch to live," was frequently quoted; though in 1584 an Englishman, Reginald Scot, pointed out that the Hebrew word for "poisoner" had been mistranslated as "witch."[9] But pagan witches, as specialists in herbal medicine and hallucinogens, were easy to slander as "poisoners," in Old Testament Hebrew as well as medieval European times; the words could have been used interchangeably. There are numerous biblical texts expressing Yahweh's hatred and condemnation of all people who could be generically defined as witches: "diviners," "pythons," "conjurers," "fortune-tellers." We know that all Neolithic Goddess-worshiping peoples were identified by the Hebrew prophets and patriarchs as "evil," "idolatrous," and "unclean"—and Yahweh wanted them all dead. Christianity's remarkably ugly record of religious intolerance begins in the Old Testament, where Yahweh's people are directed, by him, to murder anyone practicing a rival religion. The five hundred years of European Inquisition and witch-burnings had their direct inspiration and sanctification from the Holy Bible, and there is no way to avoid this conclusion. The secular motives, and secular gains, of the witch-hunts, can be credited to the imperialism of the Roman Catholic church, to the equally power-hungry fanaticism of the Protestant Reformists—and to all the other European men who obtained advantage or sick thrills from the torture and destruction of the human body in general, and women's bodies in particular. The Christian church used the Bible's divine mandate for religious murder not only to survive the political turmoil of the Middle Ages, but to expand and secure one of the largest and most powerful secular institutions on earth: Western Christendom.

We have been persuaded to believe, by Christian apologists, that the church only meant to execute the bad witches, people who cursed and poisoned their fellow beings. This is a lie. The Christian church, during the Inquisition, did make a distinction between the "good witch" and the "bad witch"—and it ordered that both kinds be destroyed. Theologians of the day wrote that the good witch was "a more horrible and detestable monster" than the wicked one; the church claimed that good witches were even more harmful to its authority than the maleficent ones. Civil law did not call for punishment of the "white witch" or "unbinding witch," as the helpful witches were called, but ecclesiastical law did. Why? Because the good witch more effectively persuaded her neighbors of the genuine power of her religion. She successfully undermined "God's will" that humans should suffer. Her cures worked!

> For a thousand years the people had one healer and one only—the Sorceress. Emperors and kings and popes, and the richest barons, had sundry Doctors of Salerno, or Moorish and Jewish physicians; but the main body of every State, the whole world we may say, consulted no one but the *Saga*, the *Wise Woman*. . . . The Priest realizes clearly where the danger lies, that an enemy, a menacing rival, is to be feared in this High-priestess of Nature he pretends to despise.[10]

And the Dominican Sprenger, he of the *Hammer,* wrote: "We should speak of the *Heresy of the Sorceresses,* not of the Sorcerers; the latter are of small account. . . . nature makes them Sorceresses." A French writer under Louis XIII wrote: "For one Sorcerer, ten thousand Sorceresses."[11] The sorceress, the town witch, was also and always the people's healer, the midwife, the skilled pharmacologist. The people needed her. Women, especially, needed her.

Christian authorities admitted that the good witches' help to the country people was of ancient tradition and good effect, but this was the *cause* for burning them. The white witch's power to cure sickness *proved* that she had a pact with the Devil. The priests could not cure; they had only punitive dogmas, abstract words, empty gestures typical of rootless ritual. If the good witch could cure, clearly she possessed superior knowledge and power—a possibility the church could not allow. Instead, it officially sourced her power in evil: "The white and the black witch were both guilty alike in compounding with the Devil." Thus, with one stroke, the priestly hierarchies eliminated both their rivals for public influence, and the living evidence that their own religion was a fraud.

As the *Witch-Hammer* spelled it out, any unexplained "power" or phenomenon was suspicious, sourced in evil; and fifteenth-century Europe was a hotbed of unexplained phenomena. There were rationalists extant who scoffed at the notion of "witchery," arguing that strange occurrences could be the result of a simple manipulation of hidden but "natural" powers—not necessarily demonic ones.[12]

But all power, however human or natural, threatened the total authority of the church fathers; and the real powers of witches—powers of nature and the human psyche, knowledge, customs, and techniques going back for millennia—were the greatest threat of all, for these were precisely the traditions the patriarchy had broken with. The *Malleus Maleficarum* called for the destruction of "the ancient and secret knowledge of poisons," or herbs and drugs, "healing and hurtful," a tradition of lore which had been handed down from the remotest time. Healing *and* hurtful. It was not the witch's "wickedness" but her effectiveness that the church wanted to destroy.

In patriarchal religion, only God has power. Power does not exist in nature, and it is not something he shares with his creatures. Dreams, faith, and energy must be strictly directed and controlled by his church. His police force on earth. And no one may fly through the night with the moon, or envision other worlds, or commune with the earth and the stars, or cure illness with herbs—without being seen as the agent of the Devil. The monks Kramer and Sprenger "prove" that any form of knowledge which is not a direct revelation of God the Father is of the Devil. And only priests had "direct revelation of God." An ordinary mortal claiming such experience was clearly possessed by Satan.

The people's ancient knowledge was, of its very nature, suspect and sinful. The "miracles" performed by Christian saints were given them "by the Grace of God," not by the power of nature. In Christianity, nature has neither grace nor power. If it appears to exhibit either, the appearance must be devilish. The saints' miracles were evidence of only antinatural power, belonging to those who deny nature and give themselves to the Father. The kind of power exhibited by the "saint" who stood before a crowd of peasants and slowly, one by one, plucked all the feathers out of the body of a wild bird; he then handed around the bloody, tortured mass as evidence that nature could not save her creatures, once God had willed their destruction at the hands of a holy man. "Since we are born of God, what wonder then that the sons of God enjoy extraordinary powers."

The daughters of the Goddess, on the other hand, were burned alive by the millions for exhibiting and using their own "extraordinary powers." And when we see that witch-knowledge was identical with agricultural knowledge—with earth, moon, and star lore—then it is no wonder that the peasants' rebellions were tied in with the witch-hunts.

> Neither shall ye use enchantment, nor observe times. Leviticus 19:26.

> Idolatry is the first of all superstitions, Divination is the second, and the Observing of Times and Seasons the third. (*Malleus Maleficarum*, Part I, Question 2)

> Seemingly Demons are readier to appear when summoned by magicians under the influence of certain stars. . . . They do this in order to deceive men, thus making them suppose that the stars have some Divine power or actual Divinity, and we know that in days of old this veneration of the stars led to the vilest idolatry. . . . (*Malleus Maleficarum*, Part I, Question 6)

> There are three superstitions: Necromancy, Geomancy, and Hydromancy. . . . (*Malleus Maleficarum,* Part I, Question 2)[13]

Three superstitions: the study of death, earth, and water. Plus the study of the stars. St. Augustine opposed cyclic theories of the moon, and Christian men could proclaim, as they did: "The Sun and Moon were made for us, how am I to worship what are my servitors . . . ?" Christianity was the abstract ideology of an urban-centered, court-hierarchic priesthood; its organization was obsessed with political power only. It knew nothing about the land, the seasons, the crops, natural energies. If the peasants listened to the church, nothing would grow!

These brilliant monks who wrote so contemptuously about "superstition," let us remember, *also* believed that the earth was flat and at the center of the universe. And that the Mother of the universe was a Man, who created the first female from Adam's rib. According to Cosmos, a sixth-century Christian geographer, Jerusalem was at the center of the flat earth—which had been created about 4000 B.C. by a Hebrew Thunder God. To doubt such Christian superstitions, during Inquisition days, meant heresy, and could lead to one being burnt at the stake.[14]

We will never know what harm was done to the human psyche by these rabid terrorisms. That Christianity destroyed books, libraries, whole cultures and their records, monuments of ancient knowledge and wonderful art—that it set the intellectual development of the human race back hundreds of thousands of years, we already know. We can only begin to guess what it did to the natural poetic psyche of human beings, the dream process itself. Ecstasy, divination, foretelling, entrancement, use of magic herbs, drugs, and shamanic-yogic techniques—powers essential to the evolutionary health and balance of the human psyche—were forbidden, punished, and driven into a guilt-ridden underground by Christian dogma. The *Witch-Hammer* reinforced the Old Testament injunction that all dreamers must be stoned to death.

> A man, or a woman, in whom there is a *Pythonical* or *Divining Spirit,* or that is a wizard, let them die: they shall be stoned. (Leviticus 20:27)
>
> Thou shalt not hearken unto the words of that prophet, or that dreamer of dreams. . . . And that prophet, or that dreamer of dreams, shall be put to death. (Deuteronomy 13:3–5)

The *Malleus Maleficarum* proclaimed:

> Those women are called Pythons, in whom the Devil works extraordinary things. . . .
>
> It is unlawful for any man to practice divination; and if he does so his reward shall be death by the sword of the executioner.[15]

The *Malleus*, and the church, denounced witchcraft as a spiritual crime; it "blasphemed" and "profaned" the Creator. Perhaps more crucial, the psychic powers tapped and activated by witches were defined as political crimes: "Witchcraft is high treason against God's majesty." Because the state acted as police, prosecutor, judge, and executioner for the church's definition of such "crime," high treason against God surely constituted a threat to its temporal power as well. "Thought police" and "dream police" are not twentieth-century atheistic inventions; they are our inheritance from the European Inquisition, which—in the joint name of God and the king—initiated the most extreme, active manipulation and politicization of the human mental processes ever known.

According to Christianity, human beings may have only one dream: the dream of redemption through Christ from the sin of being born. The entire ancient relation between the cosmos and the human mind, mediated by the dream process, was thus interfered with and distorted by patriarchal dogma. The witches were accused of riding through the night with Diana, of practicing divination, of studying the stars and observing seasons, of having knowledge of plants for medicinal and visionary purposes. In other words, they were accused of dreaming dreams and using their own minds. They were accused and found guilty of communing with the powers of the universe. And for knowing themselves to be one with that universe.

Such knowledge, such communion is a major crime in any society where a biophobic Father God rules. To this day, we in the "enlightened West" are surrounded by laws forbidding use of natural drugs like peyote and mushrooms for pythonic purposes. North American Indians, like pagan people worldwide, were punished by their conquerors for practicing peyote rituals and shamanism. As substitutes, they were handed the "white man's poisons": Christianity and alcohol. Alcohol and drugs become addictions only in cultures where ritual drug use is forbidden. Christian missionaries fight peyote and mushroom use for political reasons: They want to be in total control of human visionary experience. They want to control the contents and directions of our dreams. And where missionaries fade away, modern psychotherapists come on strong; established "mental health" doctrine views all powerful messages and visions from the "subconscious" (the Self) as undesirable symptoms of mental disturbance. Too many of our modern visionaries have been "inquisitioned" by straitjackets, the "normalizing" drugs, electroshock therapy, and lobotomies. From the torturer of the Inquisition, breaking bodies on the rack in the name of "saving souls," to the modern psychiatrist administering electroshock or sonic lobotomies for the purpose of "adjusting the mind"—there is little difference. Both are "cremators of the soul"—the soul that dreams. Both, in the name of "cure," are employed by a society that needs to adjust human beings to "*la vida sin sueños.*"

The witch-burnings didn't take place during the "Dark Ages," as we commonly suppose. They occurred between the fifteenth and eighteenth centuries—precisely during and following the Renaissance, that glorious period when, as we are taught, "men's" minds were being freed from bleakness and superstition. While Michelangelo was sculpting and Shakespeare writing, witches were burning. The whole secular "Enlightenment," in fact, the male professions of doctor, lawyer, judge, artist, all rose from the ashes of the destroyed women's culture. Renaissance men were celebrating naked female beauty in their art, while women's bodies were being tortured and burned by the hundreds of thousands all around them.

New communication technology also contributed to the witch-hunts. The printing press was established in 1450. The first major work printed was the Bible. Martin Luther was born in 1483. We know that the Protestant Reformation of the early sixteenth century was fueled, in large part, by the existence of the new mass-printing technology. The Latin Bible used by the Catholic church was an elitist handbook; few possessed it, fewer could read it. The Reformists argued for the translation of the Bible into German—into all the European vernaculars—so that the people could read "the Word of God" for themselves. This religious revolution was made possible by the new print technology. As the sixteenth century heated up, as we've said, witches were everywhere caught in the crossfire between the Catholic church and the Protestant Reformists. But there was another turn of the screw: in the sixteenth century, for the first time, people were able to read the Bible's misogyny in their own languages. Before they'd received only the Latin passages and the interpretations of priests, but now the full "Word of God" was spread before their eyes, and Yahweh's wrathful condemnation of female flesh as the unclean playing field of the Devil was quite clear. Because of their fundamentalist literalism in the following of "holy writ," the misogyny of the Reformists was often more extreme, if possible, than that of the Catholics.

Further, the new "popular press" throve on the witch-hunts. Etched plates depicting pornographic scenes of "witches" romping with satanic figures, and graphic etchings and woodcuts showing varieties of tortures, drownings, and burnings of women were printed in large numbers and broadcast through every town, large and small. Some feminists might feel these popular press images were the snuff films and *Penthouse* magazines of their day. They purported to be on-the-spot depictions of tortures and burnings, with naked and half-naked female bodies screaming and writhing in endless postures of agony, surrounded by well-dressed male judges, religious accusers, "prickers," and other righteous gentlemen of the time. There is no doubt that these mass-printed images fueled a mass-paranoia against women, against witches; they also mark the beginnings, in the West, of pornography as popular entertainment.

It is historically chilling to consider that the new print medium, before it ever served as a tool of mass education or "enlightenment," was used as a firebrand to ignite mass hysteria and murder. But this was the case. The new technology of the radio served the rising terrorist dictatorship of Adolf Hitler in the same way. And the use of the television medium by demagogic hell-raising preachers and politicians, especially in America, might give us a *frisson* of forewarning. Jerry Mander, an analyst of modern electronic communications media, points out that certain media favor certain fundamentalist types of "God" and religious worldviews.

> Religions with charismatic leaders. . . . single, all-powerful god, or individual god-like figures are simpler to handle on television because they have highly defined characteristics. Nature-based religions are dependent upon a gestalt of human feeling and perceptual exchanges with the planet, and would lose their meaning on TV.[16]

Devil projection and witch-hunting are functional parts of patriarchy; they are essential tools of mass control via mass energy diversion. If life is born out of evil, as Christians believe, then Devil-paranoia is chronic to Christian life. If we look at Western Christian history through our pagan, evolutionary glasses, we can see that demon projection and witch-hunting have never really stopped; they are endemic to Western politics. One reason the Inquisition and witch-burnings died down in Europe was that Christian European kings, governments, religious men, and male citizens had found new hunting-grounds, new scapegoats. A round world had given them new worlds to conquer, with new "heathens" to convert, use, and destroy. Europe emerged from the Inquisition of its own peoples via the Inquisition of "the dark others" across the oceans, i.e., imperialist colonialism. There were black Africans to be enslaved on their own continent or dragged in chains to the American colonies, where there were also numerous indigenous tribes of "pagan idolators," the North, Central, and South American "Indians." All of whom could be defined as "mere animals," "bestial demons," and "spawn of the Devil"—whatever it took to rationalize enslaving them, massacring them, ripping-off and cannibalizing their lands, cultures, and life-energies. Whenever we read the history of Western colonial imperialism, during the fifteenth to nineteenth centuries, we should remember that the men, the political and religious institutions and worldviews conducting it, were the same as those who conducted the Christian Inquisition and witch-hunts for five solidly sadistic centuries. Christian men, in the name of Christ, enlarging their properties, their powers, and their pieties in the same bite. Witch-hunting and devil projecting, in more-or-less subtle forms, are classic patriarchal tools; they can be picked up and used anytime, anywhere, to build the "house of God"—that exclusive clubhouse of ambitious men.

In the past decade in America, and throughout the world, there has been a resurgence of fundamentalist religious activity, or at least an increased focus on it in the media. Fundamentalism, in any Western religion—Christian, Judaic, Muslim—means a strict literalist interpretation of, and obedience to, the words of some ancient text(s) considered divinely inspired, coupled with a zealous desire to make the world correspond to these texts, i.e., "God's Word," "God's Law." In a mid-1970s poll taken by one of the popular presses, 50 percent of the Americans interviewed agreed with the statement that "all the world's troubles are caused by the Devil." And in 1980 Americans installed a president who, in public statements, seems to be stating his belief that half the world (the other half) is composed of beings who intentionally will "evil." With this upsurge of fundamentalist ontology has come increased media reports of "satanic cults," and sensationalized television dramas of such cults and related "ritual killings" in America. Undoubtedly, there are "satanic cults" in the United States, composed of both silly and dangerous people. But it must be pointed out that there is *no* historic record of mass killings by satanists anywhere, at any time.

The world record for mass killings is held by Christians. Hundreds of millions of human beings, in the past two thousand years, have been tortured and slaughtered, in an infinite number of hideous ways, in the name of Christ—and by people who believed, or who said they believed, they were exterminating "agents of the Devil," "Satan-worshipers," "dangerous idolators." We have just talked about the first holocaust, three hundred years of witch-burning in Europe. In the second holocaust, of World War II, 5 million to 6 million Jews were exterminated, along with millions of other "unclean subhumans": Communists, feminists, Gypsies, homosexuals, the physically and mentally handicapped in Germany, Austria, and France. Altogether, about 45 million people died in that war, including 22 million Russians and all the Japanese citizens who perished in the nuclear holocausts of Hiroshima and Nagasaki. World War II had several causes and secular triggers; but essentially it was one more religious war. Adolf Hitler was born and bred a German Catholic; in 1941 he stated to one of his generals, Gerhard Engel: "I am now as before a Catholic and will always remain so." In *Mein Kampf,* Hitler repeatedly states his conviction that he is working for God and Christ: "Therefore, I am convinced that I am acting as the agent of our Creator. By fighting off the Jews, I am doing the Lord's Work." At a Nazi Christmas celebration in 1926, Hitler proclaimed:

> Christ was the greatest early fighter in the battle against the world enemy, the Jews. . . . The work that Christ started but could not finish, I—Adolf Hitler—will conclude.[17]

Hitler's program was essentially a fundamentalist program. He was extremely moralistic, violently opposing "adultery," any kind of sexual liberation for women, or any roles for women outside of wife, mother, and church volunteer. He opposed abortion (though this did not keep him from killing children and pregnant women, or from allowing women's wombs to be packed with cement in "laboratory experiments"), and he opposed pornography (though this did not prevent him from creating the obscenities of Auschwitz or Dachau). The point is that, historically, it has never been "satanic cults" or "Devil-worshipers"—even when such groups exist—that have endangered the world on any large scale. The world has been endangered, and ravaged in historic times, and is endangered *now,* overwhelmingly by "righteous," fundamentalist, moralistic people who insist they are working for God, "for Christ," "doing the Lord's work"—and who manage to get large numbers of people to agree with them, in particular armed men. The mechanism of all holy war is "devil-projection": the targeting of specific groups—heretics, witches, Jews, Communists, feminists, homosexuals, "subversives"—as "demonic," "satanic agents," and the inflammatory insistence that God wills the exorcism or extermination of these devils by his chosen (i.e., self-appointed) holy men. Years or centuries of conflagration follow, the historic damage, in the West, being done not by "Devil-worshipers" but by Christians ruled by their fear and hatred of "the Devil."

We do not know how many people have died recently, in America, at the hands of satanic cults. In the past decade, there have been dozens of killings, by Christians, of other human beings believed to be "possessed by the Devil." Tragically, with few exceptions, the victims have all been little children, tortured and killed by their parents, relatives, or babysitters because these pitiful, Bible-obsessed adults believed the children "had the Devil in them." Doubtless the mid-1970s success of films like *The Exorcist* and *The Omen,* in which the Devil always sensationally picks children to inhabit, is related to this sad phenomenon.

In 1976, a Christian fundamentalist sect was involved in the beating death of a three-year-old boy, whose parents were members of the sect; they were beating "the Devil" out of the boy. In Philadelphia, in 1979, a three-month-old baby was thrown out of a second-story window by its aunt, because, she said, "the Lord told me to." In New York, in 1980, a twenty-one-month-old boy was "exorcised" by his mother while three brothers watched. The infant was scalded in boiling water and then seared to death in an oven; the mother explained to police that she had to "get the Devil out" of her baby. In 1983, a two-and-a-half-year-old California girl was held down by her father on a hot floor heater, until "the Devil left her," and she died. In 1984, in Bangor, Maine, a man killed his girlfriend's four-year-old daughter by burning her in an electric oven; he claimed the child was Lucifer, and he was performing an exorcism on her.

In Austin, Texas, in 1980, a twenty-one-year-old male was sleeping with his head against his truck window one night when his best friend drove up, saw his head, and blew his brains out with a deer rifle. The man with the gun had just been discussing Satan with his female companion, and he told police he had seen "the Devil" in his sleeping friend's head. In Hampton, Virginia, in 1979, a mother cut off her own hand, the right hand of her five-year-old daughter, and the left hand of her seven-month-old daughter, because she had been reading the Bible and thinking about "John the Baptist getting beheaded." In a small Wisconsin town in February 1985, a man calling himself "Elijah" shot and killed a priest and two church parishioners; he claimed he was following "God's will" and punishing these men for allowing a girl to read Scriptures during Mass.[18]

In American Fork, Utah, in the winter of 1984, two brothers named Ron and Dan Lafferty entered by force the home of their sister-in-law, Brenda, the wife of a younger brother, Alan Lafferty. The two brothers were founders of the School of Prophets, a breakaway fundamentalist Mormon sect. A few years earlier they had been excommunicated by the Mormon church for their behavior and beliefs, which included a return to polygamy as a "holy duty." The School of Prophets, citing Bible texts as support, claimed that wives were "property" given to men by God, and meant to obey without question all instructions from their husbands. A woman who resisted her husband's wishes, in any matter, was "a fornicator." And her children were, in the eyes of God and the Utah Prophets, "children of fornication." Brenda Lafferty had supported the wives of these two brothers in divorce suits following the men's return to "holy polygamy." Ron and Dan Lafferty had also received a revelation that called for "Six Mighty Ones" to battle for the Lord, against Lucifer. The School of Prophets was born in this revelation, composed of five Lafferty brothers—but the sixth, Alan, was discouraged by his wife from having anything to do with the self-appointed Prophets; she believed *they* were "Satanists."

When the Lafferty brothers forced their way into Brenda's home, while her husband was at work, they were acting according to another "revelation": God had told them it was "his will" that these people "be removed." Witnesses heard the men calling Brenda a "bitch," "slut," and "liar." She fought back, kicked and screamed, and begged them not to harm her child, who was in a crib. The two men stifled her with a pillow and tied a cord around her neck so that one brother could slit her throat; then they held her head back to let the blood pour from her body as a proper biblical sacrifice. The murder knife was then handed to Dan Lafferty, who went to the crib where a fifteen-month-old baby girl, Erica, was crying "Mommy, Mommy." Dan Lafferty slit the baby's throat, telling people later: "It wasn't no problem. . . . I felt the spirit. It was with me." During his trial, Dan Lafferty acted as his own lawyer, admitted the killings freely, and defended himself entirely on the basis that the murders had been commanded by God. "The state has failed to prove that a crime has been committed," he told his jury. "It could very well be fulfillment of revelation of God, not a crime." Lafferty further testified:

> Consistent with the Scripture we are told that there are going to be some frightful circumstances when the Lord's kingdom is built up and the adversary's kingdom must be torn down. We are told that will be a dreadful day. The proud will be destroyed and their children will be dashed before their eyes and there will be no pity for the infant or the suckling. I don't intend to make excuses over things I have no control of. I'm not really sorry. I'm not in the position I am because I chose

to be. We are involved in a day when the Lord has strange work to do.

A Utah jury sentenced Dan Lafferty and his brother Ron to life imprisonment. But they were not able to refute the Lafferty brothers' assertions that the Holy Bible supported their deeds.[19]

These are just a few news stories emerging from the past decade in America. All the murders and mutilations described were performed by people who saw themselves as "holy men" (and "handmaidens") of the biblical God, and of Christ the Lord. They were all "doing God's will," "smiting Devils," "smiting whores and fornicators." And "children of fornicators." The full history of such holy murders in the West, under Christianity and the influence of the biblical Old Testament, would be much longer than this account. And even more nauseating.

"The Devil is the curse of those who have abandoned the Goddess."

Finally, a word about "satanism," which has nothing to do with witchcraft. Witchcraft, we should know by now, is the ancient European pagan religion, going back to the hunting times and the Paleolithic caves. Its practitioners worship a female goddess and her consort, the Horned One, who is represented with the goat-hooves and horns of the god Pan (meaning "all"), the fertility spirit of nature. Pan goes back to the shamanic figure in the Trois Frères cave, the sorcerer dancing in animal mask and skins. This figure was interpreted by Christians as the Devil, amalgamated with their concepts of the evil principle. But Pan represented life and life energy, not evil. The witches never worshiped "evil"—which is a Christian obsession. They worshiped as human beings worshiped at the beginning of time: the Goddess, her nature, her fertility, and her cyclic life-and-death cosmos.

Satanism is a Christian heresy. (You can't believe in a "Satan" unless you also believe in Christian ontology, and the Bible.) "Satanism" is of very recent origin. The first "black mass" conducted as a parody of the Catholic mass was performed in the late seventeenth century at the court of Louis XIV. It was performed by fifty to sixty Roman Catholic priests, hired by the king, who conducted mass on a naked girl's belly as an "amatory lark" to amuse the court. The satanic black mass, dedicated to Anti-Christ and designed to worship and invoke the principle of evil, does not appear in history until the nineteenth century. It was basically a literary invention, and an amusement of decadent aristocrats and artists; and from this comes our idea of "satanism."[20]

DENIAL OF THE MOTHER: DENIAL OF THE PEOPLE

Christianity offered redemption through a single being of the male sex. Christ must redeem us from being born out of a woman. His power to do so comes from the fact that he is the son of a male God. At death, Christ does not return to the Mother Earth like earlier vegetation deities, to renew and fructify us all. Christ is a vegetation deity who refuses to be recycled. Instead, he ascends to heaven to sit as a judge at his Father's side.

In The Gospel of Thomas, the following exchange occurs in the presence of Mary Magdelen.

> Simon Peter said to them "Let Mary leave us, for women are not worthy of Life."
>
> Jesus said "I myself shall lead her in order to make her male, so that she too may become a living spirit resembling you males. For every woman who will make herself male will enter the Kingdom of Heaven."[1]

(Simon Peter was the founder of the Christian church among the Jews, and the spokesman of the Apostles. And lucky for him that women are women: The great domed Cathedral of St. Peter's in Rome was built with brothel taxes.)

Once and for all, Christ signified the end of rebirth through the Mother. He denies his mother: "Woman, what have I to do with thee?" John 2:4. Nothing, apparently; now men must be reborn through a male mother, Christ; and women must be reborn male to even be considered "worthy of life." To be wholly honest, Christ should have said: "I have come to destroy the Mother—and go about my Father's business." In apocryphal texts Jesus does say: "For I have come to destroy the works of the Female. . . . Death will prevail, as long as you, women, bear children."[2]

Such a nihilistic denial of the value of earthly life, coupled with the Christian church's imperialistic urge to control that life—specifically to control women's reproduction of it—has contributed greatly to the biophobic insanity of the past two thousand years of human existence. In the past four thousand years of patriarchy, there have been about three hundred years of comparative peace. Under Christ, the so-called "Prince of Peace," the Western world has been at continuous war—with its "enemies" and with itself. From Christendom have come doctrines of despair and alienation, theories of "master races" and "inferior blood," a daily reduction of life to stupid mechanism, grotesque paranoias about the "unconscious"—a hatred and fear of the World and all things in it as inherently evil. Most of all, Christianity has fueled men's hatred and fear of women, as being the givers of this miserable and treacherous existence. How could our ancestors have survived and evolved through more than 500,000 years of human life on earth if they had experienced life in such a consistently ugly way?

Human beings are bound to each other through the Mother. As her children, we share a blood-bond with all creation, we are all made the same: from her flesh, her desire, her dreams. Under patriarchy, this mystical blood-bond is broken. Our flesh-bond becomes the source of all evil. Under Judaism, Christianity, Islam, and State-communism—the four major Western patriarchal religions—the compulsion to control or destroy the flesh of the other has been historically stronger than the stated desire of "brotherhood." This perpetual success of war and failure of peace is then said to be "the human condition"—but it is only the condition of humans under patriarchy.

Under patriarchy, there is a literal belief that all of life is created for men to *use*. And what patriarchal men see as useable is also seen as contemptible. We suggest that the atomic or nuclear blast is man's final identification with the Sun God, the final annihilation of matter/mother—and that this is the implicit goal of all patriarchal religion. If they cannot control life utterly, they will choose to destroy it. The nuclear technician is the ultimate priest of the Father, handing us his unholy mushrooms of rigid and uncreative death, a ceremonial sacrifice of mere objective numbers—without grace, hope, rebirth, or magic immortality.[3]

Exclusive identification with the father is a way of denying dependence on the mother—who is always ultimately Mother Earth. "Taking" is a denial of dependence, and also transforms the guilt of indebtedness into aggression. The masculinity complex, the obsessive denial of femaleness, is inherently nihilistic and aggressive. Because the Christian church relentlessly uses words like "pious" and "humble" and "meek" to describe the character of Christ, such words have masked the actual historical *aggressiveness* of the church against human bodies and minds. (In fact, the Eastern Orthodox Christ Pantocrator was always pictured as quite fierce and demanding; but throughout the Christian Empire concepts of "humility" and "meekness" have been systematically used for centuries to condition submissiveness in the masses, while the ruling elites quite arrogantly and aggressively grabbed the earth's treasures for themselves.)

As John G. Jackson writes, "The story of the Dark Ages in Europe presents a chronicle of horrors almost without a parallel in human history;

and the saddest part of it is the story of the conversion of Europe to Christianity." He quotes Briffault:

> Could the full history of the *conversion* of Europe to Christianity be written, it would present a tale of horror more appalling than that of the Christianization of Spain by the Inquisition. The Christian religion has been imposed upon the people of Europe in much the same manner as it was imposed on Mexico and Peru, in the course of whose *conversion* Las Casas estimates twelve million people perished, butchered, burnt alive and tortured.[4]

Those who survived the butchery of Christian "conversion" were enslaved; as Jackson writes again:

> The Church not only perpetuated slavery, but created it where it had never existed under Roman Law. Bishop Ratherius of Verona, in the 10th century, went so far as to say: "God has mercifully destined those to slavery for whom He saw that freedom was not fitting."[5]

The medieval and Renaissance church fathers of Europe saw the institutions of private property, of coercive government, of class systems, even of slavery, as not only inevitable on this "evil earth," but desirable. They were order-imposing, elite-enforced remedies for the "corruption" of human nature. The scholastic minds of the church and its patristic theory made a distinction between the state of nature (based on natural law and expressing "God's ideal"; a world more responsive to natural order which patriarchy, of course, destroyed) and the conventional state, which is the real world (the rationalized world) sanctioned by custom. According to God's apologists, this conventional state is not the original intention of God, but has come about through human sin, as a result of the Fall. Thus the unnaturalness and exploitive coerciveness of the "real world" is blamed on human beings—few noting that this state of things was originally established to enforce "God's will" over human beings. The Christian or biblical God is never blamed for "worldly order and disorder"—his absolute will is just used to sanction its continuance. Corrupted by Original Sin, human nature supposedly demanded "restraints," which could not be found in an egalitarian order. These "restraints" are inequalities of wealth, status, and power, and the consequent "right" of a select few to rule over the many—such "restraints" were interpreted as not only the consequences of sin, but also its remedies. We are exploited, punished, and oppressed for our own good—so we are told by "God's" professional explainers. No matter how brutal, unjust, or greedy patriarchal institutions might be, they are to be understood as the whips of God on the disobedient bottoms of his mortal children.

With such fiendish "reasoning" did the church fathers build their Christian Empire. Throughout the early years of Christianized Europe, the priests and scholiasts were the only people doing such reasoning. They were the only people allowed an education; the great masses of people, with their pagan Neolithic knowledge destroyed or forbidden, were kept in profound ignorance. The church worked to ensure their minds were filled up only with Christian dogma, guilts, and fears, and Devil-superstition. When we consider that the megalithic lunar and solar-observatory builders of England and the Breton coast of France were, circa 3500 to 2500 B.C., measuring the slight periodic 0.15-degree oscillation of the moon, as well as building immense and beautiful earthworks for ritual celebration, the intellectual and cultural squalor of Europeans under the domination of the Christian church becomes truly appalling (though not, unfortunately, unique; the same mental and physical impoverishment followed the church wherever it went). As John G. Jackson points out, Europe might still be in mental darkness were it not for the periodic injections, fought tooth and nail by the church, of Arabic brilliance. Europe, says Jackson, was saved from its abysmal Christian-engineered Dark Ages not through a Greco-Roman "Renaissance" but by the entrance of Moors into Spain, and the influence of Moorish civilization in the Mediterranean and Southern Europe. He quotes Joseph McCabe:

> None of our modern sophistry redeems the squalor of Europe from the 5th to the 11th century. *And it was again the dark skinned men of the south who restored civilization.* By the year 1000, Europe was reduced to a condition which, if we were not Europeans, we should frankly call barbarism, yet at that time, the Arabs had a splendid civilization in Spain, Sicily, Syria, Egypt and Persia, and it linked on to those of India and China. We write manuals of the history of Europe, or of the Middle Ages, and we confine ourselves to a small squalid area . . . and ignore the brilliant civilization that ran from Portugal to the China Sea.[6]

The Christian church initially tried to fight the threat of this civilizing Arabic brilliance by launching Holy Crusades against it. But too many Crusaders returned to Europe trailing clouds of sensual glory from the "heathen lands," and from them created the splendidly iridescent Trouvère-Troubadour culture of Southern France. As we've seen, the Catholic church launched the Inquisition against "heretics" in 1200 by destroying these lyric Arabic influences, and for the next five hundred years the Inquisition and the witch-hunts were Christian imperial machines designed to capture every possible bit of "exotic" or pagan intelligence in trials and torture chambers, and burn it all down to gray ash. I.e., the church maintained control of Europe via a thousand years of institutionalized propaganda and terror, in which the mind of Europe was kept in darkness while all outside light was forbidden to shine in.

Almost all Christian "charity" has been motivated by spiritual self-interest. The church could piously recommend that well-off individuals help the poor—not for the sake of the poor, who after all deserved their poverty, but to help good Christians make points in heaven. Overall, the church has maintained that the order of society is as it should be. The "power of God" has been used throughout Christian history to uphold the secular status quo. This is the cruelly reactionary role played by the great imperialist church: it promises the people that it will be their guardian, only to exploit and deceive them. And when the people suffer, the church blames it on *their* sin!

Christianity's labor record is equally atrocious. It saw hard, unrelieved labor and class-inequity as fitting punishments for human sin, and necessary disciplines for innate human rebelliousness. So the church always historically and ideologically aligned itself with the boss against the workers. As Foucault writes, the Thirty Years' War in Europe caused great social upheaval and economic depression; there were three large uprisings in France between 1621 and 1639. Central to these uprisings were labor protests; new economic structures—the centralizing of capital in urban centers and development of larger and larger manufactories—were breaking the power of the medieval craft guilds, and assaulting worker's rights. The French "General Regulations" were government orders prohibitting all assemblies, leagues, or associations of workers. When some French parlements, such as that of Normandy, were reluctant or refused to prosecute guild members for political protest, the church, in its characteristic way, stepped in on the side of repression.

> . . . the Church intervened and accused the workers' secret gatherings of sorcery. A decree of the Sorbonne, in 1655, proclaimed "guilty of sacrilege and mortal sin" all those who were found in such bad company.[7]

The Church, up to the sixteenth century, was the Catholic church. Its excessive corruptions and repressions provoked the rise of Protestant Reformism—but it's hard to see how the people benefited in any way from the appearance of one more father church. Luther not only fought the papacy. During the time of the Peasant Revolt of 1500, Luther wrote ferocious pamphlets calling for the punishment of "the thieving, murderous gangs of peasants"—and 100,000 peasants were slaughtered. (Nor did all those peasants forced into the cities, into the impoverished urban labor forces, fare any better under Reformist Christianity, which was even more puritanical in its view of human labor as "God's discipline" and "God's punishment" for mortal sin.)

The peasants, and the laborers, were the people—and Christianity has always feared the people unless they were kept under strict physical, mental, and economic control. When the Black Death swept Europe in 1348, it can be seen as the psychosomatic destruction of the body resulting from the intense institutional hatred of the flesh ruling everywhere. But when the people moved to save themselves, to become healthy

Sheela-na-gig from Kilpeck, England. Church of St. Mary and St. David Corbel

and free—to revolt—the church-state was quick and ready to crush their revolt as "satanic." The continuous paranoid repression of human sexuality and creative psychic capacities led to generation after generation of bizarre social phenomena—like the "dancing-sickness" in which hundreds of people danced themselves to death.

Under the feudal system, the peasants had had a certain sense of security along with their oppression: they still lived in communal villages and retained ancient pagan customs and ritual traditions. When this system began to break down, with the rise of the centralized church-court, the peasants experienced large-scale famine, wars, poverty, uprootedness, and psychic disorientation. Europe was consumed by the belief in Satan and his black hosts, the demonic scapegoats for a rotten social and economic system, populated by a repressed and fearful humanity. During feudal times, with secular power divided among many feudal lords, as we've said, the church had never felt strong enough to move against the people, especially the country peasants, or their native pagan religion. But with growing consolidation of religious-royal power within urbanized centers, the church became politically unchallenged; it aligned immediately with the kings against the people. At no time did it even consider aligning

Swedish Freya—Nerthus, carved on stone from Gotland (island in the Baltic), circa 600 A.D.

with the people. Instead, it quickly moved to secure its power through the forceful elimination of all rival religious beliefs.

This is why pagan religion survived through at least a thousand years of Christian rule in Europe: power rested in the countryside. Missionaries were counseled by the Roman pope to accommodate pagan religion where it couldn't be overcome. Thus there are Christian churches throughout Europe built on the sites of pagan temples, and both pagan and Christian deities are pictured in many early European church reliefs. The naked Goddess, with her legs spread wide to show the origins of life, adorns the lintels of church doors, *even nunneries,* in many parts of Celtic Britain—particularly in Ireland, where she is called Sheela-Na-Gig. In the same way, Christian symbols were incorporated into the ancient pagan festivals. Christmas is the winter solstice celebration (and the Roman Saturnalia); the tree and gift-exchange are pagan customs, originating in Goddess rituals. Santa Claus originated in Siberia, in a Norse goddess named Nerthus/Hertha.[8] The Scandinavian *Jul* season (Yule in Saxon) originally celebrated the winter solstice as the "Wheel of the Year," the sun rolling back from its northernmost point; *hjul* means "wheel" in Swedish. Easter is the pagan festival of spring, the year's rebirth or resurrection. The name comes from the Saxon Goddess of spring, Oestre, who also gives her name to the female estrus-cycle. (Her name is cognate with Neolithic Near Eastern Goddesses Ostarte, Astarte, Ishtar, Ashtoreth.) The Easter rabbits, the colored eggs hidden around in the grass or rolled down the lawn, are fertility symbols of the Goddess. Finally, the Golden Number used to calculate the "movable feast" of Easter is based on lunar calculations, and on the 19-19-18 year eclipse cycle used by the Druids and earlier megalithic builders. The same number was once used to calculate the date of Christmas in relation to the winter solstice.

Christian missionaries, when they could, forbade the country people to worship their natural trees, springs, caves, and sacred stones. But they had at first no real power to enforce these taboos; and the peasants good-naturedly included some Christian reference in their own pagan ceremonies, which they continued to practice. Pagan people worldwide tend to be spiritually inclusive, not fanatic. And, after all, European pagans already worshiped the Great Mother and her magic child. Christianity could incorporate itself into this worship without much trouble, in its early days. For many centuries, it had no other choice.

But with the breakdown of the feudal system—largely through the church's ploy of sending feudal lords to fight and die in Crusades far away, in the "Holy Land," while the church was busy scheming to gain control of their homelands in Europe—the power shifted from decentralized rural/feudal to centralized city/court. Feudal lords were bankrupted by the Crusades; they returned to find urban loan sharks at their castle gates. They were unable to resist the rise of kings, their courts upheld by Rome and its priests. In the thirteenth and fourteenth centuries the church began to gather the kind of total, secularly armed power that would allow it, a couple of centuries later, to burn a significant percentage of the European population out of existence. Along with its ancient witch-knowledge, inherited from the Paleolithic caves.

In these brutal and transitional centuries, there appeared many messianic, millennial movements among the people. Though they were loosely clothed in Christian-sounding doctrine and apocalyptic imagery, the populist nature of such movements made them anathema to the church, which condemned them as "satanic." Many other movements were restless with resurgent pagan energy. There were many links, practical and symbolic, between the witches, the Knights Templar, the Gnostics, the Cabbalists, the Flagellants, and the earlier Crusades of the Poor. These Crusades were revolutions in embryo, striking terror into the hearts of the rich and privileged, whose castles and mansions were frequently burned and sacked. There were Ranters, and Diggers, and Catharites (who were among the first to be burnt for "heresy"). There were Beghards and Beguines—"The Brethren and Sisters of the Free Spirits"—women and men who advocated communal living and property, and voluntary poverty. Beguine women refused to marry, claiming freedom of sexuality and spirit as their divine right. Communities of Beguine women could be found throughout twelfth-century Europe, and many women artists, thinkers, and mystics were associated with them. These woman-cities, the largest of them located in Flanders, were self-supporting; they developed crafts and educated girl children. Nominally Christian, the Beguine women's communities refused to bow to church authority and were initially punished for their successful independence by heavy taxation and the break-up of their economies. Many Beguines, women and men, were bisexual; our word "buggering" (for male homosexuality) comes from these Boughers or Beghards . . . (who lived in the days before standardized dictionaries!). Feeling themselves to be the cosmic children of a Divine Parent (not a punitive Father), even believing they could be "living Gods," the Beghards and Beguines claimed to know nothing of "mine and thine" except the mutual ecstasy of being alive within a divine universe. Not surprisingly, they too were burnt.

There were also widespread beliefs in the coming of a female messiah. Probably this is why Joan of Arc was eliminated as a secular and divine rival of the church: she was a favorite of the people. Most of these groups and movements were wiped out by the Inquisition, or driven so far underground they gave up remembrance of their beliefs and customs. But their psychic heirs continue to spring up, everywhere and always, even to this day. Significantly, they always spring up among "the people"—the poor, the young, the outcast, women and minorities, "the mad," the artists—and they are always seen as a threat to the established patriarchal order. Rightly so: They are children of the Great Mother, struggling to regroup.

To the ancients, all things and events perceived by the senses and the intuition were interrelated, differing manifestations of the same ultimate fluid reality. The cosmos was one and inseparable, and the notion of the isolated individual self was an ego-illusion, to be transcended by ritual ecstasy and *kundalini* meditation. This was the natural holistic vision the Christian Inquisition and the witch-fires tried to burn out of the eyes of Westerners. Ironically, the Inquisition's excesses so disgusted "men of intelligence" that they turned away from the church altogether, repudiated religion, and began to build a wholly secular world on the smouldering ashes of the "holy fires."

From those fires rose Francis Bacon, calling for "the truly masculine birth of Time."[9] The "Patriark of Experimental Philosophy," as he was dubbed by an admirer, Bacon inaugurated modern science in very explicit language, calling for an aggressive male attack on nature's "secrets"—always a metaphor for female genitalia.[10] Bacon sought what he termed an "engine" of thought, the machinery of the scientific method that would allow men to "interrogate Nature with Power," to put her "on the rack," thereby uncovering the hidden processes and "secrets of excellent use. . . . still laid up in [her] womb."[11] Such metaphors were not accidental. As Bacon lived and wrote, the engines of the Inquisition were working methodically around the clock, interrogating Nature in dungeons via the naked bodies of women accused of witchcraft, interrogating all European life with the religious-judicial powers of torture and fire. Although Bacon argued against the prosecution of witches on the grounds that their "confessions" were too fantastic (i.e., unscientific) to be believed, it is very possible that he himself, as attorney general of England, was involved in authorizing arrests, trials, tortures, and burnings of accused witches. Brian Easlea, an English mathematical physicist and critic of the masculinist orientation of Western science, refers to the Baconian thesis as a "prospective gang rape" of female nature.[12] The rationalist control and exploitation of natural process launched by Bacon's method in the seventeenth century would lead to the birth of *products* as a substitute for life; this was all the enlightened European male mind could retrieve from Christianity's devastation of the original holism. To what noble end? In Bacon's words: "I am come in very truth, leading to you Nature with all her children to bind her to your service and make her your slave."[13]

Bacon was followed by René Descartes, whose extension of the theological split between mind and matter, spirit and flesh, into the realms of the physical sciences provided the intellectual whip for such an enslavement. Mind and matter became two entirely separate spheres, one "alive" and one "dead." This Cartesian division allowed scientists to treat matter as wholly inert "stuff" completely separate from themselves, and to see the material world as just so many isolated objects assembled into a huge machine—a machine that "worked," in the cosmological sense, through the sheer logic of its rigging. There was nothing inwardly alive left in Descartes's theoretical universe. As Karl Stern writes, Cartesian rationalism represents "a pure *masculinization of thought.* There is nothing childlike left in man's gaze. The hand of Wisdom, *Sophia,* the maternal, is rejected, and a proud intellect lays claim to omnipotence."[14]

As Stern also points out, Descartes's mother died in childbirth when he was a little over a year old, and his brief life was spent in physical frailty and melancholia. Intense grief was at the core of Cartesian dualism; he combated an ontological sense of loss with the precise tool of ratiocination which rendered everything dead but his own mind. In this he was a living symbol of Europe, which was killing its own ancient Great Mother with persecution and fire—and would find itself with nothing left but cold ashes, its own masculine mentation, and all the fabulous little machines it was about to construct, as a substitute for the truth of living flesh.

Newton was a master of the mechanical worldview, and made it the foundation of classical physics. From the seventeenth century to the end of the nineteenth, this "world-as-machine" philosophy dominated scientific thought, and was a model for much social and religious thought as well. A logical, technocratic God ruled the world-parts from above through the imposition of His "law," which was the impersonal law of Newtonian physics and geometry. Even nonbelievers and self-proclaimed atheist-rationalists had little trouble with this "God," who functioned as a perfect machine, doing no magic miracle tricks and demanding no devotion—beyond the application, now and then, of drops of cerebral oil. This "enlightened" way of looking at the world profoundly influenced all Western thought until quite recently. Western "man" has created his identity with his mind, instead of with his whole organism. The mind is supposed to "control" the body, while experiencing itself as something separate—this is how René Descartes handled his grief, and this is how "Western man" handles his. A method that causes an incredible fragmentation and alienation within the psyche, as well as in the organic world surrounding it.

Linearism—a wholly linear-logical concept of time and evolution—was already inherent in the biblical worldview, which pitted Hebrew historicity against the cyclicity of the pagan Neolithic Goddess religions. From the seventeenth century onwards, European linearism developed as a rational faith in "progress," which is an evolutionary accumulation of goods—property, material products, knowledge, and techniques—determined by the manly will of God. Men could fancy themselves totally emancipated from the body of the Great Mother—for didn't they have the steam engine? Didn't they have calculus and factory production? Real men were "above fate," and the imaginative energies of the soul were put away as childish toys. Nature was henceforth to be the docile handmaiden of the logical mind—the man with "know-how." That famous Western know-how which has given us, among other things, a good deal of the social, ecological, and spiritual catastrophes and crises of "our modern world."

As Foucault discovers in *Discipline and Punish*, "the sciences of nature . . . were born, to some extent, at the end of the Middle Ages, from the practices of investigation . . . . " developed by the Inquisition. The "Inquisitional technique"—that five hundred years of continuous sadistic torture of the bodies, minds, and spirits of primarily women, that Inquisition which Foucault calls "that immense invention that our recent mildness has placed in the dark recesses of our memory"—became the "scientific technique" of experimental investigation.

> These [sciences of man], which have so delighted our "humanity" for over a century, have their technical matrix in the petty, malicious minutiae of the disciplines and their investigations. These investigations are perhaps to psychology, psychiatry, pedagogy, criminology, and so many other strange sciences, what the terrible power of investigation was to the calm knowledge of the animals, the plants or the earth. Another power, another knowledge. . . . [15]

The Christian Inquisition held on the human being was to be a scientific inquisition held on all of nature, to the analytical end of turning both, nature and human being, into useful machines or functions of machines.

Notorious Western "discipline" began as a Christian monastic technique. Not a discipline of withness—of seasonal rhythm, of internal bodily rhythm and cyclicity—nor a discipline seeking illumination through the body's *kundalini* spinal energies. No: Christian monastic discipline was a rigid and deliberate program of antinaturalness, ascetically and punitively pitting the spirit against the body, against the ancient flesh. The monks established a timetable that was ideologically hostile to moon, sun, seasons, and stars; it was based instead on the Christian mind's *idea* of how mortal flesh was to be "straitened" by forcing it to go against its own biological inclinations. This monastic timetable and ascetic practice soon spread to the institutions controlled by the church: the schools and the poorhouses. These vulnerable populations were to be the first European citizens, outside of the monks themselves, to feel the systematically biophobic lashes of "God" on their brains and backsides from dawn 'til dusk. The young, the poor, the powerless—they were the ones who needed straitening. If the body was punished enough, it would be thereby weaned from nature, and then the "Christian spirit" could bloom in glorious submissiveness. So successful were these monastic programs, designed to turn human bodies into obedient machines, they spread during the seventeenth through the nineteenth centuries into the large commercial-industrial manufactories of Europe, in which the factory routine was strangely mingled with pious observation.

> The vigours of the industrial period long retained a religious air; in the 17th c., the regulations of the great manufactories laid down the exercises that would divide up the working day: "On arrival in the morning, before beginning their work, all persons shall wash their hands, offer up their work to God and make the sign of the cross." (Sant-Maur, Article I, *Reglement de la Fabrique de Saint-Maur*); but even in the 19th c., when the rural populations were needed in industry, they were sometimes formed into "congregations" in an attempt to inure them to work in the workshops; the framework of the "factory-monastery" was imposed upon the workers.[16]

To the profit of someone, we may be sure. The monastic routine was instituted further in hospitals and prisons, and achieved its ultimate success where we could predict it would: army life. In the Swedish Protestant armies of the seventeenth century, "military discipline was achieved through a rhythmics of time punctuated by pious exercises." Boussanelle, who wrote the Swedish handbook for this Christian mixture of prayer and war, believed that the military and the cloister should share the same "perfections." Through such methods the state perfected the trick of "getting rid of the peasant" and giving him "the air of a soldier."[17]

In the same way, industry turned "the worker" into "the tool," by getting rid of the human being. Thus monastic discipline, the Christian practice and urge to "free" the spirit by subjugating the body, was institutionalized throughout the Western world. And thus it led directly to the mechanization of the body, the human being turned into an appendage of the machine, a servomechanism, at work, play, love, and war. The spirit was never "freed" in this process, needless to say; it continues to share, with the body, in what Foucault calls "a subjection that has never reached its limit."[18] It has never reached its limit because the exercise of subjugation itself—the chronic submission of the human to the system and mechanism of such discipline—has become a function of profit, i.e., of world power.

The "Protestant spirit" added greatly to this process by rationalizing worldly profit as a function of Christian spirit. The fundamentalist-Protestant tautology that "wealth is a sign of God's favor because God wants you to be rich" is a perfect machine: While it grinds out "the profits of morality" for the many, it gathers in "the morality of profits" for the few; and thus Christian capitalism, where God becomes a kind of shrewd world banker in the sky, exchanging souls for dollars, and dollars for souls . . . at a terrible rate of exchange.

Foucault describes the design and construction of the nineteenth-century Panopticon, the symbolic utopian building of the Christian-Capitalist West, designed by Jeremy Bentham. This all-seeing building was based on the needs of prisons, army camps, workhouses, and factories for constant control via perpetual surveillance.

> The perfect disciplinary apparatus would make it possible for a single gaze to see everything constantly. A central point would be both the source of light illuminating everything, and a locus of convergence for everything that must be known: a perfect eye that nothing would escape and a center towards which all gazes would be turned.[19]

This is the eye of God—the God who is an eternal prison-keeper, the voyeuristic judge of morals, Big Brother. The purpose of such a building—and such a God—is, in Foucault's words, "hierarchical observation"; and we must remember that "hierarchic" comes from *hieros*, meaning "sacred," and in its first political-structural usage it referred to the positioning of the patriarchal priesthood, as the agents-spies of some remote "God," in authority above the people, over the people. God's police. This "all-seeing" structural eye of God quickly becomes the all-controlling structural eye of profit.

> This was the problem of the great workshops and factories, in which a new type of surveillance was organized. . . . "In the large factory, everything is regulated by the clock. The workers are treated strictly and harshly. The clerks, who are used to treating them with an air of superiority and command, which is really necessary with the multitude, treat them with severity or contempt; . . . "(*Encyclopedie*, article

> on Manufacture). But although the workers preferred a framework of a guild type to this new regime of surveillance, the employers saw that it was indissociable from the system of industrial production, private property and profit.[20]

Marx had seen it too.

> Surveillance thus becomes a decisive economic operator both as an internal part of the production machinery and as a specific mechanism in the disciplinary power. The work of directing, superintending and adjusting becomes one of the functions of capital. . . . [21]

Thus a kind of fascism of the eye—perpetual necrophilic control through total structural surveillance—was built into the nervous system of the West many centuries before a Hitler appeared. The West made "progress" through its willingness to turn the body into a disciplined tool, use the body as an obedient machine part, and its construction of a religious-political-economic machine which, via constant visual policing of the body's movements—work movements, sexual movements, social movements—ensured the success of this mechanization process. Success: i.e., its introjection, its internalization by a majority of its people. Today, in the modern West, mechanical surveillance is almost wholly subliminal, "a part of life." Employers, social agencies, government institutions, political and military leaders rely on constant technological surveillance as (1) a method of maintaining control and (2) a method of gathering the information needed to enforce the control. Workers and citizens have been almost perfectly conditioned to its use—i.e., few people ever question its "normalcy."

Pornography is a panoptic function. It is everything watched by a mechanical eye. With all our modern media of light, in fact—photography, cinema, television, video games—the entire West, almost the entire globe, is wired as a panoptic system. There are few places one can go to escape that "perfect eye," that "single gaze" which is modern electronic surveillance. Optics is the "genius" of the West, and voyeurism its major mechanism of control. With the spread of global or multinational corporations, and construction of "free trade zones" throughout the Third World (and soon in "undeveloped" ghetto neighborhoods of America), economic-political panopticism will be complete. "Free trade zones," which employ 80 percent to 90 percent women workers at substandard wages, often housing them in prison-like dormitories within the zones, are surrounded by cement walls usually topped by barbed wire. The women are under constant surveillance not only at work, but on their off-hours, for their *moral and political behavior.*[22] It's becoming standard practice for even well-paid, high-tech male workers in America and other major industrial countries to wear computer-sensors on their bodies throughout the work day;

these electronic sensors record the speed and efficiency of the body's work-movements in relation to each task. Sweat, skin conductivity, pulse and heartrate, muscular tension, and reaction time are all recorded by the "eye of God."

Because the West was arrogant enough, or insane enough, to believe its anal eye was truly the eye of God, its will to total dominance truly God's Will, its perpetual machinery of observation and control in fact the machinery of God—it made "progress." Western leaders, the political, religious, and economic elite, officially merged their profits with God's profits. And the Western peoples were conditioned, consistently and grindingly from the thirteenth century beginnings of the Christian Inquisition, to accept submission to this profitable machine as their moral lot.

The patriarchal denial of the Mother becomes the political denial of the people, which becomes the total mechanization, via capitalization, of the human body. And as the body moves, so does God move. The biblical-Capitalist West has created God as a prison-keeper, as a factory boss, rather than as a living cosmos. God as an assembly line rather than a dance. And this mechanical god, and the mechanism of this god, has been wired into the nervous systems of generations and generations of people.

Foucault says: "At the heart of all disciplinary systems functions a small penal mechanism."[23]

Indeed. The penal eye of God. That "single gaze," that mechanical "single vision" of the punitive, profiteering Father.

THE AMERICAN SPLIT

Americans are frequently told—especially with the resurgence of television evangelism and fundamentalist politicians—that America is "a Judeo-Christian nation, founded on biblical principles." Such a statement easily passes by all those Americans who don't know much about our own history—and most of us don't.

The English Puritans who first arrived to colonize America were highly biblical people. As Max I. Dimont points out in *The Indestructible Jews*, these Puritans regarded themselves, and were known in England, as "Hebraists." They "took the Old Testament as their model of government," and once in America, they "modelled their new homeland upon Old Testament principles." Though nominally Christian, and worshipers of Jesus, in social and political effect it was the Old Testament that served as the ideological matrix of the laws and customs the Puritans attempted to live by in the New World. The Puritans were highly influenced by the Old Testament concepts of a people chosen by the biblical God to exert his will and especially to lead the rest of the world to "righteousness." Dimont writes: "It was the [Roman] Christians who with sword in hand converted the pagans of Europe, thus bringing them their first knowledge of the Old Testament and its concept of manifest destiny."[1]

> The spirit of the frontier was merged into a political manifest destiny by the Puritans. . . . [who] transformed the Jewish concept of a religious manifest destiny into a political manifest destiny, believing it was God's will that Americans should rule the continent and the seas beyond. . . . [2]

At the founding of Harvard University in 1636, the two main languages taught were Hebrew and Latin. Governor Cotton of colonial Massachusetts wanted to make the Mosaic Code the official state law, and Hebrew the official state language. When women, and some men, were accused, brought to trial, and executed as "witches" in the colonies, it was by these Puritans, who were thus interpreting Old Testament injunctions against Neolithic Goddess religion as a colonial mandate to destroy

"New World" witchcraft, and paganism. For these Puritans, the New World was very much the biblical world of Yahweh; and when Americans began pushing at the Western frontiers, clearing land of forests—and Native Americans—all the way to the Pacific, it was the Puritan-Old Testament concept of a "manifest destiny" that fueled their drive to the West. As Dimont says, "though the political power of the Puritans was broken in 1800, their ideology became the American ethos." This Puritan ethos worked its way into fundamentalist belief and Protestant capitalism in general: A profound conviction that the political establishment of America, and later its political-economic hegemony over the entire hemisphere, perhaps someday of the entire world, were manifestations of God's will, a divinely mandated national destiny.

But Puritan religious power *was* broken in 1800. It was broken (or blocked, or rechanneled) by the second major influence on American life: the "secular" power. Who and what was this secular power? The "Founding Fathers," as they are called: Thomas Paine, Thomas Jefferson, George Washington, John Adams, James Madison, Benjamin Franklin, *et al.* The men who wrote the documents and espoused the ideas leading to the break with Britain and the American Revolution; the men who wrote the Constitution and Bill of Rights, and in general established the legal-political-ideological matrix that became American government, and American "ideals" of freedom and independence of thought and behavior.

The "Founding Fathers" were not Christian. They were Deists. Deism was an eighteenth-century rationalist philosophy, emerging from the European Enlightenment. Deists understood "God" to be the principle of organization and intelligence in the universe. This ordering principle could be discerned by rational thought and investigation, but it was not a personal deity who could be petitioned by humans. Deists considered themselves to be decent and spiritually devoted men, but when they said "God" they referred to "cosmic law," not the God of the Judeo-Christian Bible. Some Deists, including the American Deists, spent a good amount of time and energy criticizing and refuting the superstitions, dogmas, and rituals of the organized Christian churches, both Catholic and Protestant.

The major premises of Christian religions are (1) the idea of Original Sin and (2) the belief in salvation through faith. Deists totally opposed these two basic Christian principles. Instead, they espoused the eighteenth-century philosophy that defined human beings as (1) essentially good, and (2) capable of progress through knowledge, reason, justice, and liberty. Deists denied the dogmas of the virgin birth, the divinity of Christ, the concept of heaven and hell, and all ideas of damnation and redemption. Deism was, in fact, the origin of what is now called "secular humanism," and it was the practicing philosophy of the men who conducted and won the American Revolution, and became the "Founding Fathers" of the American government.

The European Enlightenment, of which Deism and the American Revolution were important elements, was a reaction against the historic collusion of court and church which had made a bloody debacle of European history. The American Deists lived on the still-raw edge of five centuries of Christian Inquisition and perpetual sectarian warfare in Europe. The historic ravages of persecution and scapegoating, the arrests, tortures, burnings, and daily terror, the confiscation of the property as well as the life of anyone accused of heresy or witchcraft—these nightmare events were still quite alive in the minds of men like Paine, Jefferson, and Adams; the Inquisition and witch-hunts were the recent history of their people. This is *why* they wrote the Constitution and Bill of Rights in precisely the way they did. The First Amendment was not a philosophical abstraction. It was an attempt, by non-Christian men, to structure a respect for religious freedom (of belief *or* nonbelief) along with a strong legal control over any church's ability to condition the minds of American citizens with the alliance of the government. The two prime virtues, for Deists, were liberty and knowledge—for white males like themselves, at least. Any church-state amalgamation threatened liberty and knowledge—which they rightly saw as enclosed in a mutual feedback system: One needs the other for either to exist. The American Deists were just one generation removed from a Europe reduced to spiritual and intellectual rubble by the power partnership of church and state. They wanted to prevent that from happening in America. They wanted the New World to have a chance to be new . . . for white men like themselves, at least.

Another strong, nonbiblical influence on the American Constitution came, of course, from the original inhabitants of this continent. "The Great Law of Peace of the Longhouse People," known as the Iroquois Confederation, or League of Six Nations, is perhaps one thousand years old, and still governs the Longhouse People of northeast America. Its intent was to unify Indian nations or tribes who spoke different languages into one communicating body as "an alliance for peace." The Deistic "Founding Fathers" were aware of this Great Law, and impressed by its sanity and practical wisdom; they incorporated much of its spirit and some of its organizational details into the U.S. Constitution. To this degree, the Constitution is a true and organic expression of the original American pagan spirit, deriving *not* from the Judeo-Christian Bible's pastoralist moralisms, nor yet strictly from European rationalism, but from the indigenous earth-oriented Indian consciousness of this land.[3]

When Thomas Jefferson said, "I have sworn upon the altar of God, eternal hostility against every form of tyranny over the mind of man,"[4] he was referring to his Deist God, the God of liberty and reason. And the tyranny he referred to was religious tyranny. Jefferson expressed admiration for the principles of the gospel Jesus, but he did not believe these principles were exemplified by organized religion. On the contrary.

> Difference of opinion is advantageous in religion. The several sects perform the office of a *censor morum* over each other. Is uniformity attainable? Millions of innocent men, women and children, since the

introduction of Christianity, have been burnt, tortured, fined, imprisoned; yet we have not advanced one inch toward uniformity. What has been the effect of coercion? To make one half the world fools, and the other half hypocrites. To support roguery and error all over the earth. . . . Reason and persuasion are the only practicable instruments. To make way for these, free inquiry must be indulged. . . . [5]

As for the biblical God, Jefferson described the Old Testament Yahweh as "cruel, vindictive, capricious, and unjust." Thomas Paine spent a good part of his adult life fighting the Bible, its God, and its ideas. This is what he had to say about it:

> Whenever we read the obscene stories, the voluptuous debaucheries, the cruel and torturous executions, the unrelenting vindictiveness, with which more than half the Bible is filled, it would be more consistent that we called it the word of a demon than the word of God. It is a history of wickedness, that has served to corrupt and brutalize mankind; and for my part I sincerely detest it, as I detest everything that is cruel.[6]

Louise Michel, one of the heroines of the French Commune, who was exiled from France after the Commune's defeat, wrote in her memoirs:

> Throughout the world there are too many minds left uncultivated. . . . Between those who know nothing and those who have a great deal of false knowledge—those warped for thousands of generations by infallible knowledge that is not correct—the difference is less great than it appears at first glance. The same breath of science will pass over both.[7]

This was the spirit of the time, the spirit of post-Inquisition Europe, when freedom-fighters saw clearly and spoke eloquently against the tyranny that had for so long been exercised, not simply over the human body, but over the knowledge-seeking human mind and the freedom-seeking human spirit, by the collusive powers of church and state. People were seeking knowledge, liberty of inquiry, "reason," "science"—as the way out, the way over that hideous tyrannous gray wall. Thomas Jefferson, the American Deist, was writing in the same spirit when he deplored "that religious slavery under which a people have been willing to remain, who have lavished their lives and fortunes for the establishment of their civil freedom."[8]

But, as Jefferson, Madison, and the other Deists saw, there were many people who *were* willing to risk their lives fighting for physical and political liberty, who then turned around and submitted their minds to religious dogma, to spiritual tyranny. Jefferson and Madison constructed the First Amendment to allow such people a "freedom of religion" to so do; but they intended the same amendment to absolutely prevent them, or any church, from imposing such mental and spiritual tyranny on anyone else.

Because of their absolute insistence on a separation between state and church, because of their Deistic beliefs in the innate goodness of human beings and the evolutionary value of reason, knowledge, and liberty of inquiry in the development of a truly human consciousness, Thomas Jefferson, Thomas Paine, James Madison, George Washington, and all the other American "Founding Fathers" could be justly called the first American secular humanists—the same type that is now being called, by fundamentalist preachers, the "enemies of America" and "those who want to destroy the American Way." This strange reversal occurs because the fundamentalists identify "the American Way" as the way of the Puritans, those pre-Revolutionary English "Hebraists" who were indeed trying to live out the mandate of the Old Testament on American soil. But the Puritans did not conduct the Revolution or write the Constitution that established the American government. *This* American Way—the way of Paine, Jefferson, Madison, and the Bill of Rights—was the way of non-Christian Deists, of men whose positive influences were not the Bible but the European Enlightenment and the very secular works of Voltaire and Rousseau. The secular humanist way, in fact, which was not the invention of twentieth-century liberals, feminists, and other "atheist pinkos," but was officially born with the birth of the American Constitution.

As many of us were growing up, "humanism" was not a dirty word. It meant a generous concern for the liberty, well-being, and growth of the entire human community. It meant a rational acknowledgment of the fact that human beings build the human world, and if we build it greedily, fanatically, or stupidly, we will all end up suffering in it. During and after World War II, it meant everything opposed to Hitlerian fascism and Stalinist tyranny. In a naive but well-meant way, during those years, "humanism" *meant* "the American Way." For the past two decades, however, Christian fundamentalist preachers and ideologues have been trying, quite loudly, to redefine "humanism" as something un-American, and even evil. In their definition, secular humanism means "putting humans at the center, rather than God." And they insist this human-centered society is to blame for all the world's crime, violence, disorder, and general unhappiness.

Socialists, and many other people, would argue that the modern Western world, led by America, is not "humanist" but "Capitalist," and that at its functional center is not the human being, but the dollar. And that it is not secular humanism but Capitalist exploitation which is causing so much of the world's violence, degradation, and destruction. Further, when we look for examples of the societies that *have* put "God at the center," what we see is appalling. We see five centuries of European Inquisition. We see the witch-hunting obsessions of our own colonial Puritans, who were not above torturing small children until they "testified" against their own parents. We see Nazi Germany, led by a crazed necrophiliac who proclaimed he was "finishing the work of the Lord," a work of mass extermination. We see contemporary Iran, ruled by "holy men," who are executing seven-year-old children, and lining their streets with the hung bodies of "traitors against God."

No human being—no preacher, no holy man, no church—can "put God at the center" of life. God is already there; we choose to perceive, or not to perceive, this fact. No one can "put God" anywhere; God is already there. What the fundamentalist preachers and self-appointed "holy men" mean is that they are going to put some man's idea of God at the center—an idea that is born of the inflated egos of these preachers and holy men themselves. It is never to God, but to men's ideas of God, and to the swollen egos of God's self-appointed policemen on earth, that millions and millions of human beings have been torturously sacrificed in all the "God-centered" societies of the past four thousand years of patriarchal earth. In all true religion, approximation to God is revealed by a steady growth of wisdom and peace. In false religion, approximation to some man's idea of God is always signaled by increasing fanaticism and bloodshed. The "God" so many contemporary fundamentalists—of any religion—want to "put in the center" of our lives is in fact a regime of total tyranny, established by mortal men in the name of God, and in name only.

The first American secular humanists, the "Founding Fathers"—and in particular Paine, Jefferson, and Madison—saw this problem very clearly, because they were children as well as students of European history. They were also children and students of American Colonial history, and had observed how quickly the old Inquisitional mind had flared up in the New World—in the habits of the Puritans. The Constitution and the Bill of Rights were their attempts to save America from becoming one more "God-centered" tyranny, ruled by "holy men" with a terrible blood-lust.

There is a third stream in North American life. It was never really on the historical surface of white American consciousness, as were Colonial Puritanism and the rational-humanist Deism of the Constitution writers. It has always been an underground stream: that of wildness, of sensual innocence, of paganism. Many Europeans did come to America with a conscious desire to "escape civilization"—a civilization of constant inequity, harsh morality, and warfare—and "return to nature." America was an entire hemisphere of pure nature. Not a few European men (this stream was mostly male) did return to wilderness in America; they joined Indian tribes, or became frontiersmen, exploring ever westward until they hit the Pacific sea-wall. Some of these people were just blindly running from "the straitened life," others were consciously pagan. This underground stream emerges as the real "American dream"—a peculiar "lust for innocence" which is always sought, never found. This pagan American search was never for the Puritan's moral God, or the Deist's rational God, but for the time of paradise before God. The garden of beasts, trees, and human souls living in harmony before Yahweh, Christ, and Descartes. There is a kind of genetic-generic memory that such a time did exist, and America briefly seemed a place where it could be refound.

In nineteenth-century America, there were many "Edenic" or "utopian" experiments in communal living, fueled by a dream of communal harmony and personal ecstasy; but the twin gods of morality and rationality always seemed to prevail, either breaking up such communes from within, or barrelling down from without, to drive them out of town. The great American tradition of "normality" has always been a public device for controlling and exorcizing these lurking demons and dreams of personal wildness. Behind every lynch mob, every cross-burning, every racist attack on "the dark other," as behind every social snobbery or "polite" rule of exclusionary etiquette, is a rationalist puritan terrorizing his or her own pagan heart. "Normal" people fear this wildness so much because it is always there, indigenous not only to this land but to our own prebiblical roots. But our conscious returns to the pagan have been sporadic and local. "Bohemian," "beat," and "hippy" communities in America have attempted it; such attempts have affected and changed our lives stylistically and politically, perhaps more than we know. But never for long enough, or inclusively enough.

The paganistic return to nature is like the Buddhistic salvation from the world wheel: nobody really does it unless, until, we all do it. North Americans, more than any other people on earth, have a hard time returning to our roots—because, for most of us, our roots are elsewhere, buried under hundreds and thousands of years of "the man's" history. We can never return to the garden of harmony and ecstasy until we know how to pass through those two fierce angels blocking its entrance: moralism and rationality. And we can never get through those patriarchal door-guards unless, until, we remember whose garden it really is.

Just as much of the rigid puritanism of Protestant fundamentalism can be traced to the biblical Old Testament, so a good deal of Catholicism's historic misogyny and zeal to convert can be traced to the New Testament's St. Paul—who was himself a fanatic convert, and a fanatic misogynist. Throughout European history, there were periodic attempts by people who saw themselves as Christian radicals to break the grip of the Old Testament and St. Paul on the established churches and over the Christian mind. These people chose to follow the gospel image of Jesus as a radical social reformer, Jesus as social revolutionary. The Templars, the Beghards and Beguins, the Albigensians and Cathari, and so forth, all tried to practice what they understood as gospel communism, a naked and ecstatic sharing of food, goods, and mutual care. Some of these medieval Christian communes tried to practice sexual equality, some extended their communal practices to the sharing of their bodies; others maintained strict marriage fidelity or practiced celibacy for Gnostic visionary purposes. All were accused by the church of social and spiritual heresy, including orgiastic sexual behavior. They all ended up at the stake.

Many of the experimental communes in nineteenth-century North America were composed of similar radical Christians, trying to live out their interpretation of the Gospels, and of the Jesus-image, as a call to return to communal living and ecstatic, nonpossessive behavior. Within a Victorian society that valued the accumulation of private property and wealth as a moral duty, the North American communalists practiced a sharing of shelter and all material goods and daily activities; within a Victorian society that covered piano "limbs" with crocheted cuffs so it was not forced to see, or even say, the fact of "legs" (in a society that had more brothels per capita than any other society on earth), the radical communalists practiced either free sex or strict celibacy, with marriage partners living as "brothers and sisters." These communal experiments in North America, like the hippie communes of the 1960s, were marginal and elitist/middle-class by necessity; there was no way for them to reach or affect the lives of large numbers of people, or to radically change the values and structure of the larger society.

All these communal or utopian experiments of Europe and North America, Christian or otherwise, saw what they considered to be social greed and injustice, and sexual hypocrisy and repression, practiced in the name of God and Christ, and they counteracted with "radical experimentation"—i.e., radical: "going to the root." Within a Christian-Capitalist context, "radical" social experimentation always means (1) communal living and sharing of goods, (2) sexual freedom and equality, (3) practice of visionary and ecstatic techniques, both communal and individual. Many of these communalists have called themselves "the *true* Christians," or considered their experimentations to be "closer" to Christ's gospel intentions than the "normal" lifestyles approved by the church. But in fact such social revolutionary communal experiments are always a reversion to pre-Christian, pagan social and spiritual structures, even though they sing and dance to gospel texts. Within a Christian-Capitalist context, "radical Christian behavior" is always a reemergence of paganism.

And this is why it is always opposed and crushed by the church. Regardless of what the Gospels may say about "the lilies of the field" and "spiritual poverty" and the virtues of not possessing wealth or worldly power, the Christian church, both Catholic and Protestant, has grown with and firmly established itself upon the practice of private property, and its existence is functionally embedded in a hierarchic framework of social classes based on wealth. The wealthy and powerful uphold the church as a major instrument of social discipline and repression, and as the most effective inculcator of the "divinity" of the status quo; the church in its turn puts "God's" seal of approval on the existing social system, conditioning people from a very early age to see nonconformity as "bad," and serious rebellion as "demonic." The Christian churches and the Western Capitalist ruling elites have always worked together as a machine, in Foucault's sense, that perpetuates and rationalizes the advantage of the few, while maintaining the many in a condition of productive repression, via ideological control and channeling of their sexual-spiritual energies.

Liberation theology began, in Latin America, with these classic conditions: the wealthy ruling elite supported by the conservative Catholic hierarchy, dominating masses of poor people. In 1956, progressive church leaders founded CELAM, the Latin American Bishops' Council, to discuss and counter these conditions with new ideas. And then came Pope John XXIII and his Vatican Council II, which proclaimed the Catholic church's "option for the poor." CELAM met in conference in Medellin, Columbia, in 1968 to find ways and means of putting Vatican II into practice in Latin America.

One of the structural ideas emerging from the Medellin conference was the "church base community," where poor people gather in self-managed parishes to discuss religion and help each other with survival problems. In Brazil, particularly, with its large population and great shortage of priests, these base communities spread rapidly; in 1984 there were about 150,000 church base communities in that country, all actively supported by the Brazilian bishops. Brazilian Franciscan and theologian Leonardo Boff, one of the architects of liberation theology, has explained that the Brazilian Catholic church needs these communities to help it face rapidly growing competition from numerous Oriental and Afro-Brazilian religions, and also from fundamentalist Protestant and Mormon churches that have been sent to Latin America, from the U.S., with President Reagan's tacit support. Boff has defended the Catholic base communities as the most creative way to compete with this "pastoral challenge"; they are the locus where the people meet together, to "read the word of God, celebrate, put into practice love of neighbor. . . . "[9]

This is the "church of the poor" in South and Central America. These base communities have spread everywhere, among millions of people who are traditionally very spiritual, and also struggling to survive oppressive conditions, as well as overthrow U.S.-backed political-military dictatorships. In *Christians in the Nicaraguan Revolution*, Margaret Randall has shown the strongly inspirational and tactical effect of the Christian base communities and liberation theology on the people of Nicaragua, who were able to harmonize their religious vision with successful armed struggle against the dictator Somoza and his U.S.-trained National Guard. This is the inspiration of liberation theology among the people, and the threat it poses to the ruling elites: when poor people read the Bible, they interpret Jesus as a social revolutionary, and liberation theologists have interwoven these popular radical interpretations with traditional theology. Boff, in particular, has applied Marxist economic analysis to the hierarchic-conservative-imperialist social and religious structures dominating Latin America; in *Church: Charisma and Power* (1981) he analyzes the Catholic church from a Marxist perspective as a "Capitalist institution." For this and his whole range of politically provocative and inspirational thought, Boff was called to Germany in September 1984, at the pope's request, to be "questioned" by Cardinal Joseph Ratzinger, the Archbishop of Munich. Ratzinger was put in charge of the Vatican's Congregation for the Doctrine of the Faith in 1981, for the express purpose of questioning and disciplining liberation theology; this Congregation is what remains in the modern world of the old European Inquisition's infrastructure.

The Vatican and conservative Catholic churchmen in Europe and Latin America have, since the early 1970s, joined together to target and denounce Christians for Socialism and liberation theology in general, as well as "Marxist infiltration" in CELAM. They claim that any use of Marxist economic-structural analysis threatens to expand into an "atheist Marxist" undermining of the human spirit (or at least the church's control over the human spirit). In fact, the church has always seen any analysis of the human condition, beyond its own, as a threat to its imperialist hegemony. It created the Inquisition in 1200 to fight "heresy," i.e., the Arabic worldview; later, in 1484, it launched its three-hundred-year-long war on "witchcraft," i.e., the pagan European worldview; now, in the mid-1980s, it fights "Marxist atheism." In all cases the church claims to "own" the true spirit, it pretends biblical-textual support for its authority, and it denounces its opponents as heretical and un-Godly. But Marxism didn't exist during the Inquisition, nor is it essentially Marxism the church is fighting. It is in fact engaged in the same, centuries-old secular power struggle against rival social visions, as well as rival religions. When it denounces "Marxist analysis" and the communalist visions of Socialist Christians, it is truly fighting its old, old war against the radical Christian vision of Jesus as social revolutionary—a vision that is always, at its ontological core, a reversion to pre-Christian paganism.

Because the Bible is not "the word of God," but the words of men—of many men, and many times—its texts can be used, like Bartlett's *Quotations*, to support just about any argument one is espousing. In Deuteronomy 5:17, Yahweh says, "Thou shalt not kill." In Deuteronomy 2:34 and 7:1–2, in Leviticus 20:1–27 (and throughout the books of Exodus, Numbers, Joshua, Samuel, Kings), Yahweh commands that his people kill a long explicit list of people Yahweh finds offensive.[10] Human sacrifice to "idols" is divinely condemned; yet, on page after page, Hebrew heroes like Samuel "chasten" their enemies by annihilating whole villages, butchering pregnant women, infants, and old people, right down to the cows and ducks and geese—and these My Lai-type massacres are, we are told, not only condoned by "God," but empowered and blessed by him. Which "Word of God" do we listen to in the crazy bowels of the night?

By the same token, there is as much biblical-textual support for the idea of Jesus as a social revolutionary, and the Gospels as a revolutionary's handbook, as there is for the maintenance of a hierarchic social system based on wealth and ruled over by a political-religious-military dictatorship in God's name. In Margaret Randall's book a Nicaraguan named David speaks:

> There cannot be a church of the rich. Christ was the first to accuse the rich, telling them it was easier for a camel to go through the eye of a needle than for a rich man to enter the kingdom of heaven.[11]

One does not need Marxist training, or Marxist analysis, to see the gospel Jesus as a spiritual and social radical breaking with the traditional hierarchy of his people and of imperialist Rome, denouncing both the wealthy Jewish and Roman ruling classes and their corrupt priesthoods, to call the human soul to rebellion against its condition: its false ontological condition, falsely rooted in an antispiritual, antiholistic social order. The Bible, like all large cosmological works of the human mind, gives to us essentially what we come looking for: The authoritarian looks for passages promising God's blessing on a fascistic status quo, and finds them; the radical seeks confirmation of an active revolutionary vision, and finds it. Certainly there are more than enough New Testament passages illustrating Jesus' radical social intuition and his desire to do away with the hardened and corrupt institutions that block and deform the aspirations of the soul, to give textual authority to the liberation theologists and their work. (And when it comes to textual authority, we have to remember that the entire establishment, structure, and worldly power of the Roman Catholic church was based on one joking pun made by Jesus, who said he would build his "church" on "this rock"—i.e., on the Apostle Peter, whose Latin name comes from *petra,* meaning "a stone." And thus Peter is legendarily the first Bishop of Rome, and all the mythic and worldly authority of the Vatican derives from this pun.)

Politics happens when people realize their daily survival problems are not caused by individual "sin" and "guilt" but *by a collective malfunctioning.* Within patriarchal Christian capitalism, this is the taboo vision. Whether it comes from Albigensian or Catharite "heretics," or pagan witches, or from twentieth-century Christian socialists or "atheist Marxists," the vision is the same, insofar as it is a collective-systemic-revolutionary approach to problems, rather than a personal-confessional-therapeutic one. While liberation theology and "the church of the poor" activate the first—the political—approach, the church encourages, as it has always historically enforced by law, when it could, the latter, personal solution. A solution which, needless to say, keeps it in business.

The conservative Catholic and official Vatican view is expressed by the German Bishop Franz Hengsbach, who since 1973 has been working through Bogotá, Columbia, with conservative Latin American clerics, to stamp out the influence of liberation theology and "the church of the poor." Hengsbach insists that Christian liberation must be solely personal—a liberation from "original sin" and "personal guilt"—not from social structures. While liberation theology seeks to free human beings from decadent and exploitive social-economic conditions, the conservative Catholic hierarchy apparently believes that hunger and poverty, forced and unrewarding labor, and massive brutal exploitation by global economic and political forces, are to be understood and accepted by "humble sinners" as God's punishment for their "sins." Or at any rate, such conditions are to be patiently endured, without revolt, while individual souls concentrate on confessing their "personal sins" on their knees—never seeking justice or mercy or fulfillment on earth, but meekly believing such "luxuries" will come to them in heaven. ("Original Sin," it seems, is the sin of being born poor—or, if not, why don't the rich, the owners, the exploiters, the bosses, the ruling political, religious, and military elites have to suffer in this way?)

Bishop Hengsbach announced, in 1977: "The so-called liberation theology leads to nothing. Its consequence is Communism." Hengsbach's opinion was important, on the secular if not the divine level. The poor Latin American Catholic churches depend on funding from the very rich West German churches; and Hengsbach was at the time the president of the German Bishops' Conference, and thus in charge of all the funding for developmental and pastoral work in poor countries, specifically Latin America. Just before making his pronouncement on liberation theology, Hengsbach had been decorated with the Order of the Condor of the Andes by President Banzer, the dictator of Bolivia. Hengsbach's view of liberation theology is similar to the Chilean dictator Pinochet's view of democracy, which he called "the breeding ground of Communism." Another major Catholic warrior against liberation theology is the Belgian Jesuit Roger Vekemans, who has denounced it, along with "the church of the poor," as a "contagious virus." In the mid-1970s, Vekemans had been reported, by the *Washington Star* and the *National Catholic Register,* to have received—on his own admission—millions of dollars in funding from the American CIA and from the Agency for International Development (AID). He had also boasted of advising then–CIA director John McCone to "let" one or two Latin American countries "go Communist," so that it would then be easy to arouse anti-Communist paranoia in the rest of the Western hemisphere.[12]

The Catholic church, as the self-defined "owner" of the true spirit, denounces Marxist analysis as "materialistic," and finds liberation theology's emphasis on social-economic problems with social-economic solutions also abhorrent in its "materialism." Apparently the desire of the world's poor to eat, to feed their children, to clothe and shelter themselves and their children, to live creative lives, to spend their days in meaningful labor rather than numbing drudgery, to earn a fair reward for their work and a future for their children—apparently all this is to be seen as "materialism." It can be seen so, by the Catholic hierarchy, only within the Christian dualistic system that separates "flesh" from "spirit," and then pretends that the lifelong degradation of one leads to the eternal liberation of the other. In fact, suffering can and does enlarge the human consciousness, but not within a dualistic, or antiholistic, system. Within Christian "civilization," the suffering of the poor, generation after generation, has served as little more than nervous titillation for the well-off; the rich derive a complacent sense of continuous self-justification by muttering "the poor we have always with us" etc., etc., and other selected phrases. Coming from the Vatican and the Catholic bishops of the wealthy German church, who have all spent most of their lives in a heady atmosphere of pearls, gold, velvet, and good wine, such a charge of "materialism" is stunning. If we wonder if any of these "princes of the church" have spent much time sweating, starving, or shaking with cold, the answer is, probably not. Nor is it "spirit" that clothes their daily lives in perpetual luxury; rather, they are liberally endowed with the accumulated material wealth of centuries.

It isn't the poor people who need "redemption," but the fabulously wealthy churches themselves. The only way the Christian institution can redeem itself, surely, is by helping the poor and the persecuted realize equity and justice. Half the world's Roman Catholics live in Latin America; that is a powerful force. Enormous changes could occur if the Catholic church, led by the Vatican, removed its holy sanctions from the exploitive systems of the rich, and denounced and renounced the ruling political, business, and military elites it has helped bring to power, and maintain in power, for over 450 years throughout Latin America. But papal lip service won't make change happen; total structural and ideological change is necessary. Liberation theology and "the church of the poor" are such real attempts at real change. And they are being called up to defend themselves before the grim persecutory shadow of the Inquisition.

Can Christianity truly be revolutionary? Can it change its institutional, ideological self and thus help change the world? What *is* Christianity? Insofar as it derives from both biblical testaments, it is a set of ontological principles, or assumptions, that must be confronted on an ontological level by anyone seeking a merger of the Christian religion and genuine world change. These principles are (1) that the creator is separate from the creation, therefore does not participate continuously in evolutionary process; (2) that the creator is pure spirit mechanically dichotomized from a creation of impure matter; (3) that human beings have committed a primal sin, or crime, of disobedience to the will of God; (4) that God has therefore condemned the entire human race to continuous suffering and punishment on an evil earth as expiation for this original crime of "our parents" in Eden; (5) that to be born, therefore, is to be born in sin; i.e., to be born through the mother who represents the "original sin" and inherent evil of flesh; (6) that, to survive in a world of sin, the male must dominate nature, while women, as embodiment of that nature and its "vessel," must undergo domination; (7) that the only way to be saved from this situation—from life on earth and life after death, both defined as hells ruled by the Devil—is through submission to Jesus Christ, who is defined by his religion as the *only* time in the history of the universe that spirit ever entered into matter, i.e., incarnated; (8) that these principles exist because the world is a mechanically structured dualism of God and Devil, pure good versus pure evil, eternally at war with each other and eternally irreconcilable, in which human life is meaningful only insofar as it functions as a battlefield for these two forces; human beings must choose one side or the other, but can never transcend the dualisms, or resolve them in holistic consciousness (which was the consciousness forbidden by Yahweh in the Genesis Garden).

Since the ontological worldview embedded in these principles is seen, by many of us, as the cause of the problem, how can radical change occur via these same principles? Can the world, or "Christian civilization," be radically changed without radically changing that world's structuring ontology? How can one find a truly revolutionary solution without radically changing the terms and cosmological assumptions of the problem?

Mary Daly is one of the few people, among feminists or contemporary thinkers in general, who has wrestled with this situation at its ontological roots; she has done so, as a feminist, in her books *Beyond God the Father, Gyn/Ecology,* and *Pure Lust.* In *Pure Lust,* in a section entitled "The Courage to Sin," she points out that "sin" derives from a Latin word meaning "to be." "To sin is to be."[13] "Sin" comes from the Old English *synn,* meaning "to sin," with the root word being Old English *es,* "to be." *Es,* the root of "being," is a basic Indo-European word root. (Interestingly enough, in Hebrew the word *sin* means "the moon.")

To *sin,* within the patriarchal religious context of Christianity, is to risk *being.* I.e., within that context, true being can only occur in the renegade spaces outside the established religion, utterly outside and beyond its terms. The Christian dream has already been written, from beginning to end. It says that only one life was worth living, and it's already been lived, and it was *his.* The best believers can hope for is an imitation of Christ. Christianity promises to save the human soul; but, in fact, Christianity exists by saving humans from the experience of our own souls. If we will forfeit our own mystical journeys through the world, if we will give up the dangerous adventure of discovering and creating our own consciousness-in-evolution, Christianity will give us, in return: a script about Jesus. And this is the only choice Christian ontology offers: One can spend one's life risking the sin of being, or one can submit, and spend one's life following a dead script. The tragedy of Christianity is that it has kept untold millions of human beings from sinning, i.e., from knowing their own souls. For it is *life* that Christianity promises salvation from—from life directly experienced, for the first time, without the stale safeguards and blinders of a prefabricated script.

Upon the machinery of sin and salvation the whole Christian ontology rests. The figure of Christ that the church is based on *is* this machinery; i.e., Christ depends on human sin for his existence. One can say that "sin" is the food of the Christian church, and it cannot keep eating it if it does not keep producing it—producing a definitive vision of life as "sin," as experiential being we must be saved from. If the world has been hell under two thousand years of Christianity, it can be said to have been so as the result of a self-fulfilling prophesy. The Christian machine is not programmed for any other result.

In Nicaragua, and in any place touched by the energy of liberation theology, the popular belief is "*Entre Christianismo y revolución—no hay contradicción*"—"Between true Christianity and people's revolution, there is no contradiction." But what is Christianity without the established

Christian church built on traditional biblical-Christian ontology? Ché Guevara said: "At the risk of seeming ridiculous, let me say to you that the true revolutionary is guided by great feelings of love."[14] This is the radical Christian vision also, the vision of Jesus as a social revolutionary; such a vision has historical precedent, going back through European Gnostic and "heretical" communalism, back through the gospel days—about two thousand years older than Marxist analysis. But, as we've said, it goes back even farther than that: to the Neolithic vision of the vegetation deity, or to the original Great Mother herself, primal beings who sacrifice themselves through love to restore and refructify all life on earth. The *radical* Christian vision is, and always was, a reemergence of paganism.

To be truly revolutionary, Christianity would have to dissolve itself. It would have to dissolve its male-dominated and celibate hierarchies, and the social class systems from which it derives its worldly power. It would have to renounce and dissolve totally the world-hatred, the flesh-hatred, the ontological misogyny which has so long provided it with fanatic energy. It would have to renounce most of the Old Testament, most of the New Testament, and *all* of Revelation, which dooms us to a grotesque apocalypse. It would have to throw out Genesis to return us radically to an image of God based on the pre-Biblical universal perception of a Great Mother—a bisexual being, both female and male in spirit and function—who *wants* us to enjoy ecstasy and to eat of the fruit of immortality. It must totally renounce and dissolve spiritual chauvinism, spiritual hypocrisy, spiritual paranoia, and spiritual tyranny, and all world systems built in the secular image of these spiritual distortions. It would have to wholly renounce and dissolve all perceptions, systems, and functions deriving from the false historical idea that some people have a "divine mandate" to coopt, convert, genocidally destroy, or otherwise imperialize others. It would have to crucify itself, *in its own terms,* as expiation for all this guilt. But, as we said, if the Christian church ever changed itself this radically, it would become pagan. To realize its most radical vision, Christianity can only reinvent paganism. So why not just, simply, *be there?*[15]

In North America, the rationalism of the Founding Fathers—the Deistic rationalism of the Enlightenment, which wrote the U.S. Constitution and the Bill of Rights—has given us a large measure of spiritual freedom, of freedom to experiment, of freedom from cradle-to-grave conditioning and control by the dogmas of any particular church in collusion with the state. We all owe more to this rational freedom than we realize; because it has worked, we take it for granted. We have no concept of what it is like to grow up under the conditions of state-enforced religious tyranny. At the same time, this very rationalism has pervaded the American atmosphere with non-ecstasy. For generations, many people have felt they stood in a very dry, pragmatic wasteland—secular America—with no genuine tradition of spiritual celebration, of communal epiphany. Americans long for this more than they know; the ersatz results are orgies of patriotism and game-fever, at parades and in football stadiums. But never quite the real thing . . . at least not as a communal experience.

In Latin America, the Catholic church (which is, chronologically and psychologically, much closer to the pagan than is anything Protestant) has allowed celebrations and customs of indigenous Indian people to remain alive, interwoven in a festive ribbon with Catholic holidays, saints' days, frequent loud celebrations of cycles and epiphanies. Latin America has this, which North America longs for in the secret places of what's left of its soul; but Latin America also bears the terrible burden of political and military dictatorships, partly (at least) established and maintained in power by almost five hundred years of domination and status-quo rationalization by one church. The death squads, the armies of terror and torture now running rampant through so many of this hemisphere's nations are in fact the leftover machinery of the Inquisition, never wholly dismantled in the Catholic tradition—and now re-oiled, updated, redesigned and modernized by the imperialist interests of the new Roman Empire, corporate America.

The American split, in raw terms, is this: nominal "freedom" without real-life ecstasy, or nominal "epiphany" without real-life freedom. Such a split is always the result when life is fed into the patriarchal dualistic grinding machine—which churns out globs of white fat, or pours runnels of blood; which turns out tasteless hamburger or the red screams of the butchered; which grinds out always one disconnected fragment or another—but never the whole feast, never holism. Never the living, gratified flesh of a true spiritual vision.

"THE DIVINE HOMOSEXUAL FAMILY"

In January 1977, the pope announced that women could never be priests in the Catholic church. The reason given was that Christ is a male, and his priests must be "imitations" of him. In the Netherlands on May 13, 1985, Pope John Paul II reiterated the Vatican's position on women to a large crowd of less than enthusiastic Hollanders: Women will never be allowed in the Catholic priesthood, he said. Liberal Protestant denominations now allow women ministers, and Conservative Jewish leaders have just opened the way for women rabbis in their synagogues; but among Catholics—as among conservative Christian churches, such as the Mormons, and Orthodox Jews—women are still not considered the proper sex to serve as "sacred ministers" or interpreters of the biblical God. The highest a woman can go in the Catholic hierarchy is deaconess, a role always subordinate to the male priest. As far as the Vatican is concerned, a priestly relation with the male Christ can only be enjoyed by another male—both of them served humbly by convent-trained nuns, as a kind of holy harem of the patriarchal spirit.

The liberal egalitarianism of the other Christian and Jewish denominations, where women ministers and rabbis are now accepted, is a very recent occurrence; it came about only via feminism, and the pressure of Christian and Jewish women for spiritual acknowledgment by their respective faiths. For most of the millennia of Christian (and Jewish) history, the biblical God Yahweh and his immaculately begotten son, Christ, have always and only been represented at the altar by a male. Quite often these males have worn skirts. And always, in all times, they have been the givers and upholders of dogmatic laws regarding women—laws telling women how to dress, how to move, how to behave, how to relate to our bodies, how to reproduce, when to reproduce, how to have sexual activities, when to have sexual activities, how to relate to our menstrual periods and our childbirths and our afterbirths, how to bow our heads, cover our hair, keep our eyes modestly averted; how, in general, to be pliant and submissive and unquestioning handmaidens in the holy back-halls, kitchens, and bedrooms of the Lord. Indeed, this strange urge of "holy men," of all patriarchal denominations, to stand there, wearing skirts, giving sermons to the world's genuine females on what it really means to be a woman . . . is a propensity that needs deep pondering. Nonetheless, it has been the history of the male God religions.

What needs deeper pondering, by all of us, is why *women* continue, today, to plead for egalitarian respect in reactionary churches that clearly, now and historically, have no interest in women as anything but followers and servants. The Catholic church's male hierarchy does not need women priests, and dismisses the very idea with celibate contempt. But the Catholic church needs women. Wherever the church exists, it is millions and millions of female believers—low-paid teaching nuns, volunteer women parishioners, catechized mothers catechizing their children—who keep the Catholic church alive.

In all Christian churches, until very recently, this was the traditional case. Women's natural religious impulse and capacity has kept patriarchal churches in business for so long. The female gift for spirituality—into which, under patriarchy, we pour so much repressed sexual energy—is used and turned against us by the male hierarchies of the male God churches; they cleverly keep women on our knees, scrubbing and scrutinizing the sacred floor, while they—a few select princes of the churches—rise upward in lofty clouds of worldly power and luxury. Religious women think they are worshiping "God"; in truth, under patriarchal religion, women believers exist only to service and inflate the institutionally ordained egos of very mortal men.

On October 7, 1984, twenty-four American nuns were listed as signers of a public statement, printed in the *New York Times.* The statement was headlined, "A diversity of opinions regarding abortion exists among committed Catholics." American nuns, in the past few decades, have been at the forefront of social action for change; in particular, regarding women's rights to control our reproductive functions—a right supported by a majority of American Catholics, it would seem—American nuns have been frequently willing to oppose or challenge the Vatican and the conservative American Catholic hierarchy. Sisters of Mercy nuns, who direct the second-largest hospital chain in the country, wanted to allow sterilization and tubal ligation in their hospitals, many of which are in isolated, tradition-bound areas where women have no other birth control options. The Vatican and a conference of U.S. bishops forced the Sisters of Mercy, under threat of dismissal from their jobs, to sign statements disavowing all surgical methods of sterilization.

The Catholic hierarchy, like all consciously patriarchal power-institutions, very much *needs* to maintain control over female reproduction. They won't allow sterilization, or birth control; they definitely oppose abortion. A large number of American (and European) Catholic lay people disagree with the Vatican on all these issues, and the American nuns have been heroically responsive to what they perceive as a desperate and legitimate need on the part of women to control the number of children we have. So the American nuns signed the *New York Times'* paid statement, which at its most radical simply pointed out that even many Catholic theologians acknowledge that abortion can be a "moral choice" in specific circumstances. The statement was signed by many prominent Catholics, including two priests, in addition to the twenty-four nuns.

How did the Vatican respond? It threatened to expel the nuns from their religious communities if they refused to recant. What this dismissal means to these women, most of whom are over forty and have given their lives to the church, is a loss of home, a loss of community, a loss of livelihood, and a loss of pensions. The nuns were not even informed of this threat of severe punishment in advance. The orders came abruptly from their supervisors; a few of the nuns heard the news on the radio, via a Vatican leak to the press, before they even had a chance to be informed by their supervisors. In the words of one of the inquisitioners, Archbishop Jerome Hamer, head of the church's Sacred Congregation for Religious and Secular Institutes (which issued the official church statement against the nuns), the nuns were "seriously lacking in 'religious submission of will and mind' to the magisterium." The two priests involved recanted; the twenty-four heroic nuns, to this date, have not.

In the words of theologian Rosemary R. Ruether, who was one of the statement's signers:

> The conservative bishops and curia were enraged that nuns would sign such a statement. Especially that celibate women were involved in an issue that shouldn't affect them. The curia can't stand the support of celibate women for women who have sex.[1]

The twenty-four nuns, in Ruether's opinion, are among the "best and the brightest in the American church." Some have national reputations for their organizational work for Central America, women's and gay rights; some hold Ph.D.s from Yale, Harvard, and the University of Chicago; some are theology teachers or authors of books on women's role in the church. They were zapped by the Catholic male hierarchy with no respect for their accomplishments, however . . . something like an enraged husband kicking out a disobedient wife. Some of the nuns felt the Vatican's threats, and mode of threatening, constituted "psychological rape."

Under Vatican II, there was great liberalization not only in the relation between the church and the poor, and in the area of social reform, but also in the customs and rules of the religious life within the church. Nuns and many priests "came out" socially, involving themselves passionately in radical issues, e.g., the antiwar movement, antinukes, Central America, women's rights. Nuns left their imprisoning *habits,* and became strong crusaders for social justice. Under Pope John Paul II, the church hierarchy has been attempting to brake and reverse this liberalizing direction, and in particular to get the "uppity" nuns back under absolute conservative male control. The media has focused on the most obvious Vatican backlash against the nuns: The attempt to force them back into their religious habits, the long thick costumes of constriction and submission. But this back-to-the-habits movement is only symbolic of something deeper. (All habits are.) In Ruether's informed opinion, the Roman Catholic curia is maneuvering back to the top-down monarchical organization of pre-Vatican II days, in which all power and authority is at the top, and all submission and obedience is at the bottom. In such a hierarchic scheme, the totally subordinate position of Catholic nuns is critical. In Ruether's words, "They are at the bottom of the chain of command, but have the essential role of passing on commands to the laity." As mothers to children. . . .

The burning question remains: Why do women continue to give our gifts—of spiritual devotion, of impassioned energy, of mental brightness, of profound social concern—to male-dominated and male-defined religious institutions which are based, structurally and ideologically, on a searing contempt and hatred for women? Why do women continue to give our physical endurance and biological endowment to patriarchal churches which exist, ontologically and practically, by attempting to dominate and control human female reproduction like a bunch of cattle breeders controlling the fertility of their cattle? What would happen, today, if all the millions of religiously active women on earth just walked *out* of their patriarchal churches, just left them flat? Better, and braver, and wiser to take our female blood-energy and brain-power and *build our own church,* within it making sacred our own experience of oneness within the Mother, between each other, and within ourselves. After two or three millennia of serving a male Godhead, and male priesthoods, in devotion and submission, could women ever take ourselves seriously enough to serve the sacredness of ourselves . . . of each other . . . of the earth, and its holy wild creatures?

No study has been made of the effect of a male Godhead on the intimate beliefs and experiences of women. Traditionally, nuns were seen as the virginal brides of Christ, serving a purely disembodied sex role in the Catholic church. The nuns also functioned as glorified housewives—polishing the church silver, embroidering altar-cloths and vestments—always the humble handmaidens and under the ultimate authority of father-confessors and male priests, serving a male God and his son—a son who had said to his mother, "Woman, what do I have to do with thee?"

In earlier centuries, where *all* the options for women were terrible, it was often a liberation for a creative independent woman to enter a cloister, instead of being forced into what usually amounted to brutal marriage and eternal childbearing. Many of the great women artists and poets of the Middle Ages and Renaissance were nuns, living in all-women environments, with freedom and time to think, read, write, and create. In the early Celtic church of Ireland, especially, many of the "nunneries" were communities of Druidic priestesses in drag, still mixing magic spells and their pagan worship of the Goddess Bride with their daily Christian duties.

As Malory told us in *Morte d'Arthur,* "Morgan le Fay was not married, but put to school in a nunnery, where she became a great mistress of magic."

"Convent" and "coven" are the same word, after all. Doubtless the psychological influence of these "witch-nunneries" contributed to the atmospheric survival of the Goddess in Ireland; according to folklorist Lewis Spence, as late as 1850, the Irish folk still worshiped her, regardless of the Catholic priesthood.

> At the well of St. Declan, Ardmore, County Waterford, . . . masses of people assembled annually on December 22, crawled beneath a hollowed stone and then drank of the well. It was surmounted by the image of a female figure which is described as being "like the pictures of Callee [Kali], the Black Goddess of Hindostan." The Catholic priests actually whipped the folk away from the spot, but to no purpose.[2]

As Kali and Cailleach are the same Goddess, after all. The whips of the priests can never turn what was into what was not; nor can failure of memory.

The Christian Trinity has been dubbed "the Divine Homosexual Family." It consists of the "all-loving" Father, his "immaculately conceived" son, and an all-male priesthood—who live in celibacy among Catholics, and among all Christians serve in some strange way as male brides to the father church. (When Christians want to blame their religion for corruption and error, they usually refer to it as the "mother church"—making sure the Father and his son are kept free of all blame for "her" material failures. Most modern Christians do not know, however, that well into the early Middle Ages, the Holy Ghost of the Trinity was seen as female by the people—another relic of Goddess worship. A crime against the Holy Ghost is, in Christian doctrine, the only unforgiveable sin; this continues the pagan matriarchal tradition that matricide is the crime without forgiveness.)

Mary, the only female now left on this divine scene, has nothing of the primal creatrix about her. She is a mere, lowly, mortal woman, "lifted up" by Yahweh's divinely disembodied attention—impregnated by it, in fact, without ever seeing or touching the man—to produce a son for the heavenly Father. (Supposedly, Mary is impregnated by the Holy Spirit; this is interesting if we interpret this fertilizing ghost as the remnants of the Great Mother.) The impregnation of Mary echoes all the classic patriarchal myths of mortal women being implanted, by more-or-less force, with the seed of the Sun God. In all the other myths, however, there is fleshly contact between God and mortal, and something that could be called sex—or rape. In the New Testament tale, there is no sex whatsoever; and it is to a divine absence that Mary acquiesces with vapid humility—an absence that uses her without even having to touch her; and Mary, in our eyes, does not even gain the simple strength of struggling or choosing. She has no identity, except as passive acquiescence to an absence. And this is how Christ is "conceived," in both his physical conception and in our conceptions of him: it is all so fastidious, so nontextural, so cerebral and unreal—so bordering on the sexually pathological, in fact. The messy femaleness of Mary is dealt with by pretending it is not there; and this has been the fate of female sexuality under Christianity: it simply is not there. It is a story of disembodied alienation and nonidentity that stretches from the Virgin Mary of the New Testament to the modern *Story of O*—in which a woman supposedly achieves complete sexual gratification by giving over her body wholly to male control, while she remains anonymous, without identity or passionate being, just *not there.* O is the twentieth-century incarnation of Mary; in both, an essentially antisexual cultural mind deals with female sexuality by using it without encountering it. For this was how Jesus Christ was conceived; and thus it becomes a major though distorted mode of eroticism in Christian culture. The faceless O undergoes daily sexual self-sacrifice and mutilation on the altar of a phallic God, just as the archetype Mary undergoes lifelong sacrifice of active self, mutilation of her conscious identity, on the altar of Yahweh and Christ. For both women, the whole purpose of existence is self-obliteration through the body: via the perpetual machine of sex, or the perpetual machine of maternity. Mary and O are bookends enclosing the history of women's lives under patriarchal religion. In their stories, they act out an alienation that is personal, social, mythic, cosmic, and total. Mary foregoes sexual consciousness, sexual pleasure, physical prowess, economic and intellectual power, cosmic risk, the ontological and evolutionary adventure of creating one's identity—she gives up her whole range of natural and magic potential, in order to become a "good mother" for her "divine son." This is the beginning and end of her meaning as a human being. Just as O's whole meaning is as a kind of sensational blob, a mass of flesh that exists to have things done to it. The biblical definition of a "good woman" is one who sacrifices herself completely to the needs and demands of others, particularly male others, while asking nothing for herself. This "good woman" is essentially the same, whether she dwells with faceless humility in the house of the Lord, or with anonymous masochism in the private rooms of the sadist.

Under patriarchal religion, maleness is made—invented, mass-produced; while femaleness is unmade, de-evolved, extincted. For over two thousand years Western biblicized women have been undergoing conditioning *out of* our natural powers and wisdoms; we grow up learning to disregard the effects of our own rhythms, which are cyclic like the moon's, the tides, the seasons. We learn the habits of ignoring them, denying them, trying to forget or overcome them, as we live under the rule of the man (without and within), who conceives of time as something that can be ordered and processed in mental-mechanical categories, regardless of the body's or the earth's phases. In this sense, all Western culture is built on ideal male homosexuality—the classic patriarchal institutions of the military, the hierarchic centralized governments, the academic, medical, and legal professions, as well as the priesthoods of the various biblically derived denominations, all being built around the male body in its relation to other males, and very explicitly to the exclusion of women's bodies, cycles, needs, and capacities.

When James Watt became head of the U.S. Department of the Interior under Ronald Reagan's first administration, the department's stationery showed a few buffalo standing on the left side of the paper, gazing eastward; Watt, a born-again charismatic Christian, had the stationery redone so that the buffalo were standing on the right side, gazing toward the west. Watt knew, intuitively and doctrinally, that *the right* is the side of the Father, as well as of neoconservative politics and free-enterprise economics. Christianity is a dextral religion in all its aspects; the sign of the cross is made with the right hand, as is the benediction. Jesus always raises his right hand in blessing, in paintings, and in heaven he sits on the right hand of the Father. Any blessing made sinistrally—with the left hand—is seen by Christians as blasphemy, part of demon-worship. The *left side* represents not only the social-political-economic left, but also the side of the Communal Mother—or, in the case of the Interior Department's stationery, communal buffalo. Watt was speaking from this same right-wing perspective when he condemned Native American tribal life as "socialistic"—i.e., it is a communally oriented life, reverent of the earth, and is thus seen by Watt as left-wing: American Indians walk and dream on the side of the Mother. In the iconography of Christian patriotism, all true Americans must be right-handed, right-wing, father-dominated, and physically male. Anything vaguely communal, leftish, and mother-dominated is viewed as sinister by the *patri*ots (*patri*: "father"). The female body, in other words, is politically subversive—or has a lurkingly treasonous potential. All patriarchy is structured, *all ways,* in militant reaction to this potential.

In ancient matriarchal society, man stood always in the relation of son to the mother. He could become divine, he did become divine, by being born out of God the Mother: by undergoing the lunar process, the twin world of the Moon God, experiencing both waxing and waning, cosmic dissolution as well as cosmic union. In this way his individual ego would transcend arrogance and exploitiveness, and become truly wise. All the ancient male heroes—even such a one as Gilgamesh of Sumer and Babylon, who defies the Great Goddess Inanna-Ishtar and is cursed by her—receive their wonderful beauty, strength, and creative-destructive restlessness from their mothers, forms of the Goddess. Their mortality comes from their human fathers; but it has no connotations of fleshly sin, guilt, or punishment—it is simply death, in the great round of life. Gilgamesh, like his Babylonian counterpart Marduk, the "son of the sun," was given the task of overcoming and slaying the Great Mother, in her form as cosmic dragon. But Gilgamesh is just at the beginning of patriarchy. Unlike the one-dimensional super-heroes of later times, he still retains some of the sensitivity, wisdom, bisexual wholeness of the ancient matriarchy. He feels and acknowledges fear and doubt; he repeats over and over that he must not bring harm or sorrow to his mother; he is depicted as often cowardly, he loves another man, and he fails in his struggle to become immortal. Gilgamesh is told, starkly and truly, that everything born must die; otherwise there can be no magic life or new beginnings. Man cannot conquer immortality by tricks, gimmicks, aggressive game-plans or armed warfare. He can only realize immortality by becoming whole. In the "Gilgamesh Epic" of four thousand years ago, the Goddess of Birth, Death, and Rebirth had not yet been subdued; she still lived as a natural process of wisdom in human minds, and in evolutionary human feelings toward an evolving universe.

The heroes of our present age, though, are something else. They are Superman, Bionic Man, James Bond, the Terminator, Rambo. They are the one-dimensional cartoon-men of children's comics and TV. These twentieth-century superheroes are fiendishly skilled in one specialty (always involving a lot of noisy smashing and silent spying), and absolutely stupid in all other ways. They don't need profound human intelligence—they have machines.[3] All presented as sex symbols for the masses, they are all eerily asexual and misogynistic; they are all just too pure, too patriotic, too damn busy, too damn dangerous, or moving too fast for one woman—or any woman. Their primary sensual relationship is with their machinery: The only *wildness* around them, thanks to the speed of the light media (cinema, television, magazine photography), is *embodied* in manmade objects, usually of shining metal. The magic swift gun, the magic swift car, the numinous technologies of spying, capture, and death: these are alive and wild. Everything else surrounding our heroes is dead meat. Clothed in steel, never born of a mother, the cartoon-heroes are true products of huge metalopolises, sky-scraping phalluses, and calculator minds that click and tick like bombs. There is not a tree or an ecstasy or a moon in sight. Some variation of Bionic Man is the ultimate twentieth-century vision, owing his life not to nature but to manmade parts, which are far superior to the original body he got from his mother; and he can be reborn with a screwdriver. This humanoid superhero is as much a product of pure male ideal homosexuality as is his prototype, Christ.

In Mary, especially within the Catholic church, the Goddess for the first time in history bows down to worship male gods as creators of life. The Christian religion (a transvestitism of the spirit?) has, from the beginning, coopted female experience, taking the victory and raw energy out of it, leaving us only an insipid view of our female selves. Christianity distorts the natural birth process into a grotesque and unnatural story of birth-through-the-male—who, twisted in this artificial creation, becomes a sadomasochistic symbol of arbitrary power and empty submission. For the whole thing centers around birth, the primeval mystery and terror and blood-rite in which women struggle alone to create and triumph within the vast unknown. Christianity, for two thousand years, has gained its energy by coopting and distorting this experience, this fact, these symbols. For while maternal suffering is unconditional, since it is ontologically inevitable—the suffering Christ is blackmail, a wretched and manipulative appeasement to a cruel, manipulative, and jealous Father God.

Mary is wife, mother, and child to the same male power-figure. She is utterly meek, abject, passive. In her, the ancient power of the Goddess is captured, chained, used, cannibalized—"metaphysically cannibalized," in Ti-Grace Atkinson's critical phrase—domesticated and tranquilized.[4] It is no accident that Mary is portrayed as giving birth in tranquility and bliss, as a reward for her asexuality and total submission (thus "redeeming" the crime of Eve)—while Christ, her son, takes on the suffering and dramatic childbearing role of the Mother. For he twists on the cross in labor, to give birth to a redeemed human race. Pierced by a soldier's sword, blood and water pour from his body—exactly as from a woman in childbirth. The figure displayed on the crucifix in Catholic churches particularly is a male parody of the female experience—of menstrual bleeding, of childbirth, of ontological physical suffering for the human race. But while Christ coopts this female experience into his own power and glory—women, who really do these things, have been forced to hide the signs of our bleeding and childbed "crucifixions" as unclean processes, and badges of corruption, inferiority, and shame. The deified male martyr flaunts his "sacrifice" everywhere, and we are supposed to bow down to it. Women, the real thing, are required by "decency" to hide our messiness out of sight.

In *The Making of the English Working Class,* E. P. Thompson describes how, among the Methodist congregations of the nineteenth-century, Christ's wounds were spoken of in a highly ecstatic, sexual, masochistic/sadistic language. His bleeding body was unconsciously identified, Thompson thinks, with the female body-role under patriarchy: long-suffering, sacrificial, the erotic-passive object of male frustrations and brutality.[5] In *Labyrinth of Solitude,* Octavio Paz explores modern sadism and torture as extreme macho attempts to get "revenge against feminine hermeticism," against passive female otherness—"a desperate attempt to obtain a response from a body we feel is insensible."[6] But the female role of insensate, passive victim-body is just that: a role. A role inculcated, enforced, and prolonged by a patriarchal religion which must keep women numb and silent while its Male God, Christ, acts out a female role: the erotic-dramatic role of bleeding and childbirth. But Christ, as a transvestite or female-imitation sacrifice to an asexual and jealous Father God, represents unbearable distortion; it is "God" itself, in this twisted person of Christ, who is maddeningly alien and alienating, ontologically insensate and eerily "other." The entire world, the entire universe is eerily other—and the sadism and torture increases daily, crazed men beating *otherness* into bloody pulp.

In such a world, where torture and brutality—or persistent threats of torture and brutality—constitute *daily facts of life* for a majority of people, sadomasochism or S/M has become a game for some people. The game is played by American heterosexuals, Lesbians, gay men, and bisexuals. S/M is seriously justified or rationalized by its participants as (1) an activity that "frees" people from sex roles by allowing them to exchange roles and "experience the other," and (2) a means of learning about "power," of acquiring "power," and of understanding "power relationships." On the first count, S/M advocates assume—wrongly, as many feminists have pointed out—that torturer and victim roles are somehow ontologically, rather than culturally, derived; and that therefore, by "experiencing" both roles, and by exchanging them in role-play, we can then learn something about our ontological selves, including our sexual selves as "female" and "male." In fact, torturer and victim roles do not represent, respectively, the ontological male or the ontological female; playing out and exchanging these roles teaches us nothing about who we are. Rather, it teaches us only about the roles a culture has imposed on us for several thousand years as a psychological-political means of confusing, coopting, and repressing our ontological energies.

Surely the major political travesty of S/M activity and its rationalizations lies in its second claim: that it seriously pretends to be telling us something about "power relationships." Surely, the whole monstrous point about power relationships is their involuntary nature: the torture victim does not volunteer for the torture experience, nor does the torturer agree to stop the procedure upon request. Power is defined and determined solely by the fact that it can be inflicted by the will of one against the will of another. But S/M advocates insist their activities are based on mutual agreement, and that this mutual agreement can teach us something about power relationships. Such an argument totters horribly on the edge of suggesting all torture is "chosen," and that all torturers are simply giving their victims the experience they really desire. The obscenity of S/M, in a political context, is that the game-players can get up and walk away from the game of pain, while real victims of real torture—i.e., of real power relationships—cannot get up and walk away. What we "learn" from one context (voluntary S/M) cannot in any way be transferred over to "understand" the other context (power relationships in the real world). S/M teaches us nothing about power. It teaches us only about certain forms of game-playing behavior in the West; and especially about the increasing inability of many of us to tell the difference between game-playing in the Western world and real life everywhere else. To transfer the contextual experience of what is essentially white, middle-class American psychotherapeutic activity (human empowerment games, est, "self-choosing" behavior) into what for most S/M players is a contextual nonexperience of brutal and unrelieved global power politics, is the epitome of self-indulgence and unreality. Such a contextual confusion is a sign of nothing but political privilege: A few well-off Americans can afford to play at torture.

The model clothed only in S/M bondage appears on the cover of *Vogue*, etc. It comes and goes as a trendy thing, something like wearing camouflage bikinis and fashion-bandoliers; something like playing at war when one has never known war.

Starting with de Sade, the whips and boots, the expensive torture-instruments designed and manufactured by highly paid artisans, the aristocratic torturers and voluntarily cringing victims of all the S/M games, do not represent "sexual liberation" in any form. They are, in the West, a sad, obsessive acting out of the Christian crucifixion ritual and social class passion—what can be called the decadent's imitation of Christ. The S/M fixation is *not* on sensuality, but on stylized coercion and humiliation. The grotesque and deliberate unnaturalness of S/M ritual reflects the Christian perversion of the natural birth/life/death process, through the total perversion of human sexual experience. The sadistic punisher is Yahweh-man-tool, the eternal sufferer is woman-womb-Jesus. All our lives are twisted on the cross of this bizarre distortion of ontological reality. S/M game-players, like Christ on the cross, are symptoms of our sexual-spiritual problem. But certainly not the cure.

In his study of the effects of Protestant Christianity on the working class of England, E. P. Thompson also speaks of how the Methodist church helped pave the way for the imprisonment of economically uprooted peasants in the urban factories of the Industrial Revolution. When Protestant Reformism merged its Calvinist belief in the complete depravity of most of humankind with the marvelous new profit-making machinery of factory mass-production, what could be called "Capitalist theology" was born. The men of wealth, the investors and factory owners, were obviously the "elect few" morally preselected by God for heaven (and righteous power, meanwhile, on earth). The masses of workers, on the other hand, had clearly been divinely prefabricated to suffer, via endless hard labor, for their innate corruption. To fit the workers to the assembly lines, to chain the many bodies together into functioning parts of an industrial machinery grinding out wealth for the few, religion was called in as always to help program living organisms into a daily condition of productive repression. In England, the Protestant religion was the right hand of the factory owners. Forced from their rural cottage industries and herded into crowded, diseased cities, the peasants were forbidden "by God" to ever again be naturally alive. They were forbidden their seasonal festivals, their dancing, their music, their singing, all those pagan communal rhythmic rites which energized the people and let them know who they were. *That* they were: living beings of a living earth. Forbidden all memory and practice of organic rhythm, the people were more readily inured to a life of mechanical rhythm. Thus the rural English peasants were reprogrammed, by the Protestant churches, into urban factory workers. The grim effects remain to this day.

(Pagan music and dance were built on erotic and melancholy modal scales and complexly sensual drum rhythms, which Protestant Christianity especially saw as "devil-inspired." It was Protestant moral-rationality that finally forced European music into the constricting framework of the major and minor scales, and the tick-tock or marching rhythms of 2/4 and 4/4 time. Interestingly, modal scales and pagan rhythms have returned to public life via rock music; and if most young people on earth are now walking around with transistor radios plugged into their brains, it is because rock-energy is the global drug of the people—a pagan resuscitation of the body in a disembodied, anti-body world. Christian fundamentalists of today, like their historic counterparts, hate rock's sound and lyrics, and denounce it as immoral Devil-music; in fact, rock is pagan music, and its rhythms and lyrics express the memory of the blood.)

With its dismissal of the worship of Mary, the Protestant church got rid of the iconic Mother altogether—and with her all organic, celebratory links to the earth and the body's rhythmic-ecstatic life. In her place, we have been given *the machine.*

THE MACHINE

Three connected phenomena are happening all around us, in the very "modern" world of the 1980s. They are (1) the rise to power of fundamentalist sects—Christian, Judaic, Islamic, Hindu, Buddhist, Confucian—and their collusion with business and military-dominated governments in directing theological and political attacks at women's rights, in particular women's right to control our reproductive capacities; (2) the growth and global distribution of reproductive technologies, everything from birth control pills, IUDs, and coercive sterilization programs dumped on Third World women, to the expensive and complex Western technologies of making sterile women pregnant through the transplantation of unfertilized eggs and embryos from the ovaries and wombs of "egg mothers" to the wombs of "host mothers," and the correlative genetic engineering of embryos to "make babies to order"; and (3) the spread of American corporate structures and advanced production technologies into "global factories," where virtually trapped workers, over 80 percent of them women, work and often live behind the barbed-wire walls of "free trade zones," at subsistence-level wages, controlled in both work and private life by a corporation-government collusion that forbids them union organization or political protest, and often extends to the economic control of their reproductive lives. (E.g., multinational corporations give preferential employment to single women without children, and with no plans to have children; in India's textile industry employers prefer women who've been sterilized through the government's population control program; and in the Bataan Export Processing Zone in the Philippines, the Mattel company offers prizes to women workers—making toys and Barbie dolls—who undergo sterilization.)[1]

These three trends might seem disconnected, even sometimes publicly antagonistic—but in truth they are profoundly linked. Their linkage can be traced back to the Bronze Age, to the practical beginnings of patriarchy at the end of the Neolithic, when men first began to organize to gain systematic control over (1) women's production and (2) women's reproduction. As we've said, the definition of the female body under patriarchy corresponds to the definition of the worker's body under private-Capitalist (e.g., American) or state-Capitalist (e.g., Soviet) production systems. At the beginning of Bronze Age patriarchy, males began to take over women's ancient inventions and "improving" them—i.e., *capitalizing* them—by turning rhythmic local qualitative handcraft work into quantitative mechanized mass-production, for trade and the building of wealth. Simultaneously, patriarchal men moved to take over and "improve"—capitalize—the most primal production of all: the female's production of children. Modeling their religious and practical notions on their new experience of cattle breeding, men redefined the ontologically and autonomously creative female body into a machine for producing wealth; that is, wealth for men via the patrifocal family in the form of children as inheritors of patrilineally controlled property, and children who could be used to make more wealth, as workers, or traded for wealth, in the form of female bodies traded as "wives." Patriarchal religion grew side by side with patriarchal wealth and secular power; the Father God's male priesthoods rationalized and sacralized the pastoralistic control and use of women's bodies as wealth-breeding machines, simultaneous with cattle breeding, spiritually programming generations of both women and men to believe that God was now a male who wanted it this way. The Neolithic Goddess religions that had supported female sexual autonomy—female control over both sexual pleasure and reproduction—were religiously "demonized" and politically destroyed. With the growth and elaboration of tribes into nations into empires, structural-systemic control of female reproduction passed from the private hands of fathers and husbands into the functional machinery of state-political economies; male rulers attempted, at least, to regulate populations according to state and business fluctuations, the need for increase or decrease in labor forces and armies, for more consumers of surplus or fewer consumers of famine, etc.

For over four thousand years now, female reproduction has not been an autonomous function of women, but an auxiliary function of patriarchal systems; and for the same time period worker production has functioned as a part of the same patriarchal-hierarchic wealth-producing machinery. Both female reproduction and worker production being rationalized and reified "by God" (i.e., religious dogmas of priesthoods and theologians) as subsidiary and inferior functions of that wealth-producing system. They are subsidiary and inferior functions in the sense that they are the disempowered many controlled by the system to the benefit of the empowered few. As far as wealth production or actual value goes, females and workers are of course not subsidiary or inferior in any way, but primary producers of all wealth.

In both cases, worker production and female reproduction, wealth is produced for the dominant males (or the dominating male system with its auxiliary "wives") by organizing what was once organically rooted sexual-spiritual activity into coerced mechanical-reproductive activity. The cyclic dance of impassioned bodies is forcibly and moralistically restructured into

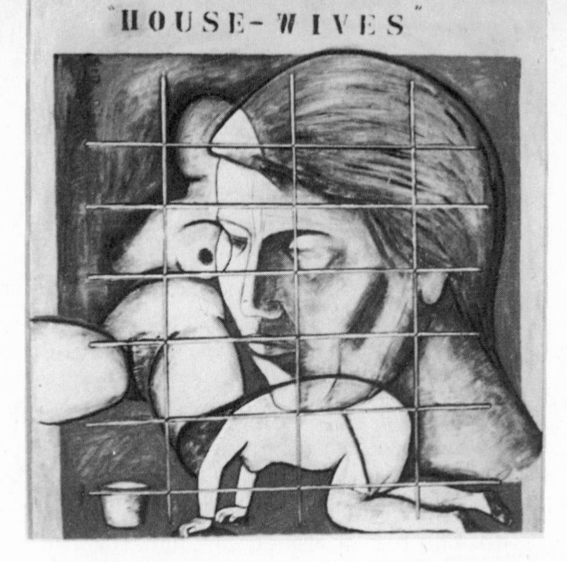

Housewives, Sjöö, 1973

the chain-gang of numbed bodies forming an assembly line, or a maternity ward. Human biological and dream energies—once numinous ends in themselves—are coopted and rechanneled into profit-making results via a collusion of religious and governmental-political ideologies that manipulate the body and the spirit of humanity away from conditions or experiences of evolutionary-revolutionary ecstasy, and into conditions and experiences of counter-evolutionary-revolutionary productive repression. Both worker production and female reproduction are controlled and directed by the same forces: sexual-spiritual ideological systems of piety and drudgery, which are themselves teleological machines producing just enough energy to rationalize themselves automatically while maintaining themselves in power. Piety and drudgery reinforce each other by dogmatically, physically, and habitually repressing energy to a mere subsistence level; a subsistence level that is capable of only piety and drudgery, i.e., incapable of the revolutionary ecstasy or creativity necessary to escape the subsistence-level system. And piety-and-drudgery is the "normative" state-of-being in which females and workers have been kept, under patriarchy, for at least four thousand years.

Finally, this condition is the result of the Bronze Age patriarchal redefinition of the female body from organic-autonomous creator to male-controlled breeding machine. Technological or systematic-ideological control of human labor could not exist if control of female reproductive labor did not preexist. For control of organic-autonomous female reproduction is structurally necessary to create the mechanical state of piety and drudgery

Women's Right to Abortion & to Dignified Childbirth/Medicine Controlled by Men, Sjöö, 1971

out of the repressed sexual-spiritual energies. (I.e., all machines, including all mechanizations, need fuel, and all fuel is originally organic energy; the subsistence-level machinery of piety and drudgery is fueled by the repressed energies of orgasmic sexual ecstasy and spiritual epiphany.) Working labor can only be controlled and exploited in a situation where female reproductive labor is equally controlled and exploited, because both exploitations are necessary to keep the exploitive machinery running; and female reproductive labor, chronologically and ontologically, is the first labor. Under world-capitalizing patriarchy, the uterus is a factory, and the factory is a uterus—and the enormous profits produced by their joint biologic-mechanical activities do not belong to the laborers, needless to say. They cannot take over their own productive-reproductive systems; they are kept too busy and too tired, functioning at the subsistence-level of mechanical piety and drudgery. (In terms of evolutionary biology, and of yoga, one could say that large masses of people are being forcibly retained, and maintained, at the level of the reptile brain—the brain of ritualized repetition and benumbed violence; *kundalini* is not allowed, by primarily moral restrictions, to rise up and illuminate this situation. Indeed, the reptile brain is kept strangely hypnotized, from the outside, by mass-produced dreams and commercial hallucinations of transcendence: the luminosity is on the entertainment screen, while the evolutionary brain sits in darkness.)

What does all this mean in relation to today's world and the three interlinked phenomena previously mentioned?

First, everywhere in the world, governments are trying desperately to control and channel their populations to meet the economic pressures being put on them by the spread of global corporate "developmental enterprise," especially the strain of domestic economies being deformed and deenergized by the enormous drain of military budgets. Pages of statistics exist to illustrate this phenomenon, but what it really means is billions of female wombs and ovaries being directly manipulated by their governments . . . and rarely in the interests of the women involved. Government heads are seeking to increase or decrease populations in the interests of their own political careers and/or to meet the demands of global corporate investors. As we've seen, a corporation like Mattel colludes with the Philippine government to promote sterilization among Filipino women workers; this ensures what corporations consider to be a more malleable and less demanding labor force in the free trade zone, and also puts numerical brakes on an increasingly revolutionary Filipino population. In Sri Lanka, Ceylon, the government also wants to reduce its population, especially of poor Tamil laborers agitating for civil and economic rights; forced sterilization occurs among female workers on the vast tea plantations. In Malaysia, on the other hand, the prime minister, Mahathir Mohamad, wants to increase his country's population to fill a labor shortage of native workers. He aims to swell Malaysia's population from 15 million to 70 million, and to do this his government has launched an all-out program of maternity promotion—including repression of feminist groups working for women's reproductive rights.[2]

In all cases, whether the plan is to increase or decrease populations, the governmental-political control of women's reproduction is directly related to the control of the labor force—in particular since women workers compose at least 80 percent of the light-assembly workforce in the global "free trade zones." Multinational corporations preferentially employ women workers because, with the collusion of the "host" government, they can pay women lower wages, and be also "assured" a "docile" population of workers, conditioned by generations of religious-social customs to obey males in authority, and to engage in long hours of boring repetitive work without complaint—i.e., women workers trained to piety and drudgery. On a global scale, therefore, it is no longer possible to speak of a labor force separate from women workers; and by the same token, it is no longer possible to analyze the management of labor production separately from the management of female reproduction. They are fast becoming one and the same; to control female reproduction and women's rights globally it is necessary to control the rights of labor populations globally, and vice versa—and the "free trade zones" are the spearheads or experimental

Women Have Only Their Chains to Lose, Sjöö, 1971

models of this total global control, with repressions of unions and political activity, along with the forced or coerced sterilization of women workers, already built into their structures. As Anna Fuentes and Barbara Ehrenreich point out in *Women in the Global Factory:*

> Crudely put, the relationship between many Third World governments and multinational corporations is like that of a pimp and his customers. The governments advertise their women, sell them and keep them in line for the multinational "johns."[3]

They do this with the help of funding received from the World Bank, the International Monetary Fund, and the United Nations Industrial Development Organization, which approve and bankroll this global arrangement. It is an arrangement by which both the world's female population and the world's labor population are legally laid out for sexual-economic use via the political and religious laws and customs of their home countries. Actual sexual coercion happens frequently in the "free trade zones," as it has always happened to women on the job, with male bosses trading continued employment for sexual favors on the work tables. But the major sexual control and exploitation is and will be a total control of female reproduction by way of the workplace, i.e., via the economic-political needs and manipulations of the multinational corporations. Indigenous male governments worldwide, to maintain themselves in funds and power, seem generally willing to "loan out" the bodies and lives of their female populations in this prostitutional way.

And what about the male populations of these countries? Unfortunately, many of them can find employment only in the national guards and police forces—and in these occupations they are frequently sent to work against the women workers: to break up labor sit-downs and organizational meetings, to destroy and punish any attempt on the part of female employees to form active unions or engage in political protest. It is the classic imperialist maneuver, to dominate a people by turning a sufficient number of indigenous males into armed guards policing and terrorizing their own people, in particular the indigenous women, thus diverting sexual energy from revolution into repression. In Guatemala, in the Dominican Republic, in Taiwan, in the Philippines, in South Korea, in Malaysia, national guards and police forces have been sent in by their governments to break up demonstrations, strikes, or simply meetings of female workers. In the Dominican Republic, the dominant multinational corporation, Gulf and Western, sponsors its own goon squad, an indigenous male motorcycle gang which "specializes in terrorizing suspected union sympathizers."

> In Inchon, South Korea, women at the Dong-Il Textile Company, a producer of fabrics and yarn for export to the U.S., had succeeded in gaining leadership in their union local in 1972. In 1978 the government-controlled, male-dominated Federation of Korean Trade Unions sent special "action squads" to destroy the women's union. Armed with steel bars and buckets of human excrement, the goons broke into the union office, smashed the office equipment and smeared the excrement over the women's bodies and in their ears, eyes and mouths.[4]

Classic labor organization strategy, long dominated by males, has been reluctant to consider the political importance of working women's issues, and has been contemptuous of the theory, put forth by some Socialist and Marxist women, that female productive and reproductive labor is the primary producer of wealth, and must be so structured into any effective labor theory and practice.[5] Classic revolutionary strategy, long dominated by males, has been equally reluctant to consider the political primacy of female issues, and equally contemptuous of the idea that a revolution should be mounted on the issue of women's oppression and liberation. With the spread of the global factory, and the consequent merger of women's reproductive issues with female workers' issues among a planetary, multinationally controlled workforce of primarily exploited women, these classic labor, left, and revolutionary-political male attitudes and positions have got to change. In the present situation, if males do not join with women workers to fight for female reproductive autonomy along with workers' rights, then males have no other place to go—except to join the National Guards, the SWAT teams, the goon squads gearing up everywhere to help colonize and exploit their own countrywomen as slave-workers and breeding-machines. These are the only two options left for political men—or, in a totally politicized world, for all men.

So long as governments can control female reproduction in any way, the workforce can be equally controlled. Vice versa, it will be possible for governments and global corporations to totally control populations of workers so long as they are able to control populations of females as breeding machines—or nonbreeding machines. No one can be free unless females are free to control our own sex and our own reproduction. If we don't control our own bodies, they are controlled by the boss—and that keeps the boss in power, forever. Some slaves can dominate and exploit the slavery of others, the classic imperialist situation; but no one will have a chance to be ontologically free. This is no longer the logic of feminism alone—it has expanded to become the inner logic of the multinational corporate marketplace, and consequently of global factory-structure and operations in relation to the international workforce.

Second, how does fundamentalist religion fit into all of this? Clearly, it was patriarchal-pastoralist religion that originally sanctified and enforced the Bronze Age designation of women as breeding machines—as cattle, yes, but cattle "for the greater glory of God." It was the male priesthoods of Father God religions who first wrote and enforced the new laws and new customs that stripped Neolithic women of all their ancient sexual autonomy, and made their sexual and reproductive functions the property of a dominating male elite—for God and profit. It was the Bronze Age priesthoods of Yahweh, in particular, who first wrote down and applied moral sanctions and religious justifications for the treatment of women as ontologically inferior beings, sacred only to the extent that we have—or should have—divine male sperm growing inside us. In the face of post-World War II feminism and a general desire on the part of many people in the Western world to liberalize their religious ideas, and in particular to "undemonize" sexuality, for both sexes, the modern fundamentalist priesthood has rebutted strongly, raising the banner of their Bronze Age counterparts of three and four thousand years ago. The basic tenets of the Bronze Age priesthood being that (1) human sex is sacred only for reproductive purposes and (2) women have nothing to say about it except "Yes, master." Woman, essentially evil, is sacralized only by lifelong sacrificial submission—to the male sex, and to reproduction. Thus speaketh the Bronze Age holy men of the 1980s.

When Curtis Anton Beseda was arrested for firebombing a feminist health center and abortion clinic in Everett, Washington, in 1984, he confessed to police: "I did it for the glory of God." In 1984, twenty-four abortion clinics or counseling offices in seven states were destroyed or heavily damaged by firebombs or arson, and there were 150 reported cases of vandalism and harassment. Don Benny Anderson, who is now serving forty-two years in a Wisconsin prison for a clinic bombing in suburban Washington, D.C., two bombings in Florida, and the kidnapping of an Illinois doctor who performed abortions, is also the man who coined the term "Army of God" to describe the fundamentalists with a mission to stop abortion in America. Referring to the bombings so far, he said: "These are just warning blasts. We are in the embryonic stages of civil war, holy war."[6]

The holy bombers of abortion clinics are utterly sincere in their beliefs; furthermore, they are right: *Their* God does call for total control, by men, over the sexual and reproductive functions of women, extending far beyond the forbidding of abortion—contraception of any kind is forbidden, or any method that might allow women to engage in nonreproductive sex, for pleasure. Their God is the Bronze Age Father God of cattle breeders, the biblical Yahweh, for whom Hebrew women of those days were to be made as pregnant as possible, to multiply his congregation; this did not spare pregnant women of other neighboring faiths, however, from having their bellies "ripped up" by holy heroes like King Menahem, before he was established on the throne of Israel by the same God (2 Kings 15:16). The Old Testament Yahweh was concerned with the fertility of the Hebrew tribes, while simultaneously he did not hesitate to command and sanctify the slaughter of other people's tribes, including other people's children, suckling infants, and fetuses. I.e., pregnancy and population control, even in the Bible, were highly political.

Be that as it may: The fundamentalist Protestant and Catholic anti-abortionists are following the ways and dictates of *their* God. The rudimentary question remains: Is their God *the* God? The feminist joke is: "If men could get pregnant, abortion would be a sacrament." The corollary to this is: "If God is seen as female, the problem does not exist." That is, the entire question of sex, pregnancy, birth control—even abortion—undergoes an ontological somersault, a revolution of basic terms. Just *what* God, *whose* God, *what* life, *whose* fertility; and who and what is defining "God"? Or "life"?

Evolutionary biology shows that the human female, alone among all earth's creatures, is designed for nonreproductive orgasmic pleasure. In her development of the menstrual cycle, and her breakaway from the estrus, or "heat" cycle of the mammalian world, the human female led the way for all the other advances of our species. *Only human beings* copulate for purposes other than species reproduction: for emotional bonding and expression, for personal pleasure, for personal confusion, personal power and glory, personal revelation—while it is precisely the poor beasts who copulate *only* to reproduce.[7] The fact that the human female can and does engage in nonreproductive copulation is exactly the fact that defines her, and her partner, as human.

How could the fundamentalist fatherhood get it so wrong? When they tell us, from the Bible's pages or the church pulpits, that human sex is sacred only if it tries to make babies, and that otherwise "the act reduces us to the level of the beasts"—how could they have got it all so mixed up, so backwards? When the preachers of all time denounce Eve, and through her all women, for our "innately lascivious and devilish" sexuality—how is it that they make the horrible mistake of confusing what demonizes us with what humanizes us? The answer is (1) because the Bronze Age priesthoods were members of pastoralist tribes, and their new patriarchal ideas of God and of human intercourse derived from cattle breeding; and (2) because female sexual autonomy represented the ancient Neolithic Goddess religion, which these priesthoods had set out to "demonize" and destroy. The biblical God was indeed a "jealous God," and it was precisely the Goddess, her women, and human pleasure that he was so jealous of. (And it was precisely because he and his priesthoods set themselves against sexual pleasure that his own people kept backsliding!) The Father Gods and Sun Gods who emerged triumphant, through force of arms and fanaticism, from the Bronze Age were concerned not with human pleasure, nor with human evolution, nor human transcendence. They—and their ruling priesthoods—were concerned with power and with control; and the way to control human beings, the way to gain power over human biological energy and the energies of the human psyche, is to dominate and control the sexual and reproductive functions of women. This is done by (1) trying to restrict sex only to reproduction (or reproductive attempts); and (2) taking the control over that reproduction away from women and handing it over to men, who then piously-mechanistically enact sex, via the female body, "as a service to God." The Christian religion historically, and biblical fundamentalists today (Christian, Islamic, or Jewish), must refute the evidence of evolution because they must refute the ontological primacy, or rightness, of the human female, *as she is*. As she is: a sexual being. Fundamentalists must (1) deny evolution, insisting instead that human beings came fully formed from the hands of Yahweh, because (2) they must deny the correctness of human sexuality the way it is; instead they must insist it results from the Fall, through the sin of Eve—and this explains why human beings are so sexual, i.e., corrupt. Through this anti-evolutionary device, the Bronze Age priesthoods thus set up their pure God (an asexual, antisexual, nonbiological God) against the sexual Goddess—who represents the ontological emergence of human beings from and through billions of years of evolution into a conscious and spiritual sexual mode unique to us. And thoroughly proper for us.

Thus the terrible irony that for centuries of human existence, in the name of distinguishing "the human spirit" from that of the lowly beasts, the fundamentalist priesthood has stupidly and brutally tried to restrict human sexual activity precisely to that of the beasts. *Is* it ironic, or has it been intentional? Sexual restriction and control, the promulgation and enforcement of moral codes based on sexual paranoia, has been the machinery by which the priesthoods have kept themselves in power, have maintained their control over human beings. Patriarchal religious power over the human mind and the human spirit has been achieved via the genitals—this is how the machinery of control and power works. The ontological coupling of female and male was broken apart, and the organic sexual energy thus released was turned into the mechanistic energy of sexual hostility. This "Adam"-splitting was done by a male priesthood who defined woman and sex as evil and dangerous, and then gave "moral control" over this evil situation to man—who was thereby rendered ontologically alien to himself, to woman, and to the entire natural world, because from that moment on he owed his life and his pleasure to something he was supposed, ever after, to see as evil, corrupt, and hostile to his "soul"—something like an animal or a plot of land he was supposed to both use and restrict, as a God-appointed exploiter and policeman. It was the classic imperialist device, activated in the Bronze Age by the power-seeking male priesthood: divide and conquer. Divide the "spiritual" man from the ontological woman, and then enrole him as her policeman, her exploiter, her colonizer, in the army of God, and for the profit of God and man. The totally colonized man (colonized by priestly ideology) is thus appeased by "giving" him the female to colonize; and his potentially revolutionary energy is thus turned into repressed/repressive hostility against woman—against his other half, his mate, his mother, his holistic self. And this is how "the divine homosexual family" of the patriarchal priesthoods maintains its power. An enormous and seemingly endless power.

The wreckage it has produced is all around us today, the results of generations of male hostility to the female, still manipulated and orchestrated by the "Holy Men" of all patriarchal systems. Reproduction-oriented sex, prohibition of birth control, the "demonization" of female sexual pleasure and autonomy, the inculcation of lifelong guilt and perpetual fear surrounding the act/the fact of sex itself—we know all this has done nothing to improve the relationship of woman and man, or of woman and woman, or man and man; on the contrary, it has, in Wilhelm Reich's accurate perception, created a bitterly deformed and deprived repressive/repressed machinery which functions as the mechanical-pathological energy source for all our "larger" human conflicts. They are "larger" only in the sense that they are the magnification of each woman's, each man's sexual-ontological pain and rage into global proportions. Perpetual seething rage and continuous violence, a world always and all ways at war, is the inevitable result when men are told, over and over from the beginning of their consciousness, that the very source of their being is evil. This is certainly *a* source of so much male aggression; while women must *be* the evil, embody it within, and this is certainly *a* source of much female depression. For male and female life roles, in patriarchal culture, are structured on the belief in this ontological evil and its embodiment in our sexual selves. In the bedroom, in the home, in the neighborhood, in the city, in the nation, in the world, all human relationships have been in some way warped and devastated by the predictable mutual hostility, grinding antagonism, fear and guilt, vicious resentment and retribution between the sexes that must result when human beings are told that God wants them to behave in their beds like breeding cattle. The lingering sour and stiff lineaments of ungratified desire that must result when both sexes are yoked together in a grim beast-of-burden union, called "sanctified marriage," functioning as pious nonecstatic cattle to reproduce herd-congregations for God and the holy church. Except the true beasts are innocent—they do not know what they do, nor what they are deprived of, nor what they suffer from the deprivation.

Equally inevitable, in such a world, are periodic eruptions into what Pope John Paul II calls our present day "hedonism"—a sexual compulsiveness that occurs, also, automatically in reaction to the antisexual compulsiveness so characteristic of patriarchal culture. The Vatican sees the rise in abortion, or in women's demands for abortion, as a sign of Western "hedonism" and material self-indulgence, a wallowing in fleshly existence and a forgetting of the spirit. More abortions occur today, certainly, because abortions have been made legal, partially legal, or safer; this does not necessarily mean the demand or need for abortions have increased—they have just become visible. Some nonfundamentalist Christians are opposed to abortion primarily because they see that other, preventive birth-control measures are available, and do not like to see surgical abortion used as a substitute for responsible birth control. No one does. But surely these thoughtful people must also understand that generation after generation of women raised in patriarchal cultures that have kept us systematically ignorant of our sexual and productive processes leaves its deep mark. Throughout Christendom, the ancient herbal contraceptives, the pagan body-knowledge, the folklore and customs of nonreproductive sex once passed on from mother to daughter were destroyed with the holy fires, or driven so far underground few Western women ever again had access to them. With all our clinical-technical knowledge of female sex and reproduction today, most teenage pregnancies occur among girls who never knew, were never taught, how their bodies work, or how to engage in sex without becoming pregnant. They do not know because their parents, their churches, their cultures still assume that ignorance equals prevention (i.e., knowledge equals sin), and this despite all the overwhelming statistics to the contrary.

But the Vatican's position, and the fundamentalist patriarchal position generally, is opposed to all birth control—to preventive mechanical and chemical contraception as well as abortion. In this opposition the Catholic church and the fundamentalist sects reveal their desire to control human sexuality by dogmatically limiting its occurrence to potentially reproductive acts only; anything else is "sin," i.e., not dominated by fear, guilt, or the actual consequence of pregnancy. In his continued insistence that nonreproductive sex is "hedonistic," and that legal abortion (or contraception of any kind) will only encourage and increase this "hedonism," the pope is repeating the celibate clergy's long-indulged myopic illusion that only single women need abortion, or birth control. I.e., that the demand for contraception and abortion is being made only by a lot of loose lascivious single women seeking to enjoy sex outside of marriage. Is it myopic illusion, or an intentional distortion? Surely the priesthood must know something of the thousand-year history of married women within its own church? Surely the Vatican must know that throughout Christian (including Catholic) history, women have always had abortions, or have tried every bizarre means thinkable to prevent pregnancies or end them. But of course they frequently risked death in doing so; or the contraception or abortion failed and they died in childbirth; or they survived childbirth and watched their children starve to death; or they saw their children grow to youth and then die as cannon fodder or rape victims or breeders for the ruling and collusive church-state wars; or they all died together of mass plagues exacerbated by the church's prohibitions on basic hygienic knowledge and witch-medicine; or. . . . Surely the church knows the common history of enormous numbers of women forced to live as breed-cows under the pious folds of its male skirts? Or how, to avoid pregnancy at all costs, they refused sex and were beaten into submission or death by their husbands with the church's blessing?

We search the Vatican's long history and find, nowhere, any faint expression of shock or outrage over this thousand-year-long saga of human wretchedness and abuse within the "sacrament" of Christian marriage. And we are forced to conclude, for one thing, that it is not contraception or abortion, per se, that the church opposes. What the Vatican and all fundamentalist priesthoods oppose is *sex without punishment* for women. Pregnancy is considered a divinely sufficient punishment for sex; contraception and abortion are opposed because they allow a woman to escape punishment: to have sex, and go scot free! But in the old days, at least, the days of witch-hunting and ignorance, contraception and especially abortion could be dangerous, life-threatening. If a woman sought abortion, and died, well *then* she was sufficiently punished too. Pregnancy or lethal abortion, it didn't matter: just so the woman was sufficiently punished for her sex.

The problem today, and the reason the pope is bemoaning mass "hedonism," is that birth control, and in particular modern abortion, have been made relatively *safe.* It is possible for a woman to have sex, and go free (relatively). It is possible for a woman to consider the possibility of enjoying sexual pleasure without facing punishment. And when this happens, women become women again. Men might even become men again. We might all become our whole selves. And lo! The patriarchal priesthood faces loss of employment: loss of control. For its hierarchic power over sexual humanity has always been in inverse proportion to the powerlessness of women and men over our own sexual lives. This is to say that there is no other choice: Either we live with sexual autonomy, or we live under sexual fascism.

Sexual fascism is a condition under which our sexual energy is sublimated for us by the automatic machinery of piety and drudgery—a machinery set in motion by the ruling elite to coopt human biological energy, to use it to run its palaces, its mansions, its gorgeous religious mausoleums, to provide it with diversionary luxuries and wars, while a large revolutionary mass of exploited people is kept in a manipulatable condition of productive repression. The machinery of sexual fascism has been running the world for three or four thousand years. And for just as long, the patriarchal priesthoods have been oiling and blessing its terrible gears. They turn, at their most hideous, under the love-beds of every woman and man on earth; until female sexual autonomy is achieved, they will continue to turn, even in the most "liberated" atmospheres, inside the hearts, the brains, the genitals of all of us. No one "escapes" unless *everyone* becomes free. That is how the machinery works.

In today's world, thousands of children starve to death every day; millions more suffer the kind of malnutrition that permanently damages the brain and the body. The priests of the world's major patriarchal religions—Christianity, Islam, Buddhism, Hinduism—do not consider this situation particularly "moral," but they do not consider it abnormal either. "The poor are always with us," "life is hell," etc.—the situation just seems to illustrate these priesthoods' biophobic case. In their ontological world-hatred and doctrinal nihilism, the "holy men" try to persuade us, and no doubt themselves, that suffering is the eternal and definitive human condition—and the daily starvation of children is just one more sad but inescapable example of our "mortal condition," of "fleshly sin and corruption," of *samsara* (the sorrow and impurity of the world), of "life on the wheel" of Buddhistic illusion. Male priesthoods of patriarchal religions—all of whom live in the maximum comfort and even luxury their cultures can afford—have been rationalizing the suffering of others for so long, throughout four thousand years of unctious droning, no doubt they've come to believe their own words—for want of hearing anything else.

One million infants die each year, of starvation and malnutrition, in India; this is considered "life" by the Hindu holy men, who preach that all of life is just "illusion" anyway. But if, this year, 1 million holy men died of starvation in India, you may be sure we would hear something about it beyond the usual *samsaric* drone. One million starved babies a year does not make headlines; 1 million starved holy men probably would. But, of course, "eternal suffering" is not the lot of the world's holy men, and never or rarely has been; "eternal suffering" is rather their property—their thing, their device, as it were, which allows them to retain employment as representatives of an "all-powerful" male God who just doesn't, somehow, seem able to help solve any of these problems. The priests blame the problems on "life," on "humanity"; they thus handily explain all this injustice and imbalance, while maintaining themselves in comfort as their beneficiaries. As holy men for whom "life's eternal suffering" is a profitable possession, they don't like "blasphemous" interference or challenge, especially from women. In the world of patriarchal piety, the only women who are rewarded, "loved," or sainted are women, like Mother Theresa, who succor the problem. Women who move to solve the problem are hated, and cursed; or worse. For example, in 1984, Kuwaiti feminist Dr. Noura Al-Falah, a sociologist at Kuwait University, was fired from her job and imprisoned for the crime of lecturing on women under patriarchal religion. She analyzed, and encouraged her students to analyze, the positions of women in Islam, Judaism, Christianity, and Greek philosophy. For this she was charged by her government with "questioning the existence of God" and "anti-Islamic activity." This is one of those governments, beloved by the fundamentalists, in which "God" is at the center. Dr. Al-Falah is now awaiting execution for her crimes.[8]

The truth is: This much suffering, this much world suffering of starvation and degradation and brutality and poverty, is neither normal, nor natural, nor ontologically given. No normal living human female, in a normal life situation, keeps having children, year after year, just to watch half of them die before the age of twelve. Women normally, and for most of human life on earth, give birth to one child at a time (this is what distinguishes *Homo sapiens* from most mammals, except the higher primates and cetaceans); and with intense and exclusive maternal care including nursing for three to six years, the mother concentrates on raising that one child to a healthy level of independent development before she has another baby. Among all "primitive," primal people, this is the normal practice. Even primates nurse one baby for three to six years before becoming pregnant again; even apes! No chimpanzee or gorilla mother is forced into bearing one baby a year, year after year, it just isn't done! Nor is it done anywhere where human females have healthy control over their own reproduction. The problem of mass poverty, mass starvation, the mass deaths of children and infants every year from a simple lack of proper nourishment, is not normal, is not "life," nor is it the fault of "human sin" or "sex" or of women. It is a condition traceable solely and specifically to patriarchal religion, and patriarchal religion's four thousand years of fascistic control over female reproduction. The problem cannot be solved, will not be solved short of mass annihilation, until and unless women regain complete sexual autonomy. And this means the priests and "holy men" must give up their unwholesome urges to possess and to explain "human suffering"—rather than to end it. They must also give up their nasty and peculiar urges to control and manipulate human genitalia and reproductive organs as holy men rather than as lovers. This too, in a normal world, just is not done.

The antiabortion movement in America calls itself "pro-life." In fact, it is "pro-fetus," period. Championing a fetus is easy—the mother's body is doing all the work. What is hard is to change the world, so that millions and millions of children have a chance for some kind of qualitative life after they are born—this is the only genuine pro-life work. If the antiabortion movement presented a consistent "pro-life" gestalt in the whole range of their political and religious beliefs, then they would be presenting an ethical position worthy of respect, if not agreement. But this is not the case. The overwhelming majority of white, Christian American "pro-lifers" display consistently biophobic voting records: hawkish on war, supportive of every Pentagon budget, supportive of nuclear proliferation, pro-Cruise in Europe; they are marked by a flag-waving, Bible-toting political-religious hostility to any idea of peaceful coexistence with the USSR, with Cuba, with Nicaragua—they tend to oppose negotiation-for-life with any government they consider "demonic" (i.e., leftish); but one cannot be pro-holy war and pro-life both, the terms cancel each other out, especially in a nuclear world. In domestic areas, the antiabortionists are consistently and militantly opposed to all social welfare programs that allow children after birth to receive decent nutrition, medical care, shelter, and education, or even a dream of social and economic equity when they grow up. Most antiabortionists, led by Ronald Reagan, are even on record in opposition to programs like WIC which try to provide minimal nutritional and medical care for poor pregnant women.[9] In February 1985, the Physicians' Task Force on Hunger in America announced that hunger—chronic malnourishment and undernourishment—has reached epidemic proportions in America; but the most visible antiabortionists align themselves on the side of a president, an administration, and a mind-set that has publicly stated that "allegations of rampant hunger simply cannot be documented," and which has pointed to the existence of very tall black basketball players and "fat" welfare mothers (i.e., women who live on cheap starch and lard) as evidence that no one is badly fed in America.[10] In 1983 in Detroit, Michigan, with depression-level unemployment in the automobile factories combined with massive state and federal cutbacks in food and medical assistance programs, the Public Health Department announced that infant mortality rates in some sections of the city had reached levels comparable to the infant-death rate in Honduras (which is one of the poorest countries in Central America).[11] Furthermore, there has been an epidemic rise in childhood cancer; once "rare," it is now the second major cause of death among children, with six thousand new cases reported each year in America—and the rise is attributable primarily to chemical pollution of the environment. But all government funding for research into children's vulnerability to environmental contamination, research that was begun under the Carter administration, was cut off totally by the Reagan administration.[12] The most visible politicians involved in the antiabortion movement have, in their voting records, supported all such budget cuts. Are the "pro-lifers" out ranting and rallying to get these budget cuts restored? No. This is not to say that abortion is the answer to all our problems of malnutrition, malregulation of industry, and maldistribution of wealth and resources. The argument is simply that to be righteously supportive of a fetus's full term within the womb, and then to entirely abandon it after it is born, is ludicrous.

When one reads the total gestalt of the antiabortionist movement in America, it is clear to see that the average "pro-lifer" is not pro-*life* at all, certainly not pro-*quality* of life. Rather, they are pro-*control*; their obsession is the old Bronze Age fundamentalist-patriarchal obsession to control female sex and reproduction. "Pro-life" men, in particular, like those who firebomb abortion clinics "for the glory of God," reveal their pastoralist belief that human life derives from divine male sperm, and that the human female is simply a "vessel" containing this life, "for God." In her research into the motivations of "pro-life" women, Faye Ginsburg, in her essay "The Body Politic: The Defense of Sexual Restriction by AntiAbortion Activists," found a more sophisticated (and secular) complex of reasons. Antiabortion women activists tend to feel that abortion rights are a key part of a whole feminist agenda that threatens their vocation as housewives and mothers.[13] In a patriarchal culture that gives women few chances for employment in interesting careers, or just well-paid jobs, the vocation of white middle-class housewife is definitely an attractive occupation; most of us, if we are honest (and have experienced a lot of the alternatives), can sympathize with these women's desire to hold onto their domestic roles, and to the mystique of these roles. But it must be pointed out that this motivation has nothing to do with the fetus; or with the problems of poor women, single mothers, or working women. It is a motivation of understandable, but limited, self-interest; further, it compounds the incorrect perception that "motherhood" and "marriage" are always synonymous, and that the "abortion problem" would be resolved if all these single, loose, and lascivious women would just stop having sex—or get married. The problem is not, nor has it ever been, this simple. Finally, no matter how deeply devoted antiabortion women activists might be to their homes, and their domestic well-being, they have never, as a group, been able to wrest enough political power away from their right-wing husbands to ensure, via adequate compassionate funding, the healthy and happy home life, nourishment, health care, education, and general well-being of all those other women's fetuses, after they are born.

The concern for the fetus alone is a blind, if not hypocritical, sentiment, easy to indulge in because it requires nothing, it demands nothing of the person indulging such a sentiment. The concern for the entire human life following birth is a genuine human passion, because it requires everything, it demands everything from us. "Pro-life" must mean more than an obsession with fetuses rolling down an assembly line of passive maternal flesh; it must mean a commitment to changing the world, so that every child who enters it enters a place worth living in. I.e., it means that every righteous antiabortionist on earth must put his or her money, time, and thought where his or her mouth is currently working all alone.

In the words of Southwest poet Will Inman:

> (where are those who call abortion murder?)
> (where do they hide the milk?)
> (how do they spend their money?)
> (what do they plant in the mouths of their young?[14])

Perhaps the hardest part of the abortion issue for women as well as men to deal with is a point that is never raised or discussed thoroughly: a woman's right to make life-and-death decisions. Certainly we live in a world in which a relative handful of ruling military, business, and political people wield life-and-death decision-making power over all of us, and over the entire continuing life of earth, all of the time. They have allocated to themselves such awesome power, with our permission. At any moment, "they" can make the decision to obliterate us with nuclear missiles, sicken and destroy us with various kinds of chemical and nerve gases, drag us off to concentration camps or torture chambers (yes, even in America), force us or our children into armies, send our sons, perhaps our daughters, off to death or mutilation in any number of dubiously necessary world conflicts. Certainly we don't like this situation, but we live with it every day; under four thousand years of patriarchal conditioning, we have come to accept it as "normal" or "given" that any number of selected groups of *men* should hold absolute life-and-death power over our lives, and over our children's lives, at least in certain designated situations—the situations defined and designated by men. We have also given power, to a larger number of people than we care to think about, to make decisions affecting the issues of diminished life, and slow death, for many, many people, including ourselves. These are issues of environmental pollution, industrial safety, chemicals in our foods, the whole universe of imperfectly tested medicines and drugs. At this moment, someone somewhere can be making a decision about putting something into the air, the water, the food chain, the school building, the automobile upholstery . . . that, somewhere down the line, twenty years from now, will kill us, or kill a child, or someone else we value and love. We all know such decisions are being made, every day, by decent and anonymous people. We prefer not to think about it; but this does not stop the decisions from being made.

For women, the issue of life-and-death decision-making power in someone else's hands is even more quotidian. Everywhere women go in this world, the male sex holds the power of life and death over us. Men can beat us, rape us, cage us in their loony bins and torture labs, force us into demeaning and life-endangering labor—sweatshop labor, factory work, street prostitution, childbearing, or illegal abortion—in exchange for our daily bread, or the lives of our living children. The life-and-death power of the male sex over the female sex has become such a substructure of every moment, act, and fact of our lives, it has come to seem "normal" to many people. Are men gods? No. But they have, over four millennia of male domination, allocated to themselves such godlike powers over us. Men rarely question their right to wield these powers. They believe it *does* come from "God"—their version of God.

In fact, the exclusive male right to decide over life and death defines patriarchal power. The "army of God" antiabortionist men who wave the Bibles in the faces of pregnant women going into clinics to have abortions, the fundamentalist men who talk so much about "God's law" in regard to female reproductive choice, are the same men who would agree absolutely with the absolute power given to biblical patriarchs, "by God," over the lives of their families. The kind of divinely mandated power that gave Hebrew fathers the right to stone their daughters to death if they were suspected of being nonvirgins before marriage; the daughter's mother had no say in the matter, she just had to stand by and watch her daughter being stoned to death. (For the great "crime" of having a nonintact hymen, perhaps; a condition occurring, doctors tell us, in about 50 percent of the female population, by mere accident.) The "God-fearing" men who are so concerned with the fetus happen to believe in a God who gave fathers the right to kill their living children at any time, if they were considered "disobedient" or "corrupt." Is this the same God who forbids a woman to abort a fetus?

Yes, it is. Because the biblical God, and the fundamentalist men who wave his holy book under the noses of pro-abortion women, are not involved in a religion of Life, but in a religion of male control. Fundamental to this religion, and this control, is a male's exclusive right to make life-and-death decisions. Abortion represents woman's right to make such decisions. And the fundamentalist men cannot bear the thought of sharing such ontological power with women. They oppose abortions not because they care mightily about the fetus—by their historic record, they show they never have—but they do care mightily about retaining this exclusive male power over life and death. For it is this power which keeps them in power.

(And it must be pointed out that, under historic patriarchy, women's nonpossession of such ontological life-and-death decision-making power has done nothing to counteract men's possession and use of such power. I.e., our "harmlessness" has not kept him from doing harm, on the historical scale of the past four thousand bloody years; our "meekness" has not influenced him to be meek, but has often, on the contrary, provoked him to greater violence. It is that "revenge against feminine hermeticism," that masculine "desperate attempt to obtain a response from a body we feel is insensible" that Octavio Paz speaks of: that "religious" female humility and nonaction against which macho sadism seems compelled to beat its fists.)

But it isn't only men who are terrified by the possibility of women regaining our ontological life-and-death deciding powers. Women fear it intensely, and for good reason: Ontological power equals ontological responsibility. A woman who is totally conscious that she is making a life-and-death decision for which she alone is cosmically answerable—such a woman can never be "a little girl" again; never again "Daddy's good little girl" or "God's sweet angel" or all the rest of the situational epithets designed to inculcate in females a chronic state of cosmic nonresponsibility, i.e., of personal nonattention to or avoidance of the universal life-and-death resonance and holistic repercussion of the effects of her choices.

I.e., she can never be a nonthinking human being again. And this is what the world needs from women: a lot of hard, ontological, life-and-death thinking that is neither distracted nor discouraged nor beaten down by four thousand years' worth of male God sermonizing about what life is, what God is, what woman is, what man is, what it's all supposed to be about in this preprogrammed, prefabricated, prearranged, and preposterous patriarchal chapter-and-verse propaganda script, which everyone has followed for too long as Holy Writ. As Paul Virilio points out in *Pure War,* women have been patted on the head and patronizingly absolved of life-and-death thinking for generations. The big man—the father, the husband, the priest, the boss, the king, the president, the military leader—takes heavy, bloody, scary life-and-death cerebration out of our hands and says: "Here, darling, let me do that for you." And now, at last—at the possible *end,* that is, of humanity—we see where this leads.[15]

If it is not to be too late for all of us, all women—on a global scale—have got to regain our ancient ontological power—and intuitive skill—for making life-and-death decisions. For they are always linked: Life-and-death-are-linked. To decide *at the root* about life—about what life is, and could be—women must also know how to decide *at the root* about death; about what death is, what death is for, what death means to Life. Millions of women worldwide, thrown into life-and-death situations of warfare, torture, mass rape, political slavery, and all the rest—millions of Third World women, and of minority women in the United States also, black, Chicano, Native American, Asian—have grown up being forced to make, and live with, heavy ontological life-and-death decisions. This is what the more sheltered average American white woman perceives as their "strength." It *is* strength, the often bitterly won authority of being utterly alone, and responsible, at the very root of things: life and death, always twining around each other like poisonous snakes—who are also lovers. All women—and maybe the highly sheltered average American white woman most of all—must begin the daily practice of wrestling with these twin, twined serpents. For that is how the ontological muscles are developed; that is how the sexual and the spiritual powers are intertwined; that is how females regain the evolutionary memory and habit of being cosmic women once again. I.e., that is how God rebecomes a female.

As women cease being passive vessels of the divine male sperm, we cease being passive vessels of male ideology—including the patriarchal priesthood's image of God. And this is probably the ultimate challenge to the Christian church, and to all the patriarchal religions which depend, for their existence, on the passive receptacleness of women: as handmaidens to male activity, as mothers who are relied on to inculcate the received male God image into their children's brains and nervous systems, as fertile proliferators of crowded and repressed—or rich and repressive—congregations. This is the real challenge presented by feminist issues, including abortion rights, to the fundamentalist religions, and to the liberal ones as well: Female sexual autonomy equals female mental autonomy, and both together add up to female spiritual autonomy. When women begin to define our own lives, including being ontologically responsible for each life we choose to bring—or not bring—into the world, then women will become fully functioning *definers of the world.* And then we will be fully responsible for the kind of world, the spiritual and physical quality of world, into which we bring new life.

And this is undoubtedly the root fear of patriarchal religions and their priesthoods and devoted followers: That someday half the world's population will get up off its knees, throw down the mops and the prayer beads and the whole dreary catechism of subliminally mumbled words, and just walk out of the house of God. For good. Leaving no one to mop the floor. And walking out into a larger world that is so inherently spiritual in its own right, just as it is—evolutionarily perceived by eyes clear at last—it will need no priests or preachers or prefabricated holy scripts to define or explain itself to us. The world and its life will then be self-evident, just as the entire living universe is self-evident—how could it be otherwise?—to itself. And if we are here at all, we are here as organic parts of itself. And the man and woman will be as gods—as gods are grains of sand tumbled by the night sea, or dustballs rolling over the church floor. And the patriarchal priesthoods will be left alone, with this, to mop their own floors.

The third point is that women must do this very soon, or we might never again—or never for a long time—be free to do it. Free, that is, in the sense of being autonomous *and* whole. Advances in reproductive technology, and the worldwide spread of technological control over female reproduction as a function of political and corporate power over worker populations, threatens all women with global exploitation as state or business-controlled breeding machines. This means having our eggs, our uteruses, our hormonal systems "engineered" and used, not in our own interests, but as functions of the global assembly line that mass produces human beings to order, along with everything else. This is not a brave new world fantasy: The basic technology exists, is in use, and is being refined and elaborated every day. Every time a Third World woman is coerced into surgical sterilization, every time "fertility-control" drugs considered too dangerous for Western women to use are dumped and pushed on populations of Third World women, every time an American "egg mother" has her eggs fertilized *in vitro* and reinserted into her womb, or her fertilized eggs transplanted into the womb of another woman, every time light-weight, Y-bearing sperm is collected in a test tube and allowed to dive quickly to the bottom, while the heavier X-bearing sperm remain floating on top, thus separating the father's male and female sex chromosomes and consequently allowing a couple to "choose" to have the woman impregnated with a male child—each incident constitutes experimental research, and is a part of a vaster research and experimental program aimed at complete technological control over human reproduction.[16] (Scientists might deny this, or call it "exaggeration," but history shows us that scientists rarely know what they are doing. They always express an ingenuous "surprise" when they finally figure out to what uses business, politics, and the military have put their "innocent" little laboratory discoveries. Further, Western scientists are themselves thoroughly enmeshed in the gears of the machinery of control which they have helped to invent; they are in fact employed by it. And they are not funded so generously by governments to be renegades, or even wise people.)

Many thoughtful members of minority populations in the United States and the West generally—black, Native American, Chicano, and Asian people—strongly oppose abortion and sterilization, and are very suspicious of all birth-control projects, because they see—correctly—that personal birth control can easily become a political tool of population control aimed at them by dominating white governments. "Population control" can effectively equal time-capsule genocide. Throughout Africa, India, Asia, and other parts of the Third World, Western "technological-humanists" promote birth control and sterilization as a key facet of industrial-economic "developmental" programs; their operating premise (or pretense) is that problems of famine, poverty, disease, lack of education and economic development, etc., are all blameable on "overpopulation," i.e., "Those savages just breed like flies." This neatly absolves their own Western imperialist cultures, and the whole machinery of political, economic, and religious colonization, from all responsibility in the creation and maintenance of these problems. Most Third World women are fully aware that the "fertility-control" and sterilization programs urged or forced on them as part of the Western economic-industrial-designed "development" programs are just a contemporary phase of the same old ongoing colonization-and-control imperialism.

It is the habit of Western white women to think of such problems as happening "elsewhere." But with the spread of the global-factory system, and the consequent "out-sourcing" of so many American jobs and industries to the low-waged countries of the Third World; with the malignant overdevelopment of military economies at the expense of domestic economies, and the consequent nondevelopment or "de-development" of Western societies to the point that Paul Virilio calls "endo-colonization"—i.e., Western nations will themselves become functional "colonies" of their own governmental, business, and military establishments now grown to politically uncontrollable global proportions;[17] and with the necessity of conducting the most elaborate and refined reproductive technology and genetic-engineering experiments initially at least on relatively affluent white Western couples, or single women, who can afford them . . . there will soon be no "elsewhere."

Further, some Western women have even welcomed the envisioned cooptation of their female biological functions by advanced reproductive technologies. Feminists such as Shulamith Firestone have expressed the idea that women will not be "free" until babies are grown entirely in test tubes, until the complete female reproductive process is taken over by medical technology.[18] (This seems to echo Christ's dictum that females will be "freed" by becoming male.) Other women believe just the opposite: that, historically, the increasing process of male control over reproduction has equalled male control over the female sex, one way or another; and, even further into sci-fi horror, once patriarchally oriented men are able to technologically-mechanically reproduce themselves, women will rapidly achieve the status of a dispensible population—these men will also be able to reproduce their own ideal sexual servomechanisms.

Both sides of this debate get lurid, because the situation calls for it. Do we become "free" by having machines and biotechnology take over all our physical functions, i.e., is "freedom" a technological state? Or is it an ontological state, achievable only when a biological-spiritual conscious organism is able to experience autonomy of all its functions (rather than substitution of its functions)?

Many contemporary Western women can sense what's going on here by considering the whole movement of pregnant women, in the past two decades, away from medical control of their pregnancies and childbirths: the reappearance of midwives, the use of herbal medications and massage and other benign techniques to ease labor, home births in low-lit, cozy atmospheres without intrusion of forceps, stirrup-position, delivery room professionalism and glare, etc. Women have become reacquainted with our own basic sexual bodies, and the experience has brought a sense of both calm and empowerment; we find that, for the most part, our bodies know what they are doing, and how to do it. Most of the time, we can trust them to perform pretty well, if not absolutely brilliantly—and when it comes to having babies we now find that *women* are doing it, rather than asking doctors to do it for us. Isn't it interesting that now, of all times, the business of reproductive technology blooms: amniocentesis; genetic screening, counseling and engineering; fetal monitoring during labor; surrogate motherhood, and all the rest. All designed to get pregnancy and childbirth back into the hands of the "experts"—i.e., highly trained intellects surrounded by machinery. Designed originally, perhaps, for special cases and emergency situations, this very expensive reproductive technology will rapidly become normative (just to pay for itself), and the day might very soon arrive when women who refuse to "take advantage" of such technologies will be considered not only "backward," but "bad mothers." With the mere existence of these technologies of reproductive engineering and control will come, inevitably, a social expectation that every child be born "perfect"; people who refuse the technologies and give birth to "imperfect" babies will be seen as morally, if not legally, guilty. And so, once more, pregnant women will be socially coerced into relying on the medical expertise of trained reproductive technologists, and will not be allowed—by their societies, their mates, their own fears—to trust or experience the wise organic autonomy of their own female bodies which, most of the time, really do know what they are doing, and how to do it.

Another lurid twist of the umbilical noose looms on the horizon: It is wrapped in the American neoconservative economic theory called "law and economics." Developed mainly at the University of Chicago's Law School under the aegis of Dr. Milton Friedman and Dr. George Stigler and their followers, "law and economics" proposes that all legal questions—including rape, murder, adoption, abortion, child custody—can be reduced to the economic terms of the free-enterprise market system. That is, all legal and moral questions can be economically quantified, and decided—by the law—in terms of their monetary value or cost to a society. For example, as "law and economics" theorist and author Richard Posner has argued, if a law like the "exclusionary rule," which forbids courts to accept evidence illegally obtained, is decided to impose too great a private and social cost on the government, then the "exclusionary rule" is not economically viable—and should be thrown out of the legal system. Other "law and economics" theorists have critiqued antitrust, workers' compensation, and minimum-wage laws on the same basis, arguing the cost to society of enforcing them outweighs their overall benefit. In other words, "law and economics" reduces legality to the market, and in so doing reduces what we think of as personal and social morality to the dollar, as well.

Richard Posner, a graduate of the University of Chicago's Law School, and currently a US Appeals Court Justice, is also one of the major definers and exponents of "law and economics" theory. He has advocated, as an example of "law and economics" in action, full legalization of medical experimentation on people in prison, arguing that such experimentation is both morally and legally justifiable "if it were shown persuasively that the social benefits of such experiments greatly exceeded the costs." In 1978, together with Elisabeth Landes, Posner published an essay in *The Journal of Legal Studies* which further elaborated his view of the extensibility of "law and economics" to our daily lives. The essay was called "The Economics of the Baby Shortage." In it, Posner and Landes argued that the current child-adoption system should be replaced by the free-market system, in which babies available for adoption would just be sold to the highest bidder. Describing the advantages of such a "baby market," Posner and Landes wrote:

> At a higher price for babies, the incidence of abortion, the reluctance to part with an illegitimate child and even the incentive to use contraceptives would diminish because the costs of unwanted pregnancy would be lower while the costs to the natural mother of retaining her illegitimate child would rise. . . . Thus the effect of legalizing the baby market would be not only to shift the marginal cost of baby production and sale downward but to move the demand curve for adoptive children upward. . . . In a regime of free baby production and sale there might be efforts to breed children with a *known* set of characteristics that could be matched up with those desired by prospective adoptive parents.[19]

What a curious mixture of Bronze Age fundamentalist moralism with the twentieth-century free-enterprise profit motive! Women who become mothers without permission (i.e., outside of patriarchal marriage) will be punished by making it economically impossible for them to keep their babies—but we will not call it punishment! We will call it economic incentive. A woman with an unwanted pregnancy will be forced to remain pregnant (for the baby-market system has eliminated abortion), but this is not punishment either: She will get paid for producing a baby! What a curious and chilling echo of the Bronze Age patriarchal priesthoods' lust to simultaneously control, punish, and exploit for profit the sexual-reproductive activity of women. Combined with the total unabashed decadence of Western capitalism's urge to reduce all life to commodity, and commodity exchange—while "human feelings," and the human spirit, are simply bought off! And when we consider the ethical characters of some of the world's wealthiest people, we can only wonder what male God is going to be there to protect the interests of the little girl and boy babies sold, by the millions, to "the highest bidders."

There is really not much more to say about "law and economics," or the economics of baby-making, except that Richard Posner is one of President Ronald Reagan's favorite jurists and legal-economic theorists. It was Reagan who appointed him, in 1982, to the Appeals Court of the District of Columbia; and when it comes time for Reagan to appoint a Supreme Court Justice (between now and 1988 Reagan could appoint as many as five new justices), Richard Posner is considered very near the top of the list of probable appointees. Posner is a young man, forty-six, and could serve on the Supreme Court a very long time.

What is *the machine?* The machine has been called man's baby, sometimes man's true lover. It is also patriarchal man's version of the World Mother. The machine is man's transformation ritual, his magic uterus of mass production. The machine is a manmade system, device, or theology-philosophy for converting world energy (animal, vegetable, mineral) into human wealth. Under four thousand years of patriarchal religious-economic systems, human wealth has meant the conversion of the energy of the many into the profit and power of the few. The primary mechanism of this energy conversion has been the control and exploitation of the female reproductive process simultaneous with the repression and punishment of female sexual autonomy. Through the energy-suppression and conversion mechanism of piety and drudgery, female sexual-biological energy has been maintained and controlled in a chronic process of productive repression; and this machine-model for controlling and using female sexual-reproductive energy has also been applied to the control and exploitation of workers' productive labor. The machine, a patriarchal-hierarchic system for exploiting and diverting female sexual-reproductive energy into wealth and profit, is now used of course to exploit and coopt the energies of most of the world's males also. The machine converts kangaroos and whales into dog food, ancient forests into toothpicks, and the oily black blood and metallic veins of earth into nuclear missiles, beer cans, and smog.

The history of humankind from Neanderthals to now has been a slow but logarithmically increasing (spatially and temporally) development of the organic into the mechanical, of the primally simple into the artificially complex. In Paul Virilio's terms, it has been a development from the gradual speed of geophysical space to the instantaneous space of electronic time. In psychoanalytical terms, it has been the his-tory of the implacable overcoming of the (matristic) oral by the (patristic) anal. The past four thousand years has been accomplished via the total physical and ideological repression of the female body. The next stage depends on the total physical and economic mechanization of the female body. The global assembly line turning out consumer junk and human consumers (and human-replacing robots) will be the great machine mother of the world—with the eggs, uteruses, and hormone systems of living women attached to it, one way or another, in servomechanistic functions. The current rage for female bodies trussed up in chains, discipline-frames, and even rubber-and-metal garter belts turns some people on specifically because it mechanizes female flesh. The media mechanizes female flesh by making it available directly to the brain via disembodied light technology. A good deal of contemporary pornography has to do, not with the eroticization of the flesh, but with the eroticization of the mechanization of the flesh—she wears all the metallic jewelry of torture. Increasing numbers of men in the world today are turned on solely, or primarily, by torture's metalloid-mechanistic thrills. The triumph of the anal-sadistic-necrophilic machine equals the total mechanization of the female body: She is screwed by machine, and she reproduces mechanically.

Patriarchal man has undoubtedly lusted after woman in his heart, as a sexual body. Even more, he has lusted after motherhood. The control of female sex and reproduction through his jealous father Gods and misogynist priesthoods has been his mode of experiencing ersatz motherhood. He has owned the female reproductive machinery, like the factory-owner owns productive machinery. (Like the pastoralist owns cows.) In modern reproductive technologies, the same lust is evident. To know the secret mechanisms of reproduction is to own the secret of life. Patriarchal-technological man has spent many centuries spying to capture the secret, as we all know. What the boss does with the factory machinery, the biotechnologist can now do in the laboratory: control and program the mechanical process of reproduction-production. I.e., he too can be "a mother"—if motherhood is defined as mechanical breeding. Early results of this machinery can be seen in fertility drugs which tend to mass-produce: sextuplets and septuplets. For life, if approached mechanistically, is certainly capable of a mechanistic response; in particular since mechanical replication is one part of the life process—as Heidegger pointed out in *The Question Concerning Technology*, it is precisely this replicative, assembly-line aspect of the life process that we keep soliciting with our technologies, and with our technologically oriented ideologies.[20] The more we relate to life as mechanisms to a cosmic machine (rather than as organisms to a cosmic organism), the more fiendishly mechanoid will be its response—the DNA will roll out like Fords and Subarus, and we will all be made by God and global corporations as production units with interchangeable parts. ("By God," i.e., this will seem normative in a mechanically self-justifying system.)

Everyone is caught in this machinery. There is nowhere to go to escape it—except inward, to a definition of life as conscious organism, rather than stupid mechanism. This is the *only* way we can stop life from becoming nothing but stupid mechanism. The process of redefinition begins with women reclaiming total sexual and reproductive autonomy; for if the female body can be controlled or used, in any way, from the outside—via exploitive definitions or systems—then so, it follows, can everything else. (The definition and use of the female body is the paradigm for the definition and use of all things; if the autonomy of the female body is defined as sacred, then so will be the autonomy of all things.) Patriarchal men have tried to pretend that males can be "free" while females can be dominated and enslaved; just as white imperialists have pretended that they can be "independent and soulful" beings in private life, while publicly colonizing and brutalizing darker peoples. Now we see that everyone involved in a dominating machine is dominated and mechanized by it; now we can also see that after four thousand years of systematic physical and ideological domination of the female sexual and reproductive processes by men, there is no free man left on earth! If the source of life is defined not as conscious autonomous organism, but as stupid useable machine, then everybody gets caught in this definitive machinery—the definers as well as the defined.

Biological beings are not analogous to machinery. Four thousand years ago, patriarchal religion and culture began forcibly defining biological beings—and primarily the female being—in mechanistic, exploitable terms. Since then, because behavior follows definition, the human world has undergone a logarithmically accelerating process of mechanization. Patriarchal religion emptied biology of spirit and of consciousness, through its machine-dualisms of fleshly body versus divine mind, of material evil versus abstract goodness—in this way it destroyed the Neolithic Goddess religion, and enslaved female beings. Patriarchal science followed with its eventually Cartesian definitions of a totally mechanoid deadness of matter being acted upon—objectively observed, manipulated—by the detached male mind. Even though modern physics and biology have once again redefined life as a magically organic process arranged and rearrangeable by subjective perception, our world religions, laws, social structures, and customs continue to follow the now *obsolete* patriarchal definition of life as stupid mechanism. So we have forgotten, or have not yet been allowed to remember, that biological beings are not analogous to machinery.

In the continuous spiraling of evolution-devolution, biology is a spiritual process—and spirit is a biological process. Spiritual energy fuels our biological organisms, and biological energy fuels our spiritual experiences.

Biology and spirituality—sexuality and spirituality—cannot be separated without destroying the living holism and producing dead mechanism: robot sex, robot piety, robot labor, robot existence. To reclaim the biological process as a numinous process is to reclaim the original process of the earth, which is a geological-biological-spiritual *being,* capable of consciousness—and of conscious relationship to its creatures. The magic is *in* the molecules, the dance of energy. Solid rock and human flesh are *in* the imagination of earth.

Women originally knew this, as did men, through tens of thousands of years of biological-spiritual experiencing of primal earth as a reciprocal Mother. Spirit and sex were not separate, dualized, or antagonistic, but experienced as twin serpents or energy flows interlocked and spiraling around each other. When women *knew* this, men knew it too. It was experienced as ontological reality. Earth and life haven't changed—our *definitions of reality have been changed*—allowing us to perceive and experience only the most mechanistic aspects of the life process. The deep structure of the imagination remains the same, where we experience biology and spirit as unified: This is where we are in dreams, with natural hallucinogens like peyote and mushrooms, and in art (sometimes). Religious ritual was once a major mode of experiencing direct communication between the sexual-spiritual imaginations of human creatures, and the evolutionarily numinous imagination of earth. Patriarchal religion turned this open channel into a blocked road, with its substitution of moralistic-necrophilious ritual for the ancient pagan rituals of biological epiphany. Now it is time to return; if we can't unblock the road with the dynamite of revolutionary consciousness, then we must build a new way back with the slower, steadier energy of consciousness-in-evolution.

Because patriarchy began by taking possession of the female body as property and as stupid machinery, the way back begins with women reclaiming full sexual and reproductive autonomy—not in pursuit of cheap thrills, or of "equality" within the present system, which is a dead system; but in pursuit of the original holism of biological-spiritual beings. Evolving sexually numinous beings, who cannot experience themselves ontologically if they are habitually being defined (and self-defined) as mechanisms—or as moralistic property.

This means that the question of whether to be pregnant, or not pregnant, must be returned to female intuition; which, when it is healthy, strong, and self-defined, is the voice of the sexual-spiritual energies interlocked and working—muscularly flowing—together. A pregnant woman, or a woman deciding on pregnancy or nonpregnancy, is not a situation analogous to any other situation. Neither male logic nor male theology apply to female reproduction, to pregnancy or to contraception or to abortion—because male logic and male theology derive from beings who never become pregnant, use contraception, give birth, or have abortions. In relation to female sex and reproduction, male logic and male theology are spectator sports; but pregnancy, childbirth, and even abortion are

Birth & Struggle for Liberation, Sjöö, 1969

participation rituals. Nor does man's busy-ness apply; female bodies are not man's business. A woman is a specialist in her own situation. In a world that worships specialists, how strange that men refuse to recognize women as specialists in our own bodies and processes, and allow us to function accordingly. The fundamentalist preachers and Catholic priests and other holy men who want to forbid women contraception and abortion, and the technological-humanist "fertility-control" experts trying to force contraception, abortion, and sterilization on Third World women, are the same mentality, and are doing the same number on women: trying to take over the female functions of organic reproduction, organic birth control, organic population limitation—and run these according to the amateurish notions of male logic and male theology. "Overpopulation" is a code word, a symptom word, for the failure of all male-dominated systems designed to control and exploit the female process for God and profit.

Women decide to be pregnant or not. Period. That is the beginning and end of "population control."

In the abortion debates, one of the questions most frequently raised is: When does life begin? The question is quasimechanistic, suggesting some ideal point on a linear scale before which abortion is "right," and after which abortion is "not right." A popular placard and slogan carried by antiabortionists in demonstrations and rallies illustrates the same mentality: A photo of a bouncing beautiful baby is shown, with the words: "If you take her life now, it's murder. If you take her life 12 months ago, it's abortion."

The problem with this reasoning is this: Life does not begin. It is always here. Nature is alive from the beginning, and prodigal. Life does not emerge *from us,* we emerge *from it.* Pregnancy and childbirth are ritual passages of eternal life through the bodies of autonomous women. From the first cell floating on the first sea at the first out-breath of the world, it has all been alive. Life does not begin with the fertilized egg, or embryo. Male sperm is alive, the female ovum is alive. Technically, as we've said, the female egg could mate with its own polar body and produce a daughter clone, all by itself. Yet each month of her life, if a woman does not become pregnant, one of these incredible eggs goes down the drain—taking with it all its potential life. With each human male ejaculation, about 2 million sperm are wasted, condemned to not become; for each single sperm that enters an egg and begins with the egg to form an embryo, 1,999,999 of its fellow sperm do not. Nature is extremely alive and extremely prodigal, and continuous waste and death occurs within a continuous sea of life.

And that continuity is both a cycle and a continuum. Thus the question "When does life begin" is asked along, and of, that continuum. A three-month fetus, if not aborted, will indeed grow into a bouncing baby. But if the continuum is reversed, and followed backward, when *does* that life begin? A three-month fetus, projected back three-and-a-half months along the continuum, separates into a female egg and a male sperm, alive within two distinct bodies of a woman and a man. Most women, especially, beginning a menstrual period, have had the experience of wondering, deeply—sometimes with overwhelming tears—just what that tiny egg might have become. Nature is prodigal, and life's potential is even more so. The female egg was once itself enclosed within an embryo, and before that was a potential egg within another egg . . . on and on and on, back through apes, forest shrews, lizards, star acorns, algae, the first molecule . . . back to the first imagination of a sea. A sea of night filled with nothing.

Where does life begin?

This is not an argument intended to prove that abortion is "right" or "wrong." It is just to say that life happens *always* along a continuum. And all the decisions we make are always decisions made along a continuum. Any "fixed point" designated along that continuum is always understood to be arbitrary. That is the best we mortals can do, if we are utterly honest with ourselves, and with life. In the abortion debate, the earnest search for that point when life begins is understandable, but futile. There will never be any final determination of the question, because the closer we look, the clearer we see that "life" does not *begin* . . . on earth it recedes to the origins of Earth, and beyond that to the origins of the universe. And certainly with the elaboration and refinement of reproductive technology, the age in months and weeks and days at which a fetus will be able to survive outside the mother's womb will also recede backward along that continuum to a point where the entire question of "beginning life" becomes as technologically inappropriate as it is now biologically inappropriate. This fixation on a logically, empirically determinable point in space, or number of days, at which life can be said to begin is another symptom of cultural-ideological fixation on mechanical quantity, rather than organic quality. It also derives from the patriarchal-pastoralist notion that life is not "divine" until male sperm enters the female womb, which from that point on is a passive container in which "God's child" grows. In the view of others, God is a woman, and the "child" is not property but embodied spirit. The continuum is also a cycle, a spiraling out and in, and what has come once—when the time is wrong—can come once again when the time is right. The point is that the entire question and answer changes—with a change of the sex of God, or the change of a straight line into a spiral.

The opposite of life is not death, but to become a mechanism. Women forced against their wills or instincts to give birth like breeding machines, in the name of "the sacred fetus," is a travesty of life. "Sacred beings" do not pass through breeding machines, nor through women tied down by the ropes of God and required to give birth to male property, or to "multiply congregations." If the mother is not a sacred, autonomous being, then the fetus is neither sacred nor autonomous. If the mother *is* a sacred, autonomous being, then she makes her own choices about what she brings, or does not bring, to birth. Sacred, holy life is not born from machinery.

In a lovely book, *Hygieia, A Woman's Herbal,* author Jeannine Parvati records the abortion experiences of several women, in the form of journal extracts, poems, letters. Few abortion experiences are shallow; whatever the method used, they are normally overwhelming psychological and spiritual experiences, even when the physical trauma seems minimal. Perhaps all antiabortionists see women as stupid cows or callow whores, from whom "the fetus" must be rescued. But most women who've undergone abortion know that the experience is indeed a participation ritual, in which a woman participates heavily and unforgettably in her own death, as well as in the death of a potential child. Few women emerge unchanged from the abortion experience, and the change is usually in the direction of greater thoughtfulness, deeper maturity, a need and a desire to listen more profoundly, gaze more intensely into the womb of one's inner experience, the bubbling crucible of life and death. Women who have not had abortions, and/or do not approve of abortion, can only be asked to consider cultivating an ontological trust of their sisters who do undergo abortion—we must begin believing, or rebelieving, that the female being, of its original nature, *knows* what it has to do, when it must be done, and why. If we reclaim this trust in ourselves, and in other women, we are reclaiming female autonomy—and this reclamation can help create a world in which much of the pain and ugliness of abortion no longer exists. This will be a world in which females are so ontologically in touch with their bodies, so tuned-in to their cycles and their hormonal activity, that the processes which Jeannine Parvati records and describes as psychic birth control and even psychic abortion can not only occur, but will predominate. Women describe experiences of being pregnant, of knowing and feeling and believing that it was not the right time or circumstance to have a child; they speak of going into meditation, or into their dreams, and speaking to the

Our Bodies—Ourselves, Sjöö, 1976

fetus as one sacred being to another: *This is not the right time or space for us to be together. Please leave now. At the right time, we will meet again.* These women practiced imaging: either of actual abortion, or simply imaging the embryonic bloodclot breaking loose from the uterine wall and flowing downward with a bloodflow. In the cases described, at least, "miscarriage" followed. This cannot always happen, but it is a beginning. The further along the pregnancy is, the harder it becomes, and the more traumatic the miscarriage; so it is very important for women to also practice meditation and dream-conversation with our entire menstrual cycles and hormonal conditions (along with, of course, many other methods of organic contraception, herbs, temperature readings, and all the rest). A woman can *know* she is pregnant, through correctly reading her own dreams, several weeks before she becomes aware of physical symptoms.[21]

Of course, the fundamentalist types might try to burn us for psychic abortions, for having conversations with our own dreams. They've done it before. And the logical-technological types will scoff and insist it can't be done, there is no objective proof, this is all subjective nonsense . . . and so on and so on. The way it goes. But each time a human female simply tries it, and finds it works . . . the community of female reempowerment grows stronger, the time of female reempowerment grows closer. We will not be empowered by way of any political, economic, or social system built on the fact of our weakness, that is certain. And all present political, economic, social, and religious systems on earth are built solidly on the fact of female weakness. Living within these systems, with no way out, we instead turn in, and find a radically different world system inside, awaiting revolution . . . that is a convolution, a turning-the-inside-out.

Female autonomy always means human autonomy—just as patriarchal domination of female reproductive labor always means patriarchal domination of human productive labor. Organism means organism, as machine means machine. We either rebecome children of the Great Mother, or we remain children of the machine. The opposite of life is not death, *but to become a mechanism.* We are now already quasimechanisms, living within a world machine. We must extricate ourselves from the machinery, which is not truly either life or death, but the absence and the travesty of both. Politics is important, social and cultural activity is important, everything that can be done should be done to change our situation; but these activities cannot extricate us from the machinery if they are still conducted in the terms of the machinery. Ontological evolution and revolution must be conducted in the mode of biology-and-the-dream. This is the mode into which machinery cannot enter. Only living beings can.

BEYOND THE MALE GOD AND HIS MACHINE . . .

■ Under Islamic law, virgins cannot be executed. So in Iranian jails, prison guards systematically gang-rape young female prisoners sentenced to death, thus rendering them fit, in "God's" eyes, for execution.

■ Pregnant women prisoners in some American jails, notably the California Institution for Women, are routinely strapped to their beds at the ankles or wrists throughout their labor and childbirth. Under twenty-four-hour surveillance, the enchained women are unable to move, turn over during sleep, or help themselves in the most minimal way to ease labor pains—though the woman in labor is not going to be, in anyone's opinion, a great security risk.

■ Hundreds of young women are killed yearly in India in the notorious "dowry-deaths," in which a young bride is set afire by her inlaws as revenge for "inadequate" or incompletely paid dowries. The new bride is doused with kerosene and then ignited with matches. This act is usually performed by mothers-in-law, i.e., women do this to other women, in acts of stupendous greed and self-hatred, conditioned by religious ideas that define sons and males generally as "spiritual beings," while daughters and other females are defined as "income property."

■ One of the most popular X-rated video games, before it was removed from circulation in response to protests from Native American and feminist groups, was called "Custer's Revenge," in which a naked General Custer scored points by raping bound Indian women. One of the most popular X-rated films ever made is the notorious South American-produced *Snuff,* in which a live woman is raped, mutilated, and disemboweled before the camera; this film has been shown throughout the world, and its popularity has spawned many "spin-offs," in which the gang rape, torture, and murder of women and also children is not simulated by actors, but really done while the cameras roll. To provide sacrificial "actresses" for these films is a function of the global slave-trade in women and young girls. *Snuff* has been shown in some American prisons, ostensibly to "entertain" male prisoners, many of whom we can assume were imprisoned for rape and killing women. In America alone, torture-pornography films are a billion-dollar business. They run the gamut from *Driller Killer,* in which women's skulls are drilled, to *Pieces,* in which college women are cut to bits by a professor with a chain-saw; the distributor of the latter hopes it will become a "cult film for kids." Despite organized protests of feminists worldwide, the production and sale of torture-and-pornography films, home videos, and video games continues to soar, with global distribution following patterns of global "development." A 1983 film called "Make Them Die Slowly" showed not only women but aborigines being tortured.

■ The National Secretary of the Moral Majority, lecturing in the early 1980s at Earlham College, a Quaker-affiliated school in Indiana, declared that the United States should have used atomic or hydrogen bombs to "win" the Vietnam war. Moral Majority and other fundamentalist American religious-patriotic groups believe that "God" gave nuclear weaponry to America, and that we have a moral right, indeed a moral duty, to use "the weapon that God gave us."

■ When new recruits are inducted into the Israeli Defense Forces, they are ceremonially handed (1) a gun, and (2) a copy of the Old Testament, in which "God" commands and justifies the righteous slaughter of thousands upon thousands of "unbelievers." The biblical Old Testament is a historic record of massive holy war conducted "in the name of God"—against Gentiles, and also in some cases against Jews, by Jews—and most of the mutilations and massacres in it, including those of pregnant women, children, and suckling infants, are considered by its patriarchal writers to be fulfillments of the will of Yahweh.

■ In the Pentagon, group Bible-reading sessions and prayer breakfasts are on the increase in the 1980s—or at least, the Joint Chiefs of Staff are more openly, under President Reagan's administration, displaying their religious beliefs. At many prayer breakfasts conducted throughout America recently, the Chairman of the Joint Chiefs of Staff, John Vessey, has urged his audiences to "enlist in God's army"; while Admiral James Watkins, the chief of naval operations, declares in public speeches that the 1983 Beirut bombing that killed 241 Marines was the responsibility of "the forces of the anti-Christ."[1]

These seven news items were not selected at random, nor do we consider them to be disconnected. They are seven facets of a world ruled by a male God, or rather by a definition of God derived from four thousand years of patriarchal ideological domination, in which countless daily acts of aggression, human degradation, and sheer ugliness not only occur but occur inevitably, as the acting-out of basic patriarchal principles and premises. All these news items record the acting-out of patriarchal ontology. The patriarchal "Godhead" of all major world religions is defined as (1) a god of righteous war; (2) a dominator of women; (3) a god of wealth and hierarchic power; (4) an imperialist god who controls vast resources of wealth and power by controlling the female body and its reproductive processes as exploitable property; (5) a sexually puritanical god who defines sex as "unclean" and "evil," and thus elicits violent pornography as the sexual punishment and *exorcism* of women; and (6) a god who thrives on "policing" and punishing life itself.

The world's definition of God is the self-definition of humanity. The Gods who rule us "from above" are simply mirrors in the sky, faithfully reflecting our own faces. The Gods who rule us "from within" might represent deep truths of the mind and heart, or they might reflect the profound self-distortions of four millennia of ontological misperception. We do not know if a "God" is a true God or a false God until we see what kind of world is created in that God's image. When we look around today at the world generated by the male Gods of patriarchal rule, we see warfare, degradation, suffering, and sadism on a scale such as earth has never seen, nor will ever see again—for of course if we don't end it, it will surely end us. Nor is it a problem of blood—of "Muslim blood," or "Hindu blood," or "Christian blood," or "Jewish blood," or "atheist Communist blood"—but a problem of ideology. If we embrace an ideology of justified holy war, we will be forever at war—and inflicting war on others. If we worship a punitive God, we will be forever punished—and punishing of others. If we believe in a religion that dualizes the human sexes into mutually hostile, dominating, and submissive categories of beings, then we, as sexual human beings, will be forever dichotomized and ravaged by hostility, within ourselves and among ourselves—and we will inflict our internal alienation and ravagement on everything we see, forever. This is all very rudimentary, but once it has been set into motion as world machinery, every living thing on earth is entangled in its gears, all our functions become definitively embodied in its functions—and it's very hard for those living inside the machinery to stop the machine, because our lives and all their ontological terms have come to depend on the ongoing machinery in all its terms.

Because, as human beings, we not only worship our gods. We become them. The God humanity follows is the kind of humanity we are and will be. What kind of God do we want as our definition? We will know the answer to this more clearly as we come to understand the kind of god which, for four thousand years, has been defining us. Has been imposing its definition on us, us human creatures, via the machinery of patriarchal religious, economic, and military systems.

The God of Patriarchy, from the beginning, has been a God of War and Economic Exploitation; incessant warfare and economic exploitation have characterized the four-thousand-year history of this male God—a timespan that is very brief relative to the 300,000 to 500,000 years of humanoid life on earth, but still long enough to make us feel, as a species, that "it has always been this way." It is no surprise that the world of today, the apotheosis of patriarchy, is a world of war and money. What else rules us, anywhere we go on earth? The paradigm of continuous, large-scale war is the institutionalized dualism of the sexes into "good, spiritual males" versus "evil, material females"—i.e., male versus female is the first holy war. The paradigm of continuous, large-scale economic exploitation is the institutionalized control of female reproduction by a ruling male elite—i.e., male controlling female reproduction is the first boss controlling worker production, the first assembly-line domination of human energy. In the modern world, we are told there are two very different and competing economic power systems, but in fact they are ontologically the same, deriving from the same God of War and Exploitation, from the same patriarchal definition of human life as a function of some larger, abstract category: "God," "the state," "the marketplace." American-based private-enterprise monopoly-capitalism defines human beings (and all of nature) as functions of the marketplace; Soviet-based public-enterprise monopoly state-capitalism defines human beings (and all of nature) as functions of the state. What is the ontological difference? To define human beings as functions, or exploitable means, rather than as sacred ends in ourselves, is to create by definition a perpetual state of war. Together, these two world machines—known politically as the US and the USSR—grind away as functions of each other, producing state economies and private economies in apparent or rhetorical conflict, both in reality subservient to one global, unified war economy which in turn serves both, and in which both collude. For perpetual war is necessary, against mock "enemies" and against one's own people, in order to maintain human beings in a perpetual condition of "exploitable means" rather than "sacred ends in our selves." This is why the patriarchal God begins, and ends, as a War God. To maintain himself in power, He must wage war against human life. His priesthoods, sacred texts, doctrines, and dogmas exist to rationalize this horrific state of incessant warfare as "man's spiritual destiny." His social and economic institutions exist to provide continuous cannon-fodder and spoils for continuous war.

A global God of War, served by the global religion of money, defines the human condition today. Our various nationalities, our sectarian beliefs, our local customs, our personal opinions, may serve as individual definitions but they no longer define the condition of the world, in which global missile systems and global factory-economic systems have rendered national, sectarian, local, and personal definitions merely soporific—and, in fact, obsolete. All humanity today lives under one global god: the God of War, who is continuously empowered and enlarged by the religion of money. The "arms race" is now the major global economy, the world economy is now a war economy, with virtually all national military systems and military budgets taking precedence over all domestic economies and domestic budgets. World Priorities, a nonprofit American research organization, in their published *World Military and Social Expenditures for 1979*, found that developing nations, with populations of 660 million people who couldn't afford basic subsistence, were yet spending over $90 billion dollars a year on military power. And this was eight years ago. In 1979, according to World Priorities, the world was investing "2500 times more in the machinery of war than in the machinery of peace-keeping"; 8 million children died in that year alone from hunger and illness related to malnutrition; America, the earth's strongest military nation, had in 1979 over 25 million malnourished people, and at least 10 million children who had never seen a doctor. In total, for 1979, "In pounds per person, the world [had] more explosive power than food."[2]

And this was eight years ago, *before* the arms race "heated up" again, *before* the resurgence of the Pentagon budget under the Reagan administration and the consequent leap in military spending in all other countries, *before* the terrible famines in Sudan, Ethiopia, and Bolivia, *before* the cutbacks in American welfare programs and the consequent diminishment of domestic priorities in governments worldwide. According to the most recent statistics, for every soldier on earth the average military expenditure is $20,000 yearly; for every school-aged child the average public education expenditure is $380. For every 100,000 people in the world there are 556 soldiers, but only 85 doctors. For every billion dollars spent to provide 28,000 jobs in military goods and services, the same expenditure could provide 57,000 jobs in personal consumption industries, and 71,000 jobs in education.[3] As Ruth Leger Sivard, director of World Priorities, writes:

> The vast development problems . . . [of the 1980s], like the unbridled arms race, must be understood in human terms. It is not the World Economy, nor the National Security, that is in danger; it is people. . . . The modern world is painfully off balance, opulently rich in arms, poor in providing for the needs of human lives. It is this social deficit that represents the most urgent threat to world security. Spending for arms not only fails to meet these needs; it intensifies them. This is the ultimate irony of the search for security through invincible military power. It threatens the society it is intended to protect. . . . In short, what the arms race means in human terms is that more people are condemned to die of hunger and of foul water; children to grow up retarded in body and mind; the special needs of the elderly to be neglected; people to live out their lives in fear and with hate. It is not only the deprived who suffer as a consequence. All of society is affected by the waste of human resources.[4]

But these are reasonable, mortal words from a reasonable, mortal woman. Looming over her, high as the sky, is *a God.* The War God. All the present-day world is in the grip of psychic and material servitude to him, and if we review the past four thousand years of human history, this makes perfect sense. Just as the underlying motivation of Bronze Age patriarchy was profit through war—war on the female, war on nature, war on human labor—so the ultimate goal of patriarchy must be the same: the profits of war. For four millennia, war has been the factual source of patriarchal power. Through the mass terror, mass rape, and mass exploitation of war, through the wartime generation of mass hysterical energy, through the war-oriented manipulation of female reproduction, through the mass conversion of human and natural resources via war into profits (for the few) and "social order" (i.e., hierarchic role-playing, organized repression, and death) for the many—the war machine has virtually created the world as we know it; i.e., as the creator of our psychic and structural world, war is God. (As both William Irwin Thompson and Paul Virilio have pointed out, the city began as a fortress; Virilio, an urban architect, claims that the city "is the result of war, at least of preparation for war"—that is, of large-scale, patriarchal professional warfare.[5])

And Gods generate not only worlds and social orders, but also belief in those worlds and social orders: a belief that overwhelms human reason. "Secular humanist liberals"—and reasonable, mortal women—have always tended to underestimate the depth and extent of the human male's identification with war as a God-experience, as well as an experience of personal empowerment. It is not accidental that the government's social programs—public welfare, health, education, the environment, transportation, art and culture, etc.—are identified as "domestic" and "female," while the defense department's programs are always promoted as "global" and "masculine"; nor is it coincidental that liberal male politicians who support the "domestic" programs are always being challenged to defend their genitals against charges of "wimpiness," "softness," and "bleeding-heartedness." (Ponder that last one.) Before the 1984 elections in the United States, support of young men for the Republicans was at an all-time post-World War II high. According to a *New York Times* article summarizing pre-election poll results, young American males (and older males too, of course) identified with the image of power projected by Ronald Reagan, in particular nationalistic warrior-power represented by a tougher military posture and increased weapons-spending vis-à-vis spending for "soft" domestic programs. One urban male professional was quoted as saying that at his workplace, "the guys stick to Reagan primarily because they see the race as women versus men, with Reagan standing for the values of men."[6] I.e., the patriarchal War God stands for (and has created) a social order that empowers men—to the degree that it gives them power over women, and over life.

As for the ruling elites, to whom patriarchy has given manipulative power over both men and women, the War God has always been a profitable machine. Fueled by their money, it not only returns wealth manyfold, it also returns social order—"patriotism" being so often a repressed form of revolutionary energy. Social order allows the ruling elite to enjoy the profits of war in relative peace. "This machinery has worked for us for four thousand years, why stop now?"—so say the owners of the machinery, as they collect the profits. In the past, war has always been something the ruling elite felt it could control, or manage, via money and political clout; that the mushrooming of the Bronze Age War Gods into a nuclear God of

Global War threatens their own continuance seems to be overlooked data, or an apotheosis they refuse to deal with. The Global War God now looms over *them,* as well as over everything else on earth; but this ontological challenge does not seem to be regulating the behavior of the war-financiers, or the people engaged in weapons' manufacture and sale. I.e., *everyone* underestimates the power of a God grown to global proportions in his material as well as psychic manifestations. As further evidence of the logarithmic growth of various patriarchal War Gods into the Global God of War is the fact that the development of the world's male populations into primarily armies, or military technicians or researchers of one kind or another, has become the major global channel of male energy; in the Third World countries, the army has also become the major mode of male survival. While women sustain agricultural and craft work in many nations (or struggle to keep themselves and their children alive in the burgeoning refugee camps created by continuous war), males are able to obtain food and shelter only by joining the army, the national guard, or other armed policing force. Thus the War God machinery perpetuates itself on three levels: that of belief, of profit, and of daily survival.

As the patriarchal War God has become the Global God of Global War, the state of holy war has become global, inevitable, and continuous. As a Christian, Paul Virilio distinguishes between the historic idea of a "just war" and the fanatic pursuit of holy war; but in the age of nuclear technology, there is no room or time left, in his opinion, for a "just war." All war today is fanatic, and also technologically devastating; all war has the potential for rapid acceleration into total war. But to maintain itself in power, the patriarchal system *must* maintain the world in a continuous, chronic state of war, of one kind or another. Holy war is all war, i.e., it is righteous war, self-justifying. Whether the war is conducted between nations, as classic "warfare," or conducted within a nation, as a national guard or "policing action" against the nation's own people, hardly makes a difference anymore. Further, as Virilio underscores, it doesn't even matter if wars occur or don't occur on any large scale: It is the preparation for war that maintains the military in power by draining the social sectors of all resources, money, and will. Whether we are fighting others, fighting among ourselves, or just chronically getting ready to fight, it makes no difference anymore: we are effectively ruled by the God of War; we are effectively living (and dying) in a habitual and structural state of perpetual war.

And what is the purpose, or result, of such a condition? As Virilio says: "Unconsciousness is the aim of pure war."[7]

But as we know, or should know, *consciousness* is the aim of evolution. So the ultimate aim, or effect, of the patriarchal pursuit of profit through war is counter-evolutionary: On a mass scale, it seeks to drag us back to a state of oblivion before human consciousness began. This correlates with the urge of patriarchal religion to force a human de-evolution back to the primate state, by controlling human reproduction as though it were the same as mammalian reproduction, and by denying the fact of human female evolution into a unique state, via the menstrual cycle, in which sex and reproduction can be separable. This female evolution away from the primates was, in a very real sense, the beginning of human consciousness. A consciousness which patriarchal religion has tried to reverse, via control of female sexual and reproductive activity—and which the patriarchal War God is now seeking to destroy, one way or another, by forcibly maintaining the human species in a state of continuous war, or continuous preparation for war.

Cui bono? We may well ask. And the answer is, ultimately: No one. But the war machinery of the War God neither asks nor answers such questions anymore. It is entirely automatic. It just keeps turning—warring, preparing for war. Like the apocryphal Christ, it says only: "I have come to destroy the works of the female." And that is seen as all of life, all of earth . . . and apparently all of human consciousness.

The other face of the patriarchal God is economic exploitation. Economic exploitation and war, as we have seen, are two faces on one head: inextricably connected. Just as the ancient shared-work and celebration-ritual groups of women were the original communalism (in which matrifocal cultures men participated also, for at least 300,000 years), so the Bronze Age patriarchal desire to control female sex and reproduction, and thus all human labor and production, was the origin of fascism. The *American Heritage Dictionary of the English Language* defines "fascism" as "A system of government that exercises a dictatorship of the extreme right, typically through the merging of state and business leadership, together with a belligerent nationalism." But throughout four thousand years of patriarchal history, "state and business leadership" have *always* been merged, and the merger has been maintained in power by "a belligerent nationalism," i.e., the war machine, always in the service of state and business interests, both at home and abroad. The only thing missing from this definition is the role of patriarchal religion (or a deified patriarchal ideology) in providing a divine rationalization, or heavenly mystique, for the fascistic apparatus. If we follow this definition, it is not too far-fetched to say that the history of patriarchy is the history of fascism; and that patriarchal economics or economic systems have always been fascistic economic systems, in which court, state, religious, military, and business ruling elites collude in mutual empowerment, and power reinforcement, to exploit human labor and earth's resources, beginning with the exploitation of female reproductive labor, and female creative-communal labor in general. Historic "revolutions" in the West have effectively done little more than add new economic groups to the collusion, e.g., the eighteenth- and nineteenth-century addition of the European bourgeoisie to the ruling elites of Europe, or the more complex twentieth-century addition of the Soviet political-military elite to the fascistic power organization of the West generally.

The wealth of the West—the wealth-making economic system, known popularly as the Western "free-enterprise system"—was built from the ground up, as we know, via brutalization of the working class, slave labor, and colonialism. Eighteenth-century *laissez-faire* "liberal" economics, now enjoying a revival as "neoconservative" economics, was solidly based and wholly dependent upon the violent exploitation of colonial resources and native or imported slave labor, as well as the forcible maintenance of indentured and sub-subsistence wage labor in the home countries. Profits occurred in the "free enterprise system" solely because the profiteers were allowed (via the fascistic collusion of state-business-military-religious elites) to ravage people and environments without paying recompense or undergoing regulation. It also had whole continents of untapped natural resources—Asia, India, Africa, the Americas—to lavishly plunder without interference. Indigenous populations of these rich continents were massacred, enslaved, "missionized," destroyed by imported diseases, or pushed further and further into uninhabitable areas (which they managed to inhabit, through sheer grit) while the colonialists ripped off all the good land. Many colonized people fought back, and sometimes won, temporarily; but they could not hold out against well-armed imperial armies, especially in a mercilessly mercenary world in which no one cared if they were slaughtered or not, and few came to their aid.

This is why the eighteenth century was the great heyday of *laissez-faire* profiteering: The world conditions were optimal for global plunder. I.e., large-scale profit taking depends on these fascistic conditions. In the twentieth century, the conditions are reversed: rapidly dwindling and polluting resources, and large "de-colonized" populations often armed and ready to throw off the yokes of Western exploitation; in this they are backed by world sympathy, and also usually by the military and economic support of one world power or another. Even if the Third World was completely depopulated, eighteenth-century-style *laissez-faire* profiteering could not be repeated for long: Due to their depletion by greed, many major world resources are due to run out, to disappear by the end of the twentieth century. The most dwindling resource of all, it seems, is the brainpower of neoconservative economists and those free-enterprise-Capitalist apologists who fail, or refuse, to see the complete reversal of global conditions, and instead suggest that the solution to the twentieth century is to return to the eighteenth and nineteenth centuries, that colonialist-imperialist paradise of unobstructed plunder, slave-trading, and labor exploitation. In fact, the Capitalist free-market system is structurally and functionally incapable of working if it pays decent wages and provides full employment; this is why it must fight against worker empowerment through unionization. Evidence that "free enterprise Capitalism" cannot work without (1) fascistic control and (2) subsistence-level wages lies in the global factory system itself. American corporate-Capitalism saved itself by leaving America—where unionized workers had fought for and won relatively high wages and decent conditions and fringe benefits—and setting up "free trade zones" throughout the Third World; where, as always, "free" is a euphemism for fascistic control over workers' lives, on and off the job, and the payment of feudal-system wages. Neoconservative economics is, in effect, the same old Fascist economics that have defined patriarchal "exploit-for-profit" social and moral systems from the beginning; the evolution of "law and economics" theory out of this mindset is inevitable, with human beings defined, from womb to tomb, as "market commodities," and all laws governing social conditions and relations rewritten to structure human life in terms of its market value. If we do not call this "neofascist" economics, perhaps "neopastoralist" would be appropriate: the breeding of human life for economic use and slaughter.

What does this have to do with women, and in particular American women? The overwhelming majority of starving, malnourished, and homeless people on earth are women and children. In the Third World, millions of women and children, and elderly people also, displaced by chronic war and related famine, are crowded into refugee camps; refugee camps have become, in fact, a permanent mode of existence for millions of people, most of them women and children. In the Western nations, more and more children and women of all ages are huddled at the bottom of the wobbling "economic ladder," ghettoized, pauperized, permanently stigmatized as "refugees" from an economic system that cannot even support its own premises, let alone support all its poor people. American women and children are joining these populations of "poverty refugees" in larger and larger numbers every year.

According to the 1980 census, more than 15 percent of Americans lived in poverty, 13 million of these children. This was *before* the Reagan administration's budget cuts. Since these cuts, at least 2 million more women have fallen below the government-defined "poverty level," and with them more millions of children. As of January 1985, one out of four American children lives in what is considered to be official poverty. Nearly 35.7 percent of the households headed by women are impoverished; among black families headed by women, 56.1 percent are impoverished.[8] As of February 1985, there were 3 million estimated homeless people in America, a number exceeding the number of homeless during the Great Depression of the 1930s. There are now 25,000 homeless people in the streets of Chicago alone, an estimated 7,000 of these being children—and a burgeoning number of the adult homeless being women. The Chicago Physicians' Task Force on Hunger, in January 1985, described childhood malnutrition in that city so severe that the children "suffered from anemia, hair loss and bloating"—i.e., "official" symptoms of starvation.[9] They also documented an alarming increase in tuberculosis; indeed, with the cutoff of medical funds and the closing of health clinics, since 1980, tuberculosis has grown to near-epidemic proportions among the poor in many major US cities, especially infecting women and children. Tuberculosis is *always* a sign of malnutrition; the Chicago Physicians' Task Force called TB "an objective marker of hunger." In midwinter of January 1985, police were rounding up 600 homeless people a night from the streets of Boston. And in Washington, D.C., capital of world capitalism, there are now between 5,000 and 10,000 homeless people walking the streets. For a while, some of the homeless got warm at night by huddling over the sidewalk gratings where heat escapes from the government buildings. The Reagan administration responded to this "free heat" situation by spending thousands of tax dollars to build cement huts, surrounded with sharp spikes, around the gratings, to ensure that no poor people would benefit from the escaping bureaucratic hot air. Demonstrations got the cement huts removed, at more expense.

Proponents of *laissez-faire* capitalism refer to the free-enterprise system as "the greatest enemy of poverty the earth has ever known." But as the "free-enterprise" system is more and more unleashed in America in the 1980s—i.e., as it is freed from the governmental restrictions and compensatory social welfare programs specifically designed, in the decades since the 1930s, to ameliorate the social and economic ravages of two centuries of unrestricted "free-enterprise" activity—the number of poor is increasing, right here in America. Faced with the statistical evidence of the increase of poverty and real hunger in America during the past six years, the administration's answer is to (1) insist that poverty is not a serious problem in America; (2) scrap all social welfare programs; and (3) turn the problem of "a few unfortunates" over to private charity. This, although all the private charity organizations in America have long ago publicly stated that the load is so enormous they are not capable of handling it, even with the welfare system still running. But "the final solution to the poverty problem" in America is, officially, to deny it exists. Or, to blame it on "lazy" women and children.

As Ruth Leger Sivard pointed out, the poverty statistics affect more than the poor, and not only by "wasting human resources." Large numbers of poor and unemployed people in a society pull the whole working-class wage level downward, and weaken the bargaining positions of working people vis-à-vis employers. Millions of working women in America are just one notch above the official poverty level; they must accept subsistence wages, unhealthy work conditions, and chronic on-the-job harassment, for fear of losing employment altogether. Sweatshop conditions are returning to major American cities—Los Angeles, Boston, New York—where "unlicensed, substandard garment shops are springing up by the hundreds."[10] Where employers can get away with employing poor women up to sixteen hours a day, seven days a week, without overtime, minimum wage rates, unemployment insurance, or even legal work-safety conditions, all workers are threatened; the entire standard of work life plummets downward. The entire "high-tech" electronics industry in America, the vaunted "leading edge" of our "economic recovery," is predicated on employing large numbers of immigrant women (40 percent), in chemically hazardous jobs, at average wages that are among the lowest in American industry. But these conditions are the only alternative for millions and millions of American

Woman, Worker, Farmer,
Sjöö, 1972

women, short of total poverty, including homelessness. Since 1980, the American divorce rate has fallen noticeably; fundamentalists think this means Americans have returned to "God and the Family"—but more likely it means that American women see less and less chance for economic survival, for themselves and their children, outside of marriage. Since 1980, reported incidents of wife-beating and child abuse have noticeably increased; i.e., the economic pressures holding all these marriages together are also increasing the violence within "the American family."

The average American woman works almost twice the hours, and receives a little more than half the pay, of the average American man. This fact has become a feminist cliché. If housewives were paid for their domestic work alone, they would earn $17,000 a year. This too has become a cliché. In lieu of payment, the average white middle-class American homemaker is patted on the head and praised for her "priceless work," a woman's work that is so important it can't have a price tag put on it. This baloney comes from men who have deliberately constructed a world in which all power over life and death is a function of money, of ascertainable wealth, period. A world of male power that is economically established on the *fact* of women's unpaid labor. But millions of married women accept this baloney, and the patronizing head-pats, because they see very clearly that unpaid labor within a marriage is still better than most of the alternatives. I.e., the effect of increasing poverty, especially of the "feminization of poverty," is to force new generations of women into accepting the old traditional terms of patriarchal marriage. American mainstream feminism's offer of "equality within the system" becomes meaningless within a rotten system. A patriarchal, Fascist economic system ontologically predicated upon the exploitation of female labor cannot possibly offer huge numbers of women anything but two choices: economic enslavement inside of marriage, or economic enslavement outside of marriage. A third choice is total poverty.

It is women, in fact—it is the *fact* of women's labor—that presents the most unanswerable challenge to the theoretical and practical claims of "free-enterprise" economics. Very simply, it is the accumulated days, years, and centuries of women's unpaid or poorly paid labor that utterly refutes the astoundingly simple-minded notion that hard work equals wealth. If hard work equalled wealth, all the world's women would be quite rich.

But clearly, the world's women are not rich. In *The Anatomy of Freedom,* Robin Morgan quotes United Nations statistics, presented by UN Secretary Kurt Waldheim in his Official Report to the UN Commission on the Status of Women in 1982:

> While women represent ½ of the global population and ⅓ of the labor force, they receive only ⅒ of the world income and own less than 1% of the world's property. They also are responsible for ⅔ of all the working hours on earth.[11]

People who put in two-thirds of the world's working hours and receive in return one-tenth of the world's income should have something to say about the idea that hard work equals wealth. They should have something very interesting to say to the neoconservative enthusiasts who insist, "Hard work is rewarded, and only the lazy are poor." The bitter truth is, under four thousand years of patriarchal "exploit-for-profit" economics, the women of the world have worked long and hard, often under the worst necrophilic conditions, to keep the human race minimally alive. In return, we receive mostly dismal statistics signifying not reward, but rip-off.

As Robin Morgan underscores in *The Anatomy of Freedom,* all those major issues labeled "world problems" are in fact women's problems. The world's starving millions are predominantly women and children. Some cultures traditionally give all their protein to men; in famine and other crises, food goes first to the male armies. It is women who are expected to stay alive on nothing, to feed infants and toddlers from their bodies as well, while gathering and preparing some kind of sustenance for everyone else . . . usually in terrain stripped of all nourishment. Over 90 percent of all the world's refugees are women and children. The world's poor are overwhelmingly women and children. And this means that most of the world's health problems, the problems of illiteracy and child abuse, are also women's problems; as is the problem of old age—of being old, and caring for the old. The major problems facing the world today are women's problems. Yet, as Morgan notes, the male "experts"—the world-analyzers, the world-developers, the world-planners—continue to list these problems in a secondary category, labeled "women's issues," i.e., consigned to the dustbin.[12] Even war, the glamorous "male issue," is a woman's problem, for global female energy keeps going into the sustaining of biological life in the face of man's technological preoccupation with death. And it is man's preoccupation that gets all the funding; it is obsessive preparation for war that drains off all the resources of will and energy needed to continue life. It takes almost ten months to make a human body, it takes a fraction of a millisecond to destroy one. Apparently war-oriented males feel this gives them a technological superiority over women, although all the superiority is on the side of death.

Morgan also discusses how technological development, spearheaded by Western—predominantly American—male experts, sets out at the very beginning to destroy Third World women's traditional farming, craft, and marketing systems by turning over all the new machinery and development plans, the urban factory and rural agricultural technologies to the indigenous men. Only men are trained to use the new high-powered machinery; further, "for the convenience of the machines," land is reallocated—the women's horticultural plots confiscated and turned over to men for large-scale, often one-crop farming. Or, the men are siphoned into urban factory centers, splitting not only families but whole cultures based on rural cooperative market systems run by women—the new "industrial power" is put in the hands of men, and the rural villages degenerate into "company towns" virtually run by multinational corporations, who even get tax credits for doing so. Morgan describes contemporary "Third World developmental programs" as "neocolonial," merely a suave continuance of the old raw colonial style, with the "developers" manipulating indigenous males into "bargains . . . made between men and over the heads of women."

> One of the most consistent inconsistencies of Man's neocolonial approach is that *where a local tradition is in the self-interest of women* (such as matrifocal land ownership or a batik industry controlled for generations by females), *Man overrides this tradition in the name of "progress." But where a local tradition is deleterious to women* (genital-mutilation practices as "rites of passage," or protein being considered a dietary taboo for women) *Man recognizes this tradition, expresses regard for it, and incorporates it into his plan for "progress."*[13]

Of course, this is not an "inconsistency" at all, but the classic imperialist ploy of dominating and manipulating a people by "giving" the men "power over women"—ideological power backed up with technological power, whether in the form of rifles or grain harvestors or textile factories. I.e., men dominate women via "superior technology." But this neocolonial maneuver not only usurps and destroys women's ancient skills and independence; it also turns a traditionally female-based communal-cooperative system into a male-dominated wage-and-profit system. Thus whole, once self-sustaining, self-articulating cultures are systematically redesigned into "company towns." And the males collecting the profits are not indigenous men, we may be sure, but the managerial elite of multinational corporations.

Seeing this process at work, again and again, can reinforce women's deeply ingrained hostility to technology; because, in our bones, we know how all machinery has been used against us, as weaponry. But, as Morgan points out, and as we have tried to show in our discussion of women's Neolithic culture, women developed most of today's technologies. Ceramic, textile, and food processing were all women's inventions, and early industries; medicines and drugs, writing, printing, agriculture itself was produced by women. It is not technology *per se* that is the enemy of women, but a specifically male-dominated use of it in a specifically male-dominated system: i.e., the patriarchal, "exploit-for-profit," Fascist economic system. Women's global task today is not to fight technology, to smash the machines and return to Stone Age handwork; rather, we must study how the most modern and helpful technologies can be used within communal-cooperative systems, not to the profit of the few but to the benefit of the many. Technologies themselves are not politically or economically biased; they can be plugged into any system. They don't have to be "profit making" in order to work. It is people who must reorient and redesign our heads, our hearts, and our social matrices so that the technologies can be plugged into cooperative life-sustaining systems, rather than the competitive, profit- and power-making systems of the past four thousand years. And this reorientation and redesign means reactivating rather than destroying women's traditional communal-cooperative patterns. And this means indigenous males everywhere refusing to be coopted by the global corporate-development system into betraying the traditional women's cooperative cultures, both in their practical organization and in their spiritual-philosophical orientation, which was, from the beginning: the people first. (Everywhere refers not only to men of the Third World; the global corporation system is planning "free trade zones" for the Bronx, and also for a two-hundred-mile strip along the Mexican-US border—and, as Paul Virilio points out, "Europe will be identified with the Third World" very shortly, as a politically disempowered entity surviving as a colonial market and enterprise zone, in the same relation to global corporate entities as Latin America is to the United States.[14] Global means global, after all; and global control refers not only to war power but to complete economic, social, and ideological power over every aspect of every human life—with instantaneous, electronic technological surveillance and enforcement.) As Morgan writes: "No one would deny that developing countries can use technological support—but such support must be keyed to the needs of *all* its citizens, not aimed at buying out half of them, a feat accomplished by selling out the other half."[15] Men worldwide must learn that every time they sell out "their women," or their women's communal systems, they are only buying a prolongation of colonial enslavement for themselves. Or neocolonial enslavement—the same specter, riding a motorcycle.

In his last book, *A GRUNCH of Giants,* R. Buckminster Fuller pointed out that since the early 1970s, humankind has "possessed" the technology to feed, clothe, shelter, sustain, and entertain all of us at a very comfortable level. The problem, Fuller said, is not the absence of the necessary and appropriate technology, but obstructions to its fair distribution and optimal use. These obstructions are created by political, business, and religious institutions and ideologies, which depend for their existence on maintaining these obstructions—e.g., national borders, exclusive markets, ideas of guilt and spiritual superiority—as modes of both profit and identity. Technologies (like earth, water, air, mineral resources) belong to the human race; the obstructing institutions, by possessing their manufacture and distribution as "private property" (or nationalistic or ethnic property), thus are able to control human beings, as manufacturers of necessities control consumers of necessities. As Fuller and others have long observed, the Capitalist system itself—the business-financial-investment system that feeds on human need and activity—is a parasitical rather than productive system. Business coopts and takes credit for human invention—what the inventors of the world create, not in a vacuum, but out of the accumulated knowledge and experience of the world's human labor and discovery—and then turns around and sells these inventions at a net profit for itself, but at a gross loss to the species. Capitalism monopolizes world technology and resources, distributes them only for profit, and in fact as a system based on calculations of greed rather than calculations of need, obstructs the existing and appropriate technologies from meeting the exigencies they would be able to meet within a radically different system of distribution and use. Fuller, certainly a master technologist, insisted that it was (1) the Capitalist market system, (2) nationalist politics, and (3) religious ideologies of guilt and punishment, ontologies of spirit-versus-flesh—these three *obsolete factors* which were alone keeping the adequate existing technologies from being mass-produced, distributed world-wide, and plugged in immediately for the greater good of all. He acknowledged this might sound utopian; but against the only and inevitable alternative of mass extermination, he offered his suggestions and calculations as hard-core realism.[16]

It is not enough for Western feminists to fight for "equality" within a rotten system. For large masses of women to be exploited side-by-side with male workers on global assembly lines paying subsistence wages, for women to be drafted into armies side-by-side with men so both can fight in corrupt imperialist wars against indigenous revolutions all over the globe . . . this is no victory for women. Nor is the entrance of a few token fems into the managerial levels and executive boardrooms of giant corporations. Both "integrations" are cooptations of female energy into the maintenance of obsolete and criminal systems. Powerful systems, yes, but nonetheless obsolete and criminal. Where women are "allowed" to share equally in their profits and advantages, we also share equally in their crimes, and in their obsolescence. If the Soviet "state-Capitalist" system has become criminal and ontologically rigid under pressure from American-based "private-Capitalism," this has happened largely because its ruling male elite stopped short of (in fact, reversed) a total sexual revolution, leaving patriarchal consciousness intact while it attempted a communalist restructuring that can only succeed in terms of matrifocal consciousness based on female sexual autonomy. Today, both major world powers are locked together in a male power dance; both systems are trapped within the terms of their own patriarchal biases: (1) control and profit via war ("defense," "security"), and (2) control and profit via labor exploitation, beginning with the exploitation of female reproductive labor and the dwindling resources of the earth. Continuous war and continuous energy exploitation have been the operating principles of patriarchal systems for four thousand years, and no patriarchal system, American or Soviet or any of their satellites, escapes the criminal stigma of these operating principles. Women must reject the constant coöptive suggestion that we have only these two choices: the man's capitalism or the man's communism. We must refute the constant diversionary suggestion that there is no precedent for a third choice: female-oriented cooperative communalism. Against four thousand years of Bronze-to-Nuclear Age patriarchy, we must set at least 300,000 years of female Stone Age precedence. During which time all the fundamental technologies and industries of human life were originated and elaborated to the benefit of all life—including the psychic-meditative-spiritual technologies which have never been improved upon, but instead have been only lost, literalized, or fascistically degraded by the world's patriarchal religions.

Remember that the Great Goddess was always a triplicity; between all dualistic choices, all warring oppositions, stood her being—a third term which mediated and synthesized the polarities into a new thing, an epiphany: the immanence of transcendence, the transcendence of immanence. The whole purpose of studying ancient women's religion and culture is to understand the great precedence for this third term, this third, alternative choice—neither the man's fascism nor the man's communism, but a radical return to the female beginning. A truly radical cooperative communalism that was at the root of human consciousness and culture. It is necessary for all of us to conceive that this female-oriented creative-collectivism existed, so that we can begin to perceive how it can be brought into being again, on this contemporary turn of the spiral. To know it existed in the past is to give its future existence not only credibility, but empowerment; we need this confidence of precedence not only as a core of spiritual vision, but as the core of our political vision. Only when we know truly

Past, Present—?, Sjöö, 1970

and accurately what human beings have been, and have done, can we begin to envision both practical and numinous modes of future being and doing. William Irwin Thompson talks about the critically important relation between history, ontology, and politics; he argues that historic extrapolation from an ontology of "man-the-territorial-possessor-and-aggressor" leads to one kind of politics, while the extrapolation from an ontology of "woman-the-creator-and-sharer-of-food" leads to quite another.

> In terms of the sociology of knowledge, one can say that one's vision of the origins of human culture affects one's political behavior in contemporary culture. If one believes that weapons and killing are the foundation of human culture, then one is inclined to accept a split in which technologically superior cultures move "forward," while "inferior" cultures are helped on their way toward extinction. Through triage a new global scientific elite determines who will survive, and through sociobiology, who should be chosen to survive. If, on the other hand, one believes with Glyn Isaacs that food sharing is the primordial act which made us human, then the global crisis would generate a vision of compassion and sharing. Ardrey's [territorial imperative, man-the-killer] vision becomes the philosophical foundation and justification for a new authoritarian and technologically managed society; Isaacs's vision becomes the basis for a totally different world culture of compassion, as the Buddhists say, "for the suffering of all sentient beings." All of which is to say that we are what we think and

> that our vision of the origin of human culture is simply another description of our perception of the present condition.[17]

The compassionate, food-sharing definition of humanity, as we've shown, has precedence in the hundreds of thousands of years of matrifocal, Stone Age culture. But of course it is not a definition exemplified by women alone. Many men have embraced this definition, argued for it, propagated it, and given their lives for it. The greatest men have always embodied it. As that reasonable and mortal man Thomas Jefferson wrote in 1809: "The care of human life and happiness, and not their destruction, is the first and only legitimate object of good government."[18] Or, in the words of the Argentinian poet and novelist, Julio Cortázar:

> . . . the moment comes when a truth becomes clear, a truth simple as it is wonderful. that of saving oneself alone is not saving oneself. or in any case it doesn't justify us as human beings.[19]

. . . THE MAGIC FLIGHT HOME

In the name of God, what patriarchy has finally achieved is "the completely profane world." What Western patriarchy has given us, in God's name, is a world wholly emptied of spirit. "The wholly desacralized cosmos is a recent discovery in the history of the human spirit."[1]

For the human spirit, and the spiritual world, existed from the beginning—as consciousness is a property of matter, and evolution is the play of spirit. By abstracting "spirit" from "flesh," by utterly demonizing the physical world and woman as its source, patriarchy has almost destroyed the home of spirit, which is sacred earth and all flesh. In its place, patriarchy has built a sordid wasteland of material products, profit and power systems, and death machines—the inevitable result of four thousand years of militant life-hatred and cynical mercantilism. Our earthly bodies themselves are mechanized and pornographized, offered up for sale as though indeed we had no souls, but existed only as exploitable units in nihilistic market and state systems. Whether we are women or men, we are all for sale in the modern world, all whores for our own survival. In the final insult, the religious fundamentalists tell us the price tags attached to our necks and groins are not travesties at all, but come from God—a "God" who, somehow, in their mercenary sermonizing, becomes the original Capitalist. And, of course, they are right. *Their* god was the first to own, control, and exploit the human female as productive property, as a head of cattle (i.e., capital). Today, as at its beginnings, patriarchy pretends to "teach" us about our souls, and offers us "spiritual salvation." In truth, patriarchy has never done anything but steal and exploit the human soul, just as, from its beginnings in mass bloodshed, repression, and plunder, it has for four millennia robbed and exploited the energies of earth and her creatures.

By setting itself against evolution, i.e., against the continuous epiphany of biological consciousness, patriarchy has set itself against life itself. For four thousand years it has plundered, pushed, and plotted its way toward the complete construction of a substitute life—an ersatz earth, à la global shopping mall, a manmade mechanical paradise. Ignoring, denying, and insulting the cosmic laws of everything growing and alive, it develops mechanoid specializations in every sphere, supposedly for our benefit. It destroys or overrides integrated living processes to turn out metalloid and plastoid *things,* deadened things which correspondingly *humanoid things* are supposed to spend our eerie lives buying and consuming. But we should know by now that human life engineered as an extension of a mechanoid vision is to the benefit of no one—except the owners of the machine. The industries and technologies of both Western capitalism and Soviet statism cannot exist without earth-rape, gross pollution of the environment, exterminations of vast numbers of animals and humans, of jungles and forests and grasslands, massive die-outs of terrestrial and oceanic life-forms—because systematic destruction is a function of the original patriarchal premise: exploit for power and profit. What can be done, under patriarchy, to one female body can be done, under world patriarchy, to the entire body of earth. The pornographic images of women trussed up in chains and barbed wire, of female flesh bruised and bloodied and beaten raw, are really our species' maps of the mutilated earth, who for four thousand years has been tortured for power and profit. The deadness of pornography is the deadness of the landscape created by patriarchy, in which nothing lives that is not hideously deformed, controlled, manipulated for the voyeur's eye, bound up for use. In such a landscape, the classic patriarchal paranoia becomes well-justified: Earth becomes indeed an ugly, hellish place in which ugly, hellish things can be done to us. Mother Earth can refuse to respond to our need, and instead begin to match our destructiveness with her own destructions.

In response, the man says "Not to worry!" and regales us with his plans for a wholly programmed, artificial life. It will be such a great improvement over the natural life, which was so encumbered with mess and error. Grass will be replaced with astro-turf, hearts will be replaced with computers. On the market right now are fluffy, purring, meowing robot pussycats, which can do all the cute things real housecats can do (catch mice?) without the cost and bother.[2] In fact everything can be replaced, including us, with those "good," efficient, obedient, nonunionized, thoroughly dreamless machines. For those still attached to the sentiment of flesh, biological engineers are probing inward with an eye to reprogramming our DNA, to eliminate perhaps our varieties as well as our mistakes, all with a vision of making us more "perfect"—which classically means more usable within the terms of specific systems.[3] For those who still gaze at stars, the man is launching out in all directions, eager to carry all these circuit boards of God to other planets, other galaxies. In all the plans to colonize space, there is a remarkable but predictable absence of any profound urge to contradict or challenge the extant patriarchal definition of the meaning of life. Moon and planets will become colonized resource stations; male and female astronauts, or the androids that replace them, will communicate with each other, with earthlings, and with galaxies in only the most linear, digitalized, and computational language.

Regardless of their siliconic sophistication, the more humans rely on machines the more we become extensions of machines. The mechanoid processes meant to "free" us are instead defining us. In his boyish enthusiasm for his own inventiveness, the man has once again thoroughly missed the point, which is this: Only fully living beings can fully experience life.

For those of us left earthbound, we live on a dying planet—a planet undergoing prolonged torture, that is, a huge, fully sensate creature being subjected to an infinite variety of murders. She is dynamited, she is strip-mined, she is gassed and sprayed with chemicals. She is riddled with wells seeking oil, her blood, determined to suck out the last black drop. Her brain, which is the sea, is dumped full of poison. The air, through which she breathes, becomes a thick toxic cloud. All the heavy metals and radioactive elements, once distributed sparsely throughout her body, are now leached into her bones, into her fleshly soil, into her womb; stored in lethal concentrations, drunk by roots, groundwater, tongues, they will pass down a more-than-necessary death to her remaining creatures for generations. A humanity starved of energy eats its own Mother. Meanwhile, nature's free and relatively wholesome, holistic energies of sun, wind, thermal heat, water, moon-tidal, human, and organic compost are ignored, rejected. Not that they are nonfeasible, but that manhood in the Western world is defined as large-scale exploitation, rather than as local cooperation.

The Western world, as we all know, is a total junkie—both in its compulsive addiction to consumption and in its foul methods of disposing its wastes. The number one drug problem in America, surely, is the twenty-four-hour-a-day addiction of "the average person" to a hundred times more artificial energy (from sugar to electricity, from mass entertainment to the bomb) than any healthy human being could ever want or need. And like any junkie threatened with a cutoff of supply, America—the Western world generally—can think and act in murderous ways. The Western world feels it is constantly threatened with having its physical power sources cut off; in response, if current political-economic trends are indicative, it will euphemistically institute and maintain a total dictatorship of the globe, in order to maintain access to energy sources which are, by most accounts, already dwindling. The alternative, for the West, is a complete change of worldview and lifestyle; but how is such a total change possible within the terms of patriarchal ontology? The Western patriarchies cannot change in any radical (i.e., *root*) way, because they are ontologically based on a *cutting off* of human roots. The patriarchal West cannot solve its energy problems because our minds and spirits were long ago cut off from the real source of energy, or creative power. This is the sexual-spiritual source of cosmic ecstasy, which patriarchy has denied in favor of manipulative moralistic and rationalistic energies; and as moral and rational energies themselves dwindle, within a lingering patriarchal framework, only the most decadent, bizarre, and vicious energies seem to erupt in their place. These criminal energies do not result from the absence of patriarchy, as the fundamentalists preach; rather, they are the corrupt residues and grotesque spasms of the dying patriarch himself.

Evil is that which prevents the unfolding of the One.

According to this definition, surely, all of patriarchal society is evil. Even in its death-throes, it attempts to pit us all against each other, as economic enemies, as political enemies, as racial enemies, as religious enemies—worker against worker, white against dark, man against woman, belief against belief—as patriarchal systems begin and end by instigating competitiveness for survival, i.e., by trying to make communalism, mutual cooperation, impossible. Ironically, even the minimal cooperation required to keep patriarchal systems going seems to be rapidly dwindling. Against the unfolding of the One—against the revelation of our oneness—patriarchy schemes ferociously to pit us against each other like many rats in a small cage, like many hungry dogs thrown only one bone. If we have to keep surviving at one another's expense, we will of course never learn, or never remember, how to live in the hope of one another's well-being. Patriarchy thrives on human discord; as a system it strives to coopt us all, buy and sell us all, one against the other. At the very heart of this divide-and-conquer strategy, we must remember, is the colonization of the indigenous female by the imperial male—the usurpation and exploitation of the original female collective by the Bronze Age patriarchal profiteer.

Among many Third World people still fighting their way out of the rubble of advanced colonialism, and among political minorities in the West generally, there is terrific suspicion and hostility toward suggestions of any "spiritual solution" to the world's real problems. This anger and doubt is understandable, and thoroughly justified. Franz Fanon wrote in *The Wretched of the Earth:* "For centuries they have stifled almost the whole of humanity in the name of a so-called spiritual experience."[4]

"They," of course, refers to the Christian West. The "so-called spiritual experience" has been that of a dominating European and American male elite (with their auxiliary "wives" and families), which has for three centuries proceeded to "realize" its pathological lust for individual power and enrichment at the expense of the rest of the world. Western patriarchy has plundered, raped, coopted, ripped off, brutalized, and massacred lavishly, always in the name of God—"God" is always available to justify what cannot otherwise be justified; the Holy Bible itself is the first written example of this phenomenon. Western Christians, throughout their long, gory history, have convinced themselves that the God of the Bible "chose" them to be spiritual imperialists. They have convinced themselves that this God virtually gave them the entire earth to use, to control, to profit from, and, in the final insult, to missionize—to teach "spirit" to!—through a rifle barrel, if necessary. It is a kind of dematerialized fairy tale Christians have long and wistfully told themselves; that the living earth is not "real" anyway, so "God" gave it to them to abstract into wealth (which is quite real). The entire planet, with its exotic varieties of peoples, lands, animals, and resources, has been viewed by Western Christianity as little more than raw material, just waiting to be appropriated and reprocessed by enterprising religious men into an ego-enhancing experience. Because, clearly, the "God" in whose name the West has terrorized the rest of the world has not been a God of Spirit, not ever, but a God of inflated, patriarchal ego; an ego so full of itself it has always been able to "spiritualize"—i.e., rationalize as "divinely ordained"—the most blatant robberies and repulsive crimes. The biblically derived Capitalist "spiritual experience," in particular, has never been an adventure of spirit, but an indulgence of extreme individualism and self-righteousness in pursuit of personal profit, personal enhancement. Always at the expense of the whole world. For only ego-experiences end up amassing profit, i.e., acts of alienation; genuine spiritual experience is always communal, i.e., an act of communication.

Just as Western biblical "spirituality" has served to rationalize imperialism, it has simultaneously served to stifle political criticism and activity against imperialism. It has been "spiritual" to colonize, brutalize, and plunder, but "not spiritual" to talk about it; i.e., "spirituality" has long been reified into an upper- and middle-class euphemistic process, in which it is considered not polite to discuss the origins of one's wealth. The origins of wealth, of course, are always very bloody, i.e., "not nice"; in the name of "refined sensibility," aka "spirituality," aka abstractness, the pursuit of bloody truth is discouraged. The paradigm for this class-evasion of the blood-origins of wealth lies in the patriarchal-evasion of the blood-origins of life. Patriarchy shamelessly colonizes, exploits, and brutalizes the female body, and then censors open discussion and criticism of this process in the name of "decency," "polite society," "civilized discourse," *et al.* In both cases, the pretense of spirit is used to cover up the fact of blood. And so, in all those parts of the world that have been ravaged by the Western Christian imperialist "experience," spirituality has a well-deserved reputation as the emblem of total hypocrisy.

This reputation continues into some "New Age" or counterculture attempts at spirituality. In particular, many activists undergoing political burn-out have made 180-degree turns to immerse themselves in apolitical spiritual pursuits—thus reinforcing the euphemistic patriarchal tradition that "spirit is above politics," "the left hand shouldn't know what the right hand is doing," "profit six days a week and go to church on Sunday," all being psychological devices to allow people to enjoy the fruits of patriarchal profit systems while avoiding responsibility for their sanguine roots. They all mean, "Don't look too closely at the origins of your wealth, including the wealth of spiritual privilege." For it is true that all spiritual exercise in the Western world is performed on a cushion of wealth—if not one's personal wealth, then the wealth of one's surrounding culture; and this wealth has been accumulated at the world's expense. For Westerners to "leave politics" and submerge themselves in "apolitical" or "transpolitical" spiritual disciplines may or may not serve personal needs and goals; on the global level, it is merely a continuance of the patriarchal-imperialist trick of "spiritualizing" one's wealth and privilege by not looking too closely at their bloody roots. Moreover, this "disappearing trick" is a lie; politics is in and of the world, and nobody leaves the world. Spiritual people "leave politics" only in the sense that rich people "leave poverty"—i.e., by being able to afford to fly off to some other place where they won't have to look at it. But poverty, like politics, is in and of the contemporary world; because most people live in poverty and in politics, not by choice but by brute force, they have become ontological conditions for the entire world. Nobody escapes them. Some people have the illusion of escaping them, for more or less prolonged periods of time. Just as during the incessant plagues, wars, and political upheavals of the early Middle Ages, rich people barricaded themselves in well-stocked castles, while hordes of the sick and starving banged—and died—at their gates. The feudal rich had the illusion they could survive as islands of life surrounded by a rising sea of suffering and death. But not for long; in most cases the castles were broken into, and the privileged few dragged out to scream and die like everyone else.

Just so, in a political world, isolated or separatist spiritual solutions are doomed. Faced with the pain and challenge of this realization, many spiritually oriented people opt for the spiritually reactionary explanations of the world's suffering: e.g., that "God" makes some people poor so that others can learn something from them, that poverty and pain are *karmic* situations brought on by one's behavior in past lives, that one chooses one's life absolutely and that some people "choose to suffer," etc. All these "explanations" are spiritual versions of blaming the victim; they derive from patriarchal religious systems which were purposely designed to rationalize hierarchies, injustice, and the status quo. All patriarchal systems are self-justifying, and the mind dwelling within these systems is capable of monstrous rationalizations in order to keep these tautologies intact. These modes of "explaining" other people's suffering are, in a very real way, acts of human sacrifice: Faced with a choice or a challenge to our religious mind-set, we are willing to sacrifice living human beings, their problems and their pain, in order to keep our worldviews intact. We are literally sacrificing people to our gods. The core of this is patriarchal ontology, which separates "spirit" from "matter," and proceeds to deny the reality of life in the name of some abstract God, or some "life-explaining" ontological system. All spiritually oriented people are prone to this trap, and it is a trap we must beware: When our desire and capacity to see the world as a sacred gestalt becomes, on another level, a monstrous justification of what must not be justified.

(When fundamentalists and some evangelicals claim that the hydrogen bomb comes from God, and that global annihilation via World War III will be a fulfillment of Revelation—a fulfillment not to be avoided at all costs but to be yearned for, in fact, as the prophesied "Rapture"—most "spiritual" people are appalled. But many of these same people will turn about and accept without critique Krishna's justification of war in the

The Goddess in Her Manifestations at Greenham Common, Sjöö, 1984

Bhagavad Gita, where the god tells Arjuna to ride into battle and slay all his relatives without remorse or hesitation—because, after all, they are all illusions anyway, and already dead, and never born . . . merely the spinnings of *maya.* One myth is prettier to us (i.e., more exotic) than the other; but in truth, what is the real difference between one patriarchal rationalization of hell and the other? All rationalizations of holy war are not spiritual; they are in fact patriarchal; and we must recognize the difference. By the same token, all spiritual rationalizations of continuous poverty, injustice, and suffering are not "spiritual" at all, but are in fact patriarchal political justifications of the status quo. And we must know the difference.)

Because "women's spirituality" in the Western world has been, or has often seemed to be, a cultural luxury of mostly white middle-class women, it too has been accused, quite justly, of "lacking a political consciousness"; or, at least, of lacking a political reference. On another level, many Lesbian and even hetero feminists who are "into the Goddess" have opted for cultural-political separatism; they have "left politics" and political solutions, that is, by blaming the world's problems on men, and then refusing to have anything more to do with "the man's world"—i.e., "Let him clean up his own mess." The glaring problem with this separatist solution is that "the man's world" is still filled with a majority population of women and children—it is women and children doing most of the suffering "out there," and to turn one's back on "the man's world" is to turn one's back on them.[5]

A genuine understanding of "the Goddess" would not allow us to do this; a true ontological experience of the Great Mother, and of the complete physical as well as spiritual bonding-together of all life on earth, would not allow us to turn our backs on "the man's world"—for we are in and of that world now, and its suffering is an extension of us, as we are an extension of it. In a true reliving of the world's first religion, we can make no distinctions between "the life of the spirit" and "the life of the flesh," for they are one. And so, we can make no separation between "spirituality" and "politics." *We are this world,* we cannot leave it. We can only work to transform it as we transform ourselves, in acts of evolution and revolution. The genius of Michel Foucault, surely, was that he showed us so clearly and so precisely how politics is everything that happens to the body. On earth, mind and spirit are definitively embodied. The notion that "mind" and "spirit" can be abstracted from the body is a patriarchal lie; and a continuance of this lie is the notion that we can indulge in a "spirituality" that is "above politics"—that somehow floats above the agony of this present earth like a little blissed-out cloud. The spirit is *within* a body—it is the conscious experience of process within that body—and the spirit evolves, or is obstructed in its evolution, depending on the body's experience of its material environment. It is patriarchy that devalues and disconnects the body from the spirit in order to make that body's energy accessible for exploitation. A feminist spirituality must begin with the *fact* of being alive as a biological body, on a living and conscious biological planet. This is the human ontological condition; this is the condition of all human evolution and all creative human activity. Those who embrace "spirituality" as an escape from politics, as a "transcendence" of political exigencies, simply do not understand what feminist spirituality means at its root: The joining of the conscious body and the conscious spirit in the ongoing epiphany of experienced evolution. Whatever represses or deforms the body's experience of itself, also represses and deforms the spirit's self-experience.

I.e., God does *not* want millions of human beings to starve and suffer and die so that a select few can undergo a "spiritual experience." Nor does the Goddess "live" solely in elite separatist retreats, dancing naked in the piney woods under a white and well-fed moon. The Goddess at this moment is starving to death in refugee camps, with a skeletal child clutched to her dry nipples. The Goddess at this moment is undergoing routine strip-and-squat search inside an American prison. The Goddess is on welfare, raising her children in a ghetto next to a freeway interchange that fills their blood cells and neurons with lead. The Goddess is an eight-year-old girl being used for the special sexual thrills of visiting businessmen in a Brazilian brothel. The Goddess is patrolling with a rifle slung over her shoulder, trying to save a revolution in Nicaragua. The Goddess is Winnie Mandela in South Africa, saying "Don't push me." I.e., the

Goddess *IS* the world—the Goddess is *in* the world. And *nobody* can escape the world. We know this, but we forget it.

In this world, at this point, no political revolution is sustainable if it is not also a spiritual revolution—a complete ontological birth of new beings out of the old. Equally, no spiritual activity deserves respect if it is not at the same time a politically responsible, i.e., responsive, activity. As Julio Cortazár says, "the moment comes when a truth becomes clear, a truth simple as it is wonderful. That of saving oneself alone is not saving oneself. Or in any case it doesn't justify us as human beings." In this world, at this point, we are at the apogee of the patriarchal project of separating flesh from spirit. (E.g., some spokesmen for the patriarchal view are actually telling us that they might have to launch World War III, even if that means annihilating the world, in order to "save the American Way"—i.e., our Christian Capitalist "souls." This thinking represents the outcome of four thousand years of patriarchal attempts to abstract spiritual from material existence.) The only meaningful political direction left now is synonymous with the only meaningful spiritual direction left now: towards the conscious re-fusion of the spirit and the flesh. This radical step might appear to be a step backward; but, in our movement along a spiral, it is in fact a step forward to the same place we began, but on the path of a larger circle of consciousness. This time it will be a global consciousness of our global oneness, and it will realize itself on a very sophisticated technological stage; with perhaps a total merger of psychic and electronic activity.

When Steve Biko defined the vision of black consciousness in Africa as a quest for "true Humanity," as a desire to define human beings as ends-in-ourselves, "not as a means" for technological development, not as mere units or functions of this economic system or that political system, "not as an extension of a broom" or pushable buttons on machines, but as "the determination of the Black to rise and attain the envisaged self"—he was articulating a spiritual vision as well as a political vision, and his articulation must be applied to all the world's people.[6] The envisaged self is the next stage in human evolution, and it will be born explicitly from the re-fusion of experienced spirit and experienced flesh—not as a "means" toward any externally established "end," but as a consciously perceived process of evolution unfolding itself. The primary urge of patriarchy has been to control and repress life toward some profitable end, rather than to allow this self-perceiving unfolding to occur. All genuine and successful revolts against patriarchy will be conjoined spiritual-political revolts; and they will occur with the organic inevitability of unfolding evolution. This is why the great political revolutionaries who end up being killed, assassinated for one ostensible reason or another, are inevitably the people who most appeal to the spirit; they are the vanguard of the inevitable re-fusion of the spiritual and material worlds, and even though they sometimes do not realize this themselves (e.g., Martin Luther King was a "Christian,"

Ché Guevara was a "Marxist," Malcolm X was a "Muslim"), their *presences,* their *beings* vibrate with this ontologically matriarchal re-fusion. For it is only within the Goddess that sexual flesh and conscious cosmic spirit can rebecome one. Steve Biko was murdered by the South African Security Police in 1977. As the future rapidly unfolds there will undoubtedly appear more and more female martyrs of the conjoined-flesh-and-spirit. Until the entire world understands that this is the next inevitable evolutionary step that *all must take.*

The fundamentalists have confused us—and have attracted many confused people—with their commercial revival of the old mechanistic-moralistic God. They have successfully integrated their literalist biblical God with the resurgent "neoconservative" economics and politics, quite brazenly offering the patriarchal cause of so many world problems as the reborn solution. While people all over the world, especially young people, are risking and giving their lives to fight for "the envisaged self," "a true humanity," the American fundamentalist preachers and politicians are trying very hard to make "humanism" a dirty word. This is the result of their Bronze Age religious heritage, in which everyday, fleshly, earthly reality had to be demonized in order to make "spirit" the property of an elite few. Also, perhaps the humanism they see in their own mirrors is not worthy of much respect. (The "secular humanist" liberals have also contributed to the problem; striving to maintain the Constitutional "separation of church and state," they have in past decades constructed program after program, government-funded housing, food commodities, food stamps, job-training and retraining programs, etc., in which the minimal needs of the body are met along with a massive disregard for the human spirit. Liberal programs failed because of their built-in spiritual deadness; like many Marxists and Socialists, American liberals fell into the trap of confusing "spirituality" with "religion.") Because we have all been trained by four thousand years of patriarchal dichotomizing to believe that "being spiritual" is qualitatively different from "being human," we refuse to see the spirit at work in so many Third World humanist political movements. For the same reason, so many people are overawed by the expensive if tacky hyper-religiosity of the modern television preachers (or "salesmen of God"): the soaring glassy churches, the golden Bibles, the patriotically positive teeth and perfect hairdos, choirs of shimmeringly otherworldly polyester . . . this definitely isn't real life, so it must be "spiritual." When the fundamentalists revive biblical arrogance in their claim to have a denominational "hot line to God," this preposterousness is believed, by millions and millions of people. This is how far we have fallen, disconnected from our primal recognition of spirit in all living things. Blatantly commercialist power-mongering can claim to be conversation with the cosmic spirit, and be believed.

True humanism, primal spirituality, and the energy of evolution must join together in a conscious force, to tell the truth about God and life.

When are we going to feel joy again?, Sjöö, 1973

The truth is that "God" is not in a book—"holy," golden, or otherwise. God is not in a church, a cathedral, a synagogue, a mosque. God is not cemented inside any manmade theological system or elitist cultural architecture. God is definitely not bursting neck-veins of righteously profitable baloney at you from the TV screen. God is not for sale, even to the highest bidder, no matter how much it indulges in nationalistic flag-waving and the bellicosity of world power.

God is the universe. We are all now living inside the body of God. There is nowhere to go to get there, we are already here. There is nowhere to go to get outside of God; there is just a forgetting of this truth. It is impossible not to be living, right now and always, within God's body. It is only possible to be aware, or unaware, of this fact.

Religions that try to block or repudiate our awareness of this cosmic fact must themselves be repudiated. Religions that try to cut us off from our long evolutionary past, moralistic-mechanistic dogmas that deny our billions of years of passionate, heroic survival crawling up from the first cell through the genetic adventures of algae, fish, land plants, insects, reptiles, birds, mammals to the complex human consciousness of now—must themselves be denied. Such religions give us a cardboard definition of life that keeps us always lonely and alienated, cut off from the creative energy and integrity of the earth's biological imagination. Religions that curse and distort our past as rooted in some dark savage "evil," which, they say, can only be "expiated" by lifetimes of guilt and suffering—must be repudiated. They cut us off from ourselves, from our origins and our destiny as creative children of an infinitely creative universe. To reduce us to something "sinful" is to reduce us to something exploitable. Religions of guilt, sin, and fear tell lies to us about who we are, in order to mechanize and exploit our beings. Religious systems that support any kind of dominance-submission social structures—primate religions that preach "holy hierarchies" based on sex, race, caste, ethnic or religious, economic or political distinctions—must be utterly repudiated. Such religions are not "visions of God" but vampire machineries that keep themselves empowered by eating our human energies and our souls. By reinforcing primate mechanisms on our unique human species, they obstruct and deform our evolution; they are counter-evolutionary. All religions that attempt to "explain" human suffering, injustice, hunger, and poverty as "manifestations of God's will" must be totally repudiated. Such religions do not speak for God, they merely reiterate patriarchal rationalizations for the status quo; such rationalizations are all self-serving for the people in power, and therefore lies told to the rest of us. Biology makes mistakes; it does not lie.

We need a new, global spirituality—an organic spirituality that belongs innately to all of us, as the children of earth. A genuine spirituality that utterly refutes the moralistic, manipulative patriarchal systems, the mechanistic religions that seek to divide us—that control and oppress us by successfully dividing us. We need a spirituality that acknowledges our earthly roots as evolutionary and sexual beings, just as we need an ontology that acknowledges earth as a conscious and spiritual being. We need this organic, global spirituality because we are ready to evolve as a globally conscious species. We are at the point where we must evolve or die. In a chilling book published in 1972, called *The 20th Century Book of the Dead,* Gil Elliot compiled statistics of all the ways we know how to die. In the twentieth century alone, according to Elliot, there have been 110 million manmade deaths, including 62 million by various forms of privation (death camps, slave labor, forced marches, imprisonment), 46 million from guns and bombs, and 2 million from chemicals.[7]

We are living in a world that practices the politics of death. And these numbers are fifteen years old; add all the wars, political murders, manmade famines since 1972. It is patriarchy that practices the politics of death. Included in these figures should be the actual deaths, perhaps also the living deaths, of all those millions of women forced by patriarchal religious systems into continuous breeding of continuous raw material for all this continuous murder and dying. Add also the vast numbers of us who will die before this century is over because of patriarchal economic systems' chemical and radiation pollution of our food, water, and air; the deaths that are in us now perhaps, the deaths that are in our children. Add finally the deaths of an entire species, if we do not learn before the end of the twentieth century to evolve out of the politics of death, into the politics of living.

The political art of living. The spiritual art of being alive. For, from now on out (from now on *in*), genuine, global spiritual awareness will be the vanguard of all successful human revolution. Political revolutions that do not follow an organic terrestrial-cosmic spiritual vision, will end up in more patriarchal death. "Religious revivals" based on obsolete patriarchal ontologies will only end in massive political deaths, the obscenities of "holy war." We are really in a trap. We must evolve or die. Clearly, patriarchal systems will be the mode of our death. What could be the mode of our evolution?

Paul Virilio speaks, in *Pure War,* about "chrono-politics and the distribution of time."

> Politics is no longer in space, in geospace, but in time. No longer geo-politics but chrono-politics. Organization, prohibitions, interruptions, orders, powers, structurings, subjections are now in the realm of temporality. And that's where resistance should be. If we fight in space instead of fighting in time. . . .

We will not find the enemy.[8] Because the enemy does not exist in space, but in time: four thousand years ago. We are about to destroy each other, and the world, because of profound mistakes made in Bronze Age patriarchal ontology—mistakes about the nature of being, about the nature of human being in the world. Evolution itself is a time-process, seemingly a relentlessly linear unfolding. But biology also dreams, and in its dreams and waking visions it outleaps time, as well as space. It experiences prevision, clairvoyance, telepathy, synchronicity. Thus we have what has been called a magical capacity built into our genes. It is built into the physical universe. Synchronicity is a quantum phenomenon. The tachyon is consciousness, which can move faster than light. So, built into our biological-physical selves evolving linearly through time and space, is an authentically magical capacity to move spirally, synchronously, multisensorially, simultaneously back and forth, up and down, in and out through all time and space. In our DNA is a genetic memory going back through time to the first cell, and beyond; back through space to the big bang (the cosmic egg), and before that. To evolve then—to save ourselves from species extinction—we can activate our genetic capacity for magic. We can go back in time to our prepatriarchal consciousness of human oneness with the earth. This memory is in our genes, *we have lived it,* it is ours.

> This we know. The earth does not belong to man, man belongs to the earth. This we know. All things are connected like the blood which unites one family. All things are connected. Whatever befalls the earth befalls the sons of earth. Man did not weave the web of life, he is merely a strand in it. Whatever he does to the web, he does to himself.[9]

These were the words of Chief Seattle, in 1852. But they are not "Indian words" alone, of one century or another. They are an articulation of *all human memory.* They are our global memory, as we all recede backward through the Christian Era, through the Bronze Age, through the Neolithic, through the Stone Age consciousness of Cro-Magnon and Neanderthal, through the primates, mammals, birds, reptiles, starfish, algae—to the first cell. By going back to our clear knowledge that the earth does not belong to us, but rather that we belong to the earth—as the cosmos does not belong to us, but *we belong in the cosmos*—we can also leap forward to that time when we know with equal clarity that we all belong together, belong equally with one another, on the earth which is our Mother and our home. Within a universe that is eternally God's body, and our home.

Such words as Chief Seattle's are not moral sentiments or emotional wishes. They are statements of cosmic law, of biological and physical law. Our consciousness is a property of our biological being. At the deepest levels of biological and of physical being, all consciousness in the universe is inextricably linked in a galactic network, or webwork, of mutual awarenesses and mutually interchanging gestalts. This mutual interaction may be described as the brain of God, in which all "thoughts" are living realities. This is where *we* live, either mutually evolving or mutually dying—just as all thoughts either realize themselves or die. Within such a living and dying cosmos, how can we make rational distinctions between "spirit" and "flesh," between "spiritual systems" and "political systems" and "economic systems" and "social systems"—clearly they are all bound together as interacting thoughts. And therefore such words as Chief Seattle's are also statements of political, social, and economic law. They tell us that, within such a cosmically extenuated webwork of mutually interacting and inter-sensing thoughts, "profit" can never be a good word, nor can individualism in pursuit of profit be a wholesome or a sane activity. Profit is always at the expense of the whole world. The "isolated individual" does not exist. "Personal profit" is an illusion of imbalance, and all rebalancing involves massive repercussion. The Western biblical-Capitalist world's individualistic denial of the interconnected webwork of all existence has not, could never, make that webwork nonexistent—it has only made its global reality increasingly painful. We are all locked in together, interlocked in mind, body, and soul together; the tremor of pain of one will eventually touch all, and become all. The degree of pain being experienced in the world today is very close to the point of global implosion; if we do not blow each other up with explosions of mutual fear and hatred, we will collapse inward in an implosion of mutually inflicted isolation and pain. As we are all connected together, there is nowhere else we can go. Whatever we do, the repercussions of our present situation will be global. The earth is implacably round.

We can change our thoughts, however. Evolution begins in the brain of any creature who experiences a need to evolve. Species can make quantum leaps of change when a threshold-number of them experience the need to change; geneticists can speak of "random mutation," but in fact gene mutations are reflections—or reflexes—of perceived needs within a species. Biology can make mistakes, but not because it is unconscious. Biology is profoundly conscious, and profoundly responsive to thought, and to perceived need. As a species, we must attain that threshold-number of conscious beings who perceive totally our need to evolve, quickly, and the optimal direction of that evolution. To do this, we must experience the spiritual as well as physical oneness of our species. Patriarchal religious, economic, and political systems are based upon the systematic inculcation of our human and irreparable differences: of sex, of color, of caste and class, of religion and nation and geographical region. The constant exacerbation of these differences (patriarchy thrives on such exacerbation) prevents us from attaining that common consciousness we need as a species in order to bring about our own evolution. Our survival, that is, via evolution.

We must *remember* the chemical connections between our cells and the stars, between the beginning and now. We must remember and reactivate the primal consciousness of oneness between all living things. We must return to that time, in our genetic memory, in our dreams, when we were one species born to live together on earth, as her magic children. These are things human beings *have known* for most of our time on earth. For at least 500,000 years of human time we have known them; for about 5 billion years of earth time we have known them; for a good 13 billion years of galactic time we have known them—and, no doubt, longer than that. Set against this long galactic, terrestrial, and human time of *knowing* our oneness, the past four thousand years of patriarchy's institutional and doctrinal *denial* of our oneness, once we see it for what it was, will appear a mere aberration. *Just a brief forgetting.*

RESPELL THE WORLD

Witches cast spells, not to do evil, but to promote changes of consciousness. Witches cast spells as acts of redefinition. To *respell the world* means to redefine the root of our being. It means to redefine us and therefore change us by returning us to our original consciousness of magical-evolutionary processes. This consciousness is within us, in our biology and in our dreams. It works on subliminal levels, whether or not we are aware of it, because it is the energy of life and imagination. When we are aware of it, it works *for us,* as the energy of destiny. And it is powerful, with the genuine power of biological life and cosmic imagination.

Perhaps ancient women had access to psychic and physical powers we have forgotten. Ancient people of both sexes, living under the Stone Age Great Mother, like those remaining of earth's primal people today, had "magical" powers—of telepathy, clairvoyance, precognition, teletransportation, of fire-walking and shape-changing, of healing and building—not because such powers were "pagan superstitions" or "of the Devil," but because they are natural powers of the earth. We know that the psychic-physical spinal techniques of illumination used by yogis and mystics, technical powers that lie dormant within all of us, were first developed by women, as natural modes of communication with the larger self, the earth, and the cosmos. During the later Paleolithic and throughout the Neolithic, sexual and spiritual powers were fused through the techniques of meditation, use of natural hallucinogens, and the spiraling, mandalic dances of creation-dissolution within the great caves, labyrinths, and stone circles. The energies generated by these techniques became power used to the benefit of all—which is the only way power can be safely used. Ancient legends speak of "the winged radiance of those who have achieved the dynamic equilibrium, the ecstatic union of the currents"—which is the description of those who have raised evolutionary energy, in the form of *kundalini,* the cosmic serpent, up through the spinal world tree of all manifest being, until it reaches the highest *chakra* of the human mind, becoming winged illumination. These beings were called "the undivided ones," of original gynandrous consciousness. With such powers, perhaps,

The Mothers, Sjöö, 1970

mountains could be moved, truly—great earth mounds could be built, great stones lifted and transported for miles, underground temples carved out of rock without the use of metal tools—i.e., great acts of physical construction could be performed, without force or slave labor, as expressions of a common consciousness and a common will. More important, acts of mental construction were performed which allowed people to live together harmoniously, in meaningful and exciting intercommunication with all the creatures of earth, earth herself, and the energy-beings of moon, sun, planets, and the stars. The time when "the mountains sang and the rivers clapped hands" was perhaps that numinous terrestrial time when all human beings were able to live harmoniously and consciously together as magic children within the living body of the cosmos.

Perhaps. We do not know. We can only look at the evidence, and imagine. We know only what we can imagine. We know only that we can imagine. That we can imagine, as no other creature on earth can do, signifies our uniqueness, both its quality and its purpose. We are the imagining animals. We are the ones who participate in the earth's evolutionary process of imagination. For what is every manifest life-form and activity on earth if not the product of earth's imagination? Imagination, which is a form of memory moving both forward and backward in time; i.e., the creative process itself.

Perhaps the greatest harm patriarchy has done to us is to stifle, coopt, and deform our powers of imagination. Moralisms, dualistic dogmas, repressive prohibitions block our imagination at its source, which is the fusion of sexual and spiritual energies. Patriarchal religions keep this fusion from happening, imagination dies, and is replaced by mechanical-linear thought patterns, i.e., indoctrination. Human beings crippled in our imaginations, or no longer able to live in the terrain of dreams, are human beings undergoing indoctrination, exploitation, colonization. Soon the only way to get there anymore is via drugs, drunkenness, madness. Or vicariously, through the art and entertainment media. Patriarchy is an anti-evolutionary and an antimagic force; by cutting us off from our long evolutionary history, and in particular by dishonestly teaching us that our prepatriarchal ancestors were "immoral savages" or stupid unrealized beings whose lives were only "nasty, brutish, and short," it blocks our access to our own blood-history—it cuts us off from millions of years of creative evolutionary energy stored up in our genes, our genetic memories, the powerhouses of imagination. It lies to us about who we are by telling us lies about who we were; it changes us from "magical" to "sinful," in order to make us believe we need patriarchy to "save" us from our own selves. By cutting us off from magic as a natural property of earth, as a conscious form of biological energy, patriarchy further tries to make us dependent upon its mechanical systems and definitions as the only modes of life that work. In its denial of magic, patriarchy creates "objectivity" as the only legitimate mode of knowledge. Objectivity, as we've said, is a spectator sport based upon the illusion that the observer is *outside* the phenomenon being observed; the "objective observer" denies his participation in the observed phenomenon by virtually killing it, by making it into a dead thing. Thus all "objective information" is analogous to autopsy studies done on a corpse. Patriarchy has tried to render and redefine the entire earth and all its creatures as dead things, in order to sustain its pretense of possessing "objective information" about all of us. "Objective information," as Foucault has also shown, is merely a tool of control and exploitation; it is one of the modes of illegitimate power, otherwise known as profit.

Subjectivity, we must know, is the only state of experience in the universe. The only state of experienced being is as the subject experiencing itself, and the world, from within. (This includes the self experiencing itself experiencing other subjective beings.) There is no such thing as "object," because there is no thing to experience *itself* as "object." We are only subjects with the illusion of experiencing other subjects as "objects." The "object" exists only, and definitively, as an aspect of the subjective consciousness; the aspect that defines "me" and "that" and some apprehension of a border between. As quantum physics shows us, this apprehension of a border is a purely subjective one, the kind of border found in cartoons and coloring books, and in the more subtle technology of the human eye. Physically, i.e., in quantum reality, no border exists. No border exists in the reality of the spirit, either, as the spirit is a conscious perception of real energy fields and interactions. The border perception is a function of the individual's experience of evolution through time and space; to initially perceive the reality of ourselves, perhaps, we need the border perception (infants, with immature eyes, don't have it). To begin to define the reality of the world, we need to erase it, to "transcend" it. *Everything touches everything in the real world,* there are no borders—and this is the fact upon which the validity of magic is based. I.e., to "objectify" us, to divide and conquer us, patriarchy needs to insist on the reality of borders while denying the reality of magic. Only in this way can we be perceptually, intellectually, systematically separated and thus weakened, while the great healing power of our common-bondedness remains repressed. This "common bond" is no moral sentiment or humanist ideal, but a biological and quantum fact. Its sheer power, when raised from the subliminal to the conscious level, could generate an energy more than equivalent to all the stored destruction of our bombs—for within us is the stored creativity of billions and billions of atoms, we know this. The thing that keeps us from activating our common creative, evolutionary power is the perceptual and intellectual habit of separateness—i.e., four thousand years of patriarchal ideology.

All patriarchal religions have their mystics, and many of them come forward now to offer humanity a "spiritual solution" to our human crisis. But all these solutions occur within the terms of the problem, i.e., they are more examples of patriarchy perpetuating itself. Male mystics, within patriarchal cultures and systems, can never reach a true fusion, in the depths of their beings, of the sexual and spiritual powers. Patriarchy's pejorative definitions of sexuality, and abstract definitions of spirit, prohibit this fusion. Patriarchal mystics are out of resonance with the earth spirit, with ecstasy, and with the dead. Most of all, they are out of contact with female energy—their patriarchal worldviews are based on a biophobic denial of this creative female energy in both women and men. All of us live in societies constructed out of this denial, societies that have attempted for four millennia to repress and destroy the bisexual nature of us all. In such nihilistic social-energy fields, no real magic can happen; in its place, in the past two decades, we have witnessed, and undergone, many morbid, sad, and narcissistic trips.[1] Mystics, and all religious people within patriarchal systems, must begin to deal honestly with the fact that patriarchy can never, ever be anything other than divided against itself—for this schizoid self-division is the basic ontological act upon which it is built. Union, or fusion, cannot happen within patriarchal terms. It is patriarchy, after all, which deliberately set out to banish and destroy ecstasy.

What is ecstasy? It is our original state of being. It is the conscious expansion of the universe into a multitude of interconnected dimensions and forms. It is her dance of being, from which all of us were born. Ecstasy is passion self-expressed through form. In the case of earth, human beings and all other creatures and biological and geological activities are the forms, cosmic energy is the passion. Ecstasy is the source and reality of all we feel, see, and are. So then: Why don't human beings exist in a state of constant ecstasy? If ecstasy is the inevitable expression of being a conscious form, or living cell, in a cosmic energy sea, why don't we cognize it or feel it? What obstructs almost all human beings beyond the age of five from knowing this experience which is physically indigenous and ontologically rooted in the very fact of the universe existing at all?

Surely we know the answer! Patriarchal systems tell us that ecstasy is impossible or wrong—except according to its terms, its alienating definitions. But ecstasy, by definition, cannot exist on patriarchal terms. Ecstasy is the complete ontological challenge to patriarchy's "explanation" of life. Where patriarchal religious and social systems cannot wholly repress ecstasy, they demonize it—ecstasy becomes an underground or forbidden activity, most often experienced "privately" accompanied by guilt, rarely in common accompanied by the whole world. But in and with the whole world is where we are supposed to feel it. *In and with and as the whole world is where our human ecstasy is born.* It is the celebration of the recognition that our spirit and flesh are One.

It is the human female who was designed by evolution itself as the *link* between sexuality and spirit, between biological energy and the cosmic soul. It is the human female, as the leading edge of earthly evolution, who was specifically, neurologically structured for the experience of ecstasy. For this reason, the first religions on earth were designed *by women,* for women, and in celebration of femaleness. For this reason, matrifocal cultures had no reason or need to deny "the Other"—for all "otherness" was a part of the Mother. In ecstasy, all "otherness" becomes the self, the One. Ancient women could not have invented, because they had no need for, paranoid divisions between psyche and body, power-hungry manipulations of spirit versus matter, dualistic exploitations of flesh versus soul. They were "the undivided *ones,*" tapping into unhindered flows of ecstatic energy, which is both "spiritual" and "biological," of earthly soil and cosmic thought together. Not needing to tell a lie-at-the-root-of-things about the origin of life—not needing to maintain this lie, by force, day and night, against the urges of all nature and its consciousness towards the truth—women's cultures would not have needed to maintain themselves by energy-repressive systems, by coercive and punitive surveillance systems based on social caste, or economic status, or skin color or eye color or dress . . . nor would there be any need for hierarchic organization, tyrannical terrors, or political frauds. All these patriarchal accoutrements are necessary to enforce a mechanical order in the absence of organic order. All these patriarchal machineries are necessary to enforce the repression of common ecstasy—an ecstasy indigenous to all cultures that exist to realize, rather than to deny, the One-at-the-heart-of-All.

A "return to the Goddess" is not a backward trip through space or time. The human race cannot really return to infancy; we are too far gone for that. We *return* to the Goddess by *remembering, redefining, respelling*—by turning, as in a dance, away from one gesture and towards another. Patriarchal ontology is based on a three-dimensional reality. Modern physics is showing us that the universe has, not four dimensions, but as many as eleven dimensions.[2] Perhaps more. The universe is undergoing ecstatic exponential expansion into eleven or more dimensions—surely, three-dimensional religions cannot keep us in touch with such a universe! If we do not want to die, then we must evolve—and that means we must dance, expand exponentially with the dancing cosmos. We return to the cosmos only by becoming lovers of life, rather than life's victims, voyeurs, and policemen. How twisted we have become, within biophobic religions, spending most of our waking hours in grotesque postures of aggression, hurry, hate, self-righteousness, resentment, paranoia, and murderousness. Under the rule of the patriarchal God, we are all gargoyles, characterized by rigid poses that reveal mostly all our terrible fears and greeds, eaten away from inside by cancerous needs. To return to harmony—to return to the Goddess, to become lovers of the Goddess once again—we must realign our gestures into those of dancers. We must become beings who do not wish to control life, but only to listen to its music, and dance it. This is not easy to do, it might be impossible. But it is our only alternative to mass death—whether by war, or by total global mechanization.

The patriarchal God has only one commandment: *Punish life for being what it is.* The Goddess also has only one commandment: *Love life, for it is what it is.*

Women, designed by evolution as the links between spirit and flesh, are perhaps also designed by the cosmos to lead the human world back, now, to the great celebration of the reconciliation of flesh and spirit. Thus, at the very edge of death, we will return to the beginning. That is, at the end of the world (where we must surely be!) we will return to the Goddess, the Great Mother of All Life, as her magic children. In a round world, the only way for human beings to survive the end is to *return* to the beginning. Thus we complete a circle; but on a spiral, we *revolve* to a larger circle.

Now is the time to make again sacred our experience.

Witch power, it is said, cannot truly die, since it is a real power of the real cosmos. It can't die, it can only be forgotten—that means it can also be *re-membered,* as the serpent can be awakened from its tranced sleep at the bottom of the spine and induced to rise, to become again the luminous flying bird of the imagining mind. Once we thoroughly understand how and why patriarchy acquired its power over us—the power of an entrenched mistake over the minds and lives of all people—once we understand and feel clearly that the fight of witch women is also the fight of earth's people everywhere against mechanical subjugation and exploitation—once we reestablish the magic link between the individual psyche and the earth's vital energy flow, between all-evolving matter and all-evolving spirit, and learn to encourage and teach others to do the same, *in a loving return to what we always were*—perhaps then, in the final time of crisis, the Serpent Goddess will shake herself loose from her deep exiled sleep in the earth's belly. Perhaps the serpent of life's flowing energy will begin to rise again, all luminous and of the earth, and the children of the Great Mother will rise up with it, and the universe will be our home again, as before. *This flight is not an escape, but a return.*

The only way for human beings to survive the end is to return to the beginning.

Listen to the words of the Great Mother.

She says: Whenever ye have need of anything, once in the month,
and better it be when the Moon is full,
then ye shall assemble in some secret place . . .
to these I will teach things that are yet unknown.
And Ye Shall Be Free From All Slavery . . .
Keep pure your highest ideas;
strive ever toward it.

Let Naught Stop You Nor Turn You Aside . . .
Mine is the cup of wine of life
and the Cauldron of Cerridwen . . .
I am the Mother of All Living,
and my love is poured out upon the Earth . . .
I am the beauty of the Green Earth . . .
and the White Moon among the Stars,
and the Mystery of the Waters.

And The Desire In The Heart Of Woman . . .

Before my face,
let thine innermost self be unfolded
in the raptures of the Infinite . . .

Know the Mystery,
that if that which thou seekest
thou findest not within thee,
thou will never find it without thee . . .
For behold

I Have Been With Thee From The Beginning.

And I await thee now.[3]
Blessed Be.

(Traditional Wiccan prayer)

NOTES

I. WOMEN'S EARLY CULTURE: BEGINNINGS

The First Sex: "In the Beginning, We Were All Created Female"

1. Helen Diner, *Mothers and Amazons* (New York: Doubleday/Anchor, 1973), 74. Diner is referring to Charles Darwin, *Descent of Man, and Selection in Relation to Sex*, volume 1 (New York: J. A. Hill and Co., 1904), 164–68; Darwin believed both sexes, originally, were maternal, and thought the prostate gland might be a rudimentary uterus.
2. Mary Jane Sherfey, M.D., *The Nature and Evolution of Female Sexuality* (New York: Vintage Books, 1973), 43.
3. Stephen Jay Gould, *Hen's Teeth and Horse's Toes: Further Reflections in Natural History* (New York: W. W. Norton, 1983), 153–54.
4. Fran P. Hosken, *Women's International Network News 2*, no. 1 (January 1976): 30–44.
5. G. Rachel Levy, *Religious Conceptions of the Stone Age, and Their Influence Upon European Thought* (New York: Harper & Row, 1963), 70.
6. William Irwin Thompson, *The Time Falling Bodies Take to Light: Mythology, Sexuality and the Origins of Culture* (New York: St. Martin's Press, 1981), 43–156.

Marx and the Matriarchy

1. Friedrich Engels, "The Early Development of the Family" (Boston: New England Free Press, n.d.); this is taken from the first two chapters of *The Origin of the Family, Private Property and the State*, originally published in Zurich, 1884; American edition by International Publishers, New York, 1942, 1972.
2. We do not intend the term "matriarchy" to suggest "patriarchy in reverse," with women in charge of an otherwise intact hierarchic-dominance system. "Matriarchy," in our usage and reference, indicates an entirely different *orientation of consciousness* around which entirely different patterns of personal, social, cultural, and spiritual relationships could—and did—occur. Some anthropological writers prefer "matrifocal

community"; Marija Gimbutas suggests the term "matristic," to indicate the "more balanced and more or less egalitarian" communities of the Paleolithic and Neolithic periods. We think these terms are better, more accurate, and less distorted by usage. The word "matriarchy" slips in by habit, really; and because it was the common term used by so many early writers on the subject. For our purposes "matrifocal," "matristic," and "matriarchal" should all be taken to mean a *communality* based on blood and spirit ties uniting all living things within the body and spirit of the Great Mother.

3. Karl Marx, *Critique of Hegel's Philosophy of Right;* quoted by Christopher Hitchens, "Laying to Rest Beliefs on Religion and Politics," *In These Times* 8, no. 2 (November 16, 1983): 27.
4. Paul Cardan, "History and Revolution, Critique of Historical Materialism," *Solidarity* 38 (London: 1971): 15 and 20. The article was reprinted from *Socialisme ou Barbarie* 36 (Paris: April 1961).
5. Keith Motherson, *Sleep Well, Father Marx* (c/o 3, Jordanston Cottages, Dwr Bach, Dyfed, Wales ST5 9RT). This manuscript, yet unpublished but widely circulated through Europe in xerox form, contains one of the most thorough and acute discussions yet of what has happened to Marxism in the contemporary world.
6. Karl Marx, *Capital*, volume 3, Untermann translation (Chicago: Charles H. Kerr, 1909; reprinted by International Publishers, New York, 1967), 954.
7. Robert Graves, *The White Goddess: A Historical Grammar of Poetic Myth* (New York: Farrar, Straus and Giroux/Noonday Press, 1966), 235.
8. Robert Briffault, *The Mothers: A Study of the Origin of Sentiments and Institutions*, volume 1 (New York: Macmillan, 1952), 478–79.

The Original Black Mother

1. John G. Jackson, *Man, God and Civilization* (New Hyde Park, New York: University Books, 1972), 217. Jackson quotes Briffault:

   > Down to the time when a dynasty of Greek rulers sought to introduce foreign usages, the conservative society of the great African kingdom [Egypt], which has contributed so largely to the material and intellectual culture of the Western world, never lost the lineaments of a matriarchal social order. . . . The functions of royalty in ancient Egypt were regarded as being transmitted in the female line. . . . Those features of the constitution of Egyptian royalty are not singular. They are substantially identical with those obtaining in all other African kingdoms.

   From Robert Briffault's *The Mothers,* one-volume edition (New York: Macmillan, 1931), 274–75.
2. Ibid, 173, 178–80.
3. Sir E. A. Wallis Budge, *Egypt* (London and New York: The Home University Library, 1925), 42; quoted in Jackson, *Man, God and Civilization*, 197.
4. Jackson, *Man, God and Civilization,* 198.

5. Ibid., 199.
6. Leo Frobenius, *The Voice of Africa,* volume 1 (London: Hutchinson and Co., 1913), 345.
7. Leo Wiener, *Africa and the Discovery of America,* three volumes (Philadelphia: Innes and Sons, 1920–1922); also *Mayan and Mexican Origins,* privately printed (Cambridge, Massachusetts, 1926). Reference to Wiener's work is in Jackson, *Man, God and Civilization*, 197.
8. Victor W. Von Hagen, *World of the Maya* (New York: New American Library, 1960), 195.
9. Jackson, *Man, God and Civilization*, 247–49.
10. Dennis Duerden, *African Art—An Introduction* (London: Hamlyn, 1968).
11. Franz Fanon, *The Wretched of the Earth* (New York: Grove Press, 1966), 170.
12. C. G. Jung, *Man and His Symbols* (London: Aldus Books, 1964; Garden City, New York: Doubleday, 1964), 82.
13. Michael Dames, *Silbury Treasure: The Great Goddess Rediscovered* (London: Thames and Hudson, 1976).
14. R. C. Morse and David Stoller, "The Hidden Message That Breaks Habits," *Science Digest* 90, no. 9 (September 1982): 28.
15. Eugen George, *The Adventure of Mankind,* translated from German by Robert Bek-Gran (New York: E. P. Dutton, 1931), 121.

Women as Culture Creators

1. Evelyn Reed, "The Myth of Women's Inferiority." This long essay originally appeared in the Spring 1954 issue of the *Fourth International Socialist Review* (New York). It has since been reprinted within the women's movement by, among others, the New England Free Press (Boston). It is also included in *Problems of Women's Liberation*, a pamphlet collection of Reed's feminist essays (New York: Merit, 1969), 22–41.
2. Evelyn Reed, *Woman's Evolution: from Matriarchal Clan to Patriarchal Family* (New York: Pathfinder Press, 1975), 109. Reed quotes Otis Tufton Mason, *Woman's Share in Primitive Culture* (New York and London: Appleton, 1911), 151.
3. Ibid., 11–12, 19–20, 143–52. Fire survey information from C. S. Ford and F. A. Beach, *Patterns of Sexual Behavior* (New York: Harper & Brothers, 1951).
4. Ibid., 121. Reed quotes Mason, *Woman's Share,* 17–18.
5. Victor W. Von Hagen, *World of the Maya* (New York: New American Library, 1960), 80.
6. Marija Gimbutas, *The Goddesses and Gods of Old Europe—6500–3500 B.C.: Myths and Cult Images* (Berkeley and Los Angeles: University of California Press, 1982), 89–111, 112–136. This is an updated edition of the original *Gods and Goddesses of Old Europe—7000–3500 B.C.: Myths, Lengends and Cult Images* (London: Thames and Hudson, 1974). This book contains a wealth of truly important, fascinating, and—until

now—virtually unknown information about early Neolithic cultures and the Goddess in southeast Europe. Reading it, people of European descent will realize how much we have not been taught about our own history.

7. Information from Merlin Stone, *When God Was a Woman* (New York and London: Harcourt Brace Jovanovich, 1976), 3, 21. Originally published as *Paradise Papers, The Suppression of Women's Rites* (London: Virago Ltd., in association with Quartet Books, 1976). Stone's research into the Goddess religion in Egypt and the Near East, and its later suppression by patriarchal religions, has become invaluable to all people interested in tracking the Goddess around the globe.
8. An interesting piece of information picked up from Erich von Daniken's *Gold of the Gods* (New York: Bantam Books, 1974), 35–36. Von Daniken's popular books were full of information, but his conclusions were somewhat insulting to the human race in their suggestion that we were from the beginning too stupid to invent anything on our own. It is not only a sexist but an imperialist assumption to believe that all great ancient cultures and earthly technologies were initiated by men from outer space.

The First Speech

1. Alexander Marshack, "Some Implications of the Paleolithic Symbolic Evidence for the Origin of Language," in *Origins and Evolution of Language,* volume 280, edited by Harnand, Steklis, and Lancaster (New York Academy of Sciences, 1976), 309.
2. William Irwin Thompson, *The Time Falling Bodies Take To Light: Mythology, Sexuality and the Origins of Culture* (New York: St. Martin's Press, 1981), 91.
3. Ibid., 88.
4. Ibid., 91.
5. According to some researchers, the corpus collosum in the female brain contains an abundance of nerve connections linking the right and left hemispheres; they found this not to be true of the male brain. Thus there is some neurophysiological evidence that males *do* tend to separate and compartmentalize "feeling" and "logic," while females tend to synthesize them. (See "Why Men Don't Speak Their Minds," *Science Digest* 91, no. 11 [November 1983]: 84.) The predictable problem is that as soon as researchers find that the male brain tends to be neurologically compartmentalized, they declare *this* brain "normal," and the synthesizing female brain then becomes a source of "aberrations": allergy, schizophrenia, phobias, depression, ineptitude in math. . . . Really and truly, there's no way to win! (See, for example, "The Battle in the Brain," *Science Digest* 92, no. 1 [January 1984]: 85.)
6. Robert Graves, *The White Goddess* (New York: Farrar, Straus and Giroux/Noonday Press, 1975), Foreword, 9–10. William Bennett, President Reagan's 1984 appointee to head the Department of Education, comes to mind. Taking over the National Endowment for the Arts in 1980, Bennett, an energetic proponent of the Great Books approach to culture, cut funding to feminist, Chicano, black, Native American, leftist, and

prison-writing publications—no doubt on the premise that all classifiably "counterculture" poetries, fictions, and thought-processes are not "real culture"; only the mental products of white male academics rate as "culture." White male academics are the 1980s American repository of the "Apollonian, rational" art process—i.e., that's where the funding goes now. Apollonians rock no boats.

7. Paraphrase of the general ideas of Rudolf Steiner, the Anthroposophist, writing at the beginning of this century in *From Jesus to Christ* (Blauvelt, NY: Rudolf Steiner Publications, n.d.). Steiner's great vision was too often blinded by Christian dualism—and worse, by white Sky God racism, which he and his followers confuse with "spirit."
8. A recent Boston University study conducted by Bradley Googins and Dianne Burden found that the average female married working parent in America today spends 85 hours a week on job, homemaking, and child-care tasks; a single female working parent spends 75 hours; a married male working parent spends 66 hours; a single male working parent spends 65 hours; and a nonparent spends 55 hours weekly on job and housework tasks. The Boston study was attempting to investigate causes of depression and strain on private corporation workers at all job levels; it found that 50 percent of the workers traced their depression to the stress of holding a job and raising a family at the same time. (Information from Suzanne Wetlaufer, Associated Press, *Arizona Daily Star,* Thursday, November 14, 1985, page 7.) A 1985 *Forbes* magazine report found that leisure time in America is rapidly decreasing, from an average of 24.3 hours of real leisure time per week in 1975, to 19.2 hours in 1980, down to 18.1 hours in 1985. (In *Arizona Daily Star Parade Magazine* section, Sunday, January 5, 1986: 5).

II. WOMEN'S EARLY RELIGION

The First Mother

1. Phillip Van Doren Stern, *Prehistoric Europe: From Stone Age Man to the Early Greeks* (New York: W. W. Norton, 1969), 95.
2. Quoted in Charles H. Long, *Alpha, The Myths of Creation* (New York: Collier Books, 1969), 39. See Mircea Eliade, *Patterns in Comparative Religions* (New York: Sheed and Ward, 1958), 242–45.
3. Ibid., 36–37.

The Organic Religion of Early Women

1. Many feminists are uncomfortable with biological explanations, or even biological influences, for anything. Among modern women growing up in patriarchal cultures, this discomfort is understandable. Under patriarchy, women's biology has been treated negatively and punitively by a male-oriented culture, and used as an excuse or "reason" for oppressing women, and denying us our share of life. Female body processes, wholly natural and life-giving, have been turned into "unclean" and "demonic" processes by the puritanic Father God religions, and thus into concrete

social, economic, and psychological disadvantages. Under patriarchy, "normalcy" is always defined in terms of the (white) male body; the differences of the female body are defined pejoratively. "Different but equal" has no possible existence under the patriarchal system, which exists by structuring all differences hierarchically, as well as moralistically. Because of this, some American radical feminists in particular have insisted that there are no significant biological differences between women and men—that observable or apparent differences are cultural projections and accommodations, rather than naturally occurring distinctions.

In fact, there are two kinds of sexual differences: (1) Those sex roles and characteristics imposed by a culture are *culturally determined* sex differences; (2) those related specifically to differential hormonal and physical-maturational processes are *biologically determined* sex differences. That is, that all human females menstruate is a *biologically determined* female trait, globally true for all females regardless of culture. The social customs and penalties, celebrations, and shames attached to the biological fact of female menstruation are *culturally determined* and variable within and between world ages, and world cultures. The common confusion between biologically and socially imposed sex traits and sex roles is easy to understand; they are intertwined intentionally at gut level, in our traumatically mixed experiences of physical-cultural conditioning and determination.

We have to look seriously at past matrifocal cultures to learn—to *remember*—that a biological difference is *not* a disadvantage unless one lives in a culture which defines that difference negatively and pejoratively, and so conditions its members to act punitively toward that difference. We all know there is no disadvantage in a black skin, a red skin, or a yellow skin *unless* one lives in a culture designed to oppress and punish these skin colors; our white culture is indeed designed just this way. Therefore it should be possible to speculate that there is no inherent or real disadvantage in a differential female biology, except in relation to a culture that defines male biology as the norm. To try to achieve justice for women by insisting there are no biological differences between women and men is to argue in embarrassing contradistinction to facts and experiences we can all ascertain. Worse, this argument plays into the terrible patriarchal assumption that we cannot all be equal unless we are all the same—a palpable impossibility that leaves a small white male elite in power (ostensibly waiting for everyone on earth to become white males).

As a corollary to their denial of biological differences between the sexes, American radical feminists tend not to believe in the existence of past matriarchies. Perhaps, seeing women as disadvantaged and negatively defined in this culture because of our biology, they are unable to imagine us ever being empowered, advantaged, or filling any creative cultural roles whatsoever as a *result* of that same female biology. That is, they see "female biology" as exclusively, and for all time, disadvantageous. The problem with this conclusion is that it is *not political*. An argument that assumes female biology has always been disadvantageous, and that women have always been in a secondary social position, is an argument that *blames nature* for women's oppression, rather than blaming a male-dominated and male-invented political, social, and ideological system. After all, men are not to blame if women have wombs—nature is. Where is the politics in this? Shulamith Firestone's desperate appeal to a male-designed technology, for the quick invention of extrauterine conception machines, to save us women from our own bodies, is the only logical result. This is not politics, it is collusion. For, at this stage of the game, how can any thinking woman believe that a male-controlled reproductive technology could ever be of benefit to women? The patriarchal mind has been working night and day for about four thousand years on just this project: to replace the human mother with a manmade machine; just as it replaced a female god and female worldview with that of a male god, thereby taking over the earth and its resources, along with women's Neolithic industries and technologies—certainly at no benefit to women. In arguing that women, due to our biology, have always been oppressed, American radical feminists seem to be involved in an ontological capitulation, an agreement at the root, with all the males who insist, "It was always this way, baby. It's a man's world. Stop fighting, submit, and enjoy it—because you've never had any other choice." This is, of course, what patriarchal men *want* us to believe: It absolves them of all responsibility. But why do American radical feminists want us to believe it? The "nature-is-to-blame" argument, further, leaves all women in the silly position of petitioning the male to please share "his" world with poor us. Who have never been able to make anything of our own, boo hoo! But this simply isn't true.

Why do American radical feminists get caught in this theoretical trap? Why do they choose to deny the abundant archaeological and mythological evidence of past matriarchies? Is it because they received their intellectual training at male-dominated colleges; and now come to us, thus militantly equipped with the Father's View of Things, to deny the Mother—in the name of *rational* feminism?

The evidence for matrifocal cultures proves that women, complete with our biology, can be primary members and creators of long-enduring cultures. It proves that our historic problem is not nature but male ideology. Pregnancy and motherhood *did not* keep Neolithic women, for example, from building Çatal Hüyük, and populating it with female priestesses, lawgivers, physicians, visionaries, artisans, architects, and traders. In such a culture—which did in fact exist—designed by women, and for women to realize their potentials in, surely female biology would not have been pejoratively defined, or structured into the culture as a disadvantage, or as any cause for oppression. The fact that such female-focal cultures existed in the past is evidence that they can exist again. It is male ideology, not our own bodies, that has oppressed us historically and oppresses us now. This is a political-ideological oppression (*not* a biological or ontological one), and it therefore has a political-ideological solution. And this should not be cause for intellectual discomfort, but for relief. Nature, after all, has gone on for a very long time, and changes slowly. Male-structured ideologies, religions, and political-economic cultures, on the other hand, appeared very recently, and really do not have the power of God, let alone nature, behind them. They have only the power of conditioned belief—so long as we choose to lend them the energy of our belief. Otherwise, like so many other recent manmade products, they show a lot of built-in obsolescence.

2. William Irwin Thompson, *The Time Falling Bodies Take to Light: Mythology, Sexuality and the Origins of Culture* (New York: St. Martin's Press, 1981), 102–3. Thompson continues:

    > For urban, civilized humanity, the work of religion is to reconnect the alienated and exploited masses in a vision of unity, or to reconnect the alienated human species with nature and the heavens. Religion is not identical with spirituality; rather, religion is the form spirituality takes in a civilization; it is not so much the opiate of the masses as it is the antidote for the poisons of civilization. . . . [Marx said the same thing.] Because religion is a response to the conditions of alienation in a civilization, religion is unnecessary in a culture of hunters and gatherers. The culture of hunters and gatherers is spiritually personified; every event is flooded with the sacred. When an entire way of life is sacred, the people do not have to build churches and sing hymns on Sundays.

    That is, it was always the imperialist Christian West that represented a profane culture, while the indigenous peoples of America, Africa, and Asia who they colonized, missionized, and brutalized—the "heathen savages"—were the ones who had been living, more or less, in a sacred way.

3. A respelling of St. Catherine of Genoa's "My me is God, nor do I know my Selfhood save in Him," in Jill Purce, *The Mystic Spiral: Journey of the Soul* (London: Thames and Hudson, 1974; New York: Avon, 1974), 18. See also Martin Buber, *Ecstatic Confessions: The Heart of Mysticism* (San Francisco: Harper & Row, 1985), 107.

4. Martin Buber, *I and Thou* (Edinburgh: T. and T. Clark, 1953; New York: Scribner's, 1970), 76–77. Buber refers to a Jewish myth that says "in his mother's womb man knows the universe and forgets it at birth."

5. Mary Long, "Visions of a New Faith," *Science Digest* 89, no. 10 (November 1981): 41. The research is being conducted by James Prescott, neuropsychologist at the Institute of Humanistic Science in Los Gatos, California.

Female Cosmology: The Creation of the Universe

1. A respelling of *The Laws of Manu*, as they were stolen from the Great Mother, as was Brahma's Golden Egg; see Jill Purce, *The Mystic Spiral: Journey of the Soul* (London: Thames and Hudson, 1974; New York: Avon, 1974), plate 65.

2. See Theodor Schwenk's *Sensitive Chaos* (London: Rudolf Steiner Press, 1971) for a beautiful exposition of the growth of life-forms from the spiraling movements of liquids and all other energy flows—the spiral dance.

3. Unpublished poem by Monica Sjöö.

The Cosmic Serpent

1. Robert Graves, *The Greek Myths*, volume 1 (New York: George Braziller, 1957), 27.
2. From Marcia Patrick's yet unpublished but fruitful manuscript *Earthly Origins* (first draft copyright 1983), 247.
3. Merlin Stone, *When God Was a Woman* (New York: Harcourt Brace Jovanovich, 1978), 199.
4. Ibid., 201.
5. Patrick, *Earthly Origins*, 249.
6. Marija Gimbutas, *The Goddesses and Gods of Old Europe—6500–3500 B.C.* (Berkeley and Los Angeles: University of California Press, 1982), 106–7.
7. Ibid., 113.
8. This really interesting piece of information—but don't try it unless you know what you're doing!—is from Stone's *When God Was a Woman*, 213–14.
9. William Irwin Thompson, *The Time Falling Bodies Take to Light: Mythology, Sexuality and the Origins of Culture* (New York: St. Martin's Press, 1981), 33.
10. Gimbutas, *Goddesses and Gods*, 152.

The World Egg: Yin/Yang

1. Hellmut Wilhelm, *Change: 8 Lectures on the I Ching* (New York: Harper & Row, 1960), 27.
2. "Dark Side of the Cosmos," *Science* 85 6, no. 1 (January–February 1985): 8. See also "Magnetic Whirlwinds," *Science Digest* 93, no. 7 (July 1985): 26; this article describes the discovery of magnetic vortices, huge, rapidly spinning spirals of electrically charged gas, or plasma, which are now believed to be as important to the shaping of galaxies and other cosmic structures as gravitation. These electromagnetic whirlpools range in size from small, half-mile-size vortices in the atmosphere of Venus to immense galactic vortices stretching across millions of light-years of space. Similar spirals, about 60,000 miles across, exist in the earth's magnetic field.
3. R. Buckminster Fuller, *Epic Poem to the History of Industrialization* (New York: Simon and Schuster, 1963), 226.

The Gynandrous Great Mother

1. Giraldus Cambrensis, *Topography of Ireland*, excerpted in *The Portable Medieval Reader*, edited by James Bruce Ross and Mary Martin McLaughlin (New York: Viking Press, 1949), 414.
2. Charlotte Woolf, *Love Between Women* (London: Duckworth and Co., Ltd., 1971). Woolf is a psychiatrist who has tried to develop a feminist analysis, "Towards a New Theory of Lesbianism."

3. M. Esther Harding, *Woman's Mysteries, Ancient and Modern: A Psychological Interpretation of the Feminine Principle as Portrayed in Myth, Story and Dreams* (New York: Bantam Books, 1971); also published by Rider and Co., London, 1971). This is an important early study (first published in 1955) of women's religions. Esther Harding is a Jungian psychiatrist and has that bias concerning archetypal "femininity" and "woman's nature"; but *Woman's Mysteries* has much useful historic, mythic, and dream information, and should not be disregarded.

4. Jean Markale, *Women of the Celts* (London: Cremonesi, 1975). Markale is himself a Celt from Brittany, and lectures in Celtic history at the Sorbonne in Paris. He sees himself as a feminist, and advocates that men return to being sons of the Great Mother. Those who might see such a return as "unmanly" should study the Celtic warriors. They fought naked of armor and often with bare hands against the invading Roman armies. They lost, of course, against the imperialist machine—and their descendents have themselves become an imperialist machine. But before they were corrupted, they were strong, just, and creatively wild. Author Rita Mae Brown, speaking of Lesbians, once said: "An army of lovers cannot lose." But in history, armies of lovers have frequently lost—e.g., the Celts, the Native Americans, the African tribes, the Thracian, Macedonian, and Libyan Amazons—when they were up against armies of machines. But this is no blotch on their courage or strength; what they all needed was modern guerilla training. For information on the tatooed peoples of Western Europe, see Lewis Spence, *The History of Atlantis* (New York: Bell, 1968), 228–30.

5. Anne Cameron, *Daughters of Copper Woman* (Vancouver, B.C.: Press Gang, 1981).

6. Mary Daly, *Beyond God the Father* (Boston: Beacon Press, 1973), 65. The remark about housekeepers was made by "a famous psychosurgeon," Dr. Freeman, called "the dean of lobotomists." The rest is from an article by Dr. Peter Breggin, "The Return of Lobotomy and Psychosurgery," which was read into the Congressional Record in February 1972. Dr. Breggin conducted investigations which showed that psychosurgery, after undergoing repudiation by social opinion if not by all doctors, began to make a comeback in the 1960s, "contemporaneous with the second wave of feminism," as Daly notes. The new wave of lobotomies was aimed particularly at "relatively well-functioning 'neurotics,' particularly women."

Mysteries of the Throne, the Cave, and the Labyrinth

1. William Irwin Thompson, *The Time Falling Bodies Take to Light: Mythology, Sexuality and the Origins of Culture* (New York: St. Martin's Press, 1981), 146–48.

2. For information on the black African cult of the throne, and on the importance of the Queen-Mother in Africa, read R. S. Rattray's *Ashanti* (Oxford: Oxford University Press, 1923); also his *Religion and Art in Ashanti* (London: n.p., 1927). Rattray was a British colonial administrator who became deeply interested in the music, religion, and culture

of the Africans; he was also aware of the African women's independent culture and their role as religious initiators.

3. For the best information on the cave as the birth womb and death tomb of the Great Mother, see G. Rachel Levy's *Religious Conceptions of the Stone Age, and Their Influence Upon European Thought* (New York: Harper & Row, 1963); originally published in Britain as *The Gate of Horn* (London: Faber and Faber, 1946). As mentioned in Part 1, Levy's book is both highly documented and quite visionary—naturally, it has been virtually ignored by academia.
4. Ibid., 159.
5. Joseph L. Henderson, "Ancient Myths and Modern Man," in C. G. Jung, *Man and His Symbols* (no comment!) (London: Aldus Books, 1964; Garden City, New York: Doubleday, 1964), 125.

The Cult of the Dead

1. Read *Les Rites de Passage* by Arnold van Gennep (Paris: n.p., 1909).
2. The perception of "gods" and other cosmic patterns via chemicals does not invalidate the existence of these gods and patterns. Ultraviolet light, X-rays, radio waves are all real phenomena; we cannot perceive them, though, without the use of special technology, which is designed specifically to tune into or capture these radiation frequencies which our human retinas or ears don't otherwise register. Similarly, our brains might be obtuse toward some real diety phenomena unless they are prepared, by specific chemical gestalts, to receive, pick up, or capture these supraretinal patterns, or gods. Ancient people used sacred mushrooms, peyote, cannabis, and other hallucinogens ritually and skillfully; they had no problems of abuse or addiction. These problems occur only when individual people use drugs to *escape* from exploitive and linear-secular cultures, not when they are *participating* communally in a sacred culture.

The Mother of Wild Animals and the Dance

1. William Irwin Thompson, *The Time Falling Bodies Take to Light: Mythology, Sexuality and the Origins of Culture* (New York: St. Martin's Press, 1981), 102. For an antidote to all the male-focused history, and a living illustration of Thompson's point, read Anne Cameron, *Daughters of Copper Woman* (Vancouver, B.C.: Press Gang, 1981).
2. Ibid., 99; also 121–22.
3. Ibid., 109.
4. It was Jessie L. Weston who traced the Grail legends back to the Sumerian and Babylonian myths of the Great Goddess, her loss of her son-lover Tammuz-Dumuzi, and her descent to the underworld to retrieve him; see her great and important book, *From Ritual to Romance* (Garden City, New York: Doubleday, 1957).
5. Jane Ellen Harrison, *Themis: A Study of the Social Origins of Greek Religion* (Cambridge: Cambridge University Press, 1927; New York: Meridian Books, 1962), 24, 31–47. This pioneering study, written in 1912,

researches the origins of early Greek religious conceptions in magico-ritual dance, mask, and rhythmic intoxication, all connected with ecstatic-oracular practices of priestesses serving the chthonic Goddess, as at Delphi. According to Rachel Levy in *Religious Conceptions of the Stone Age, and Their Influence Upon European Thought* (New York: Harper & Row, 1963), 285, "dithyramb" also meant "him of the double-door," indicating perhaps the magic and tragic son born into life, death, and immortality, again and again, through the double-door of the womb/tomb.

6. Jane van Lawick-Goodall, *In the Shadow of Man* (New York: Dell, 1971), 66.
7. *The Apocryphal New Testament*, translated by M. R. James (London: Oxford University Press, 1924), 258.
8. Quote and information from Thompson, *Falling Bodies*, 106.
9. Mary Leakey, "Preserving Africa's Ancient Art," *Science Digest* 92, no. 8 (August 1984): 57–63; 81. From Mary Leakey, *Africa's Vanishing Art* (Garden City, New York: Doubleday, 1983).
10. Robert Briffault, *The Mothers*, one-volume edition (New York: Macmillan, 1931), 248.
11. Quoted in *Technicians of the Sacred: A Range of Poetries from Africa, America, Asia and Oceania*, edited by Jerome Rothenberg (Garden City, New York: Doubleday, 1968), 361.

III. WOMEN'S CULTURE AND RELIGION IN NEOLITHIC TIMES

The First Settled Villages

1. Information on Anatolian settlements and Çatal Hüyük from James Mellaart, *Earliest Civilizations of the Near East* (London: Thames and Hudson, 1965); also *Çatal Hüyük* (London: Thames and Hudson, 1967). See also William Irwin Thompson, *The Time Falling Bodies Take to Light: Mythology, Sexuality and the Origins of Culture* (New York: St. Martin's Press, 1981), 138–48.
2. Thompson, *Falling Bodies*, 138–48.
3. Much information on Çatal Hüyük, its Goddess and women, can be found in Merlin Stone, *When God Was a Woman* (New York: Harcourt Brace Jovanovich, 1978), 16–17, 24, 44, 96, 100, 154.
4. Erich Fromm, *The Anatomy of Human Destructiveness* (New York: Fawcett Crest, 1973), 183–84.

Southeast Europe: The Bird-and-Snake Goddess

1. The evidence is collected in Marija Gimbutas *The Goddesses and Gods of Old Europe—6500-3500 B.C.* (Berkeley and Los Angeles: University of California Press, 1982). All information on the Vinča culture comes from this book.
2. Ibid., 144.

3. Herodotus, *The Histories*, book VII, translated by George Rawlinson (New York: Tudor, 1944), 389.
4. Apuleius lived in the second century A.D. He was initiated into the Mysteries of Isis, becoming a priest of Isis and Osiris as well as of Aesculapius, the God of Medicine. He was rumored to have gained knowledge of the supernatural. His account of his initiation into the Goddess's Mysteries is called *The Golden Ass—The Transformation of Lucius Apuleius of Madaura*, translated by Robert Graves (Baltimore, Penguin Books, 1950).
5. Elizabeth Gould Davis, *The First Sex* (Baltimore: Penguin Books, 1972), 49–55.
6. "Thracian Treasures from Bulgaria" (London: British Museum Publications, 1976): 25, 26, 29.

The Megalithic Tomb: The Moon and the Stone

1. See Robert Graves, *The White Goddess: A Historical Grammar of Poetic Myth* (New York: Farrar, Straus and Giroux/Noonday Press, 1966), 70. Graves did not invent these properties, or course, they are ancient biologic-mythic attributes of the Moon, or Triple Goddess.
2. Read O. G. S. Crawford, *The Eye Goddess* (New York: Macmillan, 1956) for an account of these images—her cosmic eyes—found in tombs all over Neolithic Europe and Eurasia.
3. See Erich Neumann, *The Great Mother: An Analysis of the Archetype* (London: Routledge and Kegan Paul, 1955; Princeton: Princeton University Press/Bollingen Series XLVII 1955), plates 132, 134, and 136. This book has an abundance of information concerning the different perceived aspects of the Great Mother worldwide; Neumann, like Esther Harding, is a Jungian psychiatrist, and has that bias. But a large section of the book contains great plates, images of the Goddess from all parts of the world.

The Earth Mound as Cosmic Womb of the Pregnant Goddess

1. Information in this section comes to a large extent from Michael Dames, *Silbury Treasure: The Great Goddess Rediscovered* (London: Thames and Hudson, 1976). Dames is an artist as well as a lecturer in history and art history. For a number of years he lived in the vicinity of the Silbury Mound and watched it closely during the seasons, noting its changes and its relation to moon, sun, and stars. When Monica Sjöö visited him in Birmingham, he related visionary experiences in that landscape, a sense of communication with the Goddess, which changed his life. Monica had similar experiences there; many people have.

   It is fascinating, in a hideous way, that the British government is placing cruise missile bases like Greenham Common so close to ancient sacred sites, such as Silbury Mound and Stonehenge. This practice underscores a terrible Western Christian and biblical tradition: the refusal to recognize that the whole earth is Holy Land, including the sacred sites of pagan people. In the same awful tradition, so many sacred sites of Native Americans are used by the U.S. government as dumps for toxic chemicals and radiation wastes; they are also ravaged by uranium and coal strip-mining. If all pagans were to dump our weekly garbage in the local Christian church or cathedral, perhaps some point could be made. Greenham Common, by the way, was the site of the last official witch burning in England.

2. See William Irwin Thompson, *The Time Falling Bodies Take to Light: Mythology, Sexuality and the Origins of Culture* (New York: St. Martin's Press, 1981), 264–66, for photos and diagrams.
3. For a photographic as well as written documentation of the stones, and other megalithic monuments of Britain, see Janet Bord and Colin Bord, *Mysterious Britain* (London: Garnstone Press, 1972; London: Paladin Books, 1974).
4. Elizabeth Gould Davis, *The First Sex* (Baltimore: Penguin Books, 1971), 53. Davis gets her information from Edward Gibbon, *The Decline and Fall of the Roman Empire*, volume 2 (New York: Heritage, 1946), 1562; and from Harold Mattingly, *Christians in the Roman Empire* (New York: W. W. Norton, 1967), 72.
5. Robert Graves, *The White Goddess: A Historical Grammar of Poetic Myth* (New York: Farrar, Straus and Giroux/Noonday Press, 1966), 109 (footnote).
6. Robert Silverberg, *The Mount Builders* (New York: Ballantine, 1970).

The Islands of Malta and Gozo

1. Valuable information about the ancient cultures of Malta, Gozo, Europe, the Aegean, and the Near East can be found in Sibylle von Cles-Reden, *The Realm of the Great Goddess, The Story of the Megalith Builders* (London: Thames and Hudson, 1961; Englewood Cliffs, New Jersey: Prentice-Hall, 1962). See Marija Gimbutas, *The Goddesses and Gods of Old Europe—6500–3500* B.C.*: Myths and Cult Images* (Berkeley and Los Angeles: University of California Press, 1982).
2. Quoted by Jean Markale in *Women of the Celts* (London: Cremonesi, 1975).
3. Robert Graves, *The White Goddess: A Historical Grammar of Poetic Myth* (New York: Farrar, Straus and Giroux/Noonday Press, 1966), 399.
4. John Michell, *The Earth Spirit: Its Ways, Shrines and Mysteries* (London: Thames and Hudson, 1975; New York: Avon Books, 1975), 18–19.
5. Graves, *The White Goddess*, 105.

Twelve Circling Dancers

1. From Acts of John 97–102; in *The Apocryphal New Testament*, translated by Montague Rhodes James (Oxford: The Clarendon Press, 1953), 255–56. Also see Max Pulver, "Jesus' Round Dance and Crucifixion" in Joseph Campbell, editor, *The Mysteries*, Bollingen Series XXX, Papers from the Eranos Yearbooks, volume 2 (New York: Pantheon Books, 1955), 181–82.
2. Jill Purce, *The Mystic Spiral: Journey of the Soul* (New York: Avon Books, 1974), 31.

3. See Lewis Spence, *The History of Atlantis* (New York: Bell, 1968), 84.
4. Robert Graves, *The White Goddess* (New York: Farrar, Straus and Giroux/Noonday Press, 1966), 10.
5. Elizabeth Pepper and John Wilcock, *A Guide to Magical and Mystical Sites, Europe and the British Isles* (New York: Harper & Row, 1977), 127. See also G. Rachel Levy, *Religious Conceptions of the Stone Age, and Their Influence Upon European Thought* (New York: Harper & Row, 1963), 105–6, and plate 13b. The site is called, appropriately, the Cave of the Bats.
6. Mary Leakey, "Preserving Africa's Ancient Art," *Science Digest* 92, no. 8 (August 1984): 56–63; 81.
7. C. A. Burland, *Myths of Life and Death* (New York: Crown, 1974), 155.
8. Purce, *The Mystic Spiral,* plate 59. Purce sometimes seems to assume that the primal cosmic creative energy is male; in a letter to Monica Sjöö, however, she says that this book is a portrait of female energy.
9. See Arkon Daraul, *A History of Secret Societies* (New York: Pocket Books, 1969), plate 6.
10. Purce, *The Mystic Spiral*, 30–31.
11. William Irwin Thompson, *The Time Falling Bodies Take to Light: Mythology, Sexuality and the Origins of Culture* (New York: St. Martin's Press, 1981), 106.
12. Jacquetta Hawkes, *Dawn of the Gods* (London: Thames and Hudson, 1968). In this book Hawkes writes about the Cretan religion, its goddess, and the Cretan culture and people.
13. Raphael Patai, *The Hebrew Goddess* (New York: Avon, 1978), 174.

Earth Spirit, Serpent Spirals, and Blind Springs

1. Much information for this section comes from Guy Underwood, *The Pattern of the Past* (London: Museum Press, 1969; London: Abacus, 1972); and also from John Michell, *The View Over Atlantis* (London: Sago Press, 1969; London: Abacus, 1973; New York: Ballantine, 1972) and *The New View Over Atlantis* (New York: Harper & Row, 1983); see also John Michell, *The Earth Spirit, Its Ways, Shrines and Mysteries* (London: Thames and Hudson, 1975; New York: Avon, 1975). Guy Underwood pays tribute to the Goddess and recognizes her cosmic spirit shaping and inspiring the ancient civilizations.
2. Guy Underwood, *Pattern of the Past,* 58–59.
3. Ibid., 185.
4. Erich Neumann, *The Great Mother: An Analysis of the Archetype*, translated by Ralph Manheim (Princeton: Princeton University Press/Bollingen Series XLVII, 1955), 159.
5. Michell, *The Earth Spirit,* 67. There is invaluable information in this book on sacred stones and rocking stones.
6. Ibid., 114.
7. Jill Purce, *The Mystic Spiral: Journey of the Soul* (New York: Avon, 1974), 29.

Underground Caverns and Alchemic Mysteries

1. See Janet Bord and Colin Bord, *Mysterious Britain* (London: Garnstone Press, 1972; London: Paladin Books, 1974).
2. John Michell, *The Earth Spirit, Its Ways, Shrines and Mysteries* (London: Thames and Hudson, 1975; New York: Avon, 1975), 23.
3. Ibid., plate 7.
4. Information from "Woman As Innovator (With Special Reference to Mathematics, Science and Technology)," in *Biology and Human Affairs* 40, no. 1 (London, 1974).

The Goddess at Avebury in Britain

1. Michael Dames, *Avebury Cycle* (London: Thames and Hudson, 1977), see 63, 66, and 83. This entire chapter is based on Dames's interpretation of the Avebury monuments.

Moon Time: The Great Intellectual Triumph of Women's Culture

1. Quoted in Gerald S. Hawkins, *Stonehenge Decoded* (Ney York: Dell, 1965), 138–39.
2. Alexander Thom, *Megalithic Lunar Observatories* (New York: Oxford University Press, 1971); also *Megalithic Sites in Britain* (Oxford: University Press, 1967). Thom is a Scottish engineer who confirmed ancient legends depicting the British earthworks as lunar, solar, and star observatories, with the tools of his trade: siting instruments, mathematics, and Pictish instinct.

Lunar Calendars

1. William Irwin Thompson, *The Time Falling Bodies Take to Light: Mythology, Sexuality and the Origins of Culture* (New York: St. Martin's Press, 1981), 118.
2. Information from the article "Woman As Innovator (With Special Reference to Mathematics, Science and Technology)," *Biology and Human Affairs* 40, no. 1 (London, 1974).
3. "Indian Calendar Stick," *Science 85* 6, no. 2 (March 1985): 7.
4. Thompson, *Falling Bodies*, 98.
5. Alexander Marshack, *The Roots of Civilization* (New York: McGraw-Hill, 1972), 336–37.
6. Thompson, *Falling Bodies*, 98.
7. Ibid., 99.
8. Ibid., 97.
9. Barbara G. Walker, *The Woman's Encyclopedia of Myths and Secrets* (San Francisco: Harper & Row, 1983) 560–61, 685.
10. The Pythagorean Principles were derived from ancient vibration and resonance mysteries known to the Egyptians, Persians, Hindus, and

Chaldeans, as well as the Druids; Clement of Alexandria recorded that Pythagorus learned everything from "the Gauls and other Barbarians." Neolithic monuments and rituals were structured on these principles, and we still innately respond to them; it is their abstraction from nature, and consequent exploitation of what was once "sacred engineering," that has become our historic problem. See John Michell, *The New View Over Atlantis* (San Francisco: Harper & Row, 1983), 198.

Moon Minds

1. See Elise Boulding, *The Underside of History: A View of Women Through Time* (Boulder, Colorado: Westview Press, 1976), 106.
2. Martha K. McClintock, "Menstrual Synchrony and Suppression," *Nature* 229 (January 22, 1971): 171–79.
3. Information from Louise Lacy, *Lunaception* (New York: Warner Books, 1974, 1976).
4. Quoted in John G. Jackson, *Man, God and Civilization* (New Hyde Park, New York: University Books, 1972), 108.
5. Both Merlin Stone in *When God Was A Woman* (New York: Harcourt Brace Jovanovich, 1978) and Jean Markale in *Women of the Celts* (London: Cremonesi, 1975) give examples of the Great Goddess worshiped as the sun.
6. M. Esther Harding, *Woman's Mysteries, Ancient and Modern: A Psychological Interpretation of the Feminine Principle as Portrayed in Myth, Story and Dreams* (New York: Bantam, 1973), 111, 113. Harding quotes Plutarch, *Isis and Osiris:* "The Egyptian priests style the Moon the Mother of the Universe," and "They call the moon the Mother of the Cosmical Universe having both male and female nature."
7. Sheila Ostrander and Lynn Schroeder, *Psychic Discoveries Behind the Iron Curtain* (New York: Bantam Books, 1971), 186–99.

Moon Mother

1. Erich Neumann, *The Great Mother: An Analysis of the Archetype*, translated by Ralph Manheim (Princeton: Princeton University Press/Bollingen Series XLVII, 1955), 260. It is strange that so many millions of followers of patriarchal religions know nothing of the Goddess-origins of the most sacred icons, sites, and symbols they worship. Patriarchal religions, in their basic texts, state very clearly what they are *against;* it is always the Goddess religion that preceded them. The Koran 4:116, 117 says: "God forgiveth not the sin of joining other gods with Him. The pagans, leaving Allah, call but upon female deities." Pre-Islamic Arabic worship of the Moon Goddess is clearly revealed by the crescent moon, which appears on the flags of almost all Islamic nations; just as it appears beneath the feet of the Virgin Mary in Catholic icons.
2. For a discussion of "sacred prostitution," see M. Esther Harding, *Woman's Mysteries, Ancient and Modern* (New York: Bantam, 1973), especially 158–62 and 170–82.

The Cow Goddess and New Foods

1. G. Rachel Levy, *Religious Conceptions of the Stone Age, and Their Influence Upon European Thought* (New York: Harper & Row, 1963), 101.
2. Ibid., noted in Henri Frankfort's Introduction, viii.
3. Ibid., 100. Levy writes: "The reed-bundle and therefore the looped-post, both fashioned for the insertion of a closing or binding feature to guard the tamed beasts, is the certain symbol of the Mother Goddess as the Gate of a sanctuary which is in itself (to judge by the hut-amulets) conceived as her body ('He the Lamb and I the fold'), an idea already perhaps formed in the mind of Paleolithic man." Levy refers here to the Aurignacian cave at La Pasiega in the Cantabrian Mountains near Altamira, Spain, where sketched ritual enclosures containing horned animals are approached by dotted lines resembling footprints, with large triangles, the Aurignacian symbol of female fertility, closing the corrals' entrances. See Levy, 16 and 18, figures 11 and 12.
4. See Catherine Caulfield's heroic book, *In the Rainforest: Report from a Strange, Beautiful, Imperilled World* (New York: Knopf, 1984).
5. From a leaflet published by the British Vegan Society in the 1970s.

Mother and Daughter, and Rebirth

1. Music of the Princes of Dahomey, "Festival of the Tohossu," quoted in notes by Gilbert Rouget for the *Anthology of Music of Black Africa*, Everest Records 3254/3, record 3.
2. See Jill Johnston's *Lesbian Nation: The Feminist Solution* (New York: Simon and Schuster, 1973) and her *Village Voice* articles from the 1960s when, for many of us feminists, mythic passion and political passion were still excitingly compatible.
3. From a moon legend of the African Bushmen, quoted in M. Esther Harding, *Woman's Mysteries, Ancient and Modern: A Psychological Interpretation of the Feminine Principle as Portrayed in Myth, Story, and Dreams* (New York: Bantam, 1973), 270.

The Moon Tree

1. From the *Kaushitaki Upanishad* I:2, quoted in Jill Purce, *The Mystic Spiral: Journey of the Soul* (New York: Avon, 1974), plate 44. Here's another version: "Everyone who departs from this world, comes to the moon. In the first fortnight [the moon] waxes on their breath-souls (*prana*), while in the latter half it prepares them to be born [again]; for the moon is the gateway of the heavenly world." *Hindu Scriptures*, translated and edited by R. C. Zaehner (New York: Dutton, 1966), 149.
2. See Joseph Campbell, *The Masks of God: Occidental Mythology* (London: Secker and Warburg, 1965), 9–17; published by Viking Press, New York, 1970.
3. *Mahabharata*, Mokshadharma Parva cclxxx; cited in M. Esther Harding, *Women's Mysteries, Ancient and Modern: A Psychological Interpretation of*

the Female Principle as Portrayed in Myth, Story, and Dreams (New York: Bantam, 1973), 276.

4. Inscription on the seat of Athena/Isis at Sais; see G. R. S. Mead, *Thrice-Greatest Hermes*, volume 1 (London: n.p., 1906), 273. Quoted in Harding, *Woman's Mysteries*, 215. See also G. Rachel Levy, *Religious Conceptions of the Stone Age, and Their Influence Upon European Thought* (New York: Harper & Row, 1963), 117; Levy quotes from Plutarch, *de Iside et Osiride (Isis and Osiris)*, 10: "I am all that has been, is, and shall be; no mortal has ever lifted my garment." The line was also part of the initiation ritual of the Eleusinian mysteries undergone by Apuleius in *The Golden Ass*.

The Dark of the Moon and Moon Blood

1. From Walter Krickeberg, *Märchen der Azteken und Inkaperuaner, Maya und Muisca* (Jena: Märchen der Weltliteratur, 1928), 5; quoted by Erich Neumann, *The Great Mother: An Analysis of the Archetype*, translated by Ralph Manheim (Princeton: Princeton University Press/Bollingen Series XLVII, 1955), 183. *The Great Mother* has much to say in depth about the Dark or Terrible Mother; the useful information goes through Jungian interpretation, however, which closes up so much historic reality within the mind, disconnected from raw political and economic data. The mass sacrifice of human hearts in Mexico was on the altar of the sun, and of the War God Huitzilopochtli, in the service of patriarchal Aztec imperialism.

2. Frank Waters, *Mexico Mystique* (Santa Barbara: Black Sparrow Press, 1975), 185–86. The resemblances between the Mexican Coatlicue and the Hindu Kali (and the Irish Cailleach!) are indeed uncanny. So are the similarities between European witches and the pre-Columbian Mexican witches, as described by Lewis Spence in *The History of Atlantis* (New York: Bell, 1968), 224:

   > The Mexican witch, like her European sister, carried a broom on which she rode through the air, and was associated with the screech owl. Indeed the Queen of the Witches, Tlazolteotl, is depicted as riding on a broom and as wearing the witch's peaked hat. . . . The Mexican witches too . . . smeared themselves with ointment which enabled them to fly through the air, and engaged in wild and lascivious dances, precisely as did the adherents of the cult in Europe.

   The Mexican witches were also supposed to haunt crossroads, and to use elf-arrows as their weapons, just like European witches.

3. Carlos Fuentes, *Terra Nostra.* Translated by Margaret Sayers Peden (New York: Farrar Straus, Giroux, 1976), 714. Fuentes writes:

   > You say you see her there, closed, trembling, her lips forming the sound of a mourning drum, and you tell yourself that terror is the true state of all creatures, sufficient unto itself, separate from any dynamic relationship whatsoever; terror, a state of substantive union with the earth, terra, and a desire to withdraw forever from the earth. History—this history, another, that of many, that of one

alone—cannot penetrate terrified bodies that are both paralyzed upon the earth and cast outside it.

4. Aeschylus, *Eumenides*, quoted in John Michell, *The Earth Spirit: Its Ways, Shrines and Mysteries* (London: Thames and Hudson, 1975; New York: Avon Books, 1975), 19.
5. Quoted in Alan W. Watts, *The Two Hands of God, the Myths of Polarity* (New York: Collier Books, 1969), 84. Watts takes the quote from *The Gospel of Sri Ramakrishna*, translated by Swami Nikhilananda (New York: Ramakrishna-Vivekananda Center, 1942), 619.
6. See Diane LeBow's article on the Hopi in *Women In Search of Utopia*, edited by Ruby Rohrlich and Elain Hoffman Baruch (New York: Schocken Books, 1984).
7. Philip Rawson, *Tantra: The Indian Cult of Ecstasy* (London: Thames and Hudson, 1973); New York: Bounty Books, 1974).
8. This was quoted in an article by Carol P. Christ, in *Heresies 2*, no. 1 (Spring 1978): 11.
9. Judy Grahn, the *She Who* poems, 1971–72, in *The Work of a Common Woman, The Collected Poetry of Judy Grahn, 1964–1977* (New York: St. Martin's Press, 1978), 75–109.

Menstrual Rites: Rights and Taboos

1. Penelope Shuttle and Peter Redgrove, *The Wise Wound: Menstruation and Everywoman* (London: Victor Gollancz, 1978), 208ff.

The Original Woman: Witch, Rebel, Midwife, and Healer

1. Pope Paul VI, speaking in a Catholic pamphlet published by the Vatican in 1972. The declaration against abortion claimed, "Every human being, even the child in its mother's womb, receives its right to live directly from God," i.e., the Father God.
2. "Death in Ireland," *Off Our Backs 15*, no. 3 (March 1985): 15.
3. Spoken by a New York woman cab driver to Florynce Kennedy and Diane Schulder in 1971; quoted in *Aphra: The Feminist Literary Magazine* 4, no. 3 (Summer 1973): 49.
4. Paracelsus claimed "he had learned from the Sorceresses all he knew"; see Thomas Szasz, *The Manufacture of Madness* (New York: Dell/Delta Books, 1970), 85; also Andrea Dworkin, *Woman Hating* (New York: E. P. Dutton, 1974), 139. Dr. Margaret Murray's books are *God of the Witches* (London: Faber and Faber, 1972; first published in 1933), and *The Witch-Cult in Western Europe* (Oxford: Clarendon Press, 1921). Dr. Murray is another woman scholar who has been ignored, and more often ridiculed, for claiming that European witches practiced the Dianic religion. A large number of writers and "scholars" with heavy investments in the Judeo-Christian tradition have written entire books scoffing at the idea that pagan Europeans had any significant, coherent, or continuous spiritual heritage going back to the Stone Age, and in particular denying that medieval witchcraft had anything to do with such an ancient tradition. A recent typical attack on the reality of the Old Religion

came from European historian Norman Cohn; in *Europe's Inner Demons: An Enquiry Inspired by the Great Witch-Hunt* (New York: Basic Books, 1975), Cohn makes a psychoanalytical attempt to turn all of Europe's prebiblical history, and in particular the political-religious struggles involved in five hundred years of Inquisition and witch hunts, into a mental hallucination. Some of these writers also attempt to make "pagan" synonymous with "Nazi," apparently to discourage any serious investigation by people of European descent into their own prebiblical, pre-Roman Empire cultural and spiritual roots. Since so much of the pioneering research into European pagan religion has been conducted by women—Harrison, Weston, Murray, Levy, Diner—it has been especially easy for the patriarchal upholders of the Western academic and Judeo-Christian intellectual traditions to discredit their works.

5. Heinrich Kramer and Jakob Sprenger, O.P., *Malleus Maleficarum*, translated by Montague Summers (London: Arrow Books, 1971), 171. Also, from the same source, "Midwives . . . surpass all others in wickedness"; *Malleus Maleficarum* (London: Pushkin Press, 1948), 41.
6. "Gamble (gambol?) by day, and Dance by night, better Music and more Delight." Also, "Whistle the day and Dance the night. . . . " This is an old witchy riddle; in this case, "gamble" meant "risk."
7. Martin Luther, quoted in *Aphra* (Fall 1971): 49. But the quote has also been attributed to Luther's associate Philip Melanchthon; see Sheila E. Thompson, *Misogyny In the Sweetest Story Ever Told* (Madison, Wisconsin: Freedom From Religion Foundation, 1979), 8.

   For the politics of midwifery and the church, see Monica Sjöö, "A Woman's Right Over Her Own Body—A History of Abortion and Contraception," in *The Body Politic: Writings from the Women's Liberation Movement in Britain, 1969–1972)*, compiled by Micheline Wandor (London: Stage One, 1972), 180–89.

   In *Witches, Midwives and Nurses: A History of Women Healers* (Oyster Bay, New York: Glass Mountain Pamphlets, 1974), Barbara Ehrenreich and Deirdre English independently reached many of the conclusions Monica presented in her article, concerning the links between women's ancient herbal knowledge and healing and the practice of midwifery by the witches; this was one of the major secular reasons for their persecution by the medieval male medical profession as well as by the churches.
8. See interview with Dr. Christiane Northrup, *East-West Journal* (December 1981): 34.
9. From "The Witch Manifesto," Women's International Terrorist Conspiracy from Hell, quoted in Ann Forfreedom, *Women Out of History: A Herstory Anthology* (Sacramento, California: self-published, 1972), 107.

Goddess of the Witches

1. Intensive research into Amazonian Dianic practices can be found in Florence Mary Bennett, *Religious Cults Associated With the Amazons* (New York: AMS Press, Inc., 1967); on pages 33–34 she discusses the presence of Essenes at Ephesus and their participation in ecstatic Dionysian-Dianic rites, sometimes including self-castration. She cites Pausanius (8.13) as a source among ancient historians.

2. C. De Houghton, *Man, Myth and Magic* (London: Purnell, 1970), 632.

3. Quoted in Frank Waters, *Mexico Mystique* (Santa Barbara: Black Sparrow Press, 1975), 37.

4. Christian fanatics destroyed whole cultures, whole worlds of knowledge, including the great library of fifth-century Alexandria, the repository of the ancient world's accumulated learning. The School of Philosophy in Alexandria was also pillaged; its head was Hypatia, renowned astronomer, mathematician, logician, and Neoplatonic philosopher—a brilliant, eloquent, and beautiful woman, according to all accounts, who committed the pagan audacity of lecturing to men. Fired up by the misogynist sermons of Cyril, Alexandria's Christian bishop (later St. Cyril), a Christian congregation pulled Hypatia from her chariot, stripped her naked, and dragged her to their church; there, her flesh was scooped out with oyster shells and her body fed, piece by piece, to the flames. After this, in the words of Bertrand Russell, "Alexandria was no longer troubled by philosophers." Russell's account, from *A History of Western Philosophy* (New York: Simon & Schuster, 1945) quoted in *Aphra* (Fall 1971): 52–53. See also Elizabeth Gould Davis, *The First Sex* (Baltimore: Penguin, 1971), 240.

5. Waters, *Mexico Mystique*, 42.

Crete and the Bronze Age

1. G. Rachel Levy, *Religious Conceptions of the Stone Age, and Their Influence Upon European Thought* (New York: Harper & Row, 1963), 214.

Tantra and the World Spine

1. Information on the *Tantrika* from Philip Rawson, *Tantra: The Indian Cult of Ecstasy* (London: Thames and Hudson, 1973; New York: Bounty Books, 1974); also from his introduction and catalog text for the exhibition of Tantra art at the Hayward Gallery, London, 1971.

2. Tagore expressed this theme throughout his works. Though many Western feminists dislike and reject any notion of "special female powers," traditional women's cultures throughout the world are designed to practice and preserve such powers within a hostile patriarchal context. The same Shakti energies exploited in harem systems, the business of prostitution, and in the West's commercial obsession with "glamour" might well be used, within a nonpatriarchal environment, to keep the world alive. Shakti power is, by definition and experience, an antimechanistic and antihierarchical force-field; this is why patriarchal institutions work so hard to repress or rechannel it.

3. Read more about Kerala women's massage in *Loving Hands—the Indian Art of Baby Massage* (New York: Alfred A. Knopf, 1976).

4. William Irwin Thompson, *The Time Falling Bodies Take to Light: Mythology, Sexuality and the Origins of Culture* (New York: St. Martin's Press, 1981), 115.

5. Ibid., 113.

6. Ibid., 113; also 33.
7. Siegfried Giedion, *The Eternal Present: The Beginnings of Art: A Contribution on Constancy and Change* (New York: Bollingen Foundation, 1962), 506; see page 284 for a discussion of bird-headed women and shamanism. See also Vicki Noble's discussion of the Magician card, "Dancing the Fire," in *Motherpeace: A Way to the Goddess Through Myth, Art and Tarot* (San Francisco: Harper & Row, 1983), 29–33.
8. Thompson, *Falling Bodies,* 125. Thompson refers here to a luminous book, Laurette Séjourné's *Burning Water: Thought and Religion in Ancient Mexico* (New York: Vanguard, 1956), an in-depth reading of Aztec spiritual and psychic symbols and rites.
9. See Michael Dames, *Silbury Treasure: The Great Goddess Rediscovered* (London: Thames and Hudson, 1976), 23–26; also Thompson, *Falling Bodies,* 159–208.
10. C. S. Lewis, *Surprised by Joy* (London: Fontana Press, 1959), 13.

IV: PATRIARCHAL CULTURE AND RELIGION

God as Father

1. Eugene O'Neill, *Strange Interlude,* Act II, from *Nine Plays* (New York: Random House, 1954), 524. These are Nina's lines, rearranged a wee bit by Monica.
2. Alex Shoumatoff, *A Mountain of Names: A History of the Human Family* (New York: Simon and Schuster, 1985), 39. Shoumatoff writes:

   > In the 1982 edition of Victor McKusick's *Mendelian Inheritance in Man,* a catalogue of every clearly hereditary trait then known, 115 traits unrelated to feminization are firmly assigned to the X-chromosome. But only a few traits besides the regulators for masculinity may be Y-linked: greater relative stature, tooth shape, and hairy ears, which are most prevalent among men in India. "The X-chromosome has displayed particular stability in evolution," McKusick writes. . . . Other genetic information, from the mitachondrial DNA, which transmits critical instructions on cell respiration, is exclusively inherited from the mother.

3. Alan W. Watts, *Nature, Man and Woman* (London: Thames and Hudson, 1958; London: Abacus, 1976).
4. *Tao Te Ching,* no. 25, as quoted in Jill Purce, *The Mystic Spiral: Journey of the Soul* (New York: Avon Books, 1974), 20.
5. See Mircea Eliade, *Shamanism: Archaic Techniques of Ecstasy* (London: Routledge and Kegan Paul, 1964; 1970) for detailed information, from a European perspective, on shamanic beliefs and practices worldwide, past and present.

The Olympian Male

1. Jane Ellen Harrison describes this process, in the development of Greek Olympian Gods from the old Chthonic goddesses and gods, in *Themis:*

A Study of the Social Origins of Greek Religion (Cambridge: University Press, 1927).

2. J. J. Bachofen, *Myth, Religion and Mother-Right: Selected Writings,* with an introduction by Joseph Campbell (Princeton: Princeton University Press, 1967; New York: Bollingen, 1973), 109–15. Bachofen, in the 1870s, pioneered serious Western research into ancient matriarchal religion and culture. His biases toward patriarchy reflect the nineteenth-century assumption of "inevitable progress"—the idea that what comes earlier in time must be inferior to anything coming later—a linear evaluation designed primarily by "modern" Western Christians and patriarchal rationalists to flatter themselves.
3. John G. Jackson, *Man, God and Civilization* (New Hyde Park, New York: University Books, 1972), 173, 178–80. Jackson cites anthropologists Emil Torday, Franz Boas, and A. P. Chamberlain.
4. Merlin Stone, *When God Was a Woman* (New York: Harcourt Brace Jovanovich, 1978), 94–95. It is interesting that through Iron Age Scandinavia a replica of the Goddess Nerthus, or Hertha, of the North, more ancient even than Freya, was pulled through the land, in spring, in a wagon with solar wheels; thus she brought fertility to the year. This Goddess Nerthus, bringing the gift of new life in her wagon, was the prototype of Santa Claus and his gift-bearing sleigh.
5. T. C. Lethbridge, *Witches* (New York: The Citadel Press, 1968), 77.
6. William Irwin Thompson, *The Time Falling Bodies Take to Light: Mythology, Sexuality and the Origins of Culture* (New York: St. Martin's Press, 1981), 150–51.
7. Ibid., 123.
8. Ibid., 133–34.
9. Ibid., 155–56.
10. "I turn the male to the female; I am she who adorneth the male for the female, I am she who adorneth the female for the male." From a hymn of Ishtar, quoted in M. Esther Harding, *Woman's Mysteries, Ancient and Modern: A Psychological Interpretation of the Feminine Principle as Portrayed in Myth, Story, and Dream* (New York: Bantam, 1973), 189.

Sun's Victory over the Dark Mother

1. Samuel Noah Kramer, *The Sumerians, Their History, Culture and Character* (Chicago: University of Chicago Press, 1963).
2. William Irwin Thompson, *The Time Falling Bodies Take to Light: Mythology, Sexuality and the Origins of Culture* (New York: St. Martin's Press, 1981), 162.
3. Ibid., 162–63. Thompson takes the Enki myth from Thorkild Jacobsen, *The Treasures of Darkness: A History of Mesopotamian Religion* (New Haven: Yale University Press, 1976), 112.
4. Ibid., 163.
5. *The Sumerians*, 182.
6. Thompson, *Falling Bodies*, 165–66.

7. Ibid., 198.
8. Ibid., 163.
9. J. J. Bachofen, *Myth, Religion and Mother-Right: Selected Writings,* with an introduction by Joseph Campbell (New Jersey: Princeton University Press, 1967; New York: Bollingen, 1973), 105–8. Reference to the Mysian warrior queen Hiera is on page 107, where Bachofen quotes Philostratus's opinion that Homer didn't mention the Amazon because she "might have outshone Helen."
10. For information on Amazons read Helen Diner's *Mothers and Amazons: the First Feminine History of Culture* (Garden City, New York: Doubleday/Anchor, 1973). The note on Malawi women warriors comes from Ann Forfreedom's *Women Out of History: A Herstory Anthology* (Sacramento, California: self-published, third printing 1972), 26:

    The *New York Herald-Tribune*, Paris Edition of December 2, 1964, page 10, describes an Amazon army of 5000 forming an elite body in the army of Dr. Hastings Banda, the founder and first premier of Malawi (Nyasaland). This female corps was instrumental in helping to achieve Malawi's independence and at the time of the report was guarding the crucial boundary with Tanganyika.

    A serious, and brilliant, contemporary theorist of an armed women's state is poet, dramatist, and essayist Mia Albright; see Bibliography.
11. From Robert Graves and Raphael Patai, *Hebrew Myths: The Book of Genesis* (London: Cassell, 1964; New York: McGraw-Hill, 1966), 40.
12. Ibid., 41.
13. Ibid., 40.
14. Elizabeth Gould Davis, *The First Sex* (Baltimore: Penguin, 1971), 49. The quotes are from (1) Berossus of Babylon, fourth century B.C., and (2) Polyhistor; both quoted in I. S. Shklovskii and Carl Sagan, *Intelligent Life in the Universe* (San Francisco: Holden Day, 1966), 457. Davis's is a very exciting book; but there are problems with quasi-racist notions in the glorification of blond and red-haired Celtic people as the imagined culture-bringers to the rest of the world. In Central American and Mexican myth the God Quetzalcoatl, who came from the Atlantic sea and brought learning and art to the people, was also legendarily depicted as light-skinned and blond, or red-bearded. So some have attempted to trace this legend to an actual arrival on the east Central American coast of Irish monks, perhaps—related to the legendary voyages of St. Brendan. Viracocha, the Creation God of the Peruvian Incas, was very similar to the Aztec Quetzalcoatl; both were iconically depicted as the Feathered Serpent, or magic dragon. Viracocha too was legendarily referred to as a bearded white man—and in the Chachapoyas highlands of northern Peru, there are Indians living today with blue eyes and blond hair. (See "Lost Cities of the Andes," *Science Digest* 93, no. 6 [June 1985]: 46–53.) At the same time Mayan-Olmec statues and other evidence, also recorded in world mythology, suggest that early culture-carriers to Central America were West Coast Africans. And again, jade artifacts (including Buddha figurines) originating in China have been found along the Southern California coast and foothills; and there is

also much evidence of exchange between South America and Polynesia-Micronesia. We don't know—except it is certain that ancient people traveled around a lot more extensively than we are taught. And, were it not for the fanatic (mostly Christian) book-burners and library-destroyers, we would all know a good deal more about the tremendous history of our species.

15. See Mircea Eliade, *The Myth of the Eternal Return, or Cosmos and History* (Princeton: Princeton University Press/Bollingen, 1974), 19–20.
16. Ibid., 56–57

The Sun God

1. See Merlin Stone, *When God Was a Woman* (New York: Harcourt Brace Jovanovich, 1978), 35.
2. Amalgamation of quotes from Simone de Beauvoir, *The Second Sex* (New York: Bantam Books, 1961), 149, 140, 149, 148, 164; and 138 for "carnal contingence."
3. Robert Graves, "The Divine Rite of Mushrooms," *Atlantic 225*, no. 2 (February 1970): 110.
4. Quoted in Elizabeth Gould Davis, *The First Sex* (Baltimore: Penguin Books, 1971), 206.
5. Ibid., 206.
6. Robert Graves, *The White Goddess: A Historical Grammar of Poetic Myth* (New York: Farrar, Straus and Giroux/Noonday Press, 1966). Some scholars, of the type he has described as "Apollonian," disbelieve Graves's thesis of the tree-alphabet; poets and witches don't.
7. H. R. Ellis Davidson, *Gods and Myths of Northern Europe* (Baltimore: Penguin Books, 1964), 119.
8. Tacitus, *Histories* 5:25, in *Complete Works of Tacitus*, translated by A. J. Church and W. J. Brodribb (New York: Modern Library, 1942), 672; cited in Davis, *The First Sex*, 210.
9. See Thorstein Veblen, *The Theory of the Leisure Class: An Economic Study of Institutions* (New York: New American Library/Mentor Book, 1953), 23–26, 202–206. Though not feminist in orientation, Veblen brilliantly analyzes and criticizes warfare, sport hunting, and the priesthood as "manly" occupations carried out at the expense of oppressed labor, in particular at the cost of women's lives.
10. "Our god will feed himself with them as though he were eating warm tortillas, soft and tasty, straight out of the oven." Behind the deranged mysticism, Tlacaelel very deliberately established mass human sacrifice in Mexico as a method of intimidating conquered tribes into obedience; see "Aztec Imperialism: Tlacaelel and Human Sacrifice," by Miguel Leon-Portilla, in *Aztlan: An Anthology of Mexican American Literature*, edited by Luis Valdez and Stan Steiner (New York: Vintage Books, 1972), 16; the essay is from Leon-Portilla's book *Aztec Thought and Culture, A Study of the Ancient Nahuatl Mind*, translated by Jack Emory Davis (Norman, Oklahoma: University of Oklahoma Press, 1963).

The Jealous God

1. William Irwin Thompson, *The Time Falling Bodies Take to Light: Mythology, Sexuality and the Origins of Culture* (New York: St. Martin's Press, 1981), 171.
2. Elizabeth Gould Davis, *The First Sex* (Baltimore: Penguin Books, 1971), 67.
3. E. O. James, *The Cult of the Mother Goddess* (New York: Praeger, 1959), 250.
4. Davis, *The First Sex*, 67.
5. E. O. James, *The Ancient Gods* (New York: Putnam, 1960), 91.
6. See M. Esther Harding, *Woman's Mysteries, Ancient and Modern: A Psychological Interpretation of the Feminine Principle as Portrayed in Myth, Story and Dream* (New York: Bantam, 1973), 64, 103–5.
7. G. Rachel Levy, *Religious Conceptions of the Stone Age, and Their Influence Upon European Thought* (New York: Harper & Row, 1963), 196.
8. Theodore Roszak, *Where the Wasteland Ends* (Garden City, New York: Doubleday, 1972); see especially Chapter 4, "The Sin of Idolatry," 109–41.
9. Leviticus 21:16–22:

    > And the Lord spoke unto Moses, saying . . . Whosoever he be of thy seed to their generations that hath any blemish, let him not approach to offer the bread of his God. For whatsoever man he be that hath a blemish, he shall not approach: a blind man, or a lame, or he that hath a flat nose, or any thing superfluous, or a man that is broken-footed, or broken-handed, or crookbacked, or a dwarf, or that hath a blemish in his eye, or be scurvy, or scabbed, or hath his stones broken. . . . He shall not come nigh to offer the bread of his God. He shall not eat the bread of his God, both of the most holy, and of the holy.
10. Thompson, *Falling Bodies*, 116.
11. Rosemary R. Ruether, *Religion and Sexism* (New York: Simon and Schuster, 1974), 56.
12. The Lord's nasty impatience with female "wantonness" in this passage is revealing in its hypocrisy. In biblical times Jewish virgins were forced to wear hobbles around their feet, "the purpose of the hobbles being that the hymen should not be accidentally broken by a girl's taking long strides or carelessly breaking into a run." The bells were attached to the hobbles as ornamental advertisements, announcing to the world that the girl was "cherry," a marriageable item. Thus the "tinkling" and "mincing" walk of the daughters of Zion was a direct result of the patriarchal view of young women as sexual property and tradeable goods. See *The Anti-Sex—The Belief in the Natural Inferiority of Women: Studies in Male Frustration and Sexual Conflict,* edited by R. E. L. Masters and Eduard Lea (New York: The Julian Press, 1964), 14.
13. Ruth Hurmence Green, *The Born Again Skeptic's Guide to the Bible*

(Madison, Wisconsin: Freedom From Religion Foundation, 1979), 170. Ruth H. Green, a journalist, wife, and mother, was born in the farm town of Sumner, Iowa; in her later years she and her husband lived in Lake of the Ozarks, Missouri. Nominally but not actively Christian, like many people, she first actually *read* the Bible, cover to cover, while convalescing from cancer in the mid-1970s. Her reaction, she wrote, was "increasing incredulity and horror." In her words, "the superstitious ignorance, the atrocious inhuman cruelty . . . the depravity of the Bible personalities" left her feeling "stunned." She was also overwhelmed by the Bible's cover-to-cover misogyny. After studying the Bible intensively for two years, she wrote her book. It is the wonderful, blow-by-blow reaction and response of a very smart, funny, and down-home middle-American woman to the *actual content* of the "Holy Book," with all the miasmas of conventional piety cleared away. Ruth is a joy to read, and must have been a joy to know. On July 7, 1981, faced with her third recurrence of cancer, she took her own life—after writing her own obituary. Her last years were full with writing, lecturing, and talk-show appearances. She inspired hundreds and hundreds of people to do, basically, what she had done: to read the Bible thoughtfully and critically, and to ask themselves: "Is this really the kind of 'God' and world view worthy of my intelligent respect and belief?" Inquiries about Ruth and her book can be sent to Freedom From Religion Foundation, Box 750, Madison, WI 53701.

14. " . . . *templum aedificatum super cloacum.*" Quoted in Simone de Beauvoir, *The Second Sex* (New York: Bantam Books, 1961), 156. Tertullian wrote impassioned defenses of Christianity circa A.D. 200.

Split in the Garden

1. From a sixteenth-century treatise on female temperament and educability by Juan Huerte, quoted by Swedish feminist Asta Ekenwall in *Manligt, Kvinligt (Male and Female)* (Stockholm: Scandinavian University Books, 1966). The earlier Galenos quote also comes from Ekenwall's book.
2. J. J. Bachofen, *Myth, Religion and Mother-Right: Selected Writings,* edited by Joseph Campbell (Princeton: Princeton University Press, 1967), 79, 109, and 114–15.
3. Ibid., 116–29.
4. Ibid., assemblage of quotes taken from 236–39.
5. Norman O. Brown, *Life Against Death: The Psychoanalytical Meaning of History* (New York: Vintage Books, 1959), 281–82.
6. William Irwin Thompson, *The Time Falling Bodies Take to Light: Mythology, Sexuality and the Origins of Culture* (New York: St. Martin's Press, 1981), 195.
7. Ibid., 195, 196–97.
8. John Allegro, *The Mystery of the Dead Sea Scrolls Revealed* (New York: Gramercy Publishing Co., 1981; by arrangement with Penguin Books Ltd.), 167–72.
9. Ibid., 131.

10. Ibid., 113–15.

11. According to Morton Smith, Professor of History at Columbia University, the Dead Sea Scrolls also contain plans for a sun-worshiping tower. The tower was to contain nothing but a spiral staircase leading from the ground to the roof, and was to be gilded inside and out. See *Science Digest* 93, no. 6 (June 1985): 19.

Life as a Mistake

1. "This knowledge the Holy Spirit gave me on the privy in the tower." Quoted in Norman O. Brown, *Life Against Death* (New York: Vintage Books, 1959), 202.

2. Thomas S. Szasz, M.D., *The Manufacture of Madness* (New York: Dell/Delta, 1970), 182. Szasz writes: "the objections to masturbation, like those to other types of nonprocreative sexual acts, originate from Judeo-Christian religious sources"; Szasz quotes Alfred C. Kinsey, Wendell B. Pomeroy, Clyde E. Martin, and Paul Gebhard, *Sexual Behavior in the Human Female* (Philadelphia: Saunders, 1948), 168: ". . . few other peoples have condemned masturbation as severely as the Jews have. . . . The logic of this proscription depended, of course, upon the reproductive motive in the sexual philosophy of the Jews. This made any act which offered no possibility of a resulting conception unnatural, a perversion, and a sin."

   By the same token, the religious ban on abortion also derives from old Mosaic law, which forbade any obstruction to Yahweh's command that the Jewish people "be fruitful and multiply" (Genesis 1:28). As students of the subject point out, there is no mention of abortion, pro or con, in the Gospels, nor in the early centuries of the propagation of Christian doctrine. In both Greece and Rome, law and moral opinion sanctioned the interruption of pregnancy, and it was a common practice. It was not until the fifth century that St. Augustine, attempting political control over European pagans, "renewed the old Jewish ban on abortion and condemned all forms of contraception." See Richard Lewinsohn, M.D., *A History of Sexual Customs,* translated by Alexander Mayce (New York: Bell, 1958), 84.

3. Fran P. Hosken, editor, *Women's International Network News* 2, no. 1 (January 1976): 38–39. According to Hoskens, a gynecologist involved in family planning in Ethiopia reported that "in Ethiopia the operation is meant to reduce the sexual sensitivity of the women so that they do not dominate male sexual performance." Ibid., 41.

4. Read David Cooper, *The Grammar of Living* (New York: Pantheon Books, 1974) and Rosemary R. Ruether's essays in *From Machismo to Mutuality*, with Eugene Bianchi (New York: Paulist Press, 1976).

5. St. Clement, quoted in Elizabeth Gould Davis, *The First Sex* (Baltimore: Penguin Books, 1971), 231. Aquinas, St. John Chrysostom, and Sören Kierkegaard quoted in *Aphra* (Fall 1971): 47–48. Cato of Utica cited from *Malleus Maleficarum*, included in *The Anti-Sex—The Belief in the Natural Inferiority of Women: Studies in Male Frustration and Sexual Conflict,* edited by R. E. L. Masters and Eduard Lea (New York: The Julian Press, 1964), 213.

6. Michel Foucault, *Madness and Civilization: A History of Insanity in the Age of Reason* (New York: Vintage, 1973), 59.
7. Ibid., 59. This brief rundown of European history under linked church-state power, especially in relation to the development of the poor as a class, the exploitation of labor, exploitation of women's reproductive capacity, and the invention of madness and poverty as crimes, seems important here simply because it corresponds so eerily to so much that is happening today, in the 1980s, under the resurgence of fundamentalist religious and "neoconservative" (neofascist!) economic ideologies.
8. Ibid., 55.
9. Ibid., 25.
10. Ibid., 232.
11. Ibid., 60.

The Witch-Hunts

1. This is, in fact, the origin of our "dirty words." While the Latinate terms for sexual parts and body functions (vagina, penis, urinate, defecate, fornicate, etc.) are considered "acceptable" speech, all the Old English and Teutonic words for the same body parts and functions became taboo (cunt, prick, piss, shit, fuck, etc.) Why? The "dirty words" were originally taboo not because they were "immoral" but because they were "low-class"—the speech of the people. The upper classes, gathered around the court where they hobnobbed with Catholic clerics, spoke Latin both as an amusement and as a signature of their aristocratic status. The European peasants, needless to say, did not speak Latin, but their own indigenous Scandinavian, Germanic, and Old English dialects. Fuck, shit, piss, prick, and cunt underwent social taboo originally because they were socially vulgar—i.e., the common speech of the people, native European pagan speech. To this day many of our standards of "proper speech" (not to mention the horrific Latinese of bureaucratic jargon) are dominated by the inherited snobbery of Latinized, elite Christian usage versus the communal "field talk" or "street talk" of pagan European tongues, e.g., "perspire" versus "sweat."
2. Heinrich Kramer and Jakob Sprenger, O.P., *Malleus Maleficarum,* translated and introduced by Montague Summers (London: Arrow Books, 1971; New York: Dover, 1971); the definition of *femina* is on page 117. As Ann Forfreedom writes in "The Persecution of Witches" in *Book of the Goddess*, edited by Ann Forfreedom and Julie Ann (Sacramento: The Temple of the Goddess Within, 1980/9980 A.D.A.), 194:

   > Sprenger was the Dean of Cologne University, and both men had the support of Pope Innocent VIII. The *Malleus Maleficarum* was published in 1486, republished in at least thirteen editions until 1520, republished in another sixteen editions between 1574 and 1669, and is available in paperback today. There were at least sixteen German editions, eleven French, two Italian, and several English versions. Both Catholics and Protestants accepted this book as their authority on the existence, behavior, and menace of witches.

   The extaordinary thing is that Montague Summers, a twentieth-century

Catholic, actually believes in what these two monks say about "Devil-possession." He has himself written a book called *Witchcraft and Black Magic* (London: Arrow Books, 1946, 1964), from the perspective of a Christian male sympathetic to the Inquisition. Basically, he agrees that all those witches should have been burned; and should be again, if necessary. Righteous religious men who cannot admit they enjoy sadistic pornography are quite happy when witch-hunts occur—it gives them the opportunity to watch naked women being tortured and punished under the cloak of piety.

3. Kramer and Sprenger, *Malleus,* Dover ed., 26.

4. Pennethorne Hughes, *Witchcraft* (Middlesex, England: Pelican Books, 1965), 177.

5. Forfreedom, "The Persecution of Witches," in *Book of the Goddess,* 192. The mentality that equates accusation with guilt dominated the witch-hunts. *Malleus* states: "It has never yet been known that an innocent person has been punished on suspicion of witchcraft, and there is no doubt that God will never permit such a thing to happen." From Andrea Dworkin, *Woman Hating,* (New York: E. P. Dutton, 1974), 118.

6. Ibid., 192; also Rossell Hope Robbins, *The Encyclopedias of Witchcraft and Demonology* (New York: Crown Publishers, 1970), 60. Pennethorne Hughes, *Witchcraft*, 178, quotes from *On Antichrist*, by Florimond, an author who lived at the peak of the craze:

   > All those who have afforded us some signs of the approach of Anti-Christ agree that the increase of sorcery and witchcraft is to distinguish the melancholy period of his advent: and was ever an age so afflicted as ours? The seats destined for criminals in our courts of justice are blackened with persons accused of this guilt. There are not judges enough to try them. Our dungeons are gorged with them. No day passes that we do not render our tribunals bloody by the dooms which we pronounce, or in which we do not return to our homes discountenanced and terrified at the horrible confessions which we have heard. And the Devil is accounted so good a master, that we cannot commit so great a number of his slaves to the flames but what there shall arise from their ashes a sufficient number to supply their places.

   This was the daily atmosphere of European life, a few brief centuries ago.

7. On torture and its instruments, including trial transcripts, see Robbins, *Encyclopedia,* 498–510; information on Jean Bodin, ibid., 55. Also Forfreedom, "The Persecution of Witches," in *Book of the Goddess.*

8. Forfreedom, "The Persecution of Witches," in *Book of the Goddess*, 191, 195.

9. Ibid., 194.

10. Jules Michelet, *Satanism and Witchcraft: A Study in Medieval Superstition,* translated from French by A. R. Allinson (Secaucus, New Jersey: Lyle Stuart/Citadel Press, 1939), x. This is a classic, impassioned study of the witch-persecutions, written from a pagan heart.

11. Quoted in Michelet, *Satanism and Witchcraft*, viii. See also Thomas S. Szasz, *The Manufacture of Madness* (New York: Dell/Delta, 1970), 82–94.

12. Throughout Part I of the *Malleus*, especially Questions 5–7, the Dominicans work very hard to prove that all dealings with natural phenomena—stars, water, wind, earth minerals, plants, sex, dreams—are without exception demonic and thus subject to prosecution. Before the Papal Bull of 1484, the church's official position had been that witchcraft was nonexistent. God was all-powerful, nothing could occur without his permission; therefore, a belief in the *possibility* of effective witchcraft was the legal heresy. It was Kramer's and Sprenger's task to polemically reverse this relatively benign intellectual position; the church's political control over Europe via terror was increased by simply widening the field of criminalized events into a massive paranoia.

13. Ibid., 16, 40, 19. In another paragraph, Part I, Question 2 (page 16), the superstitions are listed as: "Necromancy, the superstitious observation of the stars, and oneiromancy," or dream analysis. Part I, Question 6 warns: "Devils are attracted by various kinds of stones, herbs, trees, animals, songs and instruments of music."

14. See John Michell, *The Earth Spirit, Its Ways, Shrines and Mysteries* (London: Thames and Hudson, 1975; New York: Avon, 1975), plate 41. Lest we consider ourselves far-removed from such silliness, consider the past decade or so of fundamentalist furor over the Proctor & Gamble symbol, which features *a crescent moon and many stars.* Convinced these are Devil signs, and that Proctor & Gamble is, intentionally or naively, acting as a front for the Anti-Christ, thousands of Christians weekly bombard P & G with letters demanding the logo be changed. Poor Proctor & Gamble! They certainly have no intentions of consorting with Satan. (Those of us reading this book know what a crescent moon and many stars *really* mean!)

15. Kramer and Sprenger, *Malleus Maleficarum:* pythons, page 7; death penalty for divination, page 5.

16. Jerry Mander, *Four Arguments for the Elimination of Television* (New York: William Morrow, 1978), 324.

17. Information from "Hitler's Religion," by Anne Gaylor, in *Freedom From Religion Foundation Newsletter* (March 1982). Hitler and other Nazi leaders dabbled in "occultism." They played with pagan symbols, conducted sun-worship rituals at ancient sites, and also, as the Christian church had always done, built on recognized power points around the German countryside; they tried to use occult knowledge of ley lines and sacred sites to further their project of psychic control over their people. Himmler and the SS were quite publicly anti-Christian; the SS theoretical journal *Ahnenerbe* even attacked the church for burning so many good German women. But the SS was modeled on the Jesuit Order, the order of the Christian Knights' crusades against unclean heathens, and the order of the Sun God: power through terror. Nazi occultism was not "paganism," but the mystique of necrophilia, the flowering of Christian dualism. At the core of the Nazi vision burned the fanatic and elitist concepts that define all patriarchal religion: concepts of "power over," of

master classes and blood purity, of total control of human reproduction, of a wrathful and moralistic male god punishing the female earth and flesh for its "inferiority." Hitler was no pagan; his misogyny and brutal biophobia were in the direct biblical tradition. One of his doctors reported that Hitler had recurring dreams of battling a trio of naked Amazons riding through space on beautiful horses, and Hitler's dream-spears only shattered harmlessly against their powerful bodies. Hitler thought the Amazons were Jews; in fact, they were the Triple Goddess, laughing at the Nazis' grotesquely mechanistic ideas of earthly power. See Dr. Kurt Kreuger, *I Was Hitler's Doctor,* 276–81 (no publisher cited); referred to in Donald J. Sobol, *The Amazons of Greek Mythology* (Cranbury, New Jersey: A. S. Barnes & Co., 1973), 155.

18. Incidents of child exorcism taken from *Freedom From Religion Foundation Newsletter* (May 1979). The California and Wisconsin incidents were heard on KVNM-FM radio (Taos, New Mexico), winter 1984 and spring 1985 respectively; the Austin shooting incident is from the *Albuquerque Journal* (Winter 1983); the Bangor, Maine, killing was reported in the *Arizona Daily Star* (December 1985).

19. Story of American Fork, Utah, slaying from John Aloysius Farrell, "'Kill' Sayeth the Lord," *The Denver Post* (Sunday, January 13, 1985): 1. Ruth Hurmence Green, one of the few with the fortitude to read the Bible many times, to plow through its misogyny, sadism, revengefulness and gory slaughter in the pursuit of data, has compiled lists of all the texts in which Yahweh commands murder, massacre, and general cruelty by his "holy men" against those labeled "fornicators," "idolators," and their children. Here are a few relevant texts.

1 Samuel 15:3,7.	"Slay man and woman, infant and suckling." (Yahweh's command to Samuel)
Psalms 137:9.	"Happy shall be he that taketh and dasheth thy little ones against the stones." (Yahweh calling for the massacre of Babylonian children)
Isaiah 13:15,16.	"Their children also shall be dashed to pieces before their eyes; their houses shall be spoiled, and their wives ravished." (Revenge instructions from one of Yahweh's favorites, the bloody Isaiah)
2 Kings 2:23,24.	Forty-two children make fun of the "holy" Elisha's baldness; Elisha curses them, and in answer to his curse, Yahweh sends two bears to kill and devour the children.

2 Kings 9:8, 10:1–11. "In generational revenge against the "seed" of King Ahab of Israel, Jehu, chosen by Yahweh to succeed Ahab on the throne, arranges for the slaughter of Ahab's seventy children. After they are killed, their heads are put on display in baskets at the city gates. This act, like so many similar, fulfills Yahweh's will that someone's "seed" be destroyed.

The fundamentalists who approve such texts, as "Holy Scripture," also tend to oppose all government funding for child-abuse programs, arguing such programs interfere with the "sanctity" of the family. Indeed, within the biblical patriarchal "family," children exist as little more than property over whom the father has total life-and-death control. This derives from the Bronze Age discovery of sexual paternity and the pastoral experience of cattle breeding. Texts such as the above also reflect the Bronze Age view of children as manipulatable "counters" in the fathers' acts of revenge and war.

20. Robbins, *Encyclopedia*, 50–52.

Denial of the Mother: Denial of the People

1. *Gospel of St. Thomas*, translated by T. O. Lambdin, in *The Nag Hammadi in English*, edited by James Robinson (New York: Harper & Row, 1977), 130.
2. *Gospel to the Egyptians*, quoted in G. R. S. Mead, *Thrice-Greatest Hermes*, volume 1 (London, n.p., 1906), 153; referred to in M. Esther Harding, *Woman's Mysteries, Ancient and Modern: An Interpretation of the Feminine Principle as Portrayed in Myth, Story and Dream* (New York: Bantam, 1973), 282.
3. For a full exploration of the relation between patriarchal thought and nuclear holocaust, read Brian Easlea's *Fathering the Unthinkable: Masculinity, Scientists and the Nuclear Arms Race* (London: Pluto Press Ltd., 1983). Easlea, with a Ph.D. in mathematical physics, currently teaches science studies at Sussex University, England; he also devotes a large amount of time to speaking and writing on the dangers of the arms race.
4. John G. Jackson, *Man, God and Civilization* (New Hyde Park, New York: University Books, 1972), 261. The Briffault quote is from his book *Rational Evolution* (New York: Macmillan, 1930), 117.
5. Ibid., 261.
6. Ibid., 261–62. The McCabe quote is from Joseph McCabe, *The New Science and Story of Evolution* (London: Hutchinson and Co., 1931), 298; italics his.
7. Michel Foucault, *Madness and Civilization: A History of Insanity in the Age of Reason* (New York: Vintage, 1973), 47–48.
8. There are fascinating links between Siberian shamanism and the Santa Claus legend, including the reindeer, the red and white colors of fly agaric, used for hallucinogenic flight—even coming down the chimney,

as the shamanic trance spirit comes down and leaves through the roof hole in the Siberian hut.

9. Easlea, *Fathering the Unthinkable*, 19–22. Easlea quotes from Francis Bacon's "The Masculine Birth of Time or the Great Instauration [*sic*] of the Dominion of Man Over the Universe" in *The Philosophy of Francis Bacon*, edited by Benjamin Farrington (Liverpool: University Press, 1970).
10. Ibid., 25.
11. Ibid., 20. For "on the rack," see William Leis, *The Domination of Nature* (New York: Braziller, 1972), 57 passim. For the entire impact of Western male scientism on the female body of life, read Susan Griffin's *Woman and Nature, The Roaring Inside Her* (New York: Harper & Row, 1978).
12. Ibid., 20.
13. Farrington, *The Philosophy of Francis Bacon*, 62.
14. Karl Stern, *The Flight From Woman* (New York: Noonday Press, 1965), 104–5.
15. Michel Foucault, *Discipline and Punish: The Birth of the Prison* (New York: Vintage Books, 1977), 226.
16. Ibid., 149–50.
17. Ibid., 150; also 135.
18. Ibid., 161–62.
19. Ibid., 173.
20. Ibid., 174–75.
21. Ibid., 175; quoted from Karl Marx, *Capital* 1:313, 1970 French edition; found in Foucault, *Discipline and Punish,* 175.
22. Annette Fuentes and Barbara Ehrenreich, *Women in the Global Factory* (Boston: South End Press, 1983).
23. Foucault, *Discipline and Punish*, 177.

The American Split

1. Max I. Dimont, *The Indestructible Jews* (New York: New American Library/Signet Edition, 1971), 244. Dimont says of the Puritans: "Except for their worship of Jesus they were as Jewish in spirit as Job, who had made his way into the Old Testament as a canonized Gentile" (346).
2. Ibid., 344–49. The term "Manifest Destiny" was coined by a nineteenth-century Irish politician; the concept itself, as Dimont points out, was very biblical, and brought to America by the Old Testament-oriented Puritans.
3. See *The Great Law of Peace of the Longhouse People* (Mohawk Nation, via Rooseveltown: Akwesasne Notes, 4th printing 1975).
4. *The Living Thoughts of Thomas Jefferson*, edited by John Dewey (New York: Fawcett Books, 1957), 110.
5. Ibid., 112.
6. Thomas Paine, *The Age of Reason*, from *The Selected Work of Tom Paine*, edited by Howard Fast (New York: Modern Library, 1946), 294. By the

way, why is Tom Paine, who virtually *wrote* the American Revolution, never taught in our schools? In January 1985 the U.S. Department of Education proposed a prohibition preventing American school districts from spending any federal funds on courses determined, by that district, to be "secular humanism" in content. This proposed rule follows legislation approved by Congress in the summer of 1984; the legislation, authored by Utah Senator Orrin Hatch, represents the attempts of fundamentalists to defund "secular humanism," which was defined by a 1961 Supreme Court decision as one on a list of "religions" which "do not teach what would generally be considered a belief in the existence of God." Under this definition, the Congressional law and the proposed Department of Education rule, technically any subject, book, or idea that does *not* support the Judeo-Christian biblical texts could be defined as "secular humanist"; i.e., school districts could refuse to fund any public school that was *not*, virtually, a Bible school. The rule could definitely bar the writings, not only of Thomas Paine, but of Jefferson, Madison, Thoreau, Emerson, Whitman, Twain . . . indeed, it's hard to think of a great American thinker or writer who would not be banned under the "secular humanist" rubric. How did this one slip by Congress? "Democratic congressional aides familiar with the negotiations over the law argue that the very lack of a definition makes the prohibition harmless. . . . " It's useless to point out that the lack of clear definitions has never made religious or political censorship and thought control "harmless" in the past. (See "Proposal Would Bar U.S. Funds for 'Secular Humanism' Classes," *The Denver Post*, January 13, 1985, National News Section.)

7. Louise Michel, *The Red Virgin, Memoirs of Louise Michel*, edited and translated by Bullit Lowry and Elizabeth Gunter (University, Alabama: University of Alabama Press, 1981), 118. The Paris Commune of 1871 was inspired in many ways by the American Revolution—which has of course inspired world revolutions everywhere. Interestingly, within America, just before our Revolution, a majority of our colonial businessmen strongly *opposed* revolution, or any break with England at all—they believed it would be bad for business.

8. Dewey, *The Living Thoughts of Thomas Jefferson*, 110. Jefferson also expressed "a hope that the human mind will some day get back to the freedom it enjoyed two thousand years ago." Ibid., 124.

9. Diane Johnstone, "New Inquisition on Liberation Theology," *In These Times* 9, no. 3 (November 21, 1984): 3. For a much more intensive exposition of Liberation Theology, read Leonardo Boff, *Church: Charisma and Power* (1981); also Virgilio Elizondo, *Christianity and Culture*, and *Galilean Journey: The Mexican-American Promise.*

10. For example, Exodus 17:11, 16; 32:27. Numbers 21:25; 21:34–35; 25:4, 9; 25:16, 17; 31:7, 8. Joshua 8:1–30; 10:28–40; 11:12–17; 12:24. 1 Samuel 7:13; 14:12–20; 15:3–7. 1 Kings 20:28–30. 2 Kings 9:8; 10:1–11. . . . It's a very long list.

11. Margaret Randall, *Christians in the Nicaraguan Revolution* (Vancouver, B.C.: New Star Books, 1983), 199.

12. Information and quotes from Hengsbach and Vekemens from Johnstone, "New Inquisition."
13. Mary Daly, *Beyond God the Father* (Boston: Beacon Press, 1973); *Gyn/Ecology: The Metaethics of Radical Feminism* (Boston: Beacon Press, 1978); *Pure Lust* (Boston: Beacon Press, 1984), 150–52.
14. Ché Guevera quoted in Randall, *Christians in the Nicaraguan Revolution*, 15.
15. The suggestion that Christianity crucify itself is not so strange. The *living* part of Jesus has always been his pagan part, the mysterious birth, death, and resurrection *passion* of the vegetation deity, Green Child of the Great Mother. But where the biblical Christ is born, sacrificed, and resurrected only once, the pagan god went through this process again and again, with the cycles of the year and the universe. What Liberation Theologists should consider is that this continuous rebirth-through-self-dissolution of the pagan mystery god is analogous to the Marxian idea of "revolution in permanence." For an exploration of this idea in relation to secular feminism, see Raya Dunayevskaya, *Rosa Luxemburg, Women's Liberation, and Marx's Philosophy of Revolution* (Atlantic Highlands, New Jersey: Humanities Press, 1981); also *Women's Liberation and the Dialectics of Revolution: Reaching for the Future* (Chicago: News and Letters, 1985).

"*The Divine Homosexual Family*"

1. Information on the nuns' statement and the Vatican's reaction, including analysis and quotes from Rosemary R. Ruether, is from Beth Maschinot, "Vatican Backlash Hits Nuns' Independence on Abortion," *In These Times* 9, no. 7 (January 9, 1985), 6.
2. Lewis Spence, *The Minor Traditions of British Mythology* (London: Rider & Co., 1948), 37.
3. Or, in the case of the popular cartoon characters the Transformers, they *are* machines. How eerie that the sacred concept of *transformation*, in the mid-1980s, is presented to our children as a vision of a post-human, post-flesh world in which machinery, and machinery only, has magic life, i.e., transformative potential.
4. Ti-Grace Atkinson, "Metaphysical Cannibalism" in *Amazon Odyssey* (New York: Links Books, 1974), 56–63.
5. E. P. Thompson, *The Making of the English Working Class* (London: Pelican Books, 1963). It can be argued that pornography originates in patriarchal religious texts: the Bible, the Koran, the Greek classic myths, the Confucian texts. All texts which define nature as essentially "evil," dark, and stupid, which define the female sex as source and agent of this material evil, and which define the male sex as God's tool or policeman assigned to control, manipulate, punish, and suppress women and nature—are pornographic texts, given their *frisson* of fascination by the righteously mandated merger of piety and lechery (or at any rate voyeurism: for all men under patriarchy become voyeurs, insofar as they are given control, via God's all-seeing eye, over female reproduction and sexual activity). The attempt to eroticize slavish submission to sadistic

will did not begin with deSade; it began with patriarchy's religious project to divert revolutionary-evolutionary sexual energy into the manipulated energy of sexual repression (i.e., political and economic oppression).

6. Octavio Paz, *Labyrinth of Solitude* (New York: Grove Press, 1961), 66.

The Machine

1. Annette Fuentes and Barbara Ehrenreich, *Women in the Global Factory* (Boston: South End Press, 1983), 13.
2. See *Off Our Backs 14*, no. 10 (November 1984): 4, for information on Sri Lanka; *Off Our Backs 15*, no. 3 (November 1984): 15, for Malaysia.
3. Fuentes and Ehrenreich, *Global Factory*, 36–37.
4. Ibid., 35–36.
5. Evelyn Reed and Raya Dunayevskaya are two Marxists who are also feminists, and who have tried to integrate the feminist critique of sexual exploitation with the Marxist critique of labor exploitation. One of the best, classic essays on this integration is Mariarosa Dalla Costa's "Women and the Subversion of the Community," translated by Dalla Costa and Selma James, in *The Power of Women and the Subversion of the Community* (Bristol, England: The Falling Wall Press Ltd., 1972). Clearly, the only way to release revolutionary energy and keep it released is via release of autonomous female sexuality; this is "revolution in permanence," dissolving hierarchic structures of control over the production of value at their very root: patriarchal control of the uterus.
6. Anderson quotes and information from *The Denver Post* (Sunday, January 13, 1985): 9A, "Violence-Beset Abortion Clinics Fearful the Worst is Still Ahead." Other information, including quotes from Beseda and Webster, from *Off Our Backs 14*, no. 9 (October 1984): 9, and *Off Our Backs 15*, no. 1 (January 1985): 2. When questioned, FBI Director William Webster said, "'Army of God' is a nice name to be used."
7. This is not to diminish the beasts, whom we love! The beasts have suffered enormously under patriarchy, along with the rest of us, blamed for all kinds of things that have never been in them, but only in the alienated eyes of pious beholders. In fact, the sex life of animals is very formal; it is a dance. To miss this is to miss the epiphany of earth's imagination, and sense of humor. Homosexual, and in particular Lesbian mating behavior, has been observed among mammals and birds; and female and male mammalian mates definitely play with each other. Copulation among animals, however, has only one purpose: species reproduction.
8. *Off Our Backs 14*, no. 11 (December 1984): 13.
9. In 1985 the Reagan administration withheld $76 million that had been allocated for the Supplemental Food Program for Women, Infants, and Children, known as WIC. A House resolution forced release of the money; see *Arizona Daily Star*, September 9, 1985, A-3. But Reagan's most recent budget attempts to cut WIC's funding again, along with the elimination of subsidized school breakfasts and lunches.

10. "Hunger: Now It's Back and in Epidemic Form," *The Denver Post* (Sunday, January 13, 1985): 1.

11. *Off Our Backs* 13, no. 6 (June 1983): 13. According to a 1985 report of the private Center on Budget and Policy Priorities, over 33 million Americans are living below the federal poverty level, an increase of 4.4 million since 1981; 13.8 million of the poor are children. (Figures from *Arizona Daily Star*, November 28, 1985, H-2; *Daily World*, October 31, 1985, 8-D.)

12. Ibid., 14.

13. Faye Ginsburg, "The Body Politic: The Defense of Sexual Restriction by Anti-Abortion Activists," in *Pleasure and Danger: Exploring Female Sexuality*, edited by Carole S. Vance (London: Routledge and Kegan Paul, 1984).

14. From "Desert Child," by Will Inman, in *FIRE!* 5, 1985, edited by Rhonda Paynter, Casper, Wyoming.

15. Paul Virilio and Sylvere Lotringer, *Pure War*, translated by Mark Polizotti (New York: Semiotext(e), Foreign Agents Series, Columbia University, 1983), 110.

16. The existence of sex-determination technology, and the fact that most couples, given this choice, choose to have male babies, at least as the first child, has caused many feminists to worry about the psychological effects this would have on females, "engineered" to be always second-born, second-choice. This is a serious problem; an equally serious problem with sex-choice technology involves the genetic disadvantage that occurs when cultural selection processes interfere with biological selection. Even though the lighter-weight Y-bearing sperm swim faster, and thus have the advantage of reaching the egg first, in close to 50 percent of successful impregnations, a female is conceived. This indicates that about 50 percent of the time it is the X-bearing sperm that is most fit, under the physical conditions of that couple at that time, to reproduce itself. For those parents who continue having girls, while wanting boys, one conclusion is apparent: For this particular couple the Y-sperm is less fit, less healthy, and therefore it is genetically desirable that the X-sperm is the one that reproduces. In the unaided impregnation the selection process is based on biological, genetic fitness alone (we assume until we know otherwise). Nature doesn't care whether blue blankets or pink blankets come first. Nature doesn't care about the ideal sex-hierarchies imposed by human cultures. It cares only about the most fit genes. In the unaided impregnation, on the biological level, our own biology chooses the most fit sperm to mate with the egg, whether it is a boy- or a girl-bearing sperm. If, about half the time, a girl baby is born, then we must assume, statistically and genetically, that our biology knows what it is doing.

    Sex-determination technology would distort, or reverse, this process. In about half the impregnations involving couples seeking boy babies, it would allow the more fit X-bearing sperm to be dumped down the drain in favor of a less fit Y-bearing sperm. A biologically healthier female would be discarded in favor of a less healthy male who would *not* have successfully survived without technological help.

Human choice of a baby's sex is based on almost wholly conditioned criteria: cultural and religious biases, personal psychological needs and fears, biases and demands based on the social and political environment. On this level of manipulated consciousness, we probably cannot engineer the most appropriate genetic choice; this choice occurs on the subliminal level of biogenetic fitness. By manipulating baby sex to fit personal emotional and culturally conditioned biases—in particular since a preponderant amount of critical genetic information comes through the female—sex-choice technology poses heavy risks to the gene pool.

17. Virilio and Lotringer, *Pure War*, 91–102; this book analyzes the process of endo-colonization via military usurpation of social wealth and human energy. On page 16 Virilio quotes a Pentagon statement from 1945–1950: "Logistics is the procedure following which a nation's potential is transferred to its armed forces, in times of peace as in times of war."

    As Virilio notes, this is an "extraordinary"—and an extraordinarily clear—statement of the post-World War II Pentagon's intention to transfer America's *potential* away from the civilian-social sector and into the possession of the Defense Department permanently. "In times of peace as in times of war": *permanently*. Sixteen years before *Pure War*, this process was described with brilliant precision by Juan Bosch, the Marxist ex-president of the Dominican Republic, in *Pentagonism, A Substitute for Imperialism* (New York: Grove Press, 1968).

18. Shulamith Firestone, *The Dialectic of Sex* (New York: William Morrow, 1971).

19. This and all quotes and information on "law and economics" from John B. Judis, "Court's Worst-Case Scenario," *In These Times* 9, no. 1 (November 7, 1984): 5.

20. Martin Heidegger, *The Question Concerning Technology and Other Essays*, translated by William Lovett (New York: Harper & Row, 1977).

21. Jeannine Parvati, *Hygieia, A Woman's Herbal* (Albion, California: Freestone Collective, 1984), 195–204. Carl Sagan has suggested, in *Dragons of Eden* (New York: Ballantine Books, 1977), 195–209, that the beginning of human life can be decided at a point when the neocortex begins registering intelligence activity on an electroencephalograph. Fetuses also dream; perhaps we can define the beginning of personal life as the beginning of dream activity—although not only humans dream; all mammals do, and birds, and perhaps a recognition of this would define a standard for the killing of animals as well as the abortion of fetuses. Sagan also notes that if he pricks his finger, every drop of blood—every cell in that drop—can become a human being "if properly preserved until the time of a practical cloning technology." And he asks, page 207: "Am I committing mass murder if I prick my finger and lose a drop of blood?" When we debate abortion, we must at least begin by *talking straight about life as well as death;* and this means talking about life and death as a biological-psychological-spiritual *process*—not as "God's property," or other manifestations of the dogmas of control.

Beyond the Male God and His Machine . . .

1. News clippings picked up from 1983 to 1985. On Pentagon religiosity, "Generals More At Ease With Enlisting Religion" from *The Denver Post* (January 6, 1985). Information on IDF induction ceremony from television news during the 1982 summer invasion of Beirut. Information on X-rated films from *Off Our Backs*: "Custer's Revenge" in "X-rated Video Games Multiply," (March 1983): 27; "Outrage Against Pornography," (April 1983: 45; "Movie Snuff-ed Out in NYC," (October 1983): 14; "WAP and NOW Protest 'Pieces,' " (December 1982): 2; "Birth in Chains," (July 1984): 7. "Bride-Burnings" and "God's Bomb" clippings sent by friends, without documentation.
2. *World Military and Social Expenditures, 1979* (Leesburg, Virginia: World Priorities, Inc., Box 1003), 5.
3. *New Perspectives: Journal of the World Peace Council 15*, no. 4 (Helsinki, 1985): 16–17.
4. Ruth Leger Sivard, Director World Priorities, *World Military and Social Expenditures, 1980* (Leesburg, Virginia: World Priorities, Inc. Box 1003), 17–18.
5. Paul Virilio and Sylvere Lotringer, *Pure War*, translated by Mark Polizotti (New York: Semiotext(e), Foreign Agents Series, Columbia University, 1983), 2–3; William Irwin Thompson, *The Time Falling Bodies Take to Light: Mythology, Sexuality and the Origins of Culture* (New York: St. Martin's Press, 1981), 159.
6. "Have Gun, Will Swagger," *In These Times* 8, no. 36 (September 26, 1984): 4.
7. Virilio and Lotringer, *Pure War*, 124; the entire book makes this point.
8. "Reagan Robs Needy Again," *Off Our Backs 14*, no. 12 (January 1985): 3.
9. "The Real State of the Union is the Growing Pauperization of America," by Michael Connolly, *News and Letters 30*, no. 1 (Chicago, January–February 1985): 1 and 10.
10. Annette Fuentes and Barbara Ehrenreich, *Women in the Global Factory* (Boston: South End Press, 1983), 48–56.
11. From "Statistics Development Issue Paper No. 12, UN Development Programs," quoted in Robin Morgan, *Anatomy of Freedom* (Garden City, New York: Doubleday/Anchor Press, 1982), 20.
12. Ibid., 266–67.
13. Ibid., 263–65, author's italics.
14. Virilio and Lotringer, *Pure War*, 147. On page 122, Virilio says, "The real problematic is Pure War. It's not actual war, but logistical war. So the real problem is to oppose the war-machine *as the machine of societal non-development*." Virilio speculates that the possibility of nuclear war between the US and the USSR is smaller than that of endo-colonization;

and that it is in fact the perpetual *threat* of the first, which provides the atmosphere by which the reality of the second is occurring.

15. Morgan, *Anatomy of Freedom*, 266.
16. R. Buckminster Fuller, A *GRUNCH of Giants* (New York: St. Martin's Press, 1983). GRUNCH stands for GRoss Universal Net Cash Heist.
17. William Irwin Thompson, *The Time Falling Bodies Take to Light: Mythology, Sexuality and the Origins of Culture* (New York: St. Martin's Press, 1981), 260–61. Robert Ardrey's ideas are expressed in several books, notably *African Genesis* (New York: Delta, 1961), 9; also *The Territorial Imperative* (New York: Dell, 1966). Glynn Isaac's views are taken by Thompson from "Stages of Cultural Elaboration in the Pleistocene: Possible Archaeological Indicators of the Development of Language Capabilities," in *Origins and Evolution of Language*, volume 280, edited by Harnand, Steklis, and Lancaster (New York: New York Academy of Sciences, 1976), 309.
18. Quoted as epigraph of *World Military and Social Expenditures, 1979, 1980*, 1.
19. Quoted on a letter from The Julio Cortázar Hospital Fund, c/o Janet Brof, New York, November 14, 1984.

. . . *The Magic Flight Home*

1. Mircea Eliade in *The Sacred and the Profane*: "The completely profane world, the wholly desacralized cosmos, is a recent discovery in the history of the human spirit." Quoted in John Michell, *The Earth Spirit, Its Ways, Shrines and Mysteries* (London: Thames and Hudson, 1975; New York: Avon Books, 1975), 47.
2. "The Ultimate Yuppie Pet," *Science Digest* 93, no. 7 (July 1985): 19.
3. An example of the mechanistic approach of Western biology occurred in the treatment of the Lamarckian theory of the inheritance of acquired characteristics. To test this theory, the tails of laboratory mice were chopped off, and they were bred; when their offspring were born with tails, voila! Lamarck was disproved—the "acquired characteristic" of taillessness was not inherited. This procedure classically reflected the Western notion that nature is a stupid mechanism, rather than a conscious process. The common sense fact is, of course, that those mice did not *need* to change themselves from tailed to tailless. The chopping-off of mouse tails is not a process-acquired characteristic; it is the arbitrarily chosen infliction of a mechanical defect, from the outside. The mice had nothing to do with it! Certainly the genetic processes of nature must have built-in checks against arbitrary and abrupt changes in an entire species; species could not exist under these circumstances. Every time an animal suffered an accident—lost a leg, was blinded, lost teeth, broke off horns—offspring would be born legless, blind, toothless, hornless. This is a stupid idea, and nature is not stupid. In nature, a species changes itself when it *perceives* (or *feels*, that taboo word!) *over a period of time a generic need for change*. Species change is not dependent on random, arbitrary mutation, is not a function of sheer accident, or blind luck, but is a kind of group-willed phenomenon, in genetic response to

a species-need. In his Prologue to *Hen's Teeth and Horse's Toes* (New York: W. W. Norton, 1983), 12, Stephen Jay Gould argues that Lamarckism was finally discredited, "since the workings of DNA provided no mechanism for an inheritance of acquired characters." But, the workings of DNA are not even close to being fully known to us; and so long as scientists approach DNA mechanistically, the results they obtain will be only those definable and observable via such an approach.

4. Franz Fanon, *The Wretched of the Earth* (New York: Grove Press, 1966), 252.
5. This "don't give energy to the man by engaging in his world" attitude, in the name of the Goddess, seems most prevalent among white American women; in Europe, particularly at places like Greenham Common in England, it is very much Lesbians and Goddess-oriented women who have launched the most radical engagements with "the man's world." At Greenham Common, women have for over five years maintained a protest camp on the site of a U.S. Cruise Missile base. In the name of the Goddess, they are risking their lives to be there, right at the very missilephallic center of "his world," defying patriarchal institutions, politics, war-games and machines, defying loaded guns—they do this in defense of "the woman's world." Women's spirituality can be this powerful when it has a political consciousness of global engagement.
6. Quoted by Ida Fuller in "South African Youth in Revolt," *News and Letters* 29, no. 8 (November 1984): 11.
7. Gil Elliot, *The 20th Century Book of the Dead* (New York: Charles Scribner's Sons, 1972); data taken from the whole book. According to *New Perspectives: Journal of the World Peace Council 15*, no. 4 (Helsinki, 1985): 16, 20 million people have been killed directly in some 150 wars *since* the end of World War II.
8. Paul Virilio and Sylvere Lotringer, *Pure War*, translated by Mark Polizotti (New York: Semiotext(e), Foreign Agents Series, Columbia University, 1983), 116–17.
9. Chief Seattle quoted in "Goodbye to My West," by Richard D. Lamm, *Rocky Mountain Magazine* (Denver, Colorado, March 1982): 50. Compare this with the view of contemporary theoretical physicist Fritjof Capra in *The Tao of Physics* (New York: Bantam Books, 1977), 276: "In the new world-view, the universe is seen as a dynamic web of interrelated events. None of the properties of any part of this web is fundamental; they all follow from the properties of the other parts, and the overall consistency of their mutual interrelations determines the structure of the entire web."

Respell the World

1. And amusing trips. A number of "enlightened" New Age males have learned to acknowledge they are half-female. But then they go on to *blame* all their crazy, mean energy on that female part . . . "The Terrible Mother made me do it!" Robert Bly comes to mind: a great poet, but not a very convincing Goddess. In fact, the Terrible Mother is in women. But the crazy, violent nihilism and power-obsession and life-grabbing of

so many males derives not from their female part, but from their male part *denying association* with their female part. We are waiting patiently, boys, please get it right!

2. Paul Davies, "The Eleventh Dimension," *Science Digest* 92, no. 1 (January 1984), 72.

3. From a paper given by Robin Morgan, "Lesbianism and Feminism, Synonyms or Contradictions," at a Lesbian conference in Los Angeles, early 1970s. It is taken from *The Charge of the Goddess*, which has appeared in many versions. The original version was written by the English witch Doreen Valiente, in the mid-1950s, for use in the coven led by her and Gerald Gardner; it included several lines from Aleister Crowley's work. As oral incantation among witches, many of the lines go back many thousands of years.

BIBLIOGRAPHY

To know our history is to begin to see how
to take up the struggle again.
—Barbara Ehrenreich and Deirdre English
in *Witches, Midwives and Nurses*

Adler, Margot. *Drawing Down the Moon.* Boston: Beacon Press, 1979.

Albright, Mia. *The Arrest of an American Feminist.* New York: Ananke's Womon Publications, 1983.

———. *Feminist versus Malist Sexual-Political Philosophy*, 1978;

———. *Transcendent Politics: Feminist Apocalypse versus Malist Holocaust*, 1980; *The Nationalist Feminist Education*, 1983; *The Feminist Economy: The Social Significance of Nationalist Feminism*, 1984. Self-published: 2685 University Avenue, #26D, Bronx, New York, 10468.

———. *The Incompetent Gift of Violence Against Masters.* New York: The Print Center, Inc., 1982.

———. *A Scrap of Royal Need.* New York: Ananke's Womon Publications, 1980.

Allegro, John. *The Mystery of the Dead Sea Scrolls Revealed.* New York: Gramercy Publishing, 1981.

Allione, Tsultrim. *Women of Wisdom.* London: Routledge and Kegan Paul, 1984.

Andersen, Jørgen. *The Witch on the Wall: Medieval Erotic Sculpture in the British Isles.* London: George Allen and Unwin, 1977.

Apuleius. *The Golden Ass.* Translated by Robert Graves. Baltimore: Penguin, 1950.

Arcana, Judith. *Every Mother's Son.* London: The Women's Press, 1983.

Ashe, Geoffrey. *Ancient Wisdom.* Kent, England: Abacus Books, 1979.

———. *Avalonian Quest.* London: Fontana Press, 1981.

———. *Camelot and the Vision of Albion.* New York: St. Martin's Press, 1971.

———. *The Glastonbury Tor Maze.* Glastonbury Tor Pamphlet, 1980.

———. *The Virgin.* London: Routledge and Kegan Paul, 1976.

Bachofen, J. J. *Myth, Religion and Mother-Right: Selected Writings.* Edited by Joseph Campbell. Princeton: Princeton University Press, 1967; New York: Bollingen, 1973; originally published in 1870.

Bates, Brian. *The Way of Wyrd: Tales of an Anglo-Saxon Sorcerer.* London: Century Publishing, 1983.

Beard, Mary. *Woman as Force in History.* New York: Macmillan/Collier Books, 1971.

de Beauvoir, Simone. *The Second Sex.* New York: Bantam Books, 1961; London: Penguin, 1972; originally published 1949.

Bell, Diane. *Daughters of the Dreaming.* London: Allen and Unwin, 1983.

Bennett, Florence Mary. *Religious Cults Associated with the Amazons.* New York: AMS Press, 1967.

Bettelheim, Bruno. *Symbolic Wounds: Puberty Rites and the Envious Male.* New York: Collier Books, 1962.

Bly, Carol. *Letters from the Country.* New York: Harper & Row, 1981.

Bord, Janet. *Mazes and Labyrinths of the World.* New York: E. P. Dutton, 1976.

Bord, Janet, and Bord, Colin. *Earth Rites.* London: Granada Press, 1983.

———. *Mysterious Britain.* London: Garnstone Press, 1972; London: Paladin Books, 1974.

Bosch, Juan. *Pentagonism, a Substitute for Imperialism.* New York: Grove Press, 1968.

Boserup, Esther. *Women's Role in Economic Development.* London: Allen and Unwin, 1970.

Branston, Brian. *Gods of the North.* London: Thames and Hudson, 1955.

———. *The Lost Gods of England.* London: Thames and Hudson, 1957.

Brennan, Martin. *The Boyne Valley Vision.* London: Dolmen Press, 1980.

Briffault, Robert. *The Mothers: A Study of the Origin of Sentiments and Institutions.* Three volumes. London: Allen and Unwin, 1952; New York: Macmillan, 1952; originally published 1927.

———. *The Mothers: The Matriarchal Theory of Social Origins.* Abridged edition in one volume. New York: Macmillan, 1931.

———. *Rational Evolution.* New York: Macmillan, 1930.

———. *Reasons for Anger.* New York: Simon and Schuster, 1936.

———. *The Troubadours.* Bloomington, Indiana: Indiana University Press, 1965.

Briggs, Katherine. *A Dictionary of Fairies.* London: Allen Lane, 1976; London: Penguin Books, 1977.

Brown, Norman O. *Life Against Death.* New York: Vintage Books, 1959.

———. *Love's Body.* New York: Vintage Books, 1966.

Brownmiller, Susan. *Against Our Will: Men, Women and Rape.* New York: Bantam, 1973.

Buber, Martin. *Ecstatic Confessions: The Heart of Mysticism.* Translated by Esther Cameron. Edited by Paul Mendes-Flohr. San Francisco: Harper & Row, 1985.

———. *I and Thou.* Edinburgh: T. and T. Clark, 1953; New York: Scribner's, 1970.

Budapest, Z. *The Holy Book of Women's Mysteries*. Two volumes. Los Angeles: Susan B. Anthony Coven, 1979 and 1980.

Budge, E. A. Wallis. *The Book of the Dead: The Papyrus of ANI*. New York: Bell, 1960.

———. *Osiris: The Egyptian Religion of Resurrection*. New York: University Books, 1961.

Caldecott, Leonie and Leland, Stephanie, editors. *Reclaim the Earth: Women Speak Out for Life on Earth*. London: Women's Press, 1983.

Cameron, Anne. *Daughters of Copper Woman*. Vancouver, B.C.: Press Gang, 1981.

Campbell, Joseph. *The Masks of God: Creative Mythology*. New York: Viking Press, 1970.

———. *The Masks of God: Occidental Mythology*. New York: Viking Press, 1964.

———. *The Masks of God: Oriental Mythology*. New York: Viking Press, 1962.

———. *The Masks of God: Primitive Mythology*. New York: Viking Press, 1959.

Capra, Fritjof. *The Tao of Physics*. New York: Bantam Books, 1977.

Capra, Fritjof and Spretnak, Charlene. *Green Politics*. New York: E. P. Dutton, 1984.

Carrington, Leonora. *The Hearing Trumpet*. London: Routledge and Kegan Paul, 1977.

Carson, Rachel. *The Silent Spring*. New York: Houghton Mifflin, 1962.

Casteneda, Carlos. *The Eagle's Gift*. New York: Pocket Books, 1981.

———. *The Fire from Within*. New York: Pocket Books, 1985.

———. *Journey to Ixtlan*. New York: Pocket Books, 1972.

———. *The Second Ring of Power*. New York: Pocket Books, 1977.

———. *A Separate Reality*. New York: Pocket Books, 1971.

———. *Tales of Power*. New York: Simon and Schuster, 1974.

———. *The Teachings of Don Juan*. New York: Ballantine, 1968.

Caulfield, Catherine. *In the Rain Forest: Report From a Strange, Beautiful, Imperilled World*. New York: Knopf, 1984.

Chang, Jolan. *The Tao of Love and Sex: Ancient Chinese Way of Ecstasy*. London: Wildwood House, 1977.

Chesler, Phyllis. *About Men*. New York: Bantam Books, 1980.

———. *Women and Madness*. New York: Avon Books, 1972.

Chicago, Judy. *The Dinner Party: A Symbol of Our Heritage*. Garden City, New York: Doubleday/Anchor Press, 1979.

Childe, V. Gordon. *The Dawn of European Civilization*. London: Routledge and Kegan Paul, 1961.

———. *Man Makes Himself*. London: Collins, 1966.

Cohn, Norman. *Europe's Inner Demons: An Enquiry Inspired by the Great Witch-Hunt*. New York: Basic Books, 1975.

Cooper, David. *The Grammar of Living*. New York: Pantheon Books, 1974.

Crawford, O. G. S. *The Eye Goddess*. New York: Macmillan, 1956.

Dalla Costa, Mariarosa, and James, Selma. *The Power of Women and the Subversion of the Community.* Bristol, England: The Falling Wall Press Ltd., 1972.

Daly, Mary. *Beyond God the Father.* Boston: Beacon Press, 1973.

———. *Gyn/Ecology: The Metaethics of Radical Feminism.* Boston: Beacon Press, 1978.

———. *Pure Lust.* Boston: Beacon Press, 1984.

Dames, Michael. *Avebury Cycle.* London: Thames and Hudson, 1977.

———. *Silbury Treasure: The Great Goddess Rediscovered.* London: Thames and Hudson, 1976.

Davidson, H. R. Ellis. *Gods and Myths of Northern Europe.* Baltimore: Penguin, 1964.

———. *Pagan Scandinavia.* New York: Frederick A. Praeger, 1967.

Davis, Elizabeth Gould. *The First Sex.* Baltimore: Penguin, 1971.

Dick-Read, Grantly. *Childbirth Without Fear.* New York: Harper, 1970.

Dimont, Max. *The Indestructible Jews.* New York: New American Library/Signet, 1971.

———. *Jews, God and History.* New York: New American Library/Signet, 1964.

Diner, Helen. *Mothers and Amazons.* New York: Doubleday/Anchor, 1973.

Doria, Charles and Lenowitz, Harris, editors. *Origins: Creation Texts from the Ancient Mediterranean.* New York: Doubleday/Anchor, 1976.

Dowell, Susan and Hurcombe, Linda. *Dispossessed Daughters of Eve: Faith and Feminism.* London: SCM Press Ltd., 1981.

Du Bois, W. E. Burghardt. *The World and Africa: An Inquiry into the Part Which Africa Has Played in World History.* New York: International Publishers, 1975; originally copyrighted 1946.

Duerden, Dennis. *African Art, An Introduction.* London: Hamlyn, 1968, 1974.

Dunayevskaya, Raya. *Rosa Luxemburg, Women's Liberation, and Marx's Philosophy of Revolution.* Atlantic Highlands, New Jersey: Humanities Press, 1982; Sussex: Harvester Press, 1982.

———. *Women's Liberation and the Dialectics of Revolution: Reaching for the Future.* Atlantic Highlands, New Jersey: Humanities Press, 1985.

Durdin-Robertson, Laurence. *The Cult of the Goddess.* Huntington Castle, Clonegal, Enniscorthy, Eire: Cesara Publications, 1974.

———. *The Goddesses of Chaldea, Syria and Egypt.* Huntington Castle, Clonegal, Enniscorthy, Eire: Cesara Publications, 1975.

Dworkin, Andrea. *Woman Hating.* New York: E. P. Dutton, 1974.

Easlea, Brian. *Fathering the Unthinkable: Masculinity, Scientists and the Nuclear Arms Race.* London: Pluto Press, 1983.

———. *Liberation and the Aims of Science.* Scotland: Academic Press, 1981.

———. *Science and Sexual Oppression.* London: Wiedenfeld and Nicholson, 1981.

Ehrenreich, Barbara and English, Deirdre. *Complaints and Disorders: The Sexual Politics of Sickness.* New York: Glass Mountain/Feminist Press, 1973.

———. *Witches, Midwives and Nurses: A History of Women Healers.* Oyster Bay, New York: Glass Mountain Pamphlets, 1972.

Eliade, Mircea. *The Myth of the Eternal Return, or Cosmos and History.* London: Routledge and Kegan Paul, 1955; Princeton: Princeton University Press/ Bollingen, 1974.

———. *Shamanism, Archaic Techniques of Ecstasy.* London: Routledge and Kegan Paul, 1964; Princeton, New Jersey: Bollingen Series, 1964.

Elliot, Gil. *The 20th Century Book of the Dead.* New York: Charles Scribner's Sons, 1972.

Engels, Friedrich. *The Origin of the Family, Private Property and the State.* New York: International Publishers, 1942, 1972; originally published 1884.

Evans, Arthur. *Witchcraft and the Gay Counterculture.* Boston: Fag Rag Books, 1978.

Evans-Wentz, W. Y. *The Fairy Faith in Celtic Countries.* Atlantic Highlands, New Jersey: Humanities Press, 1978.

Fanon, Franz. *The Wretched of the Earth.* New York: Grove Press, 1966.

Forfreedom, Ann, editor. *The Book of the Goddess.* Sacramento: The Temple of the Goddess Within, 1980 (2441 Cordova St., Oakland, CA 94602).

———. *Women Out of History: A Herstory Anthology.* Sacramento: self-published, 1975.

Foucault, Michel. *Discipline and Punish: The Birth of the Prison.* New York: Vintage, 1979.

———. *Madness and Civilization: A History of Insanity in the Age of Reason.* New York: Vintage, 1973.

Fox, Robin. *Kinship and Marriage: An Anthropological Perspective.* Cambridge: Cambridge University Press, 1984.

Freer, Jean. *Toward a Reclaimed Tarot.* London: Lamia Publications, 1982.

French, Marilyn. *Beyond Power.* New York: Summit Books, 1985.

Freud, Sigmund. *Civilization and Its Discontents.* New York: W. W. Norton, 1961.

———. *Moses and Monotheism.* New York: Vintage, 1967.

———. *Totem and Taboo.* New York: Norton, 1950.

Fromm, Erich. *The Anatomy of Human Destructiveness.* New York: Fawcett Crest, 1973.

Fuentes, Annette and Ehrenreich, Barbara. *Women in the Global Factory.* Boston: South End Press, 1983.

Fuller, R. Buckminster. *A GRUNCH of Giants.* New York: St. Martin's Press, 1982.

———. *Untitled Epic Poem on the History of Industrialization.* New York: Simon and Schuster, 1962.

Galleano, Eduardo. *Memory of Fire, Part One: Genesis.* Translated by Cedric Belfrage. New York: Pantheon, 1985.

Garcia, Jo and Maitland, Sara, editors. *Walking on the Water: Women Talk About Spirituality.* London: Virago Press, 1983.

Gardner, Gerald. *The Meaning of Witchcraft*. London: Aquarian Press, 1959.

Garrison, Omar V. *Tantra: The Yoga of Sex*. New York: The Julian Press, 1964.

Gauquelin, Michel. *Astrology and Science*. London: Granada Publishing Ltd./Mayflower Books, 1972.

———. *The Cosmic Clocks*. New York: Avon Books, 1967.

Gearhart, Sally Miller. *The Wanderground*. Watertown, Massachusetts: Persephone Press, 1979.

Giedion, Siegfried. *The Eternal Present: The Beginnings of Art: A Contribution on Constancy and Change*. New York: Bollingen Foundation, 1962.

Gimbutas, Marija. *The Gods and Goddesses of Old Europe—7000–3000 b.c., Myths, Legends and Cult Images*. London: Thames and Hudson, 1974. Reprinted as *The Goddesses and Gods of Old Europe—6500–3500 b.c.* Berkeley and Los Angeles: University of California Press, 1982.

Glob, P. V. *The Bog People*. London: Faber and Faber, 1977.

———. *The Mound People*. London: Faber and Faber, 1974.

Goldenberg, Naomi R. *The End of God*. Canada: University of Ottawa Press, 1982.

Goodall, Jane van Lawick. *In the Shadow of Man*. New York: Dell, 1971.

Gould, Stephen Jay. *Hen's Teeth and Horse's Toes*. New York: W. W. Norton, 1983.

Graves, Robert. *The Greek Myths*. New York: George Braziller, 1957.

———. *The White Goddess: A Historical Grammar of Poetic Myth*. New York: Farrar, Straus and Giroux/Noonday Press, 1966.

Graves, Robert and Patai, Raphael. *Hebrew Myths: The Book of Genesis*. New York: McGraw-Hill, 1966.

Green, Ruth Hurmence. *The Born Again Skeptic's Guide to the Bible*. Madison, Wisconsin: Freedom From Religion Foundation, 1979.

Griffin, Susan. *Pornography and Silence: Culture's Revenge Against Nature*. New York: Harper & Row, 1981.

———. *Woman and Nature: the Roaring Inside Her*. New York: Harper & Row, 1978.

Hadingham, Evan. *Secrets of the Ice Age: The World of the Cave Artists*. New York: Walker and Co., 1979.

Halifax, Joan. *Shamanic Voices: A Survey of Visionary Narratives*. New York: E. P. Dutton, 1979.

Harding, M. Esther. *Woman's Mysteries, Ancient and Modern: A Psychological Interpretation of the Feminine Principle as Portrayed in Myth, Story and Dreams*. New York: Bantam, 1973.

Harrison, Jane Ellen. *Themis: A Study of the Social Origins of Greek Religion*. Cambridge: Cambridge University Press, 1927; New York: Meridian Books, 1962.

———. *Mythology*. New York: Harcourt Brace, 1963.

Hawkes, Jacquetta. *Dawn of the Gods*. London: Thames and Hudson, 1968.

Hays, H. R. *The Dangerous Sex: The Myth of Feminine Evil*. New York: G. P. Putnam's Sons, 1964.

Hitching, Francis. *Earth Magic.* New York: William Morrow, 1977.

Hite, Shere. *The Hite Report: A National Study on Female Sexuality.* New York: Macmillan, 1976.

———. *The Hite Report: A National Study on Male Sexuality.* New York: Macmillan, 1981.

Hoult, Janet. *A Short History of the Dragon.* Glastonbury: Glastonbury Tor Pamphlet, 1978.

Hughes, Pennethorne. *Witchcraft.* Middlesex, England: Pelican Books, 1967.

Huxley, Francis. *The Way of the Sacred.* New York: Doubleday, 1974.

In These Times (ITT). Chicago: Institute for Public Affairs.

———. Hitchens, Christopher. "Laying to Rest Belief on Religion and Politics." *ITT* 8, no. 2. November 16, 1983: 27.

———. Johnstone, Diane. "New Inquisition on Liberation Theology." *ITT* 9, no. 3. November 21, 1984: 3.

———. Judis, John B. "Court's Worst-Case Scenario." *ITT* 9, no.1. November 7, 1984: 5.

———. Maschinot, Beth. "A Crack in the Catholic Monolith." *ITT* 9, no.1. November 7, 1984: 7.

———. Maschinot, Beth. "Vatican Backlash Hits Nuns' Independence on Abortion." *ITT* 9, no. 7. January 9, 1985: 6.

———. Moberg, David. "Priest David Tracy Discusses Liberation Theology Dispute." *ITT* 8, no. 35. September 19, 1984: 6.

———. Morales, Jr., Cecilio J. "Popular Theology Under Attack." *ITT* 8, no. 35. September 19, 1984: 7.

———. Patricca, Nicholas A. "Pope's Instruction Guards Hierarchy." *ITT* 8, no. 36. September 26, 1984: 12.

———. Wallis, Jim. "Our Republican High Priest." *ITT* 8, no. 37. October 3, 1984: 18.

———. Weinstein, James. "Back On Track With Neo-Colonialism." *ITT* 8, no. 41. October 31, 1984: 14.

Jackson, John G. *Man, God and Civilization.* New Hyde Park, New York: University Books, 1972.

Jackson, John G. and Huggins, Willis N. *An Introduction to African Civilizations.* New York: University Books, 1970; originally published 1937.

James, E. O. *The Ancient Gods.* New York: Putnam, 1960.

———. *The Cult of the Mother Goddess.* New York: Praeger, 1959.

Johnston, Jill. *Lesbian Nation: The Feminist Solution.* New York: Simon & Schuster, 1973.

Jones, Lynne, editor. *Keeping the Peace.* London: Women's Press, 1983.

Jung, Carl G. *Man and His Symbols.* London: Aldus Books, 1964; Garden City, New York: Doubleday, 1964.

———. *Psychology and Alchemy.* Translated by R. F. C. Hull. 2d ed. Princeton: Princeton University Press, 1968.

Keller, Evelyn Fox. *Reflections on Gender and Science.* New Haven, Connecticut: Yale University Press, 1986.

Kramer, Heinrich and Sprenger, Jakob, O. P. *Malleus Maleficarum.* Translated by Montague Summers. London: Arrow Books, 1971; New York: Dover, 1971.

Lacy, Louise. *Lunaception.* New York: Warner Books, 1974, 1976.

Laing, Ronald. *The Politics of Experience and the Bird of Paradise.* Harmondsworth, England: Penguin, 1967.

Leakey, Mary. "Preserving Africa's Ancient Art." *Science Digest* 92, no. 8. (August 1984): 57–63. From Mary Leakey, *Africa's Vanishing Art.* Garden City, New York: Doubleday, 1983.

Leboyer, Frederick. *Birth Without Violence.* London: Wildwood House, 1975; New York: Knopf, 1975.

Lehman, Rosamund. *The Swan in the Evening.* London: Virago Press, 1982.

LeSueur, Meridel. *The Girl.* New York: West End Press, 1978.

———. *Harvest* and *Song For My Time.* New York: West End Press, 1977.

———. *Rites of Ancient Ripening.* St. Paul: Haymarket Press, 1975.

———. *Women on the Breadlines.* New York: West End Press, 1984.

———. *Word Is Movement: Journal Notes from Atlanta to Tulsa to Wounded Knee.* Tulsa: Cardinal Press, 1984.

Lethbridge, T. C. *Witches.* New York: Citadel Press, 1968.

———. *Gogmagog—The Buried Gods.* London: Routledge and Kegan Paul, 1957.

Levy, G. Rachel. *Religious Conceptions of the Stone Age, and Their Influence Upon European Thought.* New York: Harper & Row, 1963. Originally published in 1948 by Faber and Faber, Ltd., London, as *The Gate of Horn.*

Lewinsohn, Richard, M.D. *A History of Sexual Customs.* New York: Bell, 1958, by arrangement with Harper & Row.

Lippard, Lucy. *Overlay—Contemporary Art and the Art of Prehistory.* New York: Pantheon Books, 1983. Monica Sjöö's work is included in this book.

Logan, Patrick. *The Holy Wells of Ireland.* Gerrard's Cross, Buckinghamshire: Colin Smythe, 1980.

Long, Max Freedom. *The Secret Science Behind Miracles.* Santa Monica, California: Devorrs, 1954.

Lorimer, David. *Body, Mind, and Death in the Light of Psychic Experience.* London: Routledge and Kegan Paul, 1984.

Malinowski, Bronislaw. *The Father in Primitive Psychology.* New York: W. W. Norton, 1966.

Mander, Jerry. *Four Arguments for the Elimination of Television.* New York: William Morrow, 1978.

Markale, Jean. *Women of the Celts.* London: Cremonesi, 1975.

Marshack, Alexander. *The Roots of Civilization.* New York: McGraw-Hill, 1972.

Marx, Karl. *Capital.* Three volumes. Chicago: Charles H. Kerr, 1909; reprinted by International Publishers, New York, 1967. A new translation of volume 1 by Ben Fowkes was published in Middlesex, England, by Penguin Books in 1976; New York: Vintage Books, 1977; volume 2, translated by David Fernbach, was published by Penguin in 1978.

Masters, R. E. L. and Lea, Eduard. *The Anti-Sex: A Collection of Misogynist Writings.* New York: The Julian Press, 1964.

McCrickard, Janet. *Brighde, Goddess of Fire.* Glastonbury: Glastonbury Tor Pamphlet, 1985.

Mellaart, James. *Çatal Hüyük.* London: Thames and Hudson, 1967.

———. *Earliest Civilizations of the Near East.* London: Thames and Hudson, 1965, 1978.

Merchant, Carolyn. *The Death of Nature: Women, Ecology and the Scientific Revolution.* New York: Harper & Row, 1980.

Michel, Louise. Edited and translated by Bullit Lowry and Elizabeth Gunter. *The Red Virgin: Memoirs of Louise Michel.* University, Alabama: University of Alabama Press, 1961.

Michelet, Jules. *Satanism and Witchcraft: A Study in Medieval Superstition.* Translated by A. R. Allinson. Secaucus, New Jersey: Lyle Stuart/Citadel Press, 1939.

Michell, John. *The Earth Spirit: Its Ways, Shrines and Mysteries.* London: Thames and Hudson, 1975; New York: Avon Books, 1975.

———. *The New View Over Atlantis.* New York: Harper & Row, 1983.

Montagu, M. F. Ashley, editor. *Man and Aggression.* London and New York: Oxford University Press, 1968.

Morgan, Elaine. *The Descent of Woman.* New York: Bantam Books, 1973.

Morgan, Lewis H. *Ancient Society.* Chicago: Charles H. Kerr, 1907; reprinted in 1964 by Belknap Press of Harvard University, Cambridge, Massachusetts.

Morgan, Robin. *The Anatomy of Freedom.* Garden City, New York: Doubleday/Anchor Press, 1982.

———. *Sisterhood Is Global.* Garden City, New York: Doubleday/Anchor Press, 1984.

Motherson, Keith. *Sleep Well, Father Marx.* Circulating in xerox manuscript, © 1984; c/o 3, Jordanston Cottages, Dwr Bach, Dyfed, Wales ST5 9RT, UK

———. *Which Way Home? A Discussion Paper for the Use of Christian-Feminist Dialogue Groups.* Manchester, England: Matri/anarchy Publications, 1979.

———. *Wider We: Towards an Anarchist Politics;* published together with Monica Sjöö's *Women Are the Real Left!* Manchester, England: Matri/anarchy Publications, 1979.

Muller, Herbert J. *The Uses of the Past.* New York: New American Library/Mentor Books, 1952.

Mumford, Lewis. *The Myth of the Machine: Technics and Human Development.* London: Secker and Warburg, 1967.

———. *The Pentagon of Power.* London: Secker and Warburg, 1971.

Murray, Margaret. *The God of the Witches.* New York: Oxford University Press, 1952; Garden City, New York: Doubleday/Anchor Press, 1960.

———. *The Witchcult in Western Europe.* New York: Oxford University Press, 1953.

Neumann, Erich. *The Great Mother: An Analysis of the Archetype.* Translated by Ralph Manheim. Princeton: Princeton University Press/Bollingen Series XLVII, 1955.

Noble, Vicki. *Motherpeace: A Way to the Goddess Through Myth, Art, and Tarot.* San Francisco: Harper & Row, 1983.

Parvati, Jeannine. *Hygieia: A Woman's Herbal.* Albion, California: Freestone Collective, 1978.

Patai, Raphael. *The Hebrew Goddess.* New York: Avon, 1978.

Patrick, Marcia. *Earthly Origins.* Circulating in xerox manuscript, © 1983, c/o Box 25901, Sarasota, Florida 34277.

Paulme, Denise, editor. *Women of Tropical Africa.* Berkeley: University of California Press, 1979.

Pepper, Elizabeth and Wilcock, John. *A Guide to Magical and Mystical Sites, Europe and the British Isles.* New York: Harper & Row, 1977.

Perera, Silvia Brinton. *Descent to the Goddess.* Toronto: Inner City Books, 1981.

Petchesky, Ros. *Abortion and Women's Choice: the State, Sexuality and Reproductive Freedom.* New York: Longman Press, 1984.

Purce, Jill. *The Mystic Spiral: Journey of the Soul.* London: Thames and Hudson, 1974; New York: Avon Books, 1974.

Randall, Margaret. *Christians in the Nicaraguan Revolution.* Vancouver, B.C.: New Star Books, 1983.

Rattray, R. S. *Ashanti.* London: Oxford University Press, 1969.

Rawson, Philip. *The Art of Tantra.* Greenwich, Connecticut: New York Graphic Society, 1973.

———. *Tantra: The Indian Cult of Ecstasy.* London: Thames and Hudson, 1973; New York: Bounty Books, 1974.

Raymond, Janice. *The Transsexual Empire.* Boston: Beacon Press, 1979.

Reed, Evelyn. "The Myth of Women's Inferiority." In *Problems of Women's Liberation.* New York: Merit, 1969.

———. *Woman's Evolution: from Matriarchal Clan to Patriarchal Family.* New York: Pathfinder Press, 1975.

Reich, Wilhelm. *The Invasion of Compulsory Sex-Morality.* London: Penguin, 1975.

———. *The Mass Psychology of Fascism.* Translated by T. P. Wolfe. New York: Orgone Institute Press, 1946.

———. *The Sexual Revolution.* London: Vision Press, 1969.

Rich, Adrienne. *Of Woman Born: Motherhood as Experience and Institution.* New York: Bantam, 1977.

Robbins, Rossell H. *The Encyclopedia of Demonology and Witchcraft.* New York: Crown Publishers, 1970.

de Rola, Stanislas Klossowski. *Alchemy: the Secret Art.* London: Thames and Hudson, 1973.

Ross, Anne. *Pagan Celtic Britain.* London: Routledge and Kegan Paul, 1967.

Roszak, Theodore. *Where the Wasteland Ends.* Garden City, New York: Doubleday, 1972.

Rothenberg, Jerome, editor. *Shaking the Pumpkin: Traditional Poetry of the Indian North Americas.* Garden City, New York: Doubleday/Anchor, 1972.

———. *Technicians of the Sacred: A Range of Poetries from Africa, America, Asia and Oceania.* Garden City, New York: Doubleday/Anchor, 1968.

Rothenberg, Jerome and Quasha, George, editors. *America A Prophecy: A New Reading of American Poetry from Pre-Columbian Times to the Present.* New York: Random House/Vintage, 1974.

Ruether, Rosemary R. *Religion and Sexism.* New York: Simon and Schuster, 1974.

Ruether, Rosemary R. and Bianchi, Eugene. *From Machismo to Mutuality.* New York: Paulist Press, 1976.

Rush, Anne Kent. *Moon, Moon.* New York: Random House; Berkeley, California: Moon Books, 1976.

El Saadawi, Nawal. *The Hidden Face of Eve: Women in the Arab World.* London: Zed Press, 1980.

Sagan, Carl. *The Dragons of Eden.* New York: Ballantine Books, 1977.

Sandars, N. K., translator. *Poems of Heaven and Hell from Ancient Mesopotamia.* London: Penguin Books, 1972.

Schleuning, Neala. *America: Song We Sang Without Knowing, The Life and Ideas of Meridel LeSueur.* Mankato, Minnesota: Little Red Hen Press, 1983.

Schwenk, Theodor. *Sensitive Chaos.* London: Rudolf Steiner Press, 1971.

Séjourné, Laurette. *Burning Water: Thought and Religion in Ancient Mexico.* Berkeley: Shambhala, 1976.

Seltman, Charles. *Women of Antiquity.* London: Pan Books, 1956.

Sharkey, John. *Celtic Mysteries: The Ancient Religion.* New York: The Crossroad Publishing Co., 1975.

Shelley, Mary. *Frankenstein.* New York: Oxford University Press, 1980.

Sherfey, Mary Jane, M.D. *The Nature and Evolution of Female Sexuality.* New York: Vintage Books, 1973.

Shoumatoff, Alex. *A Mountain of Names: A History of the Human Family.* New York: Simon and Schuster, 1985.

Shuttle, Penelope and Redgrove, Peter. *The Wise Wound: Menstruation and Everywoman.* London: Victor Gollancz, 1978.

Silverberg, Robert. *The Mound Builders.* New York: Ballantine, 1970.

Sjöö, Monica. "The History of Contraception and Abortion." In Micheline Wandor, editor, *Body Politics: Writings from the Women's Movement in Britain, 1969–72.* London: Stage One, 1973.

———. *Towards a Revolutionary Feminist Art,* No. 1 and 2; *Some Thoughts of Feminist Art.* Both pamphlets edited and printed by Monica Sjöö in 1974.

Sjöö, Monica and Motherson, Keith. *Women Are the Real Left/Wider We: Towards An Anarchist Politics,* 1979.

Spence, Lewis. *The History of Atlantis.* New York: Bell, 1968.

———. *Magic and Mysteries of Mexico.* London: Rider & Co., 1930; Detroit: B. Ethridge Books, 1973.

———. *The Magic Arts in Celtic Britain.* London: Rider & Co., 1945.

———. *The Mysteries of Britain: Secret Rites and Traditions of Ancient Britain.* London: Rider & Co., 1928; reprinted in 1979.

———. *Myths and Legends: The North American Indians.* Boston: D. D. Nickerson and Co., 1914.

Stallard, Karin, Ehrenreich, Barbara, and Sklar, Holly. *Poverty in the American Dream: Women and Children First.* Boston: South End Press, 1983.

Stanton, Elizabeth Cady. *The Women's Bible.* Seattle: Coalition Task Force on Women and Religion, 1974–81.

Starhawk. *The Spiral Dance. A Rebirth of the Ancient Religion of the Great Goddess: Rituals, Innovations, Exercises, Magic.* New York: Harper & Row, 1979.

———. *Dreaming the Dark.* Boston: Beacon Press, 1982.

Stern, Phillip van Doren. *Prehistoric Europe: From Stone Age Man to the Early Greeks.* New York: W. W. Norton, 1969.

Stewart, Bob. *The Waters of the Gap.* Bath, England: Bath City Council, 1981.

Stone, Merlin. *Ancient Mirrors of Womanhood.* Volumes 1 and 2. Montpelier, Vermont: New Sibylline Books, 1979.

———. *When God Was a Woman.* New York: Harcourt Brace Jovanovich, 1978; originally published in Great Britain as *The Paradise Papers.* London: Virago Ltd., 1976.

Szasz, Thomas. *The Manufacture of Madness.* New York: Dell/Delta, 1970.

———. *The Myth of Mental Illness.* New York: Hoeber-Harper, 1961.

Taylor, Barbara. *Eve and the New Jerusalem: Socialism and Feminism in the 19th Century.* London: Virago Press Ltd., 1983.

Thom, Alexander. *Megalithic Lunar Observatories.* New York: Oxford University Press, 1971.

———. *Megalithic Sites in Britain.* Oxford: University Press, 1967.

Thompson, Dorothy, editor. *Over Our Dead Bodies: Women Against the Bomb.* London: Virago Press Ltd., 1983.

Thompson, E. P. *The Making of the English Working Class.* London: Pelican Books, 1963.

Thompson, William Irwin. *The Time Falling Bodies Take to Light: Mythology, Sexuality and the Origins of Culture.* New York: St. Martin's Press, 1981.

Tompkins, Peter and Bird, Christopher. *The Secret Life of Plants.* New York: Avon Books, 1973.

Trevor-Roper, A. R. *The European Witch Craze of the 16th and 17th Centuries.* New York: Harper & Row, 1969.

Turnbull, Colin. *The Forest People: A Study of the Pygmies of the Congo.* New York: Simon and Schuster/Clarion Books, 1962.

———. *The Human Cycle.* New York: Simon and Schuster, 1983.

Underwood, Guy. *The Pattern of the Past.* London: Museum Press, 1969; London: Abacus, 1972.

Valiente, Doreen. *An ABC of Witchcraft, Past and Present.* New York: St. Martin's Press, 1973.

Vance, Carole S., editor. *Pleasure and Danger: Exploring Female Sexuality.* London: Routledge and Kegan Paul, 1984.

Van der Post, Laurens. *The Heart of the Hunter.* London: Penguin Books, 1965.

———. *The Lost World of the Kalihari.* London: Penguin Books, 1964.

Veblen, Thorstein. *The Theory of the Leisure Class: An Economic Study of Institutions.* New American Library/Mentor, 1953.

Virilio, Paul and Lotringer, Sylvere. Translated by Mark Polizotti. *Pure War.* New York: Semiotext(e), Foreign Agents Series, Columbia University Press, 1984.

von Cles-Reden, Sibylle. *The Realm of the Great Goddess, The Story of the Megalith Builders.* London: Thames and Hudson, 1961; Englewood Cliffs, New Jersey: Prentice-Hall, 1962.

Walker, Barbara G. *The Secrets of the Tarot: Origins, History and Symbolism.* San Francisco: Harper & Row, 1984.

———. *The Woman's Encyclopedia of Myths and Secrets.* San Francisco: Harper & Row, 1983.

———. *The Crone: Woman of Age, Wisdom and Power.* San Francisco: Harper & Row, 1985.

Warner, Marina. *Joan of Arc: The Image of Female Heroism.* London: Penguin, 1983.

Watson, Lyall. *Lifetide.* New York: Bantam Books, 1979.

Watts, Alan W. *The Joyous Cosmology: Adventures in the Chemistry of Consciousness.* New York: Random House/Vintage, 1962.

———. *Nature, Man and Woman.* London: Thames and Hudson, 1958.

———. *The Two Hands of God: The Myths of Polarity.* New York: Collier Books, 1969.

Weideger, Paula. *Female Cycles.* London: The Women's Press, 1978.

Weston, Jessie L. *From Ritual to Romance.* Garden City, New York: Doubleday/Anchor, 1957.

Wilhelm, Hellmut. *Change: 8 Lectures on the I Ching.* New York: Harper & Row, 1960.

Wilhelm, Richard, translator. *The Secret of the Golden Flower.* New York: Harcourt, Brace and World, 1962.

Williams, William Carlos. *In the American Grain.* New York: New Directions, 1956.

Wittig, Monique. Translated by David Le Vey. *The Lesbian Body.* New York: Avon Books, 1976.

———. Translated by David Le Vey. *Les Guérillères.* New York: Avon Books, 1973.

Wolf, Charlotte. *Love Between Women.* London: Duckworth and Co., Ltd., 1971.

PHOTOGRAPH AND ILLUSTRATION CREDITS

Credits

British Museum: photos p. 60, p. 111, p. 118, p. 166, p. 216, reproduced by Courtesy of the Trustees of the British Museum; Photographie Bulloz, Paris, Musée du Louvre, p. 245; Photo Chuzeville, Paris, Musée du Louvre, p. 254; The Dumbarton Oaks Research Library and Collections, Washington, D.C., p. 169; Giraudon, Paris, Bibliotheque Chambre des Députés, p. 177; Giraudon/Art Resource, Musée du Louvre, p. 255; Giraudon/Art Resource, New York, Musée du Louvre, p. 265; Harvard Art Museum, Courtesy of the Harvard University Art Museums, The Fogg Art Museum, gift of William Gray (from the Francis Calley Gray Collection of Engravings), p. 156; The Henry Moore Foundation, p. 224; Michael Holford Photographs, London, The British Museum, p. 158; Lauros-Giraudon, Paris, (from Musée Antiquités Nationales, St. Germain en Laye), p. 83; The Mansell Collection Limited, London, The British Museum, p. 266; National Monuments Record, Royal Commission on Historical Monuments, London, p. 320; National Museum, Beograd, photo by Bratislav Lukic, p. 92; Popperfoto, London, p. 47; Reis, Patricia, archeological drawings: p. 45, Reis, 1986; p. 93, Reis, 1986; p. 94, Reis, 1986; p. 98, Reis, 1986; p. 102, Reis, 1986; p. 181, Reis, 1986; p. 215, from *Lost Goddesses of Early Greece* by Charlene Spretnak, illustrations by Patricia Reis, copyright © 1984 by Beacon Press, reprinted by permission of Beacon Press; p. 246, Reis, 1986; Staatliche Museen zu Berlin—DDR, Antikensaamlung, p. 274.

NAME INDEX

SUBJECT INDEX